JMK in his Treasury office the afternoon before his departure to negotiate the American Loan: Associated Press

A 'SECOND EDITION' OF *THE GENERAL THEORY*

Volume 2

Keynes had intended to write 'footnotes' to *The General Theory* which would take account of the criticisms made and allow him to develop and refine his ideas further. However, a number of factors combined to prevent him from doing so before his death in 1946.

Just as other composers have 'finished' Schubert's Eighth Symphony, these two volumes of *A 'Second Edition'* contain the work of a representative range of Keynes scholars who have written the 'footnotes' that Keynes never did.

This second volume contains essays which relate to developments in Keynes scholarship and theorizing in the years since his death and demonstrates the ongoing validity of the Keynesian tradition.

G.C. Harcourt is Reader in the History of Economic Theory (*ad hominem*) at the University of Cambridge, a Fellow of Jesus College, Cambridge, and Professor Emeritus of the University of Adelaide. He has written and/or edited 16 books and numerous articles on theoretical, applied and policy topics, including specific writings on the economics of Keynes. **P.A. Riach** is Professor and Head of Economics at De Montfort University. His research interests are in the areas of wages, employment and income distribution.

A 'SECOND EDITION' OF *THE GENERAL THEORY*

Volume 2

Edited by G.C. Harcourt and P.A. Riach

ROUTLEDGE

London and New York

First published 1997
by Routledge
2 Park Square, Milton Park, Abingdon, Oxon, OX14 4RN

Simultaneously published in the USA and Canada
by Routledge
270 Madison Ave, New York, NY 10016

Transferred to Digital Printing 2006

Typeset in Garamond by J&L Composition Ltd, Filey, North Yorkshire

British Library Cataloguing in Publication Data
A catalogue record for this book is available from the British Library

Library of Congress Cataloging in Publication Data
A 'second edition' of The general theory/edited by G.C. Harcourt and P.A. Riach.
p. cm.
Includes bibliographical references and index.
1. Keynesian economics. [1. Keynes, John Maynard, 1883–1946. General theory of employment, interest and money.] I. Harcourt, Geoffrey Colin. II. Riach, Peter Andrew. III. Keynes, John Maynard, 1883–1946. General theory of employment, interest and money.
HB99.7.S43 1996
330.15′6—dc20 96–3293

ISBN 0–415–08215–3 (set)
ISBN 0–415–14942–8 (vol. 1)
ISBN 0–415–14943–6 (vol. 2)

ISBN10: 0-415-14943-6 (hbk)
ISBN10: 0-415-40700-1 (pbk)

ISBN13: 978-0-415-14943-3 (hbk)
ISBN13: 978-0-415-40700-7 (pbk)

Printed and bound by CPI Antony Rowe, Eastbourne

CONTENTS

FIGURES AND TABLES

FIGURES

TABLES

CONTRIBUTORS TO VOLUME 1

Ingo Barens, Bergische Universität, Wuppertal, Germany
Wylie Bradford, Fitzwilliam College, Cambridge, UK
J.F. Brothwell, Univerity of Leeds, UK
Volker Caspari, Technische Hochschule, Darmstadt, Germany
Victoria Chick, University College London, UK
Robert W. Clower, University of South Carolina, USA
John Cornwall, Dalhousie University, Halifax, Nova Scotia, Canada
William Darity, Jr, University of North Carolina at Chapel Hill, USA
Robert Eisner, Northwestern University, Illinois, USA
R.M. Goodwin, University of Siena, Italy
G.C. Harcourt, University of Cambridge, UK
Kevin D. Hoover, University of California, Davis, USA
Peter Howitt, Ohio State University, USA
Marc Jarsulic, University of Notre Dame, Indiana, USA
J.E. King, La Trobe University, Victoria, Australia
J.A. Kregel, University of Bologna, Italy
M.S. Lawlor, Wake Forest University, North Carolina, USA
Robin Marris, Lingard House, London/Professor Emeritus, University of London, UK
Luigi L. Pasinetti, Universita Cattolica del Sacre Cuore, Milan, Italy
P.A. Riach, De Montfort University, Milton Keynes, UK
Colin Rogers, University of Adelaide, Australia
T.K. Rymes, Carleton University, Ottawa, Canada
Nina Shapiro, Franklin and Marshall College, Lancaster, Pennsylvania, USA
Robert Skidelsky, University of Warwick, UK
Jim Thomas, London School of Economics, UK
Christopher Torr, University of South Africa, Pretoria, SA
Warren Young, Bar-Ilan University, Israel

CONTRIBUTORS TO VOLUME 2

A.J. Brown, University of Leeds, UK
John Coates, New York
Paul Davidson, University of Tennessee, Knoxville, USA
John B. Davis, Marquette University, Milwaukee, Wisconsin, USA
Sheila C. Dow, University of Stirling, UK
Bill Gerrard, University of Leeds, UK
Myron J. Gordon, University of Toronto, Canada
Peter Kriesler, University of New South Wales, Australia
Bruce Littleboy, University of Queensland, Australia
Rod O'Donnell, Macquarie University, Australia
Brian Reddaway, University of Cambridge, UK
Jochen Runde, Girton College, Cambridge, UK
Claudio Sardoni, University of Rome, Italy
James Tobin, Yale University, USA
Alessandro Vercelli, University of Siena, Italy

PREFACE

The preparation of this work has involved the willing co-operation and support of a large number of people and we, the editors, are extremely grateful to them all. Obviously, the authors of the chapters must take pride of place. We thank them all for joining us and for making the project an enjoyable and, we hope, rewarding one for them as well as us. In addition, we would like to thank most sincerely Alan Jarvis for his great encouragement, tolerance and enthusiasm for the project since we first approached him about Routledge publishing the volume; Allan Wailoo for his expert preparation of the bibliography; Nacirah Lutton for her unfailing cheerfulness and competence in typing the introduction and handling much of the correspondence which inevitably comes with a far-flung project such as this; Samantha Watson, who also handled a lot of correspondence, and Catherine Carthy for running off copies of the chapters whenever they were needed.

G.C. Harcourt
Cambridge

P.A. Riach
Milton Keynes

NOTE ON ABBREVIATIONS

References in the text to the original edition of *The General Theory of Employment, Interest and Money* (1936, London: Macmillan) are abbreviated to *G.T.* plus the relevant page number. Similarly, references to *The Collected Writings of John Maynard Keynes*, ed. D.E. Moggridge, vols I–XXX (1971–89, London: Macmillan), are abbreviated to *C.W.* plus the volume and page numbers.

INTRODUCTION[1]

This project arose from a conversation a few years ago between the two editors (G.C. Harcourt and P.A. Riach). P.A.R. mentioned how musical compositions which are unfinished because of the death of their composers sometimes are 'finished' by other people – he cited the composer Frank Merrick, who attempted to complete Schubert's unfinished Eighth Symphony. Maynard Keynes told Ralph Hawtrey in a letter of 31 August 1936 (*Collected Writings of John Maynard Keynes* (hereafter abbreviated to *C.W.*), XIV: 47) that he was 'thinking of producing in the course of the next year or so what might be called *footnotes* to' *The General Theory*, once he had absorbed the criticisms that had arisen and he himself had become more familiar with his new self.[2] But his severe heart attack in early 1937, the Second World War and his death on Easter Morning 1946 meant that he never did write those footnotes.[3]

So the idea for these volumes materialized: we would ask a wide range of Keynes scholars, varying all the way from some of Keynes's contemporaries to younger scholars beginning to make their mark through their interpretations and extensions of Keynes's ideas, to write essays of 6,000 words or so which would have two broad characteristics:

1 accounts, based on whatever evidence was available and whatever speculation seemed reasonable, of what they thought Keynes would have written in, say, 1938 or 1939; and
2 outlines of what they had done in the post-war period on particular aspects of issues which were first raised in *The General Theory*, and of why they had done what they did.

We have thus assembled here thirty-nine chapters, most of which match the chapters in the original books of *The General Theory*. The remainder relate to extensions and developments since the publication of *The General Theory* which come under the rubric of the economics of Keynes. Some of the contributors interpreted their task as to write the first part of their essays in the form of J.M. Keynes and so we have received some fascinating 'messages' from beyond the grave through such eminent mediums as, in order of appearance, John Brothwell, Bob Clower, Chris Torr, Victoria Chick, Michael Lawlor, Jan Kregel, John King, Robert Skidelsky and James Tobin.

There are some notable absences from the list of contributors. Sometimes this was because the scholars concerned declined (politely, even regretfully) to join in; sometimes because, having initially done so, subsequent unforeseen happenings led to their withdrawal. In particular a chap called Clinton (W.) threw a spanner in our works by putting Alan Blinder and Joe Stiglitz on his Council of Economic Advisors (Blinder subsequently ceased to be a real man and became a money man by going to the Federal Reserve Board). Jim Thomas (consumption) and Myron Gordon (credit rationing) more than ably filled the considerable voids which the withdrawal of Blinder and Stiglitz opened up. Bob Solow thought the project 'a neat idea' but, with his co-author Frank Hahn, declined to contribute because of the pressure of finishing off their joint 'old man of the sea' (Hahn and Solow 1996). Edward Amadeo withdrew at a late stage because of his demanding role in the recent election of a President of Brazil. Alas, the considerable opportunity cost involved brought neither him nor us any corresponding benefit, because his candidate lost. It would probably be invidious to name further obvious omissions. We do, however, want to pay a tribute to two illustrious Keynesian scholars and wonderful human beings who were on the original list. Lorie Tarshis died in October 1993 before his chapter could be written, and his former pupil, Paul Wells, became so tragically and permanently ill that his chapter will never be written either.[4] And, sadly, Richard Goodwin, who was much loved and admired in the profession, died in Siena on 6 August 1996 while the volumes were at proof stage. Thankfully, we have his chapter (10) as a memorial.

As editors we did perhaps show some foresight at the time we planned the project in the early 1990s for it is now clear that we have reached an appropriate conjuncture in history to put Keynes and his contributions back on the agenda, sixty years on from the original publication of *The General Theory.* We have tried to do so, not in a slavish or uncritical manner, but in order to learn again, or possibly for the first time, what his insights and approach to economic theory and policy were, and what the development of his ideas by those who have been influenced by him in a fundamental way has to say about the horrendous economic problems of the world today.

It is true that Keynes said in the original preface that *The General Theory* was primarily a work of theory addressed to his fellow economists; that while the public could eavesdrop, they were not at this stage the primary audience. Nor was the argument of *The General Theory* primarily concerned with policy implications, though Keynes was such an innovative and enthusiastic man of affairs that he could not help peppering the text with ingenious asides and policy suggestions. Now, sixty years on, we hope we may widen the audience so as to include not only economists and students of economics but also that broader public of concerned citizens. Most of the chapters have been written for such an audience. Moreover, because Keynes himself seldom if ever theorized without policy in mind, the same spirit permeates many of the contributions to the present volume.

Edward Amadeo's contribution was to have been on the shifts in Keynes's thought as he moved from the *Tract* to the *Treatise on Money* to *The General Theory*. Though his contribution is dearly missed, we are lucky in that he has written a splendid book on this theme (Amadeo 1989), and, more recently, a succinct account of his interpretations (Amadeo 1994). For most of the 1920s Keynes saw himself as working within the Marshallian tradition and approach, though he found himself rebelling increasingly against certain aspects of it. In this rebellion he was, by the end of the 1920s and especially when writing *The General Theory*, most influenced by Richard Kahn. Kahn's influence was crucial because he had always been sceptical about, indeed hostile to, the quantity theory as a causal explanation of the general price level, and he had done original work on the short period as a subject appropriate for study in its own right in his 1929 fellowship dissertation (Kahn 1929). By contrast, Dennis Robertson near the end of the writing of the *Treatise on Money* was much more accommodating of Marshall's views, an attitude he kept till the end of his life. This is perhaps most clearly seen in his three volumes of *Principles* (Robertson 1957–9) which are based on his lectures while the holder of Marshall's Chair, and were published after he retired from it (see Harcourt 1992).

Keynes's change of heart was associated with a move from emphasis on the long period to emphasis on the short period, and from keeping real and monetary matters separate, at least in a long-period sense, to integrating them from the start of an analysis of a monetary production economy.[5] To reach this second position Keynes needed to liberate himself from the hold which the Quantity Theory of Money and Say's Law (in its neoclassical rather than its classical form) had on the Marshallian system *as Keynes interpreted it* and so on Keynes's own thought.

Not only was there a change of 'vision' involved, there was also a change of method. In Marshall's system the long period was the core and full equilibrium was concerned with both stocks and flows. In Marshallian long-period equilibrium, both the stock of capital goods and the supply of labour were at optimum levels for a given initial situation and set of conditions. Long-period normal equilibrium prices had as components the normal rate of profits and the long-period normal rate of wages for each industry and, by extension, for the economy as a whole. Keynes looked at economic processes in this manner in the *Treatise on Money*, examining the determination of the price of consumption goods, and of the price level of output as a whole, and so, implicitly, of the price of investment goods, both in the short periods on the way to the long period, and in the long-period position itself. This was the role of the fundamental equations which Keynes thought of as a more illuminating way of restating the Quantity Theory. They enabled him to move from the setting of prices in each short period to an analysis of their impact on profits and so on movements in employment, output and accumulation. Kahn, however, interpreted the analysis as an *alternative* theory of sectoral price levels, and the general price level to that of the Quantity Theory.

Because of the Marshallian distinction between the real and the monetary, Keynes felt that there should not be over-much emphasis on the analysis of short-period fluctuations in output and employment in a theory of money. Yet he was at the same time preoccupied with policies directed to the solution of prolonged unemployment, even in the 1920s, and, in order to tackle them, he adapted the system on which he had been brought up. But it was Marshallian analysis, in that inflations and deflations were seen to be associated with gaps between the natural rate of interest determined by the real factors of productivity and thrift and the monetary rate of interest set by the monetary authorities. The other role of the natural rate of interest was to determine the composition of the level of output associated with full employment in the labour market.

As we know, all this was to change radically once Keynes had liberated himself from the Quantity Theory and Say's Law (via the co-operative, neutral and entrepreneur economy models, which sadly did not survive in the final draft of *The General Theory*: see Barens 1990; Tarshis 1989) and had incorporated Kahn's 1931 multiplier concept into his own discussion of the consumption function. Making the money rate of interest rule the roost, defining the marginal efficiency of capital and the investment function, and replacing the Quantity Theory by Marshall's short-period pricing theory, usually with price equal to marginal cost (both suitably aggregated to economy-wide levels) completed the story. His method of analysis was the determination, for the most part, of short-period, flow equilibrium values, with long-period stocks and flows vanishing either into the background (except in Chapter 17) or altogether.[6]

BOOK I INTRODUCTION

Keynes rather disarmingly entitled the first 'book' of his *General Theory* 'Introduction'. It contains three chapters: the one-page Chapter 1, 'The General Theory', Chapter 2, 'The Postulates of the Classical Economics' and Chapter 3, 'The Principle of Effective Demand'. As we know with hindsight, Chapter 2 has been the major chapter most criticized. The received view is that it is unsatisfactory, a view to which Keynes himself was coming. Thus, Keynes wrote: 'Chapter 2 . . . is the portion of my book which most needs to be revised' (1939c: 40, n. 1). In the present volume the chapters by John Brothwell (1), William Darity and Warren Young (2) and Robin Marris (4) all relate to the difficulties and complexities of Chapter 2, some exclusively, the others as part of wide-ranging discussions. Robert Clower's and Luigi Pasinetti's chapters (3, 6) are mainly concerned with the issues of Chapter 3.

Brothwell takes up the basic theme of Keynes's contribution that employment and the real wage are determined in the product market[7] and that Keynes's exposition in Chapter 2 in terms of the classical theory of the labour market – the two classical postulates, one relating to the demand for labour, the other to its supply – obscured the vital role of effective demand. Had Keynes first expounded his theory of effective demand, then the role of expectations about an uncertain future and the crucial role of money in the determination of the rate of interest, and its role, in turn, in the determination of investment, the most vital and volatile component of aggregate demand, the contrast between the old and the new world view would have stood out clearly. In particular, he would have had to bring into his exposition the distinction between the co-operative and neutral economies, on the one hand, and the entrepreneur economy, on the other. He could then have pointed out that the old view used the first two models (implicitly), that he, Keynes, used the third model to provide the second view, and that involuntary (demand deficient) unemployment could be shown not to exist in the first view as it clearly would exist in the second. Finally, Brothwell argues that, while Keynes went a long way towards discarding the old ideas, he did not go far enough. In particular, he was reluctant to take on fully the link between oligopolistic competitive behaviour and his macroeconomic systemic behaviour, as opposed to the complementary link between perfect competition and marginal productivity in the classical real wage economy, so leaving sufficient grounds for a neoclassical revival which jeopardized his revolution – never were truer words spoken. Marris makes the link in his chapter (4) (which both summarizes and expands the work he has been doing for forty years or more, including his 1991 book and his review article in the *Economic Journal* in 1992 of Richard Kahn's 1929 dissertation).

These chapters and the chapter by Darity and Young (2) may prompt the thought: what *is* all the fuss about? If causation runs from the product market to the labour market, if activity in the product market is determined by consumption demand (itself coming from the consumption function) and investment (itself greatly affected by uncertain knowledge about an uncertain future as well by the cost and availability of finance and existing capacity) and if the vital decisions in our sorts of societies are made by people who want to make money profits rather than ensure jobs for their workers, why *should* anyone be surprised that the natural resting places of these economies do not imply full employment of labour, and therefore that involuntary unemployment is a recurring characteristic of them? On this Darity and Young are succinct and to the point. Keynes was not the economist of wage or price inflexibility, or disequilibrium, but of insufficient aggregate demand. Whatever wages were doing when there was unemployment ceased to be of major relevance – it is the elasticity (or not) of aggregate employment with respect to an increase in aggregate demand which is the key point. They document this by reference to *The General Theory* itself and to letters, lectures and articles written after its publication. To them, New Keynesianism is as much a misnomer as the arguments contained under its rubric are not those of Keynes – a point which Peter Howitt, a former New Keynesian, now 'reformed', courageously and convincingly makes in his chapter (15), 'Expectations and Uncertainty in Contemporary Keynesian Models'.

Robin Marris argues that the weakness of *The General Theory* is not to be found in Keynes's analysis of the labour market but in his analysis of the product market. Keynes gives the impression (which was successful in the short run but discouraging to the cause in the long run) that his theory was independent of the particular structure of the product market, though most of his analysis in *The General Theory* itself does imply pure or free competition (of a realistic Marshallian sort rather than the very refined notions of modern economics). Keynes seems to have done this as much for ease of exposition as for any reason of principle. He took the degree of competition as one of his givens (*The General Theory* (hereafter abbreviated to *G.T.*) 245) and cheerfully took on board the findings of Dunlop, Kalecki and Tarshis in his 1939 *Economic Journal* article (Keynes 1939c). Marris argues that this is unacceptable, that Keynes's results cannot, in the main, be obtained when perfect competition in a *general* sense is assumed to hold in the product market. Whereas if we follow Marris's lead and adopt imperfect polipoly – the term Marris uses 'for the type of large-group imperfect or non-perfect competition' – as our microeconomic foundations, we get robust results at the macroeconomic level which are recognizably Keynesian, indeed are truly the economics of Keynes. He makes a most detailed argument for this position, taking us through a number of variations of his model, variations which have to do with the nature of expectations by entrepreneurs, his market-makers in stocks, wage-earners and consumers generally. He contrasts the results from his models with those obtained by assuming perfect competition as the microeconomic foundations. He concludes his chapter by outlining the main changes his approach would make to the structure of a second edition of *The General Theory*.

There is no doubt that Marris makes a strong and, we expect for many, a persuasive case for his point of view, especially for paths for future research. Nevertheless, we should like to enter a mild defence of Keynes's procedure in a pioneering work. It was essential for him to establish that, *however* business people formed expectations as to what their sales would be

– whether they had in mind expected prices with quantity then determined by those prices equalling their marginal costs, or levels of sales at prices for which they were responsible and hoped they got the quantities correct – there would be at any moment of time a determinate *total* of expected sales in the economy which, given the conditions Keynes assumed – a given stock of capital goods, supply of different labour skills and so on – would be translated into a determinate level of employment and production. This production in turn would create an equivalent level of income which through consumption expenditure and predetermined planned investment expenditure would determine whether the expectations of prices or quantities or sales were correct. *If* they were, the economy would be at the point of effective demand, a rest state until the underlying conditions changed (which, because this is a short-period analysis, they soon would). If the expectations were not met, Keynes seems to have thought that plausible stories could be told *for all cases* (here, of course, Marris disagrees with him) whereby the economy would give out signals which would lead it towards the point of effective demand, provided that the underlying determinants of the aggregate demand and aggregate supply (?) schedules were *not* affected by the non-fulfilment of the original expectations. Marris's chapter is a thorough discussion of *all* these possibilities and his imperfect competition model is one of great originality *and* power. Moreover, whatever may be said for Keynes's procedure from an historical point of view, there is no doubt that Marris's approach is the correct way forward *now*, for it captures essential features of the modern world in a particularly illuminating manner.[8]

Thus, in his revision of the structure of *The General Theory*, Marris proposes to scrap Chapter 21, 'The Theory of Prices', and, much earlier on, have his theory of price-setting expounded as the simple, most plausible way of modelling price formation in macroeconomic theory. In doing so, he not only emphasizes his own approach as the proper way forward but reflects his shock and delight, as set out in his 1991 book, at being introduced to the similar approach taken by Kalecki in his 1936 review of *The General Theory* by Ferdinando Targetti and Boguslawa Kinda-Hass, who translated Kalecki's review into English. (The translation was published in the December 1982 issue of *Australian Economic Papers*.)[9]

Nina Shapiro has written a most thoughtful essay (5) on imperfect competition and Keynes. In an unassuming manner she draws mostly on Keynes's own writings to argue the case that it is not perfect or imperfect competition *as such* which is relevant for his results but, rather, the implications of flexibility in prices and wages for the overall workings of the economic system. Hence we have Keynes's assumption that the degree of competition may be taken as given (*G.T.* 245) because, in his view, it is not of great (indeed, of any) relevance for the theory of effective demand. The latter in turn has its roots in the impact of uncertainty on the crucial decisions relating to the accumulation of capital goods and the holding of money, which are the real sources of sustained lapses from full employment in an unregulated capitalist economy. This is especially true of investment decisions which of necessity take in *expectations* of the long term – the expected lives of the assets concerned and, here, flexibility or otherwise of prices – is relevant only in so far as it bears on the subsequent realization or not of the expectations held at the time the investments are undertaken.

This leads Shapiro to contrast the Walrasian view of decision-making, where nothing happens until all decisions have been reconciled by the auctioneer, and the real life *processes* spread out over time which Keynes analyses. They necessarily imply that decisions have to be taken even though in retrospect they may be seen to have been mistaken or misguided. Shapiro ventures the empirical judgement that a world characterized by imperfect competition *may* result in a higher level of activity on average than one characterized by perfect competition because there would be less fluctuations in prices in the first and so less *adverse* feedbacks on two key determinants of the system: the marginal efficiency of capital and liquidity preference functions. But in both worlds it is quite possible, indeed it is inevitable, to have substantial and sustained lapses from full employment. The more flexible prices of a perfect competition world, as seen by Keynes with his emphasis on ongoing processes, and the desire by the key decision-makers to make *money* profits could make the systemic performance even worse than the, admittedly imperfect, performance of a world dominated by imperfectly competitive market structures.

Of course, Nina Shapiro's views are partly at odds with those of Robin Marris, but both are extremely serious attempts to come to grips with the hard problems that have beset Keynes's scholars and analysts of real world behaviour since the publication of *The General Theory*.

We come now to Chapter 3, 'The Principle of Effective Demand'. Robert Clower (3) rewrites it as he thinks Keynes would have (up to 1946) so as to make crystal clear the outlines of the new system as Keynes saw them – in his own words, in fact. Clower next sets the scene by suggesting that Keynes was more preoccupied with problems of existence than with those of stability, in particular, the existence of a rest state with unemployment. He then examines the Marshallian base of Keynes's system. He argues that it grew straight out of Marshall's partial equilibrium demand and supply analysis with quantity leading to price rather than price leading to quantity, as in Walras, whom Clower nevertheless identifies as belonging, when Keynes was learning his trade, to the same tradition as Marshall. Clower then works through various ways in which Keynes has been interpreted, for example by Hansen, Samuelson (and, implicitly, Harcourt, Karmel and Wallace 1967), usually in terms of the Keynesian cross, relating their analyses back to Marshall's models. In the process Clower rather 'does a Marshall on Keynes', that is to say, not so much taking literally what exactly

Keynes wrote but instead interpreting him so as to mean what Clower argues he needed to say and mean: for example, about Say's Law, product market clearing and labour market clearing. Finally, Clower quotes from Chapter 18 the passage which other commentators have taken to be evidence for a long-period interpretation of *The General Theory*:

> In particular, it is an outstanding characteristic of the economic system in which we live that, whilst it is subject to severe fluctuations in respect of output and employment, it is not violently unstable. Indeed it seems capable of remaining in a chronic condition of sub-normal activity for a considerable period without any marked tendency either towards recovery or towards complete collapse.
>
> (*C.W.* VII: 249)

Clower, though, argues that Keynes's vision – as set out by Clower – is the basis for a research programme which, if successful, will constitute a second Keynesian revolution that actually does for economics what Keynes intended to do by publishing the 'first edition' in February 1936. While this is surely inspiring for the present and coming generations, we ought also to examine James Tobin's chapter (25) where he sums up a working lifetime of thinking about and contributing to Keynesian economics following his introduction to (and becoming hooked on) *The General Theory* as a freshman at Harvard in 1936. We ought also to remember Tobin's article on 'Keynesian Models of Recession and Depression' in the May 1975 *American Economic Review*. There, he pointed out that Marshall and Walras differed on the dynamics of adjustment to single-market disequilibrium: Walras assumed that prices responded, by either rising or falling, to excess demand or supply respectively at a given price while Marshall had quantitites responding when demand prices exceeded or fell short of supply prices at a given quantity. Tobin argued that in *The General Theory* Keynes was Walrasian at this juncture and the Walrasian view leads to instability of equilibrium – a point which Tobin gives Friedman credit for perceiving.

Keynes entitled Chapter 3 'The *Principle* of Effective Demand' (emphasis added), not the *theory*. Luigi Pasinetti has written a chapter (6) of sublime simplicity and fundamental insight about this distinction. As is well known, he has devoted his working life to the creation of a multi-sector growth model which could be used to analyse the major issues with which political economy has been concerned since its outset. In doing so he has distinguished between the fundamental or 'natural' relations of his system, free of specific institutions, and the consequent analysis which may operate on a lower level of abstraction, taking account of institutions, in order to get 'closer' to real world observations and behaviour. Each set of arguments is, of course, complementary to the other.

Pasinetti uses this procedure to discuss the principle of effective demand in *The General Theory*. He argues that Keynes never made completely explicit the first, institution-free account of the principle, though he gave us many hints and clues and with his adaptation of Marshallian tools to take in the concepts of aggregate demand and supply he explicitly determined the *point* of effective demand.[10]

To get to the most fundamental level of analysis, Pasinetti explains how the 45° line, which, he argues, did so much damage to the development of Keynesian analysis, is nevertheless the appropriate tool for this particular task. Pasinetti therefore banishes the time-honoured aggregate demand function from his analysis and makes the causal relationship run from expected levels of aggregate demand to corresponding levels of production. The 45° line thus ceases to be a construction line devoid of economic meaning and becomes instead a simple way of expressing the relationship between all *expected* sales in the economy at a moment of time (whether they be sales of consumption goods or investment goods *including* own sales to inventory) and the production of commodities which is generated by and corresponds to them. Provided we assume that business people never produce unless expected sales fit into one of these three categories (and we measure in the same units on both the horizontal and vertical axis), we must end up with a 45° line. Pasinetti's construction is thus the reverse of Say's Law. Finally, Pasinetti extends these ideas to the long-period development of the economy, pointing out that, for all the added complexities of technical change, relative price changes, international trade, the ultimate saturation of demand for individual products and so on in any industrial system, any institutional mechanism that may be invented for the matching of production to demand will have to rely on the same basic principle of effective demand.

BOOK II DEFINITIONS AND UNITS

As we know from Volume XIII of Keynes's *Collected Writings*, Lorie Tarshis's memories of Keynes's lectures in the early 1930s (see Harcourt 1993: 73) and from Tom Rymes's notes of a representative student (Rymes 1989a), definitions and discussion of units took up much of the exposition. The discussions themselves are mainly in Book 2 of *The General Theory*. Keynes's decision to change his definitions of saving and investment so as to make them always equal instead of only so in the long-period, full stock-and-flow-equilibrium of the *Treatise on Money*, initially caused much confusion. This was especially so because Keynes himself was not clear in his own mind, or at least exposition, about the difference between the equilibrium condition, which requires planned saving and planned investment to match (more generally, desired leakages to match planned injections) and the national accounting identities which hold good for all time but have no causal or even analytical significance. In this section of the 'second edition' there are two chapters, by Wylie Bradford and G.C. Harcourt on units and definitions (7) and Christopher Torr on user cost (8). Torr divides his chapter into two parts; in the first, the authoritative voice of Keynes is to be discerned reacting to his critics and supporters. In Part II the voice of Torr sets out some wise words on the subject.

Bradford and Harcourt argue that from his earliest times Keynes was preoccupied with philosophical questions relating to definitions, units and measurement. He also always had an aversion to the concept of the general price level as used by Cournot and Jevons and increasingly tried to develop analyses which avoided its use. He distinguished between quantities which were and quantities which were not measurable, even in principle, and put the general price level (and subsequently national output and the capital stock) in the second category. Very early on, too, he identified the puzzles that arose from the fact that definitions of things were not independent of the purpose of the particular inquiry in which they played a part.

As far as the general price level was concerned, Keynes argued that shocks to the system must of necessity have different effects on the prices of different commodities and this occurrence vitiates any attempt to give precision to the notion of the general price level and of changes in it. Moreover, he found it impossible to conceive of weights which were independent of the prices to which they were attached in the construction of index numbers.

In *The General Theory* itself he identified three precise units: money, labour and time, for the specific analytical purposes he had in hand. Yet when we go into details we find that neither labour nor time unambiguously meets his own criteria. For example, time is defeated by his own concept of 'funnels' of process; labour depends upon an assumption of the exogeneity of relativities (probably reasonable, it is true, for the short run Keynes had in mind for most of the analysis of *The General Theory*).

Nevertheless, Keynes's emphasis on definitions and precision was taken up by his younger contemporaries. We have Piero Sraffa's stringent criteria for exact theory at Corfu (Sraffa 1961: 305–6). (Sraffa was probably ahead of Keynes, or at least independently arrived at the same views as Keynes on these issues.) Also Joan Robinson's discussion of the measurement and meaning of capital and profits and the conditions under which they could be precisely defined. Again, the distinction between net and gross concepts was vital for the emerging theory of growth in the post-war period – Keynes was able to use the latter for a theory of employment in the short period. Joan Robinson was not always consistent (neither was Keynes!). Nevertheless, her distinction between precision and making do with what we have, roughly matched her distinction between the analysis of differences and of changes, as well as that between levels of abstraction at which doctrinal debates could be carried out, as opposed to descriptive analyses of processes in historical time. These issues determined the units to be used and sometimes there were neither units nor answers to be found. No one ever discussed these issues with greater clarity or simplicity than Richard Kahn.

Torr (8) has written one of the clearest accounts of user cost *ever.* As we noted, in the first part of his chapter he writes as J.M.K.; he explains the price-setting role that user cost has both in individual firms (where it is an essential component of marginal cost) and at the macroeconomic level where, because user costs have affected the level of individual prices, *any* consequent measure of the general price level must also be affected by them, that is, must continue to reflect their influence even though they have been netted out at the level of the economy as a whole. Torr also brings out the important points that we must always distinguish between *measurement* and *determination*, and that some of the worst confusions in the literature on user cost, as well as on saving and investment, arise because this distinction has not been kept clearly in mind.

In the second part of the chapter, Torr points out that, although Keynes's concept of user cost (which in turn came to Keynes from Marshall) is rarely discussed explicitly, the modern work on national accounting in all the macroeconomic texts of the last fifty years or so has taken on board the essential message about the need to avoid double-counting. Unfortunately, the role of user cost in the formation and determination of individual prices and the general price level itself has not received similar treatment.[11]

BOOK III THE PROPENSITY TO CONSUME

Historically, Keynes's own discovery of the consumption function together with Richard Kahn's conception of the multiplier were crucial events in the development of Keynes's new system (see Barens 1989; Harcourt 1994a). The two together allowed him to make endogenous the process he first set out in the parable of the banana plantation in the *Treatise on Money.* The parable was inadequate because it was only through *ad hoc* exogenous events that the process of decline (or rise) in prices, profits and activity could come to an end. Making precise the notion of the Propensity to Consume schedule also allowed Keynes to clinch (or at least make plausible) the argument that investment led and saving responded in monetary production economies.[12] Finally, the consumption function was probably the most obvious hostage to fortune in the simultaneously dawning age of econometrics.

In his chapter (9), Jim Thomas mentions how relatively unscathed the consumption function emerged from the early reviews of *The General Theory* before he discusses the criticisms of two particular authors, Hans Staehle (1937, 1938, 1939) and Elizabeth Gilboy (1938a, 1938b). The former critic wanted Keynes to put more emphasis on the distribution of income (both personal and functional); the latter looked at cross-section microeconomic studies and challenged Keynes's views on the simplicity and stability of the function. Keynes's response is presented by Thomas in terms of Keynes's views on models as a way of thinking. Keynes especially emphasized the *object* of a model as the segregation of 'the semi-permanent or relatively constant factors from those which are transitory or fluctuating so as to develop a logical way of thinking about the *latter*, and of understanding the time sequences to which they give rise in particular cases' (*C.W.* XIV: 297, emphasis added). This quotation always catches readers (the present editors, anyway) by surprise because, running ahead in their own thoughts, it could be supposed that the segregation of 'the permanent or relatively constant factors' was done in order to enable the analyst to say things about *their* relationships, having set the factors and their relationships free from effects of 'those which are transitory or fluctuating', about which theoretical generalizations were by their very nature not possible. This is of course a very neo-Ricardian response. In fact, what Keynes had done was to set out simply and succinctly the method which Kalecki and Joan Robinson ultimately were to champion in their mature work. (It is not a bad description of path dependence either.)

Thomas reviews the empirical work on the consumption function in the postwar era. He concludes that Keynes would have been out of tune with postwar developments in the discipline, especially in econometrics, even though they have proved to be more robust in the face of his criticisms of Tinbergen (on investment) than Tinbergen's own early work was thought to be (on this, see Chapter 31 by Rod O'Donnell). He points out that Keynes would have welcomed the permanent income and life-cycle hypotheses, not least because he had anticipated them in his own work in *The General Theory*. Thomas also argues that it is unlikely that these two developments will dominate all others because empirical specifications of the consumption function are usually compatible with a number of alternative theories. Hence he is able to conclude that, with broad enough specification, the consumption function remains alive and kicking sixty years on from its introduction to the world in Book III. Whether its own stability and therefore the usefulness of the multiplier for the purposes of forecasting and policy are as robust is a more vexed question. It is at this juncture that Richard Goodwin's contribution is of great relevance.

Goodwin was always lucid and succinct, and his chapter (10) is vintage Goodwin. Not wasting a word, he emphasizes why Keynes's adaptation of Kahn's multiplier was suitable for a decade in which growth and technical progress were virtually absent. Nevertheless, it was a concept less rich than Kahn's – a retrogression – and, in the more dynamic setting of the post-war world, inadequate. Goodwin draws attention to the complicated overlaps of different processes which start at different times and which take different lengths of time to complete. Such overlaps are reflected in the actual levels and rates of change of output and so on at any moment of time; they interrelate with one another in most complicated ways. Goodwin sketches the difficulties which they cause for both policy-makers and econometricians. He then discusses the application of chaos theory to economic explanation, which, he argues, allows us to forgive forecasters and econometricians their past mistakes and, at the same time, make the present generation of 'economists' more modest in their aims. That is to say, they should be glad to explain and so to illuminate and should be more careful about offering policy recommendations.

What is happening on the monetary side of the economy when the multiplier is doing its thing on the real side has long puzzled students and their teachers. Victoria Chick (11) takes us systematically through this issue, emphasizing the importance of considering existing stocks as well as new flows. First, she writes as Keynes; she brings the finance motive into the argument and responds, principally, to Dennis Robertson in stoutly defending liquidity preference against loanable funds, as well as the logical theory of the multiplier. Then she takes an independent approach, not only to make explicit the achievements as well as the muddles in the original debates, but also to throw much light on the modern debates on the same issues. (A series of exchanges on the issues started with the late Tom Asimakopulos's contribution (1983b) to the Memorial Issue for Joan Robinson in the *Cambridge Journal of Economics* of 1983.) As she had already done so (in Chick 1983), Chick makes good use of Robertsonian process analysis in order to bring out what happens to investment and saving (planned, intended and actual), and to the money supply and the banking system as the multiplier process unfolds, and to challenge effectively Asimakopulos's claim that saving may, after all, sometimes help to determine investment.

BOOK IV THE INDUCEMENT TO INVEST

Just as Book V was the core of Marshall's *Principles* so many economists regard Book IV of *The General Theory*, with its chapters on investment, long-term expectation, the rate of interest, sundry observations on capital and the peculiar properties of money as the core of *The General Theory*. Over the decades since its publication, first one and then another chapter from *The General Theory* has been in fashion. At one stage we all claimed to be Chapter 12 Keynesians; at another, Chapter 17 Keynesians. Often, of course, there were overlaps of periods and thus strong disagreements. Moreover, many would argue that while Keynes certainly identified in Book IV the right ingredients for a theory of investment, the actual recipe in which he put them together was unsatisfactory. The most cogent statements of this critique are by Kalecki (1936), Joan Robinson (1964) and Asimakopulos (1971). The interesting point about two of the contributions to a 'second edition', those by Robert Eisner and Luigi Pasinetti (12, 13) respectively, is that their authors are on the whole Chapter 11 Keynesians – and make excellent fists of explaining why.

Indeed, Eisner remains an unreconstructed Keynesian as far as the theory of investment is concerned. He sets out succinctly Keynes's own theory, the critical role which the marginal efficiency of capital (actually the marginal efficiency of investment) plays; he then examines its main determinants and what government policy can best do to bring about the optimum rate of investment (at the most fundamental level, the rate which creates and absorbs full employment saving). For Eisner, a key relationship is that growth determines investment, *not* the other way about, and therefore governments should look to the creation and preservation of high levels of effective demand – and let investment follow. Such a rate of investment would tend to be socially optimal rather than being 'too much', as it may be because of the sustained use of investment subsidies when employment and output are sub-optimal.

Eisner reviews the econometric literature on Keynesian and neoclassical theories of investment and comes down on Keynes's side. (He does have some qualms about Tobin's *q* which, he feels, is good in principle but disappointing in practice, for a number of reasons which he sets out.) Eisner argues that many of Keynes's empirical hunches concerning the elasticity of investment with respect to the rate of interest and other variables have been confirmed. In particular, he argues that modern econometric evidence confirms the low elasticity of investment demand to the rate of interest that led Keynes to 'see insufficient variation in the rate of interest and insufficient response to what variation occurred to offer hope that the economy could be self-adjusting to full employment "along these lines"'. Eisner points out that business tangible investment is only a small proportion of total investment, which includes, in addition to household and public tangible investment, vast amounts of investment, public and private, in intangible capital. It follows that policies which affect these other components of investment, particularly public investment and investment in human and intangible capital, may bring about the sort of growth which in turn may help to maintain or even increase investment. These are all down-to-earth, sensible, plausible arguments which are only to be expected from a person who has always kept his eye on the ball, regardless of what the opponents were up to.

Pasinetti (13) contributes an incisive analysis of Keynes's concept of the marginal efficiency of capital (mec) and its role in the theory of investment. He takes serious note of what Keynes himself wrote about the development of the concept – the many drafts and the much clearing up of 'immense' muddles in order to create the mec. He stresses how truly revolutionary a concept it was and, therefore, how seriously illogical a mistake it was for it soon to have been identified with the marginal product of capital and the 'process' of deepening. He relates Keynes's development of the concept to his critique of the rate of interest as being determined by the interaction of saving and investment in the 'classical' theory he was attacking. He argues that Keynes made a more successful critique of the theory of the supply of saving than of the theory of the demand for investment because he was writing before Joan Robinson's and Piero Sraffa's critique of the downward-sloping relationship between 'capital', investment and the rate of interest. Perhaps Pasinetti's most telling analogy is that Keynes's theory is akin to the theory of extensive rent in Ricardo while the 'classical' theory is akin to the theory of intensive rent. Thus, the reason why more investment may be done in a given short-period situation at lower levels of the rate of interest has nothing to do with increasing capital intensity but much to do with lower expected profitability of individual projects and higher *overall* expected profitability. In a given situation, the lower is the rate of interest, the lower is the cost of borrowing and so the greater will be the number of already existing projects thought worth doing, regardless of their capital-intensity – period. Keynes's critique of the 'classical' theories of demand and supply of investment and saving may now at least be completed, he argues, by applying the reswitching and capital-reversing results.

Some commentators have expressed reservations about Pasinetti's argument. When analysing the economy as a whole, is it legitimate, when different values of the rate of interest are considered, to suppose that nothing else will be different, *except* planned levels of investment? In particular, is it legitimate to suppose that expected prices remain unaffected? The simplest answer is 'yes' – *in a given, short-period situation*, such as the one which Keynes assumed and Pasinetti accepted.

Pasinetti also has some wise things to say about the causal nature of Keynes's own analysis as opposed to the mutually determined, general equilibrium interpretations of Keynes's system that soon followed the publication of *The General Theory*. In particular, at one level of abstraction at least, and consistently with Keynes's own method that it is necessary for each purpose in hand to regard some variables as independent, others as dependent, the rate of interest may be argued to be given *before* we determine the amount of investment in a given short-period situation. The rate of interest definitely does rule the roost, and investment, thus determined, determines income and so consumption and saving. By extensive quotation from Keynes's writings, Pasinetti sweeps aside virtually all other interpretations, especially those in the textbooks, and even that associated with Abba Lerner and the distinction between the mec and the mei. Pasinetti accepts the distinction but not the neoclassical construction of 'deepening' which went with it in Lerner's interpretation.

While the themes of Chapter 12 on the state of long-term expectation permeate virtually all of the *The General Theory* and many of the chapters of our 'second edition', it is Kevin Hoover's and Peter Howitt's chapters (14, 15) which bear most directly on them and subsequent developments in the postwar years. In Chapter 12 and the 1937 *Quarterly Journal of Economics* article especially, Keynes highlighted the importance of the effects of uncertainty on systemic behaviour. He analysed how sensible people did the best they could in necessarily uncertain environments, adopting certain conventions in the process. These had the effect of securing, if not satisfactory, then at least stable conditions for much of the time. But because of the fragile nature of the conventions, if they ceased to hold then instability and crisis could quickly emerge. In addition, behaviour within capitalist institutions such as the stock exchange in his day, and in our day the markets for property and the foreign exchanges as well, could be dominated by destabilizing speculative behaviour rather than legitimate and socially beneficial 'enterprise'. As Keynes memorably put it: 'Speculators may do no harm as bubbles on a steady stream of enterprise. But the position is serious when enterprise becomes the bubble on a whirlpool of speculation' (*C.W.* VII: 159).

Against this background Hoover has written a dispassionate and balanced account of the relationship of Keynes's own economics (as well as Keynesian economics) to the rational expectations innovations, especially those associated with Lucas and Sargent. He argues that Keynes anticipated rational expectations as far as *short-term* expectations were concerned (in the sense that he thought that *short-term* expectations were usually quickly realized and so it did no harm to assume in analysis that they were *always* realized) but never thought they were applicable to the long-term expectations which are a major determinant of the process of accumulation. This distinction has been either blurred or scrapped in the writings of the rational expectations new classical macroeconomists. While they recognize the distinction between risk and uncertainty which plays a crucial role in Keynes's analysis, they, unlike Keynes, think uncertainty cannot be modelled, and so it is left out of their models – 'Apart from that, Mrs Lincoln, how did you enjoy the play?' This makes them subject to Keynes's criticism, quoted by Hoover, regarding pretty polite techniques which treat our lack of knowledge of the future as if neither it nor the future existed.

Hoover also argues that Keynes, in his critique of Tinbergen's work on investment in the late 1930s, anticipated the Lucas critique of policy associated with the lack of stability of parameters in empirical relationships – but came to quite different conclusions. For Keynes, judgement and feel allowed policy to be effective. For Lucas, there should be abdication from policy, except perhaps on rules.

As with Keynes, so with Peter Howitt: when he is persuaded that he is wrong he changes his mind (Keynes used to add to his critics: 'What do *you* do?'). Howitt's essay (15) is a splendid account of his intellectual pilgrim's progress from his contributions in the 1970s and 1980s to the literature on co-ordination failures and sunspot equilibria (which were argued to provide rigorous demonstrations of some of Keynes's conjectures) to a plea to move outside the dominant neo-Walrasian code altogether. Instead, we should learn from Keynes's insights by taking direct account of the role of conventions and rules of thumb in coping with uncertainty and expectations. Howitt comments that even Keynes did not depart from using equilibrium analysis – in fact, he used rational expectations in the short term when doing so – but *we* should. He illustrates his new point of view with examples from the analysis of Harrodian instability and dynamic adjustments, depression and inflation. With the last topic he has fascinating things to say about the roles of historical cost accounting and the convention that the long-term value of money is constant.

The issues discussed in the chapters in Book IV – Keynes's liquidity preference theory, his account and critique of the classical theory of interest, observations on the nature of capital and the peculiar and essential properties of money – provide the background for the contributions by Jan Kregel (16), Ingo Barens and Volker Caspari (17), Colin Rogers and Tom Rymes (18), Colin Rogers solo (19) and Michael Lawlor (20). Keynes often said that the relationship between the *Treatise on Money* (he should have added the *Tract* (1923) as well) and *The General Theory* was probably clearer to him than to others (see, for example, his statement in the Preface to *G.T.*: xxi–xxii). Nowhere was this more evident than in Chapter 17, where his difficult but fundamental chapter on the theory of the forward exchanges in the *Tract* is also highly relevant. In his lectures in the early 1930s on the way to *The General Theory*, Keynes came close to praising Marx for the insights contained in his concept of the circuits of capital, for recognizing that the objective of business people was to end up with more *money* at the end of the period of production than they started with at the beginning ($M' > M$; see Sardoni's chapter (36) and the comments on it below). To do so was as important for offering employment and creating production as it was for carrying out accumulation; it was also the means by which the expectations of future prices affected present actions.

According to Kregel (16), Keynes himself combined these insights with his own theory of short-period prices, which were cut loose from the conditions of production in normal conditions. Keynes analysed the latter in the *Treatise on Money* by use of his 'fundamental equations'. Citing chapters and verse and setting out detailed arguments, Kregel makes explicit the role of these ingredients, together with the definitions of user cost and the sharp distinction between the rate of interest as determined by liquidity preference, and the mec, in Keynes's analysis in Chapter 17. He lays bare Keynes's view as to *why* the peculiar properties of money may be such as to prevent full employment of labour (and capital) *even as long-period propositions.* In this way the subtle break with Keynes's former selves (despite his own view that he was naturally evolving: *C.W.* VII: xxii) and the classics, and hence the claim for a revolution in thought, are made explicit, together with Kregel's argument that Chapter 12 is not only an integral part of the book, but is as well 'the *G.T.* in a nutshell' (see n. 6).

As we have already remarked, Chapter 17 has always been something of a mystery to Keynes observers and, indeed, even to some of his closest followers and/or admirers. Barens and Caspari trace the origins of this to the different purposes which Sraffa and Keynes had in mind in their use of the concept of own rates of interest. On the one hand, Sraffa used them essentially for an internal critique of Hayek's theoretical analysis in *Prices and Production* (1931). Keynes, on the other hand, used them as essential ingredients of a theory of the rate of interest, the essential properties of money, and the role of the money rate of interest as the ultimate barrier to attaining full employment in a world *characterized by an environment of uncertainty and missing markets.* Our authors argue that Keynes failed in this regard because own rates of interest are redundant concepts once we have spot and future (or forward) prices in the analysis, which Keynes clearly had. But, they argue, Keynes's central argument about money's role in causing unemployment does not have to be discarded just because own rates are a cul-de-sac rather than a detour.

Colin Rogers and Tom Rymes (18) have written a thoughtful account of the relationship of Keynes's arguments in Chapter 17 to recent attempts to argue that the disappearance of cash in the modern world restores the classical dichotomy and the applicability of the workings of a barter world (with an auctioneer) to the happenings of the contemporary world. Rogers and Rymes show that it is not necessary to have an *actual* commodity money in order to have a monetary economy – that money is a *convention* which is related to the fact that intertemporal decisions *have* to be made in an uncertain environment. (Rogers emphasizes this in his chapter 19 too.) There is therefore always both a need for liquidity and the inescapable fact that the resting place (*if* there is one) of a monetary production economy will always have some different determinants, and therefore different values of the relevant economic variables, than a barter world without money.

They make their argument through a reworking of Keynes–Sraffa own-rates analysis and show that liquidity and the liquidity preference function are respectively an essential variable and an essential relationship in any model, no matter how abstract, that purports to illuminate the workings of a modern economy. They argue that Keynes had already sensed this in the *Tract*, developed it much further in the *Treatise on Money* and brought it to fruition in *The General Theory*, especially in Chapter 17. Rogers and Rymes extend Keynes's analysis in the *Treatise on Money* and the concepts of own rates of interest to banking theory. They argue that the existence and conventional policies of central banks always have effects on the outputs of banks which in turn affect the output and prices in monetary economies, even in economies in which there is no fiat monetary base. They suggest on the evidence of the *Tract* that Keynes *may* have preceded Sraffa, who made explicit the own-rates analysis when he tore into Hayek in 1932, even though in Chapter 17 Keynes acknowledged Sraffa as his source for the concept. We suggest that reading the English translation of Sraffa's 1920 undergraduate dissertation (Wendy Harcourt and Sardoni 1993) could push the argument about who was first back even further![13]

Neither Joan Robinson nor Richard Kahn was happy with the arguments of Chapter 17, not least because of its long-period context and content. Increasingly over the years they were to resist the long-period interpretation of *The General Theory*. Colin Rogers (19) therefore has done us a great service by setting out, as succinctly and clearly as is to be found in the literature, the ingredients of the analysis of *long-period* under-employment equilibrium in Keynes's thought. To do this he has drawn on the work of those Keynesians who have argued for the long-period interpretation of *The General Theory*, who have stressed the role of conventions as a response to an inescapable environment of uncertainty and who, for example, the late Tom Asimakopulos (1991), have spelt out the essential Marshallian, not Walrasian, nature of Keynes's analysis in *The General Theory*: crucially, that static analysis at a high level of abstraction *necessarily* precedes dynamic analysis and that uncertainty is not a bar to determinate analysis at *this* level of abstraction.

The starting point is the claim by Harrod in his contribution to the Seymour Harris collection (1947) and in his life (1951) of Keynes (and Harrod) that the central contribution of *The General Theory* is the liquidity theory of the rate of interest and especially the notion of a 'normal' rate of interest. The latter may for decades be too high to allow full employment to be sustained, so setting an underlying level around which actual activity fluctuates with its accompanying, never disappearing, involuntary unemployment. Rogers finds this argument attractive, for he argues, correctly, that Say's Law and the Quantity Theory of Money *are* long-period propositions set at a higher level of abstraction than analysis of the trade cycle. Therefore, in order to show that classical theory is a special case of a general theory, Keynes had to set out his system at the same level of abstraction and for the long period too.

Rogers gives a careful exposition of Marshall's methods and of Keynes's description of them and of how to use them in the analysis of *The General Theory*. He then proceeds, again via modern work on the use of conventions as the means to handle inescapable uncertainty, a means which, as we have seen, sometimes works but which sometimes because of their fragility is the cause of crisis, to a Marshallian analysis of the determination of the point of effective demand in the long period. This requires identifying a long-period aggregate supply function (one with normal profits as a component of the proceeds needed to justify the various levels of employment), a long-period aggregate demand function, and their intersection. One of the determining variables is the 'normal' rate of interest, which is itself related to an assumption of *given* long-term expectations and the analysis of Chapter 17. Having thus established existence, Rogers sketches in stability in terms of sticky money-wages and inelastic expectations.

BOOK V MONEY-WAGES AND PRICES

In the first edition, Keynes concluded Book IV by summarizing his findings to date and restating his theory. Then, in Book V, 'Money-Wages and Prices', he dropped his provisional assumption of a given money-wage in order to argue in Chapter 19 that the consequences of *changes* in money-wages (he did not think that economic theory as such could ever say anything systematic or general about their *causes*) made no essential difference to his arguments or findings. He tried to establish this by asking what effect a fall (usually) in money-wages could be expected to have on the principal relations of the system – the consumption and investment functions, the liquidity preference function and the aggregate supply function.

The analysis was a verbal account of various feedback mechanisms on to the underlying relationships. It was an application of the most complicated of the three models of reality which Kregel (1976) discerned in *The General Theory* and related writings, the model of shifting equilibrium.[14] In the light of Chapter 19 and his explicit statements about his attitude to money-wages, it must never cease to amaze that so many subsequent commentators thought that Keynes's system was crucially dependent on the assumption of constant money-wages, that this was to Keynes what many commentators thought a constant capital–output ratio was to Harrod – and they were wrong on Harrod too (see, for example, Eisner 1958). That is not to say that Keynes's own arguments were entirely satisfactory, nor that there was not practical sense in a search for systemic stability to exploit any tendency in the system towards stickiness in money-wages so that a rise in real wages and the maintenance of high levels of employment could be achieved. Arthur Brown and Brian Reddaway have eminently sensible remarks to make on these themes in their chapters (26, 27); and, in his chapter (1), John Brothwell suggests that Keynes could have emphasized that his theory explained unemployment to be the result of a lack of aggregate demand (rather than money-wage rigidity) by including a preliminary discussion of the effects of changes in money-wages in the opening chapters of the second edition.

In *The General Theory* itself, Chapter 19 on changes in money-wages is followed by the rather obscure Chapter 20 on the employment function, where Keynes makes a tentative attempt to tackle aggregation problems when we consider different levels of aggregate demand. Chapter 21 is on 'The Theory of Prices'. Having scrapped the Quantity Theory Keynes, needing a theory of the general price level, transformed Marshall's short-period theory of prices in competitive industries into an economy-wide theory; he explained in the process what he now thought was the appropriate division (or divisions) of economic theory to replace the classical dichotomy (*C.W.* VII: 293–4). In both suggested divisions, uncertainty and the role and function of money were the key determinants.

It is still something of a mystery why Keynes ignored the development of the theories of imperfect competition in his explanation of prices, for he was familiar with Kahn's pioneering work in his fellowship dissertation for King's (1929), Joan Robinson's 1933 book and probably Gerald Shove's views. This issue has been extensively discussed recently in the literature (see, for example, Darity 1985; Harcourt 1987a; Kregel 1985b; and Marris 1992). Here we refer readers to Robin Marris's chapter (4), which provides a most detailed and cogent argument as to how we should proceed now in a second edition directed towards contemporary problems and their explanation.[15]

Michael Lawlor (20) has given sterling service to the volume through his examination of the fundamental theoretical issues associated with the differences, as Keynes saw them, between the classical, then neoclassical, theory of the rate of interest and his own theory. First, writing as J.M. Keynes, Lawlor rewrites the original Chapter 14, 'The Classical Theory of the Rate of Interest', in order to incorporate Keynes's subsequent writings on the rate of interest up to 1939. An implication of the revision is to make Chapter 14 into Chapter 18,[16] so as to allow the arguments on the essential properties of money and own rates of interest in the original Chapter 17 to be included. What comes out clearly is Keynes's insistence that only his theory can take in the implications of behaviour in an uncertain environment, that is, in the world as we know it, and its relevance for systemic behaviour, especially the possibility of sustained lapses from full employment. His objection to the alternative theories is that they are a hybrid of the classical theory of a barter economy and the disequilibrium analysis of transitional states between equilibria.

Lawlor then reviews in more detail the nature of Keynes's reply to his critics and the sources of his interpretation of the classical theory. He argues that Marshall is the real culprit, Marshall of his writings and lectures outside the *Principles*, despite the fact that Keynes only quoted from the *Principles* in *The General Theory* itself. Lawlor argues that Keynes neglected Irving Fisher's great contributions (especially his emphasis on the real factors of productivity and thrift as the principal determinants of the rate of interest, and on the real nature of interest), having persuaded himself that they were 'all in Marshall' anyway. Perhaps Keynes was here a victim of his extraordinary powers of identifying what the assumptions must be for a viewpoint to be valid? He then imposed them on Marshall, having learnt them from him in the first place. Whatever the reasons, while it reflects poorly on Keynes as an historian of thought, it also serves to show anew what a deep and penetratingly original theorist Keynes was, and how great was his grasp of the workings of the entire system.

VI SHORT NOTES SIXTY YEARS ON

In the last book of the first edition Keynes ranged far and wide through his 'short notes'. Here we take up specifically the trade cycle (Marc Jarsulic, 21), underconsumption (John King, 22) and social philosophy (John Cornwall, 23 and Robert Skidelsky, 24). In his chapter (21), Jarsulic describes the characteristics of Keynes's theory of the trade cycle in Chapter 22 of *The General Theory*. He compares them more than favourably with those of modern theories of real business cycles. (The latter date back at least to the writings of Keynes's greatest chum in the 1920s, D.H. Robertson, as Charles Goodhart made eloquently clear in his 1990 paper celebrating the centenary of Robertson's birth.)

After setting out Keynes's arguments, and especially his explanations of turning points, Jarsulic moves to the modern age through Goodwin's contributions in particular: he asks what the modern theories of non-linear systems and chaotic behaviour have to offer as a way forward to explain the cycle and capture in a more formal manner most of Keynes's insights.

What strikes the editors of this volume is the small to zero part played by technical progress and innovations in Keynes's story and those of most of his successors. Within this constraint Jarsulic tells a clear and lucid story, directing us to deeper explanations and suitable policy measures. Simultaneously, he reveals the basic shallowness of the structure of real business cycle theory; in particular, its failure to tell any *economic* story about the origin of cyclical fluctuations in changes in productivity and other key variables in its account of the cycle.

John Cornwall (23) eagerly took on the tasks of writing about the nature of the trade cycle and of the social philosophy which a second edition of *The General Theory* might supply. He provides a masterly account of the underlying conditions and of the institutions which made possible the Golden Age of Capitalism and Keynesianism in the post-war world. He identifies the cumulative changes that brought them to their end, as well as the immediate shocks that were also responsible. He names two types of labour market and the corresponding wage-setting institutions – adversarial, decentralized go-it-alone markets and socially conscious, relatively co-operative ones. During the Golden Age the first set currently was associated with the worse record of inflation and unemployment.

Cornwall also points to the value of the fixed exchange rate system of the Bretton Woods era. It served to reinforce employer and employee discipline regarding the setting of *money*-wages, thus helping to allow full employment, healthy rates of growth of economies and satisfactory increases in *real* wages. The disappearance of fixed exchange rates and of controls over capital movements (the maintenance of both of which is needed to keep speculation in bounds) have played a key role in the creation of what Cornwall identifies as the high unemployment equilibrium traps of many advanced countries of the last twenty years or more.

To overcome rising unemployment levels and control inflation requires co-ordination as far as fiscal and monetary policies are concerned and labour market institutions which reproduce the results of the socially co-operative regimes of the Golden Age. (It may be thought that so much damage has been done to the social and industrial relations fabric in some countries, such as the United Kingdom, that we may never get back to or be able to create appropriate labour market institutions. By upsetting pragmatic equilibria in the first place any prospect of returning to them may have been destroyed.) We also need international schemes to curb the destabilizing effects of the massive speculation associated with the deregulation of financial markets. As Cornwall says, we can only hope – the difficulties are enormous and the consequences of failure for social cohesion and reasonable life-styles for ordinary men and women are even worse.

When John King (23) rewrites as Keynes the chapter on mercantilism *et al.*, he makes Keynes much more generous than formerly to Marx and Hobson. Moreover, King very sensibly integrates the 'lost pages' found in the laundry basket at Tilton (see *C.W.* XXIX) on the co-operative, neutral and entrepreneur economies, into this section. He relates them to Marx's distinction between C−M−C′ and M − C − M′ and to how the latter sequence is the better description of the processes at work in modern capitalism. Lorie Tarshis for one had always been puzzled by the omission of the co-operative, neutral and entrepreneur economy models from the first edition. He thought they provided a much better vehicle for the explanation of the central issue of Keynes's book than his ultimately incoherent argument (in *G.T.* 25–6) that the highest Say's Law position was reached by competition between entrepreneurs.

As an interesting connection to the coming discussions by John Coates (35), John Davis (33), Bill Gerrard (32), Rod O'Donnell (31) and Jochen Runde (34) on method in *The General Theory* and in Keynes's writings generally, King refers to Harrod's and Joan Robinson's comments on the method of common sense which Keynes discovered in Malthus and others but to which Ricardo and other classicals were 'blind'. Joan Robinson was as usual more supportive than Harrod who, while he admitted the justice of the emphasis, was nevertheless reluctant to give the older pioneers any more credit than that.

Next, King does us all a service by setting out the history of underconsumption theory since 1936, starting with Otto Bauer, who was publishing at the time when Keynes was finishing *The General Theory*, and ending with the writings of Paul Baran and Paul Sweezy and of Josef Steindl. In the process he rehabilitates poor J.A. Hobson and points out that Baran's *Political Economy of Growth* (1957) was as important a contribution for the developing countries as Baran and Sweezy's *Monopoly Capital* (1966) was for modern capitalism. He shows the relationship of underconsumption to the issues tackled by Harrod (who was unsympathetic to the pioneers of underconsumption) and Domar (who recognized and was pleasant about their contributions).[17]

Following up Joan Robinson's learning curve on Marx, from her 1936 review of Strachey (1935) to her 1942 *Essay* and beyond, King argues that underconsumption theory played a vital and sensible part in Marx's theory of crisis. Finally, he recognizes the role of the profit squeeze associated with the writings of Andrew Glyn and Robert Sutcliffe in the United Kingdom, the French Regulation school, and Tom Weisskopf and others in the USA.

Finally, Robert Skidelsky (24), as befits the eminent author of the ongoing outstanding biography of Keynes, writes as though he were Keynes, looking back (from beyond the grave) at the concluding chapter of *The General Theory* in the light of both wrong interpretations and subsequent events. Inequality, the saturation of wants, the abundance of capital, the euthanasia of the rentier, the 'comprehensive socialisation of investment', state socialism and the benefits of the market mechanism – all these topics are commented upon from this vantage point. He also has Keynes critical of the excessive expansion of the welfare state, especially in the form of state consumption and transfer payments, because it serves to retard the fall in the rate of interest. Skidelsky even has Keynes making common cause with the themes of his natural opponents, the modern proponents of public-choice theory – natural opponents because their central thesis involves the denial that policy-makers ever accepted 'the presuppositions of Harvey Road'.

AN OVERVIEW: JAMES TOBIN

From the start of his undergraduate studies at Harvard, James Tobin has been an ardent Keynesian (see Harcourt 1984: 495). In his chapter (25) at the start of volume 2 he sums up a lifetime of reflecting on the messages of *The General Theory* and presents his considered judgements, many of them, of course, based on his own outstanding contributions to the development of Keynesian economics.

First, in the guise of John Maynard Keynes, he amends the original definition in Chapter 2 of involuntary unemployment in order to make it more simple, operational – and convincing. Otherwise, as both Keynes *and* himself, he remains unrepentant. Demand deficiencies rather than supply constraints bite most of the time in capitalist economies. Policy can do something about this without having radically to change either institutions or political systems. Money is integrated in the workings of the system as a whole; it is *not* a veil. Price and wage flexibility are beside the point theoretically as far as determining the levels of activity and unemployment are concerned, though there is much to be said for relative money-wage stability if we want a stable economy overall. Wage-earners do not, and do not have to, 'suffer' from money illusion to make Keynes's system 'work': their behaviour is perfectly consistent with sensible behaviour, with the balancing of pros and cons, so that it is sensible for wage-earners to resist cuts in money-wages in order to protect relative positions but not to go in for industrial unrest every time the prices of wage goods rise a little.

When we come to the mid-1990s and Tobin writes as Tobin, he argues that we have to come to grips with what we mean by equilibrium when there is unemployment. He tells us that he prefers to use the phrase 'rest state' because, clearly, the labour market is *not* clearing at the given price if, as is usually the case, there is involuntary unemployment present. He then tackles head-on the disequilibrium interpretation of Keynes. Keynesian rest states are centres of gravitation for short-period flow equilibria, given inherited stocks of capital goods, labour supplies and technical knowledge. But clearly all these change over time, some from the very attainment of short-period flow equilibrium. So we must consider the characteristics of the next period's centre of gravitation, taking into account what has happened in the previous period(s) and the implications for stocks, short- *and* long-term expectations and so on, for this period. It is an open question whether, either in fact or in theory, the disequilibrium dynamics so released will produce a succession of short-period equilibria which, left to themselves, will converge on a long-period, full stock and flow equilibrium. Tobin, like Keynes, is not sure that this is a very interesting or relevant question anyway.

SPECIFIC EXTENSIONS AND/OR MODIFICATIONS

Inflation

Though it is wrong to regard *The General Theory* as the economics of depression, it is true that its emphasis is largely on the causes of unemployment. These are systematically analysed in the book whereas the problem of inflation is mostly treated in brilliant bursts and asides. Brian Reddaway was Keynes's pupil when Keynes was writing and lecturing on the themes which became *The General Theory*. Reddaway wrote one of the most perceptive reviews of Keynes's book (Reddaway 1936). (He even 'invented' IS–LM: see the argument and the four equations on pp. 34–35, although he did not set out the argument in that form. His exposition is marked by an acute sense of the limitations of the four equations (and by implication of IS–LM) as well as their ability to give us an initial grip on Keynes's system.) Like Keynes, Reddaway is interested in theory only in so far as it bears on policy; he has, moreover, a very real sense of the complexities which characterize modern economies and the modest claims that can be made for theory in illuminating them.

In his chapter (26), 'The Changing Significance of Inflation', he expresses surprise that Keynes did not include 'Prices' in the title of his book. Though Reddaway acknowledges the presence of Chapter 21, he feels that it is not well integrated with the system of the rest of the book.

This he regards as a limitation when thinking about the post-war period in which prices have been rising 'for ever' as, thirty years ago, he himself predicted (in Reddaway 1966). Reddaway discusses how the analysis would be improved, the emphasis changed, if we take in prices and their changes as well as the determination of employment. In doing so he exhibits his robust common sense, criticizing the disgrace of incurring social and economic costs by aiming for zero inflation when there is no evidence *at all* that this is good either for employment or for growth. He explains how institutions and practices have steadily changed to take into account that we now live in inflationary times. He suggests that it is better to accept this and adjust our expectations as well as our policies accordingly, instead of permanently reducing our rates of growth (and bringing back persistent, unacceptable levels of unemployment) by chasing an imaginary will-o'-the-wisp of zero inflation.

Arthur Brown's chapter (29), 'The Inflationary Dimension', is an ideal complement to Reddaway's. Brown understands the theory of inflation and knows its history as well as anyone in the profession. He has written a masterly account of Keynes's views over his lifetime on inflation and its causes. He uses this and his own acute insights to illuminate especially the history of the post-war period, what might have been different, and what policies we needed then and still need now.

Brown shows how in *The Economic Consequences of the Peace* (1919), the *Tract* (1923) and the *Treatise on Money* (1930a, 1930b) Keynes was well ahead of his time in his understanding of the process of inflation. Especially does Brown stress – so did Richard Kahn – the cost-push, demand-pull distinction in the *Treatise on Money.* He also points out that, while Keynes was usually situation-specific in analysis and especially in his policy recommendations, he was essentially a stable prices person right up to the end of his life.

Brown discusses *How to Pay for the War* (1940b) and suggests that its lucid analysis would have been included by Keynes in any revision of Chapter 21 for a second edition. He puts to rest the canard that Keynes made a watertight distinction between rises in the general price level prior to full employment and those associated with full employment.[18] Rather Keynes recognized situations associated with more and more bottlenecks as activity became higher and higher in the short run.

Brown shows that Keynes also had the Phillips curve in an ordinal form (its only defensible form, we would argue), both as $\dot{p}$ and u, and $\dot{p}$ *and* $\dot{u}$. He gives an important role to Keynes's and to his own views on buffer stocks and primary commodity prices and output. Buffer stocks would have been of value, though probably they would not have been completely successful, in helping economies cope with the two oil price rise shocks.

Brown reminds us of the modest levels of statistical unemployment which Keynes thought would have been associated with zero involuntary unemployment. He wonders whether the Golden Age might not have been even more Golden had it been run at Keynes's levels. The great imponderable, of course, is what would have happened to 'animal spirits' in the otherwise situation. Finally, Brown reminds us that in his own researches, money had been treated as more endogenous than Keynes had it in *The General Theory* and that, still, the money-wage bargain is the vital variable to influence in order to attain and sustain full employment and steady, satisfactory growth with modest to no inflation.

Endogenous money

Sheila Dow (28) tackles the crucial issue of endogeneity of the money supply and why Keynes seemingly chose to make it exogenous in *The General Theory*, especially as in most of his other writings before and after *The General Theory* he was closer to a position associated with the money supply being endogenous. She makes the vital point that there is a difference between taking a particular variable as given for a specific purpose, on the one hand, and regarding it as truly exogenous to the economic system overall, on the other. The former, she argues, was Keynes's stance in *The General Theory*. In her own analysis she gives a very subtle interpretation of Keynes's procedure and of where the money supply, which he takes as given in the analysis of *The General Theory*, actually comes from. Another theme she emphasizes, drawing on recent work by Victoria Chick, is the various phases that have occurred in the evolution of modern monetary systems before and after the writing of *The General Theory*. The latter phases have made it more difficult to follow Keynes's procedure in *The General Theory* but have not, in her judgement, destroyed the value of the liquidity preference approach, nor opened the door for the loanable funds approach to enter and take over again. She outlines a rich modern analysis under the Post-Keynesian rubric (or one sub-division of it), which allows the modern phenomena of liability management, non-bank financial intermediaries and the internationalization of financial services to be tackled within the liquidity preference framework. Neither a horizontalist nor a verticalist be, but leave a place for credit-rationing associated with different estimations of risk as between borrowers and lenders, a Keynesian idea developed especially by Minsky. She also advocates including an analysis of the constraints on what value the rate of interest might take, given the ever-widening influence of international financial markets and trade blocs. And she highlights a distinction Keynes had already made in the *Treatise on Money*: that between the behaviour of the banking system as such and the corresponding role of the monetary authorities. This leads her to consider the nature of the liquidity preference of the *banks* as well as that of the public. Here, her discussion joins up with that of Rogers and Rymes in their chapter (18).

Her arguments are a justification for her conclusion that as long as the supply of credit is not fully demand-determined, Keynes's monetary theory retains its essential liquidity preference characteristics. For changes in interest rate expectations and in confidence concerning the predictions of these changes to lead to changes in real behaviour requires only that the money supply is constrained to some degree.

Finance and investment

As we mentioned earlier, a chap called Clinton robbed us of Stiglitz's proposed chapter on credit-rationing which was to complement Sheila Dow's chapter. We are fortunate that a pioneer in this area, Myron Gordon, has written a chapter (29) which ably fills in the gaping hole that otherwise would have been left. Starting his working life well within the orthodox Massachusetts Institute of Technology fold, Gordon soon departed. He wrote a string of articles which began with one of the earliest critiques of the Modigliani–Miller theorem. Their principal objective was to demonstrate the inadequacy of the neoclassical theory of finance and investment at the microeconomic level. Now in his eighth decade, he has written a book (Gordon 1994) that develops an alternative, Keynesian theory, explores some of the macroeconomic implications of the theory and contains the most complete statement of the critique of the neoclassical theory of finance and investment.

The central role of investment in Keynesian theory gave rise to a considerable body of research on what firms actually do. It was found that financial considerations such as internal funds, capital structure objectives, and non-price credit rationing by banks are more important than the interest rate in a firm's investment decision. Gordon's chapter shows how these financial considerations are captured in a theory of investment that recognizes the concern for long-run survival.

Gordon's chapter takes up themes which figure prominently in Keynes's own writings: the finance motive for holding money in the process of accumulation; borrowers' and lenders' risk; and the destabilizing effects of bankruptcy associated with financial structures and deflations. Gordon outlines a dynamic theory of accumulation and its finance which would have gladdened Keynes's heart – not least because in the last sections he paints on a very broad canvas indeed in the manner of Keynes in the later chapters of *The General Theory* and also that of Marx.

Keynes and the open economy

Though most of the analysis of *The General Theory* was concerned with a closed economy, Keynes usually wrote about open economies and international institutions and policy, albeit often with an eye to the interests of the United Kingdom. Paul Davidson's chapter (30) is concerned with the essential features of Keynes's analysis when applied to the world economy, and with the natural set of institutions and policies which flow from it. He starts by contrasting the experiences of inflation, unemployment and growth of, first, the Gold Standard period and, secondly, the post-Bretton Woods, deregulated foreign exchange rates period, on the one hand, with, on the other, the corresponding experiences in the Golden Age of capitalism when Bretton Woods institutions, combined with individual governments' commitments to full employment, prevailed.

Sensing that the political time is not yet ripe for the world economy to have either an international mechanism whereby to finance international trade and capital movements or a World Central Bank, Davidson designs a half-way house instead. The main features are institutional pressures which would serve to make creditor nations behave in a socially responsible manner at a world level, a 'currency' between central banks to provide liquidity and the creation of an environment wherein all countries can aim for full employment without running into external constraints. The overall aim is to reduce the contractionary bias in the world's operations without running into inflationary pressures which spread world-wide. This will allow the economies of the world to advance steadily with each allowing the others 'free lunches'. It is a scheme fittingly in the spirit of Keynes, and only the dark forces of ignorance and self-interested greed stand in the way of discussion of its principles and details – and its implementation. Now read on.

METHOD AND PHILOSOPHY

Over the last fifteen to twenty years or so there has been a welcome development whereby the link between Keynes's contributions to philosophy and his economics has been systematically examined and his views on method within a discipline such as economics have been reappraised. We call this welcome because the researches involved have revealed both a complex and a rewarding story about Keynes's views and achievements and how modern economics may be pursued more satisfactorily and productively. We are fortunate to have chapters by some of the leading pioneers in these endeavours: John Coates, John Davis, Bill Gerrard, Rod O'Donnell and Jochen Runde. We make no apology for having a number of chapters on these themes for we regard these recent developments as not only amongst the most exciting in Keynes scholarship but also as, perhaps, not as well known within the profession as they ought to be. Certainly they are not as well known as some of the other developments represented in this volume.

We start with Rod O'Donnell's contribution (31), not only because he is one of the pioneers, whose 1989 book (which grew out of his 1982 Cambridge PhD dissertation) has been acclaimed, but also because he puts to rest some of the silliest canards in the conventional wisdom concerning Keynes's attitudes to mathematics and econometrics. O'Donnell draws on his vast knowledge of the Keynes papers in order to set out Keynes's views on the use of mathematics and econometrics in our discipline. They make very sensible reading. Keynes was not in general a zealot, and though we might disagree with some of his particular judgements, such as his opinion of Marschak, his stance was both balanced and highly sophisticated. Mathematics and econometric techniques were indispensable and valuable within their own domains in economics, but misleading and dangerous outside them. Discussing logically whether the conditions which allowed their application to particular issues were present was an inescapable responsibility of the economist. Economic reasoning embraces them both – and more, for it takes in cardinal, ordinal and non-measurable concepts. Economic reasoning can by its very nature present only a sample of the full mode of thought of economists. Mathematics is helpful when used appropriately to make intelligible those samples which are presented. Especially illuminating is O'Donnell's discussion of Keynes's views on an actual use of mathematics in *The General Theory* itself. This is contained in a perceptive account of Keynes's mode of theorizing both generally and, especially, in *The General Theory*. At the close of the chapter O'Donnell outlines the modifications which his arguments suggest for the mode of exposition in a 'second edition' of *The General Theory*.

O'Donnell argues that Keynes did not have a sudden, late change of mind on the value of econometrics (as Richard Stone argued), but was always consistent in his views. He disliked inappropriate specific applications, not mathematics and econometrics as such. What could be fairer than that? From O'Donnell's account of the richness and variety of Keynes's own method and thinking on economic issues there is much that we ought to learn, especially today, when formal methods tend completely to dominate, so impoverishing our discipline and deepening its crisis. The rest of the chapters in this section are concerned with aspects of this general lesson.

Gerrard has written a thoughtful chapter (32) which is based on his sustained reading over the years of Keynes's writings, and especially of *The General Theory*, concerning Keynes's methodology. He examines the various meanings which Keynes attached to 'general' in the analysis of *The General Theory* and how they are associated with a break from previous methods. He highlights what recent commentators on Keynes have rather overlooked: Keynes's preoccupation with finding out what exactly were the assumptions, implicit, explicit or tacit, that supported theories and whether they were appropriate. In particular, can they be traced back to recognizable real world phenomena and situations? Though Keynes's own practice was often intuitive, reaching conclusions before the details of the argument were fully set out, or even sketched or known, his whole structure of thought demanded a clear, explicit, coherent chain which ran from appropriate assumptions to defensible conclusions. Gerrard analyses the details of Keynes's method and the changes it heralds when set in this particular context.

John Davis (33) takes up a theme which has become more prominent in recent years and which we have already mentioned in this introduction: the role of conventions in Keynes's thought and analysis, especially the role that conventions play in his analysis of the behaviour of stock exchanges and of the liquidity preference function in the determination of the rate of interest. Davis allies this discussion with his own researches on Keynes's changing philosophical views following Frank Ramsey's criticism of Keynes's understanding of intuition. Central to Davis's argument is the section in Chapter 12 of *The General Theory* on the analogy between the beauty contest and the determination of prices on the stock exchange. Conventions in this context are seen as interactive, as is confidence, individual and collective. An important point is that while we adopt the convention that the future will be like the present unless there are compelling reasons for expecting a change, this very proviso tends to make individuals concentrate on change, and so makes the convention itself more likely to be precarious. Nevertheless, Davis does not consider that Keynes thought reliance on conventions was irrational; rather, it was an example of sensible people doing the best they could in an environment of inescapable uncertainty.

Finally, Davis speculates that the interactive processes which serve to bring about conventions and determine confidence at a social level have contacts with Wittgenstein's later philosophy which emphasized the importance of language games. In the latter, overlaps of meaning were never the same for different people, yet communication and recognition were possible.[19] In his chapter in this volume, John Coates makes a similar point when he suggests that Keynes's ideas could be developed through the use of fuzzy set logic and analysis.

Jochen Runde has written a finely tuned chapter (34) in which he takes Chapter 12 of the *The General Theory* as the subject matter for a discussion of the relationship between Keynes's views on probability and uncertainty, rational behaviour in an uncertain environment, and his concept of economic theory (as contrasted with the dominant axiomatic theorizing of mainstream theorists). Runde examines Keynes's mode of theorizing within this chapter, which Keynes told Gerald Shove was concerned with matters the analysis of which were outside the realm of the 'formally exact' (see *C.W.* XIV: 2). Runde then relates the discussion to the approaches and contributions of two influential Post-Keynesians, the late G.L.S. Shackle and Tony Lawson, who have taken Chapter 12 and the theorizing therein as starting points for their critiques of orthodox economic theory and the positivist outlook that usually accompanies it.

Runde singles out Robert Lucas as a prominent example of a modern economist who combines the axiomatic method with the positivist methodology, and who believes that explanation and prediction are both possible through the use of toy models which are built on the basis of observed empirical regularities. Runde also mentions the more reflective views of Frank Hahn, who wonders whether empirical regularities or 'laws' will ever be found in economics. Hahn does not think prediction is possible or, at least, likely, but does think that economic theory may explain, if only by giving us a reference point (for example, the Arrow–Debreu general equilibrium model) from which to jump off in order to get back to the real world and its falls from grace.

Runde then examines Shackle's somewhat nihilistic views, especially on policy but also on explanation, and Lawson's more optimistic but complex views. Lawson draws on Roy Bhaskar's writings. Runde explains how this leads to a mutual interrelationship between societal structures and individual behaviour with each moulding and changing the other in a situation-specific manner. He concludes that Chapter 12, with its brilliant analysis of the role and the workings of the stock exchange, of confidence, expectations and conventions, is a fine example of what Lawson has in mind.

John Coates (35) draws on his profound researches into the relationship between Keynes and the Cambridge philosophers, especially Wittgenstein, and what he has dubbed 'ordinary language economics'. He discerns in Keynes's philosophy at the time of the writing of *The General Theory* an anticipation of the modern work on fuzzy logic and fuzzy sets. Coates conjectures that these recent developments may allow a bridge to be erected between the complex, multi-dimensional yet often vague concepts of economics and the powerful analytical procedures of mathematics. Fuzzy sets evidently allow us to handle in a precise analytical manner vague concepts such as 'baldness'. This is written about with feeling by both editors of the present volume, who appreciate the notion of membership or non-membership of a category which is gradual rather than abrupt.

Keynes sensed the conflict between precision and relevance due to the omission of crucial factors which was often associated with the former. Keynes also sensed what the recent developments allow. Furthermore, he understood the rich and widely ranging fund of common knowledge on which economists, by using ordinary language as much as possible, could draw. Coates's chapter is both informative about the past and a foretaste of the promise contained in future developments.[20]

Keynes and Marx

In 1987 Claudio Sardoni published a fine book on Marx's and Keynes's theories of effective demand and crisis. It was based on thorough research into what the two authors actually wrote. Reading his account, it could quickly be realized that after allowing for differences in terminology and attitudes to the survival of the capitalist system and its accompanying institutions as such, whenever these two great analysts of capitalism tackled the same questions, they came up with broadly the same answers. Yet it is known that Keynes had a very low opinion of Marx, calling him 'a very poor thinker indeed' (J.M.K. to Joan Robinson, August 1942). We think that this tells us more about Keynes than Marx and Sardoni's chapter (36) in this volume confirms our view.

Sardoni does not think that Keynes would have changed his opinion of Marx, despite Joan Robinson's attempts to make him see that coming at Keynes's puzzles through Marx's approach was a more rewarding way to tackle them. Sardoni shows how, initially, as Keynes moved towards *The General Theory* he found Marx's emphasis on the circuits of capital and the fact that entrepreneurs want to make money profits rather than produce commodities as such were the clues both to understanding how capitalism works (well and poorly) and to the critique of 'classical' economics, especially of Say's Law. These arguments were contained in the sections on the co-operative, neutral and entrepreneur economies which, as we have seen, did not make it to the published version of *The General Theory*.

Why? Because, by the time the final drafts were being written, Keynes was attacking the marginalist version of Say's Law. The latter implied the full employment of labour, and not only of capital as Ricardo and the other classical economists had it and which Marx attacked. In doing so Keynes unfortunately reduced the emphasis on the key role that capitalists played as he discussed the labour market and the role of the rate of interest in a system with exogenous money. After *The General Theory* was published Keynes brought again to the foreground the role of the banks and emphasized the effects of uncertainty on entrepreneurial behaviour. This allowed his and Marx's insight that the capitalists' ability to hoard was the clue to the emergence of overproduction and crisis. Thus, though Keynes may never have revised his opinion of Marx as such, he may have restored some of his emphasis, suggesting that Keynes's birth in the year that Marx died provided a seamless weave of profound economic sense. All those economists born in 1946 therefore ought to look to their laurels, for they have a great tradition to join!

Keynes and Schumpeter – and beyond

Joseph Schumpeter was fond of Keynes but jealous of him as an intellectual rival. In a fascinating chapter (37) on 'Keynes, Schumpeter and Beyond – a Non-reductionist Approach', Alessandro Vercelli argues that, properly understood in the light of modern developments in approaches to dynamic theory and methodology, the contributions of these two great economists may be regarded as illuminating complements to one another – as befits the contributions of two people born in the year that Marx died. In *The General*

Theory, Keynes neglected those matters closest to Schumpeter's heart, the classical problems of accumulation, growth and distribution, in order to concentrate on uncertainty, on the financial and real crises which arose out of the basic structure of monetary production systems, and on the usually unsatisfactory nature of the system's immediate rest states. Schumpeter, in turn, neglected (indeed, never really understood) Keynes's contributions. Instead, he developed his theories of longer-term development associated with the interplay of financial provisions and the innovating entrepreneurs' role of embodying new methods in production processes through the resulting accumulation.

Vercelli reviews the developments over the centuries in dynamic theories of many disciplines (including economics), showing how pre-classical views gave way to classical dynamics, which in turn was superseded by more general theories which could absorb it as a special case. He writes that Keynes's economics in *The General Theory* followed a similar path of generalization with regard to what Keynes dubbed classical theory, as did Schumpeter's economics with regard to Walras's general equilibrium system. Following an incisive critical review of the approaches and methods of different schools of modern macroeconomics, Vercelli suggests that the terrible economic and social problems of the modern world, both current and to come, would best be tackled by applying modern technical dynamic methods to aspects of the complementary contributions of Keynes and Schumpeter.

Keynes, Kalecki and *The General Theory*

Peter Kriesler, Bruce McFarlane and Jan Toporowski are currently writing the official intellectual biography of Michal Kalecki. Kriesler is also the author of the definitive book on Kalecki's microeconomics (Kriesler 1987). So he has prepared himself admirably for the task of comparing and contrasting the '*General Theories*' of Kalecki and Keynes and of comparing them in turn with the system of their classical/neoclassical rivals. Not surprisingly, Kriesler (38) is more partial to Kalecki's solution of the realization problem than to that of Keynes. The only aspect of their respective analyses in which he argues that Keynes is superior concerns the role of expectations, financial matters and especially the determination of the rate of interest. This is not to say that he does not admire Keynes. It is rather that he thinks that Kalecki's approach, which derives from Marx and the classical economists (in the non-Keynes sense), so that Kalecki's version of *The General Theory* emphasizes accumulation and cyclical growth and the role that distribution between classes plays in these processes, is a more natural way to analyse modern capitalism.

Moreover, Kalecki's realistic microeconomic foundations are superior to those of Keynes for both explaining distribution and accumulation. Finally,

Kalecki made finance and its availability the ultimate constraint on accumulation, whereas Keynes rather neglected this in *The General Theory* (though not in the *Treatise on Money*). He made amends in his subsequent work on the finance motive, thus returning to the path he was on in the *Treatise on Money*. Keynes's and Kalecki's systems in Kriesler's view (and ours) dominate that of the neoclassicals both before and after the publication of *The General Theory*. He explains why through lucid arguments and a judicious use of charts.

Littleboy on Leijonhufvud on Keynes

The publication of Axel Leijonhufvud's *Keynesian Economics and the Economics of Keynes* in 1968 had a major impact on how Keynes's message was seen and understood. Since that date a huge literature has emerged and Leijonhufvud himself has backed off from some of his major suggestions, especially on the reversal of quantity versus price movements in Marshall (and Keynes) and Walras. One of the most insightful surveyors of these developments is Bruce Littleboy, whose PhD on the topic was the basis of a well-regarded book published in 1990. In his thoughtful and wide-ranging essay in the present volume (39) he compares and contrasts Leijonhufvud's views on Keynes then and now with those of some leading Post-Keynesians, especially Shackle, whose views are discerned to be at odds with those of Leijonhufvud. Littleboy argues persuasively that in many instances this is *not* the case, and that, when it appears to be so, it is largely because the Post-Keynesians or Leijonhufvud or, most of all, Keynes have themselves been misunderstood.

CONCLUSION

We do not wish to delay further our readers' enjoyment of the chapters that follow. All we wish to say in concluding this introduction is that our authors have reinforced our belief that Keynes did provide the basic wherewithal for understanding the nature of the malfunctioning of our sorts of economies and the ingredients of sensible and effective policies for remedying them, if only the international political good will is also present. They have also set out clearly the new developments since Keynes died which will serve to reinforce these fundamental claims.

NOTES

1 The editors would like to thank the contributors to the volume, Grant Belchamber and Jörg Bibow for their helpful and supportive comments on a draft of the Introduction.
2 Keynes's suggestions for 'Footnotes to "The General Theory"'

Chapter 1 The Four Parts of the Theory:
(a) Effective demand
(b) The multiplier
(c) The theory of investment
(d) The theory of interest
2 The analysis of effective demand
3 The theory of interest regarded as the marginal efficiency of money
4 The analysis of liquidity preference regarded as constituting the demand for money
5 The limitations on the demand for capital goods
6 Statistical notes

(*C.W.* XIV: 133–4)

3 In his chapter (31), Rod O'Donnell deals briefly with Keynes's plans for books after *The General Theory.*

4 Joan Wells and Christopher Torr (whose PhD dissertation was examined by Paul) have allowed us to quote from a letter which Paul wrote to Christopher in 1983. The passage describes beautifully the aim of the volume and it is fitting that Paul's words should play a part in the volume he so enthusiastically supported:

> Keynes presented us with some fundamental and important concepts. Our job is to shape these ideas in [the] light of current conditions and experience. *The General Theory* is not a straight jacket. It is a marvellously loose book with ideas that can be shaped and reshaped as need be. And therein lies, I believe, its great power. Nobody wants to know what Keynes actually meant or wrote, etc. This is impossible. All we need to do is to take his fundamental ideas and reshape them into something sensible.

5 Paul Davidson (28 September 1995) would have us stress that 'Keynes always argued that what he was trying to write in *The General Theory* was that money mattered and was integrated with the real economy in *both* the long period and the short period'. We do not disagree.

6 Jan Kregel (3 October 1995) is worried that this may be read as implying that Chapter 17 is 'separate or different from the rest of the book'. We do *not* mean to do so; moreover, we argue that Kregel's chapter (16), which conveys the message that Chapter 17 may be interpreted as being 'the *G.T.* in a nutshell', is a profound one. Also, as Paul Davidson (28 September 1995) reminded us, Keynes had a subtle argument involving user costs which played a role in short-period equilibrium.

7 The story is, of course, more complicated than the bald statement in the text. Once quantity has been determined in the product market, the associated value of the marginal product of labour will help to determine (though not *necessarily* equal) the real wage. The schedule of the marginal product of labour is *not* a demand function for labour *but* it is a wage-setting instrument (see Riach 1995: 164–6).

8 Jan Kregel (9 October 1995) made the following qualification: the theoretical construct of effective demand itself should not be confused 'with particular or peculiar conditions of industry, that the latter should never require a special or different interpretation of effective demand' as such.

9 Keynes, of course, never knew of Kalecki's review but he did refer in his 1939 *Economic Journal* article (Keynes 1939a: 49) to '[Dr Kalecki's] brilliant article . . . in *Econometrica* [as] an important piece of pioneering work'.

10 We should mention at this point the writings of the late Sidney Weintraub who,

together with Tarshis, kept close to Keynes's own distinctive approach (see, for example, Weintraub 1957).

11 Jan Kregel has a discussion of user cost in his chapter (16) on the analysis of Chapter 17 of *The General Theory*, in which his interpretation of the concept differs from that of Torr.

12 Donald Moggridge (1992: 535) recounts the fascinating story of Ralph Hawtrey's 'discovery' of the multiplier in his comments on the proofs of the *Treatise on Money*. He rejected his discovery out of hand ever after while Keynes does not seem to have seen its significance until after Kahn's (and James Meade's) version became available.

13 In their chapter in this volume (17), Ingo Barens and Volker Caspari point out that Irving Fisher (1896) preceded them all as far as the concept, if not the name, is concerned.

14 Tom Rymes has pointed out to us that Mabel Timlin, then an assistant professor at the University of Saskatchewan in her fifty-first year (!), and thirty-five years before Kregel's article, analysed the 'system of shifting equilibrium which lies at the heart of Keynesian theory' (Timlin 1942: 7).

15 But note the reservation expressed by Kregel (see n. 8 above). Paul Davidson (28 September 1995) also argues that Keynes always wanted to show that whether competition was perfect or not, unemployment equilibrium could occur.

16 Because our trade is not an exact science, to say the least, Lawlor's chapter is in fact Chapter 20.

17 As Tom Rymes commented to us, and we agree, there is 'a huge difference between [the issues tackled by] Harrod and Domar'.

18 In the latter situation, Brown argues that Keynes not only anticipated Kaldor's 'Keynesian' theory of distribution by over twenty years but also that he would not have been as confident about a lack of fightback by wage-earners and others to rises in prices associated with excess demand.

19 Davis (1994a) is an expanded and most thorough exposition of the arguments of his chapter.

20 Rod O'Donnell has drawn our attention to a passage in the final chapter of his book (1989: 331–2) which complements Coates's contribution (though it does not mention fuzzy logic).

Part I

OVERVIEW, EXTENSIONS, METHOD AND NEW DEVELOPMENTS

25

AN OVERVIEW OF *THE GENERAL THEORY*

James Tobin

INTRODUCTION

This chapter is a contribution to a 'second edition' of *The General Theory of Employment, Interest and Money*, which celebrates the sixtieth birthday of the great book. The chapter I have been asked to write might be regarded as a revision of Keynes's Chapter 18, 'The General Theory of Employment Restated', but it is meant to be more inclusive and may appear as a preface or conclusion to a 'second edition'.

Each of the 'revised' chapters of *The General Theory* in this book is meant to be what the author thinks Keynes would have written if he had had the time and health to prepare a revised edition by 1946. These revisions, written as if by Keynes some fifty years ago, form the first part of some 'second edition' chapters. In the second part the modern author gives his or her own view of the state of the topic in the 1990s. Those are the functions of the two parts of my paper.

It is a daunting task to take on the role of Keynes. It is presumptuous too. I know I cannot write, either in content or style, as Keynes would have done. I have not tried to be a close scholar of the Keynes papers, inferring from them what his own second edition in the 1940s would have said. Although I have stuck closely to the essential themes of 1936, as I understand them, I am sure that much of what I have written is coloured by what I would like a second edition prepared by Keynes himself to have said. In the second part I discuss changes in Keynesian theory suggested by events in the world and in professional macroeconomics since the Second World War, and I argue that Keynes still has the better of the big debate.

BEHAVIOUR OF AN ECONOMIC SYSTEM WITHOUT GOVERNMENT INTERVENTION

James Tobin writing as J.M. Keynes

I take advantage of this second edition of *The General Theory of Employment, Interest and Money* to state once again the fundamental thesis of the book, and at the same time to mention some revisions resulting from my own second thoughts and from criticisms and discussions since the original publication.

The central questions before economists of our generation are: 'Does our market capitalist economy, left to itself, without government intervention, utilize fully its labour force and other productive resources? Does it systematically return, reasonably swiftly, to a full employment state whenever displaced from it?' The faith of classical economics assures us 'yes'. The answer of *The General Theory* is 'no'.

The intellectual bankruptcy of classical economics is plain to see: for the chronic mass unemployment of the last two decades, it offers neither diagnosis nor prescription. The purpose of my book is to fill the void. Our first task is to understand the sources of the systemic failures that plague us. With understanding we can design remedies. Fortunately, it appears that the remedies lie in government fiscal and monetary policies and leave intact the basic political, economic and social institutions of democracy and capitalism.

What is general about the 'general' theory of employment?

In classical theory, employment is determined jointly with the real wage, by the condition that the demand for and supply of labour hours are equal. Demand for labour, at a given time and in given circumstances, depends on the marginal product of labour, which varies inversely with the volume of employment. Supply of labour depends on the marginal disutility of work – the marginal utility of workers' alternative uses of time – in terms of wage-goods. According to the market-clearing paradigm that Marshall and his classical forebears taught us, we seek the consequences of various changes in circumstances and policies by examining their effects on those demand and supply curves and their intersection.

The general theory, quite simply, allows outcomes in which markets are not cleared, in which supplies and demands are not equal and may remain unequal for months and years at a time. In particular, for the economy as a whole, excess supply of labour is the usual condition. It takes the form of involuntary unemployment. As defined in Chapter 2, involuntary unemployment is distinguished from two other types of unemployment, frictional and voluntary, and from unemployment resulting from monopolistic or regulatory interventions that set the real wage too high.

Excess supply of any traded commodity – consumption goods, investment goods, intermediate goods, factors of production – is the difference between supply and demand at the prevailing price of the commodity, the price on which supply and demand depend. Involuntary unemployment is the excess supply of labour at prevailing real wages. This is a simpler and more straightforward definition than I originally gave in Chapter 2. The original definition also had the defect of suggesting that a reduction in the real wage would invariably be necessary to induce employers to offer more jobs. As I explain below, I now see that this need not be the case.

With given capital stock and technology, employment and output are closely linked. Labour is the principal variable factor in a closed economy, either directly or via intermediate goods. Observation suggests that excess capacity of plant and equipment moves *pari passu* with unemployment of labour. Existing capital, with the particular technologies embodied in it, is often not substitutable for labour inputs. Even when it is, user costs (Chapter 6 Appendix) may make substitution uneconomic.

In any event, involuntary unemployment of labour implies that national income is below its full employment capacity. The welfare of the society is unnaturally depressed. In my opinion, this market failure is easily the greatest flaw of capitalism.

Is involuntary unemployment an 'equilibrium'?

'Equilibrium' has several meanings. One is supply-equals-demand market-clearing. By this criterion, no situation of excess supply, specifically involuntary unemployment, is equilibrium. Only classical full employment is equilibrium. Semantics of this kind need not detain us.

A more useful concept of equilibrium is a position of rest – that is, a situation without any inherent systematic tendency to change. The general theory asserts that a multitude of outcomes with involuntary unemployment are conceivable positions of rest, no less so than the singular outcomes characterized by full employment and market-clearing. These equilibria do not, of course, exclude changes resulting from external factors: demographics, technology, government policies, individual tastes. The utility of economic analysis is precisely to reveal how those developments alter equilibria.

The general theory also assumes away some internal systematic sources of change. The equilibria described in its chapters do as a rule generate changes in stocks of capital and wealth, and these in turn affect subsequent equilibria. The theory focuses on short or medium runs, periods comparable to usual business cycles, short enough so that stock changes are too small to alter the decisive propensities governing consumption, investment and liquidity preference.

A sceptic may object that excess supply cannot be a position of rest in any market, because it is bound to trigger changes, if only in the prices of the traded commodities. In the labour market, the argument would be that competition for jobs among the involuntarily unemployed will cause the real wage to decline. This is more than a semantic question.

Chapter 2 argues that workers may not be able to reduce the real wage, even if they would like to. Markets set money prices, not real or relative prices. Labour markets set money-wages, not real wages. Conceivably a situation of involuntary unemployment could be a position of rest in real variables, like output and employment, and in real prices, wages and interest, even if not in nominal variables. That ought to be good enough for classical economists, because their theory aims to explain real variables independently of monetary 'veils'.

Aggregate demand as the constraint on output and employment

As I stressed in Chapter 3, the principle of effective demand is the central idea of the general theory. In situations of involuntary unemployment and associated under-production, output and employment are constrained by aggregate demand for the products of labour. They are not constrained by the supply of willing workers or by the capacity of the economy to produce goods and services.

Note, to avoid misunderstanding, that 'demand' in this context does not refer to the schedule of the marginal product of labour. That schedule is the 'demand' curve for labour in the classical market-clearing analysis of the labour market. Abstracting from the effects of capital accumulation and technological progress, that schedule remains in place as shifts in effective demand generate the fluctuations we know as business cycles – in employment, unemployment, national income and capacity utilization.

When the economy is operating in this demand-constrained regime, Say's Law does not apply. Supply does not create its own demand. Advances in the economy's capacity to produce will not be realized in actual production unless effective demand increases equally, and there is no guarantee that it will. Indeed, we can say 'demand creates its own supply', in the sense that businesses will be willing and able to produce more to satisfy new customers and that workers will gladly supply the needed additional labour. Increases in labour force and industrial capacity are neither necessary nor sufficient.

A full-employment market-cleared regime is quite different from a demand-constrained regime. Output and employment are supply-constrained. Additional effective demand by itself will not raise output; it will just generate price and wage inflation. In this regime, all the classical homilies apply. Thrift and industry are virtues, and the rules of efficient resource allocation come into their own. Alas, much harm is done by unthinking application of those principles in the wrong settings. The great philosopher Alfred North Whitehead warned us of the 'fallacy of misplaced concreteness', wherein abstract generalization and principles are applied in the wrong empirical circumstances.

Involuntary unemployment resulting from inadequate aggregate demand is mainly a malady of wealthy industrial capitalist economies, those of Britain, North America and continental Europe. In these economies substantial proportions of the population work for wages in large hierarchically organized groups, employed at the will of profit-seeking companies. They are dependent for their families' livelihoods on those jobs. In less-advanced lands most people are occupied in agriculture, much of it subsistence farming or share-cropping, and others are self-employed craftsmen. Economic adversities generally are deficiencies of supply and do not involve unemployment. Despite its characteristic failures, industrialization implementing the miracles of modern science and engineering is the hope for conquering poverty throughout the world. The present industrial economies can contribute greatly to this development, most fruitfully if they learn to employ productively their own populations.

Is the wage always equal to the marginal product of labour?

In Chapter 2 of the first edition, I accepted as 'indefeasible' the first postulate of the classical theory of employment and wages, namely the schedule of declining marginal productivity of labour. I accepted the implication that employment and real wages are uniquely and negatively correlated, not only in classical equilibrium but also in the movements of output, employment and wages that occur as effective demand fluctuates relative to full employment output.

In describing the classical theory of employment, I identified the marginal product schedule as one of the two blades of the Marshallian scissors. To keep my deviations from orthodox theory to the essential minimum, I accepted this blade while rejecting the other, the classical labour supply schedule. Adherence to the classical labour 'demand' curve in the first edition was natural on the assumption that competition among employing firms would keep product prices equal to marginal cost.

I leaned too far to the classical side, as I learned shortly after the book was published, thanks to the empirical studies of Dunlop and Tarshis. If the first classical postulate were correct, then we would expect real wages – measured in terms of labour's product rather than workers' consumption – to move counter-cyclically. However, Dunlop and Tarshis found that product-wages were, if anything, pro-cyclical.

This is not a fatal flaw in the general theory; quite the contrary: my essential propositions remain unscathed. All the theory requires is that there be excess supply in labour markets, whether employment-wage observations fall on the marginal product curve or below it, so long as they fall to the left of the classical supply schedule. If increases in aggregate demand can raise employment and output without diminishing real wages, so much the better! Employed workers as well as unemployed workers and capitalists will gain from higher economic activity. Nothing is lost by recognizing that imperfect competition and sluggish price adjustment may result in departures from marginal cost pricing, especially in short runs.

The principle of effective demand and the multiplier

The principle of effective demand is just common sense. Workers who are unable to sell as much labour as they would like at prevailing prices and wages have to restrict their demands for consumption goods. They do not buy as much as they would at those prices if they were not involuntarily unemployed. They cannot be confident of finding jobs in future, and even if they could be, they frequently do not have liquid assets and lines of credit enabling them to maintain their current spending. Therefore, the budget constraint on their expenditures is tighter, generally much tighter, than it would be if they were employed to the extent they would like to be at existing wages, or at the (possibly somewhat different) wages that would prevail at full employment.

Similar constraints, with similar consequences, apply to capitalists who are compelled by demand shortages to operate below capacity the lands and durable producers' goods they own.

These constraints on incomes and spending spread to sellers of consumption goods and, in turn, constrict their purchases in other markets. Demand-constrained firms limit their hiring of labour and their purchases of other inputs. The theory of the multiplier shows how an initial change in aggregate demand is magnified by chains of secondary effects on incomes and spendings throughout the economy. In demand-constrained regimes, any autonomous or unexpected increase in demand – for example, more investment spending by a business firm – has positive multiplier effects. Conversely, any decrease in demand – for example, an onset of thriftiness bringing a cut in consumption spending – tends to depress the whole economy.

The trained instincts of classical economists are to reject out of hand the idea of a reduction in *economy-wide* demand, as distinct from cuts in demands for particular commodities. Lost demand for shoes must pop up as greater demand for hats. Lost demand for consumption in total must pop up as new demand for capital investment. Or, as classical economists would put it, people may consume less today in order to consume more in future, and the investment spending that replaces current consumption is the preparation for that future bulge in consumption.

At the beginning of Chapter 16 of the first edition, I pointed out the fallacy in this view. To strengthen the connection of my argument with the principle of effective demand, I have now moved these remarks to Chapter 3. Futures markets are rare, and contingent futures markets even rarer. Decisions not to spend on goods and services now are not in fact coupled with any definite orders for future or contingent deliveries of goods and services. Typically they result in accumulations of financial assets, which can be spent on anything at any future time. The negative multiplier effects of lower current spending propensities are not offset by specific and firm expectations of higher future demands.

We know that some wage-earners, some households, some businesses are constrained not just by their wealth, including the present value of their current and future net wage incomes, but also by their liquid wealth, the part of their wealth they can at once turn into spendable cash. Binding liquidity constraints are an important but extreme form of effective demand constraint. Some wage-earners, no doubt, depend on each week's wages to buy the goods for that week's consumption.

However, the effective demand principle does not depend on such short horizons, i.e. such short periods within which expenditures are limited by cash receipts. Expectations of future spells of unemployment, enhanced by present and recent experience, can limit the current consumption spending even of long-horizon households. Liquidity constraints and prospective effective demand constraints also limit business investments. Common observation suggests that households and businesses, and governments too, differ widely in the length of the future period over which expected resources are regarded as potentially available for spending today. These horizons, moreover, doubtless change over time with circumstances and behaviour.

Do interest rate adjustments guarantee full employment?

For classical economists, interest rates are the equilibrators of capital markets. They equate saving and investment. Their adjustment is crucial to the Say's Law story, which dismisses as vulgar superficiality the notion that an economy could suffer from shortfalls in demand for commodities in aggregate. After all, classical doctrine is that the real equilibrium of the economy is independent of nominal prices, and is essentially the same as if it were the outcome of moneyless, frictionless, multilateral barter.

Can interest rates do the job? Money proper bears zero interest, and other interest rates cannot fall below that. Indeed, the rates that are relevant for investment decisions cannot fall as far. Rates on long-term securities have to compensate lenders for risks of capital losses and satisfy their conventional views of what is adequate compensation. Those rates can often exceed what entrepreneurs, given their expectations of returns of capital, can afford to pay.

Conceivably expectations of inflation could make borrowers willing to borrow at rates consistent with the zero floor on the yield of money. But in depressed economic conditions expectations of deflation are more likely. They make money and other liquid assets preferable to real capital, and thus discourage potential borrowers and investors.

Even in normal times, when rates of interest compatible with investment prospects are not so low, interest rates do not automatically maintain full employment in the face of shortfalls of effective demand. By 'automatically',

I mean without deliberate policy by the monetary authority to increase the quantity of money. The reason is that a reduction in the rate of interest will generally raise the demand for money, from which fact it follows that the rate cannot fall unless the supply of money is increased. Of course, the interest rate can fall along with a decline in economic activity and in the volume of transactions supported by the money stock. But that scenario does not restore or maintain full employment.

The issue is whether full employment will prevail in the face of a negative demand shock if the central bank 'does nothing'. I have taken a constant money supply as doing nothing, and argued that it will not suffice. Things are still worse if we recognize that if the central bank and Treasury are passive, the money stock itself will decline in periods of slack economic activity. This will surely be true if money stock is interpreted to include bank deposits. Even if the stock of currency and bank reserves is held constant, increased public preference for currency over deposits and increased liquidity preferences of banks themselves will hold down their stocks of money and credit.

Money and other liquid assets

At this point I should mention a confusion about the meaning of 'money' in my first edition, a confusion that can lead to misunderstanding even though it does not affect the central message of the book. The needed corrections have been made in the texts of Chapters 12–17.

Sometimes I seemed to refer to 'cash' in the narrow senses of currency and coin and of bank deposits actually used as transactions media. Elsewhere I obviously had in mind a broader category, including close substitutes for cash, other 'liquid' assets denominated in the monetary unit of account, safe against defaults and losses of market value, readily convertible into cash – time deposits, savings accounts, short-term Treasury bills and bankers' acceptances, and so on.

The narrow category is relevant for my transactions motive, the broader category for my precautionary and speculative motives. I am grateful to Mrs Robinson and Mr Kaldor for straightening out this matter and showing how the interest sensitivity of demand for money applies to both concepts. The interest forgone by holding cash rather than other liquid assets is the rate on those instruments. The interest forgone by holding liquid assets in general is the 'liquidity preference' premium of rates on longer-maturity bonds and illiquid loans above rates on liquid assets.

Do flexible money-wages and prices guarantee full employment?

Let us review the logic of the controversy between the general theory and classical economics. I do not interpret Professor Pigou and other orthodox theorists as saying that advanced capitalist economies can never for a moment suffer from shortfalls of aggregate demand and attendant declines in employment and industrial activity. I do interpret them as saying that these economies possess powerful natural adjustment mechanisms that will return them to full employment equilibrium – on their own, without the help of any government measures. Thanks to their faith in these adjustments, classical economists can assert that no under-employment situation is an equilibrium. Some of them, like Professor Pigou, might in special circumstances pragmatically welcome temporary government help, such as public employment projects, to strengthen and speed the adjustments. Others, fearing adverse longer-run effects of government intrusions, would trust the natural recuperative processes to take their course.

We economists have all learned, and many of us teach, that the remedy for excess supply in any market is a reduction in price. If this is prevented by combinations in restraint of trade or by government regulations, then those impediments to competition should be removed. Applied to economy-wide unemployment, this doctrine places the blame on trade unions and governments, not on any failures of competitive markets. The obvious disproportion between this explanation and the mass unemployment of the last two decades demanded a new diagnosis, and a new prescription. That was and is the purpose of *The General Theory*.

In Chapter 2 I set forth three propositions:

1 money-wages remain fairly stable in the face of fluctuations in unemployment because of the nature of labour markets, not because of monopolies or laws;
2 the stability of money-wages is no obstacle to reductions of involuntary unemployment via increases in effective demand, even if those should involve reductions of real wages;
3 downward flexibility of money-wages would not reduce real wages and increase employment.

Why the focus on money-wages? The classical theory of employment runs, of course, in terms of real wages. But in a monetary economy, offers of jobs and of work and bargains between employers and employees are expressed in terms of money. There is nothing artificial or irrational about the stability of money-wages and their insensitivity to excess supply. Money-wages are set or negotiated in thousands of decentralized markets. Employers and employees in each market are primarily motivated by their wage relative to wages elsewhere. In any one firm or industry or occupation, workers resist cuts in money-wages which they regard as damaging their status relative to those of workers in other markets. At the same time, they would not resist a universal reduction in real wages that would leave relative positions unchanged, such as would be brought about by a general rise in prices of wage-goods. Attention to relative wages imparts considerable sluggishness to money-wage adjustments throughout the economy.

The third proposition says that the analogy to price adjustments in particular markets fails for the economy as a whole. Unlike workers in a small market, the national labour force cannot lower the national average real wage. If the competition of unemployed workers actually did reduce money-wages, employers competing for sales would lower prices proportionately. The result would be that employment too would remain unchanged. All that would happen is an economy-wide proportionate reduction of money-wages and prices.

In Chapter 19 I recognized that universal price reduction, were it brought about by the impersonal forces of markets, could bring about the same results as an increase in the quantity of money by the central bank. Accordingly, it could lower interest rates, induce additional investment, and increase effective demand, output and employment. But as a practical matter, why not accomplish this result with less social trauma by monetary policy? And as a theoretical matter, there remains the possibility that an increase in the real quantity of money, by either route, will not in fact lower the interest rates relevant to real demand for goods and services and labour, because they are already as low as they can get.

To protect orthodoxy from this breach in its defences, Professor Pigou and others have advanced another argument, alleging a direct positive effect of a general reduction in money prices on effective real demand, even though interest rates are not reduced. The argument is that spending responds positively to wealth, and that the real wealth embodied in money-denominated assets is greater when money prices are lower.

A peculiarity of Professor Pigou's argument is that he gives it a long-run focus by setting it in a stationary state. One would expect that, given indefinite time to adapt, the whole structure of monetary assets and debts would have been scaled down in the same proportion as money prices and wages.

More *à propos*, it would seem, is a short-run focus, in which prices fall to levels lower than were anticipated when money-denominated securities were issued and debts contracted. A limitation of this argument, as Mr Kalecki reminded Professor Pigou, is that debt burdens are increased at the same time, and for private contracts by the same amount. It is an interesting question whether taxpayers feel burdened by government debt and feel increasingly so when deflation increases its real value. I am inclined to doubt that many people calculate in this manner. In any case, the increase in private net wealth associated with deflation must be small relative to national income. Moreover, since debtors' propensities to spend from wealth are likely to exceed those of creditors, the net change in spending could go either way. In Chapter 19 I emphasized the negative effects of increasing debt burdens, and Professor Fisher has made a convincing case that debt burdens augmented by deflation exacerbated the Great Depression in the United States.

I also agree with Professor Fisher that, whatever may be the effects of lowering the level of money-wages and prices, the process of moving to a lower level is counterproductive. Expectations of deflation are equivalent to an increase in interest rates.

For these reasons, I do not regard Professor Pigou's counterthrust as a refutation of the general theory on an abstract theoretical plane, *a fortiori* on the plane of practical policy. Indeed, I remain of the opinion that a fairly stable money-wage will result in less volatility both of output and employment and of prices.

Long-run issues and uncertainties

The general theory is not a theory of the stationary state or of long-run economic growth. Nevertheless, it does have some implications for them. These arise from the effects of accumulation of wealth and capital on saving and investment. I anticipate that improvements in productivity due to capital accumulation and technological progress will steadily raise potential per capita incomes and consumption standards. If I am right about the psychology of consumption and saving, the propensity to save will steadily rise. Accumulation of capital, faster than employment and output grow, will at the same time reduce the marginal efficiency of capital. The decline in capitalist incomes as returns on capital vanish is a consummation devoutly to be wished.

However, my theory suggests that these developments will make the maintenance of high employment more and more difficult. The problem will be to lower interest rates enough to induce investment sufficient to use the potentially large supplies of saving. Public investment and collective consumption may be necessary to prevent wasteful unemployment, and may be socially desirable as well.

I pointed out in Chapter 18 that the underemployment equilibria described by the general theory appear to be quite stable, and I attributed their stability to the relative inflexibility of money-wages. Drastic changes in the stock of money, as measured in prices or wage-units, generally do not occur. As a result, interest rates relevant to the inducement to invest are not volatile, either. Given these characteristics, the economy is vulnerable to shifts in long-run expectations and capital investment, the principal sources of economic fluctuations. My analysis of long-run developments suggests that downward inflexibility of interest rates can make involuntary unemployment an increasingly severe problem.

However, Mr Harrod's ingenious dynamic theory reaches a more optimistic conclusion, evidently because he assumes that technological progress is the equivalent of growth in the labour force and keeps the marginal efficiency of capital from falling. He also assumes that the propensity to save remains constant in the face of growth in per capita income. Thus he is more optimistic than I am for the long run, whilst his theory apparently implies greater cyclical instability. On these questions we must await further analysis and additional experience.

A 1994 PERSPECTIVE

James Tobin writing as himself

Reprise of the great macroeconomic debate

The central questions are the same as in 1936 and 1940, and so are the answers. In the meantime, the classical economics from which Keynes revolted has been reborn several times, as monetarism, new classical macroeconomics and real business cycle theory. In one or more of these reincarnations, it is riding high among professional economists, financial and business leaders, central bankers and other makers of macroeconomic policy. Classical ideas have almost regained the orthodox status they enjoyed before 1936.

The origins and rise of the classical counter-revolution can be traced in part to real-world events and disappointments. Just as the great depression of the 1930s created a receptive audience for Maynard Keynes, so the great stagflation of the 1970s fostered believers in Milton Friedman and Robert Lucas. The economics profession shared the disenchantments of the general public with government activities of all kinds, including Keynesian demand management.

Yet the counter-revolution reflected also a strong dialectic internal to the profession itself. It was a reaction against the so-called 'neoclassical synthesis' of the 1950s and early 1960s, which had made Keynesian macroeconomics an equal partner with neoclassical microeconomics in mainstream doctrine. Although the authors of the synthesis were much closer to the original general theory than the tradition that developed subsequently, they did modify what then seemed standard Keynesian doctrine, in two main ways.

One was to recognize the importance of monetary policy, relieving fiscal policy of the whole burden of demand management. The addition of an independent instrument made it possible in principle to achieve macroeconomic goals without prejudicing social and political decisions on resource allocation and income distribution. The second point was related. It was to underline the importance of neoclassical welfare economics principles in making macroeconomic policy. The fact that output is demand-constrained means that society loses nothing by putting idle labour to work, and gains the product of its employment. As Keynes said, inviting people to dig up bottles filled with banknotes – and to put others to work as they spend the banknotes – is better than nothing. He preferred intrinsically useful projects. If – and only if – they are practically feasible and politically acceptable, they are the true opportunity costs of make-work expedients, just as they would be at full employment.

Nevertheless, the marriage of Keynesian macro and neoclassical micro was always somewhat uncomfortable. Keynesian assertions of the massive market failures represented by persistent excesses of supply invited disbelief among teachers and students dazzled by the general-equilibrium paradigm. When Adam Smith's 'invisible hand', made rigorous by Arrow and Debreu, was applied to macroeconomics, Panglossian conclusions were inevitable. To many of the most powerful intellects in the profession in the last twenty-five years, that logic was more persuasive than realism.

Leading classical theorists today are more extreme and less pragmatic than their predecessors of Keynes's time. Professor Pigou and his contemporaries allowed demand-deficient departures from full employment equilibrium, while arguing that natural market mechanisms would in good time rectify them. Their successors assume that there are no such departures, however temporary. Markets are always clearing. Prices are perfectly flexible, responding instantaneously to shocks in demand or supply. Observed paths of market outcomes track these fluctuations in supply-equals-demand equilibria.

For labour markets, the implication is that there is never involuntary unemployment (other than what results from wage regulations imposed by governments or unions). Employment is always full, but the rates of employment and unemployment at 'full employment' change continuously.

Today's classical economics is much more sophisticated – methodologically, theoretically, mathematically, econometrically – than its pre-Keynesian forebear. Technical advances in the profession have provided powerful ammunition for renewed fighting on the same old battleground. The classical counter-revolution offers powerful analytical tools and challenging puzzles to use them on. These are magnets for the best young minds in the profession, just as the innovations of the Keynesian revolution were in their day.

Evidence for an empirical verdict favouring Keynes

On the central empirical issues, explaining unemployment, excess capacity and fluctuations in business activity and prescribing remedies for them, the classical economists of 1990 are no more successful than those of 1930. The moving-equilibrium model of real business cycle theory just doesn't fit the facts. In the policy arena, classical ideas have dominated European governments and central banks for fifteen or twenty years, and chronic double-digit unemployment rates are the result.

Fancy econometrics is not needed to mobilize evidence against the real business cycle theory view that observed fluctuations in output and employment are movements in price-cleared equilibrium. Here are a number of regularities of US business cycles which falsify that hypothesis:

1 *Unemployment itself* If people are voluntarily choosing not to work at prevailing wages, why do they report themselves as unemployed, rather than as 'not in labour force'?
2 *Behaviour of real wages* Real business cycle theory attributes unemployment to voluntary intertemporal choice. Workers drop out when they perceive that real wages, the opportunity costs of leisure, are temporarily low. This might be an explanation of cyclical movements in employment if real wages were strongly pro-cyclical. But there is no such systematic regularity. Nor is there empirical evidence of sensitivity of labour supply to current and expected real wages.
3 *Unemployment and vacancies* New classicals ask us to believe that the labour market is in equilibrium at 9 per cent unemployment just as truly as it is at 5 per cent. If so, there would be no reason to expect the balance between unemployment and job vacancies to differ. *Both* unemployment and vacancies would be more numerous in recessions. However, a strong negative association between unemployment and vacancy rates, as would be expected in Keynesian theory, is obvious in the USA and other market capitalist economies.
4 *Quits and layoffs* If recessions and prosperities are both supply-equals-demand equilibria, there is no reason to expect the relative frequencies of voluntary quits of jobs and involuntary separations from jobs to vary over the business cycle. But of course there are regularly many more layoffs, relative to quits, when unemployment is high and vacancies are scarce. There are many more 'job losers' relative to 'job leavers' in recessions.
5 *Excess capacity* Utilization of plant and equipment varies cyclically, parallel to utilization of labour. Presumably machines do not choose leisure voluntarily.
6 *Unfilled orders and delivery delays* These move pro-cyclically, again suggesting strongly that demand is much higher relative to potential supply in prosperities than in recessions.
7 *Monetary effects on output* According to the classical 'money is a veil' principle, monetary events and policies should affect only nominal prices. Real outcomes should be independent of them. The evidence that this is not true is overwhelming.

The GENERAL Theory: equilibrium or disequilibrium?

What is general about *The General Theory* is that it covers situations in which certain markets are not cleared at existing prices. The failure of some markets to clear affects in turn the outcomes of other markets, including those, financial markets in particular, that do clear. The theory includes economy-wide market-clearing as a special case.

The essential message is that clearing of labour markets in aggregate by prices is infrequent and exceptional; the normal case is net excess supply of labour; that is, involuntary unemployment in excess of job vacancies. In this sense Keynesian theory is definitely and definitionally not equilibrium theory.

Some general-equilibrium theorists have observed that the economy might well have two or more competitive market-clearing equilibria, some involving higher employment and social welfare than others. They suggest that Keynes meant, or should have meant, that the economy can get stuck in a sub-optimal equilibrium. They mean well, but wholly misunderstand Keynes. None of their equilibria involve involuntary unemployment, and monetary phenomena play no role.

Does *The General Theory* describe equilibrium in the sense of a position of rest? There are several possible Keynesian answers.

The first, asserted in Book I, is 'yes'. Given the parameters of the system – propensity to consume, liquidity preference, quantity of money, marginal efficiency of capital schedule, inherited money-wage, stocks of capital and wealth – all variables, both real and nominal, are determined and will not change on their own.

The second, also set forth in Book I, is a hypothetical modification of the first: suppose, contrary to fact, that nominal wages and prices do move downwards in response to excess supplies of labour and complementary inputs. Real variables will not move; the rate of involuntary unemployment will not change. Employment and output are determined by the propensity to consume and the inducement to invest, neither of which is affected by nominal variables. As students know or used to know, this argument follows from either or both of two conditions: liquidity trap, and insensitivity of consumption and investment to interest rates.

Whether or not this qualifies as equilibrium, it turns out in Book V to be a special case, embarrassing to Pigou and other classicals, to be sure, but also embarrassing to Keynes. For values of liquidity and investment parameters he regarded as normal, lower money-wages and prices would in principle be associated with higher effective demand and employment.

The third answer is not explicit in the book. There are inklings of it in Chapter 19 and in other writings of Keynes. But it is a *post hoc* alternative interpretation, and not one congenial to Keynes's trained methodological instincts. This would be to recognize the classical full-employment market-cleared outcome as *the* equilibrium, and the deviations from it as described and analysed in *The General Theory* as *disequilibria.*

This third approach involves explicit dynamic analysis, exploring the stability or instability of the classical equilibrium, and the reliability and speed of the economy's unassisted natural recuperative mechanisms. These are, after all, the central issues of the debate, then and now. In Chapter 19 Keynes's argument that the very process of deflation of money-wages and prices would tend to increase rather than decrease unemployment is a dynamic argument against the stability of the classical equilibrium. So also is Keynes's 1939 dismissal of the Pigou effect, which he, like Irving Fisher, thought would be no match for the negative demand effects of deflation due to unanticipated debt burdens and bankruptcies.

In Chapter 19 common-sense arguments like these are understated, because they do not fit into the traditional methods of comparative statics to which Keynes was committed by training and habit. Playing the game on the static equilibrium field probably lost the general theory acceptance among economists, too many of whom uncritically swallowed the Pigou effect as a decisive logical refutation.

In my opinion, a dynamic disequilibrium interpretation serves best the essential purposes of the general theory. Imagine a series of short periods, perhaps as long as two years or as short as two quarters. Keynes refers to periods of time during which we can 'take as given the existing skill and quantities of available labour, the existing quality and quantity of available equipment' and other slowly changing or exogenous circumstances and parameters. These include psychological factors underlying consumption, investment and liquidity preference; the money-wage; and the quantity of money. The equations of the theory, implicit in the book or explicit in Hicks's IS–LM exposition, then determine national income, employment, interest rate and related macro variables.

The outcomes of one period are data for the next. Saving increases wealth, investment augments capital, employment and unemployment affect money-wages and prices. Such systematic changes will alter propensities to consume and invest. In addition, external circumstances – attitudes, expectations, central bank policies – may change arbitrarily. The process goes on.

This is the structure of most empirical econometric models, used by businesses and governments for forecasting and for policy analysis. Those models are naturally Keynesian, elaborate IS–LM models of aggregate demand plus equations relating money-wages and prices to unemployment and capacity utilization.

The important issue, the one between Keynes and Pigou, is whether unemployment in any period triggers a process that raises employment next period and eventually leads to full employment. That is a question of the stability of a stationary equilibrium or of a particular dynamic path, for example a steady balanced growth path.

Keynes was aware that his theory of the determination of aggregate demand did not really lead to a position-of-rest equilibrium, because it implied saving and investment. The resulting accumulations of wealth and capital necessarily alter subsequent determinants of aggregate demand. The only true equilibrium in this sense is the stationary state, or its equivalent in the steady state of a growth model. Keynes was initially suspicious of, but ultimately intrigued by, Harrod's dynamics, in which deficient demand and unemployment would arise naturally as disequilibria, departures from the full-employment steady-state growth path.

'Disequilibrium' analysis in this sense is to be distinguished from another meaning of the word, namely to refer to the existence of excess supplies and demands. In the 1970s a school of self-styled 'disequilibrium' theorists applied the tools of static general equilibrium theory to the determination of quantities when prices are arbitrarily fixed. The equilibrium to which their models were disequilibria was that of price-cleared competitive markets. These investigators were concerned with the interdependencies of the excess supplies and demands among markets, assuming for example that actual purchases and sales would always be the smaller of supply and demand. They were, in short, extending Keynes's principle of effective demand to a multiple-market setting.

This 'disequilibrium theory' could be regarded as a multi-commodity generalization of the 'fixprice' method (J.R. Hicks's term) of macroeconomic analysis. Although some of the authors thought they were giving the general theory a formal logical structure it previously lacked, they added little macroeconomic content to Keynesian multiplier theory.

The role of imperfect flexibility of money-wages and prices

Keynes's general theory is nowadays typically described in textbooks and classrooms as crucially dependent on an arbitrary and unexplained assumption, that money-wages or product prices or both are rigid. 'Fixprice' expositions of multipliers and IS–LM models invite this caricature. Since rigidity is contrary to both theory and observation, the easy next step is to dismiss Keynesian theory in favour of its 'flexprice' competitors.

This misrepresentation is usually accompanied by another one, namely that the sources of Keynesian difficulties are nominal shocks, to the stock or velocity of money, which are converted into real demand shocks only by rigidities of nominal wages and prices. In fact, the general theory postulates real shocks to effective demand, much more difficult to absorb by flexibility of nominal wages and prices than nominal shocks.

Book V makes it clear enough that Keynes was not assuming wage or price rigidities. He believed that wages and prices were flexible, but not perfectly so. Imagine a spectrum of flexibility from perfect-flexibility – instantaneous jumps in prices sufficient to maintain continuous market-clearing – to perfect rigidity – nominal wages and/or prices wholly unresponsive to excess supplies and demands. The general theory is in the middle of the spectrum, not at either extreme. So is the real world. New classical macroeconomics is at the perfect-flexibility extreme. The real world is not.

This point is crucial to the basic debate about the efficacy of downward money-wage and price flexibility in maintaining or restoring full employment. Perfect flexibility is the only point on the spectrum that guarantees market-clearing, almost tautologically. Keynes's principle of effective demand and Keynes's multipliers apply everywhere else.

Keynesian propositions hold not just at the rigidity extreme but for imperfect flexibility as well. Once excess-supply-reducing price adjustments are acknowledged to take real time, the destabilizing effects of the process – falling prices rather than fallen prices – become important. In the context of the great macroeconomic debate, expectations of declining money-wages and prices are bad for aggregate real demand. They raise real interest rates. In comparison, the real balance effect will be at best weak and at worst wrong in sign. The only hope for stability, in the absence of active government policy and the expectation of it, is the so-called 'Keynes effect' of Chapter 19: lower prices with given nominal money stock lead to lower interest rates.

Necessary and sufficient conditions for the stability of the classical full employment equilibrium via real-time price adjustments can be shown formally. Instability is a distinct possibility. Moreover, given the non-linearities of the relevant equations, the system may be stable in the neighbourhood of equilibrium but unstable to large displacements. These possible instabilities are superimposed on other well-known dynamics, related to quantity expectations, sales, production and stocks (Tobin 1975).

The above argument concerns the possible instability of the classical full-employment equilibrium, and the time required for adjustment even if the process is stable. A still worse possibility is that no market-clearing equilibrium exists, general-equilibrium proofs to the contrary failing because markets are incomplete. The most likely scenario would be that aggregate demand falls short of potential output – saving exceeds investment – at all positive interest rates. Equilibrium would require a negative interest rate, inconceivable if inflation is non-positive. That problem could be remedied in theory by a discrete fall in nominal prices accompanied by expectations of subsequent inflation. (Keynes himself did not assert that the classical market-clearing equilibrium does not exist, only that it is just one of many positions of rest.)

Expectations, rational and Keynesian

Another criterion of equilibrium is the fulfilment of the expectations that govern economic behaviour, or, to put the same point the other way round, the formation of expectations that will be realized. Theorists have long built this condition into their models as a necessary characteristic of stationary states or steady-growth paths.

Modern rational expectations theory stresses this as a necessary property of credible models, even for non-stationary processes. Of course, Keynes's own approach to expectations was radically different. For one thing, he stressed the diversity of expectations and of estimates of probabilities among economic agents. He would not attribute these differences just to 'asymmetries of information', because he thought that there is really no possible objective 'information' about the factors that determine investment payoffs in the distant future. The uncertainties are beyond the grasp of actuarial calculus. In their ignorance people act on simple extrapolations, on social conventions, on hunches and emotions. Unpredictable changes in the psychologies of wealth-owners, entrepreneurs and investors are the main sources of fluctuations in aggregate demand, employment and output.

Rational expectations are usually invoked in competitive market-clearing models, where the expectations involved are of prices, the decisive data for individual agents' demands and supplies. In the general theory, quantities – incomes, sales, jobs – are, independently of wages and prices, important determinants of the behaviour of businesses and households. For example, if people expect with good reason that recessions in aggregate demand will be reversed, their confidence will strengthen and speed recovery. Expectations of counter-cyclical demand management could be a major source of stability. But if complacent central banks and governments do not act to overcome recession or stagnation, loss of confidence could turn recession into prolonged depression. This is a plausible interpretation of 1930–1 in the United States and of the period since 1980 in Europe.

In the last fifty years, theorists have boldly extended the neoclassical domain into remote futures and contingent states of nature. Agents' utility functions, production sets, expectations and probability estimates then determine lifetime and inter-generational consumption and investment plans. Formal general equilibrium theory, utility and all that, is stretched beyond credibility. New classical economists assert that fluctuations of economic activity which Keynesians regard as pathological are really the playing-out of rational individual and social inter-temporal programmes. Keynes would not be surprised that real business cycle theorists are not able to explain the obvious facts of cycles.

The 'Beveridge curve' and the criterion of full employment

This second edition's revision of the definition of involuntary unemployment is a welcome simplification. The hypothetical test in the 1936 definition had always been a stumbling block. Moreover, the new definition is consistent with the measurement of unemployment in sample surveys, like

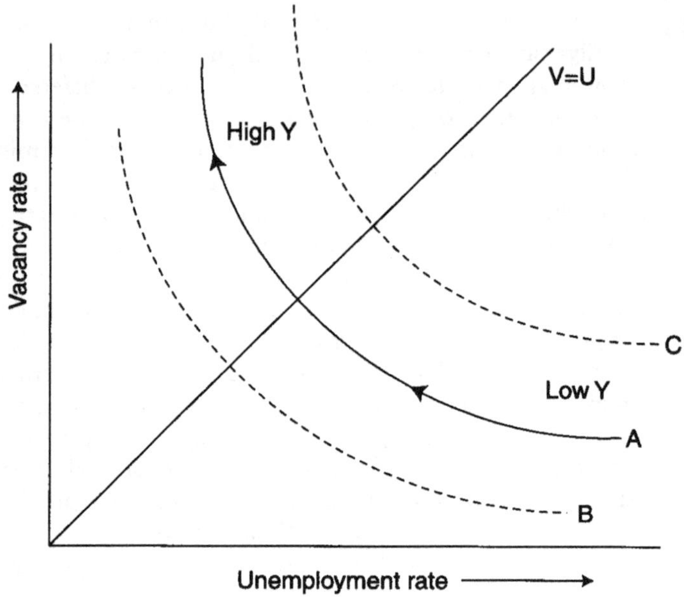

Figure 25.1 Beveridge curves, (a) in theory

Notes

1 The arrows along curve A show the path of short-run cyclical recovery, in response to increasing effective demand relative to potential real national product. Cyclical recessions follow the same curve in reverse. Inflation pressures would accentuate as the economy moves up a given Beveridge curve, such as A, and abate as it moves down.
2 The 45° V = U line is the Beveridge criterion of full employment. Points above that line meet the criterion.
3 A shift of the whole curve to B would be a favourable change in the efficiency of labour markets, reducing frictional or structural unemployment. A shift to C would be an adverse structural change.

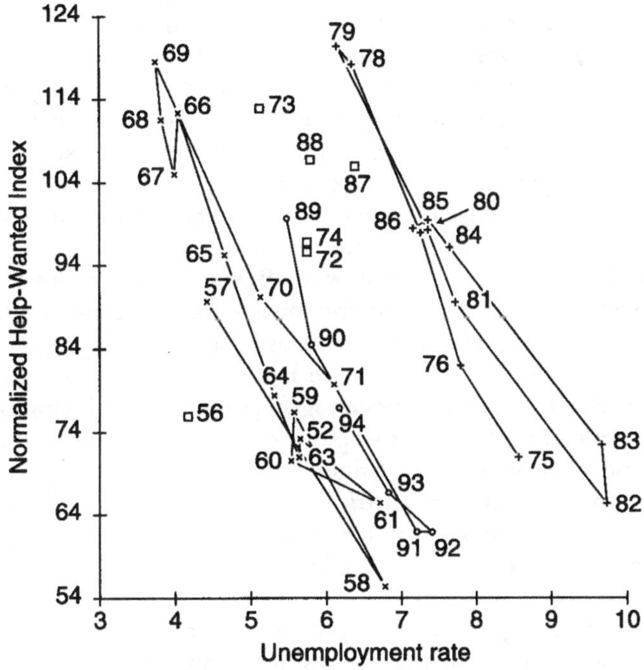

(b) United States, 1956–94

Notes

1 The unemployment rate refers to civilian workers, as reported by the US Bureau of Labor Statistics The 1994 figure is the new series, averaged over the first nine months. The proxy for vacancies is the Conference Board index (1985 = 100) of help-wanted advertising in newspapers, normalized by dividing it by the BLS series for civilian employment (1985 = 1.0). The employment series is also new in 1994 and averaged over only nine months. For this Normalized Help Wanted Index I am indebted to Professor James Medoff of Harvard University.

2 The two variables are not commensurate; therefore, it is not possible to draw a ray corresponding to the V = U 45° line in Figure 25.1(a).

3 There seem to be three clusters: I, 1957–71; II, 1975–86; III, 1989–94, plus some transitional observations in years between the clusters. Within each cluster the points have been connected sequentially, and these paths look like Beveridge curves. The shift from I to II was quite adverse, another indicator of the stagflation of the 1970s and its aftermath. The shift from II to III looks favourable, almost a return to I, but it is too early to tell. However, it suggests a decrease in the full employment rate of unemployment and a favourable shift in the Phillips curve.

the monthly population surveys of the US census, which classify persons as unemployed if they are not working and have been seeking jobs.

Defining involuntary employment as excess supply at prevailing wages and prices makes it clear that it refers to jobless persons who are willing to work at the wages employed workers of comparable qualifications are receiving. Critics who say that skilled machinists are not involuntarily unemployed if they turn down dish-washing jobs miss the point.

A measure of excess supply symmetrical to unemployment is unfilled job vacancies. Unemployment and vacancies generally exist simultaneously. Beveridge's definition of full employment for the economy as a whole makes conceptual sense: a situation in which unemployment does not exceed vacancies. In Chapter 2 Keynes acknowledges frictional unemployment but does not discuss it. Following Beveridge, unemployment matched by vacancies can be considered frictional – or, if chronic, structural.

A 'Beveridge curve' plots vacancies against unemployment, both as percentages of the labour force (see Figure 25.1). In this space, points to the left of the 45° ray meet Beveridge's criterion of full employment. The curve is generally downward-sloping, convex to the origin. Its point of intersection with the 45° ray defines full employment in the sense that the indicated unemployment is all frictional/structural. Any higher unemployment rate includes some non-frictional involuntary unemployment, Keynesian in the sense it is removable by expansion of aggregate effective demand for goods and services.

Movements along a given Beveridge curve are generated by variations of aggregate demand, north-west if positive, south-east if negative. Shifts of the Beveridge curve represent structural changes in labour markets. Outward shifts are adverse, increasing frictional/structural unemployment at the expense of unemployment remediable by Keynesian medicine.

Unfortunately, it is impossible to make commensurable measurements of unemployment and job vacancies. At unemployment rates that appear to be the minima consistent with stable inflation, measured vacancies are far fewer than measured unemployment. Empirical Beveridge curves can be drawn anyway, but the practical locus of zero excess supply lies below the 45° ray. The apparatus remains a useful framework in the frequent debates about whether observed increases in unemployment are reversible by demand expansion or are structural.

Both vacancies and unemployment can logically be determinants of money-wage increases or decreases: vacancies because they motivate employers to raise wage offers; unemployment because it motivates workers to accept lower offers. In empirical regressions, both effects are significant and important. The Phillips curve and the natural rate of unemployment are altered when the Beveridge curve shifts.

Inflation

The General Theory was written during the Great Depression. An economics student in 1996, encountering the book for the first time, will be surprised to find so little attention to inflation. But, after all, the price pathology of the times was deflation. The same reader, accustomed to contemporary worries about how to induce people to hold money and promises to pay money in the abundant quantities in which they are issued, might also be baffled to read in Chapter 17 that the basic economic difficulty is the public's voracious appetite for money and liquid near-moneys, combined with their inelasticity of supply. In that chapter those apparently riskless monetary assets are tough competition for real durable goods, given all the uncertainties of their returns.

The General Theory takes for granted that, whatever happens to money-wages and prices in short runs, people confidently expect something close to long-run price stability. They make wage bargains in the monetary unit of account, a fact that Keynes stresses in arguing that an economy's workers do not, and perhaps cannot, set real wages. Clearly, the situation would be quite different if money-wages were systematically indexed to the prices of the goods that workers produce and consume. Likewise, Keynes worries very little about the Fisherian distinction of real and nominal interest rates, except in the context of deflation.

Beginning in the 1960s, a principal battleground of macroeconomic debate has been the relation between unemployment rates and inflation. The formation and consequences of inflationary expectations have played a major role in analysis both of labour markets and of markets for money and other financial assets. A third edition of *The General Theory* would have to remedy these omissions.

In a Keynesian demand-constrained regime, output and employment will increase in response to additional real demand, whether resulting from shocks to private consumption and investment or from deliberate fiscal or monetary policies. Keynes postulated a sharp boundary, full employment, between this regime and the supply-constrained regime. Inflation is the consequence of demand expansion beyond the productive capacity of the economy.

'Full employment' is thus somewhat similar conceptually to the 'natural rate of unemployment'. Of course, it is hard to tell where the economy stands at any moment relative to full employment, or relative to the more pragmatic 'NAIRU' (Non-Accelerating-Inflation-Rate-of-Unemployment), which can be taken not as a thorough economy-wide market-clearing equilibrium but as a balance between excess-demand and excess-supply markets. These concepts are, in practice, zones rather than points.

Keynes envisaged with equanimity possible wage and price increases while employment is less than full. He was not thinking literally of a reverse

L-shaped relation between price level and aggregate output. He acknowledged in Chapter 21 that money-wages and prices could rise as sectoral bottlenecks and labour shortages are encountered. Workers' resistance to cuts in money-wages, even when they will accept cuts in real wages due to increases in prices of wage-goods, imparts in Keynes's view some inflationary bias to the economy. It is easier to make those microeconomic reallocations inevitable in a dynamic economy if the trend of money-wages, perhaps also of prices, is positive.

In the general theory, evidently, money-wages and prices are inherited from the past, possibly changed in the current period, and bequeathed to the future. The story is not so different from a Phillips curve. At high rates of utilization short of full employment, money-wages might increase repeatedly, period after period, even when output is still demand-constrained. The price path would depend also on the trend of productivity. For Keynes, this scenario is not 'true inflation', the explosive spiral associated with excess aggregate demand.

The main thing that many economists remember about *The General Theory* is the scepticism expressed in Chapter 2 on the downward flexibility of money-wages even when labour is in large excess supply. It seems irrational money illusion, the more so because Keynes asserts that the same workers would accept cuts in real wages resulting from increases in the prices of wage-goods. But the rationale Keynes offers for this apparent inconsistency is unexceptionable: workers are mainly worried about their wages relative to those of other groups. In a decentralized system of wage-setting, they bargain locally, and for money-wages, not real wages. Each group of workers fears that a cut in money-wages will turn out to be a cut in relative wages. In contrast, a rise in the cost of living, hitting all workers impartially, is acceptable.

This argument leaves unexplained how the 'inside' workers, those employed, can keep their money-wages up if unemployed 'outsiders' are willing to take their places for less. Keynes was well aware of the empirical fact that the availability of cheaper workers at the factory gate rarely lowers wages. It takes acute financial distress on the employers' side to reduce wages. But, having chosen to challenge classical theory on its own ground, pure competition throughout the economy, Keynes was not in a good position to appeal to imperfectly competitive realities. Even so, his discussions of labour markets sound more like collective bargaining than atomistic competition. Anyway, Keynesians today can invoke recent models that attribute the powers of insiders to costs of turnover and of demoralization.

Those powers are not absolute. Deep and prolonged recessions, which imperil the solvency of employer firms, endanger the jobs, seniority and fringe benefits of insiders. Barriers to downward flexibility of money-wages melt. The period 1981–3 in the United States is a recent example.

Downward flexibility at unemployment rates high enough to break established wage norms is the counterpart of upward flexibility at full employment. The upshot is a Phillips curve shaped like an elongated horizontal S. Between the two extremes of flexibility there is a long, nearly horizontal range, in which money-wages are fairly insensitive to current unemployment rates. This intermediate range is where most economies usually reside (Tobin 1955).

Nothing in *The General Theory* or in other writings of its author says that output can always be increased by events or policies that expand effective demand or by tolerating higher and higher inflation. Keynesian macroeconomic policy does not consist in riding recklessly up the short-run Phillips curve, heedless of the limitations of labour supply and productive capacity. Keynesians know the distinction between demand-constrained and supply-constrained regimes. They know that the medicines the doctor orders are, or should be, different in the two regimes. Ignoring such distinctions is the fallacy of the New Classicals, who say that, because an overdose of demand stimulus would harm a well patient, none of the medicine should be given to a sick patient either. Classical faith that demand-deficient economies will recover on their own failed theoretical and empirical challenge in Keynes's day. It fails now again, more than half a century later.

26

THE CHANGING SIGNIFICANCE OF INFLATION

Brian Reddaway

It is noteworthy that the title of Keynes's *magnum opus* (*The General Theory of Employment, Interest and Money*) includes no reference to *prices* at all. In a sense this is highly paradoxical. One may well say that the level of (real) *output* – implicitly represented in the title by 'employment' – is more important than changes in *prices*, which are 'only a paper affair': but any general macroeconomic analysis can only hope to 'make sense' if it includes prices as one of the variables, even if the investigator is not much interested in what happens to them (at least in comparison with what happens to *output*, which directly affects welfare).

The preface to *The General Theory* describes (*G.T.*: vi–vii) how the author had wrestled in his previous work (*A Treatise on Money*, 1930, *C.W.* V and VI) with the thought that he was *really* interested in output rather than prices. But he had felt bound by tradition to adopt the artificial device of seeking to explain the effects of an increase in demand as, first, producing a notional rise in prices, which would then induce a rise in output: this would, in whole or in part, prevent the rise in prices from actually happening.

Keynes did not of course leave the general price-level completely out of *The General Theory*, though he did not include any reference to prices in the title: he adapted Marshall's partial theory of prices, which he presented in Chapter 21. But this analysis is not really integrated with the general analysis of employment and so on, and has only a limited impact on his policy recommendations. One can well imagine, for example, that, in a second edition of *The General Theory*, Keynes would have recognized that an increase in demand affects *both* prices *and* production, and discussed what determines the effect on each of them. This would inevitably have been part of a very wide analysis, and the results would depend on a whole host of circumstances and assumptions: but economic life *is* a complex affair, in which a large number of factors mutually determine one another, and in which the relationships may change with changing circumstances.[1]

It is likely that in the second edition the analysis would also have been more careful to show at what points in the book the variables are assumed to be expressed in money terms, or in real terms, or in 'wage-units'. It is true that in Chapter 4 Keynes argues that for his analysis he needs only two units – money and wage-units – but this precept does not seem to be consistently followed. Moreover, in so far as 'wage-units' are employed, a further analysis is needed of what causes changes in that unit in terms of money: the hints given on (*G.T.*: 247, 301) seem to me quite inadequate.[2] It is noteworthy that when a *practical* issue was involved (in *Employment Policy* 1944, with which Keynes was much concerned), wages and prices get considerable attention.

The recognition of economic complexities – and more specifically, of the need to consider *both* prices (including the wage-unit) *and* output in a single analysis – might have avoided a great deal of rather fruitless controversy. Thus the 'Keynesian revolution' has tended to be 'simplified' by interested parties to a statement that 'output can be increased by an increase in demand up to a limit set by full employment'; and the 'counter-revolution' was similarly oversimplified to a statement that 'an increase in demand (inevitably measured in money terms) will at best have only a temporary effect in raising output, after which the effect would be wholly to raise prices'. Both the 'simplifications' ignore a whole host of other factors which cannot be dismissed by a simple assumption of *ceteris paribus* – a phrase which is capable of many different interpretations. Moreover, in many cases the results of a policy-action on demand can be made far more favourable by *combining* it with accompanying measures which are appropriate to the circumstances of the time and place under consideration; for example, by better training schemes or by special assistance to bring more of the long-term unemployed into employment.

'COST-PUSH' AND BARGAINING

Granted that macroeconomic analysis must cover a whole range of variables in a single exercise, rather than seek to discuss the effects of an increase in (money) demand on output (or prices) as a single narrow problem, what procedures can be adopted if a useful partial answer is to be sought without writing a vast tome?

In my view, the most helpful approach is to start from the idea that, while the rate of inflation is certainly influenced by the level of demand in relation to productive potential, nevertheless it is also influenced to an important extent by factors conveniently grouped as 'cost-push', rather than 'demand-pull'.[3] To my mind, these factors are greatly influenced by the fact that markets (whether for labour or for products) are not even approximately 'perfect', so that one cannot assume that every would-be buyer can buy whatever quantity (s)he wishes at an 'independently determined market price'; still less can one assume that every seller can sell whatever quantity (s)he wishes at such an independently determined market price. There are also points about *information* being imperfect, but they seem to me less fundamental.

This point about the complex working of a modern economy is so important – not only for prices, but also for output and employment – that it deserves a little elaboration at a rather basic level. It reflects in particular the extreme heterogeneity of output and of labour (and, indeed, of other productive factors) and the inevitable imperfections of markets.

In a modern economy, production of each article depends on the co-operation in a factory or other establishment of different classes of people, some of whom supply labour of various specialized kinds, whilst others supply many different kinds of capital equipment. In addition, it is essential that the teams which produce the various articles 'co-operate' with each other, both by supplying, through the market, a host of specialized intermediate products for use by the other teams, and also by supplying the general market with adequate amounts of finished goods. This intricate system of co-operation requires that the terms on which each person supplies his services, or those of his property, shall somehow be settled in an acceptable way – not only for today's activities, but also for a continuing operation over the coming weeks and months. This usually involves some sort of bargaining arrangement, in which workers typically act on a collective basis, because individuals acting on their own are in a weak position.

If an acceptable bargain cannot be agreed in any 'industry', then production will not be carried out, even though it is clearly in the national interest that it should be. (This position of stalemate is, however, usually a temporary one: it is vital that the analysis should not be too static.)

It is important to emphasize that these negotiations are usually done *sectionally*, for separate groups of specialized workers, rather than as a single collective bargain for the whole of the country's labour force. Keynes's 'wage-unit' is a convenient statistical device for many purposes, but it is not the subject of any negotiations. It has, indeed no 'real-life' existence, but is rather the almost accidental statistical outcome of a host of separate bargains, where the parties concerned are motivated by somewhat different forces from those which would apply if there were a single national bargaining table.

For each industry the evil consequences of a breakdown of negotiations – not only for the parties involved, but also for the users of the products – will loom very large, and there will be a natural tendency for many settlements to be on the high side, to ensure continuity of production: employers will hope to pass on the 'excess' wage costs to the consumers, and government influence (and public opinion) may also favour 'peace', even at a high price. The representatives of the workers have no real means of recovering any ground which they give away at the bargaining table, until the next round of bargaining.

The 'classical' or 'textbook' solution of this problem postulates that each individual supplier of a particular commodity or service (including labour of a certain kind) will compete freely with other suppliers of that item (and also with suppliers of other items); that all markets are perfect; and that everyone will accept the verdict of the market place as to the price which he receives – though he is, of course, free to decide to change to supplying something else or nothing at all. Naturally, it is recognized that the real world does not conform exactly to this simplified model; but the departures are considered negligible (except in the very short run) by those economists who believe in a simple 'market-clearing assumption', with all its beneficent theoretical results.

More pragmatic economists, with their eyes on the real world, may hope that market imperfections and heterogeneities will not prevent some sort of working agreements being reached by most sets of bargainers, which will enable production to continue without devastating interruptions. They recognize, however, that even in the labour field the bargains will be settled with little or no effective co-ordination, and that to avoid interruptions in production, settlements will tend to have an upward bias.

At the risk of labouring the obvious, it is clear that if each specialist group (including the employers) in each industry acts as a unit and 'demands' certain rates of real income on pain of a mass withdrawal of its services, and if in each industry these claims add up to more than the total output, then a breakdown is inevitable – unless, of course, some groups give way.

Fortunately, the institutional mechanisms of the bargaining process provide various elements which help to avoid a breakdown. Collective bargaining does not fix a *real* wage which must apply until the next bargain. A wage agreement is fixed in money, for a year (or other substantial period), and in an age of inflation its value in real terms is likely to be progressively decreased during the year by the actions of absent parties, such as the suppliers of consumer goods in other industries or the tax-gatherer; these future actions are not known, and uncertainty about them 'fuzzes' the exact nature of what is agreed. Moreover, no agreement is reached about the level of profits, or about the extent to which the employers may recoup higher wages by charging higher prices to another absent party – the consumer. If the bargaining really had to reach an agreement about the level of real wages and about the division of a cake of known size between the workers and the employers, the risk of breakdowns would be much greater.

Furthermore, the securing of agreements is helped by two things. First, the secular increase in productivity ensures a secular rise in real incomes for at least some of the parties to the bargains; and second, there is the *certainty* of immediate gain which any reasonable agreement will bring to the workers (as compared with yesterday) and by the thought that if this is too drastically eroded by rising prices, there will be another bargaining session in a year's time. Similarly, the employers, who suffer an immediate increase in costs, not only escape the threat of a damaging strike, but also have at least a chance of recovering these costs in the course of the year, and can reckon on being tougher next year if they fail. Once again, it is important to recognize that each bargain is only one episode in a continuous chain of bargains. Simple-minded ideas about profit-maximizing tend to treat the outcome of each bargain as if it were to apply for ever: agreements would be much harder to reach if each side thought it was a case of 'and so we will live happily (or *un*happily) ever after'.

GOVERNMENT POLICIES AND ACTION

It is manifest that macroeconomic analysis must take proper heed of government policies and actions, and it is perhaps extraordinary that so little formal attention was paid to this in *The General Theory* – and still less in the analysis of his earlier commentators, such as the protagonists of the IS–LM approach. I have, however, discussed this matter at some length in my contribution to Lekachman (1964a), so I shall not use precious space here to tackle the general issues. (In the consideration of specific problems which follows, I shall give due attention to the role of government policies.)

Some interesting problems

To start with a highly important problem, why is it that since the end of the Second World War the UK has shown a rise in prices in every single year? This is in great contrast to pre-war years, when, if we neglect war years, it was about as likely that there would be a *fall* in prices as a *rise*, and problems caused by price movements were very likely to be due to falls, rather than to rises.[4]

A first reaction to the question for some people might be to say that this is part of 'the British disease', so frequently denounced by Lady Thatcher as applying to the thirty years before she came to power. This would, however, be almost as wrong as portraying the post-war years as a period in which British output stagnated,[5] since *all* the OECD countries (including Germany) show a rise in prices in almost all post-war years – though admittedly their rises were typically below the British ones. Table 26.1 gives relevant figures for each of the G7 countries in the thirty years between 1962 and 1992: only one country recorded any annual price fall (out of the 210 movements covered by the table), and that was only 0.1 per cent (for Germany between 1985 and 1986, when oil prices fell – so the exception was not due to German austerity).

In the UK case, it seems most helpful to attribute the continuous post-war rise in prices to a combination of cost-push forces with a government pledge to seek a high and stable level of employment. It does not seem very

Table 26.1 Movements in consumer prices, 1962–92

	Germany	*USA*	*Japan*	*Canada*	*France*	*UK*	*Italy*
Ratio of index for 1992 to index of 1962	2.84	4.64	4.89	5.29	6.69	10.31	14.03
No. of years showing a fall in the index	1	0	0	0	0	0	0

Source: University of Cambridge, *Handbook of International Economic Statistics* (based on OECD, *Main Economic Indicators*).

useful to attempt to separate these two influences: it is the *combination* of the two which has been decisive.[6]

I am not competent to discuss the cases of other countries in detail, but it seems reasonable to suggest that the basic explanation was the same. Even if there was less of a formal 'full employment policy' in some of them, there was still at least a tendency to let the money supply 'accommodate' to the rise in prices which was tending to occur from the monopolistic elements in cost-push.

Why, then, did we not have ever-rising prices in the pre-war years? Essentially the answer seems to be that government policy was not then directed to 'managing the economy' in the way which has been adopted – however uncertainly – since the Second World War. *Budgetary* policy was then centred on securing a balanced budget in each year – albeit with debates over the inclusion of a regular sinking fund (to reduce the national debt), or whether certain transactions should be recorded 'below the line' and omitted from the budget balance. *Monetary* policy was centred on the maintenance of the gold standard, and the observance of certain financial 'rules'; for example, over the fiduciary issue. In practice, there was scope for some discretionary policy, but in general there was no attempt to (say) avert a price-fall if 'market forces' were tending to produce one – no matter what the effect on output and other 'real' variables might be.

Inflation and growth

Our next problem is concerned with growth as well as inflation. It is frequently asserted by government representatives that it is impossible to have good long-term growth in GDP unless inflation is kept to a low level: 'If the country is not prepared to face the temporary hardships involved in getting inflation down, any acceleration in growth (e.g. produced by a budget deficit) would only be temporary, and would worsen the inflation problems.'

A full analysis of all the possibilities, including alternative assumptions about 'other variables', would need far more space than is available. Some comments, which cast doubt on the validity of this assertion (to put it mildly), can however be supplied fairly easily:

1 The average rate of inflation in the UK, and in most other developed countries, has been far higher since the end of the Second World War than it was in pre-war years. Nevertheless, the long-term growth rate for production has been far more rapid, contrary to what the above assertion would suggest.
2 If one takes the *World Development Report* (published by the World Bank) and selects the Latin American countries which show high inflation rates over the last twenty-five years or so (typically 20 per cent per annum or more), very few fail to show a reasonable growth in GDP (measured at constant prices, and taken as an average for five years or more).
3 I have seen no convincing inter-country correlation calculation between the growth rate and the inflation rate for medium-term periods which gave a convincing negative answer, as the assertion would suggest.[7] Indeed, the very careful analysis presented by Stanners (1993) came persistently to the conclusion that there was no significant inter-country correlation between low inflation and high growth. This applied whatever grouping of countries was adopted; for example, developed countries only, or all countries for which suitable statistics were available – and also to all the periods considered.[8]

In effect, people who believe the assertion do so *in spite of* the statistical evidence, and not *because of* it. Perhaps they attribute the actual results to the strength of 'other factors' not specified in the assertion (or, usually, by them).

Weighting of objectives

My next problem is the weighting which a government should attach to the various objectives which it might seek to achieve, particularly in the macro-economic field. Since the main thesis of this chapter is the complexity of economic life and the need to consider many interacting economic variables, the treatment here is inevitably oversimplified, and any 'recommendations' need to be applied with careful consideration of the special circumstances which may arise in any specific case.

In brief, my main general approach is to stress the importance of giving great weight to *real* variables (e.g. GDP in real terms), rather than to 'financial' variables (e.g. the rate of inflation). This needs to be qualified immediately by such points as the damage which can (on relatively rare occasions) be caused by extreme or rapidly accelerating rates of inflation (if the government allows these to happen). Similarly, one should look sceptically on an objective of further reducing unemployment when it is already at a low level (e.g. Beveridge's famous 3 per cent); this point is especially important because the methods of intervention adopted may have bad (if somewhat belated) side-effects, and attempts at 'fine-tuning' may produce bad results because the data are unreliable, and 'other factors' may behave in unexpected ways.

This is of course a value judgement, but I wish to emphasize *my* strong belief that improvements in real variables are much more important than a reduction of inflation, unless one is in danger of getting into the zone of seriously accelerating inflation. Inflation undoubtedly brings some inconveniences and inefficiencies; and, if it is not reasonably well foreseen, it brings arbitrary distributional shifts of wealth. But in itself its main consequence is that people receive a rather bigger increase in money income (e.g. as wages or as pensions) than they would with no (or lower) inflation, and have to pay correspondingly bigger increases in prices: as a nation we suffer no significant 'real' impoverishment through inflation, as we do through mass unemployment – though we may lose through the forces which produced the inflation (e.g. dear oil in 1973), and if we let it get out of hand it can disorganize production.

It is perhaps worth considering the main evils which moderate inflation (say 5 per cent per annum) was traditionally thought to bring (i.e. in pre-war years). This is particularly relevant because steps have (perhaps unconsciously) been taken to mitigate many of them since inflation became a normal feature of economic life in the post-war years.

THE PRE-WAR POSITION

Before the Second World War it was normal, in developed countries, where the *average* movement in prices in peacetime years might be about zero, to regard inflation as 'unanticipated': preparations were not made in advance to deal with it if it did happen. This meant that when it did occur, various parties suffered economic losses which seemed 'unjustified', but which gave them no real scope for seeking redress as a matter of legal right – though it might mean that they could obtain some 'relief' from government or charitable sources. In general, other parties enjoyed corresponding uncovenanted gains; but these were of no benefit to the 'victims', and some hardships (as well as inconveniences) were incurred by many people. This was especially true if the movement of prices was upwards for a number of successive years.

For ease of exposition, I shall in general confine myself to the case of a closed economy and ignore cases of hyperinflation. With moderate inflation, the main sources of trouble from unanticipated inflation in pre-Second World War years (*when it occurred*) can then be conveniently divided into those arising out of the use of money as a *medium of exchange* and those arising from its use as a *unit of account*.

Medium of exchange

Very briefly, if the quantity of money was being increased at an excessive pace and prices were rising in consequence, then the creators of the money gained immediate purchasing power (though in the case of bank money they incurred a consequent debt). The main losers were wage- and salary-earners whose (money) incomes did not rise as fast as prices, together with rentiers (whose money income often did not rise at all). Entrepreneurs in general gained from a 'shift to profit', because their selling prices rose faster than their costs.

If views about future movements in prices were not much affected by past history (as was broadly the case), this process might go on for some years, as long as the forces for inflation continued to work (possibly with temporary gaps). The unorganized process of sectional wage-fixing might prevent the average loss of real wage from getting progressively bigger – indeed, rising productivity usually kept the average real wage rising on a historical basis, albeit interruptedly – but some people (notably those said to be on 'fixed salaries') never recovered their initial loss. This would also be the typical result for rentiers holding fixed-interest bonds, and for many pensioners there was no system for adjusting their income in the light of rising prices. (That is, however, getting into the territory of the unit of account.)

Unit of account

Many debts – including notably government bonds – have traditionally been fixed in terms of money, with a rate of interest which was often fixed for the whole term of the debt. 'Unanticipated inflation' produced an unintended revision of the real terms of the contract in favour of the borrower.[9]

The important question was then whether the creditors' losses in years of inflation would be roughly balanced by gains in years when prices fell. In practice this might happen in pre-war years, but for particular individuals it was a case of very rough justice indeed; moreover, there was in many cases a risk of default in years when prices fell. Even, however, if things did balance out in the long run, and even if there was much special pleading in the individuals' stories of 'gloom and doom', it is apparent that a world *without* unanticipated inflation (and deflation) would, *ceteris paribus*, be preferable to what actually happened. The real question was whether this could be achieved at all, and if so, whether it could be done without sacrificing other important objectives.

The post-war years

After the end of the Second World War it took more than a decade before there was a thorough recognition that things would be very different from pre-war on inflation (and indeed on many other macroeconomic variables). This showed up very clearly in the capital market, where the relative prices of bonds and ordinary shares continued to reflect the old principle that the immediate yield on the latter should be higher than that on the former, to compensate for the 'riskiness' of ordinary shares.[10]

Since about 1960, however, relative prices of equities and bonds have moved in such a way that the old 'yield gap' has disappeared and has been replaced by a 'reverse yield gap', with the immediate yield on long-dated bonds now being about double the immediate income received on equities (as 'compensation' for the virtual certainty that, in real terms, the income from bonds will fall progressively, while that on equities might well rise).[11]

This somewhat belated adjustment in the market place is one way in which things have changed, so as to keep down the damage caused by inflation; purchasers of bonds or investors in building societies receive a reasonable compensation for the fall in the real income from the original purchase, because the initial money income is high. There are, however, other ways in which the apparent imperfection of money as a unit of account in the post-Second World War world of inflation has been mitigated. The most direct has been the introduction of index-linked bonds, under which both interest and redemption money are adjusted for the rise in prices since the date when the bonds were issued. The basic rate of interest on these bonds is of course much lower than on conventional bonds, and is indeed usually at about the old level which prevailed on bonds in Victorian days, when the possibility of price-changes (in either direction) was virtually ignored.

Another device – much used in the field of life assurance – is virtually to take money as such out of the contract (except to fix the premium). The funds received are largely invested in equities rather than bonds, and the payment to the policy-holder at the end of the contract reflects the value of the resultant assets – essentially a development of the old 'with-profits' policy. (Alternatively the final payment is fixed at the outset in terms of the price of some well-known unit trust as numeraire.)

There is, to my mind, scope for further useful developments in this field. But wealth-holders (and borrowers) already have a substantial choice of methods by which the deficiencies of money as a unit of account can be rendered tolerable. It would of course be *nice* if we could follow the practice of using money as the unit of account without fears of serious loss through price changes; but the community should not pay more than a token price (e.g. through higher unemployment) to get an improved unit of account.

The post-war world has also seen many other ways in which action has been taken to limit the inequity which might be caused by 'rising prices for ever'. Wage settlements (and even salaries) are revised much more regularly, and a major consideration is the rise in prices since the last settlement. Pensions (including state pensions) and many welfare benefits are typically index-linked; this may or may not be formally part of a contract, but at least there is a presumption in favour of raising the payment in money so as to preserve the *real* benefit. Tax rules (including the famous Rooker–Wise provision about the amount of income to be free of tax) have been put on the basis of a *presumption* in favour of preserving the 'real' position in the face of inflation. (A cynic might say that the government now has the best of both worlds: the 'norm' is to preserve the 'real' position, but a cut in real terms can be called a freeze if the government wants to economize.)

Under these circumstances I find it rather odd that so much attention is paid by governments and other authorities to the case for the (virtual) 'elimination' of inflation. Under John Major, the present UK government is supposed to be attaching a lot of importance to 'growth', but its *actions* are much more concerned with getting inflation down to a very low level. There is not even a *target* for growth (to 'balance' the target of '1 per cent to 4 per cent and falling' for inflation).

Considering that the norm for growth of GDP in real terms is about $2\frac{1}{2}$ per cent per annum, it is really pathetic that GDP in 1993 should still, despite the much-heralded 'recovery' in output, be below the level of 1990: 'par for the course' in 1993 would be about 7 per cent above the actual level, and there seems little chance of having such a rise (over and above the normal increase) before the end of the century.

Since a modern economy is a very complex affair, it is impossible in this chapter to do the comprehensive analysis needed for detailed policy prescriptions. But the damage caused by inflation of less than 5 per cent per annum seems to me so small (given the way that our institutional arrangements have adapted) that a sustained increase in growth should be given overriding priority over a further campaign against inflation.[12] Price *changes* on individual items, which cause 'disturbance', would be almost as numerous with inflation at 1 per cent per annum as with 4 per cent.

As part of the policy for growth there needs to be a set of measures to improve the balance of payments on current account – even if that includes a lowering of the exchange rate, which would tend to raise many prices. The improvement of the BOP would directly help with growth, as well as being needed in the interest of external solvency.

In the famous words of Franklin Roosevelt, on the question of priority to be given to a coherent policy to establish a higher growth path for output, 'there is nothing to fear but fear itself'.

NOTES

1 Keynes was usually more interested in actions than in pure analysis, and at the time his book appeared the main problems were insufficient demand and unemployment: hence his analysis was developed primarily to deal with that problem, and his policy prescriptions up to the war were mainly directed to it (notably *The Means to Prosperity*, 1933b). But when war led to the danger of overheating, the same general ideas led to *How to Pay for the War* (1940b) as a means of reducing effective demand. I share Keynes's preference for discussing practical issues, and some of my ideas are reflected in the 'Keynes Lecture' which I delivered to the British Academy (Reddaway 1983).

2 This chapter provides a few tentative ideas on what such a discussion might have included but does not attempt the wide-ranging analysis which is really needed.

3 The same is of course true of the level of output. Moreover, there are inverse relationships from the levels of output and inflation to the other variables: it is a true case of 'mutual determination'.

4 This point is of special significance to one who started to study economics in 1931.

5 In fact, it advanced more rapidly in each decade from 1950 to 1980 than in any earlier decade for which statistics exist. See my chapter in Shepherd, Turk and Silberston (1983).

6 What has popularly been referred to as 'full employment policy' was never as unconditional as this name might suggest, and various governments have whittled it down. But the basic idea of government action has persisted, with an understandable bias in favour of expanding demand so long as unemployment was undesirably high in relation to political expectations. In view of the cost-push factors, this was likely to keep inflation positive, despite rising productivity. I discussed these matters in an article in Reddaway (1966). The main conclusion was that the question mark in the article's title should be deleted: we *are* likely to have rising prices 'for ever'.

7 As a very simple example, the rank correlation between the rise in consumer prices for a country in any period (shown in Table 26.1) and the rise in GDP in real terms for the same period is practically nil.

8 The reader is strongly recommended to read this careful article, which also considers other approaches, besides inter-country comparisons, such as analysis for a single country, correlating inflation and growth over single years (or a series of short periods).

9 In the classic cases where inflation became wildly accelerating (e.g. in Germany in 1923) the holders of bonds found that their savings had been wiped out: but the German nation had a corresponding gain in the destruction of the national debt, so private losses were offset by public gain. (This is not, however, the sort of 'pre-war norm' which I am trying to analyse.)

10 I am glad to say that in 1953 the investment committee of my college decided to change its portfolio of Stock Exchange securities from 100 per cent bonds to 100 per cent equities. This reflected our view that, in money terms, the income from bonds could not rise, whereas that on equities was likely at least to keep pace with inflation, which we thought would be consistently positive. (Our typist showed good economic understanding by recording our decision 'not to hold any g*u*ilt-edged securities'.) For a discussion of this and related issues, see Reddaway (1992).

11 On the strength of this reverse yield gap, the investment committee of my college now has a small holding of bonds. This reflects its ignorance about

which type of security would yield a higher average real income in the long run and a desire to spread our risks. (We have, however, a firm rule that a first charge on the cash income from the bonds in each year is an allocation to capital to make good the fall in its real value caused by inflation during the year. The cash income received on the additional bonds roughly keeps the 'spendable' income at the same level as for equities.)

12 As I wrote this chapter, *The Times* had a headline to an article which nicely reflected my views: 'Inflation obsession blinds policy makers to other ills' (see article by Janet Bush, 25 August 1994).

27

THE INFLATIONARY DIMENSION

A.J. Brown

What can we mean by the 'inflationary dimension' of a revision of *The General Theory*? No one is likely to think of the *General Theory* of 1936 as a book about inflation – very much the opposite; its central theme is underemployment, which, at that time at least, was associated with deflation. But, by the same token, its policy implications have generally been taken as expansionary, and its critics, both on its first appearance and since, have maintained that Keynesian policy would lead (or has led) to inflation. From where we now stand in the 1990s it is plain that the sinking of Keynesian policies from favour in the last two decades, after a quarter of a century during which the practice of or lip-service to them went with unprecedentedly full employment and with unprecedentedly rapid and uninterrupted growth in the main industrial market economies of the world, was largely due to their being also associated with unprecedented peacetime inflation, which eventually came to replace unemployment as the chief focus of popular and official economic anxieties.

In this chapter, I propose to examine three questions. First, what was Keynes's attitude to inflation? Was he 'soft' towards it? Second, what changes relating to inflation does it seem likely that he would have introduced into *The General Theory* if he had prepared a revision of it towards the end of his life? Third, what revisions relating to inflation seem to be required now, half a century on?

KEYNES'S ATTITUDE TO INFLATION

Many members of Keynes's generation were, by the early 1920s, highly sensitive to threats of inflation. They had been brought up in a world where that threat was remote; therefore, before the war, they had not learned to guard against it by trusting to judicious assortments of equities, rather than to good quality bonds, as vehicles for their savings, or by insisting where possible on indexation of wages and salaries. (The tying of wages in a few industries to the prices of the product was a different matter: that had turned out badly for wage-earners in the last quarter of the nineteenth century, and had been abandoned.) The First World War and its immediate aftermath had doubled the cost of living in this country and had led to much worse inflations in Central and Eastern Europe, turning in some cases into true hyperinflations, of which that in Germany in 1922–3 was the most spectacular.

Keynes not only shared this experience of his generation but, by virtue of his interest as an economist, his position in the wartime Treasury and various special concerns (notably his membership of the Committee of Experts on the stabilization of the German Mark in 1922), was more intimately aware of such matters. Indeed, as early as September 1915, he had written a memorandum on the mechanism of wartime inflation ('The meaning of Inflation' *C.W.* XVI: 125) which, with its emphasis on the way in which inflation could supplement taxation in gathering resources for the government, was well ahead of its time. In its insistentce on the instability of this process – its dependence on, and its erosion of, confidence (especially abroad) in the value of sterling, it was also far from comforting; it closed with the characteristically Keynesian remark: 'When this happens in Brazil, Brazil is said to be bankrupt.'

In *The Economic Consequences of the Peace* (*C.W.* II) published in 1919, the role which he attributed to wartime and post-war inflation was again a destructive one. Inflation raised profits at the expense of other factor incomes, turning the rest of society against the 'profiteers' on whose role as entrepreneurs economic progress nevertheless depended. He quoted Lenin (it has been suggested by Fetter 1977, cited by Moggridge 1992, that he invented the quotation) to the effect that the best way to destroy the capitalist system was to debauch the currency, adding: 'Lenin was certainly right' (*C.W.* II: 149). In the *Tract on Monetary Reform* (1923 and *C.W.* IV) he dwelt again on the arbitrariness and injusticies of the income redistributions that inflation caused, especially its victimization of those who, by the received standards of economic conduct, had been the most prudent. In short, his attitude to inflation in the earlier half of his career was clear – he was against it. It is true that already in the early 1920s he was also against deflation, on the twin grounds that it could operate successfully (that is, bring down costs of production) only through unemployment and labour disputes, and that it would shift the distribution of income unacceptably to the advantage of rentiers, whose large war debt holdings already made them potential objects of hostility. Either of those dislocations would strain the fabric of capitalist society, then seen in the light of events in Russia and Central Europe as being fragile. The *Manchester Guardian* once attacked him as an 'inflationist' on the ground of his criticism of the bank rate increase of early 1923. In fact, his object at that time, as he claimed, was neither inflation nor deflation, but a stable general level of prices.

Does this claim still hold good, however, for his more considered views half a dozen years later, as expressed in the *Treatise on Money* (1930, *C.W.* V and VI)? There are important features of that work which certainly raise the question. Its central theoretical distinction so far as inflation is concerned was that between 'income inflation' and 'profit inflation', the former consisting of a rise in the prices of the hired factors of production; the latter, as its name suggests, in a rise in the return to entrepreneurship. (This is, in effect, a distinction between 'cost-push' and 'demand-pull' inflation, a point to which we shall return.) Profits being both the incentive for productive investment and the source of much of the funding for it, profit inflation tends to go with rapid growth and high employment; profit deflation (its opposite) and income inflation are unfavourable to growth and employment. Keynes elaborated this in his 'Historical Illustrations' (*C.W.* VI: ch. 30). The influx of gold into Europe in the sixteenth century produced profit inflations associated with rapid growth (which enabled us, as he rather incautiously added, to 'afford Shakespeare'); the British return to gold in 1925 induced a profit deflation with the opposite effect. He suggested that the great growth-spurts of economic history owed more to profit-inflation (and hence to forced saving) than to voluntary 'thrift'.

We might deduce from this that Keynes advocated inflation, so long as it was profit-inflation, as the means to growth and prosperity. Indeed, he quotes F.P. Ramsey's work on the optimum rate of saving and investment as suggesting that everyone, including wage-earners, who suffer an immediate real income loss from profit-inflation, might be better off in the long run with some such inflation generating, as Keynes assumes it would, increased investment (*C.W.* VI: 144–5). In a passage that seems, in the light of hindsight, to look forward to *The General Theory* concept of the income multiplier, he suggests that higher employment and output resulting from a higher current rate of investment might compensate wage-earners for the forced saving imposed upon them by profit-inflation. All this seems to be an argument for profit-inflation. His summing-up, however, does not support such an inflationary bias: 'Nevertheless, I am not converted, taking everything into account, from a preference for a policy which, while avoiding Deflation at all costs, aims at stability of purchasing power as its ideal objective'. (*C.W.* VI: 145).

That was presumably his position in September 1930, when the *Treatise on Money* went to press. But although the price fall of the Great Depression had been under way for about a year, it had proceeded only half as far (less than half for dollar prices) as it was to go by 1933, and by then Keynes was insisting on the need to raise prices to something like the level of 1929. That he did this in spite of having argued against attempts to reverse the price inflation of 1914–20 could perhaps be taken at first sight as evidence of 'softness' towards inflation. Was his general doctrine: avoid both inflation and deflation if you can, but if they happen nevertheless, it may be expedient to reverse a deflation, but not to reverse an inflation? This, of course, would turn out to be an inflationary doctrine in the long run. But Keynes's views should be taken in the contexts in which they were expressed, and not be over-generalized. A substantial part of his ground for objection to deflation in the early 1920s, as I have noted above, was the existence of a huge burden of war debt, which stood to be magnified by every fall in prices – though the difficulties of forcing money-wages downwards were also in Keynes's mind. In the early 1930s, a large part of his concern was less with the general price level as such than with the low relative level of primary prices, which had the effect of extinguishing primary producing countries' demand for manufactures (especially investment goods). To have corrected this maladjustment by further reduction of the prices (and costs) of manufactures would have been socially and politically impossible, bearing in mind that they had already been heavily reduced and that the real burden of debts of all kinds had thereby been substantially increased. Moreover, a deflationary attempt to remedy the situation would only have made it worse, since prices of primary products were more sensitive to demand than those of manufactures – the fact from which much of the change in the terms of trade had arisen.

Keynes was always sensitive to contemporary problems and conditions. In the First World War and its immediate aftermath he was concerned about inflation, giving at least full value to its disruptive social and economic consequences. (After sixty years of continuous inflation which has left the capitalist system in greater general favour than before, we may think that his anxieties were excessive.) In the times of the Cunliffe deflation, the over-valued pound and the Great Depression, he was concerned principally about the costs of deflation. The outbreak of the Second World War brought concern about inflation to the fore again, though not to the exclusion of some attention to the dangers of deflation and unemployment that he saw as lying ahead in the post-war world. As a matter or principle, he was a stable-prices man, in spite of his formulation of the connection between profit-inflation and prosperity, and his advocacy of specific rises in the general price level was limited to special conditions, such as the trough of the Great Depression and certain wartime or post-war situations in which he thought controlled prices could not be held down with advantage.

INFLATION IN *THE GENERAL THEORY*

Before considering what changes relating to inflation Keynes might have introduced into *The General Theory* if he had revised that work, we should perhaps note what is said about inflation in the work as it stands. Although it is far from being the book's central theme it is, in fact, brought into the picture, mostly in Chapter 21 ('The Theory of Prices'). Because the book's main emphasis is on what Pigou called 'lapses from full employment' and the differences between the analyses appropriate to the fully employed and incompletely employed economies, it is not surprising that Keynes starts from a firm distinction between price rises that go with the drawing of unemployed resources into use and those that take place when full employment has already been achieved. In connection with the former, he mentions the usual reasons for expecting rising unit costs – notably differences in efficiency between different establishments and between different individual operatives – but he does not regard as 'true' inflation this price rise caused by the rising marginal costs that go with fuller utilization of resources. He prefers to reserve the name for price increases caused by excessive money demand in conditions of full employment, when output could not be increased further by drawing in spare factors of production – such spares not being available. The practical importance of this distinction, of course, is that rising prices attributable to bringing into action less-efficient marginal units of labour and/or equipment is generally tolerable; it goes with an increase in aggregate real income, and the scope for it is limited, whereas 'true' inflation is, by hypothesis, not automatically accompanied by a rise of real income, and the scope for its continuation is unlimited. Indeed, there are mechanisms, such as a flight from the currency and an increasing lag of government tax revenues behind expenditures, by which 'true' inflation may accelerate itself into hyperinflation.

Keynes recognized, however, in the chapter in question, that the distinction between the responses to rising money demand in conditions of non-full and full employment is somewhat blurred. First, since factors of production are not homogeneous, rising output is liable to encounter a series of 'bottlenecks': full employment of particular kinds of skill or plant which will cause the relevant prices to rise, in so far as they are market-flexible, even though substantial amounts of different kinds of skill or plant capacity remain idle. Second, mainly because wages are largely fixed by collective, not individual bargaining, money-wage rates may rise even while substantial amounts of the relevant kinds of labour remain unemployed:

> Since each group will gain, *cet.par.*, by a rise in its own wages, there is naturally, for all groups, a pressure in this direction, which entrepreneurs will be more ready to meet when they are doing better business. For this reason a proportion of any increase in effective demand is likely to be absorbed in satisfying an upward tendency of the wage unit.
> (*C.W.* VII: 301)

In these two sentences, it may be claimed that Keynes anticipated, though in an ordinal rather than a cardinal form, the relation which a generation later was associated mainly with the name of A.W.H. Phillips (1958). The first of Keynes's sentences supports the essential Phillips relation: a negative one between unemployment (which can be seen as an inverse indicator of business prosperity) and the rate of wage inflation. Indeed, it gives a considerably more convincing explanation of the relation than did Phillips and most of those who came after him. They suggested that wage rates moved towards equilibrium with a speed that varied directly with their distance from it: a proposition which is less than clear if we consider how awkwardly the notion of a full-employment equilibrium price for labour sits with the facts of collective bargaining. Keynes was nearer to the earth. The second of Keynes's sentences quoted above suggests, however, a relation different from that implied in the first, namely, one that should manifest itself in a negative relation between wage inflation and the rate of change rather than the level of the unemployment percentage. This relation, in fact, was also noted by Phillips in his 1958 article as a subsidiary one – wage inflation was promoted by *falling*, as well as by *low* unemployment.

Keynes's interest in the mechanisms of wage inflation was limited, for the purposes of *The General Theory*, to the conditions in which they begin to operate, and having made the point that they do so some way short of full employment (even if one excludes short-period decreasing returns and, presumably, the normal frictions of the labour market), he turned to other matters, without noting the difference between his two relations or the fact that the second of them follows from the first (as he seems to imply) only at those levels of unemployment low enough to go with a rise rather than a fall in wages. In a revision intended for a world in which inflation was either a more recent memory or a more menacing threat than it appeared to be in 1935, he might well have developed these insights which appear only as throw-away remarks in his great book as it stands, along with other relevant ideas which appear in his writings – not least those elicited by the Second World War and the events immediately after it which he lived to witness.

AFTER *THE GENERAL THEORY*

In fact, of course, the threat of full-blooded inflation under wartime full employment soon presented itself, and Keynes gave his attention to it in *How to Pay for the War* (1940b, *C.W.* IV and XXII). In the course of this work he describes what would happen if, starting from a situation of full employment, where total output cannot be further raised, the government increases its purchases of that output without engineering a corresponding reduction of expenditure by the private sector. The analysis is essentially a multiplier one, except that, as total expenditure increases, it is prices and not output that rise. Keynes suggests that, in practice, sellers may be reluctant to raise prices, in which case there will be queues and empty shops; but in his main analysis the assumption is that prices are flexible, and that they and money incomes (profits in the first instance) rise enough to generate extra savings and tax revenue to match the government's extra purchases. The inflation necessary to produce this result is reduced by the fact that both the marginal rate of taxation on profits and the marginal rate of saving out of them are likely to be high. It is simply what is needed to reduce real incomes in the private sector sufficiently to make their receivers go without the extra resources that the government has decided to buy. Kaldor later used a similar mechanism to formulate his 'Keynesian theory of distribution', in which the share of profits in income has to rise or fall to bring savings to equality with investment. Keynes recognized, however, that contrary to the assumptions of Kaldor's model, some income-receivers in the private sector can fight back. Wage and salary earners bargain for increases to match the raised cost of living, while sellers of final goods and services put up their prices to protect their real profits – a price–wage spiral augments the multiplier process. It is, of course, a spiral that can become explosive, because there is not enough real income (even after allowing for rises in productivity) to satisfy all parties, and each party is in a position to do something about it at the expense of others. The explosiveness is naturally mitigated by such delays as occur in the processes of wage and price adjustment.

The account I have thus tried to summarize of a demand-led inflationary process under full employment conditions (*C.W.* IX: 416–22) is a gem of lucid Keynesian exposition, and is what Samuelson probably had in mind when he remarked that *How to Pay for the War* should always be read as an appendix to *The General Theory* to correct the latter's bias towards conditions of non-full employment. One can well imagine that, if Keynes had prepared a new edition after inflation had re-emerged into the limelight, he might have included a few pages giving a version of this account in Chapter 21.

With such an addition, *The General Theory* would emerge more clearly as the fountain-head of practical macroeconomic policy, and particularly of the concept of the *ex ante* inflationary gap, which was perhaps its main conceptual instrument. It appears unnamed in the passage referred to above in *How to Pay for the War*: it was named as 'The Gap' in Keynes's note dated 3 March 1941 (*C.W.* XXII: 289–94) in preparation for the 1941 Budget, and was a key concept in the Chancellor's Budget Speech (as well as a feature, represented by a hole in the floor, in a David Low cartoon published on Budget Day). It was the key concept, again, in the post-war Economic Surveys prepared in 1945–7 by the Economic Section of the Cabinet Office. Keynes was critical of the use made of it in the draft 1947 Survey, prepared shortly before his death (see Cairncross 1985: 413–15). The fact remains, however, that it was essentially his child, and is still the prime instrument for diagnosing threats of inflation – or deflation – originating from differences between aggregate intentions to spend on the national output and the value, at present prices, of the national output likely to be available.

Not all threats of inflation came from that quarter, however. I have mentioned above the distinction made in the *Treatise on Money* between 'profit' inflation and 'income' inflation. Broadly speaking, the inflationary gap is an estimate of the threat of the former, or, in the language of a later period, of 'demand-pull' inflation. 'Income' inflation, or 'cost-push', comes from rises in the prices of the country's inputs; mainly, that is to say, of its labour and its imports. Rises in wages (and salaries) may, of course, be 'induced' by rises in the cost of living, themselves originating in import-price increases, earlier wage-increases, or earlier profit inflation due to excess demand (an earlier inflationary gap); but they may also be of the apparently more spontaneous kind due to the 'constant pressure' to which Keynes referred in *The General Theory*, and the willingness of entrepreneurs to concede to it when they are doing good business. In *How to Pay for the War*, Keynes remarks that, in wartime conditions, including the existence of Excess Profits Tax, 'it will not cost [employers] much to share their profiteering with their employees'. As for import prices, they are decided mainly in world markets rather than by the importer's national policies, though excess demand may raise prices to him by lowering his currency's external value.

In the early part of the Second World War, when Keynes was concerned with his deferred pay scheme, published in *How to Pay for the War* and partly realized in the 1941 Budget, he was well aware of other inflationary threats, beside those connected immediately with the inflationary gap. One was the rise of import prices, which had occurred because of increased shipping and insurance costs, widespread desire to build up stocks against possible interruptions of supply later, and a fall in the external value of sterling. His attitude to this was at first sight a little complex. He urged the government not to keep controlled prices down too rigidly in the face of world market price increases, because that would divert demand from imports to home products, and because such a policy would mean that 'the Government would have to take over the importation of almost everything and then sell the stuff at a stupendous loss to the Treasury' (*C.W.* XXII: 5). Instead, he advocated allowing the wholesale price index to rise by about 35 per cent (more for imports, less for home-produced goods), which he though could be made consistent with a rise in the cost of living of about 10 per cent – and that this, in view of the longer hours of work, would keep real wage incomes at about their 1937 level.

When, early in 1940, the government announced that it was subsidizing the prices of some goods included in the cost of living index, he wrote that this would be desirable only as part of a wider policy (presumably one designed to close the inflationary gap) of which no sign had been given. By the time of the 1941 Budget, however, a wider view was being taken, and he advised that keeping down by subsidy the prices of the (largely rationed) goods entering into the (then existing) index would assist in moderating wage demands without making consumers' real disposable purchasing power too high in relation to available supplies – and also without detailed control of wages, which he thought undesirable as likely to incur the hostility of the trade unions. The goods included in the index of that time (obsolete as a sample of normal peacetime consumption) were on the whole such as could be regarded as 'necessities', on the cost of which claims for the maintenance of an austere wartime standard of life could legitimately be based. When the war was over, he recognized that these conditions ceased to apply; consumers became less willing to accept that their claims on the economy should be limited to 'necessities', especially as these were represented in a thirty-year-old index. Moggridge (1992) records that Keynes, immediately before his death in April 1946, was drafting a memorandum arguing *inter alia* that a controlled rise in British prices was required rather than continued subsidization. In the meantime, the wartime subsidization policy had worked well.

So much for limiting 'induced' income inflation by the use of subsidies to offset rises in (largely) import prices. About import prices before subsidy, less can be done by the importing country alone (though in wartime the United Kingdom used such bargaining power as it had in making purchasing agreement with its suppliers), but already in 1939 Keynes's mind had turned to a subject of some relevance to inflation in world markets, namely what he considered to be the excessive short-term variability of primary commodity prices, and the possibility of reducing this by a policy of government storage – an extension of the policy, then recently announced by the President of the Board of Trade, of storing essential foodstuffs and raw materials as a measure of war insurance (*C.W.* XXI: 456–70). Later, in the course of discussions about post-war relief and reconstruction, he urged the advantages of a co-ordinated scheme for international controls of the principal primary products, under the supervision of a General Council for Commodity Control – a scheme which he attached, in the first instance, to his Clearing Union proposals. It did not survive – the Bank of England was an important objector to it – though pale ghosts of it appeared in the General Agreement on Tariffs and Trade and in the guidelines drawn up in 1947 by the Economic and Social Council of the United Nations for its Interim Committee on International Trade Agreements (see *C.W.* XXVII: Part I, *passim*).

Richard Kahn, who had shared so much of Keynes's thought and who in 1943–4 served in the Raw Materials Department of the Ministry of Supply, became interested in buffer stock schemes, and after the war worked on such schemes for tin and sugar. In the post-war generation, however, with the terms of trade moving mostly against primary products, there was a tendency for the improvement of those terms rather than price stability to be the aim of control schemes. The United Nations Conference on Trade and Development, beginning in 1964, worked up in the succeeding decade to an Integrated Programme for Commodities, in which price stability and buffer stocks had a place; but, partly because UNCTAD's objectives were wide – 'a New International Order', no less – and partly because of the differences of interest inseparable from attempts to change the terms of trade, little was achieved.

The obvious relevance of Keynes's thinking on these matters is to reduction of short-term price fluctuations and to reduction in fluctuations of activity through judicious anti-cyclical purchases and sales, rather than to inflation as such. Had inflation and its prevention been at that time his main preoccupation, however, it would probably have occurred to him that upward impulses to prices and wages generally, from the primary commodity markets, tend to be responded to more strongly than do downward impulses. It is always easier to raise money-wages, in particular, than to reduce them. And this being so, fluctuations in primary prices exercise something of a ratchet effect on the price-level of final goods and services; there is a presumption that less of the former would mean less inflation of the latter. In the discussion of control schemes during the post-war decades, however, this point was only intermittently seen as important.

A KEYNESIAN REVISION

What, then, might the treatment of inflation in a revision of *The General Theory* made by Keynes towards the end of his life have looked like? Much of it would have been little changed from what we have in print. The distinction between decreasing returns and 'true' inflation would probably have remained. I like to think that he might have re-introduced the essence of the distinction between 'profit inflation' and 'income inflation' which he had made in the *Treatise on Money*. How excess demand causes profit inflation, and how that induces income inflation which, money supply permitting, induces price increases to restore profits and hence a price-wage spiral (which may be convergent, but which may be divergent and even lead to hyperinflation) would have been explained on the lines of section IX of *How to Pay for the War*. The existing references to factor prices beginning to rise short of full employment, and to the upward pressure of wage demands that are increasingly likely to be granted at more prosperous levels of business (Keynes's 'Phillips curve') would presumably have remained, and might have been amplified. Keynes's remark in a letter of June 1945 to S.G. Macfarlane, an Assistant Secretary to the Australian Commonwealth Treasury, that 'One is also, simply because one knows no solution, inclined to turn a blind eye to the wages problem in a full employment economy' (*C.W.* XXVII: 385), reads more like a statement of worry than of dismissal. And surely, in the light of wartime experience, he would have said something about rises in the prices of imports as inducers of domestic inflation. He would almost certainly not have advocated subsidies to offset them in peacetime, but he might well have made some reference in connection with them to the problems of worldwide commodity control schemes, to which he had devoted so much thought; just as he might have referred to hopes that the International Monetary Fund and the Economic and Social Council of the United Nations would help to promote some degree of stability in the world prices of primary commodities generally by facilitating appropriate management of aggregate demand in the world economy.

THE VIEW FROM 1994

If this can be taken as a reasonable estimate of Keynes's views of inflation, in the general macroeconomic context of *The General Theory* towards the end of his life, what can we say of it now, nearly half a century on?

For about half of that half-century we lived in what could be described as a Keynesian Paradise or Golden Age of full employment and rapid growth in all the main industrial countries, discussed under 'Golden Age' titles in Marglin and Schor (eds) (1990), and in Cairncross and Cairncross (1992). The median of the annual average unemployment rates (standardized by Maddison 1982) over the sixteen main OECD countries from 1950 to 1974 (inclusive) was 3.1 per cent against about 7.5 per cent for the period 1920–38. (The corresponding figures for the UK are 3.0 per cent against 9.2 per cent.) Unemployment rates in the 1950s and 1960s may not have been very much lower than before the First World War (the median annual average rate for the UK, the USA and Germany over the years 1900–13, according to Maddison's data, was 3.8 per cent) but the growth rate was probably something like twice as fast – Maddison gives, for his sixteen OECD countries, an average rate of 4.9 per cent for 1950–73, against 2.5 per cent for 1870–1913. The Keynesian Golden Age was, indeed, characterized by the fastest growth of real income in the developed world as a whole that has ever been recorded, or reliably estimated, for a period of substantial length.

The serpent in this Eden was, of course, inflation. It will be useful to think of it in two parts: that which was led, on a world scale, by the mostly market-determined prices of primary commodities, and that, largely in particular countries rather than in the world as whole, which proceeded without that leadership. There were two main primary product booms in the Golden Age and another after its demise; respectively, the Korean War boom of 1950–1, the commodity boom of 1973 merging into the first oil shock, and the second oil shock of 1979–80, which ushered in what seems to be a new era of fresh Juglar (roughly ten-year) trade cycles, from the depression phase of the second of which we are only just, as I write, beginning to recover – with inflation still unbroken, though moderated.

These primary product price booms led into acute bursts of inflation in the more developed countries. That of 1950–1 was due to causes with which Keynes would have been familiar from his memories of 1914 and 1939: a rise in costs of shipping and insurance, and a desire of dealers and governments to accumulate stocks of foodstuffs and raw materials while they were still available and transportable. They might have been moderated if the policy of government storage which he had supported in 1938 had been continued, and if the co-ordinated buffer stock schemes on which he had worked during the war had been adopted. In the event, raised primary prices set off price–wage spirals in the industrial countries, which continued to operate for some time after primary prices had started to fall. The raised money incomes in the industrial sector resulting from these spirals naturally prevented primary prices from falling subsequently to their starting levels. This interaction of mainly market-determined primary prices and mainly cost-determined prices of manufactures, combined with the ability of wage-earners and profit-receivers to take some effective action in defence of their real income, is essentially a multiplier mechanism such as Keynes had described in *How to Pay for the War*, though in a somewhat different context.

The boom of 1973, before the oil shock, was in some degree due to a failure of demand management in the main industrial countries taken together; a number of national booms coincided. The peak of demand would not, however, have been very serious by itself. To exacerbate its effects there were important shortcomings on the supply side, notably a harvest failure in the Soviet Union, and the institutional changes of the time were unhelpful; in strong contrast to the kind of arrangement that Keynes had sought to promote for the post-war world, the collapse of the International Wheat Agreement had caused stocks to be too low for such an emergency.

But it was, of course, the oil shocks that created the main havoc. Crude oil production accounted for probably more than 1 per cent of the value of gross world product. By the cartel action of OPEC, crude oil prices were virtually quintupled within a year and increased some seventeen-fold within a decade. The power, already referred to, of wage- and salary-earners in the non-primary sector to resist reduction in their real incomes and the passing-on of cost increases into prices ensured a multiplication of the primary inflationary impulse. Also, the drawing-off of purchasing power into the oil-producing countries produced a shortage of it elsewhere, which was supplemented by the action of many governments and monetary authorities in pursuing restrictive (or at least not completely accommodating) monetary and fiscal policies against the prevailing price inflation. So 'stagflation' on an unprecedented scale was engendered. In a general sense, this was an extreme case of the kind of disruption, initially from the supply side, against which Keynes had devised his world commodity scheme; but it was a very special case. Given the existing Middle Eastern political conflicts, to visualize a benevolent buffer stock scheme, subject to a world authority created and surviving in the place of OPEC, demands unusual imaginative powers. Nor can the political events in Iran, from which the second oil shock (of 1979–80) arose, be regarded as disturbances against which an enlightened control scheme, with appropriate consumer representation, would have been wholly proof. We cannot say that the inflationary impulses from primary commodity markets in the last half-century would have been totally or even mainly avoided if Keynes's schemes for this department of the post-war world economic institutions had been adopted by the United Nations in 1945; but it is hard to see what other lines of action could be envisaged that might mitigate the severity of similar impulses in the future.

The other main elements in world inflation, besides impulses from the prices of primary products, has been the propensity of the non-primary sectors of the various national economies to sustain wage–price and wage–wage spirals. These have amplified other inflationary impulses, whether from primary product prices, import prices generally or excessive spending intentions of the kinds that might have been diagnosed as positive inflationary gaps. It is not always easy to separate the initiating impulses from the ensuing spiral-driven inflation. We can, however, point to cases where inflation has reached considerable rates without the help of any impulse from primary product prices, and with no very obvious propulsion of the inflationary gap type. In other words, an apparently self-propelled wage–price or wage–wage spiral has been the culprit.

From 1953, when the Korean war peak was already well past, to 1958, the dollar price index of internationally traded primary products followed a falling trend (9 per cent over the fifteen years), but the corresponding index of traded manufactures rose by 9 per cent, and the consumer price indices (in national currencies) of the main countries also rose by amounts varying from 30 per cent in the United States to about 75 per cent in France and Japan (the UK increase was 56 per cent). Thus, a gentle fall in the dollar prices of primary inputs went with increases in consumer prices (even in the land of the dollar) which were in some cases sufficient to cause intermittent anxiety and some anti-inflationary measures.

This raises one of the most discussed questions about the inflation of the Keynesian Golden Age: was it (or much of it) an inevitable consequence of achieving low levels of unemployment, amounting to actual labour shortage – in other words, does the Phillips curve genuinely depict limits to Keynesian high-employment policies, which were transgressed with inflationary consequences?

At this point, we may be tempted to put the question whether the low unemployment of this time (and for a few years longer) was the consequence of Keynesian policies. It is a difficult question which I have insufficient space to do justice to here. It would be hard to deny an important influence to the widespread acceptance of Keynesian doctrine at this time and to the effects of it embodied in 'full employment' legislation in a number of countries. Though in the UK, at least, it was private capital formation and to some extent exports rather than public spending that acted as the main propellants of high activity, the 'animal spirits' which fuelled them were largely sustained by perceptions that prosperity was virtually government-guaranteed. For my present purpose, however, it seems adequate to confront the question posed in the preceding paragraph as being important and interesting in itself, without considering further how the high and stable activity of the period was produced.

To return, therefore, to the Phillips curve: an important point to be noted about it is that most of the changes in unemployment and wage inflation to which it was fitted were cyclical changes between boom and depression and back again, and that it should not therefore be taken uncritically as giving information about the effects of changing the average level at which unemployment stands over a substantial period – which is what is relevant to questions concerning the Keynesian Golden Age as a whole. If, from Phillips's original data, averages are taken over each of the trade cycles that he distinguished, we find that these averages for the cycles from 1861 to 1913 vary only over small ranges, and do hardly anything to help in defining the curve. The averages for inter-war cycles confirm that high unemployment goes (or went then) with low wage-growth (though not with actual decline over a whole cycle), and the post-1945 cycles naturally show low unemployment going with high wage-inflation; that is the extent of the evidence of these data, once we deal with cyclical averages rather than annual figures. To this limited extent, it supports Keynes's generalization that employers will be more willing to concede money-wage increases when business is good.

In this connection, it is worth remembering that Keynes's idea of the minimum level of unemployment corresponding to 'full employment' was relatively modest. In his June 1943 draft on the size of the post-war national income (*C.W.* XXVII: 335) he wrote: 'We cannot regard the unemployment problem as substantially solved so long as the average figure is greater than 800,000, namely 5% of the wage-earning population, or rest content without resort to drastic changes of policy so long as it exceeds one million.' These figures were based on the results of an official survey in 1935 which placed frictional and structural unemployment at 760,000, or 6 per cent of the insured (roughly, the wage-earning) population. Keynes suggested that, in the light of more recent information, this might be reduced to 5 per cent. But between 1953 and 1957, the unemployed numbered only about 300,000 altogether.

Does this suggest that, if the British economy had been run at a rather lower temperature in the 1950s and at least the earlier 1960s, so as to keep unemployment at the level regarded by Keynes as the practical minimum, the rate of wage inflation (and price inflation) would have been substantially lower? Phillips's curve suggests a reduction in wage inflation of somewhere about three percentage points a year, which would have brought it down to a level at which productivity growth could have covered most or all of it. And further, if this had been so – if we had escaped most if not all of the inflation that we experienced in the first fifteen years or so of the Keynesian Golden Age – should we also have escaped a substantial part of the inflation that we have suffered since?

The answers to these questions are not straightforward, even as the answers to hypothetical questions go. First, there is some doubt about the comparability of the pre-war and post-war unemployment percentages that Phillips used. When Maddison (1964) came to compile a long series, he reported (p. 221): 'For 1950–60, we have raised the registration figures [which Phillips used] by 1 per cent [one percentage point] because they do not cover all categories of unemployed and the discrepancy from the 1951 census was of this size.' If this is justified, it steepens the Phillips curve at the 'Golden Age' levels of unemployment, and to that extent strengthens the expectation that higher unemployment would have meant less wage-inflation. Or again, the fact that unemployment in this period, even after Maddison's correction, was lower than the minimum that Keynes had thought possible may suggest that employers were behaving differently, their confidence in business prospects and their perception of recruitment difficulties leading them to hoard labour which they could have done without for the time being (Brown 1958). But though this may imply a different relation between overt unemployment and wage inflation from that in slacker times, it seems likely to go with a propensity to make concessions to labour demands. Perhaps its main significance is that it suggests a tendency towards local instability in the relevant part of the Phillips curve; that when unemployment is pushed down to some level at which recruitment difficulties are perceived or expected, the remaining available labour (or most of it) will be very quickly taken up for precautionary reasons. There will thus be some range of low unemployment rates which it is difficult to maintain, and this may well be the range in which the ideal point of 'full employment' is situated. It may be that, in the Golden Age, we were drawn on to the inflationary side of this ideal point by some such mechanism.

Of course, a more fundamental instability has been attributed to the Phillips relation by Milton Friedman (1968), and some empirical colour has been given to this attribution by the fact that in most countries the curve has apparently, from some date mostly in the later 1960s, flown away to the north-east. The theoretical argument is that, if all parties agree in expecting a particular rate of inflation, the curve will be raised by that amount; the total wage-inflation rate in the coming period will be the sum of this expected inflation and what we might call the 'Phillips' inflation – that generated by the excessively high level of employment without the help of inflationary expectations. 'Phillips' inflation thus serves to accelerate the inflation rate – to keep it that much faster than the expected inflation which is taken to be that experienced in the previous period. With 'Phillips' inflation at zero, total inflation is not necessarily zero, but merely constant, and the unemployment rate needed to achieve this constancy is the 'non-accelerating inflation rate of unemployment' (NAIRU). The Phillips curve as a static relation between unemployment and wage inflation thus disappears, leaving a single point of equilibrium at the NAIRU, with an acceleration to infinity on the left of it (at least superficially plausible from experience of hyperinflation), and an infinite plunge of accelerating price and wage deflation (in which nobody has been found actually to believe) on its right.

Like many logically coherent models, this one is helpful to our understanding of the possibilities, but it is not quite so useful for interpreting actual experience. Phillip's curve, as drawn in 1958, did demonstrate some striking regularities in the British economy, over almost a century, which are hard to reconcile with Friedman's model. The pattern then changes. Sir Henry Phelps Brown has conjectured that what he calls 'the Hinge' – the surge of wage inflation in the later 1960s, shifting nearly all national Phillips curves to the north-east – has something to do with the attainment within working populations of majorities whose memories of the job-insecurity of the 1930s were dim or non-existent. One could offer a corresponding suggestion about memories, or lack of memories, of any year-on-year fall in annual averages of consumers' prices. (At the time of writing, there are no members of the British population of working age who can remember such a decrease, unless perhaps as precocious five-year-olds: the last such occurrence was in 1932–3.) Nothing like this run of a general price indicator consistently in one direction has ever happened here before. It would be surprising if, somewhere along the road, such experience had not created a general acceptance of inflation as a virtual certainty, requiring annual wage-increases as a matter of course – quite a different thing from the fine-tuning of expectations to current short-term experience or to the predictions of some model, which is sometimes assumed.

Some of the north-eastward shift of the Phillips curve in the UK and some other countries, which begins in the later 1960s, can be explained by increasing imperfection in labour markets or increasing completeness in the recording of unemployment. Up to about 1980, this is only a small part of the shift; in the 1980s a larger amount of structural, largely regional unemployment has to be added (see Worswick 1991: ch. 6). The rest seems to correspond to a general increase in expected inflation, smaller than that which would reflect the inflation currently experienced, either in its short-term variations or in its level (Brown 1985: ch. 8). Evidence on the state of expectations about inflation in the UK, whether from direct survey evidence or from indirect testimony based on interest rates and asset yields, suggests that 2 per cent or 3 per cent a year began to be anticipated in the 1950s, with further additions of about the same amount in the late 1960s and the mid-1970s, and with various short-lived scares of higher rates. Realized rates were, nevertheless, generally underpredicted (Brown 1985:

chs 5 and 8). The broad conclusion seems to be that something like a Phillips relation between pressure in the labour market and the rate of wage inflation survives as a partial relation, after the effects of changes in expectations have been eliminated, and, if the unemployment rate is used as an inverse measure of labour market pressure, provided that its shortcomings for that purpose are corrected. And expectations have to be taken as bearing not a simple but a complex relation – partly long-term and cumulative, partly short-term – to experience of inflation.

The cycle of 1979–90 might be regarded as providing a test of what higher unemployment (more than 9 per cent on average over these years) can do to reduce wage inflation, but there are complications – most notably the fact that the cycle began with the second oil shock of 1979–80, a fact mainly responsible directly and indirectly for a 20 per cent rise in British import prices, reactivating the price–wage spiral. It took a second depression, after 1990, with unemployment again over 10 per cent and assisted (until October 1992) by stationary import prices, to bring wage inflation below the level at which it had stood, with less than 3 per cent unemployment, in the Golden Age. The extra unemployment of the 1990s may be partly due to greater imperfection in the labour market (more regional unemployment – though I doubt whether this makes much difference to the bargaining process). Most of the extra slack in the economy that it now takes to contain wage inflation may result from more firmly established inflationary expectations, built on longer inflationary experience. But however that may be, one does not need the reforming zeal of a Keynes to feel that there must be a better way of doing things.

On the international scale, experience since Keynes's time has shown that the operation of the price–wage spiral, and thus the position of the Phillips curve, is very different in different countries, apparently for reasons connected with political and labour market institutions. Bruno and Sachs (1985) have suggested that the spiral was more subdued in countries where wage determination was more highly centralized, and there does seem to be a tendency for the more 'centralized' countries (Australia, Germany, Austria and most members of the Scandinavian group) to enjoy more favourable combinations of unemployment and inflation than the United Kingdom, for instance – but the character of institutions is not easily captured by a single attribute. In so far as institutions do influence outcomes, one has hope that reform of them may be a road to improvement in economic performance. Temporary wages policies (or policies that turned out to be temporary because of difficulties in operating them) have been repeatedly tried in this country (see Brown 1985: ch. 8 and relevant references therein) with results that, although less negative than it has been fashionable to claim, were less than inspiring.

Keynes, as already noted, was against interference with wage-bargaining in wartime (he said its freedom was 'the Ark of the Covenant' to the trade union movement – a description that has remained largely valid), but that was in the context of wartime pressures making for restraint and of the policy, surely practicable (and backed by him) only in wartime, of stabilizing a basic 'cost of living' by subsidy. Our experiences since the war have given us much more evidence of the difficulties (and dare one say the possibilities?) of treading in this sacred area.

CONCLUSION

To sum up, then, what can be said about the 'inflationary dimension' of a revision of *The General Theory*? First, Keynes was himself in no way lacking in anti-inflationary zeal (though he repeatedly insisted that deflation was worse, because it brought unemployment and a relative absence of growth and prosperity). Had he revised his great book at any time when the danger of inflation, from war or otherwise, was visible on the horizon, it is likely that he would have echoed some of the warnings of the economic and social damage it can do which appear in the *Consequences*, the *Tract* and *How to Pay for the War*, and would at least have hinted at the analysis, by way of multiplier and price–wage spiral, which he set out in the last-named work. We can reasonably assume, also, that his throwaway remarks, already in *The General Theory*, about inflation beginning short of full employment and wage inflation rising as business improves (his anticipation of the Phillips curve), would have remained, with or without elaboration. A Keynesian revision of *The General Theory*, written further from the shadow of the Great Depression, would probably have given a more balanced treatment of the inflationary and deflationary ailments to which the modern economy is heir.

What further amendments would we want to add half a century on, after a continuous inflation the beginning of which (in a cyclical recovery) actually ante-dates *The General Theory*'s first appearance and after more than half a generation of renewed high unemployment, which has still not broken the run of ascending annual retail price indices? We would, I think, have to note that the British economy, among many others, was run during the war and for some twenty years after it at a level of unemployment below that which Keynes had judged to be that corresponding to 'full employment'. Had it been otherwise, it is possible that the period of continuously rising prices, starting in 1933, would not have reached the length of more than thirty years which was perhaps necessary (along, no doubt with other factors) to generate the assumptions on which the wage explosions of the late 1960s seem to have been based. Possible, but by no means certain. And we would have to add, I think, that the ideal 'full employment' point of effective demand, between perceptions of labour-scarcity leading to labour-hoarding and unemployment which by the standards of that time would look substantial, may be an unstable one, which we avoided by sitting on the inflationary side of it.

A modern revision would also have to recognize more explicitly the nature of 'wage-push' (in excess of productivity growth) and its consequences. Each employer stands to lose by yielding to it alone, because profits are thereby compressed or his competitive position weakened, or both; but if employers in the rest of the economy are yielding at a similar average rate, then nothing is changed except the value of money. If the supply of money is rigid, then, of course, the value of the total stock of it will be reduced and real demand and output will be squeezed. The supply of money – of credit, at least – has proved, however, to be generally elastic.

This is, indeed, a further respect in which Keynes's analysis requires revision. He believed that central banks could effectively control the supply of money, in the broad sense. Experience of attempts to do so has revealed difficulties, and the analysis of Dow and Saville (1990), among others, has thrown further light on them. It would indeed be surprising if lending by commercial banks, which generates the bulk of the money supply, was not positively sensitive to demand for credit and expectations of profit, both of which are positively correlated with the nominal GNP. Central banks can exercise some influence on the ability of the commercial banks to lend, but it is a limited influence. Bankers' deposits at the Bank of England are a small part of what commercial banks regard as their reserves. In a crisis, the failure of the central bank to act as a lender of last resort could be utterly disastrous. The normal influence of the Bank of England is through its control over interest rates, and this, too, is a limited control. A considerable literature, including Kaldor (1970, 1980), Rousseas (1986), Moore (1988), Goodhart (1989), and Wray (1990), as well as Dow and Saville referred to above, has grown up around the proposition that money supply in the modern economy is largely if not wholly endogenous, determined by market forces rather than at the discretion of the authorities. My own examination of the six principal OECD countries from (roughly) 1950 to 1980 (Brown 1985: ch. 6) pointed to the conclusion that 'the greater part of (monetary) growth in our sample countries seems to have taken place as either a full or a partial response to demand rather than with supply running ahead'.

Keynes probably also attached too much importance to interest rates as the determinants (along with the marginal efficiency of capital) of investment and thus of expenditure. Empirical studies, as well as reflection on the importance of risk premiums for investment decisions, suggest that the significance of interest rates for those decisions is heavily concentrated on long-term projects with relatively high degrees of certainty attached to their outcomes. The Dow and Saville proposition that monetary policy is more effective in controlling the exchange rate than in influencing internal expenditure directly also seems to deserve attention – but these are wider questions, not specifically related to 'the inflationary dimension' of *The General Theory*.

After sixty years of continuous inflation, we have to ask whether the established expectation of its further continuance is a major obstacle to bringing it under control. The traditional remedy of letting depressions take their course has proved absurdly expensive, leaving us in the early stages of recovery from the second major depression in a dozen years, with a rate of inflation similar to that which we had thirty years ago when unemployment was at a third of the present level. If nothing could be done except to continue with policies as deflationary as those of the last decade or more, it would make sense to ask whether inflation really is such a scourge – whether it is as bad as Keynes seems consistently to have believed.

All the main economies of the world have now experienced, over nearly half a century, peacetime inflation which, while a long way from the spectacular hyperinflations associated with defeat in war or its aftermath, have been more severe than in any previous equally widespread peacetime episodes. In economic growth or the quality and development of social relations, has this period been notably disastrous? On the contrary, it has been sufficiently prosperous to alert informed opinion for the first time to the ecological problems of rapid economic growth, and perhaps the worst that can be said about it is that, in its later stages the growing impatience with inflation has caused governments to accept an increase of unemployment, poverty and inequality as lesser evils. The worst of the recent brand of inflation, on any rational calculation, is that it makes people do silly things.

That, however, is a consequence of inflation which cannot be ignored – in addition to the fact that it is always at least a general nuisance and involves some injustice (though much that may immediately flow from it is remediable). Fortunately, there are other lines of approach to the problem of inflation. They lead through the labour market. They are not unexplored, and much of the previous exploration has come up against difficulties. For that reason, such exploration has been out of fashion for the last decade or so. But now that we know how cost-ineffective our recently fashionable approaches to the problem have been, the time may be coming when the necessary reform of labour market institutions can be approached with the required sense of urgency. Meanwhile, any revision of Keynes's great book should emphasize that the labour market holds the key to unchaining prosperity from its dark companion.

28

ENDOGENOUS MONEY

Sheila C. Dow

> If this explanation is correct, the quantity of money is the other factor, which, in conjunction with liquidity-preference, determines the actual rate of interest in given circumstances. Liquidity-preference is a potentiality or functional tendency, which fixes the quantity of money which the public will hold when the rate of interest is given; so that if *r* is the rate of interest, M the quantity of money and L the function of liquidity-preference, we have M = L(*r*). This is where, and how, the quantity of money enters into the economic scheme.
>
> (*Collected Writings* VII: 167–8)

INTRODUCTION

The quantity of money was important to the argument of *The General Theory* as the factor, along with liquidity preference, determining the rate of interest and thereby effective demand. The subject of this chapter is the determination of the quantity of money, first as expressed by Keynes and second in the modern literature which reflects the evolution since Keynes's day of monetary behaviour and institutions. In the process the conventional wisdom that Keynes in *The General Theory* understood the money supply to be exogenous is challenged. Furthermore, the argument is developed that the determination of the stock of money and liquidity preference are interdependent, and that this interdependence is evident in Keynes's thought.

Keynes specified three 'ultimate independent variables' (*C.W.* VII: 246–7) which underpinned *The General Theory*. One of these was the money supply. Not unnaturally, the conventional wisdom developed that Keynes understood the money supply to be exogenous. Nevertheless, an exploration of Keynes's other writing reveals an understanding of the process of money creation through bank lending, and of the limitations on the scope for control by the monetary authorities. This has been taken (for example, by Moore 1988 and Wray 1990) as indicative of Keynes's endogenous-money leanings. But was Keynes's treatment of the money supply in *The General*

Theory an aberration, or can it be understood as being consistent with his overall system of thought?

Whatever was in fact in Keynes's mind at the time of the writing of *The General Theory*, his treatment then of the money supply as being controllable by the monetary authorities was influential in determining the path taken by the neoclassical synthesis. Furthermore, it led to an apparent bifurcation between Post-Keynesian monetary theory which focused on liquidity preference and that which focused on endogenous money. A resolution between these two approaches is only now being worked through.

Had Keynes written a second edition of *The General Theory* in 1938 or 1939, it is not clear that he would have expressed himself very differently with respect to the money supply. A reconsideration of *The General Theory* in the next section suggests that Keynes's money supply assumption was not an aberration. Rather, it is a misunderstanding of his treatment of money in *The General Theory* which has led to a false dichotomy between liquidity preference theory on the one hand and endogenous money theory (in its extreme, horizontalist form) on the other.

However, the banking system has undergone significant evolution since the 1930s, in a way which has particular implications for the question of money supply endogeneity. In other words, the theoretical treatment of the money supply appropriate to the 1930s may well not be appropriate to the 1990s. This view is quite consistent with Keynes's view that 'Economics is a science of thinking in terms of models joined to the art of choosing models which are relevant to the contemporary world' (*C.W.* XIV: 296). Keynes's treatment of the money supply in the 1990s would thus probably have been different. But, in my view, it would have been different in a way which would have enhanced rather than detracted from the theory of liquidity preference.

In the third section we consider the evolution of the banking system since the 1930s, with a particular focus on developments in money supply determination; this section draws heavily on the insights developed in Chick (1986). The following section is devoted to the current expression of endogenous money theory and its implications for Post-Keynesian monetary theory. In particular, the issue of the relationship between endogenous money theory and liquidity preference theory is addressed. Contrary to the conventional view of the 1980s that the two are incompatible, attention is drawn to work, inspired by Minsky, which combines the two in a constructive way. This approach draws on the explanation in the second section for Keynes's 'given money supply' stance in *The General Theory*. It also represents the kind of theoretical extension of Keynes's work which is consistent with what we know of his views on money.

KEYNES ON THE ENDOGENEITY OF THE MONEY SUPPLY

The passage in *The General Theory* which explains the conventional interpretation of Keynes as assuming the money supply to be exogenous (see, for example, Moore 1988: 195) is in Chapter 18, where he specifies his three 'ultimate independent variables'. Of these, the third is: 'the quantity of money as determined by the action of the central bank' (*C.W.* VII: 247).

To put this passage in perspective, it is important first to understand Keynes's methodology. Keynes was not trying to develop a closed, deterministic general equilibrium system in which the selection of variables as being endogenous or exogenous is absolute (see Dow 1990). Rather, he was constructing partial systems, bearing in mind the implications of limited knowledge. Thus the passage should be interpreted as taking the money supply to be *given*, not *exogenous*; the process by which that *particular* supply should have arisen is up for discussion and further analysis. Indeed, the passage is followed by the qualification that '[t]he division of the determinants of the economic system into the two groups of given factors and independent variables is, of course, quite arbitrary from any absolute standpoint' (*C.W.* VII: 247).

Elsewhere in *The General Theory* (in the body of the analysis as it were) he places less emphasis on the role of the monetary authorities. He refers (*G.T.*: 84) to 'the amount of cash that the banking system has created', for example. Indeed, he commonly uses the term 'the banking system' in *A Treatise on Money* as the determinant of the money supply. The 'banking system' refers solely to the private sector; it is distinguished from the monetary authority (see, for example, *C.W.* VII: 205).

In Chapter 15 of *The General Theory*, Keynes explicitly raises the issue of how a change in the money supply comes about. He considers the possibilities: that money increases either as a counterpart to increased income (to gold-miners, or from money-financed state expenditure), or 'by a relaxation of the conditions of credit by the banking system' (*C.W.* VII: 200). He suggests that, since both are associated with changes in income and the rate of interest in opposite directions, a 'change in M can be assumed to operate by changing *r*, and a change in *r* will lead to a new equilibrium partly by changing M2 [the speculative motive] and partly by changing Y and therefore M1 [the transactions and precautionary motives]' (*C.W.* VII: 200–1). This passage makes clear that Keynes was very conscious that the money supply is not exogenous in the sense of helicopter money; it only changes as part of a larger process.

For the money supply to be regarded as exogenous to the private sector, there must be a belief in the capacity of the monetary authorities to control it. In terms of the passage quoted above, the authorities must be able to control the conditions of credit. It is clear from *A Treatise on Money* that

Keynes did not see the capacity for control as complete, and indeed saw it as varying with the different institutional arrangements in different countries (see *C.W.* VI: Book VII). That argument is summarized in *The General Theory* (*C.W.* VII: 205–8), including Keynes's extreme hypothetical case of the liquidity trap where the authorities are powerless.

Keynes did demonstrate confidence that the monetary authorities have a considerable degree of influence over the banking system, so that assuming full control might be regarded as a reasonable approximation. But it is clear that Keynes saw the money supply as being determined by the authorities in conjunction with the banking system. Moore (1988: ch. 8) and Wray (1990: ch. 4) supply ample quotations from *A Treatise on Money* and elsewhere to demonstrate Keynes's understanding of the process of credit creation. But this understanding is simply taken for granted in *The General Theory*. As Keynes says in the Preface to *The General Theory*, in explaining its evolution from *A Treatise on Money*: 'whilst it is found that money enters into the economic scheme in an essential and peculiar manner, technical monetary detail falls into the background' (*C.W.* VII: xxii). Indeed, it seems that Keynes chose to represent the consequences in terms of a given money supply rather than a given interest rate merely as a matter of convenience; in his 1933 lectures, for example, before proceeding to assume a 'determined quantity of money', Keynes is quoted as pointing out that 'it is just as reasonable to assume that they fix the rate of interest and allow the money supply to change "or it can do a bit of both"' (Rymes 1989a: 124–5). In fact, in *The General Theory*, Keynes generally discussed monetary policy in terms of interest rate management, rather than control of monetary aggregates (see, for example, *C.W.* VII: 164).

The conventional Post-Keynesian view of Keynes's given money supply assumption in *The General Theory* is that it was an aberration from his general theoretical stance. This is the argument of Moore (1988), G.P. Foster (1986) and Wray (1990), although Foster points out that Keynes gave the monetary authorities considerable influence even in *A Treatise on Money*. Joan Robinson (1971a: 81–2) suggested that the assumption was adopted purely for strategic reasons (see also Harcourt 1987a). By carrying over the orthodox assumption of a fixed money supply, Keynes rendered his argument about liquidity preference more palatable.

The essentials of Keynes's monetary theory revolve around the concept of liquidity preference. As long as the supply of credit is not fully demand-determined, that is, as long as supply is independent of demand to any extent, then Keynes's monetary theory retains its essentials. Liquidity preference changes with changes in interest rate expectations and with changes in confidence in predictions of interest rate changes. An increase in liquidity preference puts upward pressure on interest rates, which in turn puts downward pressure on output and employment, as long as the money supply is constrained to some degree. Keynes put this theory in starkest focus by talking in terms of a given supply of money. But it would apply as long as the money supply function had an upward slope with respect to the interest rate; it only loses force as the function approaches the horizontal position of the modern endogenous money theorists.

Suppose Keynes had chosen instead to assume a given interest rate rather than a given money supply. Would this have implied an unlimited willingness on the part of the banks and the monetary authorities to meet the increased demand for liquidity? Clearly, from the statement that the public do not determine the money supply, Keynes would not have taken that view. What would make more sense in relation to Keynes's view of the banking system is that the jointly determined interest rate would not necessarily stay constant, but would be increased in response to the increase in liquidity preference, with the same real outcome as noted above. But it involves a more complex account than if the money supply is taken as given (see Arestis and Howells forthcoming), so that it should not be surprising that Keynes chose the simpler (and strategically more effective) route. As we shall see in the fourth section, some explicit unravelling of the credit market from the money market is required in order to analyse the consequences of an increase in liquidity preference for the availability of credit.

That Keynes saw the banks as not in general accommodating changes in the demand for money is evident from the first 'special characteristic' he specified for money: that its elasticity of production by the private sector (not the monetary authority) be zero or very low (*C.W.* VII: 230). Keynes is referring here to physical production; the characteristic is necessary not only to preserve the value of money as such, but to preclude the possibility that unemployment due to an increase in liquidity preference be eliminated by means of the production of money. But Keynes states that the inelasticity of supply of 'an inconvertible managed currency' (*C.W.* VII: 230) means that the condition with respect to production is strictly satisfied; in other words, he is treating the supply of deposit money as a special case of production (one which involves negligible labour input).

None of this interpretation of Keynes's view is affected in any essential way by the developments of 1937. Moore (1988: ch. 8) draws attention to the debate with Ohlin about his liquidity preference theory of interest. He quotes Keynes's apparent shift in emphasis to the power of the banks: 'Unless the banking system is prepared to augment the supply of money, lack of finance may prove an important obstacle to more than a certain amount of investment decisions being on the tapis at the same time' (*C.W.* XIV: 209); 'the power of the banks through their control over the supply of money' (ibid.: 211); and again, 'in general, the banks hold the key position in the transition from a lower to a higher scale of activity . . . The investment market can become congested through a shortage of cash. It can never become congested through a shortage of saving. This is the most fundamental of my conclusions within this field' (ibid.: 222). Keynes qualifies the argument by noting the scope for demand for credit to be satisfied by unused overdraft facilities, but (unlike Moore 1988) he does not see this qualification as implying a general passivity of the banks in the face of credit demand. Rather than supporting the notion that the supply of credit is demand-determined, these passages affirm Keynes's view that it is not – that there may be a 'shortage of cash'. Indeed, if it is a necessary characteristic of money that its supply has a low elasticity, then the logical consequence of complete demand-determination would be that whatever was the money-asset would cease to be acceptable as such.

Further, Keynes affirmed in his 1937 writings the importance of the theory of liquidity preference and its interrelationships with investment; indeed, in the 1937 *Quarterly Journal of Economics* article (*C.W.* XIV: 118) he explicitly pointed out that the conditions which increase liquidity preference 'as a rule' are also those which induce pessimism about future yields. Far from making concessions 'under heavy pressure' (as Moore 1988: 204 puts it) by referring to the power of the banks, Keynes was simply affirming his view that the supply of credit is not demand-determined. This was an integral part of the theory of liquidity preference.

But further, in the December 1937 *Economic Journal* article (*C.W.* XIV: 215–23), Keynes extended the scope for the theory of liquidity preference by applying it to the banks themselves. Here he refers explicitly to the liquidity preference of the banks (ibid.: 220), and to 'the rate of interest as being determined by the interplay of the terms on which the public desires to become more or less liquid and those on which the banking system is ready to become more or less unliquid' (ibid.: 219). This particular expression of Keynes's theory of interest resulted apparently from a suggestion from Dr Herbert Bab. But it finds echoes in Keynes's earlier writing about banks, for example in 1931 when he was writing about 'The Consequences to the Banks of the Collapse of Money Values' (*C.W.* IX: 150–8). Here he discusses the behaviour of bankers in terms of conventions under uncertainty, just as he discusses the origins of liquidity preference in the 1937 *QJE* article (*C.W.* XIV: 114).

Keynes is not explicit as to what he means by banks' liquidity preference. The wording in the 1937 *Economic Journal* article suggests that he was thinking in terms of the disposition of the asset side of the banks' balance sheet, in the same way as he expressed households' liquidity preference in terms of the disposition of household assets. Banks would express liquidity preference by curtailing credit creation (loans being their least liquid asset) and placing any free resources in investments. Just as the expression in aggregate of household liquidity preference pushes down the value of household assets, so the expression in aggregate of liquidity preference by the banks reduces the volume of credit and thus money in the system as a whole. The result is a paradox of liquidity, on a par with the paradox of thrift (see Dow 1993: ch. 10). This interpretation in terms of the asset side of the balance sheet is consistent with the banks' relative passivity at that time with respect to liabilities; in taking these ideas forward in the fourth section, account will be taken of the banks' more activist modern role with respect to liability management, which suggests that the concept of banks' liquidity preference now be considered explicitly in terms also of the size of the banks' balance sheet itself.

It is shortly after the passage about banks' liquidity preference that Keynes refers to the banks as holding 'the key position'. He did not spell out the nature of this position in terms of banks' liquidity preference; but the preceding passage implies that he had in mind the way in which an increase in banks' liquidity preference would aggravate the consequences of an increase in the non-bank public's liquidity preference by curtailing the supply of credit. This point strengthens, without altering the thrust of, the theory of liquidity preference as expressed in *The General Theory*. But the theory of liquidity preference is conveyed most straightforwardly in relation to a given supply of credit and thus of the money supply. Thus Keynes would probably have continued in 1938 to abstract from bank liquidity preference. It would have prevented continuing confusion of interpretation if he had referred to the quantity of money as jointly determined by the actions of the central bank and the banking system; but this was not the focus of the 1937 exchanges.

As far as Keynes's views about the scope for central bank influence on the banks are concerned, there is no evidence of any significant shift by 1938. The strength of that influence for Keynes was a matter specific to the context under study, and that context did not change between 1936 and 1938. The change in context since the 1930s, however, means that the application of Keynes's ideas to the 1990s requires attention to that change. There is the question of the capacity of the monetary authorities to influence credit conditions, and the question of the willingness of the banking system to accommodate demand for credit. These we consider in the next section. In the light of this consideration we proceed in the following section to set out a theory of money and credit which retains the essential features of Keynes's theory of liquidity preference and his understanding of the banking system, while incorporating subsequent developments in banking. This account draws on the modern endogeneity theory, but also on theoretical developments which can be traced directly back to Keynes.

EVOLUTION OF THE BANKING SYSTEM SINCE THE 1930s

Chick's (1986, 1993b) stages of banking development framework is addressed to the changing causal processes within banking as it develops, and how that affects the choice of theory appropriate to different stages.

This framework is thus ideally suited to the questions at hand. Further, while the framework can be adapted to different national banking systems, its initial expression refers to the English (latterly British) banking system.

Seven stages are identified, of which Britain had reached number four by the 1930s. Progression through the stages can be characterized by the increasing capacity of the banking system to create credit. Up until stage four, the banks have been able to increase the bank multiplier, and the speed with which the multiplier operates; but the multiple is still constrained by a given volume of bank reserves. Stage four represents a crucial shift. It is at this stage that the central bank accepts the role of lender-of-last-resort in order to maintain confidence in the banking system. Now the banks are no longer constrained by a given stock of reserves. They are still subject to reserve requirements, and the central bank can influence the demand for reserves by manipulating interest rates. But if the banks are prepared to pay the required interest rate to borrow reserves, then there is no limit on their credit creation.

This was the situation in which Keynes was writing; the question of judgement was about the strength of central bank influence, since the days of a given stock of reserves were gone. But of course Keynes was not addressing the modern conventional preoccupation with limiting the volume of credit. He was most concerned with expanding credit to satisfy increased liquidity preference; then the question was whether the central bank could induce banks to borrow more reserves – Keynes was relatively pessimistic on that score. But overall, Chick (forthcoming) endorses Keynes's judgement that, in general, the central bank had a significant degree of influence over the banking system at that time. The causal chain started with demand for credit, which was supplied by the banks and backed by an increase in borrowed reserves. The demand for credit could in general be discouraged by an increase in interest rates. The difficulty in the 1930s was in inducing the demand for credit in the first place. But even up to the 1960s banks had to be wary of stepping out of line in credit expansion relatively to the other banks because of the need to expand deposits (at a time when banks did not engage in competition over deposit rates).

The fifth stage of banking evolution occurred in the USA in the 1960s and in Britain in the 1970s with the onset of fierce competition among the banks over market shares. This was the era of liability management. Banks now more actively sought out lending opportunities, taking care of the deposit funding by competing over deposit rates and by making increased recourse to the wholesale market. This period can be seen as close to the modern endogenous-money account, with banks accommodating credit demand. But even then, the banks could not be said to have been passive, in that they were themselves creating much of the credit demand by opening up speculative opportunities in the wholesale market. Further, attempts by monetary authorities to curtail the growth of credit, if anything, further fuelled the process; the massive growth of the Eurodollar market can be seen to have resulted in large part from attempts to evade monetary control in Britain and the USA (see, for example, Wojnilower 1980).

Subsequent developments have demonstrated the conjunctural nature of the massive credit expansion of the 1970s; banks chose to meet credit demand which was not deterred by rising interest rates. Banks then found in the 1980s that their loan portfolios were unsustainable, and the monetary authorities turned their attention from reserves as the fulcrum of influence to capital. Monetary policy thus consisted of attempts to manage market interest rates and the setting of capital adequacy ratios. Curiously, this development introduced a new element of endogeneity into the credit-creation process, in the sense of increased private sector determination. But, rather than increased control by borrowers, it is the equity market as the supplier of capital which now ultimately determines the limits to bank credit creation; the equity market may be unwilling to capitalize what it sees as unwarranted credit expansion. Thus the sixth stage of securitization in the 1980s saw banks attempting to liquidate some of their loan portfolios to reduce risk exposure, and to meet capital adequacy requirements as the equity market became less willing to supply capital.

The disintermediation of stage six could be interpreted as a shift away from the world of liquidity preference to the world of loanable funds, as banks withdrew from lending in favour of securities markets (see Chick 1993a). But the developments of the seventh stage throw some doubt on this conclusion. This stage can be characterized as the stage of market diffusion (see Gardener 1988). The divide between banks and non-banks has been eroded by deregulation, as well as by market forces. This has direct relevance for how we classify the money whose supply we are concerned with here. Building society deposits are now highly liquid and used in transactions, so that building societies can create credit; these deposits are thus part of the money supply. But the legal-restrictions theorists argue that there is no reason other than regulation why liabilities of other non-bank financial intermediaries should not also count as money; large corporations, for example, may settle debts with securities rather than with deposit money. Thus, counteracting the disintermediation process of stage six, we now have the possibility of the liabilities of a wider range of institutions becoming so liquid as to be treated as money, so we need to consider their credit-creation behaviour as well.

Since 1936, therefore, we have seen the growing capacity of the private sector to create credit. The increasing range and sophistication of financial instruments as well as the increase in international transactions have made it more difficult for the monetary authorities to exert their influence on the volume of credit. This phenomenon is attested to by those with experience of central banking, such as Goodhart (1989) and Dow and Saville (1990). To that extent the supply of credit, and thereby of money, has become more endogenous over the last few decades. But the private sector is not homogeneous; there is no necessary reason for the banks (or credit-creators, however one defines that category now) to accommodate all demand at the market interest rate. While they may have chosen to do so in the 1970s, it is clear that this is no longer the case. Moore's focus on overdraft facilities as proof of passivity in the face of demand points to further evidence of reduced willingness to lend. It is noticeable how the proportion of bank lending through overdrafts has declined; in the UK, for example, from 1984 (the first year for which the data were published) to 1992, the proportion had fallen from 22 per cent to 14 per cent. This development raises the question of availability of overdraft facilities themselves; the evidence suggests that these, like the volume of credit as such, may also be rationed (see Morgan 1991).

The diffusion of stage seven also has direct consequences for the way in which liquidity-preference theory is expressed. In 1936 the portfolio behaviour of banks, non-bank financial intermediaries, non-financial firms and households was quite distinct. This is no longer the case. The divide between financial and non-financial firms has been eroded, with some firms internalizing banking functions and others providing them for customers; firms now therefore compare much more directly the expected returns on physical investment with the expected returns on financial investment, since these are now direct alternatives. Further, with rising standards of living, a rising proportion of consumer spending on durables is subject to considerations similar to those traditionally reserved for firms. Returns on physical and financial investment, the cost of borrowing and the uncertainty surrounding their future thus affect all sectors (see Dow and Dow 1989).

ENDOGENOUS MONEY SUPPLY AND LIQUIDITY PREFERENCE

The endogeneity of the volume of credit to the private sector is now widely recognized, although it is rarely incorporated in standard, orthodox macroeconomic models. There is a strong New Keynesian strand of theory inspired by Stiglitz and Weiss (1981) which emphasizes credit rationing, but its theoretical foundations are very limited (see Dow forthcoming). The longer-standing endogenous money approach, which is also closer to the Keynesian tradition, is most closely associated with Kaldor (1982) and Moore (1989) (see also Rousseas 1986; Wray 1990; Arestis 1992: ch. 8; and Lavoie 1992: ch. 4). Kaldor's strongest argument for the passivity of the monetary authorities in the face of expanding credit is that this is what inspires the confidence in the financial system which allows it to flourish; if the authorities were to contemplate refusing to supply reserves on demand, the entire financial system would be threatened by a crisis of confidence.

Moore further has catalogued and analysed the ways in which banks have managed to evade attempts at monetary control; in other words, his argument is that the authorities could not control the volume of credit even if they wanted to do so (see also Wojnilower 1980).

But, according to this approach, the monetary authority plays a key role in setting the interest rate. The fundamental difference between Keynes and the modern endogeneity theorists thus does not relate so much to the capacity for central bank control as such, that is, the scope for exogenous determination of credit conditions. Both see the central bank as a dominant player in the financial sector. The fundamental difference arises over the influence of the non-bank sector. For Keynes, 'the quantity of money is not determined by the public' (*C.W.* VII: 174). Rather, it is determined by the banks as (heavily) influenced by the central bank. It is important to distinguish the two senses of endogeneity: that the money supply is endogeneous to the private sector as a whole (determined by the non-bank public through the banks), on the one hand, and that the money supply is endogenous to (i.e. determined by) only the banks, on the other hand. The modern endogeneous-money theorists in the horizontalist mode affirm the first, while Keynes affirmed the second (see Davidson 1988 for a discussion of this distinction).

Both Kaldor and Moore deny any role for liquidity preference in determining either the money supply or the interest rate; indeed Kaldor (1983a) argued forcefully that Keynes had committed a serious error by insisting on his theory of liquidity preference and a *given* money supply. It follows from the argument that credit is demand-determined that there cannot be a 'shortage of cash'; Keynes's 'fundamental conclusion' would be invalidated. The importance of money would rest simply on the rate of interest set by the monetary authorities, and its effect on planned investment.

But some have questioned the willingness of banks to supply credit indefinitely at this rate (see Davidson 1972; Rousseas 1986; and Jarsulic 1989); this structuralist approach raises the possibility of central bank influence on the volume of credit (see Pollin 1991). Others have extended the notion of liquidity preference to corporate finance (see Mott 1985–6; Dow and Dow 1989), while others have, further, analysed bank behaviour itself in terms of liquidity preference (see Kregel 1984–5; Dow and Dow 1989; Wray 1990; and Chick forthcoming). Thus, in this work, not only are banks (and thereby the monetary authorities) given some control over the volume of credit (as Keynes himself had emphasized) but the theory of liquidity preference has been extended in a way Keynes only hinted at in 1937. This extension has broken loose from Keynes's original statement of liquidity preference in *The General Theory* with respect to a given portfolio to encompass changes in the size of portfolio, as is entailed, for example, by banks choosing to expand credit (see Dow 1993: 165–8). Minsky (1975, 1982) has provided much of the inspiration for these developments, by following up on Keynes's mention of borrower's risk and lender's risk, by developing Keynes's theory in the context of the business cycle, and by putting a direct focus on the issue of firms' financial structure.

The following is an account of a theory which combines the causal force of the demand for credit and the difficulties of the monetary authorities in controlling total credit, on the one hand, with liquidity preference manifested in all markets, on the other. The influence of the non-bank public on the creation of credit is thus incorporated with that of the banks and the monetary authorities. This representation is offered as one which not only is consistent with, or at least derives from, the Keynes of *The General Theory*, but also demonstrates where the misunderstanding arose over Keynes's assumption of a given money supply. The key is to separate the two sides of the banks' balance sheet. The finance motive demand for money is shown as a demand for credit in the credit market while the preference to hold assets in liquid form (liquidity preference) is shown in the money market (see Graziani 1984). Wray (1990) distinguishes between demand for money and liquidity preference; he does not make clear, however, that liquidity preference also involves a demand for money.

Figure 28.1 shows the money market and the credit market separately. The volume of credit and the loan rate, r_l, relative to a base rate, r_b, are determined in the credit market. The demand for credit is a function of the expected yield on investment, r_k, and liquidity preference, LP, expressed as a choice about whether or not to undertake debt in general and long-term investment in particular. The supply of credit is a function of the cost of funds, represented by the base rate, of liquidity preference expressed as a choice about the proportion of loans in the banks' portfolios, and the default risk perceived to be attached to those loans. The money market shows demand for and supply of money as a function of the differential between the wholesale rate, r_w, and the deposit rate, r_d. The diagram can be applied to a closed or open economy. If the economy is open, the curves will be more elastic, given alternative sources of credit and liquid assets; in addition, the base rate will be established by the authorities with reference to international rates. Exchange rate expectations introduce an additional source for revision of expected returns. The analysis would thus be different for closed and open economies, but the fundamentals of the argument developed below are the same for both.

Starting in the upper part of the diagram, the demand for credit is shown as negatively related to the loan rate, while the supply of credit is positively related to the loan rate. The less than perfect elasticity in the former reflects increasing borrower's risk as borrowing increases, while in the latter it reflects increasing lender's risk. Perceptions of risk depend on how much confidence is held in the forecast of returns on which the loan is based. In an economic upturn the two curves will be very elastic (the demand curve just below the expected yield of investments, r_k, and the supply curve just

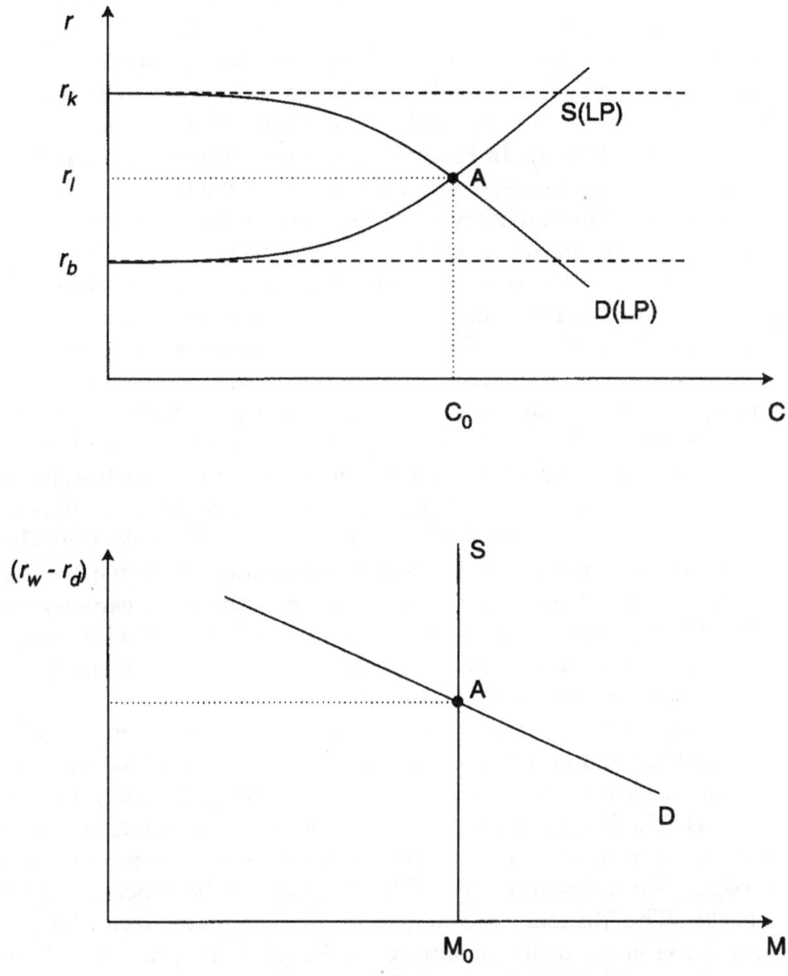

Figure 28.1 The credit market and the money market

above the cost of funds, r_b) as perception of risk falls. Then the mark-up on the base rate is minimal and the credit supply curve is close to horizontal. But in a downturn, the curves will become quite steep, curtailing the supply credit and increasing the mark-up. All demand for credit at the base rate is not accommodated. This representation finds confirmation in Rousseas' (1986) empirical work which finds the mark-up on the Federal Funds rate to be countercyclical. It is also confirmed by Pollin's (1991) finding that interest rates are determined jointly by the authorities and the banking system, not by the authorities alone.

The volume of credit is determined by the intersection of the two curves; this in turn determines the supply of money, shown in the lower part of the diagram as a vertical line. This, I would argue, is what Keynes meant by a given money supply; it was determined by the banks' willingness to extend credit, as influenced by the monetary authorities; their influence is exerted most directly through their r_b. In Keynes's day it would be the rate on borrowed reserves which had the most direct influence on the base rate; now the rate will also reflect rates in wholesale markets, which the authorities also seek to influence through the short-term securities market. But the base rate alone does not determine the volume of credit; the perception of lender's risk is also a powerful determinant of banks' willingness to meet credit demand, and it may be subject to indirect influence by the monetary authorities.

Liquidity preference enters also in the demand-for-money function. Liquidity preference can be characterized as a preference for short- over long-term assets. Now that retail deposits earn interest, 'the interest rate' needs to be expressed as the additional interest rate which induces asset holders not to hold money. There are several interest rates which could serve this purpose, but here we use the rate on wholesale term deposits. The import of recent stages in banking evolution is that whatever constitutes money has increased in scope, in turn extending the capacity to create credit. This representation sticks to the traditional one of classifying credit as bank credit and money as bank deposits, but there is a strong case for future work to go beyond this tradition.

There is a direct feedback to the credit market through the wholesale rate, since the latter enters into the determination of the base rate, which in turn influences the supply of credit. At this stage in the argument, the limitations of a diagrammatic representation of a non-deterministic organic process become very clear. This framework is being offered here as an aid to thought, but it can only cope with one phase of the process, not with the feedbacks. The difficulties inherent in diagrammatic representation are exactly the same as those accounting for the false interpretation of Keynes's representation of the money supply as exogenous rather than given (see Dow 1993: ch. 8 for a fuller discussion, albeit in a different context).

The horizontalists' argument is that the top part of the diagram is the important one, and the fact that the counterpart of credit is money is incidental; there is no point in adding the bottom diagram. As Lavoie (1985: 76) puts it: 'Keynes' liquidity-preference theory is well known. Post-Keynesians do not abide by it anymore, however.' Those who do not subscribe fully to horizontalism (Chick, Davidson, Weintraub, Dow and Earl) are simply charged by Lavoie with 'confusion'. The issue then is whether a change in liquidity preference can have any demonstrable effect on credit-creation, with the influence of the authorities limited to interest rates.

Suppose that there is an increase in liquidity preference in the sense of a wish to switch from long-term to short-term assets (see Dow and Dow 1989 for a discussion of liquidity preference with respect to household behaviour). Households will be unwilling to undertake debt, and will withhold consumption demand, as they attempt to build up stocks of liquid assets. Firms will find their profits squeezed, will revise downward their investment plans, and will likewise be unwilling to undertake new debt while trying to build up liquid resources. Banks will find the riskiness of their loan portfolios increasing, will perceive increased lender's risk attached to new loan requests, and will for both reasons favour holding placements over new lending. The effects are shown in Figure 28.2, where the curve labelled LP_0 refers to the initial state, and LP_1 refers to the state of increased liquidity

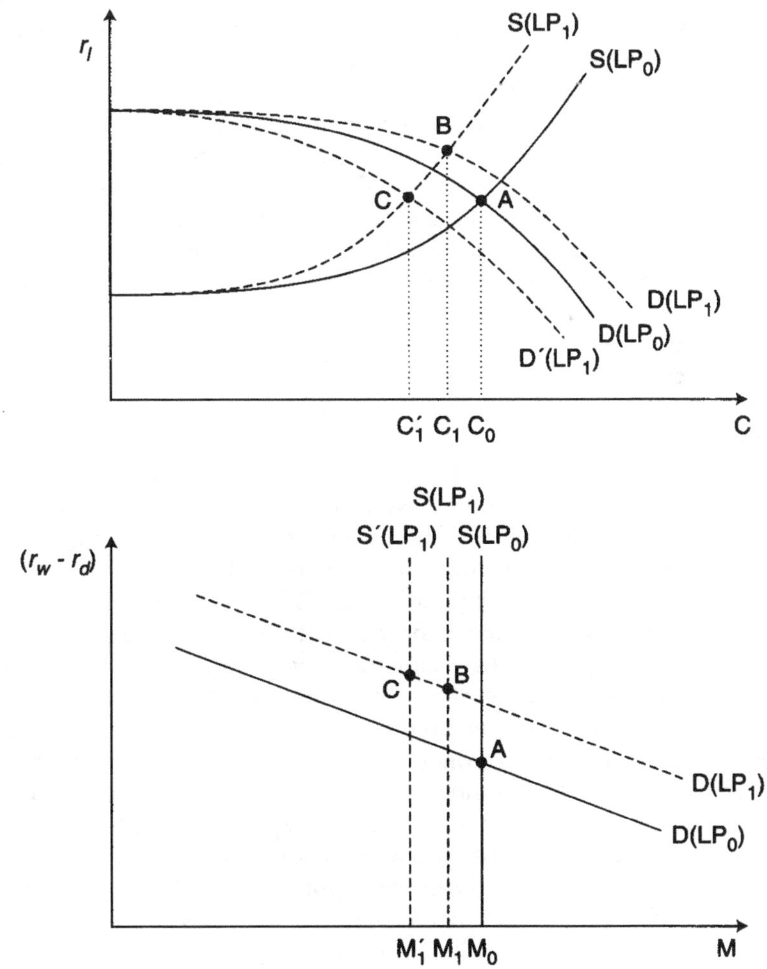

Figure 28.2 A shift in liquidity preference

preference. While the effect on the supply of credit is unambiguously in the direction of a cutback, the effect on demand for credit is less clear. Initially, firms facing a profits squeeze may prefer not to borrow, but may be forced to do so to maintain working capital. The demand curve thus shifts out, adding further upward pressure to the mark-up on base rate, represented by a movement from A to B. But as financially weaker firms go bankrupt in the downturn, distress borrowing tails off, and the unwillingness to undertake debt (because of reduced expected returns on investment) takes over; this is shown as a shift in the demand for credit schedule to $D'(LP_1)$, allowing the mark-up to fall back to point C on the new supply schedule.

The effect on the money market is shown in the lower part of the diagram; the volume of credit does not change the money stock dramatically initially, but eventually reduces it significantly. But the increase in liqudity preference has in the meantime shifted up the demand-for-money curve, putting further upward pressure on $(r_w - r_d)$. The money market moves from point A to point B to point C. There is now a feedback to the credit market, which is shown in Figure 28.3. As wholesale rates go up, r_b is pushed up. As a result, the credit supply curve shifts up, further reducing the volume of credit and increasing loan rates, which in turn reduce the money supply and push $(r_w - r_d)$ up further, as represented by point D in both diagrams. A 'shortage of cash' has raised interest rates and discouraged investment, just as in *The General Theory*.

Finally, the framework can be used to illustrate the influence of the monetary authorities through interest rates – an influence which is not absolute. The authorities can exert their influence through bank rate, which determines the cost of reserves. Or they can operate in the securities markets to manipulate securities' yields, and thereby the wholesale market. In the money market, this would have to be represented as a shift down in the demand for money curve; if the monetary authority is treated as one (influential) actor in financial markets, then a purchase of securities represents a fall in aggregate liquidity preference. The purchase has no effect on the money supply, since banks simply substitute the injection of cash for reserves which they would have borrowed anyway. Both monetary policy routes affect the banks' base rate, which directly affects the credit supply curve. But the elasticity of the credit demand and supply curves and the position of the demand-for-money curve depend on the state of expectations, which the monetary authority can also influence. A reduction in base rate, for example, would have a much more expansionary impact if it were accompanied by assurances of a policy of maintaining interest rates steady at a low level; not only would the credit supply curve shift down, but both it and the demand curve would flatten out, and wholesale rates would move down further because of reduced liquidity preference. The monetary authorities have scope for influence, but it is not a deterministic one, depending crucially on the state of expectations.

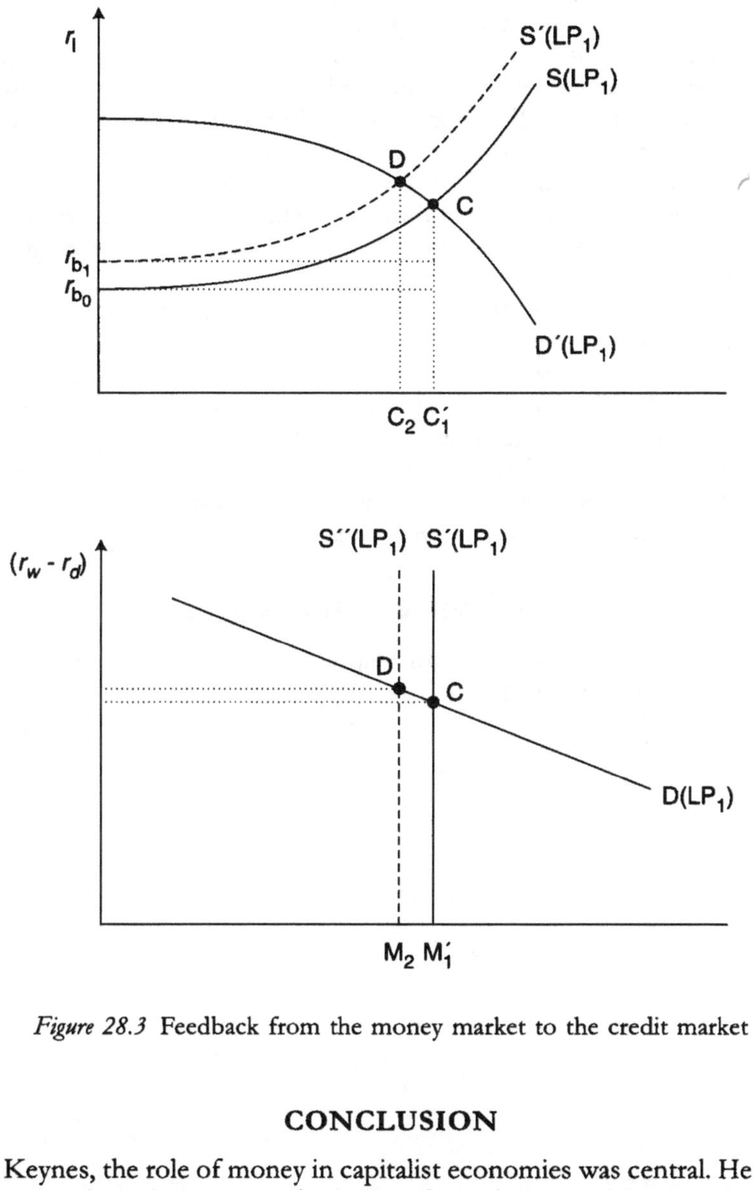

Figure 28.3 Feedback from the money market to the credit market

CONCLUSION

For Keynes, the role of money in capitalist economies was central. He chose to express this role in terms of a theory of liquidity preference, juxtaposed to a given money supply. While he mentioned the complementarities between liquidity preference of the non-bank public with investment plans and with bank behaviour, these do not appear in the formalization of his monetary theory which was picked up in the neoclassical synthesis.

His ascription to the monetary authorities of power over the money supply and the separation of liquidity preference from the rest of the theory were in fact reasonable in the context in which he was writing. But they are no longer reasonable. Post-Keynesians are united in putting emphasis on the causal power of credit demand, and the lack of power of the monetary authorities to control the money stock. But a wide range of opinion has built up between those who see credit as solely demand-determined, at an interest rate set by the central bank, with no influence for liquidity preference, on the one hand, and those who still regard the theory of liquidity preference as central, and compatible with money supply endogeneity, on the other.

A representation has been offered here which shows liquidity preference as playing an active part in determining the volume and price of credit, together with a limited role for the monetary authorities. The volume of credit is thus shown to be jointly determined by the central bank, the banks and the non-bank public. This represents the views at the latter end of the spectrum. But the representation is offered, not only as capturing the nature of the modern capitalist system, but also as a continuation of Keynes's thinking in *The General Theory.*

ACKNOWLEDGEMENT

The chapter has benefited from helpful comments and suggestions from Philip Arestis and Paul Dalziel.

29

A KEYNESIAN THEORY OF FINANCE AND ITS MACROECONOMIC IMPLICATIONS*

Myron J. Gordon

Capitalists, who here include proprietors, portfolio investors and corporations, may be looked on as members of a species, a socio-economic species if not one in nature. Like any other species, the primary concern of capitalists is long-run growth and survival. That means avoiding bankruptcy; and growth, it will be seen, is a necessary condition for avoiding bankruptcy. This chapter presents a theory of finance, that is of saving and investment, which recognizes the concern for survival.[1] The saving behaviour that recognizes this concern is captured by Keynes's consumption function. Investment is where we break new ground. Keynes was highly critical of the neoclassical theory (he called it classical theory) of investment because it failed to recognize and deal with the fact that the future is uncertain. However, Keynes did not go beyond pointing out the unfortunate consequences of that failure, probably because he could not make use of the important developments in capital theory under uncertainty and risk aversion since the end of the Second World War. I believe that Keynes would have considered the theory of investment presented here a satisfactory solution to a problem that he left unsolved.

The first section provides a macroeconomic setting by reviewing the role of investment in the neoclassical and Keynesian theories of the level and growth in output. The next section presents and criticizes the string of assumptions that have been adopted with the objective of making the neoclassical theory of investment under certainty remain true when uncertainty and risk aversion are recognized. The next two sections present our growth and survival theory of investment and explore some of its macroeconomic implications. Finally, we outline how differences among economic systems in their ability to satisfy the need for growth and security explain their rise and fall. The ideas presented here summarize and in some respects carry forward the treatment of these subjects in Gordon (1994).

MACROECONOMIC BACKGROUND

The two central problems in macroeconomics are the current levels of employment and output and their future growth rates. Before Keynes, neoclassical economic theory found a solution to these two problems that was simple and elegant. To summarize that solution: with the capital stock given at the start of each short period, the level of output is determined in the labour market, where the real wage rate equates the supply and demand for labour. Consequently, everyone finds and provides the employment they desire at the prevailing real wage rate, so that involuntary unemployment is logically impossible in this system. With the level of output determined in the labour market, the capital market determines its future growth by determining the allocation of the output between consumption and investment. Saving is an increasing function of the interest rate and investment is a decreasing function of the interest rate, so that there is some rate that equates the supply and demand for capital, that is saving and investment. Notice that everyone makes the allocation of income between current and future consumption that they wish (just as time is freely allocated between work and leisure) on the basis of the prevailing interest rate, while the independent investment of these savings generates the matching future income. The simplicity and elegance of the theory are very appealing. Unfortunately, however, the theory has little empirical relevance.

This ideal economic system requires the assumptions that all labour, capital and product markets are perfectly competitive and that the future is known with certainty.[2] The considerable gap between the world we live in and this theoretical construct has not gone unrecognized by neoclassical economists, but it has been attributed to 'market imperfections' such as trade unions, mismanagement of the money supply and lack of information. Hence, to the degree that these market imperfections are eliminated, perfection is realized. Economic theory therefore provided a more attractive vision of the future and rationalization of the status quo than our great religions. To reach the paradise of a great religion we have to overcome the imperfections within us, but to reach the paradise of neoclassical theory we need only overcome market imperfections.

The genius and authority of Keynes combined with the Great Depression of the 1930s led to the development and acceptance of an alternative theory of short-run employment and output. His most important contributions here were the two related propositions that (a) output is determined by aggregate demand and not the conditions of supply except as an upper bound, and (b) consumption is a function of income. It follows that the level of output in a closed system is not determined in the labour market. Instead, it is the sum of consumption and investment demand; and with consumption a function of income, *the current level of output as well as its growth rate are determined in the capital market.* Investment demand is the all-important variable.

Keynes's third important contribution was to demonstrate the inadequacy of the neoclassical theory of capital. Under that theory the firm maximizes its current market value, and it does so by making the investment that equates its marginal rate of return with the interest rate. The marginal rate of return, also called a project's internal rate of return, is the 'rate of discount which would make . . . the returns expected from a capital-asset during its life just equal to its supply price' (*G.T.*: 135). Keynes did not explicitly reject this proposition and present an alternative theory. What he did in Book IV was to argue at great length that the consequences of uncertainty about the future leave investment largely unexplained by this theory. The marginal efficiency of capital depends materially on 'the state of confidence' with respect to our knowledge of the distant future, and that knowledge 'is usually very slight and often negligible' (*G.T.* 149). Investment will be adequate only when 'reasonable calculation is supplemented by animal spirits' (ibid.: 162). Once the precautionary and speculative motives for holding money are recognized, the rate of interest becomes a highly psychological phenomenon. Keynes responded to four critiques of his book, for the most part by elaborating on his rejection of neoclassical investment theory under certainty. He concluded: 'Thus the fact that our knowledge of the future is fluctuating, vague and uncertain, renders wealth a peculiarly unsuitable subject for the methods of the classical economic theory' (Keynes 1937c: 213).

Keynes left economists with two related questions with regard to the short-run behaviour of a capitalist system. How should his work be incorporated in macroeconomic theory, and what should be done to recognize the presence of uncertainty and risk aversion in the theory of investment? The widely accepted answer to the first question was found in the synthesis of Keynesian and neoclassical theory that grew out of Hicks (1937). The synthesis combined the theory of aggregate demand and the consumption function due to Keynes and the neoclassical theory of investment. That synthesis will not be reviewed here, nor the debate that followed on the usefulness of monetary policy in controlling investment and, if it is useful, how it should be used.

On the second question, the consequences of uncertainty and risk aversion for investment, there has been a very large post-war theoretical literature, but the Keynesian contribution has been relatively small. Post-Keynesians, including Shackle (1955) and Davidson (1991), have argued that no solution is possible for the problems raised by Keynes. Specifically, the nature of the uncertainty involved in the investment decision makes it unsuitable for rational scientific analysis by means of probability theory.[3] The major Keynesian effort has been by Tobin. Tobin (1958) demonstrated that liquidity preference is behaviour towards risk, and Tobin (1980a, 1982) explored the macro implications of that proposition. However, to this day the widely accepted two-way classification of assets in macroeconomics is money and all other assets, whereas it should be loans free of default risk which includes money, and assets for which the future nominal cash flows are uncertain. If we consolidate financial statements over all persons in a closed system, we are left with the government debt and the stock of real assets. The former may be called the supply of economic security that is peculiar to capitalism.

On the empirical level there has been a significant Keynesian literature that was either inspired or anticipated by Kalecki's (1937a) principle of increasing risk. Starting with Meyer and Kuh (1957) it has been found that investment is determined by retained earnings and concern for capital structure as well as the profitability of investment opportunities. More recently, Fazzari *et al.* (1988) and Chamberlain and Gordon (1989) provide further evidence that 'financial considerations' influence investment.[4] For the most part, however, Keynesians have not found it necessary to find an alternative to the neoclassical theory of investment. They have been satisfied with the evidence that, with or without the aid of monetary policy, the market alone cannot be relied upon to generate the full-employment level of investment in the short run. In addition, many of them share the view advanced by Keynes that an increasing share of the capital requirements in a mature capitalist economy cannot be satisfied by private investment, and the economy faces secular stagnation unless government investment financed with debt is used to employ a large fraction of private savings (see Eisner, Chapter 12 in Volume 1 of this work).

The post-war literature on investment has come to be dominated by the neoclassical theory of finance that grew out of the work of Franco Modigliani and Merton Miller (1958), one a Keynesian and the other a neoclassical economist. According to them, uncertainty and risk aversion leave the investment decision substantially unchanged. The decision still equates the marginal rate of return on investment with the interest rate. The only change is to add a risk premium to the risk-free interest rate in arriving at the cost of capital. That is to be expected, since risk is now a cost no less than waiting.

According to this theory, the risk premium in the discount rate that is used to choose among projects may vary among the projects with their risk, but it is independent of any property of the firm, including its overall financing and investment policies. Otherwise the choice among projects and the overall level of investment would depend upon the distribution of wealth and of investment opportunities among capitalists. That would violate the Utopian properties of neoclassical theory. Furthermore, little if anything can be said about what happens over time to the risk premium in the macro cost of capital. Hence, the recognition of uncertainty and risk aversion in macro models since Keynes is little different from their recognition before him.

NEOCLASSICAL THEORY OF INVESTMENT

Unfortunately, the validity of the neoclassical theory of investment under uncertainty and risk aversion requires the truth of five propositions. They are:

1 real persons hold only securities while corporations hold all the real risky assets of the system;
2 at each point in time corporations follow the financing and investment policies that maximize the current market value of their shares without regard for the subsequent probability of bankruptcy;
3 a corporation's market value is independent of its capital structure;
4 a corporation's market value is independent of its dividend policy; and
5 most importantly, a corporation's investment opportunities are independent of its history, that is of anything the corporation may do.

These propositions in total are shown below to be almost as far-fetched as the assumption that the future is certain.

Rarely if ever are the assumptions of a theory in the social sciences strictly true in reality, so that empirical evidence is also considered in deciding whether or not a theory is true. However, not only are the assumptions far-fetched, but the theorems on behaviour, on the valuation of securities and on the investment decision are quite opposite to what we observe. Why these propositions are necessary for the truth of the theory and why they are empirically false are demonstrated briefly below and in greater detail in Gordon (1994: chs 2, 4, 5 and 6).

Why does the neoclassical theory of investment require the first proposition, that real persons only hold securities, while corporations hold and invest in all the real assets of an economy? Real persons maximize utility and not wealth, but the two result in the same decision under certainty. With uncertainty, however, utility maximization may result in an investment that departs from the wealth-maximizing decision. Hence, real persons must be divorced from the investment decision.

Under proposition 1, real persons are portfolio investors who allocate wealth between a diversified portfolio of shares and a risk-free bond to maximize utility. No one knows what that allocation will be since it is quite impossible to articulate a person's utility function, let alone its aggregate over all persons in an economy. That is no problem, however, since all investment in real assets is by corporations, and investment in real assets is what concerns us.

The first proposition is the least objectionable of the five in advanced capitalist countries at the present time. Over the last 150 years in these countries, the proprietorship has declined considerably relative to the corporation as a form of business organization, and nominal assets have become the predominant form of personal wealth. However, real assets still represent a very substantial fraction of personal wealth, so this proposition is far from being completely true.

Proposition 1 leads directly to the second proposition, that the sole objective of the corporation in its financing and investment decisions is the maximization of its current market value. That is exactly what portfolio stockholders want corporations to do. An investment or financing decision by a corporation that raises the price of its shares may change the risk and return on shareholder's portfolio, but that is of absolutely no concern to her or him. The shareholder enjoys the increase in net worth that results from the price increase, and a few minutes on the telephone to a broker creates a portfolio that restores the previous or achieves any other risk-return position on the net worth.

Corporate managements have the legal obligation to serve stockholders, but at least as long ago as Berle and Means (1932) it was recognized that the separation of ownership and control creates a principal–agent situation. That is, a corporation's management has considerable freedom of action to subordinate stockholder interests to its own interest. A corporation's management does not hold a well-diversified portfolio of jobs, so bankruptcy is very costly to management. It will be shown shortly that maximizing share price today is accomplished by very high debt ratios and dividend payout rates that create a high probability of bankruptcy tomorrow. Hence, self-interest persuades corporate managements to follow conservative leverage and dividend policies.

What is at stake here is not merely the narrow self-interest of a corporation's management. At stake is the long-run growth and survival of the corporation, and with it the welfare of all its employees and other stakeholders. More conservative capital structure and dividend policies than those which maximize current market value are necessary conditions for long-run survival. On the other hand, it may be no less damaging to the welfare of the corporation and its service to society to leave a management in complete and uncontestable control of its corporation. The considerable literature devoted to the ground rules that should govern the 'market for corporate control' is evidence that either extreme is no solution. Further evidence on this point is the reluctance of mutual funds, pension funds and other such financial institutions in the United States to exercise their latent power to take control of corporate boards of directors. They could then impose on corporations their objective of maximizing current market value.

The assumption that corporations maximize their current market values leads directly to the third and fourth propositions, that value is independent of financial policy. Value must be independent of capital structure and dividend payout policies, because a corporation may not make the investment that maximizes its current market value, if the financing policy used to undertake the investment also influences value. These financing propositions have been the primary concern of neoclassical financial economists.

In their famous 1958 paper Modigliani and Miller (hereafter MM) argued that the value of a corporation is independent of its capital structure because personal leverage is a perfect substitute for corporate leverage. That paper also found the evidence consistent with the theorem. In 1963, however, they acknowledged a theoretical error in the 1958 paper: the tax system makes the value of a corporation rise with leverage up to 100 per cent debt in otherwise perfect capital markets. This gave rise to a search for other market imperfections that would make a finite capital structure optimal. Otherwise, value maximization and/or the leverage theorem would be false, since we do not observe 100 per cent debt ratios.

In 1966 MM argued that their tax-adjusted theorem is empirically true. However, comments on this paper and other empirical work, including Brigham and Gordon (1968), contradicted their results. Value increases with leverage by more than the tax-adjusted MM theorem. One reason, as Gordon and Kwan (1979) pointed out, is that personal leverage is through margin loans, while corporate leverage is available through long-term loans. It follows that personal leverage is in fact a very poor substitute for corporate leverage. Not only does value increase with leverage up to very high debt ratios, but profitable corporations have much lower debt ratios than those which maximize value. This record of failure in reconciling theory and evidence culminated in a collection of papers that celebrated the thirtieth anniversary of the theorem by acknowledging that the theorem is in fact not true! (See Miller 1988; Ross 1988; and Stiglitz 1988.) Stiglitz (1988: 126) concluded that there has been 'a reexamination of [the theorem's] standard assumptions. That reexamination is still going on.' Perhaps it is time to look elsewhere for the explanation of capital structure.

Turning to dividend policy, Miller and Modigliani (1961) argued that it has no influence on a corporation's value because the sale of shares is a perfect substitute for the retention of earnings in financing investment. In fact, taxes, transaction costs and other imperfections make the sale of shares a very imperfect and costly substitute for retained earnings. Modifying the theory to incorporate these imperfections leads to the conclusion that to maximize value, corporations should pay no dividends and make distributions only through share repurchases. Also, share issues should only take place by firms that retain 100 per cent of earnings.

The evidence on dividend policy and its influence on price is quite opposite to these predictions. Most corporations pay dividends regularly, they rely little on share repurchases, and dividend-paying corporations also issue shares. Furthermore, over a wide range the value of a corporation increases instead of decreasing as its payout rate rises. These facts are obvious to the naked eye as well as being confirmed by econometric analysis. Some neoclassical financial economists, such as Black (1976), find the facts puzzling. Others manage to find the evidence consistent with the proposition that value is independent of payout, or value decreases as payout is increased. Others accept that there is covariation between payout and value, but they attribute it not to the value of dividends but to information that the dividend provides about earnings. For more on the efforts to make the facts consistent with the theory on capital structure as well as dividend policy, see Gordon (1994: chs 4 and 5).

What we have just done is to look at four of the five propositions in the neoclassical theory of finance. They are: real investment is by corporations; they maximize current market value in their financing and investment decisions; and value is independent of capital structure and dividend policies. We have seen that all four propositions are more or less false. Only the most devout disciples maintain that these propositions are true. For the most part, finance research looks for 'market imperfections' that reconcile theory and fact. However, the neoclassical theory of investment depends upon the truth of these propositions, and the theory is invalid to the degree that market imperfections violate the truth of these propositions. What is most damaging to the theory is that modifying it to recognize these so-called imperfections still fails to explain the facts, as noted above.

The last of the five assumptions necessary for the truth of the neoclassical theory of finance and investment is by a wide margin the most important and the most unrealistic. The value of a firm, according to the theory, is the sum of the present values of (a) the expected future income on its existing assets, and (b) the excess of the expected rate of return on its future investments over its cost of capital, that is the risk adjusted interest rate (see Miller and Modigliani 1961: eq. 12). This valuation model leads directly to the neoclassical theory of investment, where the value of the firm is maximized by the investment that equates the marginal rate of return on investment with the cost of capital.

At first glance, this valuation model may seem reasonable, but implicit in it are two highly unreasonable and empirically false assumptions. One is that the yield that investors require is independent of the size of the investment plan. The other is that the discovery of investment opportunities that offer excess returns is independent of the firm's history. The latter may be called the equal-opportunity assumption.

The first assumption is contradicted by the well-known fact that growth stocks are risky. As a firm's expected return on investment and its investment rate rise, bankruptcy becomes less likely but its shares become more of a growth stock. As that takes place its beta factor or risk to shareholders increases, and the expected or required return at which the stock sells rises (see Fewings 1979).

The equal-opportunity assumption is even more unreasonable. It implies that a corporation does nothing to create its investment opportunities. They are due to good fortune or other accidents of nature. In particular, they are independent of the firm's investment history. Another way of stating this assumption is that corporations, like portfolio investors, do not discover opportunities to earn abnormal rates of return (see Gordon and Gould 1978).

An alternative valuation model, described in Gordon (1962) and Gordon and Gould (1978), does not require the above two highly implausible assumptions. This model follows directly from the fundamental theorem of finance that the value of an asset is the present value of its expected future payments. For a share, the payment expectation is its dividend expectation, and that expectation may be represented by a current value and an expected growth rate. Gordon (1994: ch. 6) demonstrated that this simple model does a far better job than the MM model in explaining how price varies among shares, and it does a far better job of arriving at the investment policy that maximizes share price. Important features of the model are widely used in the teaching and practice of finance (see, for example, Ross *et al.* 1993: chs 6 and 14; and Elton and Gruber 1991, ch. 16). The model is useful because it can be implemented and because a corporate management is concerned with the price of its stock. However, as stated earlier, corporate managements do not simply maximize current market value. Their primary concern is the growth and survival of the firm, and we turn now to the behaviour that serves these objectives.

A SURVIVAL THEORY OF BEHAVIOUR

Our theory of saving and investment under uncertainty is best introduced by considering the consequences of uncertainty for a competitive, closed, stationary capitalist system. Such a system is the starting point from which Marx's as well as the neoclassical model of a capitalist system has been developed. It will be seen, however, that such a system breaks down when the presence of uncertainty about the future is recognized. The problem is that an increasing fraction of the capitalists go bankrupt over a relatively short period of time. Recognizing what capitalists do to achieve tolerable prospects of long-run growth and survival is the basis for our theory of finance.

For concreteness, assume a competitive system with a large number of proprietors, in which the net worth of the jth proprietor at the start of period t is W_{jt} and his or her debt is L_{jt}. Interest at the rate r is paid (earned) on the debt if it is positive (negative). The proprietor has a stock of risky assets or capital of $k_{jt} = W_{jt} + L_{jt}$ on which the profit rate is a random variable, with x_{jt} the actual value for the jth proprietor in period t. For simplicity, it may be assumed that the expected value or mean of the x_{jt} for all proprietors in all periods has the same value μ. The expected value for the jth proprietor's return on net worth in t at the start of t is:

$$k_{jt} = \mu + (\mu - r)\, L_{jt} / W_{jt} \tag{29.1}$$

and the realized value is:

$$y_{jt} = x_{jt} + (x_{jt} - r)\, L_{jt} / W_{jt}. \tag{29.2}$$

Risk aversion guarantees that $\mu > r$, but the proprietor faces $x_{jt} \gtreqless r$. Hence, k_{jt} which is the mean of y_{jt} increases with L_{jt} / W_{jt}, the proprietor's debt–equity ratio. The proprietor's risk, which is measured by the variance of y_{jt}, increases with the variance of x_{jt} and with L_{jt} / W_{jt}.

The necessary but not sufficient condition for a proprietor to remain in a stationary state is that consumption in each period is equal to income; that is, $C_{jt} = y_{jt}W_{jt}$. However, a proprietor is not able to set $C_{jt} = y_{jt}W_{jt}$ with the future uncertain. In fact, $y_{jt}W_{jt}$ may be negative. The best a proprietor can do is set $C_{jt} = k_{jt}W_{jt}$, in which case wealth changes by the difference between actual and expected income, that is, by $(y_{jt} - k_{jt})\, W_{jt}$.

Under this policy the system as a whole may remain in a stationary state, but that is not true of each proprietor. The arithmetic mean growth rate in net worth for each proprietor is zero, but the geometric mean growth rate falls below the arithmetic mean by an amount that increases with the variance in the return on net worth. The policy that maximizes the geometric mean growth rate has been advocated on the grounds that the actual growth rate converges on its geometric mean as time goes to infinity. However, the variance in the growth rate becomes infinite as time goes to infinity. See Merton and Samuelson (1974) for other objections to the policy. Of course, what happens as time goes to infinity is of absolutely no empirical relevance. Over a finite horizon the actual growth rate varies over a wide range among proprietors, a majority experience negative growth, and both the size of that majority and the fall in net worth increase with the variance in the return on net worth. Furthermore, sooner or later practically every proprietor will find consumption to be intolerably low under the consumption rule that it be equal to expected income, since there is a minimum consumption below which starvation takes place. The minimum below which consumption will not be allowed to fall, as long as there is wealth that can be consumed, is raised by the terms under which a proprietor believes that taking a job or going on the dole is an acceptable alternative to remaining in business.

With C_0 a proprietor's minimum consumption, bankruptcy becomes practically certain soon after net worth falls below the level at which $k_{jt}W_{jt} = C_0$. Sooner or later every proprietor who consumes expected income as long as $k_{jt}W_{jt} > C_0$ finds $k_{jt}W_{jt} < C_0$, so sooner or later all proprietors go bankrupt. C_0 is an absorbing barrier. With the high variance of return that exists in a competitive system, a great majority of the proprietors will go bankrupt within twenty-five years, a relatively short period of time.[5]

It may be argued that the bankruptcy of proprietors on the micro level is of no concern for the survival of the system. The system remains in a stationary state from one period to the next, since consumption is equal to actual income at the macro level. That would be true if there were some process to bring the required number of new proprietors into the system as old ones consume expected income and go bankrupt. However, proprietors are quite unlikely to accept such a fate passively. Biological analogies have become popular in the social sciences, and the one suggested at the start of this chapter seems appropriate. Proprietors may be looked upon as a socio-economic species, with long-run survival and growth the primary concern of each member of the species. Hence, we should consider what a proprietor is compelled to do in order to achieve more attractive prospects for long-run survival and growth.

It can be shown that our proprietor's probability of long-run growth and survival, that is, of not going bankrupt over a finite horizon such as twenty-five years, increases as the arithmetic mean rate of growth in net worth rises and as the variance in that growth rate is diminished. There are three things that a proprietor can do to raise the mean and/or reduce the variance in the rate of growth in net worth. The first is represented by the Keynesian consumption function

$$C_t = C_0 + \alpha Y_t \tag{29.3}$$

where C_t = consumption in t, $Y_t = k_{jt}W_t$ = expected income in t, $C_0 > 0$ and $0 < \alpha < 1$. Clearly, the lower are the values of C_0 and α for any one proprietor, the lower is the value of C_t/W_t, and the higher is the mean rate of growth in net worth. However, the extent to which the C_0 and α are reduced for all proprietors, aggregate demand and the growth rate in their net worth are reduced. We have seen why a proprietor must have a minimum consumption, in which case the stationary-state policy of α = 1 will not be followed. With $\alpha < 1$, as argued by Keynes, the saving (and growth) rate rises as wealth rises. In other words, as expected income rises, consumption rises, but the fraction of expected income consumed falls in order to reduce the probability of bankruptcy in the future. (For more on the reasons why $C_0 > 0$ and $\alpha < 1$, see *G.T.*: chs 8 and 9.)[6]

The second way in which a proprietor raises the mean and reduces the variance of the rate of growth in net worth is through the pursuit of monopoly power. Proprietors behave in the manner described by Kalecki (1954: 11–27). Monopoly power does this by raising the mean and reducing the variance of the rate of return on net worth. The systematic pursuit of monopoly power and its necessity for avoiding bankruptcy are revealed most clearly by the behaviour of the modern large corporation. It does not engage solely in production; it also engages in a wide range of non-production activities that include research and development, marketing and selling, and influencing government by various means. These activities may be socially beneficial, benign or malignant. What they have in common is that they make production profitable by increasing sales or by increasing the margin of price over production cost. Without the monopoly power obtained through product differentiation, by one means or another, the rate of profit has such a low mean and such a high variance as to make the probability of long-run survival very low, regardless of consumption (dividend) policy and investment policy.

The third way in which a proprietor can raise the mean or reduce the variance in the growth rate is through investment policy. Investment is the purchase of risky real assets, and the amount by which investment is above (below) saving raises (reduces) debt. At the start of each period a proprietor has a desired stock of capital, and investment in the period is intended to bring the actual stock closer to the desired stock. Investment expressed as a fraction of net worth may therefore be given by the expression:

$$I/W = \lambda\ [\hat{K} - K]/W, \tag{29.4}$$

where $\hat{K} - K$ is the excess of the desired over the actual stock of risky real assets, and $0 < \lambda < 1$ is the speed of adjustment in moving K to $\hat{K}$. The desired ratio of capital to net worth is:

$$\hat{K}/W = \beta_0 + \beta_1\ (\mu - i) + \beta_2 v + \beta_3 W \tag{29.5}$$

Here, $\mu - i$ is the excess of the expected return on capital over the interest rate, v is the variance in the return on capital, and W is net worth. A proprietor who maximizes the probability of long-run survival has $\beta_1 > 0$, $\beta_2 < 0$, and $\beta_3 < 0$. Only the last relation, $\beta_3 < 0$, is open to question, since the variation in $\hat{K}/W$ both with the mean and inversely with the variance of the return on capital are consistent with the neoclassical theory of investment. There, covariation in $\hat{K}/W$ with $\mu - i$ and inverse variation with v take place in order to maximize current market value by equating the marginal rate of return with the cost of capital. Here, the explanation is different. The objective here is long-run survival.

The inverse relation between $\hat{K}/W$ and W in equation (29.5) means that when W is very low the proprietor's $\hat{K}/W >> 1$. He wants a very high debt–equity ratio. As W rises, $\hat{K}/W$ falls towards one and then below it, and an increasing fraction of net worth is devoted to risk-free loans. In other words, when net worth is small the proprietor adopts the 'go for broke' policy involved in a high mean and variance, since it is the only policy that offers some chance of escaping bankruptcy in the near future. On the other hand, as net worth rises, the proprietor increases investment as well as consumption, but an increasing fraction of income and net worth are devoted to increasing security. First, the debt–equity ratio is reduced, and then the fraction of net worth in risk-free loans is raised as net worth rises.

With the mean and variance of the return on capital given, this policy reduces the mean as well as the variance of the return on net worth. However, when net worth is very large, the negative impact on long-run survival of the lower rate of return is more than offset by the lower variance. What we have done here is to carry forward the principle of increasing risk, recognized long ago by Kalecki, to show how concern for financial strength and survival makes the ratio of saving to investment rise with net worth. The empirical work of Fazzari *et al.* (1988), Chamberlain and Gordon (1989) and others before them make clear that the debt–equity ratio is not constrained solely by creditor concerns.[7]

MACROECONOMIC IMPLICATIONS

The investment behaviour just described is our important innovation in a Keynes–Kalecki model such as the one presented by Asimakopulos (1977). There, investment varies with profitability, and vice versa, so that only the interest rate prevents the system from moving indefinitely in the direction of an initial shock. Here, the inverse relation between investment and net worth incorporated in equations (29.4) and (29.5) absorbs the shock. Incorporating this investment behaviour in the Keynes–Kalecki macro model leaves it unchanged otherwise. For instance, it matters not whether workers are left out of the model, are included with consumption equal to income, or, more realistically, are included with consumption equal to a constant plus a fraction of income. The choice influences the macro values of the parameters of equation (29.3), the consumption function, but we still have $C_0 > 0$, and $0 < \alpha < 1$. The important difference between proprietors and workers is that the latter do not invest, so their debt–equity ratios are equal to minus one. Apart from worker investment in housing, whatever net worth they have is invested (hopefully) in risk-free loans. The workers who periodically become proprietors commonly move immediately to the highest debt-equity ratio allowed by their creditors. New small firms go bankrupt at a high rate because they cannot obtain the credit needed for optimal growth and to survive losses in the early period.

Perhaps the manner in which the equality between saving and investment on the macro level is realized should be explained. A proprietor with a net worth of W and an expected return of k has an expected income of kW. Equation (29.3) describes her or his decision to consume C and save $S = kW - C$. The proprietor also decides to invest I with $I \gtreqless S$, planning to lend or borrow the difference. The actual return on net worth will be $y \gtreqless k$, and under the reasonable assumption that C + I will be as planned, actual saving will be $\hat{S} = yW - C$. The proprietor will lend (or borrow) $\hat{S} - I$ if it is positive (negative). In aggregate, but not for each proprietor, we must have $\hat{S} \equiv I$, and the values of yW aggregated over all proprietors will adjust to satisfy this condition. However, some proprietors become more secure while others move closer to bankruptcy.

We now turn to some interesting macroeconomic implications of the theory of saving and investment presented here. First, it makes even clearer why Say's Law, that the supply of output creates its own demand, is not true of capitalist systems. In pre-capitalist systems people dealt with the problem of uncertainty about future harvests and about supply in general by storing the objects of consumption. Hence, supply generated its own demand, whether it be for consumption or for storage. Storage also takes place in capitalist systems, but such storage is specialized in firms that do so for profit and not for security. These firms, like all other firms and like individuals, find security by increasing the fraction of wealth held in the form of loans, both interest-and non-interest-bearing loans, that are free of default risk. The supply of output in order to acquire such assets does not generate its own demand for output.

Risk-free loans are a wonderful instrument for security on the micro level. Holding them earns a positive instead of a negative interest rate. Furthermore, they have negative betas, in that their real value rises as the economy declines, at which time investors may need to call or sell the loans in order to supplement current income. However, the use of nominal risk-free loans for economic security wreaks havoc with the relation between supply and demand. In a closed system the desire to increase economic security as wealth increases is satisfied most effectively by an increase in the public debt. Unfortunately, the demand for economic security does not generate its own supply of output, and that is what makes excess supply a chronic problem of capitalist systems. They experience secular stagnation without the more or less regular introduction into the system of new capitalists who have extraordinarily profitable investment opportunities and who borrow like mad to take advantage of them. The next section describes how this took place in the transition from feudalism to capitalism. On the other hand, the enormous stock of liquid risk-free loans held by real and corporate persons along with their borrowing capacity make it possible for demand to be an enormous multiple of supply over any short interval of time. This becomes painfully clear during periods of hyperinflation. As long as that does not take place, capitalist systems fluctuate in a fairly narrow range due to the saving and investment behaviour described earlier.

To elaborate, recall that investment varies with the rate of profit and inversely with the level of wealth. A rising rate of profit, therefore, raises investment, income and wealth, but the fraction of wealth devoted to reducing debt also rises with wealth. Consequently, the rise in wealth moderates and then ends the rise in investment, income and the profit rate. The rise in wealth continues and the increasing fraction devoted to loans makes investment, income and the profit rate turn down. Conversely, as these variables fall, the rise in wealth is moderated and then reversed, and the decreasing fraction devoted to risk-free loans moderates and reverses the decline in investment, income and the profit rate.

Gordon (1994: ch. 8) presents a macroeconomic model that captures these relations in a system where investment is by corporations and their owners are portfolio investors. Income is the sum of consumption and investment demand, and consumption is a Keynesian function of income. Corporations are allowed to behave according to neoclassical theory, equating the marginal return on investment with the cost of capital, but the latter must adjust to persuade portfolio investors to hold the outstanding stock of risky shares and risk-free bonds.[8] These portfolio investors allocate their wealth to maximize the probability of long-run survival, in which case the cost of capital fluctuates so as to make the investment by corporations vary with its rate of return and inversely with wealth. There is a unique set of values for the model's parameters, under which investment and related variables fluctuate in cycles of fairly constant amplitude. Departures from these values, however, result in the explosive growth, decline or other unrealistic time paths that take place with multiplier accelerator models that are represented by second-order difference equations.

The deranged behaviour described above took place because a representative agent was used for each class of persons in the system. This implies, for instance, that in each period either no corporation goes bankrupt or all corporations do so. Most important, the equality of income and expenditure and of saving and investment that are true on the macro level for a closed system are forced on each person on the micro level. Kirman (1992) discusses other limitations of macro models that employ representative agents.

Gordon (1994: ch. 9) presents a macro Keynesian model with a superior microfoundation in that the system has a large number of proprietors; each one makes Keynesian consumption and investment decisions; and macro values of the variables are *simply aggregates over the proprietors of their micro values*. Each proprietor's consumption and investment is determined by his or her wealth and its expected rate of return. The actual rate of return is its expected value plus or minus a random variable with mean zero. In addition, the income of each proprietor is scaled up or down by a fraction of the amount needed to make aggregate expenditure and income equal. They need not be equal on the micro level, and each proprietor lends or borrows the difference. There is an upper limit on a proprietor's debt–equity ratio, so that negative or low rates of return over a number of periods can wipe out a proprietor's net worth and lead to bankruptcy.

Simulation results obtained with this model are interesting. Under the consumption policy that is a necessary condition for a stationary state, about 90 per cent of the proprietors go bankrupt within fifty years, notwithstanding the assignment of a very low variance to the rate of return on capital. Under the Keynesian consumption and investment policies described earlier, the rate at which proprietors go bankrupt is reduced materially, and the probability of bankruptcy over any horizon for a proprietor is lower the more conservative are the proprietor's consumption and investment policies. A conservative consumption policy has a small minimum consumption C_0 and a small income coefficient in equation (29.3). A conservative investment policy has the coefficients of the excess return and of net worth, β_1 and β_3 in equation (29.5), both small in absolute value. However, to the degree that all proprietors follow more conservative policies, aggregate demand is reduced, and the average survival rate of all proprietors is also reduced. Keynes made this clear with respect to consumption policy many years ago.

Quite the opposite takes place when $\beta_3 = 0$ in the investment equation. Proprietors then behave according to the neoclassical theory of investment. The simulation results have all the variables moving rapidly toward zero or growing at rates that increase explosively. Hence, without the restraint imposed by the desire for security, the growth in the nominal values of the variables could be accommodated only by runaway inflation or deflationary collapse.

The above results were obtained for a closed system in which there are no new proprietors entering the system, no government and no financial relations with foreign systems. Under these conditions, practically every proprietor goes bankrupt sooner or later, regardless of the consumption and investment policies followed. Withdrawal of these assumptions has interesting consequences. The periodic introduction of new proprietors who start with a small net worth, and who have a return on investment with a high mean and a high variance, benefits the system. A large fraction go broke very soon, but a significant minority soon become securely established. In addition, the wealth and the survival rate of the old proprietors both rise with the rate at which new proprietors are introduced. The moral is that it pays to encourage small business.

Growth in the government debt at a modest rate increases the stock of risk-free assets, and that, as one might expect, is quite beneficial. The survival rate of proprietors is raised over any given horizon, and the real as well as the nominal wealth of proprietors is raised. A most fascinating question is the consequences of international trade and financial relations, since we do not merely get specialization and exchange. If foreign proprietors are wealthier, they force the domestic proprietors to become debtors and their survival rate is reduced on average. Differences in profitability may also influence capital flows, growth and survival rates.

The model described above still does not capture many important features of actual capitalist systems. Inventory investment which includes the excess of the quantity sold over production is not recognized. The same is true of the quantity of money, the interest rate, changes in relative prices and changes in the general price level. Expanding the model to recognize these variables in a realistic way may improve our understanding of what happens to actual capitalist systems over time.

LONG-RUN DEVELOPMENT

The theory of economic behaviour presented earlier can be used to provide a plausible explanation of the changes in Europe's economic systems over the last 1,500 years. These economic systems have exhibited remarkable diversity and change: tribalism, feudalism, capitalism and socialism are the terms used to describe them. Another remarkable feature of this experience is that these systems have not been imposed from abroad, but have appeared and evolved in response to the progress of technology and other developments within Europe. Furthermore, the major economic changes elsewhere in the world over the last few hundred years have been imposed or inspired by forces that originated in Europe.

The starting point for our explanation is the same natural law that is the basis for the theory of investment presented in the previous sections. For a people, just as for a person, long-run survival and growth depend upon the security of their income no less than upon its average level. No matter how large an annual level of consumption may be, it results in death if it is enjoyed for only one-half of the year. The related additional proposition on which our theory of economic development relies is that an economic system well-suited to provide growth is ill-suited to provide security, and vice versa. The consequence is that the progress of a people under a system that is designed to provide growth requires the adoption of laws, institutions and other arrangements that provide security. However, the compromises in the direction of security undermine the old system at the same time as they make possible continued progress under that system. At some point the 'contradictions' involved in modifying the growth system to provide security for its people become unmanageable, and the society collapses or there is a complete transition to a system that is designed to provide security. Progress under that system then requires introducing and expanding the alien institutions of still another system, one that provides growth.

To make the story concrete, feudalism arose in the centuries following the fall of the Roman Empire in order to provide security against the raids of marauding tribes. Tribalism was the alternative economic system at the time. The typical feudal manor was a closed system that also provided economic security through its technology of production and social arrangements. The peace and community achieved under feudalism increased both the population and the excess of its production over subsistence requirements. The optimal use of this surplus was to support an increasing population of artisans in the production of handicrafts.

However, the feudal manor could not use the surplus efficiently in this way for two reasons, one technological and the other social. First, it was not a large enough economic entity to support the production of the wide range of high-quality handicrafts that were becoming available. The other and perhaps more important problem was that specialization and exchange according to the privileges and obligations of the feudal manor was a very ineffective way to organize the production and exchange of a wide range of high-quality handicraft objects. Money, exchange through markets and terms of employment that could encourage the development of skilled craftsmen were all alien to the feudal economy.

The towns with their merchants and craftsmen offered a far more attractive use of the agricultural surplus than the support of artisans on the feudal manor. However, these towns could not be made part of the system of feudal obligations and privileges. They could function only with specialization and exchange through markets, and therefore they required independence or at least a special place in the feudal system. Furthermore, both serf and lord could take advantage of the towns and use them for foreign trade only by accepting their method of doing business – exchange through markets.

Nowhere is the contradiction in the development of a system more vivid than the role of capitalism in the development of feudalism. The towns made possible the realization of the surplus being produced on the feudal estates, but they did not merely embellish feudal life by providing it with more attractive products for consumption. The size of the feudal armies, the period of time that they could be mobilized for war, and the quality of their armaments all depended on the development of the towns and their activities. Where the towns were suppressed or failed to develop for other reasons, feudal power stagnated and became vulnerable to defeat.

None the less, the towns were an alien growth on the feudal order that made impossible the realization of the ideal feudal order contemplated by the Catholic Church. Since intercourse between town and manor had to be carried on under the terms that suited the town – through markets – both serf and lord wanted money. Hence, market arrangements between serf and lord came to replace the feudal obligations and privileges. The serf was transformed into a rent-paying tenant or a farm labourer, while the lord was transformed into a large-scale farmer or landlord.

Efforts by feudal lords to destroy the towns or exploit them through excessive taxes and other charges were self-defeating, since feudal progress was tied to the growth of the towns and cities. Furthermore, the merchants and craftsmen sought freedom from feudal oppression by financing the rise of national monarchs and eventually nation states. The contradictions in this process transformed, corrupted and ultimately destroyed feudal society. It culminated in the transition to capitalism between the fifteenth and eighteenth centuries. This was a unique and remarkable event, since that transition did not take place under roughly similar circumstances in other times and places.

Capitalism with its market relations is a wonderful engine of economic growth, but it is also a terrible engine of economic insecurity, and without high growth the insecurity is intolerable. The insecurity was moderated during the transition from feudalism to capitalism in two ways. One was the growth made possible by the transition, since feudal and other non-capitalist systems were the source of labour and resources needed for high growth rates. The other was the cushion of security provided by the underlying fuedal society. However, once the transition was completed in England by the end of the nineteenth century, that country was to come as close as it ever would to a pure competitive capitalist system. In such a system there is complete private ownership and control of capital, and complete reliance on markets to organize and administer economic activity. England's failure to eliminate the market imperfections that stood between it and a pure capitalist system may seem surprising, in view of the fact that capitalism was immensely successful, capitalists were all powerful, and they were firmly committed to the virtues of markets and private ownership. In addition, with few exceptions economists were to follow Adam Smith in establishing the features and extolling the merits of such a system.

The continued development of capitalism during the nineteenth and twentieth centuries in England and elsewhere as a closed competitive capitalist system proved to be quite impossible. The insecurity and instability of such a system proved intolerable for both labour and capital and for national survival as well. Progress did take place but it was made possible by means of the socialization of economic relations in all sectors of the economy. This was true in labour markets, in agriculture, in the growth of large corporations, in the growth of the public debt and, most of all, in the rise of the welfare state – pension plans, unemployment compensation, socialized medicine, housing subsidies, deposit insurance and other measures to protect income or wealth from one contingency or another. Incorporating the socialist relations, perhaps we should say social democratic relations, of the welfare state in a capitalist system undermines the system while making possible further progress under it.

At one time it was widely believed that the contradictions in the process of capitalist development would be resolved in the long run, if they could be resolved at all, through a transition to socialism. Now it is widely considered quite ridiculous even to entertain the possibility of a transition to socialism, given what has taken place in Eastern Europe and the former Soviet Union. The transition of China to a 'market socialism' economy and the resurgence of capitalism everywhere else is considered further evidence.

Before speculating on what these recent events mean and what the future will bring, our theory of economic development must be explained further. The model of a capitalist system developed earlier is different from Marx's in a number of important respects, but the theory of economic development that emerges here is quite Marxist. What Marx had to say on the latter subject is summarized in the following widely quoted passage:

> In the social production which men carry on they enter into definite relations that are indispensable and independent of their will; these relations of production correspond to a definite stage of development of their material powers of production. The sum total of these relations of production constitutes the economic structure of society – the real foundation, on which rise legal and political superstructures and to which correspond definite forms of social consciousness. The mode of production in material life determines the general character of the social, political and spiritual processes of life. It is not the consciousness of men that determines their existence, but, on the contrary, their social existence determines their consciousness. At a certain stage of their development, the material forces of production in society come in conflict with the existing relations of production, or – what is but a legal expression for the same thing – with the property relations within which they had been at work before. From forms of development of the forces of production these relations turn into their fetters. Then comes the period of social revolution. With the change of economic foundation the entire immense superstructure is more or less rapidly transformed. (Marx 1904: 11–12)

Two propositions advanced here are especially noteworthy. One is the primary role assigned to technological progress in transforming socio-economic institutions 'from forms of development . . . into their fetters'. The other is that the progress of technology is fairly steady, while socio-economic institutions are 'more or less rapidly transformed' by a social revolution.

The evidence, however, is that change in socio-economic institutions is no less gradual than the change in technology. The radical changes in the economic system carried out when the revolutionary socialist governments took power in the Soviet Union and China seem to confirm Marx's prediction. However, the counter examples are plentiful. For instance, the transition from feudal to capitalist organization of economic activity in England took place more or less continuously over the fourteenth to the eighteenth centuries, while the next two centuries witnessed the more or less steady adoption of collective or socialist methods of organizing economic activity. Furthermore, the highly centralized systems adopted when the socialist governments of the Soviet Union and China came to power are explained better by political considerations – maintaining power in a hostile capitalist world – than by the state of technology. Both countries have been forced to retreat, in one case abandoning socialism altogether it seems.

The welfare state in its social democratic as well as its socialist manifestations is in retreat everywhere. National responsibility for welfare is faced with increasing difficulties in advanced capitalist countries as well as in the poor ones. The internationalization of capital, real capital via the transnational corporations and nominal capital via financial markets, is eroding very rapidly the ability of national governments to maintain the welfare state, even to manage their affairs. Inequality of income and unemployment are increasing everywhere, in the rich countries due to competition with the poor ones, and in the poor countries due to the rationalization of agriculture or the inability to compete.

We are fast approaching, if we have not already arrived at, a world capitalist system in which membership is compulsory, in which transnational corporations take over the control of international trade and are looked upon as the engines of economic progress. Government is increasingly seen as a bureaucracy that can serve society only to the degree that it contracts. Hence, wherever there is prosperity capitalism can claim victory, and wherever the economy declines and civil society collapses, capitalism suffers defeat. Regardless of how one weights the victories and defeats, it is clear that the only threat to the system as a whole lies within the system. There is nothing to fear as long as the United States and other advanced capitalist countries enjoy increasing income for the managerial, professional and property class that represents a substantial minority of their population.

In the long run, however, there is a good reason to believe that the world's most serious problem is the environmental destruction due to the increasing consumption by the rich and the increasing numbers of the poor. It seems that the solution to this problem requires a substantial reduction in consumption in the rich countries, a substantial reduction in inequality and unemployment everywhere, and a massive shift in investment to poor countries to provide the technology needed for resource conservation. It is not clear how this solution will be realized through a world order in which growth, monopoly power and financial strength are necessary for survival. Consumption and competitiveness are glorified, and the people as well as the resources of each country must be thrown ever more aggressively into the arena of international competition. Success, it would seem, contributes to the destruction of the environment, unless the increasing poverty and civil disorder taking place in Africa and elsewhere is considered a solution to the problem.

NOTES

* The author benefited from comments on an earlier draft by G.C. Harcourt.

1 Finance is frequently defined narrowly to include only the trading of securities in secondary markets such as stock exchanges. Keynes (*G.T.*: ch. 12) discussed how this activity could have a disruptive influence on saving and investment, leading some people to believe that the suppression of financial activity would improve the process by which saving and investment are determined. However, in a capitalist system, we do not have each person investing his or her own

saving, and finance is the process by which savers and investors are brought together. The process is served by the existence of secondary markets in real and financial assets. In pre-capitalist systems, wealth transfer takes place through gifts, theft and other non-capitalist methods.

2 Perfect markets in neoclassical theory are those in which (a) the number of participants on each side of the market is so large that no participant has any influence over the price, and (b) all participants have identical information about future prices, quantities, etc. When the future is uncertain, and decisions are made on the basis of parameters of a probability distribution, everyone knows the values of these parameters. However, the definition of perfect markets has been enlarged to include whatever the writer finds necessary to arrive at the Utopian properties of the neoclassical capitalist system. See Fama (1978).

3 Davidson (1991) and others have questioned the empirical relevance of theorems on investment under uncertainty on the grounds that investors have little or no knowledge of probability theory and of the probability distributions for events such as the price of a share one period hence. However, the word probability is used here to mean likelihood, so the investor is only required to believe that bankruptcy is more or less likely under one policy than another. In addition, the conclusions reached in this chapter require only that the investor assign values to the mean, variance and possibly also the skewness of a variable. The manner in which the investor is presumed to estimate these parameters from historical data is specified, so that our theorems have empirical content.

4 The empirical work of Jorgenson and Siebert (1968) found the data consistent with the neoclassical theory of investment, but Eisner and Nadiri (1970), Chamberlain and Gordon (1989) and others cited in the latter paper found their methodology seriously flawed and could not replicate their results. I know of no other work that has found the neoclassical theory of investment empirically true.

5 Keynes dismissed concern for the long run with the statement that in the long run we are all dead. However, when the biological or economic conditions for a long life are not satisfied, death or bankruptcy may take place very quickly. The necessary if not sufficient conditions for long-run economic survival will be stated shortly. Here we shall only note that a very small fraction of newly established firms survive more than five years. A new firm without some degree of monopoly power, that is product differentiation, has practically no chance of survival.

6 Notice that equation (29.3) has consumption as a function of expected income, kW, and not actual income, yW. What we call expected income, Friedman called permanent income. As he argued $(y-k)$ W is added to net worth and is not consumed. However, neither his so-called permanent income theory of consumption nor the data invalidate the Keynesian consumption function.

7 It is clear that with the future uncertain a firm is not free to borrow at the risk-free interest rate to finance all investments with a higher expected rate of return. It is also true that lenders frequently find credit rationing a more effective means of dealing with the problem of default than raising the nominal interest rate (see Freimer and Gordon 1965 and Stiglitz and Weiss 1981). However, credit rationing is for the most part self-imposed in order to minimize the risk of bankruptcy. By making the fraction of net worth in risk-free loans rise with net worth, the firm is in effect increasing the debt capacity in good years in order to survive the 'lean' years.

8 It was argued earlier that corporate managers are concerned with the long-run growth and survival of their corporations so that their dividend–investment

decisions are like the consumption–investment decisions of proprietors and portfolio investors. What we show here is that the macro values of the variables behave over time in the same way as they would in a system of proprietors, even though the corporations ignore the problem of survival and maximize current market value in their investment decisions. This takes place because the discount rate that enters into their dividend–investment decisions is determined by portfolio investors who are concerned with survival.

30

THE GENERAL THEORY IN AN OPEN ECONOMY CONTEXT

Paul Davidson

Keynes's *General Theory of Employment, Interest and Money*[1] is developed primarily in a closed economy context. Keynes did, however, introduce an open economy analysis when he noted that: (a) trade could modify the magnitude of the domestic employment multiplier (*G.T.*: 120): (b) a reduction in money-wages would worsen the terms of trade and therefore reduce real income, while it could improve the balance of trade (*G.T.*: 263): and (c) stimulating either domestic investment or foreign investment can increase domestic employment growth (*G.T.*: 335).

In a world where governments are afraid that deliberately stimulating any domestic spending will unleash inflationary forces, export-led growth is seen as a desirable alternative path for expanding domestic employment. A 'favourable balance [of trade], provided it is not too large, will prove extremely stimulating' (*G.T.*: 338) to domestic employment, even if it does so at the expense of employment opportunities abroad.

In a passage that is particularly appropriate for today's global economic setting, Keynes (*G.T.*: 335) noted that:

> in a society where there is no question of direct investment under the aegis of public authority [due to fear of government deficits *per se*], the economic objects, with which it is reasonable for the government to be preoccupied, are the domestic interest rate and the balance of foreign trade.

If, however, nations permit free movement of funds across national boundaries, then

> the authorities have no direct control over the domestic rate of interest or the other inducements to home investment, [and] measures to increase the favourable balance of trade [are] . . . the only *direct* means at their disposal for increasing foreign investment
>
> (*G.T.*: 336)

and domestic employment.

Keynes was well aware that the domestic employment advantage gained by export-led growth 'is liable to involve an equal disadvantage to some other country' (*G.T.*: 338). When countries pursue an 'immoderate policy' (ibid.) of export-led growth (e.g., Japan, Germany and the newly industrialized countries (NICS) of Asia in the 1980s), this aggravates the unemployment problem for the surplus nations' trading partners.[2] These trading partners are then forced to engage in a 'senseless international competition for a favourable balance which injures all alike' (ibid.: 338–9). The traditional approach for improving the trade balance is to make domestic industries *more competitive* by either forcing down nominal wages (including fringe benefits) to reduce labour production costs and/or by a devaluation of the exchange rate.[3] Competitive gains obtained by manipulating these nominal variables can only foster further global stagnation and recession as trading partners (or rivals) attempt to regain a competitive edge by similar policies. Indeed, Keynes noted that 'The remedy of an elastic wage unit, so that a depression is met by a reduction of [money-] wages . . . [is] a means of benefiting ourselves at the expense of our neighbours' (ibid.: 339n).

Unlike the classical theorists of his day (and our day as well[4]), Keynes recognized that 'the mercantilists were aware of the fallacy of cheapness and the danger that excessive competition may turn the terms of trade against a country' (*G.T.*: 345), thereby reducing domestic living standards so that, as President Clinton noted in his 1992 campaign, 'people are working more and earning less'.

Keynes realized that if *every* nation did not actively undertake a programme for public *domestic* investment to generate *domestic* full employment, then the resulting *laissez-faire* system of prudent fiscal finance in tandem with a system of free international monetary flows would create a global environment where *each* nation independently sees significant national advantages in a policy of export-led growth even though pursuit of these policies simultaneously by many nations 'injures all alike' (*G.T.*: 338–9). This warning of Keynes, however, went virtually unrecognized in the 1980s while mainstream economists waxed enthusiastic about the export-led economic miracles of Japan, Germany and the Pacific Rim NICS without noting that these miraculous performances were at the expense of the rest of the world.

In a *laissez-faire* world, when governments do not have the political will to stimulate directly any domestic component of aggregate spending to expand output growth and reduce unemployment, 'domestic prosperity [is] directly dependent on a competitive pursuit of [export] markets' (*G.T.*: 349). This is a competition in which all nations cannot be winners! When, in the late 1980s, the United States began to take steps to reduce its huge trade deficit with the 'miracle economies' of the early 1980s by both depressing its domestic demand and trying to make its industries more competitive in order to gain a larger share of existing world markets, the whole world was plunged into a stagnating slow-growth recessionary era.

For a nation to break out of a global slow-growth stagnating economic environment, the 'truth', Keynes insisted, lay in pursuing a

> policy of an autonomous rate of interest, unimpeded by international preoccupations, and a national investment programme directed to an optimum level of employment which *is twice blessed* in the sense that *it helps ourselves and our neighbours at the same time.* And *it is the simultaneous pursuit of these policies by all countries together which is capable of restoring economic health and strength* internationally, whether we measure it by the level of domestic employment or by the volume of international trade.
>
> (*G.T.*: 349, emphasis added)

From 1982 to 1986, the Reagan administration unwittingly pursued this Keynesian truth by increasing military (public investment) spending and cutting taxes to stimulate consumption. By mid-1982, the Federal Reserve helped by reducing interest rates to avoid a massive international debt default. As a result of the US acting as the 'engine of growth' between 1982 and 1986, most of the OECD nations rapidly recovered from the greatest global recession since the Great Depression. Unfortunately, as recovery occurred, most of the major trading partners of the USA did not engage in a 'simultaneous pursuit of these policies' of increasing public spending and reducing interest rates. These nations neither remembered nor understood Keynes's recommendation that only by the concurrent investment policies of all nations could global economic health and strength be restored.[5] Instead, some of America's trading partners took advantage of Reagan's 'Keynesian' policy, which stimulated US demand for imports, to pursue an export-led growth policy.

Until we understand the lessons of Keynes's *General Theory* in an open-economy context, we are doomed to repeat the past errors encouraged by 'the inadequacy of the *theoretical* foundations of the *laissez-faire* doctrine' (*G.T.*: 339) and by 'orthodox economists whose common sense has been insufficient to check their faulty logic' (*G.T.*: 349) which presumes global full employment so that free trade must increase the global wealth of nations by reducing each nation's aggregate supply constraints through the law of comparative advantage.[6]

In a passage that is amazingly prescient for the economic environment since Bretton Woods, Keynes warns that the law of comparative advantage is only applicable *after* all nations have domestic demand management policies ensuring full employment. Whenever nations operate under a *laissez-faire* mentality that produces significant global unemployment, then

> if a rich, old country were to neglect the struggle for markets its prosperity would droop and fail. But if [all] nations can learn to provide

themselves with full employment by their domestic policy . . . there need be no important economic forces calculated to set the interest of one country against that of its neighbours. There would still be room for the international division of labour and for international lending in appropriate conditions. But there would no longer be a pressing motive why one country need force its wares on another or repulse the offerings of its neighbour, not because this was necessary to enable it to pay for what it wished to purchase, but with the express object of upsetting equilibrium in the balance of payment so as to develop a balance of trade in its own favour [i.e. export-led growth policy]. *International trade would cease to be what it is, namely, a desperate expedient to maintain employment at home by forcing sales on foreign markets and restricting purchases, which, if successful, will merely shift the problem of unemployment to the neighbour which is worsted in the struggle*, but a willing and unimpeded exchange of goods and services in conditions of mutual advantage.

(*G.T.*: 382–3, emphasis added)

Unfortunately, as is evident from the political slogans that surrounded the successful conclusion of the NAFTA agreement and the Uruguay Round of the GATT talks in 1993, most governments have been led by mainstream economists to believe that free trade *per se* is job-creating globally. Keynes's *General Theory* suggests otherwise.

The post-Bretton Woods international payments system has created perverse incentives that set trading partner against trading partner to perpetuate a world of slow growth (if not stagnation). Generalizing Keynes's *General Theory* to an open economy provides a rationale for designing an international payments system that creates incentives for each nation to pursue domestic demand policies that ensure full employment without the fear of a balance of payments constraint. Only then will the gains from the law of dynamic comparative advantage become relevant.

KEYNES'S *GENERAL THEORY* AND AN OPEN ECONOMY

A consistent theme throughout Keynes's *General Theory* is that classical logic has assumed away questions that are fundamental to a market-oriented, money-using economy. These problems are particularly relevant for understanding the current international payments relations that involve liquidity, persistent and growing debt obligations, and the importance of stable rather than flexible exchange rates.

An example of the sanguine classical response to Post-Keynesians who raise these issues is Milton Friedman's response to me in our 'debate' in the literature. Friedman (1974: 151) stated:

A price may be flexible . . . yet be relatively stable, because demand and supply are relatively stable *over time*. . . . [Of course] violent instability of prices in terms of a specific money would greatly reduce the usefulness of that money.

It is nice to know that as long as prices or exchange rates remain relatively stable, or 'sticky', over time, there is no harm in permitting them to be flexible. The problem arises when exchange rates display volatility. Should there be a deliberate policy that intervenes in the market to maintain relative stability, or should we allow a free market to determine the exchange rate? Keynes helped to design the Bretton Woods Agreement to foster action and intervention in order to stabilize exchange rates and control international payment flows. Friedman sold the public on the beneficence of government inaction and the free market determination of exchange rates.

Nowhere is the difference between the Keynes view and the view of those who favour *laissez-faire* arrangements more evident than in regard to these questions of international capital movements and payments mechanisms and the desirability of a flexible exchange rate system. The analysis of Keynes's *General Theory* suggests that government monitoring and, when necesary, control of capital flows is in society's interest. Such controls are not an infringement of the freedom of economic agents any more than the control of people's right to shout 'fire' in a crowded theatre is an infringement of the individual's right of free speech.

CAPITAL MOVEMENTS

Old Keynesians (such as Samuelson and Tobin) as well as New Keynesians have little to say about exogenous capital movements and their potentially detrimental effects on the balance of payments and global employment.[7] Keynes, by contrast, recognized that large unfettered capital flows can create serious international payments problems for nations whose current accounts would otherwise be roughly in balance. Unfortunately, in a *laissez-faire* system of capital markets there is no way of distinguishing between the movement of floating and speculative funds that take refuge in one nation after another in the continuous search either for speculative gains or precautionary purposes, or for hiding from the tax collector, or laundering illegal earnings *vis-à-vis* funds being used to promote genuine new investment for developing the world's resources or to finance legitimate trade flows.

The international movement of speculative, precautionary or illegal funds (hot money), if it becomes significantly large, can be so disruptive to the global economy as to impoverish most, if not all, nations who organize production and exchange processes on an entrepreneurial basis. Keynes warned: 'Loose funds may sweep round the world disorganizing all steady business. Nothing is more certain than that the movement of capital funds must be regulated' (*C.W.* XXV: 25).

One of the more obvious dicta that follow from Keynes's revolutionary vision of the importance of liquidity in open economies is that

> There is no country which can, in future, safely allow the flight of funds for political reasons or to evade domestic taxation or in anticipation of the owner turning refugee. Equally, there is no country that can safely receive fugitive funds which cannot safely be used for fixed investments and might turn it into a deficiency country against its will and contrary to the real facts.
>
> (*C.W.* XXV: 87)

Even in these days of global electronic communication, nations can monitor and control international capital flows *if* they have the will and the necessary co-operation of other nations to do so. Monitoring and control of capital fund movements are technical matters involving the reporting of records that are kept in the accounting system of every banking community. As long as governments have the power to tax and central bankers have the power to audit and regulate their respective domestic banking systems, large-scale international capital flows can be monitored and regulated provided there is international co-operation in this matter. As long as currency is issued only in small denominations, the physical bulkiness of moving large currency sums secretly across borders cannot be a major threat to any capital monitoring and control policy.

In recent years, however, governments' willingness to avoid capital fund monitoring has made it easy to hide not only legally earned income and wealth from tax collectors but also profits from drug and other illegal activities from law enforcement agencies. This *laissez-faire* attitude encourages uncivilized behaviour by self-interested economic agents – and thereby imposes an important, if often neglected, real cost on society. During the 1980s flight, capital drained resources from the relatively poor nations towards the richer ones, resulting globally in a more inequitable redistribution of income and wealth.

Co-operation between nations in monitoring, reporting and controlling disruptive capital funds movements among nations can be readily accomplished by the international payments mechanism described in this chapter.[8] Moreover, the successful implementation of the proposed international payments scheme in co-ordination with some rules for co-ordinating incomes policies among nations would insure very inelastic expectational elasticities regarding the rates of exchange among various nations' monies. These inelastic expectations would mean that individuals would no longer be impelled to engage in disruptive international speculative and precautionary financial transactions. Thus, within a very short span of calendar time after a new payments scheme similar to the one proposed here is implemented, problems of speculative and precautionary 'hot money' flows, as well as the international movements of income and wealth to avoid the tax collector or law-enforcement officers, should quickly shrink to relative insignificance.

The free world embarked on its great classical experiment of floating rates in 1973. Since 1973 there have been periodic bouts of great inflation, increasing rates of global unemployment, a persistent growth of international debt, and an increasingly inequitable international distribution of global income and prosperity. Some of the rich nations grew richer, while most of the poor nations became poorer and suffered huge 'flight capital' losses.

Moreover, since 1982, one nation – the United States – has been able to take advantage of the existing international payments system to obtain a 'free lunch', that is, to run massive perpetual trade deficits. Although residents of most other nations may resent the ability of the United States to use the present system to obtain this 'free lunch', they are hesitant to change a system that is heralded by modern classical economists as the only mechanism that permits everyone the freedom to choose. To be against the existing system is considered to be anti-free-market and for controls by government; this is a particularly unpopular position in these days when state planning has apparently failed so spectacularly in Eastern Europe. In the absence of a complete collapse of the international monetary payments system, however, unless an attractive feasible alternative to the current system is put on the public agenda for discussion and development, the status quo will remain. It is an old adage in political science that 'you can't beat somebody with nobody!'

Any suggestions for reforming the international payments mechanism should build on whatever advantages the current system possesses, while providing rules to prevent any one nation from enjoying a free lunch – unless the free lunch is available to all. It is possible to provide all with a free lunch (that is, increased global employment) if a new payments system has a built-in expansionary bias that encourages all nations to operate closer to full employment than the existing system does.

Before developing the suggestion for an international payments scheme which does provide such an expansionary bias, it is necessary to elaborate on why the existing flexible exchange rate system tends to encourage national policies that inhibit efforts to achieve global full employment and, instead, imparts a slow-growth, deflationary bias.

FLEXIBLE EXCHANGE RATES AND EXPORT-LED GROWTH

Because of the success of the Keynesian revolution in stimulating domestic full-employment policies between the end of the Second World War and the mid-1960s, the problem of wage-cost inflation became endemic to most of the developed countries of the world. Without the persistent threat of large-scale unemployment, workers in many OECD nations, and labour unions especially, became more truculent in their wage demands. By the late 1960s many developed nations were forced to pursue so-called 'stop–go' policies that generated small, planned recessions to reduce the market power of labour to demand inflationary wage increases. These recessions were then followed by expansionary, domestic-spending, Keynesian policies that moved the economy back towards full employment until the next round of inflationary wage demands was tabled by workers. Hence the nomenclature of 'stop–go' policies.

In a flexible exchange rate system, successful export-led growth policies permit a nation to export to its trading partners not only its unemployment but also any inflationary tendencies. In a fixed exchange rate system, export-led growth policy does not provide to a nation any advantage in permitting more employment and growth *with lower inflation rates* compared with Keynesian policies that stimulate domestic aggregate demand to achieve greater employment. Moreover, under a fixed exchange rate system, it is possible for all nations simultaneously to pursue co-ordinated growth-oriented policies by stimulating domestic components of effective demand without necessarily running into balance of payments difficulties as long as the ratio of each nation's growth rate relative to its trading partners' growth rate is equal to the ratio of the elasticity of demand for its exports compared to its elasticity of demand for imports (according to Thirlwall's Law[9]).

In other words, a flexible exchange rate regime guarantees that for every 'successful' economy that pursues a mercantilist trade surplus policy which can promote employment growth without significant inflation, there must be one or more offsetting 'failure' nations importing inflation and unemployment while being plagued with persistent trade deficits. For every winner on the flexible rate system, there must be one or more losers. A fixed exchange rate regime in tandem with intelligent domestic demand and incomes management policies, by contrast, can provide entrepreneurs with profitable expansionary market opportunities in a global environment where all nations are winners. A fixed exchange rate system combined with intelligent international co-operative Keynesian policies, therefore, holds out the promise that all nations can be winners of a free lunch.

In a world operated according to classical axioms, export-led growth should be no more desirable in terms of generating employment without inflation than internally generated demand growth. Classical economics assumes that the economy will track the long-run full-employment growth trend no matter what the primary source of demand growth. Yet the facts of the 1980s demonstrate that all 'successful' economies tend to pursue export-led growth rather than domestic demand-induced expansion. Nations such as West Germany, Japan, Taiwan, Singapore, Hong Kong and South Korea are not only applauded for their economic miracles by leading monetarist and Old and New Keynesian scholars, but are held up as shining examples of the proper functioning of a classical economy operating free from oppressive government intervention.[10] Yet there is nothing in classical theory that justifies relying primarily on export-led growth.

WHY THE PREFERENCE FOR EXPORT-LED GROWTH?

In a flexible exchange rate world, governments can have an incentive to pursue export policies rather than stimulating internal components of aggregate demand if growth without inflation is an objective. To demonstrate the existence of this incentive, let us for simplicity assume that labour is the only variable factor of production. The money-wage (w) divided by the marginal product of labour (MPL) is equal to the marginal cost of domestic industry (MC). Accordingly in a purely competitive economy:

$$(w/\mathrm{MPL}) = \mathrm{MC} = \mathrm{P}_d \qquad (30.1a)$$

where P_d is the price level associated with domestic output. If there is a given degree of monopoly (m) at any level of employment, where $0 \leqslant m < 1$, then $\mathrm{P}_d > \mathrm{MC}$, and

$$(w/\mathrm{MPL}) = \mathrm{MC} = (\mathrm{P}_d)\ (g) \qquad (30.1b)$$

or

$$\mathrm{P}_d = w/\ [\ (\mathrm{MPL})\ (g)\ ] \qquad (30.1c)$$

where g equals one minus the average degree of monopoly in the system.[11] In a purely competitive system where $m = 0$, $g = 1$, the more general equation (30.1b) is reduced to the specific case of equation (30.1a). If $m > 0$, then $g > 1$. Consequently $g \geqslant 1$.

Equation (30.1b) can be rewritten as:

$$(w/\mathrm{P}_d) = (\mathrm{MPL})\ (g) \qquad (30.2)$$

Mainstream economists claim that the aggregate marginal productivity of labour curve is the demand curve for labour when $g = 1$. Post-Keynesians have argued that the marginal productivity of labour curve (multiplied by any value for the scalar g) can be envisioned as a real wage-determining curve, or in Patinkin's terms a 'market equilibrium curve', rather than a demand curve for labour (see Brothwell 1983; Davidson 1983). This is not the place to revive this analytical dispute. In either case, it appears that the real wage at each level of employment is related to the marginal product of labour schedule.[12]

A downward-sloping MPL curve means that industry 'is subject to decreasing returns . . . so that the marginal product . . . necessarily diminishes as employment increases' (*G.T.*: 17). Accordingly, marginal costs for domestic industries are rising as domestic employment increases. Accordingly, if industries are operating under diminishing returns, the

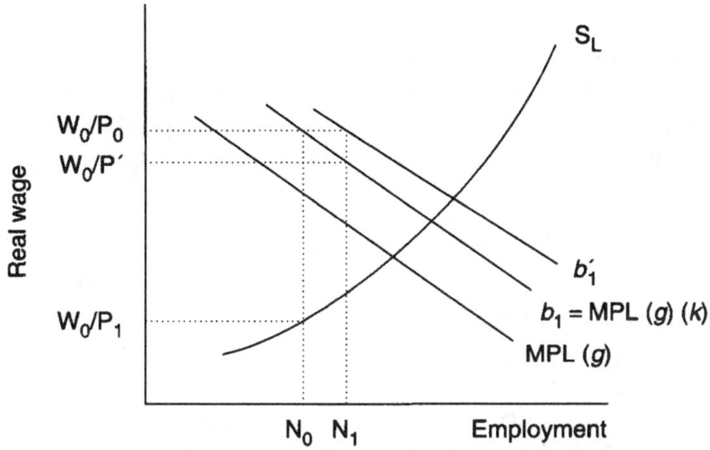

Figure 30.1 Diminishing marginal labour productivity and labour supply schedules

marginal product curve will be downward-sloping and the curve that relates the real wage with alternative employment levels (in Figure 30.1) will be equal to the downward-sloping marginal product curve multiplied by g (where $g \geqslant 1$) for domestic output. If production occurs instead under constant returns, then the marginal product and the MPL (g) curves will be horizontal (as shown in Figure 30.2).

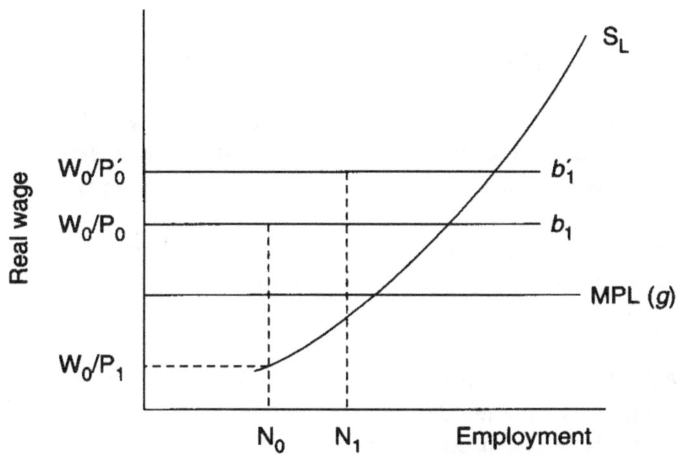

Figure 30.2 Constant marginal labour productivity and labour supply schedules

As far as labour is concerned, its real wage is determined by its money wage divided by the price level (P^c) of the consumer products (wage goods) bought by labour. In other words, the equation for the real wage, whether the economy is open or closed is:

$$w_r = (w/P^c) \tag{30.3}$$

where w_r is the real wage. As a first approximation, we may assume that the price level of domestically produced consumer goods (P^c_d) is equal to (P_d), the price level associated with all the domestically produced goods (i.e. the GDP price deflator).[13] Hence, *for a closed economy*, equation (30.3) can be written as:

$$w_r = (w/P^c) = (w/P^c_d) = (w/P_d) = (\text{MPL})\ (g) \tag{30.4}$$

In an open economy, on the other hand, the price level associated with domestic consumption expenditures (Pc) is given by:

$$Pc = (P^c_d)\ (1 - \phi) + (P^c_m)\ (\phi) \tag{30.5}$$

where P^c_m is the price of consumer good imports in terms of domestic currency and ϕ is the proportion of aggregate domestic consumption expenditures spent on imports. Assuming $P^c_d = P_d$, substituting equation (30.5) into equation (30.3), the real wage in an open economy is:

$$w_r = w/P^c = \frac{w}{P_d\ (1 - \phi) + P^c_m\ (\phi)} \tag{30.6}$$

$$= \frac{w}{(P_d)\ (1/k)} \tag{30.7}$$

where

$$(1/k) = [(1 - \phi) + (P^c_m/P_d)\ (\phi)]. \tag{30.8}$$

Since the prices of imported goods are necessarily lower than the prices of domestic goods that they replace in domestic markets, then P^c_m/P_d is necessarily less than one, and therefore according to equation (30.8), $1/k$ must be less than unity.

Substituting the right-hand side of equation (30.1c) for P_d in equation (30.7) gives the real wage rate in an open economy as:

$$w_r = \text{MPL}\ (g)\ (k) \tag{30.9}$$

where $k > 1$. Thus, in Figure 30.1, S_L is the aggregate supply curve of labour while the real-wage determining equation (30.2) in a closed economy is drawn as MPL(g). Comparing equation (30.9) with equation (30.2), it is obvious that the real-wage determining curve in an open economy (b_1 in Figure 30.1) will be some multiple (k) of (MPL) (g). This b_1 curve lies above the MPL(g) curve as the price level of imported goods is lower than the price level of domestic goods at any employment level and $\phi > 0$. Moreover, the more open the economy (the greater is ϕ), *ceteris paribus*, the greater is the vertical distance between MPL(g) and MPL(g) (k). If the exchange rate appreciates, and imported products become even cheaper, then *k* will be even larger and the real-wage determining curve will shift upwards to b'_1, even if the proportion of imports purchased (ϕ) is unchanged.

Consequently, for any given proportion of imports in total domestic expenditure, there will be a higher real-wage determining curve for each employment level, the more the exchange rate appreciates. In Figure 30.1, at N_0, the real wage W_0/P_0 exceeds the minimum real wage required to bring N_0 workers[14] into the labour market W_0/P_1. Given the existence of involuntary unemployment in the system, if the government (or the central bank) initiates a policy of domestic expenditure expansion so that employment expands to N_1 in Figure 30.1, then the real wage would fall to W_0/P_0' as the average price level rose (inflation) due to the law of diminishing returns. As drawn in Figure 30.1, N_1 is still a less-than-full employment level, but the economy is experiencing a higher price level with every increase in employment because of diminishing returns. If, moreover, workers insist on cost-of-living adjustments (COLAs) as prices rise, then the resulting money-wage inflation will exacerbate the inflationary problem induced by domestic demand expansion.

If the government were to wait for export-led growth (due to an initial expansion in one's trading partner's economy), then the real-wage determining curve would shift upwards from b_1 to b'_1 as the improved export–import relationship of the domestic economy leads to an appreciation of the exchange rate.[15] In Figure 30.1, the real wage remains at W_0/P_0 (by construction) as employment rises from N_0 to N_1. Thus, even though domestic output prices rise due to diminishing returns, the domestic consumer does not experience inflation in the price level of the market basket of goods purchased as the rise in the cost of living is offset by lower import prices.

Accordingly, there would be less pressure for higher money-wages for COLAs as the domestic economy expands. Moreover, the appreciating exchange rate improves the competition of foreign firms with domestic producers while making potentially cheaper foreign workers available to multinationals currently operating factories domestically. These competitive factors threaten domestic workers and thereby weaken their bargaining power for higher money-wages. Simultaneously, it strengthens any anti-labour resolve of the government and consumers to resist giving into strikers' demands for higher money-wages. Finally, previously employed workers (N_0) do not experience any decline in their real wage as additional workers are employed. Hence they are not likely to become restive.

Export-led growth can, therefore, lead to expansion without inducing any inflationary pressures that might otherwise arise if a domestic component of demand were to be exogenously increased. Simultaneously, export-led growth weakens the ability of labour unions (and the rank and file's desire) to raise money–wages.[16] Internally stimulated growth in aggregate demand, by contrast, would lead to expansion with inflation due initially to diminishing returns which lower real wages and may then induce wage–price inflation as workers vainly attempt to re-establish the original real wage through COLAs.[17]

In sum, in a flexible exchange rate system, export-led growth can permit policy-makers in any one nation to achieve higher employment without inflation provided some trading partner is willing and able to take on the task of acting as an initial engine of economic growth. In a world of fixed exchange rates, there can be no exchange appreciation and therefore the price of imports will not fall when the nation experiences a trade surplus. In Figure 30.1 under a fixed exchange rate regime, employment expands only through a movement down the b_1 curve. Consequently, there would be no significant difference in the rate of inflation experienced in the nation whether growth was due to being export-led or whether it was driven by some increase in an internal component of domestic demand.[18]

The story does not change significantly if domestic industries operate under constant returns rather than diminishing returns. If, in a flexible exchange rate system, the economy's MPL curve is horizontal, as in Figure 30.2, then export-led growth that results in exchange rate appreciation leads to higher real wages and a falling price level for the consumer's market basket, as long as money-wages are unchanged. For example, as the economy moves from N_0 to N_1 under export-led growth in Figure 30.2, the real wage would rise from W_0/P_0 to W_0/P'_0. In this constant-returns case, export-led growth leads to simultaneously rising real wages, rising employment and falling prices.[19] This situation may resemble West Germany's experience between 1985 and 1989.

Of course, this delightful situation of rising employment, real wages and little or no inflation that the export-led growth nation enjoys does not imply that global inflation and unemployment problems have been resolved. These problems are, as in the card game of Old Maid, merely being passed on as the Black Queen to some other players in the international economy. Inflationary tendencies (and unemployment if the authorities undertake orthodox policies to stop inflation) will appear in those trading partners whose rising trade deficits lead to depreciating exchange rates. This may merely exacerbate inflationary tendencies if the deficit nation tries to maintain employment and workers demand real wage protection either through cost-of-living adjustments or catch-up negotiations in new labour contracts.

From a global perspective, the existence of flexible exchange rates can encourage each nation to try to resolve problems of unemployment and inflation by merely pushing them off, in an uncivilized way, to others. If all act in this way, then the result can be a global recession and stagnation (or even global stagflation). If, however, one nation acts as the engine of growth, as long as it continues to expand – even as it runs a balance of payments deficit – the trading partners who pursue export-led growth will experience an economic miracle that they may attribute to their virtuous ways and even to their superior central bank which would willingly accept a recession rather than permit any wage inflation.

THE FACTS VS. THE THEORY OF FLEXIBLE EXCHANGE RATES

Since the breakdown of Bretton Woods, it has been popular to assume that freely fluctuating exchange rates in a *laissez-faire* market system are efficient. Every well-trained mainstream economist, whose work is logically consistent with a Walrasian, Arrow–Debreu microfoundation, 'knows' that the beneficial effects of a freely flexible exchange rate include (a) the impossibility of any one country running a persistent balance of payments deficit; and (b) the proposition that each nation is able to pursue monetary and fiscal policies for full employment without inflation, independent of what is occurring in its trading partners' economies.[20]

The facts since the breakdown of Bretton Woods, however, do not appear to be consistent with these Panglossian promises. Between 1982 and 1990 when the United States (perhaps unwittingly) took over the engine-of-growth role for the global community, it has run persistent annual deficits; and these, barring a Great Depression, are expected to continue into the twenty-first century. Also, since 1980 the major trading nations of the developed world have felt a greater necessity to co-ordinate monetary and fiscal policies, rather than run independent policies. When, in September 1987, the United States and Germany publicly clashed over incompatible monetary policies, the great October 1987 crash of world financial markets followed. This experience has reinforced the idea among the central bankers of the developed nations that if they do not all hang together they will all hang separately.

Finally, flight capital has drained resources from the relatively poor nations towards the richer ones, resulting in a globally inequitable redistribution of income and wealth, thereby increasing the immiseration of a majority of the people on this planet.

In sum, then, during this period of floating rates, the world has not achieved the state of economic bliss promised by classical theory. If anything, the economic situation for a majority of the world's population has deteriorated.

REFORMING THE INTERNATIONAL PAYMENTS SYSTEM

The current international payments system does not serve the emerging global economy well. The *Financial Times* and *The Economist*, both previously strong advocates of the existing floating rate system, have acknowledged that it is a failure and was sold to the public and the politicians under false advertising claims.[21] Can we not do better?

Too often, professional economic discussions on the requirements for a good international payments system have been limited to the question of the advantages and disadvantages of fixed versus flexible exchange rates. Although this issue is important, the facts of experience plus Keynes's revolutionary analysis indicate that more is required than simply a choice between fixed and flexible exchange rates if a mechanism is to be designed to resolve imbalances and simultaneously promote global full-employment economic growth and a long-run stable international standard of value.

The post-war world has conducted two experiments with the international payments system. For a quarter of a century after the war, there was a fixed, but adjustable, exchange rate system (1947–73) set up under the Bretton Woods Agreement. Since 1973, we have operated under a flexible exchange rate system.

The 1947–73 period was 'an era of unprecedented sustained economic growth in both developed and developing countries' (Adelman 1991: 15). The growth in real gross domestic product per capita in OECD nations escalated to 2.6 times that of the inter-war period (4.9 per cent annually compared to 1.9 per cent). Moreover, this real growth rate was almost double the previous *peak* growth rate exhibited by the industrializing nations during the period from 1820 to 1914, while the growth in productivity during the Bretton Woods era was more than triple that of 1820–1914 (ibid.).[22]

This unprecedented prosperity was transmitted to developing nations through world trade, aid and foreign investment. The real per capita GNP growth rate for *all* developing nations rose to 3.3 per cent, more than triple the growth experienced by the early industrializing nations between 1820 and 1914. Real total GNP growth of developing nations was almost the same as in developed countries (ibid.: 17).

During the Bretton Woods epoch, free economies experienced unprecedented real economic growth. Moreover, during this period, there was 'a much better overall record of price level stability' *vis-à-vis* either the post-1973 period or the previous era of fixed exchange rates under the gold standard (1879–1914) (McKinnon 1990).

The free world's economic performance in terms of both real growth *and* price-level stability during the Bretton Woods period was unprecedented. Moreover, even the record during the earlier gold-standard–fixed-exchange-rate period was better than the experience during the 1973–91 period of flexible exchange rates. The dismal post-1973 experience of recurrent unemployment and inflationary crises, slow growth in OECD countries, and debt-burdened growth and/or stagnation (and even falling real GNP per capita) in developing countries contrasts most sharply with the experience during the Bretton Woods period.

What can we surmise from these facts? First, several hundred years of experience support the thesis that a fixed exchange rate system provides an international environment that is more compatible with greater real economic growth and price stability compared to what was experienced under a flexible exchange rate regime. To reduce entrepreneurial uncertainties and the possibility of massive currency misalignments, Keynes recommended the adoption of a fixed, but adjustable, exchange rate system. More significant, however, is that the superior performance of the free world's economies during the Bretton Woods fixed-rate period compared to the earlier gold-standard–fixed-rate period suggests that there must have been an additional condition besides exchange rate fixity that contributed to the unprecedented growth during the 1947–73 period.

That additional condition had been described by Keynes, in developing his proposals for an international payments scheme. The 'main cause of failure' of any traditional payments system – whether based on fixed or flexible rates – was its inability to foster continuous global economic expansion when persistent current account imbalances among trading partners occurred. This failure, Keynes wrote:

> can be traced to a single characteristic. I ask close attention to this, because I shall argue that this provides a clue to the nature of any alternative which is to be successful.
>
> It is characteristic of a freely convertible international standard that it throws the main burden of adjustment on the country which is the *debtor* position on the international balance of payments – that is, on the country which is (in this context) by hypothesis the *weaker* and above all the *smaller* in comparison with the other side of the scales which (for this purpose) is the rest of the world.
>
> (*C.W.* XXV: 27)

Keynes concluded that an essential improvement in designing any international payments system requires transferring 'the *onus* of adjustment from the debtor to the creditor position', and aiming 'at the substitution of an expansionist, in place of a contractionist, pressure on world trade' (ibid.: 176). In other words, to achieve a golden era of economic development requires the combining of a fixed, but adjustable, rate system with a mechanism for requiring the surplus trading nation(s) to initiate most of the effort necessary to adjust a payments imbalance, without removing all discipline from the deficit trading partner.

During the first half of the Bretton Woods era, the world's major creditor nation, almost accidentally, accepted responsibility for curing deficits in the current account balance via the Marshall Plan and other forms of foreign and military aid.

After the Second World War, the economic recovery of the free capitalist world required the Euorpean nations to run huge import surpluses to feed their populations and rebuild their stock of capital. Under the rules of free market economies, this implied that the United States would have to provide enormous credits to finance the required export surplus to Europe. The resulting European indebtedness would be so burdensome that it was unlikely that, even in the long run, the European nations could ever service this debt. Moreover, US policy-makers were mindful that reparation payments after the First World War were financed by US investors lending to Germany foreign exchange, and that Germany never repaid these loans. Given this history and the existing circumstances, it was obvious that private lending facilities could not be expected to provide the credits necessary for European recovery.

Under the fixed exchange rate system of Bretton Woods, the only mechanism available for redressing this potentially lopsided global import–export trade flow was for the debtors to accept the main burden of adjustment by 'tightening their belt' and reducing their demand for imports to what they could earn from exports.[23] The result would have been to depress further the standard of living of western Europeans. This could have induced political revolutions in most of western Europe.

Instead, the United States produced the Marshall Plan and other foreign grants and aid programmes. The Marshall Plan provided $5 billion in aid in eighteen months and a total of $13 billion in four years. (In 1991 dollars this was equivalent to over $100 billion.)

Marshall Plan transfers represented approximately 2 per cent per annum of the GNP of the United States.[24] Yet no US resident felt deprived of goods and services. Real GNP per capita in the United States during the first year of the Marshall Plan was still 25 per cent larger than in the last peacetime year of 1940. Per capita GNP continued to grow throughout the 1950s.[25] There was no real sacrifice associated with this export surplus. These exports were produced by employing what otherwise would have been idle resources. For the first time in its history, the United States did not suffer from a severe recession immediately after the cessation of a major war. The world experienced an economic 'free lunch' as both the potential debtors and the creditor nation gained from this 'give-away'. It was the failure of the Bretton Woods system after the 1950s to perpetuate this creditor-nation action that led to its ultimate abandonment and the end of the golden era of economic development.

By 1958, although the US still had a goods and services export surplus of over $5 billion, US governmental and military transfers exceeded $6 billion, while there was a net private capital outflow of $1.6 billion.[26] The post-war US surplus position on current account was at an end. As the US current account swung into deficit, other nations began to experience current account surpluses. These nations converted a portion of their dollar current account surpluses into gold. For example, in 1958 the US lost over $2 billion in gold reserves. These trends accelerated in the 1960s, partly as a result of increased US military and financial aid responses to the construction of the Berlin Wall in 1961 and later because of the USA's increasing involvement in Vietnam. At the same time, a rebuilt Europe and Japan became important producers of exports so that the rest of the world became less dependent on US exports.

The USA maintained a positive merchandise trade balance until the first oil price shock in 1973. More than offsetting this trade surplus during most of the 1960s, however, were foreign and military unilateral transfers plus net capital outflows. The Bretton Woods system had no mechanism that would automatically force the emerging surplus nations to step into the adjustment role played by the USA since 1947. Instead, they continued to convert some portion of their annual dollar surpluses into calls on US gold reserves. The seeds of the destruction of the Bretton Woods system and the golden age of economic development were sown as surplus nations drained gold reserves from the United States.

When the USA closed the golden window and unilaterally withdrew from Bretton Woods, the last vestige of Keynes's enlightened international monetary approach was lost – apparently without regret or regard as to how well it had served the global economy.

A NEW INTERNATIONAL PAYMENTS SYSTEM

The following proposal for an international payments system builds on Keynes's proposals that proved successful for producing the expansionist pressure on world trade and development during the 1947–73 period.

In an interdependent world economy, some degree of economic co-operation among trading partners is necessary. The proposal, however, does not require the establishment of a supranational central bank to create a unionized monetary system (UMS) – even if this were believed to be desirable on other grounds. Keynes's original 'bancor' plan for the post-Second World War environment was developed around the idea of a single supranational bank. At this stage of the evolution of world politics, however, a global UMS with a supranational central bank is not feasible.[27] The suggestion is more modest and is aimed at obtaining an international agreement that would not require the surrender of national control of local banking systems and fiscal policies.

Keynes provided a clear outline of what was needed when he wrote:

> We need an instrument of international currency having general acceptability between nations . . . We need an orderly and agreed upon method of determining the relative exchange values of national currency units . . . We need a quantum of international currency . . .

[which] is governed by the actual current [liquidity] requirements of world commerce, and is capable of deliberate expansions . . . We need a method by which the surplus credit balances arising from international trade, which the recipient does not wish to employ can be set to work . . . without detriment to the liquidity of these balances.

(*C.W.* XXV: 168)

What is required is a *closed*, double-entry bookkeeping, clearing institution to keep the payments score among the various trading regions plus some mutually agreed-upon rules to create and reflux liquidity while maintaining the international purchasing power of the international currency. The eight features of the clearing system suggested in this section meet the criteria laid down by Keynes. The rules of our proposed system are designed:

1 to prevent a lack of global effective demand[28] due to any nation(s) either holding excessive idle reserves or draining reserves from the system;
2 to provide an automatic mechanism for placing a major burden of payments adjustments on the surplus nations;
3 to provide each nation with the ability to monitor and, if desired, to control movements of flight capital;[29] and finally,
4 to expand the quantity of the liquid asset of ultimate international redemption as global capacity warrants.

Elements of such a clearing system would include:

1 the adoption of the International Money Clearing Unit (IMCU) as the unit of account and ultimate reserve asset for international liquidity, all IMCUs being held *only* by central banks, and not by the public;
2 the commitment of each nation's or UMS's central bank to guarantee one-way convertibility from IMCU deposits at the clearing union to its domestic money. Each central bank would set its own rules regarding making available foreign monies (through IMCU clearing transactions) to its own bankers and private-sector residents.[30] Since central banks would agree to sell their own liabilities (one-way convertibility) against the IMCU only to other central bankers and the international clearing agency while they simultaneously held only IMCUs as liquid reserve assets for international financial transactions, there could be no draining of reserves from the system. Ultimately, all major private international transactions would clear between central banks' accounts in the books of the international clearing institution;
3 the exchange rate between the domestic currency and the IMCU would be set *initially* by each nation – just as it would be if an international gold standard were instituted. Since enterprises that were already engaged in trade would have international contractual commitments that would span the changeover interval, then, as a practical matter, the existing exchange rate structure (with perhaps minor modifications) could be expected to

provide the basis for initial rate-setting. Points 7 and 8 below indicate when and how this nominal exchange rate between the national currency and the IMCU would be changed subsequently;

4 the denomination of contracts between private individuals would continue to be in whatever domestic currency was permitted by local laws and agreed upon by the contracting parties. Contracts to be settled in terms of a foreign currency would therefore require some announced commitment by the central bank (through private sector bankers) on the availability of foreign funds to meet such private contractual obligations;

5 an overdraft system to make available short-term unused creditor balances at the clearing house to finance the productive international transactions of others who need short-term credit, the terms to be determined by *pro bono publico* clearing managers;

6 a trigger mechanism to encourage any creditor nation to spend what is deemed (in advance) by agreement of the international community to be *'excessive' credit balances accumulated by running current account surpluses.* These excessive credits could be spent in three ways: (a) on the products of any other member of the clearing union; (b) on new direct foreign investment projects; and/or (c) to provide unilateral transfers (foreign aid) to deficit members.

Spending by way of method (a) forces the surplus nation to make the adjustment directly through the balance on goods and services; spending by way of method (c) permits adjustment directly by the current account balance; while method (b) provides adjustment by the capital accounts (without setting up a contractual debt that would *require* reverse current account flows in the future).

Consequently, point 6 would provide the surplus country with considerable discretion in deciding how to accept the 'onus' of adjustment in the way it believes is in its residents' best interests. It would not, however, permit the surplus nation to shift the burden to the deficit nation(s) through contractual requirements for debt-service charges, independent of what the deficit nation could afford.[31] The important point would be to make sure that continual oversaving[32] by surplus nations could not unleash contractionary forces and/or a build-up of international debts so encumbering as to impoverish the global economy of the twenty-first century.

In the unlikely event that the surplus nation did not spend or give away these credits within a specified time, then the clearing agency would confiscate (and redistribute to debtor members) the portion of credits deemed excessive.[33] This last-resort confiscatory action by the managers of the clearing agency would make a payments adjustment via unilateral transfer payments in the current accounts.

Under either a fixed or a flexible rate system, nations might experience persistent trade deficits merely because their trading partners were not living up to their means – that is, because other nations were continually hoarding a portion of their foreign export earnings (plus net unilateral transfers). By so doing, these over-savers would be creating a lack of global effective demand. Under point 6, deficit countries would no longer have to deflate their real economy merely to adjust their payment imbalance because others were over-saving. Instead, the system would seek to remedy the payment deficit by increasing opportunities for deficit nations to sell abroad.

A further element would be:

7 the development of a system to stabilize the long-term purchasing power of the IMCU (in terms of each member nation's domestically produced market basket of goods). This would require a system of fixed exchange rates between the local currency and the IMCU that changes only to reflect permanent increases in efficiency wages.[34] This would assure each central bank that its holdings of IMCUs as the nation's foreign reserves would never lose purchasing power in terms of foreign-produced goods, even if a foreign government permitted wage–price inflation to occur within its borders. Consequently, the rate between the local currency and the IMCU would change with inflation in the local money price of the domestic commodity basket.

If, however, increases in productivity were to lead to declining nominal production costs, then the nation with this decline in efficiency wages (say of 5 per cent) would have the option of choosing either (a) to permit the IMCU to buy (up to 5 per cent) fewer units of domestic currency, thereby capturing all (or most of) the gains from productivity for its residents while maintaining the purchasing power of the IMCU; or (b) to keep the nominal exchange rate constant. In the latter case, the gain in productivity would be shared with all trading partners. In exchange, the export industries in this productive nation would receive an increasing relative share of the world market.

By altering the exchange rate between local monies and the IMCU to offset the rate of domestic inflation, the IMCU's purchasing power is stabilized. By restricting use of IMCUs to central banks, private speculation regarding IMCUs as a hedge against inflation is avoided. Each nation's rate of inflation of the goods and services it produces is determined solely by the national government's policy towards the level of domestic money-wages and profits margins *vis-à-vis* productivity gains, i.e. the nation's efficiency wage. Each nation would therefore be free to experiment with policies for stabilizing its efficiency wage to prevent inflation. Whether a nation is successful or not, the IMCU would never lose its international purchasing power. Moreover, the IMCU would have the promise of gaining in purchasing power over time, if productivity grew more rapidly than money-wages and each nation were willing to share any reduction in real production costs with its trading partners.

Point 7 produces a system designed to maintain the relative efficiency wage parities among nations. In such a system, the adjustability of nominal exchange rates would be primarily (but not always: see point 8 below) to offset changes in efficiency wages among trading partners. A beneficial effect that follows from this proviso is that it would eliminate the possibility of a specific industry in any nation being put at a competitive disadvantage (or securing a competitive advantage) against foreign producers solely because the nominal exchange rate changed independently of changes in efficiency wages and the real costs of production in each nation.

Consequently, nominal exchange rate variability could no longer create the problem of a loss of competitiveness due solely to the overvaluing of a currency as was experienced, for example, by the industries in the American 'rust belt' during the period 1982–5. Even temporary currency appreciation can have significant permanent real costs, e.g. industries may abandon markets and the resulting idle existing plant and equipment may be cast aside as too costly to maintain.

Point 7 would also prevent any nation from engaging in a beggar-thy-neighbour, export-thy-unemployment policy by pursuing a real exchange rate devaluation that did not reflect changes in efficiency wages. Once the initial exchange rates were chosen and relative efficiency wages locked in, reductions in real production costs associated with a relative decline in efficiency wages would be the main factor (with the exception of point 8 below) justifying an adjustment in the real exchange rate.

Under point 7 of the proposal, the IMCU would provide its holders with an invariant international monetary standard, no matter whether the domestic rates of inflation in the various nations converged (or not) or accelerated (or not).

Although point 6 prevents any country piling up persistent excessive surpluses, this does not mean that it would be impossible for one or more nations to run persistent deficits. Consequently, the following point provides a programme for addressing the problem of persistent export–import deficits in any one nation:

8 a country at *full employment* and still having a tendency towards persistent international deficits on its current account would provide *prima facie* evidence that it does not possess the productive capacity to maintain its current standard of living. If the deficit nation were a poor one, then there would surely be a case for the richer nations in surplus to transfer some of their excess credit balances to support the poor nation.[35] If it were a relatively rich country, then the deficit nation must alter its standard of living by reducing its relative terms of trade with its major trading partners. Rules, agreed upon in advance, would require the trade-deficit rich nation to devalue its exchange rate by stipulated increments per period until evidence became available to indicate that

the export–import imbalance had been eliminated without unleashing significant recessionary forces.[36]

If the payment deficit were to persist despite a continuous positive balance of trade in goods and services, then there would be evidence that the deficit nation might be carrying too heavy an international debt-service obligation. The *pro bono* officials of the clearing union should then bring the debtor and creditors into negotiations to reduce annual debt service payments by (a) lengthening the payments period; (b) reducing the interest charges; and/or (c) debt forgiveness.[37]

If any government were to object to the idea that the IMCU provisions provided governments with the ability to limit the free movement of 'capital' funds, then that nation would be free to join other nations with a similar attitude to form a regional currency union (UMS), and thereby assure a free flow of funds among the residents of the currency union.

CONCLUSION

These proposals for a new international payments system are not unalterable for practical reasons. Instead, they should provide the basis for starting a sound analytical discussion of how to prepare for a twenty-first-century international monetary system.

The problems facing the international payments system are not easily resolved. If we start with the defeatist attitude that it is too difficult to change the awkward system we are enmeshed in, then no progress will be made. We must reject such defeatism at this exploratory stage and merely ask whether these particular proposals for improving the operations of the international payments system to promote global growth will create more difficulties than other proposed innovations. The health of the world economic system will not permit us to muddle through.

APPENDIX: THIRLWALL'S LAW – AN EXTENSION OF KEYNES'S MULTIPLIER

Professor A.P. Thirlwall (1979) has developed Keynes's multiplier mechanism into a demand-driven model of economic growth that does not make the classical presumption of continuous global full employment:

$$X_a = (P_d/P_f)^z Y^{erw} \tag{A30.1}$$

$$M_a = (P_d/P_f)^u Y^{ea} \tag{A30.2}$$

where X_a and M_a are exports from nation A and imports into A during a period, (P_d/P_f) is the ratio of domestic prices to foreign prices expressed in terms of the domestic currency of A, z is the price elasticity of demand for A's exports, u is A's price elasticity of demand for imports, e_a is A's income elasticity of demand for imports, and e_{rw} is the rest of the world's income elasticity of demand for A's exports. If either z and u are small and/or relative prices do not change significantly, then, as a first approximation, substitution effects can be ignored and income effects be concentrated upon. Taking the natural logs of equations (A30.1) and (A30.2) and ignoring substitution effects, we obtain Thirlwall's Law of the growth of income that is consistent with an unchanged trade balance as:

$$y_a = x/e_a \qquad \text{(A30.3)}$$

where y_a is the rate of growth of nation A's GNP, x is the rate of growth of A's exports, and e_a is A's income elasticity of demand for imports. Since the growth of exports for A depends primarily on the rest of the world's growth in income (y_{rw}) and the world's income elasticity of demand for A's exports (e_{rw}), i.e.:

$$x = (e_{rw})\ (y_{rw}) \qquad \text{(A30.4)}$$

equation (A30.3) can be written as:

$$y_a = [e_{rw}\, y_{rw}]/e_a \qquad \text{(A30.5)}$$

The rate of growth that a nation can maintain without running into a balance of payments problem depends on the rest of the world's growth and the relevant income elasticities for imports and exports. If the growth of imports is to exactly equal the growth in the value of exports:

$$e_{rw}y_{rw} = y_a e_a \qquad \text{(A30.6)}$$

then

$$[y_a/y_{rw}] = e_{rw}/e_a \qquad \text{(A30.7)}$$

the ratio of the growth of income in nation A compared to growth in income in the rest of the world is equal to the ratio of the income elasticity of demand for A's exports by the rest of the world to A's income elasticity of demand for imports. Thus, for example, if $e_{rw}/e_a < 1$, and if growth in A is constrained by the need to maintain balance of payments equilibrium, then nation A is condemned to grow at a slower rate than the rest of the world.

If, for example, less-developed nations (LDCs) of the world have a comparative advantage in the exports of raw materials and other basic commodities for which Engel's curves suggest that the developed world will have a low income elasticity of demand, while the LDCs have a high income elasticity of demand for the manufactured products of the developed world, then for most LDCs

$$[e_{rw}/e_{ldc}] < 1 \qquad \text{(A30.8)}$$

Accordingly, if economic development and balance of payments equilibrium are left to the free market, the LDCs are condemned to relative poverty, and the global inequality of income will become larger over time.

Moreover, if the rate of population growth in the LDCs (p_{ldc}) is greater than the rate of population growth in the developed world (p_{dw}), that is, if $p_{ldc} > p_{dw}$, then the rate of growth of GNP per capita of the LDCs will experience a greater relative decline to the standard of living of the developed world, i.e.:

$$[y_{ldc}/p_{ldc}] << [y_{dw}/p_{dw}] \qquad \text{(A30.9)}$$

In the absence of Keynesian policies to stimulate growth, the long-term growth rate of the developed world taken as a whole tends to be in the 1–2.5 per cent range. As long as the developed world's population growth is less than its long-term growth rate, however, these nations can still enjoy a rising living standard.

If, however, we accept the reasonable values for the parameters implied in inequality (A30.9), then, since $y_{ldc} < y_{dw}$, while $1 < y_{dw} < 2.5$, a dreary prognostication for the global economy emerges. As long as the world permits the free market to determine the balance of payments constraint on each nation, then a shrinking proportion of the world's population may continue to get richer (or at least hold their own), while a growing proportion of the earth's population is likely to become poorer. Moreover, the slower is the rate of growth in income of the rich, the more rapidly are the poor likely to sink into poverty.

Thus, there is an obvious case to explore whether there are some policy interventions that can be developed to prevent market-determined balance of payments constraints from condemning the majority of the world's population to increasing poverty. Only if the rich can achieve the historically high real rates of growth experienced in the first twenty-five years after the Second World War (when Keynesian rather than free market policies were actively pursued domestically and internationally by the developed world) can we hope to improve significantly the economic lot of the poorer nations of the world.

Since the USA has apparently not been significantly constrained by payments deficits, equation (A30.8) can be interpreted in a different light for the USA. Given the US rate of growth under Reagan since 1982, then, if we assume that the import and export income elasticities of demand (e_{rw} and e_a) are fixed, solving equation (A30.8) for y_{rw} yields the income growth that would have been required of the USA's trading partners in order to eliminate the US trade deficit. Alternatively, if y_{rw} is presumed unchanged, then solving for e_{rw} would be the required income elasticity necessary to avoid a US trade deficit.

Thirlwall's analysis demonstrates that international financial payment imbalances can have severe real consequences, i.e. money is not neutral in an open economy.

NOTES

1 John Maynard Keynes, *The General Theory of Employment, Interest and Money*, New York: Harcourt, 1936. All page references to passages from this book will be cited in the text of this chapter accompanying the relevant quote or discussion, abbreviated to *G.T.* plus page number.

2 Nations with banking institutions which make it difficult for foreign authorities to obtain information regarding bank accounts held by their residents are likely to encourage the influx of funds trying to escape national tax collectors, criminal investigators, and the central banks of nations that try to limit capital outflows. Thus, it is not surprising that exchange rates often reflect speculative and flight capital flows rather than purchasing power parities.

3 For example, in 1977, the Carter administration attempted to 'talk down the dollar'. In the spring of 1993, Secretary of the Treasury Bentsen tried to talk up the yen. In January 1994, the *New York Times* quoted Secretary Bentsen as saying that 'allowing the yen to decline would not be an acceptable way for Japan to try to escape from its recession'.

4 Most mainstream economists were appalled by President Reagan's boasts regarding the higher dollar that was achieved in the early years of his administration.

5 Even in the 1990s, as this is being written, nations are still ignoring this Keynesian 'truth' to the detriment of over 38 million unemployed people in the OECD nations and many more in eastern Europe and the former Soviet EU.

6 In this matter, Keynes pointed out, 'we, the [orthodox] faculty of economists, prove to have been guilty of presumptuous error' (*G.T.*: 339).

7 As I point out in my book, *Post Keynesian Macroeconomic Theory* (Davidson 1994), both Old and New Keynesian analysis is based on the restrictive classical axioms that Keynes threw out in developing his *General Theory*. It is no wonder, therefore, that these 'Keynesians' subscribe to the classical view of international trade.

8 To argue, from the outset, that international co-operation in sharing records and helping to enforce capital flows cannot be achieved is unduly pessimistic. It paints a picture of the human condition where nations are willing to co-operate in military wars at a cost of the lives of a large portion of their youth, but unwilling to co-operate even if it costs the recipient nations a 'fast buck'.

9 For a discussion of Thirlwall's Law, see the Appendix to this chapter.

10 Of course, they are not *laissez-faire* economies.

11 See Davidson and Smolensky (1964: 128–39) where it is demonstrated that profit maximization requires that $P(1 - m) = MC$. Thus, if the degree of monopoly (m) equals zero, $P = MC$. If the $m > 1$, then marginal cost must be negative, while if $m = 1$, marginal cost is zero. These latter two cases are unlikely. Consequently, as long as the firm faces some marginal positive cost, $0 \leq m < 1$.

12 Nothing of substance would be lost if less than perfect competition were analysed; all that would be required is that the MPL curve be multiplied by a scalar whose magnitude is less than unity.

13 This is likely to be true as long as the economy is at less than full employment, so that any increase in output is associated with an expansion of production in both the consumer goods sector and the other sectors of the system. At full employment, however, if consumption is reduced to permit expansion of investment goods and both the consumption and investment sectors are operating under diminishing returns, then the productivity of labour in the

consumer goods sector will rise as production contracts, while productivity in the investment sector will decline with expansion in the face of diminishing returns. Accordingly, in this case of 'forced savings' at full employment, consumption and investment sector price levels may move in different directions or at significantly different rates.

14 This situation is consistent with Keynes's definition of involuntary unemployment (*G.T.*: 128).

15 If there is some substitutability of imports for exports, the higher exchange rate would increase the openness of the domestic economy as the proportion of spending on foreign products increased *at each level of employment.* This would increase the magnitude of ϕ, thereby shifting the real-wage determining curve further upwards. For simplicity, we shall ignore this further factor increasing the real wage with export-led growth, since this would only increase the force of the argument developed here.

16 As the domestic currency appreciates, the cheaper imports yield higher real wages without labour having to demand higher money-wages at the bargaining table.

17 If some other nations are tied to this nation via a common market which maintains fixed exchange rates, then these common market partners can share in the benefits of an appreciating exchange rate that raises real wages in the common market *at the expense of the rest of the world.*

18 There might be some small *ceteris paribus* differences, if the rate of diminishing returns differs in the foreigners' export industry compared to the diminishing returns experienced in the domestic industries.

19 Or if money-wage rates are rising, less inflationary pressure.

20 In 1968, Professor Harry Johnson wrote: 'the basic argument for floating exchange rates is so simple that most people have considerable difficulty in understanding it . . . a floating exchange rate would save a country from having to reverse its full employment policies because they lead to inflation and deficit' (*The Times*, 12 September 1968).

21 *The Economist* magazine (6 January 1990) indicated that the decade of the 1980s will be noted as one in which 'the experiment with floating currencies failed'. Almost two years earlier (17 February 1987), the *Financial Times* admitted that 'floating exchange rates, it is now clear, were sold on a false prospectus . . . they held out a quite illusory promise of greater national autonomy . . . [but] when macropolicies are inconsistent and when capital is globally mobile, floating rates cannot be relied upon to keep the current accounts roughly in balance'.

22 Depressions disappeared, recessions were minor and exports grew more than 50 per cent faster than GDP.

23 The 'scarce currency' clause of the Bretton Woods Agreement permitted European nations to discriminate against American imports. But this would not resolve the problem since there was no other major source of the goods necessary to feed and rebuild Europe.

24 In 1991, Japan's export surplus was running at approximately 2 per cent of her GNP, while 2 per cent of America's GNP was equal to $111 billion.

25 Only in the small recessions of 1949 and 1957 did per capita GNP stop growing. But even during these brief periods, it never declined.

26 Figures obtained from *Statistical Abstract of the United States 1959*, Washington, D.C.: US Bureau of Census, 1959, p. 870.

27 This does not deny that some groups of trading partners may wish to integrate their central banks and banking systems into a regional UMS common market.

Implicit in much of 'Europe 1992' planning is the belief that 'ultimately' there will be a single currency among the European community of nations governed by a single supranational central bank. If some nations were willing to develop an inter-regional UMS they would be free to develop their own UMS clearing mechanism which would operate as a single unit in the larger global clearing union proposed below.

28 Williamson (1987) recognizes that when balance of payments 'disequilibrium is due purely to excess of deficient demand', flexible exchange rates *per se* can not facilitate international payments adjustments.

29 This provides an added bonus by making tax-avoidance and profits from illegal trade more difficult to conceal.

30 Correspondent banking will have to operate through the international clearing agency, with each central bank regulating the international relations and operations of its domestic banking firms.

Small-scale smuggling of currency across borders, etc., can never be completely eliminated. But such movements are merely a flea on a dog's back – a minor, but not debilitating, irritation. If, however, most of the residents of a nation hold and use (in violation of legal tender laws) a foreign currency for domestic transactions and as a store of value (e.g. it is estimated that Argentinians hold close to US$5 billion), this is evidence of a lack of confidence in the government and its monetary authority. Unless confidence is restored, all attempts to restore economic prosperity will fail.

31 Some may fear that if a surplus nation is close to the trigger point it could short-circuit the system by making loans to reduce its credit balance *prior* to setting off the trigger. Since preventing unreasonable debt-service obligations is an important objective of this proposal, a mechanism which monitors and can restrict such pre-trigger lending activities may be required.

One possible way of eliminating this trigger avoidance lending loophole is as follows: an initial agreement as to what constitutes sensible and flexible criteria for judging when debt-servicing burdens become unreasonable is established. Given these criteria, the clearing union managers would have the responsibility for preventing additional loans which push debt burdens beyond reasonable servicing levels. In other words, loans that push debt burdens too far could not be cleared through the clearing union, i.e. the managers would refuse to release the IMCUs for loan purposes from the surplus country's account. (I am indebted to Robert Blecker for suggesting this procedure.)

The managers would also be required to make periodic public reports on the level of credits being accumulated by surplus nations and to indicate how close these surpluses are to the trigger point. Such reports would provide an informational edge for debtor nations permitting them to bargain more successfully regarding the terms of refinancing existing loans and/or new loans. All loans would still have to meet the clearing union's guidelines for reasonableness.

I do not discount the difficulties involved in setting up and getting agreement on criteria for establishing unreasonable debt service burdens. (For some suggestions, however, see the second paragraph of point 8.) In the absence of co-operation and the spirit of goodwill that is necessary for the clearing union to provide a mechanism assuring the economic prosperity of all members, however, no progress can ever be made.

Moreover, as the current international debt problem of African and Latin American nations clearly demonstrates, creditors ultimately have to forgive some debt when they previously encourage excessive debt burdens. Under the current system, however, debt forgiveness is a last-resort solution, acceptable only after both debtor and creditor nations suffer from faltering economic growth. Surely a more intelligent option is to develop an institutional arrangement which prevents excessive debt servicing burdens from occurring in the first place.

32 Over-saving is defined as a nation persistently spending less on imports plus direct equity foreign investment than the nation's export earnings plus net unilateral transfers.

33 Whatever 'excessive' credit balances are redistributed shall be apportioned among the debtor nations (perhaps based on a formula which is inversely related to each debtor's per capita income and directly related to the size of its international debt) to be used to reduce debit balances at the clearing union.

34 The efficiency wage is related to the money-wage divided by the average product of labour; it is the unit labour cost modified by the profit mark-up in domestic money terms of domestically produced GNP. At this preliminary stage of this proposal, it would serve no useful purpose to decide whether the domestic market basket should include both tradeable and non-tradeable goods and services. (With the growth of tourism, more and more non-tradeable goods become potentially tradeable.) I prefer the wider concept of the domestic market basket, but it is not obvious that any essential principle is lost if a tradeable-only concept is used, or if some nations use the wider concept while others use the narrower one.

35 This is equivalent to a negative income tax for poor fully employed families within a nation. (See Davidson 1987–88 for further development of this argument.)

36 Although relative prices of imports and exports would be altered by the change in the terms of trade, the adjustment is due to the resulting income effect, not a substitution effect. The deficit nation's real income would fall until its import surplus disappears.

37 The actual programme adopted for debt-service reduction would depend on many parameters, including: the relative income and wealth of the debtor *vis-à-vis* the creditor; the ability of the debtor to increase its per capita real income, etc.

31

KEYNES AND FORMALISM*

Rod O'Donnell

'But, as you know, my practice is not to have second editions. When I have got something further to say, I would rather have a new book.' Thus Keynes responded in 1939 to his publisher, expressing a preference for further reprints of *The General Theory* rather than a new edition.[1] Earlier, in 1936, he had declared to Hawtrey that 'Of course, in fact, the whole book needs re-writing and re-casting' (*C.W.* XIV: 47). Had the 1937 heart attack not drastically curtailed his output, we may well have had a new statement of *The General Theory* which, if not a second edition in the ordinary sense, would have been a reorganized and recomposed version. That some new books were in the offing is evident from four plans (never fulfilled) for clarifying, re-presenting and extending his economic masterpiece. The first (July 1936) was to be a popular version of *The General Theory* focusing on its economics and politics; the second (August 1936), entitled *Footnotes to the General Theory*, was to deal with specific issues and criticisms raised by economists; the third (May 1937) was for a short controversy-free book giving a clear statement of what he thought it all amounted to; while the fourth and most ambitious (*circa* 1938) was a ten- or twelve-volume educational work, *An Introduction to Economic Principles*, covering both micro- and macroeconomics from the perspective of *The General Theory*.[2]

The point of this brief excursus into Keynes's thoughts on revising and extending *The General Theory* is both historical and methodological. It reaffirms Keynes's frequent acknowledgment that the work was not particularly well organized or expounded, and that it could be improved by recomposition (propositions with which many continue to concur).[3] It also clarifies why no new edition appeared. In a broader context, it raises issues relating to the improvement of existing works. Improvements depend on notions of deficiencies, and notions of deficiencies depend, *inter alia*, on theoretical frameworks and intended audiences. What appears as deficiency in *The General Theory* to a neoclassical economist may appear as a strength to a non-neoclassical, and what is appropriate in a book addressed to 'fellow economists' might be quite out of place in one intended for the lay public. The relevance of these points will emerge below.

From the many themes in Keynes's broad methodological canvas, I have selected one: his position on the use of formalism in economics.[4] By formalism I mean symbolic representation, mathematics, and statistical inference or econometrics. Any 'second edition' or restatement of *The General Theory* needs to address this topic because of its important influence on exposition, and because of the desirability of basing the restatement on an informed interpretation of his position.

Understanding Keynes on the role of formalism in economics is important from three standpoints. In the history of economic thought, satisfactory representations of a writer's views are a primary concern. In methodology (particularly the vexed issues of the use of formalism and what counts as 'science' in economics), the value of Keynes's writings, both philosophical and economic, is that they provide a constructive conceptual framework for approaching formalism and science which is *alternative* to that underpinning the modern mathematical economics mainstream.[5] The presupposition that there is only one conceptual framework for the deployment of mathematics in economics to be accepted or rejected according to personal taste or ability is mistaken, for there is clearly a choice between competing conceptual frameworks. The final standpoint is that of the Keynesian tradition. Keynesians who value the sensible use of formal tools need no longer be embarrassed by the traditional portrayals of Keynes's views, but can reject them in favour of a more informed account which reveals the totality of his position, its reasoned nature and its reasonableness. Depending on their own stances, they may then choose to endorse, criticize or reformulate Keynes's position.

The chapter opens by reviewing the current state of interpretation and the two main positions – here called the 'traditional account' and the 'revised account'. Its central contentions are that the revised account (a) provides a superior understanding of Keynes's general stance on the use of formalism in economics as well as an explanation of the inadequacies of the traditional account; (b) reveals that Keynes's remarks on, and use of, formalism are elements of a unified framework which are not in basic conflict with his consideration of non-formal factors; and (c) permits, in any reworking or extension of *The General Theory*, an increase in formalism over and above the level actually chosen by Keynes in 1936, provided always that formalism is appropriately used and interpreted. A 'second edition' of *The General Theory* could therefore take advantage of these opportunities without neglecting Keynes's warnings.

THE CURRENT STATE OF INTERPRETATION

Two broad positions may be identified: the traditional account originating in the 1940s and 1950s, and the revised account which emerged in the 1980s. At present, the traditional viewpoint is shared by more writers but supported by less evidence and argument, while the revised viewpoint has fewer adherents but greater evidential support and analytical depth.[6] The clash often reduces to one between prejudged or uninformed readings and careful readings.

According to the traditional account, Keynes was *either totally or preponderantly hostile towards the use of mathematics and statistical inference in economics.* This viewpoint, advanced in various forms and arenas, has been dominant for more than four decades and remains influential in many quarters. In the literature up to the 1980s, it took the following forms. Samuelson (1946: 197) contended that Keynes had an 'antipathy toward the use of mathematical symbols', while Leontief (1954: 215) suggested that Keynes equated mathematical economics with 'mere concoctions'. Stone (1978: 58–60), the most extreme exponent of the traditional stance, portrayed Keynes as motivated by a violent 'hostility to the use of mathematics in economics' and an 'eagerness to belittle both its difficulties and its potential usefulness', such animosity carrying through unabated from the 1920s to *The General Theory.* In relation to econometrics, Schumpeter judged that Keynes 'disliked genuinely econometric work', and that his 1939 'attack' upon Tinbergen implied 'wholesale condemnation' of *any* kind of econometric effort (1946a: 195).[7] Lawson (1985b: 129–30, 132) has portrayed Keynes's 'opposition to econometrics' as virtually total. Similar or related viewpoints may be found in Blaug (1980: 90) and Skidelsky (1983: 222, 228). A minority, such as Sweezy (1963: 314) and Patinkin (1976a: 22; 1976b: 1093–4), departed from the traditional interpretation, but their remarks, while perceptive, made little headway against prevailing opinion.

During the 1980s, however, the traditional understanding was criticized as superficial and misleading because it is based, not on all the relevant evidence, but on scattered and partial selections which overlook a large quantity of crucial material in Keynes's writings. Accompanying this critique was a comprehensive investigation of Keynes's position on the use of formalized techniques which argued that it is far more sophisticated and reasonable than the traditional portrait suggests.[8] The two keys to this deeper understanding are (a) Keynes's *philosophical thought,* and (b) the evidence provided by *all* his economic writings.[9] Since no extended study of the links between Keynes's philosophical and economic writings was available before 1982,[10] and since the *Collected Writings* and his 1932–5 lecture notes only appeared during 1971–89, it is unfair to be excessively critical of the originators of the traditional conception. But knowledge of the philosophical foundations of Keynes's thought and a vastly expanded information base have now given us a far better overall conception of Keynes's position and an understanding of the earlier errors.

The central thesis of the revised account is that Keynes accepted that *formal techniques have useful but limited roles in economics.* His position, discussed at length below and summarized later (pp. 156–7), is thus relatively complex because it *both endorses and constrains* the use of formal methods in economics. Characteristically, it seeks a reflective middle position which avoids the dogmatic extremes of outright hostility and unthinking zealotry. From this standpoint, misinterpretations arise from incomplete recognition of the two aspects of his position and their complementarity. The traditional viewpoint ignores the endorsing aspect, for example, and exaggerates and misrepresents the constraining aspect.

Two responses to this recent work may be discerned. One is continued support for the traditional account, albeit without investigation of its general validity. Lawson (1990a: 988) reasserts it,[11] while Mini (1991) contends that the whole thrust of Keynes's thought was opposed to mathematics and econometrics. Although Stone's (1991) later view is less monolithic than before, it remains cut from the same cloth – he still sees Keynes as exhibiting 'virulence and asperity' towards econometrics in 1938–9, though admitting that a 'puzzle' arises because of the apparent evaporation of this hostility by 1944–5.[12] Hahn (1992b) declares that Keynes was 'scornful of the mathematics employed by his contemporaries' and 'did not begin to make a case', while Moggridge (1992: 622) views Keynes as calling 'the whole econometrics enterprise into question'. The second response is to move to a halfway house between the two accounts. This may take the form of accepting elements from each viewpoint without seeking to weld them into a consistent whole.[13] Or it may implicitly adopt the view that tensions exist between the formal and non-formal elements of Keynes's thought, thus converting the external conflict between Keynes and formalism of the traditional account into an internal conflict within Keynes's thought itself. One of the objects of this chapter will be to show that both conflicts are illusory and that Keynes's remarks belong to a unified framework.

All accounts should address the same tribunal, the total body of available evidence. A major fault of the traditional account is its dependence on a small and highly selective portion of this evidence, chiefly certain remarks from *The General Theory* and the Tinbergen controversy. The revised account, on the other hand, aims at consistency with all of Keynes's known writings and his biography. Consistency here means that his writings either positively support the account or do not contradict it. It also means that any first impressions of apparent conflict can be shown by closer analysis to be deceptive.

Accounts also need to be based on careful, contextual and informed readings of Keynes's remarks. This is the only route to sound interpretations of his views because his prose, especially if colourful or provocative, sometimes has a tendency to mislead on a first reading. Insufficiently careful reading and analysis is the second important fault of the traditional account, whether by overlooking key words, failing to probe the text with questions, paying little or no attention to context, or neglecting wider knowledge of Keynes's writings.

In addition, it is important to recognize that the philosophical framework underpinning Keynes's position is not the same as that informing modern mathematical economics. Keynes's framework derives from his *Treatise on Probability* (1921) in at least five ways – the development of a general theory of non-conclusive logic which includes deductive and 'formal' logic as a special case; the use of a general theory of quantity embracing cardinality, ordinality and non-measurability; the presentation of probability primarily in conceptual terms without neglecting its formalization for the probability calculus or a role for formal techniques in the analysis of problems; the recognition that non-algebraic or non-numerical factors are often essential to the understanding of problems which other approaches seek to analyse completely by formal means; and the adoption in statistical inference of the twofold task of exploring valid argument and discrediting invalid argument. A failure to recognize the existence of differing philosophical frameworks is a third main source of error in approaching Keynes. If it is assumed that only one framework exists, that of 'mathematical economics', then a rejection by Keynes of any part of this framework can easily be read as implying a rejection of the whole enterprise of using mathematics to assist economics. But if the existence of different frameworks is recognized, then a rejection of one part of the 'mathematical economics' framework by no means implies rejection of the view that mathematics can contribute to economics.

Modern economics gives formalization maximum scope and treats it as the *sine qua non* of rigorous economic science. By contrast, Keynes's position reduces its priority, terrain and authority. This reduction does not signify antagonism, however, but a realignment of roles. Demotion within a framework is not the same as a declaration of hostility. Logic, always the master with Keynes, still incorporates and requires the services of mathematics and econometrics. The large differences between Keynes and modern economics are thus not an argument in favour of the traditional account; to assume that they are is to commit the error of thinking that there is only one possible philosophical framework for formalism in economics.

Unfortunately, there has been relatively little debate between the rival accounts. Rather than retrace ground covered in previous discussions, however, I shall concentrate on advancing *new* evidence and argument for the revised account, chiefly from the post-1930 period and including vital unpublished correspondence.[14]

THE PERIOD 1905–14

Since Keynes's writings on formalism prior to 1932 are not the primary concern of this chapter and since they have been discussed in some detail elsewhere, readers interested in this period are encouraged to consult the relevant literature.[15] The purpose of this section is to provide additional items of evidence from the initial phase of Keynes's career as an economist, such items identifying his early focus on the topic, the influence of Marshall, and the strong threads of continuity in his position.

Marshall's lectures to Keynes, 1905

In late 1905, during attendance at Marshall's lectures, Keynes took the following note under the heading 'Economics and Mathematics':

> Mathematical *language* supreme within its scope.
> The influence of Jevons and mathematical reasoning has been the great enemy of *overstatements*.
> Bentham's fundamental confusion – saying that one thing is greater than another, when the two differ in quality.[16]

Each remark is significant. The first indicates that mathematics is sovereign but only within its own domain of application. The second prefigures the recurrent idea in Keynes's later writings that one of the useful but negative functions of mathematical methods is the detection of errors of reasoning (*C.W.* VIII: 125; X: 186; and Rymes 1989a: 101–3).[17] The final remark anticipates the philosophy of quality and quantity of the *Treatise on Probability* in which mathematical relations (whether cardinal or ordinal) have restricted domains over real phenomena because of differences in kind rather than degree.[18]

An unwritten textbook, 'The Mathematical Organon of Economics'

On 31 January 1909, Keynes composed a list of proposed writings, most of which were never written. Last on the list was a textbook entitled 'The Mathematical Organon of Economics'. Clearly, he viewed the matter as worth writing about in an educational context. Given his other writings, possible topics might have been the relevant types of mathematical technique, the question of the superiority of some methods over others, and the value and limits of mathematics in economics. Significantly, the title entails the existence of a mathematical organon of economics. The wording recalls his 1907 fellowship dissertation where he explicitly accepted the existence of an 'organon' of correlation theory while at the same time criticizing the *particular* analysis of its foundations by Pearson. Argument by analogy suggests that rejection of particular usages of mathematics in economics does not imply rejection of the entire apparatus.[19]

This plan for a textbook on mathematics in economics provides informative background for later comments. In 1924 he lamented that 'we still, after fifty years, lack the ideal textbook' for the purpose of making diagrammatic analysis in economics 'available to students in the fullest and clearest form possible' (*C.W.* X: 188 & n. 3).[20] Much later (*c.*1938), he referred to mathematics in another written work, 'An Introduction to Economic Principles', the opening volume of which was to discuss, ***inter alia***, the 'techniques' of economics and their relations to 'other moral, mathematical and natural sciences'.[21]

The Cambridge University Political Economy Club

In October 1909 Keynes founded a weekly discussion club for his economics undergraduates, papers being given with Keynes summing up at the end. In his initial list of topics, the third item was 'The use of mathematical reasoning in Economics' which again indicates his definite interest in the subject and his desire to acquaint students with the issues.

Keynes's lecture notes, 1910–14

Keynes lectured on 'The Principles of Economics' from 1910 to 1914. In his introductory lecture, after listing the main areas to be covered, his notes appended the comment: 'while treating of fundamentals perhaps introduce a series of special topics: – e.g. . . . use of mathematics'. Some pages later he expanded on this:

> With regard to the use of mathematics: –
> The line taken by Marshall in his preface to be agreed with: –
> 'The chief use of pure mathematics in economic questions seems to be in helping a person to write down quickly, shortly and exactly some of his thoughts for his own use . . . but when a great many symbols have to be used, they become very laborious to anyone but the writer himself.' See also Appendix D with regard to long trains of reasoning.
> A mathematical mind rather than mathematical technique.
> Very easy quâ mathematics, and of very limited usefulness.
> Diagrams on the other hand rather useful.
> In these lectures I shall make some use of diagrams, but not – with one or two exceptions – of algebraical mathematics.[22]

Naturally, Keynes's views reflect the contemporary state of mathematical and economic knowledge. But the two general messages conveyed to his students are those that later occur in his writings – the primary one that mathematics has a useful but limited role in economics, and the secondary one that diagrammatic analysis tends to be a more useful form for teaching than algebraic manipulation.

This evidence from the early stages of Keynes's career indicates that he was much influenced by Marshall in this area (as he was in others).[23] I now turn to his mature views of the 1930s which, as will be seen, provide strong lines of continuity with his earlier thought.

THE PERIOD OF *THE GENERAL THEORY*

This period will be discussed under two heads: Keynes's lectures whilst formulating *The General Theory*, and *The General Theory* itself.[24]

Keynes's lectures, 1932–5

As a result of Rymes's (1989a, 1989c) valuable work in collecting and compiling lecture notes taken by ten different people over 1932–5, we now possess good insight into the methods Keynes adopted in presenting his new ideas.

One notable feature of the lectures is the extent to which Keynes employed mathematics in presenting and organizing his thought. The mathematics itself is unremarkable – simple algebra, functional equations and derivatives – but what deserves attention is its steady usage and its role in relating key variables. This is not to suggest that Keynes thought or wrote as a mathematical economist would, either in the 1930s or the present. It does, however, show that he proceeded in a manner consistent with the view that mathematics has a role in economic theory even if this is much less pervasive than that suggested by mathematical economists. The lectures further demonstrate the unsustainability of the traditional notion that Keynes was antipathetic, dismissive or violently hostile towards the use of mathematics in economics.

The notes also bring out the priority of conceptual thinking over mathematical thinking in Keynes's framework. In 1933, after writing down a set of equations determining the level of employment, he observed:

> These equations are merely a means of exposition, and not a productive tool. The real tool is thought, and they are not a substitute for it, but at most a guide, or embodiment.
>
> (Rymes 1989c: G35)

That is to say, mathematical equations may assist exposition by acting as an embodiment of, or guide to, thought. Above all, the essential, creative and productive tool in economics is 'thought', or logical thinking in conceptual terms.[25]

Another distinctive feature of the lectures is the proposition that mathematical reasoning, as an aid to thought, has greater value in its *symbolic* capacity than in its algebraic or numerical capacities. This view may be traced back to philosophical reflections in the *Treatise on Probability* where, reacting against the notion that the moral sciences could be brought completely under the sway of numerical or algebraic methods, he observed that 'mathematical reasoning now appears as an aid in its symbolic rather than in its numerical character' (*C.W.* VIII: 349), a principle put into practice in that work.[26] In the lead-up to *The General Theory*, Keynes likewise used symbols to denote variables which are central to his analysis but which do not have clearly defined numerical counterparts. One instance occurred in 1932 in relation to liquidity preference (ρ being the rate of interest, A the state of liquidity preference, and M the quantity of money):

> One point re equations . . . used:
> e.g. $\rho = A.(M)$
> This is a symbolic equation not an algebraic equation – It is only [a] shorthand method of stating [the] relations between various complexes. This is better because to use algebra we must [make] . . . simplifying assumptions.[27]

Sometimes in this context Keynes also refers to 'catalogues' as well as 'complexes' of prices, indicating that these are not to be viewed as indexes or single numbers subject to 'a machinery of calculation' (Rymes 1989c: D19, I22; 1989a: 76). A second instance is his use in 1933 of w to indicate 'a given state of the news' in connection with the liquidity preference equation.[28] A third example is E, denoting 'the state of confidence or long term expectation' in a 1934 draft of *The General Theory* (*C.W.* XIII: 440–4), E also being non-numerical in Keynes's scheme.[29]

This interesting aspect of Keynes's stance may, I think, be clarified as follows. Mathematics can serve useful functions in economics in two ways. One way is the *algebraic*, where variables either clearly possess numerical or mathematical properties or can have these attributed to them by means of simplifying assumptions so that relevant mathematical manipulations may be performed. On this level, variables meet the requirements of strictly defined mathematical operations. The other way is the *symbolic*, where mathematical formulation provides a general way of expressing and thinking about relationships between concepts. The concepts do not necessarily possess mathematical properties such as cardinality, but can represent unstructured complexes of numbers, or non-numerical factors which bear significantly on magnitudes capable of being expressed numerically. This level of thinking, more suited to new theoretical work, is more open than the algebraic in encompassing a greater range of possibilities, and more general in that it includes the algebraic as a particular case. Keynes saw this mode of thinking as important not just in economics but in mathematics itself: 'Even in mathematics, when it is a matter of original work, you do not think always in precise terms. The precise use of language comes at a late stage in the development of one's thoughts' (Rymes 1989c: G7).

The 'algebraic' mode of mathematical analysis is related to 'scholasticism'. Both are characterized by formal precision and rigour and as a result have contributions to make to economics; but, for exactly the same reason, both have only limited carrying power because economic phenomena do not possess those characteristics (displayed by certain natural science phenomena) which facilitate the use of precise techniques. On the other hand, the 'symbolic' mode of mathematical usage is related to the 'quasi-formal style' or 'symptomatic thinking', to be discussed further below, that Keynes thought most appropriate in the analysis of economic phenomena. This approach, based on logic applied to complex material exhibiting variable mixtures of change and constancy, aimed at a 'middle way' between scholasticism (or completely formal or watertight thinking) on the one side, and woolliness (or confusion or obscurity) on the other.

Keynes's symbolic approach illustrates again his underlying proposition that mathematics has useful but limited roles in economics. In this instance, the usefulness stems from the assistance rendered to thought, while the limitations arise from the equations not being able to serve the cause of mathematical elaboration. The difference on this score between Keynes and mathematical economists lies *not* in the use of symbols, but in their interpretation. Mathematical economists seek to deploy symbols in a mathematically precise manner and would be unsympathetic to undifferentiated 'complexes' of numbers as the referents of symbols – an order or pattern needs to be imposed so that the complex assumes some mathematically operational form, as with a matrix. To those who believe that the essentials of economic behaviour can be theorized rigorously only in mathematically operational terms, this aspect of Keynes's approach will appear vague, woolly, unscientific or literary. But to those for whom at least some of the essentials are not captured by strict conformity with the precise methods of existing branches of mathematics, Keynes's approach may appear as a fruitful way of thinking about economic behaviour without committing oneself at the outset to the narrower sets of assumptions presupposed by strictly mathematical formalizations.

The General Theory

Formalism is an explicit component of *The General Theory* and a matter that receives methodological comment. Although far from the dominant language, it is nevertheless a crucial carrier of the analytical argument at key points. But to understand its role, we must first clarify Keynes's *general model of reasoning* in the theoretical parts of the work. This model, which encompasses *both* formal and non-formal elements, may be described as follows. In economic theory, formalism normally plays an important part in the investigation of a topic (though not always, as with the subject of expectations). In such cases, theory commences with analysis based on a functional relationship between key variables. This relationship then provides a structure for the subsequent discussion of factors influencing the function and its variables. But at some point the use of formalism is discontinued, and non-formalized argument takes over. Formalism has exhausted its usefulness, either because vital factors in the theory are not formalizable, or because its further development does not advance understanding, or because it is premature to crystallize the theory in particular forms at a certain stage. The model thus has *two broad phases – formalized beginnings and non-formal elaborations* – each of which is essential to theory. Since the model is mostly implicit throughout *The General Theory*, the purpose of the following discussion is to bring it clearly into view.

The most important role of formalism in *The General Theory* is the representation of relations between concepts in functional form as a means of systematically ordering thought. It commences its work at the very beginning when Keynes advances his central objective, a theory of output (and employment) as a whole. The two blades of his giant scissors, aggregate supply (Z) and aggregate demand (D), are presented as 'functions' of the quantity of employment (N), the 'point of intersection' of $Z = \phi(N)$ and $D = f(N)$ defining effective demand and determining equilibrium employment. This succinct formalized statement is presented as 'the substance' of the general theory of employment, and the rest of the work is primarily devoted to examining 'the various factors upon which these two functions depend', such discussions also deploying formalism (*C.W.* VII: 25).

The analysis of consumption begins with, and is structured around, a functional relationship. The propensity to consume is defined as 'the functional relationship χ' between consumption and income expressed in wage units: $C_w = \chi(Y_w)$ (ibid.: 90). But C is also influenced by other factors so that χ is a 'portmanteau function' silently capturing all non-income determinants as well. Given that income is the primary influence and other factors secondary, the propensity to consume also becomes 'a fairly stable function' in given situations. The next question, that of 'the normal shape' of χ, receives a mathematical answer: 'dC_w/dY_w is positive and less than unity' (ibid.: 95–6). After this, the non-formal investigation of the unrepresented influences on C, the so-called 'objective' and 'subjective' factors, then becomes the main purpose of the remaining discussion. Mathematical treatment is also inevitable in handling the corollary to consumption theory. The investment multiplier (k) is a 'definite ratio' or 'precise relationship' given by $\Delta Y_w = k\Delta I_w$ where $k = 1/(1 - dC_w/dY_w)$ (ibid.: 113–15). The discussion of the remaining multiplier theory draws on a mixture of mathematics and non-formal considerations.

The analysis of investment (I) commences with a piece of formalism which provides entry points for the non-formal elements that complete the theory. The marginal efficiency of capital (MEC) is defined by equality between the current supply price of a capital asset and the present value of the prospective returns (Q_i) over its lifetime:

$$\text{Supply price} = \sum_{i=1}^{n} Q_i/(1 + MEC)^i$$

Aggregation over types of capital produces the investment demand schedule, with a further equality between *MEC* and the market rate of interest determining the level of *I* (ibid.: 135–6). That two other formalizations lead to the same answer is also noted: equality between the demand and supply prices of capital assets, and Fisher's rate of return over cost (ibid.: 137, 140). The remainder of Chapter 11 is primarily concerned with shift factors for the *MEC* schedule, in all of which expectations are crucial (ibid.: 141–6).

Chapter 12 then subjects the expectations-dependence of investment to closer scrutiny in a non-formal elaboration of the previous discussion. It carries the theory beyond the basic formalism of Chapter 11 by focusing on two topics that introduce *additional* considerations absent from that formalism. (It also moves to a different level of abstraction, one closer to empirical observation than pure theory.) The first topic is a theory of (long-term) expectations formation, or rationality under uncertainty, which emphasizes the precariousness of our information base and the inadequacy of exact calculations of prospective yields. The additional factor here is the human urge to action, so that the real foundation of enterprise is a combination of 'reasonable calculation' and 'animal spirits' (*C.W.* VII: 149–50, 161–3). The second topic is the influence of the stock exchange on investment decisions. Individually rational activity in this market ('speculation') competes with, and may dominate and distort, the firm's proper task of estimating prospective yields ('enterprise') (ibid.: 150–61). These new topics, which introduce human nature and institutions, supplement and enrich the formal beginnings in Chapter 11 without subverting them.

It is not until the third chapter on the rate of interest that Keynes fully describes his liquidity preference theory. Immediately the motives of money demand have been outlined, he constructs, for the purposes of *further analysis* (his phrase), the following equation:

$$M = L_1(Y) + L_2(r)$$

where M is the quantity of money, L_1 expresses transactions and precautionary demand as a function of income (Y), and L_2 expresses speculative demand as a function of the interest rate (r) for a given state of expectation (ibid.: 199–200). This equation then determines the three matters investigated in the ensuing discussion: (a) the relation of ΔM to Y and r, to which the general answer is that an increase in M lowers r and raises Y so that L_1 and L_2 both increase until a new equilibrium is reached; (b) the shape of L_1, the general answer being that it is a positive function of Y which is virtually linear in the short run but more variable in the long run; and (c) the shape of L_2, to which the general answer is that for a given state of expectation L_2 is an inverse function of r (ibid.: 200–2). These answers were earlier anticipated with the observation that 'As a rule, . . . the schedule of liquidity preference relating the quantity of money to the rate of interest is given by a *smooth curve* which shows the rate of interest falling as the quantity of money is increased', this reasoning being based on transactions demand rising 'more or less proportionately' with income and speculative demand rising as the interest rate falls (ibid.: 171–2, emphasis added). Two observations are pertinent at this point. The variable, r, does not signify a single rate, but a 'complex of rates of interest' (ibid.: 167 n. 2, 168, 205), this 'symbolic usage' harking back to earlier themes (the *Treatise on Probability* and his 1932–5 lectures). The second point is that the function L_2 (r) may be viewed as a corollary of a more complex relationship, L_2 ($r - r^*$), where r^* is the expected safe level of r (ibid.: 201–2). The remainder of Chapter 15 then extends the discussion to issues of monetary policy and stability. In this context, Keynes distinguishes between movements along, and shifts of, the liquidity preference schedule, though this is not his exact terminology. The first arises when ΔM produces Δr along a given function, while the second occurs when changes in expectation shift the function itself and produce Δr in the absence of ΔM (ibid.: 197–8).[30]

Keynes's chapter criticizing orthodox interest rate theory is notable for containing the only diagram in *The General Theory*. Although its main purpose is to undermine orthodox theory, this should not obliterate Keynes's willingness to portray functions as curves and to reason diagrammatically. The downward-sloping curve of I as a function of r represents both Keynes's MEC schedule and the classical capital demand curve (ibid.: 178, 180), the critique then depending on a shift in the I curve producing indeterminacy of r because the relevant saving curve is unknown until the new Y is determined. But there is an even more telling fact to be considered. Keynes's statement, 'This diagram was suggested to me by Mr R.F. Harrod' (ibid.: 180 n. 1), might easily be interpreted to mean that Harrod drew the diagram and passed it on to Keynes. Investigation of the background correspondence, however, reveals that although the *idea* of the diagram originated with Harrod, it was Keynes who produced the *drawing*. In his letter of 30 August 1935, Harrod described, particularly in a final note, a diagram without actually drawing it (*C.W.* XIII: 553–7). Keynes was so pleased with Harrod's suggestion that he converted it into a diagram using his own symbols.

> I think the construction in the note . . . is *both correct and very useful as a help to exposition*, and I shall [*sic*] like to appropriate it. . . .
>
> Let me start out from your note *which I understand as follows*: –
> [Here Keynes presented his drawing]
> . . . I should like to point out that what the diagram does show (*and most elegantly*) is the relation between the rate of interest and the level of

income, given the schedule of the marginal efficiency of capital and the propensity to consume.

(*C.W.* XIII: 557–8, emphases added)

In short, Keynes positively embraced the diagram as an expository device and retained an amended version in *The General Theory*.[31]

Keynes's exploration of the aggregate supply side of his theory, expressed inversely as 'the employment function', contains considerable mathematical elaboration.[32] On the assumption of a unique distribution of effective demand between industries, the employment function for the economy as a whole is obtained by simple aggregation of the individual industry functions (*C.W.* VII: 282):

$$\Sigma N_r = \Sigma F_r(D_w) \qquad \text{or} \qquad N = F(D_w)$$

A considerable amount of algebra and calculus follows, investigating how employment, output and prices respond to changes in effective demand, the results being expressed in terms of various elasticities (e). Assuming the existence of a satisfactory unit for measuring output, one main conclusion in money terms is

$$e_p + e_o(1 - e_w) = 1,$$

which indicates how an increase in effective demand is expended between proportionate changes of price (e_p), output (e_o) and wages (e_w) (ibid.: 284–5). However, this sort of analysis is based on imprecise and restrictive assumptions and Keynes turns directly to non-formalized discussion of a broader range of considerations, including non-constant division of effective demand between industries, the role of time, and income distrtibution effects (ibid.: 286–91).

Chapter 21 extends the above discussion to Keynes's quantity theory of money which links short-run changes in the price level (p) to changes in the money supply (M). His first step is to use further restrictive assumption to construct a simple version based on linear relationships (*C.W.* VII: 295–6). This is followed by non-formalized discussion which relaxes several of these assumptions and warns of interdependencies between factors, matters easily overlooked in purely mathematical manipulation. His third step is a return to formalism to derive the following equation for 'a generalised quantity theory of money' expressed in terms of elasticities (ibid.: 305):

$$e = (dp/p)/(dM/M) = e_d\,(1 - e_e\, e_o + e_e\, e_o\, e_w)$$

This states that a percentage increase in M will produce a generally different percentage increase in p, the magnitude of which depends on the response of D to ΔM (e_d) and the responses to the resulting ΔD of employment (e_e), output (e_o) and money wages (e_w). The derivation is again immediately followed by warnings (discussed below, pp. 147–8) as to its limitations. The final section of the chapter is a non-formal discussion of whether some simpler relation between *p* and *M* might exist over long time periods.

During Book V, which contains the most detailed mathematics of *The General Theory*, Keynes passes two remarks which seem at first sight to support the traditional account and undermine the revised account. These remarks thus need to be addressed. It turns out, however, that careful, logical analysis completely changes these first impressions.

The first remark occurs in the opening footnote of Chapter 20: 'Those who (rightly) dislike algebra will lose little by omitting the first section of this chapter' (*C.W.* VII: 280 n. 1). Superficially, this favours the traditional account. In fact, the sentence is poorly expressed and ambiguous, and its only sensible meaning conforms to the revised account. The first problem word is 'rightly'. If it is omitted, ambiguity disappears and the sentence serves its main apparent purpose, that of advising readers that the algebra of the first section may be skipped without great loss. But whether parenthetical inclusion was a quick afterthought or not, we cannot ignore it, with the result that we are faced with two different meanings depending on how we interpret the second problem word, 'algebra'. If it means 'algebra *per se*', then what is being said is that it is right to dislike a branch of mathematics, a proposition which merely concerns personal preferences about mathematics that have nothing to do with economics. The remark becomes pointless in an economics book, so that this interpretation may be reasonably discarded. What seems far more probable is that 'algebra' stands for 'the use of algebra in economics', for this connects the word to its context.

Why, then, is it right to dislike the use of algebra in economics? At least four answers can be suggested: (a) because algebra should never be used in economics; (b) because its unreflective usage without awareness of pitfalls is misleading; (c) because it is inferior to graphical (or other) methods; or (d) because verbal discourse is generally superior to the algebraic as a means of conveying economic understanding. The first proposition, a variant of the traditional account, may be eliminated because it does not exist anywhere in Keynes's writings and is contradicted by his own practice (including *The General Theory*). The remaining three propositions do occur in his writings before, during and after *The General Theory*, and are also consistent with his practice. It is one or more of these senses, I suggest, that captures the meaning of his sentence, one possible rephrasing of which is: 'Those who (rightly) dislike the unreflective use of algebra in economics will lose little by omitting the first section of this chapter.'

Logical dissection thus reveals that far from bolstering the traditional account, the footnote actually favours the revised account. Quite apart from its opacity, however, Keynes's judgement in adding it may be questioned. For something *is* lost by omitting this section, in terms of both economic theory and his second contentious remark about mathematics to which I now turn.

From the viewpoint of formalism, the most famous (or most notorious) passage in *The General Theory* occurs in the last analytical chapter of the book. Through unreflective reading, frequent selective quotation and neglect of context, the traditional account has relied heavily on this paragraph in winning currency and acceptance. It is therefore necessary to expose its pitfalls by careful analysis, consideration of context, and reference to other relevant sections of *The General Theory*.

The last two sentences of the paragraph are those cited, in full or in part, as overwhelming evidence of Keynes's hostility towards the use of mathematics in economics:

> It is a great fault of symbolic pseudo-mathematical methods of formalising a system of economic analysis, such as we shall set down in section VI of this chapter, that they expressly assume strict independence between the factors involved and lose all their cogency and authority if this hypothesis is disallowed; whereas, in ordinary discourse, where we are not blindly manipulating but know all the time what we are doing and what the words mean, we can keep 'at the back of our heads' the necessary reserves and qualifications and the adjustments which we shall have to make later on, in a way in which we cannot keep complicated partial differentials 'at the back' of several pages of algebra which assume that they all vanish. Too large a proportion of recent 'mathematical' economics are [*sic*] merely concoctions, as imprecise as the initial assumptions they rest on, which allow the author to lose sight of the complexities and interdependencies of the real world in a maze of pretentious and unhelpful symbols.
>
> (*C.W.* VII: 297–8)

Now this is certainly an attack, but exactly *what* is being attacked? Two entities are mentioned: (a) *pseudo*-mathematical methods in economics, and (b) a certain type of 'mathematical' economics (the inverted commas are Keynes's). What is not being attacked, and cannot be without gross inconsistency,[33] is the use itself of mathematical methods in economics. But *why* are these entities attacked? Pseudo-mathematical methods are criticized because they 'expressly assume strict independence between the factors involved' and ignore 'complicated partial differentials'. And a certain type of mathematical economics is rejected because it is based on imprecise assumptions and produces concoctions of symbols which obscure the interdependencies of the real world. Notice Keynes's central concern with the issues of interdependency and partial differentiation. Notice also that the first criticism echoes his earlier objection to Pigou's procedures in the *Theory of Unemployment*:

> The pitfalls of pseudo-mathematical method, which can make no progress except by making everything a function of a single variable and assuming that all the partial differentials vanish, could not be better illustrated. For it is no good to admit later on that there are in fact other variables, and yet to proceed without re-writing everything that has been written up to that point.
>
> (ibid.: 275–6)

Further light on the real object of Keynes's hostility is cast by his 1933 letter to Robertson criticizing Pigou's method of using mathematics. After deprecating the mathematical expressions and functions defined in the *Theory of Unemployment*, Keynes concluded as follows:

> The whole thing turns on a completely bogus use of the mathematics of a single variable. The apparatus is, from start to finish, nonsense apparatus. He arbitrarily takes two items, namely employment and real wages, out of a complex, but presumably determinate, system and then treats them, without proof or enquiry, as being analytic functions of one another. But they are not independent variables. . . . [Pigou] produces as great a sense of bedlam in my mind as Hayek does. Are the undergraduates to be expected to take it seriously? What a subject!
>
> (*C.W.* XIII: 312–13)

It is likely that Keynes had Pigou's book in mind as a prime example of that type of recent 'mathematical' economics, composed of obfuscating concoctions and imprecise assumptions, which so exasperated him.

Though two entities are delineated in Keynes's attack, they are both species of the wider genus, the inappropriate use of formalism in economics. Consistent with his position at other times and places, *this* is the target of his hostility, not the appropriate use of formalism.

Additional reasons for concluding that the conventional reading of the passage is hopelessly wrong derive from its context and a striking remark in its depths. The context is the development of a generalized quantity theory of money. Having used simplified assumptions to establish crude linear relations between the price level and the quantity of money, Keynes then introduces five complicating factors which generate a more realistic non-linear relationship (*C.W.* VII: 295–7). Each of these factors is to be considered in turn, but before doing so in the following section (ibid.: 298–303), Keynes issues a warning, a word he himself uses when referring back to this section (ibid.: 305).

The warning that is the subject of the paragraph in question may be stated as follows. When factors are considered on a case-by-case basis, interdependencies between them must not be neglected. The *ceteris paribus* procedure that is initially so useful must be abandoned in subsequent stages. For the 'nature of economic thinking' is (a) 'to provide ourselves with an organised and orderly method of thinking out particular problems', *and* (b) after reaching 'a provisional conclusion by isolating the complicating factors one by one, . . . to go back . . . and allow, as well as we can, for the probable interactions of the factors amongst themselves'. 'Any other way of applying our formal principles of thought', Keynes declares, 'will lead us into error' (ibid.: 297).[34] It is at *this* point that Keynes launches into the attack quoted above. Pseudo-mathematical methods and the certain type of mathematical economics do *not* obey this fundamental principle of economic enquiry and are therefore roundly catstigated – the former assumes 'strict independence between the factors involved' and the latter loses sight of the 'interdependencies of the real world'. They are the methods of 'blind manipulation' that Keynes had rejected earlier in the paragraph.[35]

The striking remark, buried parenthetically in the middle of the paragraph and intended as an aside aimed (unsuccessfully) at preventing misunderstanding of his views, is that '*without [our formal principles of thought] . . . we shall be lost in the wood*' (ibid.: 297, emphasis added). This proposition, that formal principles of thought are *essential* to economics, must surely alert readers to the difficulties of supporting the traditional argument that Keynes was deeply antagonistic to formalism in economics.

Careful readers will also note that in the middle of the paragraph Keynes refers to an example of pseudo-mathematical method from his own pen. It is presented in section VI of the same chapter (ibid.: 304–6), which should obviously be read in conjunction with the notorious paragraph. The example arises when he returns to formalized methods to derive his formula for a generalized quantity theory of money, $(dp/p)/(dM/M) = e_d\,(1 - e_e e_o + e_e e_o e_w)$. Although some meaning can be read into this equation (as Keynes indicates), it is not particularly informative as it stands and hints of a concoction. He summarizes his attitude to it as follows:

> I do not myself attach much value to manipulations of this kind; and I would repeat *the warning, which I have given above*, that they involve just as much tacit assumption as to what variables are taken as independent (partial differentials being ignored throughout) as does ordinary discourse, whilst I doubt if they carry us any further than ordinary discourse can. Perhaps the best purpose served by writing them down is to exhibit the extreme complexity of the relationship between prices and the quantity of money, when we attempt to express it in a formal manner.
>
> (*C.W.* VII: 305, emphasis added)

These reasons for his lack of enthusiasm amount to a restatement of his earlier criticisms of pseudo-mathematical methods.[36]

One final methodological comment, arising out of the opening chapter of the formative but relatively neglected Book II, is relevant. Before he could find a satisfactory voice for *The General Theory*, one of the problems

Keynes had to overcome was that of 'units of quantity' appropriate to theorising the economy as a whole (ibid.: 37). 'Obviously', he declared, 'our quantitative analysis must be expressed without using any quantitatively vague expressions' (ibid.: 39). Such concepts had to satisfy certain conditions: they had to be capable of (a) providing a basis on which to 'erect a quantitative science'; (b) developing a 'causal analysis' which requires 'perfect precision' (in theoretical terms at least); and (c) generating suitable 'material for the differential calculus' (ibid.: 38–40). Traditional aggregate concepts (real output, real capital stock and the general price level) were judged defective, and were replaced with an alternative set (the labour-unit and wage-unit) which could fulfil these objectives. Though not set out explicitly, the propositions underpinning Keynes's discussion are that economic analysis has a quantitative side, that this side is an essential element of economic science, and that foundations in unit-satisfactory concepts are required to generate material for rigorous theorizing which includes mathematical methods. The entire argument supports formalism as having a positive role in economics.

Keynes's general model of reasoning in *The General Theory* and the actual substance of his criticisms of the inappropriate use of formalism reveal that the various elements of his position fit together as a coherent whole and do not represent conflicting or inconsistent tendencies. In particular, they reconcile the formal and non-formal aspects and hence eliminate recourse to psychologically oriented hypotheses such as, for example, that Keynes only adopted the tools of his opponents the better to persuade them, or that putative conflicts in this area were suppressed by his force of character or multiple motivations.[37]

AFTER *THE GENERAL THEORY*

This section concentrates on two episodes for which there is unpublished correspondence of vital importance to Keynes's views on formalism. It does not attempt a complete survey of his writings for this period, many of which have been discussed elsewhere, nor does it implicitly depend on partial selection of supportive evidence, for all his writings are consistent with the revised account.

Letters from Keynes to Harrod and MacDougall, July 1936

In 1936, G.D.A. MacDougall submitted to the *Economic Journal*, with Harrod's encouragement, an article on prime and supplementary cost which was apparently highly mathematical. Extracts from Keynes's correspondence set out his reflections, first to Harrod, then to MacDougall:

> Undoubtedly it is a very able piece of work. I am not yet perfectly convinced that he is really an economist rather than some kind of

mathematician or logician. I have had the same kind of doubt as I have had about a good deal of Champernowne's work. I feel increasingly that one cannot think as an economist unless one's method of thought is capable of handling material which is not completely clear-cut and which is, so to speak, symptomatic thinking (I do not know if that quite expresses what I mean) rather than completely formal, watertight thinking. What one hopes from people like Champernowne and MacDougall is that they may learn to be mathematicians and economists simultaneously, capable of keeping in their minds at the same time formal thinking and shifting uncertain material. But it is a very difficult thing to do, and they are always in danger of producing something which is jejune, and of wasting a lot of time and space on stuff which they have to discard as soon as they get down to the real topic in hand. Obviously, however, MacDougall should have been given a First.

(Keynes to Harrod, 2 July 1936)

I think I understand why you have written it in the form which it has taken. There is indeed a certain aesthetic quality in your mode of presentation which partly depends upon its extreme detail and completeness. Nevertheless, there is, in my opinion, a good deal in it which leads to very little, and I believe you could make your central points whilst saving much space. To give an example of what I mean, take the function which you set forth on page 16, and the footnote attached. Its generalised form is, of course, somewhat arbitrary. That might be justifiable, if you were going to make any use of it. But, in fact, you are quite naturally not able to make any material use of it, and in due course you have to equate to zero all the coefficients except c_1. Has anything really been gained by the introduction of the longer expression and all the complications which that involves? Practically all your abstract propositions apply equally, and indeed are more intelligible, if this elaborate expression is discarded.

Again I am not sure, though you will probably differ from me and are thoroughly entitled to, that the mode of presentation is not excessively formal. If the completely formal treatment could be maintained to the bitter end, then it would be well worth while. *But in economics it is in the very nature of the case that at a fairly early stage in the argument it has to be discarded. As a rule it is impossible to pursue an economic argument to a point where it is useful whilst maintaining so high a standard of formalism as you have set yourself. Thus just when one reaches the stage where formalism might save one from mistakes it becomes necessary to throw it away.* It is my belief that the fundamental conditions which, on your view of things, the definitions of Prime and Supplementary Cost must satisfy could be expressed far more shortly. There would be some loss of aesthetic satisfaction I agree. But, on the other hand, it would be much easier for most readers

> to grasp the substance of your point.
>
> I am not completely convinced that the above criticisms are well taken. It may be that, if you attempt to do what I ask, the article will lose some of its virtue, undoubtedly some of its virtuosity. Nevertheless, I should be grateful if you would make the attempt; – for the two reasons, first, that space is scarce, and secondly, that I have an aversion to superfluous formalism in economics unless it is quite clear that it is required for the accurate statement of the ideas involved.
>
> If you would be so kind as to attempt another version, it would be easier for both of us to come to a conclusion whether or not it is an improvement.
>
> (Keynes to MacDougall, 2 July 1936, emphasis added[38])

Keynes's letters are highly informative. It is evident that his hostile remarks are again not directed at formalism in economics but at superfluous or irrelevant formalism. Nowhere does he suggest that mathematical work has no place in economics. Indeed, his hope is that mathematically trained people like MacDougall and Champernowne can be *both* mathematicians and economists, so that economics can benefit from (but not be subsumed under) mathematics.

A second theme is that economic phenomena are not ideally suited to analysis by formal methods. The material of economics is susceptible to shift and change, while the methods of mathematics are invariable and precise. This friction between *material and method*, however, does *not* imply the abandonment of the latter, but rather its reflective use. The difficult task of the good economist is to create modes of thinking in which the properties of mathematical methods and economic material are judiciously combined. MacDougall and Champernowne should become 'mathematicians and economists simultaneously'. His 1930s lectures expressed similar themes. In 1933 his answer to the question, 'What degree of precision is advisable in economics?', was typically twofold: precise modes of thought provide important benefits, but economics as a whole cannot be grounded on a 'mechanical logic'.[39] Thus 'In a complicated subject like economics the thing to do is avoid woolliness on the one hand, and scholasticism on the other' (Rymes 1989a: 101–2). The goal is clear, logical modes of analysis which respect the complex nature of economic material and do not seek to treat it as if it invariably possessed precise properties. The friction between method and material emerges in his succinct comment of 1934: 'Economic theory tries to apply precise methods to things themselves vague' (Rymes 1989c: H12, O8). Formal techniques are thus certainly part of the economist's toolkit, but such tools are generally not perfectly suited to the material worked upon, or capable of carrying jobs through to completion.

The above exposes deficiencies in one line of argument used to support the traditional interpretation. On this line, the essential themes of *The*

General Theory – ignorance and uncertainty, sudden appearances of new information, mass psychology and temporal inconstancy, for example – are prevented from incorporation in formal models by the very nature of mathematics. Hence Keynes rejected mathematics in economics because it excluded the central features of his system.[40] There are, however at least two major flaws in this line of argument (quite apart from the question of whether mathematics can handle such issues or not). One is that it is a highly partial representation of *The General Theory*. Keynes's system certainly includes the above factors, but it also includes, without falling into inconsistency or collapsing into orthodoxy, factors such as stability, knowledge, rationality, causality and adjustment mechanisms, all of which may be amenable to mathematical treatment. The second flaw is logical confusion. Factors which *limit* the use of mathematics in economics are confused with factors which *exclude* it. Even if certain central aspects of *The General Theory* cannot be mathematized, it does not follow that all important aspects fall into this class. The proposition that mathematical models cannot capture all significant aspects does not reduce to the claim that they capture none. 'Not all' implies 'some' and, as the evidence indicates, it is with 'some' that Keynes took his stand.

A third theme is that excessive formalism generates loss of substance, and this leads to loss of usefulness. Dictatorship by the mathematical mode creates analyses which are deficient in economic content, and the greater this lack of substance the more purely mathematical analysis moves towards irrelevance in economics. The economist who wants useful conclusions to emerge will employ mathematics up to a certain point but will not generally persist with formalism to the bitter end (a proposition consistent with the model of reasoning in *The General Theory*). The idea that extended formal analysis can become empty harks back to earlier stances. In 1931 Keynes was disappointed in the development of formal logic by Russell, Wittgenstein and Ramsey (*C.W.* X: 338) which was sharply opposed to his own treatment of logic in the *Treatise on Probability*. In 1932 he declared that 'Those writers who try to be strictly formal, generally have no substance' (*C.W.* XXIX: 38), while in 1933 he observed that scholasticism could 'precise everything away', leaving 'a comparative poverty of meaning' (Rymes 1989a: 102). These views are in stark contrast with that of modern mathematical economics, the general presupposition of which is that higher degrees of technical sophistication lead to greater explanatory power, not greater emptiness.

Fourth, Keynes is evidently grappling with words to capture his view of the appropriate mode of thought for the economist. He suggests the phrase 'symptomatic thinking', in contrast to 'completely formal, watertight thinking', but the suggestion is tentative. It appears that Keynes never succeeded in creating a term that suitably expressed the notion for which he was struggling. His quest here is continuous with earlier remarks. Theoretical economics, he declared in 1932, 'often has a formal appearance where the reality is not strictly formal. It is not . . . logically watertight in the sense in which mathematics is' (*C.W.* XXIX: 37–8). But the comments which perhaps most closely relate to what Keynes meant by 'symptomatic thinking' occur in 1933 and 1934. In his 1933 lectures he remarked that since it was impossible to obtain a generalization to cover everything, thinking in economics was 'thinking by sample, not by generalisation' (Rymes 1989a: 101–2).[41] And in a 1934 draft preface to *The General Theory*, after first describing the best available means for writing economic theory as a 'quasi-formal style' which generates neither verbally complete and exact documents nor logically complete proofs, he advanced his view of 'the essential nature of economic exposition':

> [I]t gives, not a complete statement, . . . but a sample statement, so to speak, out of all the things which could be said, intended to suggest to the reader the whole bundle of associated ideas, so that, if he catches the bundle, he will not in the least be confused or impeded by the technical incompleteness of the mere words.
>
> (*C.W.* XIII: 470)

Thus, just as a quasi-formal style presents sample statements as indicators of a larger associated body of ideas, so symptomatic thinking may be conceived as presenting statements as symptoms or indicators of the same larger body of thought.

Finally, it is worth noting that although requesting significant revision, Keynes acknowledged MacDougall's high ability, and did not seek dogmatically to impose his views on the author. Whilst outlining his stance, he gave MacDougall several opportunities to disagree with his criticisms. The overall message of the letters may be summed up as cautionary: mathematics is certainly of assistance to economics but is to be kept firmly in harness. It is the economist who is to be in the saddle, not the mathematician.

During 1937–8, when Keynes commented on issues such as Harrod's accelerator–multiplier analysis (*C.W.* XIV: 170–8), Kaldor's note on Pigou's views on wages and unemployment (ibid.: 240–8), and Harrod's new growth theory (ibid.: 320–50), his stance was continuous with that shown before and during *The General Theory*. In all cases mathematics formed a natural part of the discussion, without ever dominating and without ever being more than a servant to the economic analysis. It also informs his 1938 letter to Harrod on methodology which contains the illuminating but not always well-understood comment that in economics 'to convert a model into a quantitative formula is to destroy its usefulness as an instrument of thought' (ibid.: 299). This is *not* further evidence of Keynes's hostility to the use of mathematical methods in economics. His criticism is actually of Tinbergen's and Clark's *assumption* that empirically estimated economic magnitudes remain temporally constant in the same way as natural science constants do, regardless of phases in the credit cycle. The objection is neither to the use of mathematical models (which the above quotation accepts as having a usefulness as an instrument of thought), nor to the econometric estimation of variables such as the multiplier, but simply to an assumption which wrongly treats economic material as always 'constant and homogeneous' (ibid.: 300).

Econometrics

Keynes's criticisms of Tinbergen's work are famous. Both his published comments of 1939 and 1940 have been reproduced in the *Collected Writings* along with informative background correspondence *prior* to the interchange (*C.W.* XIV: 285–320). On a quick reading these documents seem to support the traditional view that Keynes was predominantly antagonistic to statistical and econometric work. Read more carefully, however, they constitute a prime exemplar of Keynes's more sophisticated approach. They show, first, that Keynes's main target was Tinbergen's specific methodology rather than econometrics in general, and second, that Keynes accepted the usefulness of econometric techniques when properly applied. The *Collected Writings*, however, only presents relevant correspondence up to September 1938. It omits a crucial letter written in the aftermath, which puts the central issue beyond reasonable doubt.

Shortly after publishing Tinbergen's rejoinder in the March 1940 issue of the *Economic Journal*, Keynes received a submission from Lange and Marschak which was also critical of his review of Tinbergen's book.[42] In considering whether to print it, he wrote to Pigou for advice:

> 2) In my own opinion, Tinbergen's reply is of far higher quality than this one. He really does try to meet my specific points to the best of his ability and says some very interesting and important things about them, whether or not one considers him convincing. This document, on the other hand, seems to me very largely a mere expression of opinion. On most of the main issues the authors tell us what their view is but do not give their reasons. Tinbergen was not guilty of this particular fault.
>
> 3) *In the first two or three pages there is a wild misunderstanding of what I am saying. I have, of course, never said anything to the effect that no business cycle theory can be tested statistically. I was dealing solely with Tinbergen's very special method of analysis. The early part of the article is written on the assumption that I was disputing the validity of any conceivable statistical method. It is sometimes useful to have a controversy about something which one has said, but it can never be of interest to the general public to have a controversy about something which one has not said.* However, this is not important, as I could no doubt persuade the authors to modify this particular point.
>
> 4) One of the most interesting points they raise, which is definitely

not in Tinbergen, is on page 12, where they attempt to deal with my 'suspicion that the assumption of linearity rules out cyclical factors'. I think there may be something in what they say there. My intuition cannot, however, see clearly. But, however this may be, the example they actually give is not a good one, and this is important because the argument, as expounded, depends solely on the force of this example. The example is not a good one because, if one calculates the series backwards according to their formula, one finds that $p_{t-2} = 120$ and $p_{t-3} = -40$. A formula which results in a negative price is obviously incorrect.

5) There seems to me a grievous inconsistency between what they claim for Tinbergen and what they admit on page 14. Every single case to which Tinbergen has applied his method assumes that the same formula is valid over a long period of years. If this is never the case, then it is hardly worth while to bother about the details of this method. However, I agree that that does not destroy the academic interest of a great deal of the argument.

6) My main feeling after reading this article is that I am not a penny the wiser. I did not feel that at all after reading Tinbergen's reply. There is something extraordinarily candid and conscientious about Tinbergen and, however much one disagrees with him, he really does try to deal with the points which have been raised. There are three or four points in this article which could have been put in a useful way in three or four pages. But an awful lot of it seems to me just parlez-vous. But perhaps I am prejudiced. I have a very poor opinion of Marschak and only a moderately good one of Lange. Although Lange signs the letter, I suspect a lot of Marschak in this article. I should say that it was quite up to Marschak's usual level, but not up to Lange's.

Well, at any rate, I should like to know what you think! Do not reply that you are not an authority on statistical theory, for who is? Certainly not the professional statisticians.

(Keynes to Pigou, 29 March 1940, emphasis added[43])

In the present context, the letter is vital. It demonstrates, in the italicized paragraph, two important propositions. The first is that Keynes's critique of Tinbergen's work was only a critique of a 'very special method of analysis'. Although this proposition may be inferred from Keynes's previously published writings, it is unambiguously confirmed by the letter. One of the features of Tinbergen's very special method was the assumption that the same formula was valid over a long period of years, an issue related to several of Keynes's criticisms in his 1939 review.

The second is that the object of his attack was *not* the validity of all conceivable statistical methods, including those for statistically testing the business cycle. That component of the traditional viewpoint which contends that Keynes expressed wholesale condemnation of, or opposition to econometrics, and which seemingly draws its strength from his review of Tinbergen, can now be laid to rest. As suggested elsewhere, Keynes's stance in relation to Tinbergen is fundamentally similar to that adopted in his *Treatise on Probability* of nineteen years earlier, namely, the *double* task of discrediting *invalid* statistical arguments and of exploring the foundations of *valid* statistical inference (*C.W.* VIII: 362).[44] Both propositions are also abundantly clear in Keynes's reply to Lange of 10 April 1940 which sought to remove misunderstandings of his views to avoid 'unnecessary controversy'.[45]

There is thus no support for the suggestion thrown out by Stone of a late change of mind by Keynes as regards econometrics. Both letters indicate that in 1938–9 Keynes was not virulently opposed to econometrics in general, so that the need to postulate a change of position to explain his acceptance of the Presidency of the Econometric Society in 1944–5 disappears.

Also noteworthy is Keynes's willingness to cede ground by admitting that one of his original propositions might have to yield to criticism. The matter was not settled, but he accepted that even though the particulars of his critics' argument were faulty, there may nevertheless be something to be said against his view that linearity assumptions might rule out cyclical factors. This open-mindedness in a new area was characteristic of Keynes, and is consistent with his object of understanding the conditions of applicability of econometric techniques. Finally, and just as consistently with his other writings, the letter underlines Keynes's high opinion of Tinbergen's attitude to intellectual discussion, despite not always finding him convincing on applications of statistical theory.

AN OVERVIEW OF KEYNES'S POSITION

It will draw the threads of the previous discussion together and assist in clarifying the methodology of formalism to be deployed in a restatement of *The General Theory*, if the main propositions of the revised account are summarized in general terms. On this view, Keynes's alternative stance on the use of formal methods in economics reposes on the following interrelated ideas:

1 Logical analysis necessarily *precedes* formal analysis. One role of logical analysis is to investigate the applicability or otherwise of formal analysis to a given topic. Another is to propose general relationships between variables prior to detailed investigation of functional forms.
2 Formal methods are perfectly legitimate in economics whenever they are *properly applied*, both mathematically and in relation to economic material. What deserves censure is not the careful reflective use of such techniques, but unthinking assumptions about the applicability of formal

analysis, and the use of mathematics in ways which ignore or suppress key characteristics of economic variables. (The mis-specification of the real object of Keynes's scorn is one of the central errors in the traditional account, and largely explains why his scathing remarks have so often been misinterpreted.)

3 In a general theory of quantitative reasoning there exist *three types of ordering relationships* between magnitudes: cardinal ordering, ordinal ordering, and complete incommensurability. Which of these obtains in a given situation is a matter to be decided by prior logical analysis. The fact that neither cardinality nor ordinality is universal clearly places *limits* on the scope of mathematical methods.

4 One of the critical factors affecting the applicability of formal methods is the *nature of economic material.* It may or may not be amenable to formalization (to some degree) or to quantification (in some form), and it may or may not exhibit a sufficient degree of constancy or 'homogeneity' over time.

5 Not only is the inappropriate application of formalism to be criticized, but also the notion that formalization always represents the *most fundamental,* most profound or most useful vehicle for economic discourse.

6 Logical *verbal thought* is a generally superior medium of understanding in economics to purely formalized thought. The former embraces a wider range of phenomena, while the latter, a sub-set of the former, requires additional assumptions which typically narrow applicability.

7 The value of mathematics as an aid to thought in economic theorizing lies more in its *symbolic* character as an expression of general relationships between variables, than in its *algebraic or numerical* character which often necessitates particular simplifying assumptions.

8 Formalism can provide a useful *check on intuitions* arrived at by other means.

9 Generally speaking, the capacity of mathematics to generate *useful* conclusions in economics is inversely related to its degree of technical elaborateness – useful here meaning informative about reality, both theoretically and practically. Increasing degrees of formal sophistication usually result in decreasing usefulness so far as understanding and influencing the actual economy is concerned. The characteristics which make for more powerful formal analysis are thus not the same as those that make for more powerful economic analysis.

10 *Scientific thought* in economics is not universally reducible to formalized thought. Formalization assists economic science but is neither its precondition nor criterion of demarcation from non-science.

11 When formalism is used, economic theory typically proceeds best in *two phases* – formalized beginnings followed by non-formal elaboration.

12 The *same general principles* apply to the use of all formal methods in economics, that is, to both mathematics and econometrics.

IMPROVING *THE GENERAL THEORY*

Given that *The General Theory* needs much rewriting and recasting, what proposals might one make, from the viewpoint of formalism, to improve its exposition in a 'second edition'? In the initial stages of the Keynesian revolution, Keynes defended his 'comparatively simple fundamental ideas' more strongly than the 'particular forms' of embodiment chosen in *The General Theory*, trusting that 'time and experience and the collaboration of a number of minds' would 'discover the best way of expressing them' (*C.W.* XIV: 111). These initial stages are long past, and the task now is to press on with identifying the best modes of expression for comprehension, dissemination and intellectual advance. Formalism is a nearly universal language in economics and its appropriate deployment can be harnessed as an effective vehicle for communication and growth. We are not time-locked by the particular (and provisional) choices Keynes made in expositing his ideas in 1936. Expanding the use of formalism will involve no rupture or inconsistency with his methodological position provided its boundaries are respected. Remember his observation in 1938 that models possess usefulness as instruments of thought. And without desiccating the richness and pleasure of prose, we can also draw on some of the good qualities of textbooks: well-organized structure, logical and sequential analysis, the use of all relevant techniques of exposition, and open-mindedness on unresolved issues.

Several suggestions for improvement are advanced below, these presupposing fidelity to Keynes's general methodological framework (as outlined above) and an audience with some academic training in economics – professional economists, graduates and later-year undergraduates. (It is also partly based on, but not inherently confined to, the type of comparative statics analysis that Keynes often employed, a richer and more sophisticated usage than the mechanical approach of many textbooks):

1 Inclusion of a new chapter (in Book II) dealing with methodological matters such as
   (a) the general role and properties of formalized language as one of the languages of economic argument, referring particularly to the lines between appropriate and inappropriate usages; and
   (b) the basic model of reasoning pursued, clarifying the role of formalism within the two phase process of formalized beginnings and non-formal elaborations.

   In other words, the issues that Keynes had on his mind in 1909 and 1938 need to be explicitly, rather than implicitly, addressed.
2 Reorganization of material so that the order of presentation in individual chapters is more easily related to the underlying model of reasoning, as well as being more logical across the book as a whole. For example, Chapter 12 on investment is quite jumbled and needs reordering so that

its component parts and their relations to Chapter 11 are more clearly seen. And with respect to the labour market, those parts of the discussion in Chapter 2 that are irrelevant to the main objective of Book I should be transferred to Book V to facilitate treatment along formal and non-formal lines.

3 Diagrams should be used whenever possible to allow visualization of the posited 'functional relationships' and 'curves', their shifts, and their interconnections in the overall system. The aggregate-supply–aggregate-demand ($Z-D$) apparatus of Chapter 3 cries out for a diagram,[46] the use of which would have helped to dispel the impression that *The General Theory* is only demand-side economics. Diagrams relating to consumption, investment, the interest rate and the more complicated labour market would also greatly improve exposition.

4 Further specification of algebraic equations would clarify the (short- and long-run) determinants of key variables, eliminate ambiguities and remove sources of misrepresentation. This has several dimensions:

(a) the inclusion of determinants as shift variables (or exogenous parameters) in equations. For example, the dependence of consumption on Keynes's 'objective' and 'subjective' factors can be brought more vividly to mind by a list of arguments in the function. And the use of E to denote the state of expectation in equations would emphasize the key dependence of Keynes's system on this factor;

(b) ambiguities can be cleared up as to whether a change in an endogenous variable is due to a change in a shift parameter or a change in the functional form (or both). Keynes's frequently used phrase, 'a change in the propensity to consume', is ambiguous between a change in C on given χ or a change in C due to a change in χ itself, in each case the ultimate cause being a change in an exogenous parameter;

(c) the applicability of equations can be specified. The influence of a variable, such as the rate of interest, may depend on whether it has a small or large range of variation;

(d) in general, equations (and their arguments) may be interpreted symbolically as instruments for ordering thought, or they may be capable of algebraic interpretation if variables can be quantified in the necessary ways.

Although the adoption of these suggestions would significantly alter the *form* of presentation of *The General Theory*, it would not change its basic theoretical content nor be antithetical to Keynes's methodology. Provided it is accompanied by necessary comment concerning the role of formalism, the assumptions involved, conditions of applicability and modes of interpretation, the greater use of formalized techniques in the manner outlined would improve the clarity and exposition of the book and accelerate the further development of its economic framework. Specifiying relationships in diagrams and equations maintains their usefulness as *instruments of thought* (when interpreted appropriately), *and* increases their usefulness as *instruments of communication and intellectual progress.*[47]

CONCLUSION

Although Keynes clearly made no striking technical contributions in the area of formalized economics, his views on the subject are worthy of attention. He possessed, as a result of his broad intellectual formation in mathematics, philosophy, probability and economics on the one hand, and his engagements in theoretical investigation, debate and the editorship of the *Economic Journal* on the other, an interesting, intelligible and intelligent position. One does not have to subscribe to all aspects of his stance to accept that methodological reflection is logically prior to usage, that formal tools have domains of application, and that formalism is not the sole scientific language in economics. But among exponents and advocates of mathematical economics there is a relative paucity of such reflections because of a clear preference for getting on with technical problem-solving rather than the sort of prior philosophical and methodological analysis that preoccupied Keynes. And even when the protagonists do engage in fundamental reflection, as in Stigum's massive (1990) prolegomena directed at placing all sciences (including economics) on 'a formal unitary methodological basis', the enterprises rest on philosophical and methodological assumptions significantly different from Keynes's. The conceptual terrain does not divide into 'all or nothing', where any criticism of the use of formalism in economics implies ditching the 'all for formalism' party in favour of the 'totally against formalism' party. There is at least a third position, one which is more intelligent and reasonable than the two extremes and which facilitates progress in economics.

To understand Keynes's stance, the traditional account needs to be abandoned in favour of the revised account (or some better variant of it).[48] It is no longer adequate to repeat the presuppositions and mistakes of the past, or to accept uncritically the opinion of authority, no matter how eminent elsewhere. We now have a wealth of information, published and unpublished, that was never available to the originators and early disseminators of the traditional view and it is extremely difficult to see how such information could possibly be used to sustain their position. Far too much evidence exists to the contrary, and an alternative account consistent with all the evidence is available.

To sum up: Keynes's position reposes, not on a general hostility to the use of formal tools in economics, but on an acceptance of their usefulness provided they are legitimately deployed, and on an insistence that their usage be economics-driven rather than mathematics-driven. It thus opens up opportunities for the further development of his economics, especially that of *The General Theory*, without conflicting with a proper concern for non-formal considerations.

NOTES

* An earlier version of this chapter was delivered to the Australian Conference of Economists at the University of Melbourne in 1992 (O'Donnell 1991b). I am indebted to King's College, Cambridge, and Professor David Papineau for permission to quote from Keynes's papers, and to the Australian Research Council for financial assistance. I should like to thank Peter Kriesler, Craig Freedman, Geoff Harcourt, Flavio Comim and Colin Rogers for helpful comments.

1 J.M. Keynes to Daniel Macmillan, 18 March 1939 (British Library, Add. Ms. 55204). Though reprints were common, none of Keynes's books ever went to second editions.

2 For further information on these four unwritten books, see O'Donnell (1992).

3 As Harrod perceptively remarked in August 1935, 'the new book will be understood by almost as many people as understood the *Treatise* [*on Money*]. . . . It means that still another work, a Manual of Elements, will be wanted' (*C.W.* XIII: 534).

4 Hahn's (1992a, 1992b) provocative advice to the young – to give little or no thought to methodology, and to avoid discussions of mathematics in economics like the plague since they are pointless – will be disregarded, not because my youth has passed but because the advice is silly.

5 Hayek (1978: 288–9) even went so far as to suggest that the future of Keynesian theory would be settled in the methodological arena, though his understanding of Keynes's methodology and writings was sometimes lamentable.

6 Many writers have also discussed issues without adopting a definite stance.

7 The overall thrust of the judgement was maintained in Schumpeter (1946b: 496), albeit in slightly softened form: 'Though never definitely hostile to mathematical economics . . . [Keynes] never threw the weight of his authority into its scale. The advice that emanated from him was almost invariably negative. Occasionally his conversation revealed something akin to dislike.'

8 See O'Donnell (1982: 174–9, 1989: ch. 9, 1990b, 1991b); Harcourt (1987a); and Vercelli (1991: 222, 242).

9 Keynes's philosophical thought includes his published and unpublished papers, two unpublished fellowship dissertations, and the *Treatise on Probability* (1921). His accessible economic writings embrace the thirty volumes of the Royal Economic Society's *Collected Writings of John Maynard Keynes*, a large quantity of unpublished material destined to appear in *The Further Collected Writings of J.M. Keynes*, and his now–published lecture notes of 1932–5 (Rymes 1989a, 1989c).

10 See O'Donnell (1982), a revised and expanded version of which appeared as O'Donnell (1989).

11 Three misunderstandings in Lawson (1990a) may also be cleared away. First, the revised account nowhere advances or relies on the proposition that Keynes was 'opposed to mathematics *per se*'. Criticisms based on this proposition have no bearing on the revised account. Second, although setting out to defend the traditional viewpoint, Lawson concludes with a proposition which is contrary to it and entirely consistent with the revised viewpoint, namely, that 'Keynes appreciated the beauty and intricacies of mathematical

reasoning, while simultaneously being vociferous and uncompromising in his condemnation of what he regarded as its inappropriate application'. Finally, it is *not* part of the revised account that Keynes was 'methodologically all things to all people'. The view that mathematics has a useful but limited role in economics is a distinct and coherent position, and does not possess whatever internal inconsistency is required for the simultaneous satisfaction of all conflicting opinions.

12 In partial explanation of this 'puzzle', Stone returned to the same psychological form of explanation he used in 1978: a focus on Keynes's *personal* characteristics rather than his *analytical* remarks. On the revised account, the puzzle ceases to exist. The more illuminating course of focusing on Keynes's analytical position reveals that his views exhibit internal coherence as well as basic consistency over time. This avoids the two problems in Stone's account of (a) an (unexplained) change of viewpoint late in Keynes's life, and (b) the suggestion that at the same time as he was attacking econometrics in print he was actively supporting the econometrically oriented work of the Cambridge Research Scheme and the formation of the Department of Applied Economics.

13 Skidelsky (1992) appears to appeal, rather inconsistently, to both sides of the debate. On the one hand, he states that 'Keynes's scepticism about the use of mathematics in economics grew rather than diminished with age, though it was present from the start', while on the other, that Keynes 'did not retreat from the attempt to capture important elements of . . . complexity in models' (pp. 412–13). He describes how Keynes accepted Harrod's 1935 suggestion of a diagram because it showed 'most elegantly' one of the relations of his new theory, but later writes that Keynes 'acquiesced in the mathematisation of *The General Theory* for pedagogical and policy purposes' (pp. 535, 610). Finally, he writes of Keynes's 'objection to econometrics' and his 'diatribes' against it, but also contends, rather unclearly, that Keynes objected 'not to econometrics as such, but to the method of econometrics' (pp. 619–20), the accompanying footnote referring the reader simply to two works with opposed viewpoints (O'Donnell 1989 and Mini 1991).

14 Although absent from *The Collected Writings of John Maynard Keynes*, they will be included in a multi-volume supplementary edition of Keynes's writings, *The Further Collected Writings of J.M. Keynes*, currently in preparation by the author; see O'Donnell (1995a).

15 See, for example, O'Donnell (1989: ch. 9, 1990b).

16 Keynes Papers, UA/3, King's College, Cambridge.

17 The other advantage of formal methods that Keynes recognized was their ability to compel authors to make their ideas precise (*C.W.* VIII: 125).

18 One of the stimuli for this idea, absent from Keynes's earliest 1904 essay on probability, may thus have been this comment by Marshall on Bentham.

19 See O'Donnell (1989: 185–8).

20 In a sympathetic obituary of 1935, he noted that Henry Cunynghame had written the 'first article on mathematical economics' in the *Economic Journal* in 1892 and had been a champion of geometrical methods in economics. One of Cunynghame's arguments which Keynes thought still had 'great force' and was worth 'calling to the attention of contemporary writers', was his grounds for preferring graphical over algebraic methods. As well, Cunynghame's attempts to develop more generalized supply and demand curves to overcome the limiting assumptions of the usual curves were sympathetically treated. He also described Cunynghame's *Geometrical Political Economy* as 'an excellent little book' and recalled his 'delight' on reading it thirty years earlier (*C.W.* X: 298–305).

21 See O'Donnell (1992) for Keynes's unwritten books and papers from 1909 to 1938.

22 Keynes Papers, UA/6/7–10, King's College, Cambridge. Marshall's *Principles* is the work referred to.

23 Marshall held distinctive and interesting views on the role of mathematics in economics(essentially that it has useful but limited functions), the general thrust of which was endorsed by Keynes. Keynes's position, however, differed from Marshall's in being less draconian. In 1924, for example, Keynes suggested that Marshall may have 'gone too far' in his reaction against excessive mathematization (*C.W.* X: 188). And while Marshall proposed burning the mathematics after their translation into English (Groenewegen 1995: 412–13), Keynes, it seems, would have withheld a considerable selection from the conflagration.

24 Other relevant material produced in the lead-up to *The General Theory* supports the revised account but is not discussed; see, for example, *C.W.* XIII: 286–7, 310–12, 374–5, 396–405, 425–7, 439–42, 480–4, and XXIX: 37–8, 65, 68–72, 110, 151–6.

25 The distinction drawn here between 'conceptual thinking' and 'mathematical thinking' is intended to refer only to the domain of economics, and not to the domain of mathematics where it has little or no meaning.

26 A clear example is the formula in Chapter 26 for combining weight of argument (w) and probabilities (p, q) as a possible resolution of an issue in the theory of rational conduct (*C.W.* VIII: 348). Since weight and most of Keynes's probabilities are non-numerical, the equation can only be interpreted symbolically and not algebraically. More generally, Keynes's symbolic approach is relevant to Part II of the *Treatise on Probability* where he brings his logical theory to bear on the standard probability theorems. Because his formalization is not to be restricted to numerical probabilities, Keynes is required to define addition and multiplication in a particular way and to take these definitions as axioms. A meaning can then be given, even when some probabilities are non-numerical, to equations for adding and multiplying probabilities (*C.W.* VIII: 144–9).

27 Bryce's notes as reproduced in Rymes (1989c: A39); words in square brackets are provided by Rymes, including an amendment to the last sentence. See also ibid.: 122–3; Rymes (1989a: 76–7); and O'Donnell (1989: 199–200). In a 1932 draft chapter for *The General Theory*, Keynes indicates that ρ refers to a 'complex' of rates of interest (*C.W.* XIII: 398 & n. 1).

28 This now became $M = A(w, \rho)$. See Rymes (1989c: B57–59, E15, G33–34, J36–7, M19, N16–17; 1989a: 125–6).

29 For a further example, see his 1932 equation for the price of capital assets, $P_2 = B(\rho)$, where P_2 = price complex of capital assets, B = complex of quasi-rents, and ρ = complex of rates of interest, such price complexes not being equivalent to a price index or to an average price (*C.W.* XIII: 397–400). See also Rymes (1989a: 78, 1989c: A40, D19).

30 Interestingly, he observes that open market operations may affect r through *both* channels.

31 The version of the 1935 diagram given in the *Collected Writings* (*C.W.* XIII: 557) is unfortunately incorrect; see O'Donnell (1995b) for the correct version and the genesis of the two diagrams.

32 It deserves to be read in conjunction with the preceding Appendix on Pigou because on the supply side there is little difference between the 'classical' theory and Keynes's.

33 Because of Keynes's considerable use of functional relations in explaining his own theory, and because of a remark in the same paragraph discussed below.

34 An instance of this two-stage procedure occurs in Keynes's analysis of the impact of reduced money wages (W) on employment (N). The first stage asks whether reduced W produces increased N, *ceteris paribus* (that is, with χ, MEC and r constant). The second stage then investigates whether reduced W will affect N through its repercussions on χ, MEC and r (*C.W.* VII: 260). At a more general level, Keynes's two stages of economic enquiry can be seen as related to his general model of reasoning outlined above.

35 For the Marshallian background to Keynes's static method of analysis, see the chapter by Rogers in this work: Vol. I, Chapter 19.

36 Space does not allow discussion of the pertinent issue of the mathematical derivation of Keynes's formulae.

37 See, for example, Skidelsky (1992: 610–11).

38 Harrod Papers, Chiba University of Commerce. MacDougall evidently made major alterations to his article, for an almost entirely non-mathematical paper on the subject appeared in the September *Economic Journal* (MacDougall 1936).

39 There are important parallels here with the *Treatise on Probability.* Although it explicitly included formal theorems, Keynes's general theory of logic was always grounded on judgement and intuition and never on mechanical applications of logical theorems and formulae. Similarly, in advancing his principle of indifference, he stressed the element of judgement so as to avoid reliance on a purely mechanical approach which had been part cause of the errors of the principle of non-sufficient reason (*C.W.* VIII: 56–7, 63).

40 See, for example, Mini (1991: 180): 'Now these facts and characteristics [with which Keynes was concerned] cannot be dealt with in mathematical models – the new information coming from outside the model cannot be "endogenized", coefficients determining the reactions by a crowd in the grip of mass psychology are meaningless. Mathematics [imposes] its rationality on . . . agents, demanding certainty, ruling out the unexpected and re-enthroning classical ways of thinking. . . .'

41 This proposition does not conflict with Keynes's search for general theories.

42 'Mr Keynes on the Statistical Verification of Business Cycle Theories', by Oscar Lange and Jacob Marschak, sent from Chicago on 15 February 1940.

43 Keynes Papers, EJ/1/6, King's College, Cambridge.

44 See also O'Donnell (1989: 200–3, 1990b: 44–5). Care needs to be taken, however, in interpreting Keynes's usage of the term 'testing' in econometric contexts; see O'Donnell (1989: 231–2).

45 The relevant paragraph of this letter reads as follows:

> 1) There are some passages in the first two or three pages which seem to me to misunderstand the general character of my criticism. *I do not remember having said anything whatever to the effect that no business cycle theory can be tested statistically. Certainly that is not my opinion, and any words which have seemed to you to carry that interpretation have been misunderstood. I was dealing solely with Tinbergen's very special method of analysis. That part of your article which is written on the assumption that I am disputing the validity of any conceivable statistical method is quite misconceived.* I emphasise this because, whilst it is sometimes useful to have a controversy about something one has said, it can never be of interest to the general public to have a controversy about something which the author himself does not admit having said and which, however that may be, he certainly does not believe.
>
> (Marschak Papers, Box 103, UCLA, emphasis added)

46 See King (1994b) for an early history of diagrammatic analysis of the aggregate supply–aggregate demand model.

47 This is not the place, however, to survey the many attempts to formalize Keynes's theory (with varying degrees of fidelity to *The General Theory*) since the IS–LM model of 1936.

48 Alternatively, those still wishing to defend the traditional account (or a variant of it) need to do so with arguments that (a) address *all* the evidence and (b) reveal why the revised account is inferior.

32

METHOD AND METHODOLOGY IN KEYNES'S *GENERAL THEORY*

Bill Gerrard

INTRODUCTION

The exact nature of the Keynesian revolution remains a matter of much debate. One key aspect of this debate is the *level* of Keynes's contribution. Is Keynes's *General Theory* to be considered primarily as a contribution at the level of theory or does it also make a contribution at the more fundamental level of method? Even amongst those who adopt a radical interpretation of Keynes's *General Theory* there is still no widely agreed view on the level of Keynes's contribution. Chick (1978) and Milgate (1982), for example, offer two contrasting views on the issue. Chick, in criticism of Clower's neo-Walrasian interpretation of Keynes, states that:

> the formal nature of the 'Keynesian Revolution' . . . involved the complete overthrow of the static method of solving a set of simultaneous equations, in favour of analysing the results of decisions which are taken in a well-defined sequence, on the basis of information available at the time and forecasts of an uncertain future.
>
> (Chick 1978; as reprinted 1992: 77)

Harcourt (1987a) also makes the case for a change in method in *The General Theory*. Milgate, by contrast, in arguing for a neo-Ricardian interpretation of Keynes, writes:

> The central conclusion, put very broadly, is that Keynes made no fundamental departure from his predecessors at the level of *method* but that he broke away radically from the orthodox marginalist *theory*.
>
> (Milgate 1982: 8; emphasis in original)

The aim of this chapter is to set out Keynes's views on methodology and method as expressed in *The General Theory*. An 'instantaneous picture' of Keynes's views is presented on the assumption that a consistent approach to economic theorizing had emerged in Keynes's economic writings by the time of the publication of *The General Theory*. There is no attempt to trace the 'dynamic development' of Keynes's views on methodology and method, in particular the links with Keynes's earlier 'philosophical' writings, especially *A Treatise on Probability* (1921). These issues form part of the 'new' Keynesian fundamentalist research programme associated with Carabelli (1988) and O'Donnell (1989) amongst others. (See Harcourt 1987a; Gerrard 1992, 1994a, for a discussion of new Keynesian fundamentalist issues, particularly the links between *A Treatise on Probability* and *The General Theory*.)

The main proposition of the chapter is that Keynes's views on methodology and method form a cluster of radical beliefs with much relevance for contemporary economic theorizing. In particular, Keynes's concern for a causal analysis based on realistic assumptions offers a radical alternative to the 'black-box' instrumentalist methods of neoclassical economists. Furthermore, Keynes's emphasis on the need to encompass existing (neo)classical theory within a more general framework is central to the post-classical interpretation of Keynes's *General Theory* presented in Gerrard (1995).

The structure of the chapter is as follows. The next section deals with Keynes's methodological views on the objectives and structure of economics, theory appraisal, progress in economics and the socio-political context. Keynes's rhetorical style is then considered, followed by details on Keynes's method of analysis. Nine aspects are considered: the encompassing approach; the macro–micro structure; causal analysis; the monetary context of behaviour; rationality; analytical methods; equilibrium and dynamics; the mathematical method; and the units of analysis. The penultimate section provides an assessment of Keynes's views as a radical cluster of methodological beliefs with much relevance for contemporary economic theorizing, and the chapter closes with a summary and some conclusions.

KEYNES'S METHODOLOGY

The objectives of economics

Keynes distinguished between two objectives: the theoretical and the practical. The theoretical objective relates to the explanation of observed phenomena. The practical objective relates to providing advice to policy-makers as to the most appropriate course of action in any given situation. *The General Theory* is primarily a theoretical work, seeking to provide the explanatory underpinning for appropriate policies to solve the problem of involuntary unemployment. Keynes stated the theoretical nature of *The General Theory* in the opening sentences of the Preface:

> This book is addressed to my fellow economists. I hope that it will be intelligible to others. But its main purpose is to deal with difficult questions of theory, and only in the second place with the applications of this theory to practice.
>
> (*C.W.* VII: xxi)

Providing the explanation of the causes of involuntary unemployment was the necessary prerequisite for developing appropriate policy measures. Indeed, Keynes considered the achievement of his theoretical objective to be necessary for re-establishing the credentials of economics as a subject of great practical signifiance. He sought to overcome 'the deep divergences of opinion between fellow economists which have for the time being almost destroyed the practical influence of economic theory, and will, until they are resolved, continue to do so' (*C.W.* VII: xxi). Hence, for Keynes, the theoretical objective was motivated by the practical objective. He developed his theory with its practical implications very much in mind. But Keynes believed that the task of designing specific policy measures for dealing with involuntary unemployment lay beyond *The General Theory* and required quite a different type of book: 'It would need a volume of a different character from this one to indicate even in outline the practical measures' (*C.W.* VII: 383).

In re-establishing the link between theory and practice, Keynes saw himself as breaking away from the Classical School and following more in the spirit of the mercantilists:

> as a contribution to statecraft, which is concerned with the economic system as a whole and with securing the optimum employment of the system's entire resources, the methods of the early pioneers of economic thinking in the sixteenth and seventeenth centuries may have attained to fragments of practical wisdom which the unrealistic abstractions of Ricardo first forgot and then obliterated.
>
> (*C.W.* VII: 340)

Keynes believed that classical theory 'cannot solve the economic problems of the actual world' (*C.W.* VII: 378). It did not provide an economic theory of the actual economy in which we live 'with the result that its teaching is misleading and disastrous if we attempt to apply it to the facts of experience' (ibid.: 3). Keynes set himself the objective of developing a general theory which dealt with actual economic behaviour and, hence, could provide 'practical wisdom' and a 'contribution to statecraft'.

The structure of economic theory

Keynes viewed economic theory as possessing a two-tiered structure: a set of basic assumptions and a theoretical superstructure. Given the basic assumptions, economic theory develops by deducing the theoretical implications of these assumptions as applied to different aspects of economic behaviour. The basic assumptions are the fundamental characteristic feature of a particular school of thought. Keynes considered that these basic assumptions are often implicit, hence forming a tacit dimension to economic theory. These tacit assumptions need to be made explicit and subject to critical evaluation. Indeed, as Keynes observed in the case of various schools of thought in trade cycle theory, it may not be possible to make sense of a specific theory without supplying these tacit assumptions (*C.W.* VII: 329).

One of the first analytical tasks of *The General Theory*, in Chapter 2, is the clarification of the characteristic tacit assumptions of classical theory. Keynes detected three logically equivalent tacit assumptions of classical theory; (a) the real wage equals the marginal disutility of employment; (b) no involuntary unemployment; and (c) Say's Law, that supply creates its own demand (*C.W.* VII: 21–2). Later, in his discussion of the rate of interest, Keynes detected another logically equivalent tacit assumption, that the actual rate of interest is the neutral rate of interest (i.e. the equilibrium or 'natural' rate of interest consistent with full employment). It is these tacit assumptions which firmly ensconce classical theory in what Kevnes called the 'Ricardian world' (ibid.: 244).

Theory appraisal

Keynes can be viewed as adopting a three-stage process of theory appraisal, each stage involving quite different criteria for the evaluation of economic theory: logical consistency, realism of assumptions, and empirical testing. The first criterion of theory appraisal is the purely internal requirement of logical consistency: is the theoretical superstructure logically valid with respect to its basic assumptions? This is a formalist evaluation dealing with the internal logical properties of economic theory. There is at this stage no evaluation of the empirical claims about the real world *per se*.

The empirical claims of economic theory are evaluated at the second and third stages. The second stage of theory appraisal is the degree of realism of the assumptions. Given his theoretical and practical objectives, Keynes adopted a realist approach to economic theory. (See Lawson 1989 for a discussion of the realist approach in economics with particular reference to Keynes's critique of Tinbergen's use of econometric methods.) Economic theory should try to explain the causal mechanisms which generate observed economic phenomena. Hence the basic assumptions have to be realistic in the sense of reflecting the actual causal mechanisms which the theorist believes to exist. The assumptions must reflect empirical reality, not vice versa: 'A scientific theory cannot require the facts to conform to its own assumptions' (*C.W.* VII: 276). Thus Keynes can be interpreted as rejecting the instrumentalist strategy of choosing assumptions on the grounds of predictive power. The choice of assumptions is a matter of experience. Thus Keynes also rejected the deductivist approach that the basic assumptions are axioms that are true *a priori*.

These two criteria of theory appraisal are evident in Keynes's evaluation of classical theory. Keynes concluded that classical theory is logically valid but based on special assumptions with limited empirical relevance. This assessment of classical theory is clearly stated in the Preface to *The General Theory*:

> For if orthodox economics is at fault, the error is to be found not in the superstructure, which has been erected with great care for logical consistency, but in a lack of clearness and of generality in the premisses.
>
> (*C.W.* VII: xxi)

For Keynes, the error of classical theory lies, not in its logic, but in its assumptions, which are lacking in clearness because of their tacit nature and in generality because they are not realistic. This evaluation is repeated in the final chapter:

> Our criticism of the accepted classical theory of economics has consisted not so much in finding logical flaws in its analysis as in pointing out that its tacit assumptions are seldom or never satisfied, with the result that it cannot solve the economic problems of the actual world.
>
> (Ibid.: 378)

Keynes considered that classical theory had become a purely formal analysis with little empirical relevance. He traced the roots of this back to Ricardo:

> Ricardo offers us the supreme intellectual achievement, unattainable by weaker spirits, of adopting a hypothetical world remote from experience as though it were the world of experience and then living in it consistently. With most of his successors common sense cannot help breaking in – with injury to their logical consistency.
>
> (Ibid.: 192)

This is what Keynes deemed, perhaps unfairly, to be the 'Ricardian heritage' of classical theory: logical consistency but applied to a hypothetical world far removed from the everyday world of experience. It is this lack of realism and, hence, inappropriate conclusions, which Keynes sought to correct in his own more general (i.e. more realistic) theory.

Keynes's realist critique of classical theory is exemplified by his discussion in Chapter 2 of the accepted theory of labour market. Throughout this chapter Keynes raises objections to classical assumptions on the grounds that 'ordinary experience tells us, beyond doubt' (*C.W.* VII: 9). For example, Keynes rejected the classical assumption that labour supply is a function of the real wage alone on the evidence that workers tend to resist money-wage cuts but not small rises in the price of wage-goods. He also rejected the classical assumption that the wage bargain determines the real wage, claiming that such an assumption shows that 'there has been a fundamental misunderstanding of how in this respect the economy in which we live actually works' (ibid.: 13).

Keynes contrasted the logical consistency but empirical irrelevance of classical theory with mercantilism. He considered there to be an 'element of scientific truth in mercantilist doctrine' (ibid.: 335). The limitation of mercantilism was its lack of an adequate theoretical analysis:

> The mercantilists perceived the existence of the problem without being able to push their analysis to the point of solving it. While the classical school ignored the problem, as a consequence of introducing into their premisses conditions which involved its non-existence; with the result of creating a cleavage between conclusions of economic theory and those of common sense.
>
> (*C.W.* VII: 350)

Similarly, Keynes considered Malthus's vehement opposition to Ricardo's doctrine of the sufficiency of aggregate demand had been in vain because Malthus failed to provide a clear explanation as to why effective demand could be deficient (ibid.: 32).

Keynes also explained the incompleteness of Gesell's theory as the main explanation of the neglect by academics of his original and profound work (*C.W.* VII: 356). You need a theory to defeat a theory. Yet despite their theoretical failings, Keynes aligned himself with 'the brave army of heretics . . . who, following their intuitions, have preferred to see the truth obscurely and imperfectly rather than to maintain error, reached indeed with clearness and consistency and by easy logic but on hypotheses inappropriate to the facts' (ibid.: 371). Keynes's task in *The General Theory* was to furnish the necessary theory to support the intuitions of Malthus and the other heretics on the possibility of a general deficiency of effective demand.

The third stage in the appraisal of economic theory is the empirical testing of its implications. Keynes recognized that empirical testing cannot provide conclusive evidence for or against any economic theory: 'in economics (along with the other moral sciences) . . . it is often impossible to bring one's ideas to a conclusive test either formal or experimental' (*C.W.* VII: xxiii). But, although empirical testing cannot be conclusive, Keynes held that confirmation (or attempted refutation from Popper's falsificationist perspective) of theoretical results by the empirical evidence is a necessary requirement for economic theory to be accepted, particularly by those outside the profession. He considered that classical theory had been a 'signal failure' as regards 'scientific prediction' and this had 'greatly impaired . . . the prestige of its practitioners' (ibid.: 33):

> For professional economists, after Malthus, were apparently unmoved by the lack of correspondence between the results of their theory and the facts of observation; – a discrepancy which the ordinary man has not failed to observe, with the result of his growing unwillingness to accord to economists that measure of respect which he gives to other

> groups of scientists whose theoretical results are confirmed by observation when they are applied to the facts.
>
> (Ibid.)

Classical theory could not claim to be scientific in the sense that it did not appear to respond to a lack of correspondence between theory and observation. Its theoretical results were not 'confirmed by observation' and it failed 'for purposes of scientific prediction'.

Keynes himself used empirical evidence to criticize the implications of classical theory. For example, Keynes claimed that the classical conclusion that unemployment in a depression is due to money-wage rigidity 'is not clearly supported by the facts', citing the experience of the United States in 1932 (*C.W.* VII: 9). He also quoted empirical evidence in support of his own theory, for example, Clark's estimates of investment in Great Britain, 1928–31, and Kuznets's data on capital formation in the United States, 1925–33, in support of his effective-demand explanation of the depression (ibid.: 102–4). Keynes was also open to empirical criticism of his own theory. The most obvious example of this is his recognition of the need to revise his initial assumption of short-period diminishing returns in the light of the empirical evidence on the movements of real and money-wages produced by Dunlop, Tarshis and Kalecki (Keynes 1939c).

Keynes's recognition of the inconclusiveness of empirical testing was related in part to his recognition that the units of analysis are quite different between the theoretical domain and the empirical domain (see Chapter 7 by Bradford and Harcourt in Volume 1 of this work). The choice of units is discussed in Chapter 4. Keynes argued that the three units widely used by economists – output, the capital stock, and the general price-level – are unsatisfactory. The theoretical difficulties in their definitions, arising from their very nature as aggregates of heterogeneous objects, cannot be resolved. But Keynes did not see that this presented any problems for economic theory. These three units have 'no relevance to the causal sequence of economic events' (*C.W.* VII: 39). Hence they had no place in his quantitative (i.e. theoretical) analysis. However, this did not mean that these units had no value:

> The fact that two incommensurable collections of miscellaneous objects cannot in themselves provide the material for a quantitative analysis need not, of course, prevent us from making approximate statistical comparisons, depending on some broad element of judgment rather than of strict calculation, which may possess significance and validity within certain limits.
>
> (*C.W.* VII: 39–40)

Thus aggregate measures of output, the capital stock and the general price-level could be used as part of a statistical and historical analysis despite their theoretical indeterminacy. This statistical analysis, in turn, could be used to confirm, or otherwise, the empirical status of the theoretical analysis. But the theoretical analysis itself must be conducted in terms of theoretically precise units with causal significance. In this respect, Keynes argued that the theory of employment required two fundamental units: quantities of money-value and quantities of employment.

Progress in economics

Keynes recognized two modes of development in economics. The first is that of progressive evolution as the theoretical superstructure associated with a given set of basic assumptions is developed. This is largely a process of cumulative development, characterized by continuity. In contrast, the second mode of development is that of the revolutionary overthrow of one set of basic assumptions by another set of basic assumptions. Keynes's recognition of two modes of development bears many similarities to Kuhn's distinction between normal science and revolutionary science (Kuhn 1962).

Keynes described the progress of classical theory in the Preface to the French edition of *The General Theory* as follows:

> For a hundred years or longer English Political Economy has been dominated by an orthodoxy. That is not to say that an unchanging doctrine has prevailed. On the contrary. There has been a progressive evolution of the doctrine. But its presuppositions, its atmosphere, its method have remained surprisingly the same, and a remarkable continuity has been observable through all the changes.
>
> (*C.W.* VII: xxxi)

Keynes described that orthodoxy as the 'Classical School' by which he meant 'the *followers* of Ricardo, those, that is to say, who adopted and perfected the theory of the Ricardian economics, including (for example) J.S. Mill, Marshall, Edgeworth and Prof. Pigou' (*C.W.* VII: 3 fn. 1). Keynes recognized that he was perpetrating a solecism in including the neoclassical economists in his definition of the Classical School but he wanted to stress the continuity between the early classical economists such as Ricardo, Say and J.S. Mill and the later neoclassical economists. The marginalist revolution had led to a significant change in the form of the theoretical superstructure of classical theory but the basic assumptions had remained the same, particularly the belief in Say's Law.

Keynes saw *The General Theory* as a revolutionary break from the classical set of assumptions:

> The classical theorists resemble Euclidean geometers in a non-Euclidean world who, discovering that in experience straight lines apparently

> parallel often meet, rebuke the lines for not keeping straight – as the only remedy for the unfortunate collisions which are occurring. Yet, in truth, there is no remedy except to throw over the axiom of parallels and to work out a non-Euclidean geometry. Something similar is required to-day in economics.
>
> (*C.W.* VII: 16)

Say's Law was to be regarded as classical theory's 'axiom of parallels'. It had to be discarded to permit the development of a general theory allowing for the possibility of deficient effective demand and involuntary unemployment.

Keynes understood well the powerful hold which classical theory exercised on the profession. Progress in economic theory is not just a matter of rational evaluation of existing theories. He recognized that many were strongly wedded to the classical theory. He himself had held to it with conviction and had to go through 'a long struggle of escape' (*C.W.* VII: xxiii). The power of the Classical School showed itself in the lack of controversy:

> Ricardo conquered England as completely as the Holy Inquisition conquered Spain. Not only was his theory accepted by the city, by statesmen and by the academic world. But controversy ceased; the other point of view completely disappeared; it ceased to be discussed.
>
> (*C.W.* VII: 32)

It also showed itself in the dismissal of mercantilism: 'we were brought up to believe that it was little better than nonsense. So absolutely overwhelming and complete has been the domination of the classical school' (ibid.: 335). Similarly, the power of the Classical School had led to the writings of non-orthodox economists such as Gesell to be treated 'as being no better than those of a crank' (ibid.: 353). One implication of the power of classical theory is, as discussed above, that empirical criticism is insufficient on its own to result in the overthrow of classical theory. There needs to be an 'alternative construction' to replace classical theory. This, in turn, has implications for the rhetorical style adopted by Keynes in *The General Theory*, as discussed below. The non-rational aspect of the dominance of classical theory is conveyed in Keynes's frequent use of religious analogies:

> I remember Bonar Law's mingled rage and perplexity in the face of economists, because they were denying what was obvious. He was deeply troubled for an explanation. One recurs to the analogy between the sway of the classical school of economic theory and that of certain religions. For it is a far greater exercise of the potency of an idea to exorcise the obvious than to introduce into men's common notions the recondite and the remote.
>
> (*C.W.* VII: 350–1)

In a similar vein, in the Prefaces to the German and Japanese editions, Keynes likened his own development to that of a priest of the Catholic faith becoming a Protestant (*C.W.* VII: xxv, xxix). As noted above, he also described non-orthodox economists as a 'brave army of heretics' and compared the dominance of Ricardian economics to the Holy Inquisition.

The socio-political context of economic theory

The dominance of classical theory is discussed by Keynes as the result of the convergence of a number of factors which favoured its acceptance by professional economists, the business world and political leaders:

> The completeness of the Ricardian victory is something of a curiosity and a mystery. It must have been due to a complex of suitabilities in the doctrine to the environment into which it was projected. That it reached conclusions quite different from what the ordinary uninstructed person would expect, added, I suppose, to its intellectual prestige. That its teaching, translated into practice, was austere and often unpalatable, lent it virtue. That it was adapted to carry a vast and consistent logical superstructure, gave it beauty. That it could explain much social injustice and apparent cruelty as an inevitable incident in the scheme of progress, and the attempt to change such things as likely on the whole to do more harm than good, commended it to authority. That it afforded a measure of justification to the free activities of the individual capitalist, attracted to it the support of the dominant social force behind authority.
>
> (*C.W.* VII: 32–3)

The remoteness and mathematical beauty of classical theory, particularly the work of Edgeworth and Walras, added to its attractiveness to the professional economist but its dominance was also based on the wider socio-political context of *laissez-faire* capitalism.

Keynes also considered that the socio-political context would play an important role in determining the acceptance of *The General Theory*. He recognized differences between countries. For example, he believed that German readers would be less resistant since classical theory was less well established there and there was no tradition of dominance by purely formal theories (*C.W.* VII: xxv). Similarly, Keynes considered French economists as 'eclectic' and 'without deep roots in systematic thought' (*C.W.* VII: xxxii).

Another aspect of Keynes's concern for the socio-political context of economics was his belief that economic ideas have considerable power to influence our lives, more so even than vested interests in the long run:

> the ideas of economists and political philosophers, both when they are right and when they are wrong, are more powerful than is commonly understood. Indeed, the world is ruled by little else. Practical men, who

believe themselves to be quite exempt from any intellectual influences, are usually the slaves of some defunct economist. Madmen in authority, who hear voices in the air, are distilling their frenzy from some academic scribbler of a few years back. I am sure that the power of vested interests is vastly exaggerated compared with the gradual encroachment of ideas. Not, indeed, immediately, but after a certain interval . . .

(*C.W.* VII: 383)

KEYNES'S RHETORICAL STYLE

In reading *The General Theory* it is important to appreciate Keynes's rhetorical style. In particular, who was Keynes's intended audience? what modes of argument did he use? why did he use these modes of argument?

Keynes's intended audience was his fellow professionals, not the general public, as he made clear in the Preface:

if my explanations are right, it is my fellow economists, not the general public, whom I must first convince. At this stage of the argument the general public, though welcome at the debate, are only eavesdroppers at an attempt by an economist to bring to an issue the deep divergences of opinion between fellow economists . . .

(*C.W.* VII: xxi)

That his 'fellow economists' were his intended audience, not the general public, has much significance for the interpretation of Keynes's modes of argument. First, it explains why *The General Theory* is primarily presented in the mode of abstract theoretical analysis rather than more generally accessible language:

This book is chiefly addressed to my fellow economists. I hope that it will be intelligible to others. But its main purpose is to deal with difficult questions of theory, and only in the second place with the applications of this theory to practice.

(Ibid.)

Keynes sought to resolve the deep theoretical divisions in economic theory as the prerequisite for developing a practical economics for application to the real world. He hoped that *The General Theory* would be 'intelligible' to others but this was not a primary objective.

Another mode of argument used by Keynes is controversy. Throughout *The General Theory* Keynes not only presents logical criticisms of classical theory but he also ridicules classical theory for its lack of understanding of the real world. Thus, for example, he wrote:

The celebrated optimism of traditional economic theory, which has led to economists being looked upon as Candides, who, having left this

> world for the cultivation of their gardens, teach that all is for the best in the best of all possible worlds provided we will let well alone . . .
>
> (*C.W.* VII: 33)

Elsewhere, Keynes, wrote that: 'The part played by orthodox economists, whose common sense has been insufficient to check their faulty logic, has been disastrous . . .' (ibid.: 349). These and other similar attacks provide some of the most memorable passages in *The General Theory*. But why did Keynes intentionally seek to generate controversy in this way since the hostile reaction it was likely to provoke, and indeed did, from those being criticized, namely, the majority of his 'fellow economists', could make it even more difficult to get his ideas across to his intended professional audience? One possible interpretation is that Keynes was using controversy as an appeal 'above the heads' of economists to the general public, particularly policy-makers. But Keynes himself gave explicitly quite a different justification for his use of controversy as a necessary tactic in presenting his ideas to his 'fellow economists':

> I cannot achieve my object of persuading economists to re-examine critically certain of their basic assumptions except by a highly abstract argument and also by much controversy.
>
> (*C.W.* VII: xxi)

The use of controversy by Keynes followed from his methodological views on the nature of economic theory as a logical superstructure derived from a conventional foundation of basic, often tacit, assumptions held with conviction. In such circumstances, controversy is a necessary 'shock of the new' device to provoke economists into re-examining their theoretical convictions. Keynes did recognize the inevitable dangers of using controversy:

> My controversial passages are aimed at providing some material for an answer; and I must ask forgiveness if, in the pursuit of sharp distinctions, my controversy is itself too keen. I myself held with conviction for many years the theories which I now attack, and I am not, I think, ignorant of their strong points.
>
> (Ibid.)

Yet he deemed controversy as necessary and unavoidable, especially given his own previous classical convictions. It was his stated intention to initiate a conversation with his 'fellow economists': 'The writer of a book such as this, treading along unfamiliar paths, is extremely dependent on criticism and conversation if he is to avoid an undue proportion of mistakes' (ibid.: xxiii). Controversy was Keynes's chosen device to provoke classical theorists into recognizing the need for a conversation.

Subsequently, in the Prefaces to various translations of *The General Theory*, Keynes reconsidered his use of the controversial style of argument. In the

Prefaces to the German and Japanese editions, written in September and December 1936 respectively, Keynes defended his use of controversy as unavoidable, given his own past beliefs:

> My emphasis . . . upon the points of my divergence from classical theory has been regarded in some quarters in England as unduly controversial. But how can one brought up a Catholic in English economics, indeed a priest of the faith, avoid some controversial emphasis, when he first becomes a Protestant.
>
> (*C.W.* VII: xxv; see also p. xxiv)

However, by the time Keynes wrote the Preface to the French edition three years later in February 1939 he had become critical of some of the rhetorical style in *The General Theory*, not only his use of controversy but also his concentration on the audience of 'fellow economists':

> I . . . have felt myself to be breaking away from . . . orthodoxy, to be in strong reaction against it, to be escaping from something, to be gaining an emancipation. And this state of mind on my part is the explanation of certain faults in the book, in particular its controversial note in some passages, and its air of being addressed too much to the holders of a particular point of view and too little *ad urbem et orbem*. I was wanting to convince my own environment and did not address myself with sufficient directness to outside opinion. Now three years later, having grown accustomed to my new skin and having almost forgotten the smell of my old one, I should, if I were writing afresh, endeavour to free myself from this fault and state my own position in a more clear-cut manner.
>
> (*C.W.* VII: xxxi)

Keynes reiterated that the use of controversy was partly due to his 'own state of mind' in 'breaking away' from classical theory and his not yet having 'grown accustomed' to his 'new skin'. Three years on, these reasons no longer existed. In addition Keynes had come to view his use of controversy as explaining 'certain faults' of *The General Theory*, implying that he had changed his evaluation of the gains and losses of provocation. Thus, if Keynes were ever to rewrite *The General Theory* a less controversial style would be used. Any rewrite would also be directed at a wider audience with the implication that there would be more emphasis on the practical objective. Hence a second edition of *The General Theory* would differ in its rhetorical style due to the changes in the intended audience and objectives. But, despite his later criticisms of his rhetorical style in *The General Theory*, it is evident that Keynes adopted that style, particularly the use of controversy, for what he considered at the time to be good reasons.

KEYNES'S METHOD

The encompassing approach

Keynes considered *The General Theory* to be 'general' in at least two senses. First, it is general in the sense that it attempts to encompass classical theory within a more general framework. Second, it is general in the sense of dealing with the aggregate behaviour of the economic system (i.e. macroeconomics) rather than the behaviour of individual agents (i.e. microeconomics). The two senses are closely related.

The need to encompass classical theory is stated by Keynes in Chapter 1 of *The General Theory*: 'I shall argue that the postulates of the classical theory are applicable to a special case only and not to the general case, the situation which it assumes being a limiting point of the possible positions of equilibrium' (*C.W.* VII: 3).

Keynes considered classical theory as a 'special case' applicable only to a particular position of equilibrium. He identified the classical equilibrium as the special case of full employment. The uniqueness of full-employment equilibrium in classical theory is derived from the theory of the labour market (as summarized in the two fundamental postulates) and Say's Law. Keynes sought to develop a more general theory that could allow for a range of 'possible positions of equilibrium'.

The encompassing approach involves determining the limits to the domain of relevance of the existing theory by clarifying the range of applicability of its basic assumptions. These assumptions may be tacit and, therefore, require to be made explicit. Once the restrictive nature of these assumptions has been clarified, a more general theoretical framework is developed incorporating alternative theories to deal with the implications of relaxing the restrictive 'special-case' assumptions. Encompassing implies revolutionary but progressive change with the existing theoretical framework being retained, not rejected, but re-interpreted within a more general framework. The process of generalization has a transcendental quality, a characteristic feature of the encompassing approach.

Keynes identified the tacit assumptions of classical theory as implying the assumption of a full-employment equilibrium. This led him to define the domain of relevance of classical theory as follows: 'it investigates what laws will govern the application and rewards of the community's productive resources subject to this assumption' (*C.W.* VII: 244).

Keynes saw classical theory as dealing with the allocation of a given quantity of resources. Within this domain of relevance, he considered classical theory to be valid:

> Regarded as the theory of the individual firm and of the distribution of the product resulting from the employment of a given quantity of resources, the classical theory has made a contribution to economic

thinking which cannot be impugned. It is impossible to think clearly on the subject without this theory as a part of one's apparatus of thought.

(Ibid.: 339–40)

Keynes repeated this evaluation of classical theory in Chapter 24:

> if our central controls succeed in establishing an aggregate volume of output corresponding to full employment as nearly as is practicable, the classical theory comes back into its own from this point onwards. If we suppose the volume of output to be given i.e. to be determined by forces outside the classical scheme of thought, then there is no objection to be raised against the classical analysis of the manner in which private self-interest will determine what in particular is produced, in what proportions the factors of production will be combined to produce it, and how the value of the final product will be distributed between them.
>
> (Ibid.: 378–9)

Classical theory explains how a given quantity of employed resources will be used and the distribution of income. But Keynes did not believe that classical theory could explain the determination of the level of employment of available resources. He viewed the determination of the level of employment as a non-allocative process and, hence, beyond classical theory. Thus, he saw a need to encompass classical theory within a more general theory that could explain the level of employment. The non-classical theory of employment would be able to explain a new non-allocative phenomenon, that of involuntary unemployment. In contrast, classical theory could only explain frictional and voluntary unemployment, the two types of unemployment that may arise in the allocation of a fixed quantity of labour services between alternative uses including leisure.

The macro–micro structure

The General Theory is general not only in the sense of encompassing classical theory but also in the sense of being concerned with the macro behaviour of the economic system. 'This book . . . has evolved into what is primarily a study of the forces which determine changes in the scale of output and employment as a whole' (*C.W.* VII: xxii). This latter sense of 'general' is made clear in the Preface to the French edition:

> I have called my theory a *general* theory. I mean by this that I am chiefly concerned with the behaviour of the economic system as a whole, – with aggregate incomes, aggregate profits, aggregate output, aggregate employment, aggregate investment, aggregate saving rather than with the incomes, profits, output, employment, investment and saving of particular industries, firms or individuals. And I argue that important

> mistakes have been made through extending to the system as a whole conclusions which have been correctly arrived at in respect of a part of it taken in isolation.
>
> (*C.W.* VII: xxxii)

The two senses of 'general' come down to the same thing. Keynes believed that classical theory is the microeconomic theory of allocation of a given quantity of resources. It could not adequately explain the macroeconomic question of the determination of the aggregate level of employment of the available resources. He sought to encompass classical microeconomics in a more general framework which could also deal with macroeconomic phenomena. Classical theory had to be generalized beyond the special case of full employment of available resources.

The need for generalization through the development of an adequate macroeconomic analysis of employment arose because 'important mistakes had been made'. These 'important mistakes' constitute the fallacy of composition: 'extending to the system as a whole conclusions which had been correctly arrived at in respect of a part of it taken in isolation'. This fallacy of composition is detailed in Chapter 19 in the analysis of the effects of changes in money-wages:

> In any given industry we have a demand schedule for the product relating the quantities which can be sold to the prices asked; we have a series of supply schedules relating the prices which will be asked for the sale of different quantities on various bases of costs; and these schedules between them lead up to a further schedule which, on the assumption that other costs are unchanged (except as a result of the change in output), give us the demand for labour schedule in the industry relating the quantity of employment to different levels of wages, the shape of the curve at any point furnishing the elasticity of demand for labour. This conception is then transferred without substantial modification to industry as a whole; and it is supposed, by a parity of reasoning, that we have a demand schedule for labour in industry as whole relating the quantity of employment to different levels of wages.
>
> If this is the groundwork of the argument . . . , surely it is fallacious. For the demand schedules for particular industries can only be constructed on some fixed assumption as to the nature of the demand and supply schedules of other industries and as to the amount of the aggregate effective demand. It is invalid, therefore, to transfer our assumption that the aggregate effective demand is fixed. Yet this assumption reduces the argument to an *ignoratio elenchi*. For, whilst no one would wish to deny the proposition that a reduction in money-wages *accompanied by the same aggregate effective demand as before* will be associated with an increase in employment, the precise question at issue

> is whether the reduction in money-wages will or will not be accompanied by the same aggregate effective demand as before measured in money, or, at any rate, by an aggregate effective demand which is not reduced in full proportion to the reduction in money-wages (i.e. which is somewhat greater measured in wage-units). But if the classical theory is not allowed to extend by analogy its conclusions in respect of a particular industry to industry as a whole, it is wholly unable to answer the question what effect on employment a reduction in money-wages will have. For it has no method of analysis wherewith to tackle the problem.
>
> (*C.W.* VII: 258–60)

The fallacy of composition occurs in the move from the microeconomic analysis to the macroeconomic analysis. The microeconomic analysis of the demand for labour in an individual industry is based on the assumption of a fixed level of aggregate demand. In moving to the macroeconomic analysis of the aggregate demand for labour for industry as a whole Keynes believed that classical theorists had maintained the assumption, tacitly, of a fixed level of aggregate demand. 'The idea that we can safely neglect the aggregate demand function is fundamental to the Ricardian economics' (ibid.: 32). This neglect of aggregate demand is formalized in Say's Law that supply creates its own demand. It arose, Keynes believed, 'by a false analogy from some kind of non-exchange Robinson Crusoe economy' (ibid.: 20). Classical theorists presume that there is always sufficient aggregate demand and hence that 'we can safely neglect' the demand-side when analysing the effects of changes in money-wages. But, as Keynes recognized, this implies that classical theory can only deal consistently with the special case of full-employment equilibrium. Any shift from that equilibrium due to a change in money-wages would have implications for aggregate demand, thereby rendering the existing aggregate demand-for-labour schedule inappropriate. Hence, as Keynes concluded, classical theory 'has no method of analysis wherewith to tackle the problem'.

Keynes saw the fallacy of composition as running throughout classical theory. In his discussion of saving and investment in Chapter 7, Keynes stressed 'the vital difference between the theory of the economic behaviour of the aggregate and the theory of the behaviour of the individual unit, in which we assume that changes in the individual's own demand do not affect his income' (*C.W.* VII: 85). In particular, individuals may change their saving decisions but at the aggregate level equilibrium requires that desired saving must equal the given level of investment, with this equality being brought about by changes in aggregate income. Similarly, individuals may change their demand for money but, in aggregate, equilibrium requires that the demand for money equals the fixed money stock with the adjustment mechanism again involving changes in aggregate income.

Thus, for Keynes, classical theory could provide an analysis of the partial equilibrium effects of changes in individuals' decisions but it could not deal with the aggregate implications of such behaviour. Classical theory, through its attachment to the Ricardian view of the unimportance of aggregate demand, had no macroeconomic analysis of the aggregate consequences of individual behaviour. Keynes's *General Theory* is an attempt to provide a more general theory that extended economic theory to the problems of aggregate outcomes other than the special case of full employment.

In generalizing economic theory beyond the basic assumptions of classical theory, Keynes recognized that this would require a fundamental restructuring of economic theory. He saw classical theory as being divided between the theory of value (i.e. the demand-and-supply theory of price determination) and the theory of money and prices (i.e. the quantity theory of money). He believed that there had been little attempt to relate these two components of classical theory and this had, inevitably, created confusion:

> We have all of us become used to finding ourselves sometimes on the one side of the moon and sometimes on the other, without knowing what route or journey connects them, related, apparently, after the fashion of our waking and our dreaming lives.
>
> (*C.W.* VII: 292)

Keynes considered that: 'The division of Economics between the Theory of Value and Distribution on the one hand and the Theory of Money on the other is, I think, a false division' (293). He proposed an alternative dichotomy:

> The right dichotomy is, I suggest, between the Theory of the Individual Industry or Firm and of the rewards and the distribution between different uses of a *given* quantity of resources on the one hand, and the Theory of Output and Employment *as a whole* on the other hand.
>
> (Ibid.: 293; emphasis in original)

Thus, Keynes believed that the appropriate structure of economic theory is a dichotomy between the microeconomics of the allocation of a fixed quantity of resources and the macroeconomics of aggregate employment. Classical theory provided the starting point for the former. Keynes sought to develop the latter. Keynes's micro–macro structure did not maintain the classical dichotomy between the demand-and-supply theory of price determination and the quantity theory of money. Rather, Keynes believed that both individual-level and aggregate outcomes are the result of the interaction of demand and supply. Hence he sought to generalize demand-and-supply theory by developing a complementary aggregate demand-and-supply analysis of price determination to replace the quantity theory of money.

Causal analysis

One of Keynes's principal criticisms of classical theory is its lack of realism. He believed that classical theory does not explain the actual causal mechanisms operating in the macro economy. Thus, for example, in the appendix to Chapter 19 on Pigou's *Theory of Unemployment*, Keynes rejected Pigou's analysis on the following grounds:

> we may regard his book as a non-causative investigation into the functional relationship which determines what level of real wages will correspond to any given level of employment. But it is not capable of telling us what determines the *actual* level of employment; and on the problem of involuntary unemployment it has no direct bearing.
>
> (*C.W.* VII: 275)

In contrast, in his own analysis, Keynes adopted a realistic approach to economic model-building. His method of analysis involved trying to set out the causal mechanisms which result in the observed economic phenomena. Keynes proceeded by first identifying the determinants of individual decisions and then considering the likely aggregate consequences of any changes in these determinants. Thus his causal analysis begins with the microfoundations before moving on to the macro implications. The macro analysis considers two types of effects: direct and indirect. Direct effects are the initial aggregate impact of any specific change without any feedback effects through induced changes in the three variables: the propensity to consume, the marginal efficiency of capital and the rate of interest. The indirect effects (or repercussions) are the feedback effects through the induced changes in these three variables.

This method of analysis is used in Chapter 19 to consider the effects of a reduction in money-wages:

> Let us, then, apply our own method of analysis to answering the problem. It falls into two parts. (1) Does a reduction in money-wages have a direct tendency, *cet. par.*, to increase employment, '*cet. par.*' being taken to mean that the propensity to consume, the schedule of the marginal efficiency of capital and the rate of interest are the same as before for the community as a whole? And (2) does a reduction in money-wages have a certain or probable tendency to affect employment in a particular direction through its certain or probable repercussions on these three factors?
>
> (*C.W.* VII: 260)

This method of analysis is also used in Chapter 8 in the discussion of the likely consequences for the propensity to consume of a change in the rate of interest (ibid.: 93–4).

Throughout *The General Theory* Keynes is critical of the classical theory's assumptions about the causal processes in the actual economy. In Chapter 2 Keynes rejects the classical labour supply function on the grounds that 'ordinary experience tells us, beyond doubt' that the wage bargain determines the money-wage and labour reacts differently depending on whether a fall in the real wage is due to a rise in the general price-level or a fall in the money-wage. This asymmetry is seen to arise from labour's concern with relative wages. In Chapter 11 Keynes criticizes the implicit assumption in classical theory of a static state which 'imports into it a large element of unreality' (*C.W.* VII: 146). Keynes believed that his concepts of user cost and the marginal efficiency of capital would rectify this, 'bringing it back to reality'.

Keynes's concern with basing his theory on realistic assumptions which relate to the actual decision-making processes of individuals is apparent in his focus on consumption and investment, rather than saving:

> Clearness of mind on this matter is best reached, perhaps, by thinking in terms of decisions to consume (or to refrain from consuming) rather than of decisions to save. A decision to consume or not to consume truly lies within the power of the individual; so does a decision to invest or not to invest. The amounts of aggregate income and of aggregate saving are the *results* of the free choices of individuals whether or not to consume and whether or not to invest; but they are neither of them capable of assuming an independent value resulting from a separate set of decisions taken irrespective of the decisions concerning consumption and investment.
>
> (*C.W.* VII: 64–5)

A causal analysis has to begin with consumption and investment decisions since these decisions are 'within the power' of individuals. Saving and income are 'results', that is, outcomes caused by the consumption and investment decisions of individuals. This causal analysis ensures that saving and investment are not treated as equivalent in causal terms. As Keynes points out in Chapter 16, it is a fallacy to treat the desire to hold wealth as a desire to hold capital. This fallacy is fundamental to the Ricardian tradition of Say's Law and the neglect of aggregate demand. 'Saving . . . is a mere residual' (ibid.: 64) and not to be identified with investment.

Keynes saw a similar confusion in the classical treatment of saving and the demand for money. The decision to reserve some current income for future consumption is causally quite distinct from the decision as to the form in which this command over future consumption will be held. In Keynes's analysis the theoretical structure is developed with respect to the causal distinction between the two decisions. The first decision is modelled by the consumption function, the second by the liquidity preference function.

The context of behaviour

A key element in Keynes's analysis is his recognition of the significance of the monetary context of behaviour. Keynes believed that 'money enters into the economic scheme in an essential and peculiar manner' (*C.W.* VII: xxii). In particular, Keynes viewed money as having a vital role in the dynamic adjustment of the economy through time: 'For the importance of money essentially flows from its being a link between the present and the future' (ibid.: 293). The role of money in linking the present and the future gives rise to the characteristic feature of a monetary economy: 'A monetary economy . . . is essentially one in which changing views about the future are capable of influencing the quantity of employment and not merely its direction' (ibid.: xxii).

Thus, for Keynes, it is the monetary context of behaviour that creates the possibility of expectations about the future causing involuntary unemployment. Understanding the causal significance of the monetary context is, therefore, a necessary prerequisite for understanding the importance of uncertainty in *The General Theory*. (See Gerrard 1995 for a more detailed discussion of the importance of the monetary context of behaviour in Keynes's analysis.)

Rationality

In analysing the behaviour of individual agents, Keynes found the classical assumption of rational economic agents a useful starting point. In particular, in retaining the first fundamental postulate of classical theory that the wage is equal to the marginal product of labour, Keynes implicitly retained the assumption of profit-maximizing firms. The first postulate is the condition for profit-maximiziation given pure competition. The profit-maximization assumption is explicitly stated in Chapter 7: 'the volume of employment (and consequently of output and real income) is fixed by the entrepreneur under the motive of seeking to maximise his present and prospective profits' (*C.W.* VII: 77). But Keynes encompassed the classical conception of rationality within a much thicker analysis of individual behaviour which allows for the psychological and habitual aspects of economic behaviour. These aspects are given much prominence in his analyses of consumption, long-term expectations and the rate of interest.

In his analysis of consumption, Keynes distinguished three principal determinants: (a) income; (b) 'other objective attendant circumstances' including changes in the wage-unit, windfall changes in capital values, changes in the rate of time-discounting, and changes in expected future income; and (c) 'the subjective needs and the psychological propensities and habits of the individuals' (*C.W.* VII: 91) and the distribution of income. Keynes detailed these subjective factors in terms of eight motives for saving, including precaution, foresight and bequest. Keynes also listed some of the determinants of these habitual motives: race, education, religion and current morals, and present hopes and past experience. In the short period, Keynes believed, the subjective factors could be taken as given except in abnormal or revolutionary circumstances. But changes in subjective factors would have to be allowed for in longer-period historical studies.

The most important contribution of Keynes's emphasis on the psychological aspects of consumer behaviour is his proposition that the marginal propensity to consume is less than unity:

> The fundamental psychological law, upon which we are entitled to depend with great confidence both *a priori* from our knowledge of human nature and from the detailed facts of experience, is that men are disposed, as a rule and on the average, to increase their consumption as their income increases, but not by as much as the increase in their income.
> (*C.W.* VII: 96)

This fundamental psychological law is based on both introspection as well as empirical evidence. Keynes considered this law to be primarily a short-period phenomenon when individuals tend to maintain their habitual levels of consumption in the face of cyclical fluctuations. Keynes contrasted this short-period habitual behaviour with 'more permanent psychological propensities' when individuals have 'time enough to adapt themselves to changed objective circumstances' (ibid.: 97).

In his analysis of the determinants of investment, Keynes encompassed the profit-maximizing assumption within a more general framework. (See Gerrard 1994b for a more detailed discussion of Keynes's analysis of investment, particularly the role of animal spirits.) The marginal efficiency of capital represents the calculation of the internal rate of return on the basis of the prospective returns from capital projects. The prospective returns depend on the state of long-term expectations comprising the most probable forecast and the state of confidence. Keynes considered the state of confidence to be of much importance in determining actual investment behaviour but that it had been given little attention by economists since '[t]here is . . . not much to be said about the state of confidence *a priori*' (*C.W.* VII: 149). As a result, the state of confidence needs to be studied by 'actual observation of markets and business psychology' (ibid.).

Given the 'extreme precariousness of the basis of knowledge on which our estimates of prospective yield have to be made' (ibid.), Keynes believed that behaviour depends on the convention that 'the existing state of affairs will continue indefinitely, except in so far as we have specific reasons to expect a change' (ibid.: 152). The recognition of the essential conventional aspect of long-term expectations implies that investment cannot be modelled purely on a choice-theoretic basis:

> human decisions affecting the future, whether personal or political or economic, cannot depend on strict mathematical expectation, since the basis for making such calculations does not exist; and . . . it is our innate urge to activity which makes the wheels go round, our rational selves choosing between the alternatives as best we are able, calculating where we can, but often falling back for our motive on whim or sentiment or chance.
>
> (*C.W.* VII: 162–3)

Investment behaviour needs to be modelled partly as (rational) calculation but also partly as the outcome of other motives including 'animal spirits – of a spontaneous urge to action rather than inaction' (ibid.: 161).

Psychological aspects also play a key role in Keynes's analysis of liquidity preference and the rate of interest: 'It is evident . . . that the rate of interest is a highly psychological phenomenon' (*C.W.* VII: 202). Rather than 'highly psychological', Keynes considered the rate of interest to be more accurately described as 'highly conventional' in that 'its actual value is largely governed by the prevailing view as to what its value is expected to be' (ibid.: 203). Again, the recognition of the conventional element in the determination of the rate of interest implies that the method of analysis cannot be purely deductive but must also involve empirical investigation of actual behaviour.

There is also an implicit view on the limits to rationality in Keynes's distinction between voluntary and involuntary consequences. Voluntary consequences are the immediate results of individual actions whereas involuntary consequences are caused by the feedback from the aggregate effects of individual actions. Thus, for example, voluntary unemployment is caused directly by the labour supply decision, specifically, labour's refusal to accept a wage equal to its marginal product. Involuntary unemployment, on the other hand, is caused indirectly by the lack of effective demand resulting from aggregate outcome of individual consumption and investment decisions. Thus, for Keynes, rationality relates to the direct effects of individual actions, not the total effects, direct and indirect.

Analytical methods

Keynes was acutely aware that he needed to develop a method of analysis that could cope with the analytical difficulties created by the 'complexities and interdependencies of the real world' (*C.W.* VII: 298).The complexity of the economic system rules out a very mechanistic approach in which economic behaviour is modelled formally in a very precise and rigid manner: 'in a study so complex as economics . . . we cannot hope to make completely accurate generalisations' (ibid.: 247). Rather, Keynes adopted a much more open-ended approach in which the emphasis is on providing a method for clear thinking that could be applied to a range of theoretical questions:

> The object of our analysis is, not to provide a machine, or method of blind manipulation, which will furnish an infallible answer, but to provide ourselves with an organised and orderly method of thinking out particular problems; and, after we have reached a provisional conclusion by isolating the complicating factors one by one, we then have to go back on ourselves and allow, as well as we can, for the probable interactions amongst themselves. This is the nature of economic thinking. Any other way of applying our formal principles of thought (without which, however, we shall be lost in the wood) will lead us into error.
>
> (*C.W.* VII: 297)

Keynes's 'organised and orderly method of thinking' is a logical analysis which builds up through a number of stages. In the early stages the analysis is conducted on the basis of temporary assumptions of strict independence between the variables perceived to be the causal determinants. At a later stage in the analysis these temporary assumptions are relaxed to allow for possible interactions between the causal determinants. The aim is to identify the possible causal mechanisms and the likely direction and importance of their effects. From this analysis, provisional conclusions can be drawn about the causes of observed phenomena and the policy implications.

The key step in Keynes's analysis is to isolate the variables in any analytical problem and to classify these variables into one of three types: dependent variables, independent variables and given factors. Dependent variables (or *quaesitum*) are the variables to be explained. In *The General Theory*, Keynes identified two dependent variables: the volume of employment and the national income measured in wage-units. His analysis sought to detail the causal processes which determine these two variables.

Having identified his two dependent variables, Keynes classified the causal determinants as independent variables or given factors, outlining the basis of this classification as follows:

> The division of the determinants of the economic system into the two groups of given factors and independent variables is, of course, quite arbitrary from any absolute standpoint. The division must be made entirely on the basis of experience, so as to correspond on the one hand to the factors in which the changes seem to be slow or so little relevant as to have only a small and comparatively negligible short-term influence on our *quaesitum*; and on the other hand to those factors in which the changes are found in practice to exercise a dominant influence on our *quaesitum*.
>
> (*C.W.* VII: 247)

Independent variables are those factors which exercise a 'dominant influence' on the dependent variables. In contrast the given factors are 'slow' to change or 'so little relevant'. Another characteristic of the given factors is that they 'influence our independent variables, but do not completely determine them' (ibid.: 245–6). This latter characteristic is implied by the definition of independence. If a variable is completely determined by given factors then it is not an independent variable. The division between independent variables and given factors is context-specific. It depends on the dependent variables to be explained as well as actual experience as to which causal determinants are 'dominant' or 'slow' or 'so little relevant'.

In *The General Theory*, Keynes identified seven given factors (ibid.: 245):

1 'the existing skill and quantity of available equipment';
2 'the existing quality and quantity of available equipment';
3 'the existing technique';
4 'the degree of competition';
5 'the tastes and habits of the consumer';
6 'the disutility of different intensities of labour and of the activities of supervision and organisation'; and
7 'the social structure', particularly its effects on the distribution of income.

With the exception of consumer tastes and the social structure, the given factors are supply-side influences which determine the aggregate supply function, the labour supply function and the employment function. In particular, these supply-side given factors determine the relationship between employment and any given level of effective demand measured in wage-units. Given the supply-side conditions, the volume of employment depends on the level of effective demand which, in turn, is determined by the independent variables. Thus, the division between independent variables and given factors is fundamental to the analysis. The proposition that involuntary unemployment is caused by insufficient aggregate demand is the inevitable conclusion of Keynes's fundamental belief that employment is the dependent variable to be explained by the independent demand-side variables with supply-side factors taken as given.

Initially, under the temporary assumption of strict independence, Keynes identified three independent variables: (a) the propensity to consume; (b) the marginal efficiency of capital; and (c) the rate of interest. Taken together, these three independent variables determine the level of effective demand and, hence, the volume of employment. Keynes criticized classical theory for failing to identify these independent variables:

> the traditional analysis is faulty because it has failed to isolate correctly the independent variables of the system. Saving and investment are the determinates of the system, not the determinants. They are the twin

> results of the system's determinants, namely, the propensity to consume, the schedule of the marginal efficiency of capital and the rate of interest. These determinants are, indeed, themselves complex and each is capable of being affected by prospective changes in the others. But they remain independent in the sense that their values cannot be inferred from one another. The traditional analysis has been aware that saving depends on income but it has overlooked the fact that, when investment changes, income must necessarily change in just that degree which is necessary to make the change in saving equal to the change in investment.
>
> (*C.W.* VII: 183–4)

Keynes believed that classical theory treated investment and saving as independent variables but, from the perspective of his analysis, investment and saving are not independent since the multiplier process ensures that any change in investment causes an equal change in saving. Thus Keynes focused attention on the underlying independent determinants of investment and saving, namely, the propensity to consume which determines saving and the marginal efficiency of capital and the rate of interest which together determine investment.

But, as Keynes pointed out, these three independent variables are themselves capable of further analysis. Keynes recognized that changes in any of these independent variables could affect the other independent variables. For example, Keynes considered the rate of interest as one of the 'other attendant circumstances' which could influence the propensity to consume. This led Keynes to move beyond the temporary independence assumptions in order to discover the 'ultimate independent variables'. Keynes discovered three such variables: (a) 'the three fundamental psychological factors, namely, the psychological propensity to consume, the psychological attitude to liquidity and the psychological expectation of future yield from capital-assets'; (b) 'the wage-unit as determined by the bargains reached between employers and employed'; and (c) 'the quantity of money as determined by the action of the central bank' (*C.W.* VII: 246–7). However, these ultimate independent variables should not necessarily be assumed to be the ultimate starting point of the causal process under analysis; further analysis of the ultimate independent variables is possible: 'But these again would be capable of being subjected to further analysis, and are not, so to speak, our ultimate atomic independent elements' (ibid.: 247). Thus, for example, when Keynes considered the likely consequences of changes in the wage-unit, he recognized that changes in the wage-unit could affect the other ultimate independent variables, namely, the three fundamental psychological factors.

Keynes also suggested a further classification of the causal determinants with regard to the practical objective of developing policies to achieve desired aggregate outcomes: 'One final task might be to select those variables which can be deliberately controlled or managed by central authority in the kind of system in which we actually live' (ibid.). In addition to his assumptions with regard to the classification of variables, Keynes also made several simplifying assumptions. These simplifying assumptions are not realistic in the sense of being judgements based on experience about the degree of relevancy or speed of change. Rather, the simplifying assumptions are unrealistic, used to abstract the analysis from irrelevant complications. He made four principal simplifying assumptions, either explicitly or implicitly: (a) profit maximization; (b) pure competition; (c) correct short-term expectations; and (d) homogeneous labour supply. The first three of these simplifying assumptions are implicit in Keynes's retention of the first fundamental postulate of classical theory that the wage equals the marginal product of labour. In Keynes's analysis this postulate implies a unique relationship between the real wage and the volume of employment. It has no causal significance as in classical theory where the first postulate represents the demand-for-labour schedule. The implicit assumption of correct short-term expectations is a reflection of Keynes's concern with explaining involuntary unemployment. Incorrect short-term expectations are one of the 'various inexactnesses of adjustment' which cause frictional unemployment and, therefore, are irrelevant for Keynes's analytical task. Subsequently Keynes stated that he would make this assumption explicit in any new edition of *The General Theory*:

> I now feel that if I were writing the book again I should begin by setting forth my theory on the assumption that short-period expectations were always fulfilled; and then have a subsequent chapter showing what difference it makes when short-period expectations are disappointed.
> (*C.W.* XIV: 181)

Thus Keynes's analytical method provides 'an organised and orderly method of thinking' in which the dependent variables, independent variables and given factors are identified and the causal processes analysed initially under temporary assumptions of strict independence which are subsequently relaxed. This gives a framework in which the effects of a change in one of the independent variables can be analysed. The first stage of the analysis is to consider the direct effects of the change under the *ceteris paribus* assumption of no changes in the other independent variables. The second stage is to relax the *ceteris paribus* assumption to analyse the indirect effects. This is the approach which Keynes applied in Chapter 19 to the effects of a change in the wage-unit. Up to that point in his analysis Keynes had treated the wage-unit as a fixed independent variable. In Chapter 19 he outlines the possible causal processes that may be initiated by a change in the wage-unit. His concern was to discover whether or not a change in the wage-unit will affect the level of effective demand measured in wage-units and, in turn, the volume of employment. Keynes suggested seven possible indirect effects of a change in the wage-unit: 'This is not a complete catalogue of all the possible reactions of wage reductions in the complex real world. But the above cover, I think, those which are usually the most important' (*C.W.* VII: 264). After further analysis of these causal processes he concluded that there is 'no ground for the belief that a flexible wage policy is capable of maintaining a state of continuous full employment' (ibid.: 267). A similar analytical method is used in Chapter 8 to consider the effects of changes in objective factors on aggregate consumption.

Equilibrium and dynamics

For Keynes, *The General Theory* represented a move away from the predominantly static analysis of his *Treatise on Money* towards a dynamic analysis able to deal with changes in the volume of output and employment. Keynes considered his failure to deal with changes in the volume of output and employment in the *Treatise on Money* to be 'the outstanding fault of the theoretical parts of that work':

> My so-called 'fundamental equations' were an instantaneous picture taken on the assumption of a given output. They attempted to show how, assuming the given output, forces could develop which involved a profit-disequilibrium, and thus required a change in the level of output. But the dynamic development, as distinct from the instantaneous picture, was left incomplete and extremely confused.
>
> (*C.W.* VII: xxii)

The General Theory represented Keynes's attempt to provide an analysis of the 'dynamic development' of the economy. He saw the emphasis on static equilibrium rather than the dynamics of disequilibrium as a failing of classical theory which he traced back to Hume:

> Hume began the practice amongst economists of stressing the importance of the equilibrium position as compared with the ever-shifting transition towards it, though he was still enough of a mercantilist not to overlook the fact that it is in the transition that we actually have our being . . .
>
> (Ibid.: 343 fn. 3)

In developing a dynamic analysis, Keynes retained the concept of equilibrium as part of his 'organised and orderly method of thinking'. In particular, he sought to show how the macro economy could move towards a stable equilibrium characterized by a volume of employment less than full employment.

Keynes distinguished between two types of equilibrium: stationary equilibrium and shifting equilibrium (see Kregel 1976). The difference between these two types of equilibrium depends on the nature of the state of expectations about the future. A stationary equilibrium is the equilibrium outcome 'in a world in which our views concerning the future are fixed and reliable in all respects' (*C.W.* VII: 293). Keynes viewed classical theory as a theory of stationary equilibrium concerned with the distribution of (fully employed) resources between different uses. The fundamental equations of the *Treatise on Money* characterized a stationary equilibrium. Keynes further divided the types of stationary equilibrium depending on whether the economy is 'stationary' or 'non-static'. These distinctions were first introduced in Chapter 8 in his discussion of the propensity to consume and were discussed further in Chapter 21 on the theory of prices. In the case of a non-static economy, that is, an economy subject to change, stationary equilibrium requires that 'all things are foreseen from the beginning' (ibid.).

The theory of shifting equilibrium, in contrast, is concerned with 'the problems of the real world in which our previous expectations are liable to disappointment and expectations concerning the future affect what we do today' (*C.W.* VII: 293–4). The theory of shifting equilibrium deals with situations of imperfect foresight in which the state of expectations may change in the light of realized results. Changes in the state of expectations affect current outcomes, particularly the volume of employment. This causal link between the future and the present is created by the monetary context of behaviour. Keynes saw the theory of shifting equilibrium as a development of demand-and-supply theory:

> our method of analysing the economic behaviour of the present under the influence of changing ideas about the future is one which depends on the interaction of supply and demand, and is in this way linked up with our fundamental theory of value. We are thus led to a more general theory, which includes the classical theory with which we are familiar, as a special case.
>
> (*C.W.* VII: xxii–xxiii)

The theory of shifting equilibrium represented a generalization of the classical theory of stationary equilibrium to allow for 'the influence of changing ideas about the future'. In particular, the state of long-term expectations affected the level of investment which, in turn, affected the level of effective demand and, hence, the volume of output and employment.

An important implication of Keynes's view that the appropriate theory of shifting equilibrium is a form of demand-and-supply theory is that his concept of equilibrium has two dimensions, as in classical theory. Equilibrium represents both a point of rest and market-clearing. However, unlike classical theory, market-clearing in Keynes's analysis is relevant only in the context of the goods market (aggregate demand equals aggregate supply), the money market (the demand for money equals the supply of money), and, by implication, other financial markets. Equilibrium does not imply full employment in the neoclassical sense of market-clearing in the labour market with the demand for labour equal to the supply of labour. In Keynes's analysis, employment is not determined by an allocative process in which the real wage adjusts in response to labour market conditions. In effect, Keynes denies the relevance of the concept of an aggregate market for labour. (See Gerrard 1995 for a more detailed discussion of this point.)

Within the dynamic theory of shifting equilibrium, Keynes differentiated three stages of analysis. These are set out in Chapter 5, 'Expectation as Determining Output and Employment'. The first stage of analysis is to determine the long-period equilibrium associated with a constant state of expectation:

> If we suppose a state of expectation to continue for a sufficient length of time for the effect on employment to have worked itself out so completely that there is, broadly speaking, no piece of employment going on which would not have taken place if the new state of expectation had always existed, the steady level of employment thus attained may be called the long-period employment corresponding to that state of expectation. It follows that, although expectation may change so frequently that the actual level of employment has never had time to reach the long-period employment corresponding to the existing state of expectation, nevertheless every state of expectation has its definite corresponding level of long-period employment.
>
> (*C.W.* VII: 48)

The long-period employment is that volume of employment associated with a state of expectation that has existed for a sufficient period of time such that there has been full adjustment. It is a centre of gravitation towards which the system is tending. However, in the actual course of events, the state of expectation is likely to change before the existing adjustment process is complete, leading to a new long-period centre of gravitation for the economy and a new adjustment process. In a footnote Keynes acknowledged that the level of long-period employment need not necessarily be constant. In a non-static economy 'the only condition is that the existing expectations should have been foreseen sufficiently far ahead' (*C.W.* VII: 48 fn. 1) (see Harcourt 1981).

The second stage of analysis is to consider 'the process of transition to a long-period position due to a change in expectation, which is not confused or interrupted by any further change in expectation' (*C.W.* VII: 48–9). The process of transition is the dynamic analysis of the sequence of movements from one long-period position to another. As an example, Keynes sketched out the process of transition to a new long-period position with a higher level of employment, suggesting that initially employment may change little but subsequently may increase to a level higher than the new long-period level to which it would eventually fall back.

The final stage of the dynamic analysis is to consider the actual course of events which will consist of a complex of different processes of transition due to changes in the state of expectation:

> An uninterrupted process of transition . . . to a new long-period position can be complicated in detail. But the actual course of events is more complicated still. For the state of expectation is liable to constant change, a new expectation being superimposed before the previous change has fully worked itself out; so that the economic machine is occupied at any given time with a number of overlapping activities, the existence of which is due to various states of expectation.
>
> (*C.W.* VII: 50)

This method of dynamic analysis is applied by Keynes in his discussion of the multiplier in Chapter 10. Here Keynes distinguished between 'the logical theory of the multiplier, which holds good continuously, without time-lag, at all moments of time' and 'the consequences of an expansion in the capital-goods industries which take gradual effect, subject to time-lag and only after an interval' (ibid.: 122). The 'logical theory of the multiplier' is a long-period theory which determines the change in long-period output and employment consequent on a permanent change in investment. The 'consequences of an expansion in the capital-goods industry' relates to the process of transition to the new long-period position. This process of transition depends crucially on the degree to which the expansion is foreseen.

Keynes distinguished between the long period and the short period in two senses. First, the long period, as discussed above, is the period required for full adjustment to the equilibrium position associated with a constant state of expectation. In this case the short period refers to the process of transition to the new long-period position. Second, the long period is also used by Keynes as the period over which the given factors may change. In the short period the given factors remain constant. This second sense of the distinction is used, for example, in the discussion of the consumption function. In the short period psychological, social and other given factors are constant so that changes in consumption are due to changes in income and not changes in the propensity to consume. Keynes also used this second sense of the distinction in his theory of prices in Chapter 21. In the short period, changes in the price level are a consequence of changes in the level of employment which affects marginal prime costs. In the long period changes in the price level are due to changes in the given factors, specifically new techniques and new equipment.

Keynes also used the notion of the long run in the context of the long-run relationship between the price level and the quantity of money. Keynes described this long-run relationship as 'a question for historical generalisation rather than for pure theory' (306). Keynes used the term 'long run' to describe actual historical outcomes over a relatively lengthy time period whereas the short period and long period are theoretical constructs for the analysis of hypothetical changes in the state of expectations or given factors (see Harcourt 1981).

The state of expectations consists of short-term expectations of immediate market conditions relating to the pricing and output decisions which are revised on a 'daily' basis and long-term expectations of the more distant future relating to the investment decision. (See Gerrard 1994a for a more detailed treatment of Keynes's analysis of the state of expectations.) Keynes considered both short-term and long-term expectations to be primarily based on the convention that 'the existing state of affairs will continue indefinitely except in so far as we have specific reasons to expect a change' (*C.W.* VII: 152). However, the difference in the term of the two types of expectations means that they are evaluated in fundamentally different ways. Short-term expectations are revised 'daily', by which Keynes meant 'the shortest interval after which the firm is free to revise its decision as to how much employment to offer' (ibid.: 47 fn. 1). Short-term expectations can be checked at short intervals against realized results, so much so that Keynes believed that short-term expectations could be 'approximately eliminated or replaced by realised results' (ibid.: 51). Long-term expectations, however, by their very nature cannot be fully checked at short intervals and hence cannot be modelled by realized results. Thus long-term expectations are one of the 'ultimate independent variables' in Keynes's analysis with a crucial role in determining investment and, hence, the volume of output and employment.

The mathematical method

Within *The General Theory* Keynes made use of the mathematical method to derive expressions for aggregate demand (Chapter 3), aggregate supply (Chapter 4), the multiplier (Chapter 10), the employment function (Chapter 20) and the relationship between the price level and the quantity of money (Chapter 21). The mathematical method provides a powerful tool with which to formally model economic behaviour and to deduce the implications. However, Keynes was very critical of how the mathematical method was being used in economics. He referred to these misuses as 'pseudo-mathematical methods':

> It is a great fault of symbolic pseudo-mathematical methods of formalising a system of economic analysis . . . that they expressly assume strict independence between the factors involved and lose all their cogency and authority if this hypothesis is disallowed; whereas, in ordinary discourse, where we are not blindly manipulating but know all the time what we are doing and what the words mean, we can keep

'at the back of our heads' the necessary reserves and qualifications and the adjustments which we shall have to make later on, in a way in which we cannot keep complicated partial differentials 'at the back' of several pages of algebra which assume that they all vanish. Too large a proportion of recent 'mathematical' economics are merely concoctions, as imprecise as the initial assumptions they rest on, which allow the author to lose sight of the complexities and interdependencies of the real world in a maze of pretentious and unhelpful symbols.

(*C.W.* VII: 297–8)

'Pseudo-mathematical methods' are characterized by their use of the assumption of strict independence between the determinants. This leads to mathematical models of the economic system which are too limited and obscure 'the complexities and interdependencies of the real world'. Keynes was particularly critical of Pigou's *Theory of Unemployment* as an example of 'the pitfalls of a pseudo-mathematical method, which can make no progress except by making everything a function of a single variable and assuming that all the partial differentials vanish' (ibid.: 275). Pseudo-mathematical methods sacrifice realism and complexity for simplicity and tractability. Mathematical methods could deal with multivariate functions and partial differentials but the analysis is much more complicated and less tractable. Hence Keynes believed that it may be more useful to deal with real world complexities by using a much more informal approach, 'an organised and orderly method of thinking', with the mathematical method limited to those parts of the analysis which can be usefully simplified. The usefulness of the mathematical method is determined by the object of analysis not vice versa.

The units of analysis

Keynes discussed the nature of the appropriate units of analysis in Chapter 4 of *The General Theory*. (See Chapter 7 by Bradford and Harcourt in Volume 1 of this work.) He was much concerned by the difficulties associated with the three traditional units of analysis at the aggregate level: real income, the capital stock and the general price-level. Keynes believed that all three units involve aggregation problems for which there are no solutions. But Keynes did not consider these difficulties as a barrier to aggregate analysis:

these difficulties are rightly regarded as 'conundrums'. They are 'purely theoretical' in the sense that they never perplex, or indeed enter in any way into, business decisions and have no relevance to the causal sequence of economic events, which are clear-cut and determinate in spite of the quantitative indeterminacy of these concepts. It is natural, therefore, to conclude that they not only lack precision but are unnecessary.

(*C.W.* VII: 39)

The aggregation problems associated with the traditional units of analysis could not be solved. Hence these units of analysis are vague concepts which may be used for the purposes of historical and statistical comparisons:

> The fact that two incommensurable collections of miscellaneous objects cannot in themselves provide the material for a quantitative analysis need not, of course, prevent us from making approximate statistical comparisons, depending on some broad element of judgment rather than of strict calculation, which may possess significance and validity within certain limits. But the proper place for such things as net real output and the general level of prices lies within the field of historical and social description, and their purpose should be to satisfy historical or social curiosity, a purpose for which perfect precision . . . is neither usual nor necessary.
>
> (Ibid.: 39–40)

But the traditional units of analysis could not be used for theoretical purposes since they lack the necessary precision of definition. Furthermore, their exclusion from the theoretical analysis presented no difficulties since the traditional units of analysis have no causal significance.

Keynes proposed instead that aggregate analysis should be based on two fundamental units:

> In dealing with the theory of employment I propose, therefore, to make use of only two fundamental units of quantity, namely, quantities of money-value and quantities of employment. The first of these is strictly homogeneous, and the second can be made so.
>
> (Ibid.: 41)

Keynes measured the quantity of employment in labour-units (with appropriate adjustments for the heterogeneity of labour) and quantities of money-value in wage-units, where the wage-unit is defined as the money-wage of a labour-unit. Keynes believed that these two units are free from the theoretical difficulties which plagued the traditional units of analysis. He also recognized a third fundamental unit of analysis, namely, time.

KEYNES'S METHOD AND METHODOLOGY: AN ASSESSMENT

Keynes's views on methodology and method as expressed in *The General Theory* can be considered as embodying a radical cluster of methodological beliefs which allow for the development of economic theory beyond the limitations of neoclassical theory. In contrast, orthodox theorists tend to be wedded to a more conservative cluster of methodological beliefs which, from the perspective of Lakatos's methodology of scientific research programmes, provide a protective belt and associated immunising strategems with which to defend the characteristic hard-core beliefs of neoclassical theory, especially the notion of full employment as a unique and stable point of equilibrium.

In broad terms, Keynes's radical cluster of methodological beliefs is characterized by three main elements: (a) realism; (b) empiricism; and (c) openness.

Realism

Keynes's method of analysis aims to explain the causal mechanisms underlying observed economic phenomena (see Lawson 1989). Causal analysis requires realistic assumptions. It contrasts sharply with the instrumentalist methods advocated by Friedman (1953) in which the usefulness of economic models is judged by their predictive power. From the instrumentalist perspective the realism of assumptions is an irrelevant consideration since the objective of the analysis is not to explain causal mechanisms. The realistic aspect of Keynes's method is exemplified by his treatment of rationality. Keynes made some use of traditional rationality assumptions such as profit maximization as convenient theoretical devices, but his emphasis throughout *The General Theory* is on the actual behavioural patterns of individuals, especially the motivating psychological propensities. Keynes's realistic approach to individual behaviour has much in common with the behavioural approach of Simon (1976), who distinguished between the neoclassical theoretical assumption of substantive rationality and the more realistic assumption of procedural rationality.

Empiricism

Keynes's method of analysis is characterized by the use of logical methods, including mathematics, to deduce the aggregate implications of individual behaviour patterns. But Keynes did not embrace the apriorism of classical theory associated with J.S. Mill in which the truth of economic theory derives from its axiomatic foundations. Keynes applied logical deduction to assumptions justified on empirical grounds as realistic representations of actual behaviour patterns. He adopted the scientific method but recognized the difficulties of conducting conclusive empirical tests. In modern terms, it can be argued that Keynes was aware of the Duhem–Quine thesis of the underdeterminacy of empirical tests (see Cross 1982). Furthermore, Keynes's methodological views have much in common with the 'new view' of science (see Gerrard 1990), particularly his concern with the structure of economic theory, the revolutionary nature of his contribution and the recognition of the socio-political aspect to the dominance of orthodox economic theory. These concerns have obvious parallels with Kuhn's notion of paradigms, scientific communities and scientific revolutions

(Kuhn 1962). Also Keynes's awareness of the rhetorical aspects of *The General Theory*, especially the use of controversy, is a theme in the methodology of economics to which McCloskey (1983, 1986) has drawn much attention recently.

Openness

Keynes's method of analysis is open-ended in order to be able to deal with the 'complexities and interdependencies of the real world'. Analytical methods, by their very nature, imply that the object of analysis is assumed to be atomistic in the sense that the causal determinants are treated as independent variables. The validity of analysis does not depend on whether or not the economic system is deemed to be ultimately atomistic or organic. Rather, it depends on whether or not it is useful to impose temporary independence assumptions in order to gain some partial understanding of the causal mechanisms. Keynes developed an 'organised and orderly method of thinking' with which to investigate a complex economic system. This method of thinking involved distinguishing between dependent variables, independent variables and given factors. The dynamics of the causal processes are analysed in stages, moving from the long-period (shifting) equilibrium to the process of transition, then on to the actual course of events. Keynes's method is also open-ended in the sense of encompassing both classical theories of the allocation of resources as well as non-classical theories of the level of employment of resources. This 'post-classical' synthesis is no mere eclecticism, a 'pick-and-mix' approach to economic theory. Rather, it represents the attempt to generalize classical theory by defining the limits to its domain of relevance and encompassing it within a more general framework incorporating non-classical theories also with well-defined domains of relevance. It is a pluralism which Dow (1985) has described as the Babylonian mode of thought. This type of pluralism stands in stark contrast to the orthodox reliance on a unitary framework in which all economic behaviour is interpreted as allocative decisions by rational agents. (See Gerrard 1995 for further elaboration of the post-classical nature of Keynes's *General Theory*.)

In summary, Keynes's views on methodology and method form a radical cluster of methodological beliefs characterized by an emphasis on realism, empiricism and openness. As such, they provide an important exemplar of an alternative approach to economic theorizing in contrast to the defensive emphasis on deductivism and instrumentalism in neoclassical economics.

SUMMARY AND CONCLUSIONS

This chapter has provided a detailed review of Keynes's views on methodology and method as set out in *The General Theory*. Keynes has been portrayed as possessing a radical cluster of methodological beliefs emphasizing realism, empiricism and openness. Keynes's method of analysis provides an exemplar of how to approach the study of the dynamic macro behaviour of a monetary production economy in which uncertainty about the future plays a crucial role in determining the level of aggregate activity:

> the *The General Theory* presents a model of a *production* economy, using *money*, moving through *time*, subject to *uncertainty* and the possibility of *error*.
>
> (Chick 1978; as reprinted 1992: 59; emphasis in original)

Hence, with regard to the question of the nature of the Keynesian revolution posed at the outset of this chapter, it is concluded that Keynes's contribution is to both theory and method. His theoretical contribution is to have shown that the demand side is an independent determinant of both the point of equilibrium and the path of adjustment with the implication that there is no automatic tendency to full-employment equilibrium in a monetary production economy. But associated with this theoretical contribution is Keynes's development of an appropriate method of analysis which can furnish a means of understanding the causal nature of a monetary production economy. Thus Keynes's *General Theory* has continued significance for current economic theorizing. A constructive reading of *The General Theory* can provide crucial insights not only into the behaviour of the macro economy but also the appropriate methods of analysis.

ACKNOWLEDGEMENT

I should like to thank Victoria Chick, Sheila Dow and the editors of this volume for many useful comments on an earlier draft of this chapter. The usual disclaimer applies.

33

J.M. KEYNES ON HISTORY AND CONVENTION

John B. Davis

In 1938, two years after the publication of *The General Theory*, Keynes read a paper to the Memoir Club gathered at Tilton entitled 'My Early Beliefs', in which he criticized many of his early philosophical attachments. He confessed that when it came down to disagreements between his friends over knowing which states of mind might be thought intrinsically good, it was not 'a matter of direct inspection, of direct unanalysable intuition about which it was useless and impossible to argue', but '[i]n practice' a matter of 'who could speak with the greatest appearance of clear, undoubting conviction and could best use the accents of infallibility' – G.E. Moore being the acknowledged master of the art (*C.W.* X: 437–8).[1] Keynes's 1938 critique, however, was not only aimed at the early concept of intuition he had inherited from Moore's *Principia Ethica.* In his early attachment to intuition as certain, unfailing direct insight into the nature of what was real, Keynes had also gone on to deny that general rules and conventions played any significant role in judgement: 'we repudiated entirely customary morals, conventions and traditional wisdom' (*C.W.* X: 446). This was hardly in keeping with the answer he had recently given in *The General Theory*, in his famous twelfth chapter on long-term expectation, to the question, 'How then are these highly significant daily, even hourly, revaluations of existing investments carried out in practice?': 'In practice we have tacitly agreed, as a rule, to fall back on what is, in truth, a convention' (*C.W.* VII: 152, 152). Here I shall not attempt to account for how Keynes came to abandon his early philosophical thinking about intuition and judgement, a task I have pursued at length elsewhere (Davis 1994a). Rather, I shall set out Keynes's new philosophical thinking about convention as it appears in *The General Theory*, and then attempt to chart the likely post-*General Theory* path of development of the concept of convention in Keynes's thinking. This is arguably a task of considerable importance in the interpretation of Keynes's later economics, since the genuinely revolutionary positions found in *The General Theory* appear to depend in important respects upon the new views Keynes developed there regarding history and conventions.

The concept of convention is the primary philosophical concept of Keynes's later philosophical thinking. Yet because it emerged in Keynes's overall thinking more as a product of decisions made regarding non-philosophical matters, in connection with the problems of argument encountered in the writing of *The General Theory* in the 1930s, the concept of convention never received the systematic investigation from Keynes that his early philosophical notions had when philosophy and ethics were his chief preoccupation. As a result, because the concept has always been seen as an economic concept – and then with an uncertain pedigree – it has gone unappreciated as a specifically philosophical contribution of *The General Theory*. The lack of attention the concept of convention received from Keynes may also be due to his being influenced by Ludwig Wittgenstein's thinking about convention. Keynes may have felt that Cambridge was already producing a clear philosophical understanding of the nature of the concept, and that Wittgenstein was better suited to take on primary responsibility in that effort. I explore the connections between Keynes and Wittgenstein in regard to the concept of convention briefly at the end of the discussion below (pp. 218–21). In any event, whatever the relationship between Keynes and Wittgenstein, Keynes's failure to take rules and conventions seriously in his early philosophy left him without a clear account of the nature and workings of convention when he turned to the topic in *The General Theory* and was chiefly concerned with economic argument. In a second edition of the book he might have chosen to amplify those passages where the operation of conventions was central to his argument. But what was ultimately most needed was a careful elaboration of the central ideas he believed were involved in the concept. On account of his early death and the tremendous demands upon his time of policy and economic debate in his last years, this elaboration never occurred. Accordingly, it is necessary to reconstruct how Keynes's argument and thinking about convention might have proceeded in light of the foundations laid down for the concept in *The General Theory*.

I undertake this project in a number of steps. First, turning to the passages of *The General Theory* where convention is central, I map out the structure of the concept there, making very brief reference to the changes in Keynes's philosophical thinking that were afoot subsequent to his earlier exchange in the 1920s with Frank Ramsey on the meaning of probability. Second, I discuss how Keynes's treatment of the concept of convention was opaque yet also susceptible of some clarification. The topic here lends itself to the idea of a second edition of *The General Theory*. In such a work it would surely have been Keynes's intention to preserve the essential integrity of the original work so as to maintain the power of its conclusions. Though the concept of convention is very central to Keynes's later economic thinking, most readers would no doubt have seen further discussion of the concept as a distracting digression. As has long been appreciated, the basic ideas of the book were too revolutionary to be easily absorbed, and thus it would not pay to complicate an argument which many already found difficult.[2] Third, I proceed to further possible developments in the concept of convention that Keynes might have undertaken in a more peaceful later life. 'My Early Beliefs' signals Keynes's intention to set the record straight about his early philosophical thinking, but it goes little beyond this. Moreover, Keynes's post-*General Theory* writings do not add significantly to our understanding of Keynes's thinking on the subject. Thus, my strategy in this section of the chapter is to examine the shortcomings of Keynes's *General Theory* view of convention together with indications of the likely direction of his thinking to construct a case for the development of his later thinking on the subject. Finally, in the last section of the chapter, the influence of Wittgenstein and the confluence of Keynes's and Wittgenstein's thinking on convention are investigated in an effort to isolate key philosophical issues involved in the concept.

THE STRUCTURE OF KEYNES'S *GENERAL THEORY* CONCEPT OF CONVENTION

To understand the role the concept of convention plays in Keynes's thinking we need to understand how Keynes believed that less than full employment equilibria were possible in the economy. This in turn is perhaps best understood in the context of the principal misinterpretation of Keynes's thinking in the years after the publication of *The General Theory*. Economists trained in what Keynes had called classical thinking, yet who label themselves Keynesians (or neoclassical Keynesians), generally agree that equilibrium unemployment is only possible when there are frictions or imperfections in the economy. This mistaken interpretation of Keynes's views centres most often upon the labour market (but also the bond market) where it is typically said that workers may suffer money illusion, or an inability to distinguish real and money-wages. However, in the 1980s this view was found unpersuasive by many economists when rational-expectations theorists argued that rational agents would not make systematic expectational errors. Without systematic errors in expectation, it was then argued, equilibrium unemployment simply could not occur, and Keynes's equilibrium unemployment view (or what it had been taken to be by neoclassical Keynesians) was said to be based upon a misunderstanding of the process of expectation formation.

Overlooked in this history of reception was the fact that Keynes himself had never employed the idea of money illusion or indeed argued that economic agents, rational or otherwise, made systematic expectational errors.[3] Indeed, in Keynes's view, if workers were willing to reduce their money-wage demands in pursuit of employment, worker incomes might well fall sufficiently that firms would withdraw employment in the face of falling sales. In such circumstances, the economy was, as it were, locked into a low-level circuit of wage payments and consumption expenditures that still left a portion of the workforce unemployed. An additional source of demand was consequently needed if full employment were to be achieved; and among the questions that preoccupied Keynes during the time he was working through the drafts of *The General Theory* in the 1930s were: why investment expenditure could not be counted on to provide the additional demand a full employment economy required, and how this investment insufficiency related to the character of investment as a form of conventional activity. In important respects, then, Keynes's understanding of unemployment equilibria depended upon his thinking about conventions. Accordingly, we need to be able to explain how conventions functioned, and how they determined levels of activity among individuals making investment decisions, to be able to explain unemployment equilibria for Keynes. This in turn suggests that, because conventional behaviour is by nature an interactive sort of activity, we need to begin by looking at how Keynes understood behaviour generally.

Before turning to what Keynes had to say in *The General Theory* about the behaviour of economic agents in a general sense, it will be helpful to review briefly his well-known exchange with Ramsey over Keynes's understanding of intuition in his 1921 *A Treatise on Probability*. At issue is Keynes's theory of judgement, an important component of a theory of decision-making and action, and a topic which received serious attention in the *Treatise on Probability*. In his early philosophy Keynes had applied the theory of intuition, developed first by Moore and then by Bertrand Russell at the beginning of the century, to the analysis of probability judgements. In Keynes's view he believed himself to be extending Moore's and Russell's philosophical revolution against the philosophical idealism of F.H. Bradley, Bernard Bosanquet and J.E.M. McTaggart. But Keynes's view was also original in departing from the then widely accepted frequency theory of probability, which made probability judgements out to be empirical statements about the relative frequencies of events. Keynes argued first in his early unpublished Apostle paper, 'On Ethics in Relation to Conduct' (1904) and later in the *Treatise on Probability* that the frequency theory presupposed general rules whose application itself presupposed acts of judgement. This seemed to give a special place to direct, unmediated intuitive judgement, or intuition, and Keynes went on to conclude that probability judgements were ultimately founded upon our intuiting abstract but real probability relations. Ramsey, however, was altogether sceptical of both the idea of intuiting metaphysical relationships and of the notion that individuals possessed a capacity for insight into the nature of the real. He concluded that

> a fundamental criticism of Keynes's views, is the obvious one that there really do not seem to be any such things as the probability relations he

> describes. He supposes that, at any rate in certain cases, they can be perceived; but speaking for myself I feel confident that this is not true. I do not perceive them, and . . . moreover I shrewdly suspect that others do not perceive them either . . .
>
> (Ramsey 1978: 63)

When Keynes finally came to reply after Ramsey's death, he simply agreed: 'I think he is right' (*C.W.* X: 338—9).[4] This does not imply, it should be emphasized, that Keynes overthrew the whole of his early reasoning in the *Treatise on Probability* about the forms assumed by probability judgements. As argued by Jochen Runde (1994b, 1994c), Keynes almost certainly retained his general comparative probability conception that emphasized ordinal comparisons, while discarding the Platonic relations metaphysics meant to explain the meaning of probability, which Ramsey had found an easy target.

The significance of this for Keynes's later economics and thinking about convention is that abandonment of a role for intuition in the Platonic sense changed the conceptual foundations of Keynes's philosophical thinking about decision-making and action. Since the judgement involved in agent decision-making could not be explained in terms of an unmediated intuitive apprehension of timeless qualities and relations, it necessarily possessed a historical character. Judgement exercised by individuals in economic life reflected their being historical individuals reasoning in terms of concrete circumstances created by past patterns of events. Practically speaking, this meant that we looked to individuals' dispositions, tendencies and propensities to explain their behaviour. The social economic world exhibited a variety of forces and causes operating upon individuals, and we could at best sort out individuals' tendencies to respond to these forces and causes. Keynes was clear about this in his summary of his model, in Chapter 18 of the *General Theory*, 'The General Theory of Employment Re-stated'. We begin, he asserts, by identifying the factors that are given, the independent variables, and the dependent variables, where chief among the 'ultimate independent variables' are 'the three fundamental psychological factors, namely, the psychological propensity to consume, the psychological attitude to liquidity and the psychological expectation of future yield from capital assets' (*C.W.* VII: 246–7). These variables of course reflect levels or states of activity associated with demand in different spheres of the economy. Thus to understand aggregate demand we needed to understand the dispositional character of human behaviour as a set of tendencies to respond to the complex historical forces impinging upon individuals.

In *The General Theory*, then, Keynes turned away from the more episodic conception of judgement and behaviour that he had adhered to in his early philosophical intuitionism. In its place, he drew upon another tradition in philosophy at Cambridge that regarded economics as a moral science.

Writing to Roy Harrod in 1938 in a letter critical of Lionel Robbins's natural science conception of economics, Keynes stressed the need to understand the complex character of human motivation to explain the distinctively social behaviour studied in economics:

> I . . . want to emphasise strongly the point about economics being a moral science. I mentioned before that it deals with introspection and with values. I might have added that it deals with motives, expectations, psychological uncertainties. One has to be constantly on guard against treating the material as constant and homogeneous.
>
> (*C.W.* XIV: 300)

Contrary to Robbins's view that a few simple principles were involved in economic behaviour, decision-making in economic life was a complex affair with many factors entering into individual judgement. The determinacy natural science seeks in its conclusions is unavailable in economics, which as a moral science combines analysis of human motivation with an account of the historical circumstances in which individuals find themselves. Thus, there is no simple account of human judgement available to us, as Keynes had once thought possible in regarding judgement as intuition. Historical individuals' intuitions, in fact, were 'intuitive' in the ordinary sense of the term: rather unpredictable responses to complex circumstances resulting from a variety of competing motives.

From this perspective, we can see why Keynes drew back from his early confidence in the powers of individual judgement, and charged himself and his early friends at the 1938 Memoir Club meeting with mistakenly thinking they could 'judge every individual case on its merits, and [with] the wisdom, experience and self-control to do so successfully' (*C.W.* X: 446). That view, Keynes confessed, had been based upon 'an *a priori* view of what human nature is like, both other people's and our own, which was disastrously mistaken', when the conclusion which experience taught was that the 'human race' did not simply consist of 'reliable, rational, decent people, influenced by truth and objective standards, who can safely be released from the outward restraints of convention and traditional standards and inflexible rules of conduct' (*C.W.* X: 447). Indeed, it was best to assume, Keynes emphasized, that 'civilization was a thin precarious crust erected by the personality and will of a very few, and only maintained by rules and conventions skilfully put across and guilefully preserved' (ibid.). Rules and conventions, that is, anchored individual behaviour, whether in ethics, politics or economic life, and we thus only grasped the behaviour of individuals fully when we understood how it came to be subsumed under society's rules and conventions.

Economic behaviour, in this respect, was thus in important ways interactive. Keynes had indicated as much in his letter to Harrod when he had emphasized that economics made use of introspection and judgements of value. That is, just as economists might analyse the behaviour of individuals using introspection and judgements of value, so individuals in the economic world also used these methods to evaluate each other's responses to complex conditions that faced all. Since, *contra* Robbins, economic behaviour was neither constant nor homogeneous, individuals typically lacked clear strategies of response to the circumstances in which they found themselves. One way of addressing this would be to examine the behaviour of other individuals in like circumstances. By observing another's actions and through introspection and judgements of value imputing a motive to that individual for those actions, we could reinforce or revise our own opinions regarding desirable courses of action in similar circumstances. I have argued at length elsewhere (Davis 1994a) that this form of interaction implies a conception of individual judgement that is best termed interdependent judgement, and that, as a historical, concrete mode of judgement replacing Keynes's earlier view of judgement as abstract intuition, it operates in Keynes's various analyses of convention. Perhaps the most vivid example of this is Keynes's metaphorical representation of professional investment as a newspaper beauty contest.

Recall that the question Keynes raised regarding placements was: 'How are these highly significant daily, even hourly, revaluations of existing investments carried out in practice?' (*C.W.* VII: 151). Keynes's answer, that this process of revaluation depends upon a convention that 'the existing state of affairs will continue indefinitely, except in so far as we have specific reasons to expect a change' (ibid.: 152), only invites us to wonder when there are indeed reasons to expect a change; or, as Keynes puts it, how precarious the convention regarding any given set of investments might be. Not very reassuringly, Keynes goes on to assert that a 'conventional valuation . . . is established as the outcome of the mass psychology of a large number of ignorant individuals' (ibid.: 154), or:

> professional investment may be likened to those newspaper competitions in which the competitors have to pick out the six prettiest faces from a hundred photographs, the prize being awarded to the competitor whose choice most nearly corresponds to the average preferences of the competitors as a whole; so that each competitor has to pick, not those faces which he himself finds prettiest, but those which he thinks likeliest to catch the fancy of the other competitors, all of whom are looking at the problem from the same point of view.
>
> (*C.W.* VII: 156)

The idea that it is not the prettiest but those most likely to be thought the prettiest nicely captures the change in Keynes's view of judgement. No longer does the individual intuit the real quality of beauty, but rather proceeds to draw a judgement interdependently about what others facing the same dilemma may choose. Each contestant, in effect, uses introspection to consider his or her own opinion, compares that to an opinion imputed to others, makes adjustments for judgements of value, and comes up with an individual judgement bearing the strong imprint of social opinion. Placement, which at any time involves considerable speculation, is in Keynes's view little different. Individual investors cannot know through intuition the true value of an investment, and thus rely upon their abilities to gauge the mass psychology of the public and especially the temper of other investors. The convention governing investment, therefore, may be defined as a temporarily settled state of opinion that derives from a mass of interdependent judgements made by different individuals.[5]

This, of course, does not tell us much more about the precariousness of the convention governing investment. Indeed, if anything, Keynes's characterization of convention only raises more questions about the dividing line between the stability and instability of investment expenditure, since the business of imputing motives to others (though we regularly do it) is clearly fraught with considerable difficulty. Here, however, we begin to see the state of development and status of Keynes's philosophical thinking about the concept of convention. What Keynes was clear about on the concept was that a convention is a structure of interdependent judgements across individuals that both contributes to the determination of different individuals' respective judgements and results from the interaction of different individuals making their respective judgements. In the other locations in *The General Theory* where the concept has a role, this view can well be seen at work. Admittedly, in no instance is as much attention given to the notion as in Chapter 12 on long-term expectations, though there are interesting things said, some explicit and some more implicit, about bonds and the rate of interest (*C.W.* VII: 202–4), about relative money-wages and wage bargaining (ibid.: 264 ff.), about producer price expectations (ibid.: 46–51), and about what Keynes calls the subjective factors influencing consumption (ibid.: 107–12).

Unfortunately, in the secondary literature on the interpretation of Keynes there is some confusion about what the concept of convention concerns. Some writers have been quick to link conventional behaviour and irrational behaviour, often thinking in the latter instance of Keynes's reference to 'animal spirits' (*C.W.* VII: 161). George Shackle (1967, 1974) did much to encourage this sometimes popular view, which has more recently been defended by Ted Winslow (1986) in connection with Keynes's interest in Freud. Three points are in order. First, while for Keynes conventional behaviour sometimes simply involves individuals unreflectively observing conventions as rules of thumb, it more often involves their operating within patterns of activity that contribute to the structuring of their behaviour. Second, Keynes clearly believes much decision-making is what is generally termed rational (e.g. in connection with his chapter on the marginal efficiency of capital). Third, Keynes also treats the existence of irrational behaviour separately from his treatment of conventional behaviour in both 'My Early Beliefs', where conventions actually control irrational impulses, and in Chapter 12 of *The General Theory*, where conventional behaviour is a (second-)best response to the dilemma of determining a good investment in an uncertain world. This latter point has been emphasized by a number of recent contributors to the topic of Keynes and convention. Anna Carabelli (1988: 224) argues that conventional behaviour for Keynes involves 'practical techniques . . . for facing the future in a situation of limited knowledge'. R.M. O'Donnell (1989: 251) sees investment conventions as a form of weak rationality. Tony Lawson (1985b, 1993) treats conventional behaviour as a rational strategy, and adds that conventions are an important form of social knowledge. Of course, much turns in this on the meaning of 'rational'. If 'rational' is taken in the Platonistic sense of intuiting essential relations and qualities (as in O'Donnell), the term seems mistaken and inappropriate. But if 'rational' is equated with reasonable judgement in the sense of being a cognitive process of deliberation set in a historical context and influenced by individual values and motives (as in Carabelli and Lawson), then it seems that conventional behaviour can well be thought 'rational'.

The position here is that because conventional behaviour is an interactive activity, it needs to be understood on its own terms, apart from the issue of whether behaviour is rational or irrational. Some authors have emphasized views of this sort. Oliver Favereau (1988) makes interactive behaviour and conventions central to his interpretation of Keynes's probability thinking in terms of possible-worlds reasoning. Similarly, Bruce Littleboy (1990: 29) argues that 'one of Keynes's most important innovations lay in the realization of the significance of conventions that arise when transactors, confronted by an uncertain environment, are psychologically disposed to act in a manner in which they study and imitate the actions of others'.[6] A. Orlean (1989) advances a formal analysis of imitative interaction between professional speculators to account for a number of ideas in Keynes's Chapter 12 discussion of professional investors. Of course, imitative interaction is only one (relatively simple) form of conventional behaviour, and to argue that individual decisions tend to converge in an imitative process requires strong assumptions about the patterns of interaction between individuals that Keynes did not always make himself. Indeed, though Keynes was much concerned with conventions as a basis for explaining behaviour in ways that went beyond simple aggregation of individual behaviours, he did not go very far in *The General Theory* towards explaining the various different ways in which conventions operated and changed.

What, then, was Keynes not clear about in *The General Theory* in his treatment of convention? Aside from not developing the distinctions between different kinds of conventions, Keynes does not tell us much about the stability or instability of conventions, whether those that govern investment or other domains of the economy, and thus his account of the dynamics of conventions remains to be developed. We do find in connection with his discussion of investment in Chapter 12 a treatment of the issue of investor confidence, a matter Keynes had puzzled over from the time of his writing *A Treatise on Money*. Thus it seems fair to suggest that were Keynes to have produced a second edition of *The General Theory* he would have at least attempted to say more about how confidence affects the stability or instability of the convention governing investment. This extension might in turn serve as a model for how the dynamics of other conventions operating in money markets, labour markets and elsewhere might begin to be explained. With this conclusion, we thus turn to changes Keynes might have pursued in a 'second edition' of *The General Theory*.

CONVENTION IN A 'SECOND EDITION' OF *THE GENERAL THEORY*

To see how Keynes might have re-tailored his exposition in his twelfth chapter on long-term expectations to allow more illumination to fall on the topic of confidence, it is necessary to look more closely at how he understood the convention governing investment as a structure of interdependent judgements. For Keynes, conventions helped to determine the levels or states of activity taken on by the psychological propensities and attitudes at work in the economy. But strictly speaking, since these psychological propensities and attitudes manifest themselves in varying degrees in different individuals, it is more accurate to say that conventions act to structure different individuals' propensities and attitudes in relation to one another. This becomes clearer if we think of a convention as a structure of interdependent expectations (expectation being a form of judgement), and note Keynes's special emphasis upon average expectation in his treatment of the convention governing investment. What constitutes a good or bad investment, Keynes tells us, is 'governed by the average expectation of those who deal on the Stock Exchange as revealed by the price of shares' (*C.W.* VII: 151), where average expectation, from the perspective of the beauty contest metaphor, is determined according to 'what average opinion expects average opinion to be' (ibid.: 156).

An average expectation of an investment's worth, however, must subsume a set of different individual expectations, since different individuals have different views regarding a given investment's worth. Different individuals might thus be said for Keynes to position themselves in investment markets relative to average opinions in those markets. In doing so, they compare average expectation and their own individual expectations regarding various investments, considering the weight they feel they should ascribe to overall market opinion as embodied in average expectation relative to the weight they feel they want to ascribe to their own individual opinions and expectations. Each dimension of expectation has its own plausibility, and yet each also lacks certain advantages that the other possesses. Average expectation reflects the judgement of many investors, and thus carries a certain guarantee against individual errors in judgement. Yet it is not a guide to making gains in the market since that requires anticipating the movement or the market ('to outwit the crowd'; *C.W.* VII: 155). Individual expectations, in contrast, often reflect special knowledge or opinion relevant to a given investment ('by reason partly of differences in environment and . . . partly of differences in knowledge and interpretation of the situation'; ibid.: 198–9), and thus at least hope of gain. But, of course, trying to beat the market also carries the possibility of loss. Investors, Keynes noted, are always intent on 'foreseeing changes in the conventional basis of valuation a short time ahead of the general public' (ibid.: 154). Thus individual and average expectation both figure in investor behaviour, and we may suppose that central to the stability of an investment market and the convention governing it is whatever balance is achieved between individual and average expectation, where average expectation is continually likely to be changed by individual profit-seeking.[7]

Keynes approached this question of balance or precariousness in terms of the concept of confidence. There are three cases to distinguish to understand the role he gave to confidence. First, apart from the question of the dynamics or movement in a given investment market, a conventional valuation might be stable if fluctuations in price around an average value tended to leave price within a certain range. In this instance, confidence would tend to manifest itself in a conviction on the part of individual investors that average expectation was likely to prevail and individual views about an investment's value added little to average opinion. Second, in investment markets where price moved significantly but then fluctuated around a new average value, confidence would manifest itself differently during the price movement and afterward: initially confidence would appear as a conviction on the part of investors that some individuals (with one view of the investment's price movement) had expectations superior to average opinion (causing average expectation to continually shift); later, when price came to fluctuate in a given range, confidence would appear as a conviction that average opinion was again a better guide to price. The third case is the one that often concerned Keynes most, namely, that situation where instability seemed to rule in a given market valuation, and where the market seemed likely to move without a clear destination. In this case, confidence is generally undermined, and fails even to be manifest in investor conviction that an orderly movement in the market driven by superior individual expectations is afoot. Of course, Keynes knew that markets cannot be driven by 'bear' or 'bull' expectations indefinitely. But he was unable to say why a market would ultimately re-settle into some new range of values, or why confidence re-emerged after a period of turmoil in opinion.

What we can thus say about Keynes's thinking about confidence is that it turned on a balance between individual and average expectation. What does this imply? From a psychological perspective, confidence is an affective state of mind in which an individual brings closure to a cognitive process of investigation by regarding any conclusions reached as adequate and satisfactorily final. Lack of confidence is reflected in indecision regarding the boundaries appropriate to a thought process, and an inability to complete a course of judgement. It would not be reasonable, it seems, to expect Keynes to have developed a psychological analysis of individual reasoning, so as to be able to say how individuals actually became confident about one thing or another. What, however, it seems it was appropriate for Keynes to have done in his attention to confidence in *The General Theory* was to set out an account of the conditions associated with states of confidence obtaining across individuals in various markets. That is, what were the circumstances that in his view allowed confidence to emerge? In this respect, he would have built on his account of conventions as a form of interactive activity where an interdependence of individual judgements explained levels of activity of his independent variables. This, at the same time, would probably have gone beyond the modest sorts of changes a 'second edition' of *The General Theory* would have permitted.

In a 'second edition' of *The General Theory*, then, Keynes might have proceeded by drawing more attention to the role of confidence in determining particular patterns of conventional judgement. To the extent that this can be understood as a question of individual confidence, Keynes did indeed emphasize the fragility of individual expectation in his reference to conventional judgement in a subsequent paper. In his response to his critics in his 1937 *Quarterly Journal of Economics* paper he drew attention to this theme:

> Knowing that our own individual judgment is worthless, we endeavour to fall back on the judgment of the rest of the world which is perhaps better informed. That is, we endeavour to conform with the behaviour of the majority or the average. The psychology of a society of individuals each of whom is endeavouring to copy the others leads to what we may strictly term a conventional judgment.
>
> (*C.W.* XIV: 114)

Moreover, as many commentators have noted, Keynes also took this occasion to emphasize the radical uncertainty associated with decisions facing the future, a circumstance that could be expected to heighten the sense of indecision and the fragility of the state of confidence in an investment community. But if these points were made more strongly in a re-issue of *The General Theory* they would not have taken the reader much further towards an understanding of what might settle states of confidence. And, since Keynes advanced an equilibrium theory of unemployment, he needed this further element in his analysis, if conventions were to be seen as central to the explanation of the economy. Thus we turn in the following section to how Keynes's argument might have been further developed beyond the framework of *The General Theory*.

BEYOND *THE GENERAL THEORY*

That Keynes's basic understanding of a convention depends upon viewing individual judgement as interdependent, where the imputing of motives to others involves conjecture and speculation, suggests that confidence is central to the very process of judgement itself. Indeed, when individuals introspectively examine their own motives and compare them to those they think are justifiably imputed to others, unless they possess some measure of confidence about their thinking, they seem as likely to doubt their conclusions as think them reasonable. Every individual of course is a relatively autonomous being in the sense of possessing a private thought process. Yet we customarily do make confident claims about what we suppose others to feel and think. How, then, can individuals be confident that they correctly impute motives and beliefs to others whose thoughts and feelings are, as it were, hidden from view? Traditionally there are two general answers to this question, one of which figures prominently in Keynes's thinking. First, through powers of inference we read individuals' motives from their observed actions and behaviour. Confidence in imputing motives to others in this instance depends upon making reference to widely accepted patterns of connection between action and motive. Second, we also consult with one another, and then adjust our opinions accordingly. Keynes would have cited both of these explanations, but had special grounds for noting the latter. In his characterization of the pursuit of average opinion in connection with the beauty contest metaphor, he emphasized the implicit, successive iterations involved in individuals trying to anticipate how others might anticipate (how others might anticipate, etc.) what average opinion would be:

> It is not a case of choosing those which, to the best of one's judgment, are really the prettiest, or even those which average opinion genuinely thinks the prettiest. We have reached the third degree where we devote our intelligences to anticipating what average opinion expects the average opinion to be. And there are some, I believe, who practise the fourth, fifth and higher degrees.
>
> (*C.W.* VII: 156)

Yet how many iterations such a process might involve is less the point here than noting what is involved in the very possibility of there being higher iterations. That is, to the extent that an individual is able to imagine higher degrees of anticipation, then that individual is able to implicitly confirm lower degrees of anticipation in others.[8] Confidence emerges, consequently, if not quite by consultation, then by an interaction between individuals commonly involved in attempting to establish each other's motives on a common subject, where that interaction leads to successive degrees of anticipation. On Keynes's view, therefore, because individuals engage in interdependent judgement of often considerable complexity, they are able to establish some confidence about one another's motives.

But to fully understand interdependence between individuals, it needs to be remembered and emphasized that the process of imputing motives to others is a many-sided one engaged in by many different individuals simultaneously. When Keynes speaks about the practices of the Stock Exchange, he is not thinking only of his own case as one investor, but rather of many like individuals interacting with one another on roughly the same basis. Thus the iterative process of anticipating others' views is being carried out by many individuals whose respective success in imagining higher iterations of anticipation not only confirms each individual's separate opinions about others, but also tends to confirm the entire collection of individuals in their conjectures about investor motives in the market. Put simply, confidence for Keynes is shared confidence. In effect, because judgement is interdependent in the manner described, confidence emerges between individuals. This means that if we are to extend Keynes's thinking about conventions in *The General Theory* we must delineate the different conditions under which shared confidence develops. For Keynes, the issue truly concerns states of confidence obtaining between groups of individuals.

Recall, then, that our discussion of the precariousness or stability of investment – the topic where the state of confidence is at issue for Keynes – distinguished three cases according to the way in which confidence develops or declines. In the first case, the market was relatively settled and average expectation was dominant. Here shared confidence coalesces in a widespread conviction that individual expectations are quite similar, and that individual motives vary little. In the second case, where price changes but then re-settles into a new range, there is initially a pattern of re-evaluation of investor motives carried out by each individual in the market, at least until the direction of price change and likely full movement becomes clear. Confidence in this case is shared at best by smaller collections of investors who agree on the nature of the change in the market (such as 'bulls' or 'bears'). Individual expectations are, however, obscure across groups, and individuals lack confidence about their own opinions more generally. The third case involves an unstable market that may fluctuate wildly or appear to be moving in one direction without sign of re-settling. It might be thought that such a situation exhibits high levels of confidence if many individuals ultimately agree on the direction of the market (as in a crash). But it could also be argued that what confidence individuals possess about each other's views is not deep in the sense of involving higher degrees of anticipation, and that little confidence really exists between groups or individuals regarding where the market is ultimately headed. Individual expectations, then, are not especially coherent, confidence is fragile, and the convention that things will remain the same indefinitely is, as Keynes warned, precarious.

For Keynes, then, the conditions associated with states of confidence concern the success or lack of success with which individuals come to assess each other's opinions about markets. However, given the complexity of a process of interdependent judgement, where the subjects involved and associated motives may be diverse and vary continuously over short periods of time, explaining the conditions underlying different states of confidence may be quite difficult. It would certainly be a mistake to suppose, then, that Keynes hoped or thought individuals' different judgements in any market would ultimately converge, or that the distribution of individual expectations about an average would in the long run be small. 'Bulls' and 'bears' or otherwise constituted divisions in opinions were desirable and inescapable dimensions of an economy built upon individual decision-making and action. Keynes, none the less, would still have liked to see less instability in placement markets, since this seemed to depress investment expenditure and consequently levels of aggregate demand. Thus as a long-term policy proposal, Keynes recommended 'a somewhat comprehensive socialisation of investment' (*C.W.* VII: 378), whereby public and semi-public boards and agencies such as universities, port authorities, redevelopment corporations, and so on, would direct a larger share of total investment expenditure. This institutionalization of investment would in his view create conditions for better communication and understanding among individuals within organizations having shared purposes, and, on the grounds that like minds would conceivably exhibit higher states of confidence, lead to more stable investment rates in part of the economy. The investment community at large, Keynes believed, was simply too atomistic to avoid the regular swings in confidence that lent the convention surrounding investment its periodic instability, and accordingly a long-term policy sensitive to the conditions of confidence was in order.

The concept of shared confidence, then, would have required new texts and another venue subsequent to any re-issue of *The General Theory* to be adequately developed. Much of what the notion involves was implicit in Keynes's treatment of convention as a structure of interdependent judgement, and much of what is involved in the idea of creating a stronger climate of confidence was explicit in Keynes's writings for many years both before and after *The General Theory*. Indeed, Keynes's own personal confidence that there were always steps that could be taken to reduce unemployment demonstrates the importance he placed on the idea that the conditions of confidence were central to the operation of the economy. Of course, Keynes may not ever have chosen to direct his energies towards this more social philosophical aspect of his thinking. The direction of his intellectual development for many years had been away from philosophical argument, and it is difficult to imagine an individual so involved in practical affairs taking time away from his many commitments to elaborate upon such concerns. It would have required, no doubt, a very peaceful and extended retirement.

KEYNES AND WITTGENSTEIN

It may none the less be possible to speculate about Keynes's later philosophical thinking regarding convention by considering ideas he may have shared with Wittgenstein. It is well known that Keynes and Wittgenstein knew each other at Cambridge, and it seems that they were also acquainted with each other's work (Coates 1990). Indeed, their intellectual histories followed certain common paths. Both made significant contributions to the early twentieth-century Cambridge philosophy initiated by Moore and Russell – Wittgenstein in his *Tractatus Logico-Philosophicus* and Keynes in his *A Treatise of Probability* – and both later abandoned many of their early ideas in revolutions in thinking that fundamentally influenced philosophy and economics respectively. Moreover, Wittgenstein joined Ramsey in criticizing Keynes's probability relation,[9] and Keynes indicates that he had opinions about Wittgenstein's later philosophy in correspondence. What is there, then, in Wittgenstein's later thinking that has links to Keynes's later philosophical thinking?

One important dimension of Wittgenstein's *Philosophical Investigations* is its abandonment of the view held in the earlier *Tractatus* that language is ultimately composed of names, the meanings of which are simple objects. In the *Investigations* Wittgenstein substituted the view that the meaning of an expression is its use, as reflected, as he put it, in the language game in which that expression is used. Keynes had held a view similar to the meanings-as-names view in his own early work where he used Moore's notion of there being an indefinable simple quality of goodness that we know intuitively in accounting for the meaning of the term 'good' (see Davis 1994a: ch. 1). And, like Wittgenstein, he later came to emphasize (in 'My Early Beliefs') the importance of social rules and conventions such as would be involved in a language game in Wittgenstein's sense to account for what might be thought to be good. Each, then, reasoned that social practices, each having a relative autonomy, played an important role in determining the meanings of the objects and activities of the world. For Wittgenstein this also meant that one could not typically produce a rationale for the rules a language game or practice exhibited. One rather grasped their function and purpose by, as it were, playing the language game or participating in the practice. Much the same opinion enters into Keynes's discussion of convention in *The General Theory*. The convention governing investment may be said to have rules in the interaction among individual investors, but these implicit rules only have meaning within the framework of that conventional behaviour.

It might be thought, however, that Wittgenstein's thinking about language games really concerns matters essentially little related to what preoccupied Keynes in his attention to convention in *The General Theory*. Keynes wanted to account for patterns of interaction between individuals in different domains of the economy, in order to explain aggregate demand and unemployment equilibria. Wittgenstein was interested in re-explaining language meaning as part of a more general project of redeveloping our theory of mind and conception of philosophy as an intellectual enterprise. Yet Keynes's conception of the operation of a convention actually shares more of Wittgenstein's project about language games than it initially appears. The determination of an investment's value in the form of a community of investors' average expectation constitutes a meaning of sorts for the activity of making that investment for individual investors. While market values are not meanings in the ordinary sense of language meanings, they none the less bear sense interpretable by individuals who are part of the practice in which they are defined. Indeed, Wittgenstein's abandonment of the idea that meanings are names itself encourages a new view of what sorts of entities meanings are. The traditional view of meanings as linguistic items that bear relations to various features of the world is replaced by the view that meaning is a product of a social practice. Thus, on this broader view, an investment value is a meaning not in the sense of a number that simply compares a flow of possible earnings and capital goods purchase costs, but rather in the sense that those earnings and costs reflect a social practice embedded in certain historical opportunities, investor sentiments and patterns of market development.

From this perspective, Keynes's view that average expectation emerges from the play of individual expectation, where an inherited or reigning average value represents a point of departure for individual investors, can be seen to bear interesting connections to Wittgenstein's concept of 'family resemblance'. Wittgenstein's idea was that in every case where things are called by the same name there is not a single quality or set of qualities common to all these things, but rather 'a complicated network of similarities overlapping and criss-crossing: sometimes over-all similarities, sometimes similarities in detail' that he termed 'family resemblances' (Wittgenstein 1953: 32e). On this view, a name does not represent quite the same thing to all individuals, though generally individuals who understand a name somewhat differently can appreciate each other's usages through participating in language games where the name is employed. Keynes's treatment of a convention involves essentially the same understanding. Individual expectations regarding investments are typically distinguished from average expectations, the analogue of a common name. Yet individual investors, though they may doubt one another's investment strategies, can still appreciate that each is, as it were, playing the same game. Thus just as the meaning of names is established for

Wittgenstein in a practice that distributes features of that meaning across a variety of games or usages, none of which possess all those features, so for Keynes the meaning of an investment is distributed across a variety of individual expectations each of which reflects some insight into an investment's worth, but none of which fully captures that range of insights.

One further comparison between Keynes and Wittgenstein seems in order. Wittgenstein is well known for his argument that there cannot be a private language in the sense of a set of meanings that individuals might allocate apart from interaction with others through acquaintance with inner streams of consciousness. More broadly, Wittgenstein believed that descriptions of our mental acts and states of mind were governed by criteria that made reference to the circumstances, behaviour and dispositions of individuals. Keynes, we saw above, approached individuals' behaviour dispositionally, and then in his moral science remarks made this a matter of individuals' 'motives, expectations, and psychological uncertainties' (*C.W.* XIV: 300). But it is important here to understand Keynes's view of the linkage between psychology and behaviour. When individuals consider the motivations of others in order to understand their actions, they introspectively establish what motives they themselves would have were they to pursue similar actions, because they wish to have some basis for explaining other individuals' observed behaviour in terms of possible motives. Thus if an individual were to satisfy him or herself that another individual had some motive where a certain action was observed, an understanding of the circumstances, behaviour and dispositions of individuals – observable behaviour generally – would be the key to comparing individuals' unobservable motives. Keynes, then, seems to share a conception of psychology and behaviour similar to the one Wittgenstein employed. Indeed, since Keynes had held in his *A Treatise on Probability* that one could be directly acquainted with one's inner sensations (among other things), but gave up this view with his abandonment of intuition as a source of direct insight into the world, it seems that a case could also be made for saying that Keynes would have agreed with Wittgenstein that private languages were not possible.

Of course, the points outlined here about the philosophical connections between Keynes and Wittgenstein are speculative, and would require more careful discussion to make either a case for their having shared views or the particular interpretation suggested here of Keynes's later ideas (cf. Davis 1996). But it is not unreasonable to attempt such an argument, since not only were Keynes and Wittgenstein aware of the way each other's work had developed from a number of common beginnings, but both shared a climate of intellectual development at Cambridge in the 1930s that must have reinforced many of the views they each developed separately. Certainly this latter development, that of the intellectual climate in which they operated, is sometimes neglected in intellectual histories which chart each individual's path in isolation from the larger social and intellectual world and the connections between the different disciplines. Further thinking about Keynes's later philosophy, which received little elaboration by Keynes in his later years, would seem to require greater attention to this wider sphere of intellectual development.

NOTES

1 Keynes added that this 'was hardly a state of mind which a grown-up person in his senses could sustain literally' (p. 422). All references to Keynes's works are by volume number to the *Collected Writings of John Maynard Keynes.*
2 One good measure of the difficulty of interpreting Keynes's argument is the difficulty of determining the standing of IS-LM analysis in Keynes's thinking. See Young (1987) for a valuable account of the early problems of interpreting *The General Theory.*
3 That Keynes did not assume rigid money-wages is clearly apparent in Chapters 2 and 19 of *The General Theory.*
4 See Cottrell (1993) for a good discussion of this important exchange.
5 For an influential, recent philosophical account of convention emphasizing interdependent judgement that is very close to the analysis here, see Lewis (1969). For a discussion about the proper concept of convention to attribute to Keynes, see Runde (1994c).
6 Littleboy goes on to advance for Keynes a theory of macroeconomic dynamics based on the interaction of different conventions in different spheres of the economy (Littleboy 1990: 289ff.).
7 Keynes's discussion of 'bears' and 'bulls' in money markets is particularly appropriate: '[t]he market price [that is, average expectation in the language of Chapter 12] will be fixed at the point at which the sales of the "bears" and the purchases of the "bulls" are balanced' (*C.W.* VII: 170).
8 Lewis (1969) is especially clear on the iterative nature of anticipation in a convention.
9 In his 1935 Lent Term Lectures, Wittgenstein was recorded by Alice Ambrose as saying:: 'Keynes claimed to discover a probability relation which was like implication. But logic is a calculus, not a natural science, and in it one can make inventions but not discoveries' (Ambrose 1979: 138–9). Wittgenstein later credited Ramsey and Sraffa, another friend of Keynes, in the preface to his *Philosophical Investigations* with being the chief influences on the development of the ideas in that influential book.

34

KEYNESIAN METHODOLOGY*

Jochen Runde

Although some authors have singled out what they take to be the distinctive method of *The General Theory*, notably Hicks (1936) and Kregel (1976), it is probably more accurate to describe it as Dow (1990: 147) does, as an assemblage of approaches which tackles issues 'simultaneously with a range of different chains of reasoning' (see also Harcourt 1987a).[1] Rather than attempting to analyse Keynes's methodology as a unified body of ideas, then, I shall focus on the methodological approach employed in one specific part of *The General Theory*, his famous Chapter 12 on long-term expectation.[2] My primary reasons for doing so are that this chapter seems to me an example of Keynes at his best and because it has provided much of the inspiration for the 'Keynesian' contributions to economic methodology discussed later in this chapter. But it is especially relevant for at least three further reasons. First, much of recent work on the philosophical foundations of Keynes's thought focuses on the relation between his earlier *Treatise on Probability* and his later work in economics. As Chapter 12 marks a return to one of his central concerns in the *Treatise on Probability*, the question of rational conduct under uncertainty, it is an obvious focal point (Meeks 1991a).[3] Second, as Chapter 12 covers many topics that continue to receive a great deal of attention in Economic Theory – uncertainty, expectations, mimetic and speculative behaviour in asset markets – its subject-matter remains as topical as ever. And finally, while many who have taken an interest in Keynes's methodology regard his Chapter 12 as significant in this regard, I suspect that most modern (neoclassical) Keynesians would deny that it contains any methodological lessons worth learning (e.g. Mankiw 1992). The purpose of this chapter is to give some reasons why such denials might be unfounded.

The first half of what follows reviews some characteristically Keynesian themes on probability, uncertainty and the analysis of asset market behaviour. The discussion contains little that is new and is intended to convey something of the flavour of the Keynes-philosophy literature and to highlight some epistemological and ontological issues that arise in Keynes's account. The second half is devoted to the metatheoretical positions advanced by two authors influenced by Keynes's writings on uncertainty and economic analysis, G.L.S. Shackle and Tony Lawson respectively. I shall focus on Keynes's intuition, shared by both these authors, that the analysis of investor behaviour is somehow not amenable to formal Economic Theory.

FROM A *TREATISE ON PROBABILITY* TO CHAPTER 12

Although I shall come back to more specific issues below (pp. 228–40), it is useful to begin with a brief sketch of the argument in Chapter 12 and its links with *A Treatise on Probability*. The reader should be warned that the account I offer here is my own rather than a summary of any consensus in the Keynes-philosophy literature (but see Carabelli 1988 and O'Donnell 1989). Moreover, the themes I draw out are largely independent of Keynes's controversial early position on the existence of objective logical probability relations. The review which follows therefore bypasses the controversy over the impact of Ramsey's (1926) famous critique on Keynes's later views on these questions,[4] and avoids prejudicing the alternative approaches discussed below.

At bottom, Keynes's theory is one of judgemental probability in which binary comparisons of the form $h_1/e_1 \geqslant^* h_2/e_2$ are fundamental. The term h_1/e_1 reads 'hypothesis$_1$ relative to evidence$_1$' (the Keynesian probability relation) and $\geqslant^*$ is the qualitative probability relation 'at least as probable as'. The relation $\geqslant^*$ is transitive and amounts to what we would now call a weak partial order relation. Keynes's theory is often characterized as a contribution to the 'logical' approach to probability because he analyses rational degrees of belief as arising out of the apprehension of a relation of (partial) implication between hypotheses and evidential propositions. Yet he has rather little to say about the probability relation itself, which he presents as an indefinable that cannot be analysed in terms of simpler ideas. He is more concerned to develop the structure of $\geqslant^*$, an exercise which presupposes no more of judgements of probability than that they can sometimes be compared. Given some such comparisons, he shows how further comparisons and, under certain conditions, numerical probabilities may be derived.

Three key themes in Keynes's theory of probability resurface in his later writings on investment behaviour. The first and most distinctive is his insistence that while it may be possible to compare some probabilities by $\geqslant^*$, others are not comparable at all. In such cases, then, neither $h_1/e_1 \geqslant^* h_2/e_2$ nor $h_2/e_2 \geqslant^* h_1/e_1$. Keynes thus insists on the distinction between judgements of indifference between, and non-comparability of, probability relations.

The second theme is the familiar Keynesian one about how seldom it is possible to determine numerical probabilities. Numerically definite probabilities, in the framework sketched above, are derived from judgements of equiprobability based on the Principle of Indifference. Keynes's formulation of this principle provides criteria by which the alternatives to which numerical probabilities are to be assigned may be judged to be equiprobable and indivisible or 'atomic' (i.e. not be capable of being divided into sub-alternatives of the same form). Given that such equiprobable and indivisible alternatives are exhaustive and exclusive, the probability of any one of them is $1/n$ (where n is the total number of possible alternatives). Keynes's theory of numerical probability, then, is essentially a refinement of the classical interpretation of probability. The implication is that numerically definite epistemic probabilities can only be determined in situations which approximate games of chance (save perhaps for what Keynes regards as the rare cases in which numerical probabilities can be assigned on the basis of a knowledge of statistical frequencies).

The third theme I wish to emphasize is Keynes's concept of evidential weight. This is a complex and controversial idea, but what he has in mind here is that in using probability as a guide to conduct we should not only be interested in the probability (relative to the evidence) of the propositions concerned, but also in the *extent*, in some sense, of the evidence on which such probabilities are based. Keynes suggests, as with judgements of probability, that it will only sometimes be possible to make qualitative comparisons of weight. Other things being equal, he argues, when using probabilities as a guide to conduct, we should prefer those based on the body of evidence which is 'more complete'.[5]

We are now in a position to trace these themes in Chapter 12 of *The General Theory*. As is well known, the aim of this chapter is to provide an explanation of the precariousness of real investment demand. Now the demand for assets depends, amongst other things, on investors' expectations of their prospective yields. Keynes argues that the considerations that inform such expectations are based partly on a knowledge of existing facts (such as the existing stock of capital equipment relative to what could profitably be employed on the basis of existing demand) and partly on facts that can only be forecasted with more or less confidence (such as future changes in the stock of capital equipment and demand). The 'state of psychological expectation' of which these forecasts form part are what he calls the state of long-term expectation. Central to his account is that the state of long-term expectation depends not only on the most probable forecasts that investors make but also on the confidence with which they make them. I shall return to this point below.

We have seen that on Keynes's theory of probability, the conditions under which numerically definite probabilities can be determined are stringent and unlikely, if ever, to be met in investment decision situations. This is one of his points of departure in Chapter 12, that we cannot

> rationalise our behaviour by arguing that to a man in a state of ignorance errors in either direction are equally probable, so that there

> remains a mean actuarial expectation based on equi-probabilities. For it can easily be shown that the assumption of arithmetically equal probabilities based on a state of ignorance leads to absurdities.
>
> (*C.W.* VII: 152)[6]

As investors generally do not have statistical frequencies to go on either, Keynes denies that it is possible to assign numerical probabilities to the possible outcomes of current investment decisions. This in turn means, and this is central to his argument, that such decisions cannot be based on calculated mathematical expectations.[7]

Thus far we have only reached the point where *A Treatise on Probability* leaves off and, as Coddington (1982) notes, it is not sufficient for Keynes's purposes merely to invoke uncertainty.[8] Keynes does go on to provide an argument from uncertainty to the instability of investment demand, however, which, contrary to what is often maintained, includes a theory of expectations formation. These expectations are obviously not 'rational' in the sense of conforming to the axioms of expected utility theory, but this is not to say that they have no basis in reason (Lawson 1991, 1994a; O'Donnell 1989; Orléan 1989). Central to Keynes's account is that, in situations of uncertainty, investors fall back on certain 'conventions'. Chief amongst these are the practices of assuming that the existing state of affairs will continue except in so far as there are specific reasons to expect a change, of taking current market valuations as 'correct' relative to existing knowledge and of copying the behaviour of others who are in a like situation.

Early in Chapter 12, Keynes shifts emphasis from investment in real capital goods to investment on the stock market. As has often been pointed out (e.g. Matthews 1991: 104–5), his account of the connection between stock market activity and real economic activity is rather cursory.[9] But given this connection – a modern account would stress the impact of share price movements on firms' capacity to raise finance for investment in capital goods – Keynes shows how his conventional methods of calculation may have an important negative impact on investment demand. The problem, as he sees it, is that they are so easily disturbed. There are a number of reasons for this. The first is epistemic: as investor expectations often have distant and perhaps indefinite time horizons, they tend to be unduly influenced by the agent's current situation. As Keynes puts it, 'the facts of the existing situation enter, in a sense disproportionately, into the formation of our long-term expectations' (*C.W.* VII: 148). Here, there is an explicit parallel with the weight of evidence when it is low, that expectations formed on the basis of information that is relatively incomplete (by comparison to that which will be acquired over time) will be subject to undue fluctuation with changes in the 'news'. Keynes is here invoking the converse of his observation in the *Treatise on Probability*, that 'the more we know about any phenomenon, the less likely, as a rule, is our opinion to be modified by each additional item of experience' (*C.W.* VIII: 82). He describes the investment community as having beliefs, not only about the forecasted outcomes of different investments, but also about the general firmness with which such forecasts are held. This suggests that it may be possible for there to be a decline in investment demand due simply to a decline in confidence in existing forecasts, even without substantial changes in their content.

The second source of instability is the self-referential nature of the 'conventional' methods of calculation (see Davis 1994a), namely that they may involve market participants 'putting themselves in the shoes of others' on the lines described in Keynes's famous beauty contest example. The problem with practices of this kind is that they may drive a wedge between market valuations and the 'genuine' prospects of the enterprises concerned. Where opinions about certain assets (or classes of assets) change in market situations in which everyone is following everyone else's lead, expectations may be self-fulfilling, with the potential to generate dramatic price-changes. Knowledge about the strategic aspects of stock market activity, in Keynes's view, also encourages short-termism and gambling instincts which further exacerbate instability. This is of course not to deny that existing conventions, as long as they hold, may be consistent with a significant degree of price stability. The point is merely that the balance is a delicate one.

Third, Keynes points to institutional features of financial markets. He remarks that in earlier times owners of enterprises tended to be of 'sanguine temperament and constructive impulses' who embarked on business as a way of life, rather than relying on precise calculations of profit, and made investment decisions that were largely irrevocable. With the advent of the separation of ownership and management and the stock market, however, investors were given the opportunity frequently to revise their asset-holdings. The property of liquidity provided by organized assets markets makes it possible for investors to realize their investments at short notice and thereby ensures a greater flow of investment funds than would otherwise be the case. The downside is that, in facilitating the frequent revision of portfolios, liquidity promotes short-termism and, thereby, asset-market instability. Keynes points to various factors that exacerbate this influence, the excessive effect that day-to-day fluctuations in profits have on prices, the impact of mass psychology, mimetic behaviour, and so on.

Finally, there is the matter of 'irrational' psychological motivations. Keynes begins by arguing that enterprise depends on more than cold calculation, that it also requires a 'spontaneous urge to action rather than inaction' (*C.W.* VII: 161). If such 'animal spirits' should wane and 'spontaneous optimism' falter, so too will enterprise. The theme is a familiar one and I shall say no more about it here, other than to note that it is only one component of Keynes's theory of investment demand. At the end of the relevant section he writes:

> We are merely reminding ourselves that human decisions affecting the future, whether personal or political or economic, cannot depend on strict mathematical expectation, since the basis for making such calculations does not exist; and that it is our innate urge to activity which makes the wheels go round, our rational selves choosing between the alternatives as best we are able, calculating where we can, but often falling back for our motive on whim or sentiment or chance.
>
> (*C.W.* VII: 162–3)

Although arbitrary 'irrational' factors play a role in Chapter 12, they are certainly not its central theme.

Uncertainty, the practices that investors adopt to cope with it and the institutional environment in which they operate, on Keynes's account, all contribute to the tendency towards asset price instability and, with it, to the instability of real investment demand. The emphasis is on the word 'tendency', however. Keynes does not deny that 'the state of long-term expectation is often steady, and, even when it is not, the other factors exert their compensating effects' (*C.W.* VII: 162). The fact that this steadiness is not firmly rooted, however, is never far from investors' minds. If existing conventions should become shakier (for reasons that may at first be real or imagined), according to Keynes, this may precipitate significant price movements with a corresponding impact on the level of real investment demand.

AFTER *THE GENERAL THEORY*

Keynes's correspondence with Hugh Townshend (*C.W.* XXIX: 288–94) suggests that his views on the epistemics of the investment decision were, by the end of the 1930s, much as he had expressed them in Chapter 12. The three themes from *A Treatise on Probability* noted above (non-comparability of probability judgements, non-numerical probability and evidential weight), moreover, are strongly in evidence:

> Moreover the economic problem is, of course, only a particular department of the general principles of conduct, although particularly striking in this connection because it seems to bring in numerical estimations. One arrives presumably at the numerical estimation by some system of arranging alternative decisions in order of preference, some of which will provide a norm by being numerical. But that still leaves millions of cases over where one cannot even arrange an order of preference.[10]
>
> As regards my remarks in my *General Theory*, have you taken account of what I say at page 240, as well as what I say at page 148 [the places he refers to the *Treatises on Probability* and the link between confidence and the weight of evidence] . . . I am rather inclined to associate risk

> premium with probability strictly speaking, and liquidity premium with what in my *Treatise on Probability* I called 'weight' . . .
>
> Generally speaking, in making a decision we have before us a large number of alternatives, none of which is demonstrably more 'rational' than the others in the sense that we can arrange in order of merit the sum aggregate of the benefits obtainable from the complete consequences of each. To avoid being in the position of Buridan's ass, we fall back, therefore, and necessarily do so, on motives of another kind, which are not 'rational' in the sense of being concerned with the evaluation of consequences but are decided by habit, instinct, preference, desire, will, etc.

Chapter 12 itself does not appear to have attracted much criticism from Keynes's early reviewers, many of whom single it out as one of the better parts of the book (Hicks 1936: 242; Knight 1937: 113, Pigou 1936: 131). It is therefore all the more noteworthy that Keynes chooses to emphasize this part of his argument and its methodological implications in his 1937 *Quarterly Journal of Economics* reply to his critics. As before in *The General Theory*, he goes on to elaborate on the theme of 'conventional methods of calculation' as surrogates for mathematical calculation, and the ways in which the conventions he notes contribute to financial market instability (*C.W.* XIV: 112–15, also 106–7, 124–5). All this suggests that he would have left unchanged, or possibly even strengthened, this part of his analysis had there been a second edition of *The General Theory*.

KEYNESIAN METHOD

Although Keynes is explicit that Chapter 12 is more philosophically orientated and proceeds at a different level of abstraction from the rest of the book, he gives no more than the occasional hint about why and in what way this is so. A theme which does recur in various asides, however, is that its subject matter is somehow not amenable to formal analysis. This idea is anathema to Economic Theory and therefore seems a suitably controversial peg on which to hang a discussion of 'Keynesian methodology'.[11] By Economic Theory I mean the orthodox method of proceeding from some set of premises (which include statements of general laws or 'axioms') and then using the rules of logic and set theory to deduce their consequences, the so-called 'axiomatic-deductive' method.

The remainder of what follows considers two metatheoretical perspectives on Chapter 12 that share Keynes's aversion to formalism in the study of social phenomena, those of G.L.S. Shackle and Tony Lawson respectively.[12] I have chosen to concentrate on these two authors for two reasons. First, their methodological concerns seem in both cases to have been precipitated by an initial interest in Keynes's treatment of expectations and uncertainty. Second, and although their opposition to Economic Theory is based on similar grounds, they represent two interesting and increasingly influential alternatives to positivism in the social sciences, hermeneutics (Shackle) and scientific realism (Lawson).

Choice and empirical regularities

Shackle and Lawson occupy very different philosophical positions and have very different views on the possibility of economics as a science. But they stand united on two important points. Both agree on the futility of the search for sharp empirical regularities in economics and both locate one reason for this in their understanding of human choice. Their arguments proceed at different levels, however. Whereas Shackle departs from the existing state of affairs within economics, Lawson argues from a more general philosophy of science perspective. I begin with Shackle, since the most developed statements of his argument owe relatively more to Keynes.

Shackle argues that Economic Theory developed as it did because the simplest way to apply reason to the study of human conduct is to assume that human conduct is itself based on reason. This assumption begs an important question: if economic phenomena are to be understood by supposing that agents apply reason to their circumstances, then one must surely ask what they know about their circumstances. Economic Theory, in Shackle's view, proceeds by applying reason to circumstances assumed to be fully known by the agent(s) concerned and then introduces problems of risk, uncertainty, ignorance, and so on, as refinements of the theory. These refinements tend to be such as to allow reason to continue in its pursuit of determinate (equilibrium) model solutions. The tactics are familiar enough. For example, 'uncertainty' might be introduced by having agents maximize subjective expected utility *à la* Savage, rather than simply maximizing utility.

The trouble, according to Shackle, is that devices such as the subjective expected utility model assume far more knowledge than agents could ever have in practice, when many important economic phenomena stem from the absence of such knowledge. It is here that the influence of Chapter 12 and Keynes's 1937 *Quarterly Journal of Economics* article become apparent in his writings. Following Keynes, Shackle argues that agents' knowledge of their circumstances often falls short of that required to decide the best course of action open to them. He thinks of the problem in terms of an incompleteness of the body of premises that would be necessary for the agent to determine a uniquely optimal course of action.[13] Such ignorance is irreducible, in his view, as it is rooted in the fact that an agent's circumstances depend in part on the unknowable (future) actions (and interactions) of other agents. He lays particular emphasis on the point that agents will often not even be able to imagine some of the consequences of their actions.[14]

For Shackle, then, there is an *epistemic gap* between agents' circumstances and their actions, that reason cannot bridge. It is the question of how agents fill this gap which, in one way or another, occupies most of his writings. His central thesis is that agents perceive their situation before they react to it, and act not so much on what they perceive as on what they infer. Choice, for Shackle, is not a reaction to past stimuli but to expectations of the possible consequences of different courses of action. As expectations are the constructions of agents' imaginations, they are, when acted upon, a constant source of 'new trains of events' in the social world. In short, Shackle's notion of the 'creative' economic agent lies at the heart of his scepticism about the existence of sharp empirical regularities in the economic realm.

Closed systems and economic theory

Lawson, as I have already indicated, takes a more general *realist* perspective and begins by positing a world composed not only of events and our experience of them, but also of mechanisms and structures that give rise to and govern such events.[15] He argues that events are typically not synchronous with the mechanisms that give rise to them, since they are usually the outcome of multiple causal mechanisms (some of which may impede or override others). Following Bhaskar, Lawson demonstrates by argument that event regularities or 'closed systems' arise only in situations in which some mechanism operates in isolation from any factors that might disturb it, something which occurs most often in situations of experimental control.[16] Experimental activity, from this perspective, is an attempt to isolate a causal mechanism by insulating it from possible disturbing factors (so that it can be empirically identified), rather than creating the situation in which some empirical law is put into effect. Causal mechanisms, when triggered, are thus regarded as operating in the same way in open and closed systems alike. The difference is that their effects are not always realized in a regular way in open systems.

Lawson offers two arguments in support of his view that the social world is open. The first is simply the claim that 'significant' event regularities have yet to be found in the social world. Since science is so closely associated with the goal of prediction and is so widely held to be successful, however, it seems unlikely that this observation would command sufficient agreement to clinch the issue. There is also the problem that deciding the question of whether or not something qualifies as an event regularity presupposes agreement on (a) the criteria for deciding on what are to count as the relevant events; and (b) whether or not the regularity must hold without exception for it to qualify as such or, if not, what would count as it being 'sufficiently reliable' for it to do so. Lawson does not have much to say about either of these issues. His second argument is more compelling, however, and, as in the work of Shackle, turns on the human capacity for choice. The argument rests on the idea that it is analytic to the notion of choice that the agent could always have acted other than he or she did. Because a necessary condition for this to be so is that events could really have been different, it follows that choice is possible only in an open world. Given only that choice is real, then, Lawson concludes that the world must be open (Lawson 1994c).[17]

The question which now arises is how the presumption of an open world bears on Economic Theory. Again, Shackle and Lawson press the same point: that Economic Theory is strongly wedded to event regularities, both as a condition for and goal of science. Since their accounts are so similar, I shall run them together. The terminology, however, is mostly Lawson's.

Lawson characterizes Economic Theory in terms of its commitment to what he calls 'deductivism'. By deductivism he means the covering-law model of explanation (Hempel 1965). To explain an event of interest in terms of this model is to deduce that (type of) event from a set of statements of initial conditions and at least one general law. Implicit in Economic Theory, then, is an adherence to the thesis of 'regularity determinism', that 'for every economic event or state of affairs y there exists a set of events or state of affairs $x_1, x_2 \ldots x_n$, such that y and $x_1, x_2 \ldots x_n$ are regularly conjoined under some (set of) formulation(s)' (Lawson 1994c: 19). The objection that Lawson and, as we shall see, Shackle raise against Economic Theory is that an adherence to regularity determinism is hardly justified in a fundamentally open social world.

What, then, are the theoretical restrictions that would justify this adherence? Lawson and, indirectly, Shackle (1972: 74–6) offer three. The first is a condition placed on the individual units of the analysis, the consumer, firm, investor, etc., to ensure that each is so constituted or organized that under the specified set of initial conditions $x_1, x_2 \ldots x_n$ the same outcome y always follows. This may be called the *intrinsic* condition for closure. An obvious requirement for this condition to be met is that the individual units of the analysis exhibit a constant internal structure, that they always behave the same way under the same circumstances. The arguments discussed above, that choice is an act of the creative imagination (Shackle) or that it presupposes that the agent could have acted other than he or she did in a given situation (Lawson), suggest that this requirement is often violated in the social world. But intrinsic constancy alone is not enough. It is also necessary that the outcome y be *reducible* to the set of initial events or states. For even if the individual units of analysis display the requisite degree of internal constancy, a given set of initial conditions need not always lead to the same outcome. Without reducibility indeterminacy remains a possibility.

The second fundamental condition is some principle of composition or *aggregational* condition for closure. This is to ensure that regularities at the level of the individual units of analysis translate into regularities at the aggregate level. Shackle too anticipates the need for a condition of this sort where he warns of the 'sources of dissolution' to which aggregative variables fall prey:

> for individuals are imitative and suggestible, and will swing off together on new courses rather than give an effect of consistency through the mutual independence of their responses and the 'law of large numbers' . . . aggregative variables, indispensible if a general model is to be interpretable and meaningful to intuition, have their own capacities for generating inconsistencies. Their composition can change and thus the relative weights of diversely behaving components.
>
> (Shackle 1972: 75)

The aggregational condition for closure tends to be met, in Economic Theory, by one of a number of possible assumptions. Most familiar, perhaps, are the hypothesis of perfectly competitive equilibrium, the various solution concepts of game theory and the practice of sidestepping the aggregation problem altogether by modelling the 'economy' as a representative agent. In general the aggregational condition for closure requires a detailed specification of the rules of interaction of the individual units of analysis.

Finally, the third fundamental condition which, if satisfied, contributes to ensuring an event regularity, the *extrinsic* condition for closure, is that the system is effectively isolated from the factors not explicitly taken into account in the analysis itself. Shackle refers to such external factors as sources of dissolution 'which affect the model as a whole' and remarks in this connection that '*Ceteris paribus* is a mere pedagogic device or means to insight, and cannot be turned into practical experimental insulation' (Shackle 1972: 75). The extrinsic condition for closure is met if all extrinsic factors are either (a) physically isolated from the system; (b) impact on the system in a constant way; or (c) impinge on the system in a way that is constant on average and is not correlated with those explicitly taken into account in the analysis.

Yet Economic Theorists would presumably deny that it follows, from the presumption of an open world and the closed nature of their models, that their project is a misguided one. It is therefore useful to consider two obvious possible responses to the points just raised. The first is to argue that it is, or will one day become, possible to effect the necessary closures. The second is to accept that economists have yet to find significant empirical regularities but to argue that Economic Theory is nevertheless useful in some way.

A prominent proponent of the first view is Lucas (1981), who offers what might be called the 'analogue-system' justification for Economic Theory. The purpose of Economic Theory, according to Lucas, is to provide a mechanical test-bed for economic policy, 'fully articulated, artificial economic systems that can serve as laboratories in which policies that would be prohibitively expensive to experiment with in actual economies can be tested out at much lower cost' (Lucas1981: 271). More specifically, he writes:

> Our task as I see it . . . is to write a FORTRAN program that will accept specific economic policy rules as 'input' and will generate as 'output' statistics describing the operating characteristics of time series we care about, which are predicted to result from these policies. For example, one would like to know what average rate of unemployment would have prevailed since World War II in the United States had M1 grown at 4 percent per year during this period, other policies being as they were.
>
> (Lucas 1981: 288)

It is hard to imagine a clearer statement of the regularity determinism thesis. What, then, about the closure conditions? Lucas seems to be aware that something on these lines is needed and begins by noting that it is necessary 'to gain some confidence that the component parts of the program are in some sense reliable prior to running it' (ibid.). This confidence is to be earned in the following way:

> The central idea is that *individual* responses can be documented relatively cheaply, occasionally by direct experimentation, but more commonly by means of the vast number of well-documented instances of individual reactions to well-specified environmental changes made available 'naturally' via censuses, panels, other surveys, and the (inappropriately maligned as 'casual empiricism') method of keeping one's eyes open. Without such means of documenting patterns of behaviour, it seems clear that the FORTRAN program proposed above cannot be written.
>
> (Lucas 1981: 288–9)

This passage assumes that the stable patterns are there to be found, however, rather than presenting an argument as to why individual responses should be expected to display the requisite stability. Clearly, the idea that agents will respond in a predictable way to specified changes in their environment does presuppose some intrinsic constancy, the typical assumption being that they have only one intrinsic state (namely that they are rational maximizers). Lucas does not consider the possibility that people often do seem to behave differently in the same circumstances, however, whether this be for reasons of lack of attention, emotional turbulence, a taste for variety, changes in tastes, etc., and proceeds on the assumption that the problem of documenting the 'reliable' behaviour he has in mind has been solved:

> Suppose, on the contrary, that such means are available, or that we have some ability to predict how individual behaviour will respond to specified changes. How, if at all, can such knowledge be translated into knowledge of the way an entire *society* is likely to react to changes in its environment?
>
> (Lucas 1981: 289)

This brings us to the aggregational condition for closure. Lucas sounds on firmer ground here, appealing to competition and, more specifically, 'the hypothesis of competitive equilibrium which permits group behaviour to be predicted from knowledge of individual preferences and technology without the addition of free parameters' (Lucas 1981: 290). Again, however, the hypothesis of perfect competition is hardly one that can be said to be descriptive of, or even an approximation to, the world. (Lucas does not consider the extrinsic condition for closure here. But it is difficult to see how, in a world subject to wars, natural disasters, rapid technical progress and ceaseless variation in political, diplomatic and trading arrangements, it could ever expect to be met.)

The second and somewhat weaker justification of Economic Theory is to interpret its models as 'theoretical' or 'ideal' closures, as thought-experiment analogues to laboratory experiments (see Maki 1992). Although economic analysis is couched in terms of closed systems (models), on this view, it would simply be naive to confront these with 'the data'. Perhaps the most prominent advocate of this view is Hahn (1984, 1985), who is critical of Lucas's brand of positivism and sceptical about the possibilities of finding 'laws' of economics at the systemic level:

> Indeed it is one of the great virtues of theorising in economics that it leaves the practitioner with a suspicion that, what I suppose was once a programme for economics, may be impossible to carry out. It goes of course without saying that economics is not like physics. But I rather think it may not be much like meteorology either. The law of large numbers does not self-evidently operate in the social world in which customs and views of some contaminate those of others. It is not just that there are many variables and complex interactions: it is that the constraints on what is possible seem much weaker than is the case with physical processes studied in meteorology. A theorist then will be surprised if there are 'laws of economics', in the sense of propositions holding universally, to be discovered. He will be surprised if deep knowledge of 'affairs' were to reveal some fundamental or invariant structure of an economy.
>
> (Hahn 1985: 26–7)

Although Hahn appears to draw attention to the possible failure of the intrinsic and aggregational conditions for closure here, he nevertheless appears to remain of the view that the root of the problem is an epistemological rather than an ontological one. That is to say, he seems to believe that if it were possible to cope with the complexity of economic phenomena and have the analysis go 'deep' enough, then prediction would again be feasible. He certainly does not deny that empirical regularities are there to be found:[18]

> For I do not wish to deny that there are empirical regularities of human economic behaviour awaiting discovery. But I claim that these will be, as it were, much deeper down, more elementary and closer to the form in which axioms are postulated than are the complex, institution and history dependent 'facts' of the econometrician.
>
> (Hahn 1984: 332)

Both Lucas and Hahn remain wedded to deductivism in their formal theoretical work. They differ in that Lucas, who is optimistic about the possibility of prediction in economics, is able to remain consistent with the covering-law model of explanation in his more reflective writings on Economic Theory. In particular, Lucas has no need to distinguish between explanation and prediction, which merge in terms of this model.[19] Hahn (1984: 4–5), however, who is rather less optimistic about prediction in economics, is forced to make this distinction in his methodological writings. For if Economic Theory were to be found wanting on explanatory as well as predictive grounds, this would appear to leave it with little justification at all.[20] However, and although his examples sometimes seem to suggest that he has in mind explanation in the sense of giving a causal account of how some phenomenon arises, Hahn's argument is more oblique than this. What Economic Theory provides, in his view, is an aid to 'understanding' or 'orderly thinking', a common precise language in which economic question can be discussed (Hahn 1985: 10–28). Unfortunately, Hahn is not particularly explicit about what it might be to understand something. A criterion which he does seem to consider important, however, is the extent to which particular statements or instances of Economic Theory models cohere with, complement and extend existing theoretical 'successes'.[21] Since its practitioners involved invariably invoke rather dramatic idealizations decided prior to the investigation (such as atomistic agents characterized in terms of no more than preferences that conform to certain more or less fictitious postulates of 'rational' choice), the extent to which this approach might yield causal explanations of concrete economic phenomena would seem to be rather limited. It is surely no accident that the word 'explanation' is so notably absent in Hahn's methodological writings.

The two arguments for Economic Theory considered thus reduce to interpreting it as offering (a) predictions/explanations in the empiricist regularity-between-events sense (Lucas); or (b) as a tool that facilitates 'understanding' but which in itself offers neither predictions nor much, if anything, in the way of causal explanations (Hahn). As (a) presupposes closure conditions that are unlikely ever to be met in practice and as (b) does not appear to offer the possibility of explanation in anything but an extremely restricted sense, this suggests that it may be useful to consider some alternative approaches to economic explanation. I now turn to the positive proposals of Shackle and Lawson.

Hermeneutics, critical realism and Chapter 12

Thus far I have concentrated on the ground Shackle and Lawson share in their opposition to Economic Theory. In order to sketch their proposed alternatives, however, it becomes necessary to emphasize the points on which their positions diverge. A key difference lies in that Shackle is a methodological dualist, someone who sees a fundamental difference between the natural and the social sciences. Lawson in contrast holds that, at the level of explanation, there is a basic unity between the sciences. As the positivist philosophy they are reacting against has tended to lead the argument for a monistic view of science, it may appear that Shackle's position represents more of a departure from positivism than does Lawson's. I shall argue that this is not so.

Proponents of methodological dualism tend to accept the positivist view of the natural sciences, and with it, the associated conception of knowledge as consisting largely of events given in experience, and general (scientific) knowledge, of constant conjunctions of such events. Shackle is no exception. He writes, for example, that 'Knowledge and constancy are so intimately related in all science, that we can say that science is merely the recognition and description of constancy' (1972: 18), and that what is fundamental in science is no more than a refinement of what we use in everyday living:

> The ultimate indispensable permissive condition of knowledge is the repitition of recognizable configurations. These patterns or stereotypes form a hierarchy in our minds. A pattern of sense-impressions, perhaps from more than one sense, is pinned down as an object or an event. The occurrence, over and over again, of similar objects or events establishes a class of objects or events, a *concept*. Such concepts themselves can then form the building blocks of more complex and inclusive configurations. Science tells us what to count on, what to rely on. But in doing so it merely imitates and refines the process by which we build, each of us for himself, the homely technology of everyday living. The means of its doing so is the power of survival and reappearance of types of configuration.
>
> (Shackle 1972: 6–7)

As we have seen, however, Shackle's distinctive contribution to economics is chiefly concerned with situations in which this conception of knowledge is inadequate, where there are no salient patterns or event regularities to guide conduct. He accordingly proceeds to analyse such situations by invoking agents' subjective view of their circumstances and reasons for action, using, in effect, the hermeneutic method of empathetic understanding or *Verstehen*: 'If the economic theoretician is to organize his subject as a manifestation of human nature, and to trace it back to the operation of feelings and of thought, he must exhibit its events and situations as flowing from men's construction of their opportunities and their choices amongst these conceptions' (Shackle 1974: 76). In effect, then, in advocating that economic analysis be conducted in terms of how agents themselves conceive their situations, Shackle is proposing an epistemological solution to what he regards as an epistemological problem. Agents' conceptions are not to be explained, merely to be grasped and taken as starting points in arguments that trace economic phenomena (e.g. unemployment) as the (often unintended) consequences of the actions to which such conceptions give rise.[22]

In many ways, all this does represent a break with the positivist image of science. In particular, it requires an ontology of more than atomistic objects and events (and regularities between them) given in experience, but also an ability to grasp the contents of agents' minds, their feelings, thoughts and conceptions. In his emphasis on agents' capacity to 'create' the future, moreover, Shackle goes beyond the conception of human behaviour supported by positivism, of agents as passive sensors of events and their constant conjunctions. However, and this is an important caveat, the category of experience is still primary in Shackle's account. His break with positivism is incomplete on this count, and makes it difficult for him to accord a role to phenomena that are not, and cannot be reduced to, objects of experience. It comes as no surprise, then, that Shackle's expositions of Chapter 12 concentrate almost exclusively on the subjective experience of the investor. For example:

> I think that what Keynes had in mind is an aspect of what elsewhere I have ventured to call his kaleidic account of the economic process of history. By the kaleidic theory I mean the view that the expectations, which together with the drive of needs or ambitions make up the 'springs of action', are at all times so insubstantially founded upon data and so mutably suggested by the stream of 'news', that is, of counter-expected or totally unthought-of events, that they can undergo complete transformation in an hour or even a moment, as the patterns of a kaleidoscope dissolve at a touch; the view that men are conscious of their essential and irremediable state of un-knowledge and that they usually suppress this awareness in the interest of avoiding a paralysis of action; but that from time to time they succumb to its abiding mockery and menace, and withdraw from the field.
>
> (Shackle 1974: 42)

Now Shackle is surely correct that investor uncertainty is an important and perhaps even the key factor underlying the instability of investment demand. It cannot be denied, moreover, that his many contributions on this topic yield a rich and insightful impression of the impact of uncertainty on investor behaviour and the texture of economic affairs. Nevertheless, it is a mistake to argue that the investor's subjective experience and uncertainty is *all* that matters in accounting for the instability of investment demand, something he sometimes comes close to doing:

> Chapter 12 is a curiously unsatisfying chapter. It loses sight of what in the end Keynes saw as its profoundly important meaning, and spends many pages discussing the possible advantages of abolishing the joint-stock company, or at any rate greatly reducing the marketability of its shares.
>
> (Shackle 1967: 132)

The trouble is that the things Shackle here dismisses as mere distractions from Keynes's main theme are in fact integral to the behaviour and practices described in Chapter 12. For example, the idea that uncertainty might lead investors to 'withdraw from the field' (i.e. move into liquid assets) presupposes the existence of all manner of irreducibly social phenomena, the joint-stock company, organized asset markets and so on. These exist and operate quite independently of any individual investor's conception of them (a conception which may in any event be inadequate or simply false). In the absence of such institutions investors would presumably continue to labour under significant uncertainty, but equity values might be considerably less subject to fluctuation than they are under existing institutional arrangements. The point is that an analysis which is restricted to elaborating agents' conceptions of their situations and activities, while perhaps the most obvious for someone for whom '*being* consists in continual and endless fresh *knowing*' (Shackle 1972: 156), will often be inadequate in so far as it ignores the influence of the (often unacknowledged) material aspect of social life.

Lawson, in contrast, and while accepting the insights that hermeneutics might afford, offers an account which can accomodate both individual action (agency) and the material aspect of social life (structure).[23] I have already said something about his distinction between events and the mechanisms and structures that give rise to and govern them. Central to Lawson's account is that these mechanisms and structures are (a) irreducible to events or *structured*, and (b) *intransitive*, existing and acting independently of their identification.[24] Now if the world is open it follows that the goal of science can no longer be the discovery and elaboration of event regularities. Instead, Lawson urges, science must be explanatory, and that explanation, properly conceived, consists in the movement from the phenomenon to be explained to the mechanisms and structures that give rise to and govern it. This approach, *retroduction* combined with inference to the best explanation (Lipton 1991), applies in the natural and the social sciences alike. Of course, the different sciences have different objects of knowledge, and in the case of social science these are human practices and their consequences. The explanation of human practices thus involves identifying the mechanisms and structures that make them possible. This includes identifying and understanding the 'unacknowledged conditions of these practices, their unconscious motivations, the tacit skills drawn upon, as well as their unintended consequences' (Lawson 1995b).

Lawson (1990b, 1995b) portrays Chapter 12 as an exemplar of this mode of explanation. The phenomenon to be explained, of course, is the propensity for fluctuations in the level of real investment demand, and this, to repeat, is to be achieved by 'going behind' it, by identifying and elaborating the mechanisms and structures that give rise to and govern it. The first step of the argument, then, is to establish the connection between real investment demand and stock market instability (*C.W.* VII: 150–1). The second step is to identify the human activities that precipitate this instability, namely, the frequent revaluation of existing assets on the stock exchange. These activities, of course, are the focus of Chapter 12.

Lawson identifies the main 'underlying' structures and mechanisms that Keynes invokes in his explanation as the organization of modern investment markets, the 'nature of and structure of uncertainty' and the prevalence of psychological motivations. His account of the structure of Keynes's argument is similar to the one implicit in the review given above, albeit with different points of emphasis. The picture that emerges is one of a causal explanation in which neither individual agency nor social structure predominate, but in which the object of analysis is explained as emerging out of the interplay and (often recursive) relations between them.

I have left out here considerable detail and the many ways in which Lawson develops Keynes's argument. But I hope I have succeeded in relaying the case for Chapter 12 as an example of a coherent and rigorous (albeit discursive) analytical approach that transcends some of the difficulties encountered by Economic Theory. Finally, it does not follow, on the view just outlined, that scepticism about event prediction has nihilistic implications for economic policy.[25] It merely requires a different view of policy, not as directed at exploiting 'laws', but as directed at changing the social structures and motivations that give rise to and govern human behaviour. A full discussion of this issue must be left for another occasion, but Keynes himself provides an illuminating example of how a change in the existing institutional framework, while it would not determine the particular actions of investors, would induce them to take a longer, and hence more socially beneficient, view in deciding their investments:

> That the sins of the London Stock Exchange are less than those of Wall Street may be due, not so much to differences in national character, as to the fact that to the average Englishman Throgmorton Street is, compared with Wall Street to the average American, inaccessible and very expensive. The jobber's 'turn', the high brokerage charges and the heavy transfer tax payable to the Exchequer, which attend dealings on the London Stock Exchange, sufficiently diminish the liquidity of the market (although the practice of fortnightly accounts operates the other way) to rule out a large proportion of the transactions characteristic of Wall Street. The introduction of a substantial government transfer tax on all transactions might prove the most serviceable reform available, with a view to mitigating the predominance of speculation over enterprise in the United States.
>
> (*C.W.* VII: 159–60)

CONCLUDING REMARKS

It may seem strange that a chapter on methodology should be silent on standard debates in the philosophy of science about the possibilities of induction, verificationism, falsificationism, and so on. The reason I have had nothing to say about these debates is that they are family disputes within the positivist tradition. They are largely irrelevant to the alternative conceptions of social science I have been discussing, turning as they do on epistemological issues concerning empirical regularities between events.

Chapter 12 of *The General Theory* is an example of a mode of economic analysis that neither depends on nor reflects the positivistic conception of science and its associated emphasis on event prediction. It is this feature, perhaps, that has secured its place in the non-mainstream methodological literature. I have argued that Shackle and Lawson, two of its most prominent expositors, are largely at one on why the positivist programme must fail in economics and, accordingly, in their view, on the need for an alternative to Economic Theory. But Shackle's positive proposals only partially succeed, as his hermeneutic gloss on Keynes's analysis ultimately reduces to a subjectivist version of the position he seeks to transcend. This is of course not to deny the importance of question of knowledge and uncertainty in social life, problems that also occupy Keynes in his philosophical work and later analysis of investor behaviour. But there is more to economic explanation than the grasping and elaboration of individual agents' subjective conceptions of their situations and their activities. For economic action and its consequences also have a material aspect in their dependence on social structures that are independent of any individual agent's conception of them. The strength of Keynes's Chapter 12 analysis is that it can give due weight to both.

NOTES

* I am grateful to Vicky Chick, John Davis, Geoff Harcourt, Tony Lawson, Bruce Littleboy, Rod O'Donnell, Steve Pratten and Arnis Vilks for their comments on earlier versions of this paper.

1 It has been suggested that this methodological diversity may be attributed to the fact that *The General Theory* is written with more than one purpose in mind. Skidelsky (1992: 540) refers to its 'double character' as at once 'enquiring into the nature of economic life and providing a tool of policy' and suggests that 'Keynes acquiesed in the mathematisation of *The General Theory* for pedagogical and policy purposes' (ibid.: 610). It certainly seems plausible that Keynes's eagerness to convert the profession accounts for why he conducts part of the argument in the style of his 'Classical' opponents. Nevertheless, and rhetorical devices aside, it remains hard to reconcile the more formal and mechanistic parts of Keynes's analysis with his views on the 'specious precision' of many of his fellow economists and his continued insistence that the proper analysis of many of the key social phenomena identified in *The General Theory* lies 'outside the realm of the formally exact'.

2 This is, of course, not to say that the approach adopted in Chapter 12 is unique to it. Substantially the same approach is adopted in Chapters 8, 9, 13, 15, 16, 17, 22 and 24.

3 My emphasis here will be on Keynes's analysis of (rational) conduct under uncertainty rather than on his views on statistical inference and econometrics (on which, see Lawson and Pesaran 1985; Carabelli 1988; Lawson 1989; O'Donnell 1989, and Chapter 31 in this volume; Bateman 1990a; and Conniffe 1992).

4 The debate turns on the extent to which Keynes accepted Ramsey's criticisms, an issue with obvious implications for work aimed at grounding Keynes's economic writings on uncertainty in his writings on probability. Advocates of the continuity view include Carabelli (1988), Lawson (1985a, 1987) and O'Donnell (1989); and of the discontinuity view, Bateman (1987) and Davis (1994a). My own position is that Keynes later gives up his ontology of logical probability relations, but that he continues to regard qualitative probability comparisons as basic to epistemic probability (Runde 1994b). See also Bateman (1990b, 1991); Cottrell (1993); Gillies (1988, 1991); O'Donnell (1990c); Moggridge (1992); and Skidelsky (1992).

5 Although the concept of evidential weight is a relatively unfamiliar one in modern decision theory, it has links with issues raised in the 'probability ambiguity' literature precipitated by Ellsberg (1961). See Brady and Lee (1989a, 1989b) and Runde (1994a).

6 The 'absurdities' Keynes mentions here seem to be the paradoxes to which the principle of indifference leads when applied to alternatives that are not indivisible. These paradoxes are discussed at length in Chapter 4 of the *Treatise on Probability*. See also van Fraassen (1989: 293–317).

7 Investors may of course yet be able to decide the 'most probable forecast' (*C.W.* VII: 148).

8 Investors might respond to uncertainty in the current period by repeating whatever they did in the preceding period, for instance, which would promote stability rather than the reverse. Whether or not such behaviour would translate into a stable level of employment, however, would of course depend on other conditions being met (such as productivity levels remaining unchanged, for example).

9 But the daily revaluations of the Stock Exchange, though they are primarily made to facilitate transfers of old investments between one individual and another, inevitably exert a decisive influence on the rate of *current investment*. For there is no sense in building up a new enterprise at a cost greater than that at which a similar enterprise can be purchased; whilst there is an inducement to spend on a new project what may seem an extravagant sum, if it can be floated off on the Stock Exchange at an immediate profit. Thus certain classes of investment are governed by the average expectation of those who deal on the Stock Exchange as revealed in the price of shares, rather than by the genuine expectations of the professional entrepreneur.

(*C.W.* VII: 151)

10 In *A Treatise on Probability* Keynes suggests that it may sometimes be possible to make use of 'inexact' numerical probabilities derived from comparison with some numerical standard or interval-values between which they are judged to lie (*C.W.* VIII: 176–80). See Brady (1993).

11 A number of the people have commented that my use of the term 'Economic Theory' cedes too much to the orthodoxy. As I have no wish to deny the possibility of non-deductivist economic theory, I shall use upper-case letters to denote the orthodox deductive variant.

12 The main sources I draw on in this section are Shackle (1967, 1972, 1974, 1979) and Lawson (1994a, 1994b, 1994c, 1995a, 1995b). Lawson's position, in turn, owes much to the philosophical writings of Roy Bhaskar (1978, 1979, 1986, 1989). Shackle makes no reference to specialist philosophers.

13 Shackle (1972: 25). The underlying intuitions and formal properties of Shackle's measure of potential surprise are remarkably similar to those of Keynes's measure of evidential weight (Runde 1993).

14 Economic Theory has of course developed considerably since the 1970s and there are now formal models of many of the economic phenomena that feature in Keynes's writings: sunspots and self-fulfilling expectations (Woodford 1992); conventions and mimetic behaviour (Orlean 1989); liquidity (Jones and Ostroy 1984; Makowski 1990); as well as a plethora of models of choice under uncertainty that do not assume point probabilities (Kelsey and Quiggin 1992; Runde 1995). There have even been steps towards incorporating Shackle's 'residual hypothesis' (i.e. unimagined choice outcomes) into the standard probability framework (Kreps 1992; Madan and Owings 1988). The emphasis on reason, it appears, is as strong as ever in economics. But whereas reason once promised determinacy, recent theoretical work has increasingly become characterized by indeterminacy, that is, by too many (and often a continuum) of equilibrium outcomes.

15 Events are defined as instances of the possible (which may or may not be the objects of direct experience).

16 Event regularities are defined as the object of statements of the form 'whenever event (type) *x* then event (type) *y*'.

17 Lawson (1995a) does not deny that there may be 'local' closures in the social realm, such as regular annual holidays, school opening and closing times, etc. These, however, will usually have been consciously brought about.

18 Hahn turns the fact that Economic Theory tends not to yield single-valued predictions into an argument in its favour: that it serves as a warning that certainty is not to be had and that many things are possible (e.g. Hahn 1984: 341–2). In a recent survey, however, Hahn (1991) hints that Economic Theory has become overly permissive in this sense and predicts an increasing resort to

specific psychological, historical and sociological postulates to counter the problem of multiple equilibria.

19 In terms of the classical covering-law model, explanation is symmetrical with prediction: every full explanation is a prediction and vice versa. The difference between the two is purely pragmatic, depending on whether the relevant event occurs before or after the argument that accounts for it is proposed.

20 This leaves the 'benchmark' argument that Hahn (1984) invokes in various places, that general equilibrium theory may be regarded as a normative ideal for policy purposes. The trouble with this argument, as Mittermaier (1986) points out, is that it does not sit easily with the 'base camp' hypothesis, that the 'student of GE believes that he has a starting point from which it is possible to advance towards a descriptive theory' (Hahn 1984: 137).

21 Hahn's favourite example of such a success is the Arrow–Debreu model, which he regards as an 'ideal reference point' without which he believes it would be difficult to comprehend 'realistic' phenomena such as externalities, imperfect competition and increasing returns (Hahn 1985: 20–21).

22 Shackle occasionally seems to take the radical hermeneutic view that economic analysis should itself take on some of the mutability, imprecision and variegated meanings of agents' perceptions and constructions of their world (e.g. Shackle 1974: 73–5).

23 On Lawson's account, neither agency nor structure can be reduced to the other. Instead, he adopts a 'tranformational' view of social activity in terms of which agents both draw on (but are not determined by) social structures in acting, and reproduce (and perhaps transform) such structures in drawing on them. Social structure, in other words, is both a condition for and dependent upon human agency (see Bhaskar 1986: 118–36; and for an alternative account, Giddens 1984).

24 The terminology is Bhaskar's. Following Bhaskar, Lawson also identifies an epistemological or *transitive* dimension consisting of the cognitive materials of science, theories, models, hypotheses, etc. This dimension is transitive in the sense that it is always open to revision. Scientific progress is thus conceived as an ongoing process of updating the transitive dimension.

25 Shackle, in contrast, who does not have an ontology of generative mechanisms and structures, is driven to precisely this conclusion. See especially Shackle (1983).

35

KEYNES, VAGUE CONCEPTS AND FUZZY LOGIC*

John Coates

The issues that dominated Cambridge philosophy during the 1930s still to a certain extent dominate contemporary philosophy. For it was at that time that the fundamental divide between theorists of formal semantics, such as Russell, and theorists of communication-intention, such as the latter Wittgenstein, first took shape. It is therefore a fairly straightforward exercise to map the thought of a Cambridge philosopher on to current debates. Wittgenstein and Russell are, so to speak, still players to be dealt with. Keynes too was a philosopher involved with later Cambridge thought, and the ideas he penned in letters, manuscripts and lecture notes at that time find a home context in today's debates in the philosophy of the social sciences. He came to focus on one of the issues which occupied Wittgenstein and Ramsey: they drew attention to the inevitable vagueness of ordinary language and to how this property challenged the analytic project of constructing a fully formalized language based on predicate logic. However, none of these philosophers were bothered by the failure as they came to recognize that vague concepts paradoxically could be more efficient than formalized ones, particularly, as Keynes argued, when analysing complex entities such as social reality. There is today a great deal of work being done on the compatibility of classical logic with vague predicates and on alternative, fuzzy logics. Keynes's ideas on the role of vague concepts therefore have a contribution to make to this discussion, particularly since few philosophers have pursued the issue within the social sciences.

KEYNES AND LATER CAMBRIDGE PHILOSOPHY

Keynes's involvement with the ideas of the later Wittgenstein and Ramsey has not been dealt with fully because most attention has been focused on his earlier *Treatise on Probability*. The problem with confining attention to this book is that it is an artefact from early Cambridge philosophy, when analytic techniques and assumptions dominated. But Cambridge thought underwent a revolution at the time of Wittgenstein's transitional *Blue and Brown Books*, indeed, it repudiated most of the tenets of analytic philosophy. If we are to argue that Keynes's early philosophical work continued to dominate his thought, we must impute to him an uncharacteristic lack of curiosity concerning the work of his close friends, Wittgenstein and Ramsey. This is highly unlikely. Few people in Cambridge were unaffected by the new ideas. Another difficulty in focusing exclusively on his earlier work on probability is that Keynes rarely returned to the subject after the mid-1920s. In his later writings on the philosophy of the social sciences he addressed the same questions on formalization as those with which Wittgenstein was dealing.

Wittgenstein returned to Cambridge in 1929 when doubts concerning his earlier work, the *Tractatus*, brought him back to philosophy and to a new line of thought which transformed Cambridge philosophy. At the time of his return Keynes was perhaps his closest friend. Wittgenstein stayed with Keynes for several weeks, during which time Keynes got him re-elected to the Apostles. Ray Monk has recently argued that the two drifted apart after a few weeks, and that their friendship was confined to purely practical affairs after that. But the biographical evidence indicates the opposite. The discussions which began early in 1929 were regular and intense, as he complained to Lydia: 'I must not let him talk to me for more than two or three hours a day.'[1] Moreover, these discussions continued through 1933, as Keynes regularly referred to the 'visits from Ludwig'.[2] Wittgenstein was somewhat single-minded in his philosophizing, so it must be assumed that during these meetings Keynes and he were discussing Wittgenstein's new ideas. Skidelsky asks, 'What did they talk about for two or three hours a day?' and similarly concludes that 'Much of the conversation must have been philosophical' (Skidelsky 1992: 292). He also claims that Wittgenstein's return to Cambridge 'had rekindled Keynes's love of philosophy' (ibid.: 380). Keynes was certainly aware of the various manuscripts Wittgenstein was working on as he offered financial assistance on one occasion to help publish the *Brown Book*;[3] and later he was one of the first to read through Part 1 of the *Philosophical Investigations* (Wittgenstein 1974: 138, 139).

The influence of the discussions manifests itself as an echo in Keynes's writings of Wittgenstein's analysis of vague concepts. Wittgenstein and Russell had earlier tried to construct a logically perfect language. A central assumption of this project was the Fregean view that concepts must have sharp boundaries; clearly defined concepts were to logic what rigid bodies were to geometry. Wittgenstein came to question both the possibility and the utility of such concepts. Central to his reappraisal of logical atomism was the discovery of an unbridgeable gap between the formalized constructs of predicate logic and the irreducibly vague concepts of natural language. In the *Philosophical Remarks*, written around the beginning of the 1930s, Wittgenstein wrote:

> The moment we try to apply exact concepts of measurement to immediate experience, we come up against a peculiar vagueness in this experience. But that only means a vagueness relative to these concepts of measurement. And, now, it seems to me that this vagueness isn't something provisional, to be eliminated later on by more precise knowledge, but that this is a characteristic logical peculiarity.
>
> (Wittgenstein 1975: 263)

Keynes in an early draft of *The General Theory*, written around the same time, criticized formal methods in much the same words as Wittgenstein:

> Much economic theorising to-day suffers, I think, because it attempts to apply highly precise and mathematical methods to material which is itself much too vague to support such treatment.
>
> (*C.W.* XIV: 379)

The issue of vague concepts was thus on both their minds. Largely as a result of Wittgenstein's work much effort has been spent trying to square formal logic with vague predicates. Max Black's (1949: 28) definition of vagueness is the starting point for most discussions of the issue: 'A symbol's vagueness is held to consist in the existence of objects concerning which it is intrinsically impossible to say either that the symbol in question does, or does not, apply.' The term 'bald', for example, is vague: while it is possible to state decisively that the term applies to someone who is hairless and does not to someone with a full head of hair, it is impossible to say exactly when a rapidly receding hairline turns into baldness. The same problem occurs with other words which measure properties along a scale, such as big–small, hot–cold. In all these cases there is a fringe or penumbra of objects, borderline cases, over which decisive judgement is impossible. Moreover, this failure is not due to the lack of information about the objects; no new evidence would clear up the matter. The problem also exists for singular terms. Black imagined a museum lined with chairs, objects running from a Chippendale, which is universally recognized as a chair, down to a lump of wood, which is not. In between there are intermediate objects where 'personal uncertainty is a reflection of objective lack of agreement' (ibid.: 33). The attendant difficulties are rife, for the property is pervasive; as Russell (1923: 90) said: 'all language is more or less vague.'

The type of vagueness Wittgenstein focused on is analytically different from those discussed by Russell and Black. This type of vagueness is entailed by his cluster theory of meaning: there are a number of independently sufficient conditions for the application of words, not just one, a common property shared by the objects subsumed. This makes definition difficult. Wittgenstein recognized that definitions can be given, and misunderstandings can be cleared up by legislating the boundaries of words. But these definitions cannot circumscribe all that we normally consider, say, a game, or a number. William Alston distinguishes vagueness stemming from the absence of a cut-off point along a scale, as is found with size and age, from vagueness which is caused by a term's having 'a number of independent conditions of application' (Alston 1964: 87). He calls these 'degree' and 'combination of conditions vagueness' respectively (ibid.). Russell and Black focused on degree vagueness while Wittgenstein emphasized combinatory vagueness. In the example of games, we find not a single defining feature, but several: a game may be played for amusement, although war games are not; it may involve the display of skill, but flipping a coin is a random procedure; it may involve competition between players, but the card game solitaire does not. All those practices we call games display many defining features, but they do not display any common one. Wittgenstein called this property family resemblance. Hjalmar Wennerberg (1967) interprets Wittgenstein by considering five objects classified by eight properties; he thinks the idea of family resemblance includes cases where no features are shared by two objects, yet they are considered samples of the same concept. Wennerberg illustrates this possibility with the series

e	d	c	b	a
ABCD	BCDE	CDEF	DEFG	EFGH

Here objects e and a have nothing in common. The family resemblance holding a series together acts locally, like links in a chain, and not globally by means of a common unifying property. Here definition cannot be done by generalizing common properties; it is rather the practice of choosing a sample object to stand as a paradigm case. But such a definition will inevitably render a word vague because we cannot say definitely which properties, or how many, are required for a word to apply to an object. This distinction between identifying a common property to objects, that is, the process of generalization, and proposing a sample from a diverse population of objects was central to Keynes's understanding of the nature of definitions and models.

Wittgenstein had stressed that the property of vagueness did not prevent us from using words in a manner perfectly suited for their purposes. Just because our everyday sentences cannot be interpreted in a manner similar to formal semantics does not mean that they are inherently prone to mislead us. Keynes also made this point. In a series of lectures given in 1932 dealing with the core ideas of *The General Theory*, he began by discussing 'The difficulty of choosing convenient terminology' (*C.W.* XXIX: 35). And in this lecture he made much the same point – 'one of great practical importance to anyone who essays to write an intricate work on economics' (ibid.: 36) – as Wittgenstein was making at the time:

> A definition can often be *vague* within fairly wide limits and capable of several interpretations differing slightly from one another, and still be perfectly serviceable and free from serious risk of leading either the author or the reader into error . . .
>
> (*C.W.* XXIX: 36, original emphasis)

Keynes here displayed an acceptance of several key Wittgensteinian notions: the idea that words have a variety of interlocking uses, each of which differs slightly from the others, but all of which bear a family resemblance to one another; the use of the term 'vague' to refer to this property of words; and the understanding that vague concepts can be perfectly serviceable without being analysed. The vagueness Keynes wrote about here is combinatory vagueness, and he appreciated how difficult it is to formalize concepts displaying this property.

Wittgenstein and Keynes also questioned the utility of a Fregean language. To begin with, demanding exactness from ordinary language is a touch pedantic: we can always demand more precision: 'But has this exactness still got a function here: isn't the engine idling?' (Wittgenstein [1953] 1958: s. 88). And what if we could effect a revision of our language? Would this contribute to easing communication? A broom, for example, might in the first instance be analysed into broomstick and brush:

> Then does someone who says that the broom is in the corner really mean: the broomstick is there, and so is the brush? . . . Suppose that instead of saying 'Bring me the broom', you said, 'Bring me the broomstick and the brush which is fitted on to it'! – Isn't the answer: 'Do you want the broom? Why do you put it so oddly?' – Is he going to understand the further analyzed sentence better? – This sentence, one might say, achieves the same as the ordinary one, but in a more roundabout way.
>
> (Ibid.: s. 60)

The ideal language of the *Tractatus* can be seen rather as a particularly cumbersome form of discourse compared to everyday language, which is ideally suited for its uses. This leads to an apparently paradoxical conclusion: words in our natural language are inherently vague, and since this means that more goes into a word than can be made explicit in a definition, we are led to the conclusion that there is a precision in vagueness. Strictly circumscribed concepts, at least when dealing with problems formulated in natural language, will leave too much out of account, or will be too cumbersome to achieve their goal of facilitating understanding; our vague concepts, in contrast, are implicitly understood by native speakers. The more precise statement, by analytic standards, if it did not confuse with its foreign terminology, might achieve the same as an ordinary statement 'but in a more roundabout way'.

Keynes had hinted at such a conclusion in the *Treatise of Probability* where he criticized the reductionist symbolism of *Principia Mathematica*, and questioned in what sense it was preferable to everyday language in exposing fallacious reasoning:

> Confusion of thought is not always best avoided by technical and unaccustomed expressions, to which the mind has no immediate reaction of understanding; it is possible, under the cover of a careful formalism, to make statements, which, if expressed in plain language, the mind would immediately repudiate. There is much to be said, therefore, in favour of understanding the substance of what you are saying *all the time*, and of never reducing the substantives of your argument to the mental status of an *x* or *y*.
>
> (*C.W.* VIII: 20 fn. 1)

This doubt as to the utility of formalization was to move from the status of a footnote to become during the 1930s an outright critique of formal methods in the social sciences. He often argued that rather than being a more sure-footed route for inquiry to follow, a symbolic treatment could disguise faulty reasoning. And he too questioned the *a priori* belief in the economy and efficiency of more formalized languages. Just as Wittgenstein had pointed out that analysed statements communicate their meaning 'in a more roundabout way' as ordinary language, so too Keynes argued that:

> If an author tries to avoid all vagueness, and to be perfectly precise, he will become so prolix and pedantic, will find it necessary to split so many hairs, and will be so constantly diverted into an attempt to clear up some other part of the subject, that he himself may perhaps never reach the matter at hand and the reader certainly will not.
>
> (*C.W.* XXIX: 36)

He returned to the issue in his lectures of November 1933, which were addressed to the question 'What degree of precision is advisable in economics?' (Rymes 1989a: 101). His students noted that, 'on the matter of precise definition of terms, there is some question as to the utility and propriety of the scholastic exercise in trying to define terms with great precision in a subject like economics' (ibid.: 102). A danger of this approach 'is that you may "precise everything away" and be left with only a comparative poverty of meaning' (ibid.). Here Keynes pointed out the problems that ensue from defining with an artificial precision concepts that are characterized by combinatory vagueness, for the precise definition will leave out of account too much of what we intuitively intend when using the concept.

Keynes repeatedly commented on 'the appalling state of scholasticism into which the minds of so many economists have got' (*C.W.* XXIX: 150). Ramsey had made the same point about the arcane logical ideals of the

Tractatus when he wrote: 'The chief danger to our philosophy, apart from laziness and woolliness, is *scholasticism*, the essence of which is treating what is vague as if it were precise and trying to fit it into an exact logical category' (quoted in *C.W.* X: 343, original emphasis). Keynes quoted this passage in his anthology of Ramsey's works, and it shows up as well in the lecture of 6 November 1933 where he said: 'In a complicated subject like economics the thing to do is avoid woolliness on the one hand, and scholasticism on the other' (Rymes 1989a: 102). Lorie Tarshis, one of the students recording the lectures, wrote of scholasticism, '"the essence of which is treating what is vague as what is precise"' (ibid.: 101). The fact that he put this passage in quotation marks indicates perhaps that Keynes made it clear that he was quoting, obviously from Ramsey. Keynes was thus picking up an analysis of vague concepts from both Wittgenstein and Ramsey.

Keynes's appreciation of the dangers involved in formalizing concepts displaying combinatory vagueness led him to choose definitions that did not sever the concept's connection to the vague penumbra of tacit understanding that surrounds our use of words. He took great pains to define his terms in accordance with common usage. For example, while recognizing that 'In common parlance the term *income* is somewhat vague' (*C.W.* XIII: 424–5), he decided on the proper definition in the following way:

> But finally I have come to the conclusion that the use of language, which is most convenient on a balance of considerations and involves the least departure from current usage, is to call the actual sale proceeds *income* and the present value of the expected sale proceeds *effective demand.*
>
> (Ibid.)

This practice is repeated throughout Book II, where Keynes distilled from the various uses of a term a definition which involved 'the least departure from current usage' (*C.W.* VII: 61). Every definition is thus chosen because it corresponded with actual usage of the terms involved. He defended his definition of 'net income' by referring to common practice:

> It will be seen that our definition of *net income* comes very close to . . . the practices of the Income Tax Commissioners . . . For the fabric of their decisions can be regarded as the result of the most careful and extensive investigation which is available, to interpret what, in practice, it is usual to treat as net income.
>
> (Ibid.: 59, original emphasis)

He concluded that 'The above definitions of income and of net income are intended to conform as closely as possible to common usage' (ibid.). Similarly, in dealing with 'savings' he pointed out: 'So far as I know, everyone agrees in meaning by *saving* the excess of income over what is spent on consumption. It would certainly be very inconvenient and misleading not to mean this' (ibid.: 74). And then of 'investment': 'In popular usage it is common to mean by this the purchase of an asset, old or new, by an individual or corporation' (ibid.: 74–5). Thus Keynes's 'own definition is in accordance with popular usage' (ibid.). Throughout, he meant saving and investment to be 'taken in their straightforward sense' (ibid.: 81). According to these new definitions, as opposed to those used in his *Treatise on Money*, 'saving and investment are, necessarily and by definition, equal – which, after all, is in full harmony with common sense and the common usage of the world' (*C.W.* XIV: 427). This approach to concept formation has some fruitful contributions to make to philosophical debates today.

VAGUE CONCEPTS AND FUZZY LOGIC

Vagueness poses grave difficulties for traditional philosophy in that it throws doubt on such doctrines as metaphysical realism, which requires determinate entities, and on the applicability of classical two-valued logic to the material world. Specifically, the law of the excluded middle, according to which every statement is either true or false, does not hold when dealing with vague predicates, for it is not always possible to say definitely, for example, that a man is or is not bald. Vagueness is also an impediment to the construction of a fully extensional language, the long-time research project of formal semantics. This requires that a number of idioms in natural language be reformulated so as to leave only the quantification and truth functions of the predicate calculus. Any idiom which admits referentially opaque contexts, i.e. contexts where the substitutivity of identicals does not hold, must be reparsed. Thus a truly scientific notation cannot admit tense, quotation, vagueness or the propositional attitudes. Alternatively, the theory cannot be committed ontologically to entities lacking clear identity conditions; it must eliminate, as Willard Quine (1960: 228) says, all 'sources of truth-value fluctuation'. If vagueness is rife and inevitable it is difficult to see how this language is possible.

The same problem occurs in the formalization and operationalization of concepts in the social sciences. This is apparent when focusing on the complexity or combinatory vagueness that characterizes many of their concepts. These concepts, like the word 'game' analysed by Wittgenstein, commonly have many criteria which jointly or individually determine the application of the term. Alston illustrates the combinatory vagueness with the example of religion. There are a number of criteria that can be used in deciding if some institution or belief system constitutes a religion. These might include belief in a god, an ontology, ritual, prayer, a divinely ordained moral code, and an organization of believers. The problem arises in deciding which criteria are necessary and sufficient to identify a religion. Quakers abstain from ritual; and for some Unitarian and Buddhist sects a supernatural being plays little or no role. At the same time, many of these criteria are satisfied by political or philosophical movements such as Marxism or humanism. The criteria clearly apply to paradigm cases such as Catholicism; but they also leave many cases undecidable, 'even', adds Alston, 'when all the "facts" are agreed on' (Alston 1964: 89). Many of the central concepts in the social sciences are of this nature, and that means that operationalized definitions and formalization in these fields may narrow the application of concepts so drastically that the results of research cease to be interesting.

Wittgenstein's cluster theory of meaning has inspired cognitive psychologists to examine our native practices of definition. Eleanor Rosch conducted experiments into our ability to determine class membership, and found that we do not assign membership in a digital manner, based on a definition (see, for example, Rosch 1975). However, we do operate with prototypes in mind when using a word. A prototype is an object that most clearly exemplifies a concept, one that displays the largest number of characteristic features: a kitchen chair for a chair, say, or Catholicism for religion. The existence of these prototypes gives the illusion of a defining feature, but their role is not as a manifest definition. They serve rather as convenient summarizing devices. As such they give the appearance of definition to what is essentially a vague concept. They are, as Keynes termed his own concepts, samples rather than generalizations. If these concepts are of central concern to the social sciences, it must be asked how we can formalize concepts which in important ways have no definition.

This question can be approached through a more general discussion of attempts to wed classical logic with a recognition of vagueness. Two broad alternatives present themselves. We can try to decrease vagueness in our concepts and retain classical logic. Or we can accept the vagueness and turn to many-valued or fuzzy logics. Quine points out that science is pulled in two directions by its loyalty to system and evidence, and that the simplicity of theory is bought at the expense of links to observation. He chooses to retain classical logic, but cautions: 'We stalwarts of two-valued logic buy its sweet simplicity at no small price in respect of the harboring of undecidables' (Quine 1981: 32). He retains 'the law of excluded middle in logical analysis simply by proceeding as if all the terms concerned were precise' (Quine 1987: 56). Quine's assumption is not as heroic as it may seem if we also accept Rosch's finding that reasoning in natural language employs paradigm cases, because here the problems attendant on vagueness are minimized.[4]

Others have taken the opposite tack and have introduced many-valued and fuzzy logics to solve the problem. Black, for one, proposed a measure of the consistency of application of a term and suggested that instead of the one-place propositional function $L(x)$ we use $L(x, c)$, which says that L applies to x with consistency c (Black 1949). According to Carl Hempel (1939), Black has shown how to replace vague terms by metrical expressions. This in other forms has been a standard strategy of eliminating vagueness: transforming polar property-words such as hot–cold, hard–soft, into relative or metrical terms. 'Hard' is characteristically vague; but the relation 'harder than' can be more easily specified by an experiment showing that one substance can scratch another but not vice versa. Recourse to this relation thus diminishes vagueness. Similarly, the polar words hot and cold are simply replaced by measurements of temperature. This has been a successful strategy in science, and its appeal in the social sciences is obvious. Polar terms in political life are often freighted with emotional weight, something which might be diminished if the participants had recourse to more metrical terms. Such a view no doubt lies behind many attempts to quantify the terms used in political science and sociology.[5] Indeed, we could argue, if we were a naively optimistic positivist, that the chronic lack of consensus in the social sciences and political conflict generally, stemmed from the insoluble debates over the application of vague polar terms. Natural language could thus be seen as subversive, the source of political disagreement. If we could retreat behind this veil of words to the numerical scales behind we could, as Leibniz hoped, when disagreement arose merely say, 'Let us calculate'.

However, there is a serious logical difficulty with the project of replacing vague terms with metrical ones. Many of the concepts used in the social sciences display combinatory vagueness rather than degree vagueness, and it is not clear that these can be replaced by metrical terms.The problem can be illustrated by considering the example of attempts to determine the effect of economic development on religioius belief and practice. Such studies commonly involve the construction of an index of religious belief and correlating this with variables of economic growth. The exercise is purely quantitative, but the results will undoubtedly hide the combinatory vagueness we have seen attends the concept of religion. If we are unable to specify the necessary and sufficient conditions for the presence of a religion then the index's technical rigour will be spurious. Alston makes the same point with the example of studies which correlate racial prejudice with degrees of acceptance of oneself: the results 'are subject to all the indeterminacy that attaches to questions of the form, "Does Jones accept himself?"' (Alston 1964: 93).

It could be argued in response that our focus on the peripheral vagueness is a touch pedantic. The study on religions could confine itself to the paradigm cases, and then the correlation, while limited in its implications, could still impart information. As could a broader study which attempted to incorpoarate less clear-cut cases; these could still teach us something. Perhaps. But if the question at issue here is one concerning the preferable degree of formalization for the social sciences then it is doubtful that these experiments carry the methodological implications they are often intended to – that metrical terms necessarily contribute to intersubjectively shared results. In fact, quite often the opposite is the case. Alston considers the thesis that city living contributes to psychological stress. Both variables are vague, but if we try to eliminate that attending the word 'city' by specifying the number of inhabitants that constitute one, then we arrive at the more precise statement that life in a community of, say, more than 50,000 people causes psychological strain. But we may accord this new version less credence than the original vague statement, since we find it hard to believe that the strain is noticeably different in a community of 49,000. Alston concludes: 'There are . . . theoretical advantages to vagueness. Often our knowledge is such that we cannot formulate what we know in terms that are maximally precise without falsifying the statement or going far beyond the evidence' (ibid.: 86). In many such cases of definition in the social sciences we find that vagueness contributes to accuracy, while precision detracts from it. Specifying a sharp definition of a concept by legislation may eliminate some borderline cases and make it operational and precise, but by chopping off cases of application that are intuitively justified the concept becomes inaccurate.[6] In short, there may be a zero-sum relationship between accuracy and precision. We may define religion in a narrow enough way so as to permit operationalization, but then the concept no longer encompasses all those belief systems and institutions we intend to speak of when discussing religion. In this case of definition, as with other words displaying combinatory vagueness, the undefined word in natural language permits more accuracy in discussions of religion. Quine recognizes that 'good purposes are often served by not tampering with vagueness', and, borrowing I.A. Richards' analogy of the results achieved by a painter as compared with a mosaic worker, says: 'the skillful superimposing of vaguenesses has similar advantages over the fitting together of precise technical terms' (Quine 1960: 127).

This analysis of vagueness suggests the conclusion that no definition is possible at all in the social sciences. If we are interested in examining religion, say, from a sociological perspective, any operationalized or formalized definition will inevitably leave out of account some phenomena in which we are intuitively interested. Any definition, in short, seems to involve changing the subject. There is something to this argument, and it points to the trade-off between relevance and precision. One exit from this nomenalist nightmare is provided by the theorists of fuzzy logic. Lotfi Zadeh, for one, has greatly extended the work of Black, Wittgenstein and Lukasiewicz. He sees words as summarizing tools, approximations, and as such they do not operate according to the digital rules of classical set theory; words are 'labels of fuzzy sets, that is, classes of objects in which the transition from membership to non-membership is gradual rather than abrupt' (Zadeh 1973: 28). To handle this fact Zadeh proposed extending set theory by permitting partial membership. So instead of having to decide whether a belief system is or is not a religion, i.e. whether its membership is 1 or 0, we assign it a degree of membership. Through a polling process we might find that people view Catholicism as 1.0 a religion, Quakerism 0.8, the Church of Scientology 0.5, and Communism may receive 0.4 membership. By permitting graded membership, he claims, the logical core of the paradoxes arising from having to say when a man is or is not bald, or when sand does or does not form a pile is removed. The digital approach is replaced by a scale and no paradox remains. This fuzzy logic incorporates classical logic as a special case where membership values are either 1 or 0. Zadeh (1975: 409–10) characterizes it as 'a fuzzy extension of a nonfuzzy multi-valued logic' such as that of Lukasiewicz. He believes that this fuzzy logic is the one habitually used in natural language. He claims that its use in engineering can afford us more-efficient control mechanisms. And he also recognizes its potential utility in the social sciences, since the concepts we use in political and social life defy formalization along traditional lines. He too makes the point that there may be a zero-sum relationship between precision and accuracy:

> Essentially, our contention is that the conventional quantitative techniques of system analysis are intrinsically unsuited for dealing with humanistic systems or, for that matter, any system whose complexity is comparable to that of humanistic systems. The basis for this contention rests on what might be called the *principle of incompatibility*. Stated informally, the essence of this principle is that as the complexity of a system increases, our ability to make precise and yet significant statements about its behaviour diminishes until a threshold is reached beyond which precision and significance (or relevance) become almost mutually exclusive characteristics.
>
> (Zadeh 1973: 28)

Our natural conceptual scheme is admirably suited to the task of summarizing complexity, so Zadeh suggests that we move 'away from the use of quantified variables and toward the use of the type of linguistic descriptions employed by humans' (ibid.: 29). His own form of analysis is, however, not strictly verbal since his fuzzy sets permit mathematical manipulation. His variables are what he calls 'linguistic variables', variables, that is, whose values are sentences taken from natural language. It has in fact been claimed that fuzzy logic's ability to deal mathematically with vague concepts could permit a bridging of the divide between quantitative and qualitative social science.[7]

Keynes as well provided some ideas on the problem of concept formation now being discussed by philosophers such as Alston, Crispin Wright and the theorists of fuzzy logic. He had pointed out the problem in his lectures of 1933: 'Many economists in making their definitions so precise, make them too rigid. This is the danger of scholasticism' (Rymes 1989a: 102). In other words, precise definitions leave too much out of account. But in theoretical work some sort of definition is required if we are to build models. 'Amidst the welter of divergent usages of terms', he said, 'it is agreeable to discover one fixed point' (*C.W.* VII: 61). He took the prototypes as the cases from which to extract a definition for use in theoretical manipulation. Keynes used the term 'sample' to make this point, and said that 'Generalising in economics is thinking by sample, not by generalisation' (Rymes 1989a: 102). These samples or prototypes he found in our common understandings, or in the practices of specialists such as tax commissioners (*C.W.* VII: 59). However, there is an important distinction between Keynes's use of prototypes and their use by others who have taken these paradigm samples as the basis for operationalization or a formalized definition: Keynes, while directing attention to prototypical samples to clarify his intended meaning, remained on the level of everyday language when using the concepts. By so doing he allowed us to take account intuitively of the wider application of the concept, something that is easily lost when formalizing these prototypes: 'in ordinary discourse, where we are not blindly manipulating but know all the time what we are doing and what the words mean, we can keep "at the back of our heads" the necessary reserves and qualifications' (ibid.: 297). Ordinary language recommended itself to Keynes on the grounds of economy and accuracy.

Many of the philosophers now working with the problem of vagueness share with Keynes an appreciation of the utility of the ready-made summaries we find in ordinary language for handling a complex subject matter. Keynes was thus the first to work out the implications of Wittgenstein's analysis of combinatory vagueness for the language of the social sciences. This led him to conclude that formalization runs the risk of leaving behind the subject matter we are interested in. Formalization thus also runs the risk of increasing rather than decreasing muddle. Put another way, he had recognized the trade-off between precision and accuracy. In his later writings he developed more fully the view that the vagueness of ordinary language was a valued property in simplifying theory of a complex system. His frequent reminder that ordinary language allows us to draw on a vast amount of tacit knowledge displays an understanding of the vague penumbra of cases that surround the prototypes we have in mind. This account of concept formation leads to a very cautious approach to formalization: when, in the name of scientific method, everyday concepts are replaced by more formal ones and the familiar is explained in terms of the unfamiliar we should be candid in appraising whether the new language leads to a loss of information. However, Keynes did not intend his methodological view to be a blanket prescription for all social sciences. The method we use will depend on the question being asked, and some questions can be fruitfully handled with formal methods. However, the extreme complexity of historical reality and the instability of expectations with which macroeconomics must grapple led Keynes to conclude that this branch of the social sciences is unpromising material for formal techniques.

Keynes's views thus stand as an interesting response to the theorists of formal semantics and positivist social science. They have argued for the need for the simplifying role of formal techniques. For both, simplicity is served by admitting only those entities entering into quantification, a stipulation that precludes entities lacking clear identity conditions. Keynes, though, presents a compelling case for the view that without vague terms social theory would be unmanageably cumbrous. A formal treatment that attempts to make explicit even part of what goes into our commonsense understanding of an issue can be 'prolix and complicated to the point of obscurity'. The properties of economy and simplicity are valued in scientific discourse, and these virtues for many questions in the social sciences at any rate are paradoxically served by the vague concepts of our natural language.

NOTES

* The material for this chapter is drawn from my book *The Claims of Common Sense: Moore, Wittgenstein, Keynes and the Social Sciences* (Cambridge: Cambridge University Press, 1996).

1 Letter of 18 January 1929. Letters to Lydia, 1928–30. Keynes Papers, Kings College Library, Cambridge, PP/45/190.

2 Letter of 4 December 1933. Letters to Lydia, 1933–4, ibid.

3 See letter to G.E. Moore, dated 6 March 1935. Keynes papers, King's College Library, Cambridge, PP/45/349.

4 This point is argued by Margolit (1976: 216).

5 The principle may in fact be flawed, as well as impractical. If the theorists of complexity at the Sante Fe Institute are right about the occurrence of emergent properties and phase changes in social phenomena then the hope of quantifying properties, particularly along a linear scale, may be considerably more difficult than has been appreciated.

6 Margolit makes this case (1976: 211–12).

7 See Smithson (1988: 12–15). Claude Ponsard has done pioneering work on fuzzy logic and economics (see Ponsard 1985).

Part II

KEYNES AND OTHERS

36

KEYNES AND MARX*

Claudio Sardoni

INTRODUCTION

Soon after the publication of *The General Theory*, Keynes manifested his dissatisfaction with the 'final product' of the intellectual process which had started in 1931–2 and he stated an intention to recast his ideas in a clearer and more satisfactory way. Joan Robinson thought that starting from Marx, rather than orthodox economics, would have saved Keynes 'a lot of trouble' (1964: 96). The object of this chapter is to inquire into the possibility that Keynes could have rewritten *The General Theory* by giving Marx more attention and more credit than he did in the 1936 edition of the book.

The interest in this issue does not derive, however, from any evidence that Keynes changed his opinion of Marx after 1936: it remained highly critical. Such interest, rather, derives from the fact that, in the quest for a clearer formulation of his fundamental ideas, Keynes, in my opinion, could have chosen to go at least partly 'back' to the approach that he had followed earlier on in the process which led to the publication of *The General Theory*. In fact, at a relatively early stage (1933) of this process, Keynes's analysis of a capitalist economy and his critique of the orthodox view had come close to Marx's approach.

Keynes soon abandoned his 1933 approach and, in *The General Theory*, he formulated the critique of orthodox economics in a different way from Marx. In the chapter, I argue that the reason for the change may be found in the fact that the economic theory criticized by Keynes was significantly different from the Ricardian theory to which Marx referred. In particular, a satisfactory criticism of the marginalist version of Say's Law and its implications required the development of some theoretical issues that Marx was not compelled to take into consideration.

After a brief exposition of those aspects of Marx's analysis that could be fruitfully developed along Keynesian lines (pp. 262–8), the chapter proceeds by looking at Keynes's general opinion of Marx before, in and after *The General Theory* (pp. 268–9). The next section deals with Keynes's analysis in 1933 by pointing out the similarities with Marx, following which the possible reasons why Keynes abandoned this analytical approach are examined and discussed. The final section looks at the evolution of Keynes's ideas after 1936 and his dissatisfaction with *The General Theory*. In particular, attention is focused on the relationship between Keynes's position in his 1937 articles and his position in 1933.

A general conclusion of the chapter is that it seems quite unlikely that Keynes, in recasting his ideas more clearly, would have explicitly taken Marx into more serious consideration. However, he could have come closer to Marx by partly returning to his previous approach, the main merit of which was to provide a lucid and concise analysis of the basic laws of the functioning of a capitalist economy and a critique of the orthodox view which was aimed at its very foundations.

MARX'S THEORY OF EFFECTIVE DEMAND AND THE CRITIQUE OF SAY'S LAW

Joan Robinson's conviction that Keynes should have started from Marx derived from her comparison between Keynes's and Kalecki's theories of effective demand. She held that Kalecki offered more general and more robust results than Keynes because he had the advantage of being little influenced by orthodox economics and well acquainted with Marx. One of the factors that, for Joan Robinson, made Kalecki's theory of effective demand more satisfactory than Keynes's was that the former started from the Marxian schemes of reproduction.[1]

Marx expressed the essential characteristic of the capitalist process of production and circulation with the formula

$$M - C - M' \qquad (36.1)$$

The objective of capitalist entrepreneurs is to produce and sell goods in order to obtain more money than they advanced to buy means of production and hire workers. In other words, they produce in order to make money profits.

Two relevant analytical issues stem from this. On the one hand, Marx set out to study the conditions under which the capitalist thrust to produce for profits can give rise to an orderly process of production, circulation and growth; on the other hand, he analysed how the same capitalist drive for profits can lead to crises, characterized by a general overproduction of commodities and unemployment of labour. Marx developed his analysis of social circulation in the second book of *Das Kapital* (1956) through his schemes of reproduction. The problem of crises was analysed, above all, in the second volume of *Theories of Surplus-Value* (1968), where Marx criticized Ricardo's theory, which denied the possibility of general overproduction crises being due to an insufficient level of effective demand.

Let us look at Marx's schemes by concentrating on the monetary aspects of his analysis[2] and by considering an economy in which there are only two sectors (the consumption-goods sector and the investment-goods sector) and only two classes (capitalists and workers). Commodities exchange according to their values (embodied labour); money is gold, so prices of commodities are expressed in terms of the value of gold. The price of the ith commodity is

$$p_i = \frac{v_i}{v_g} \tag{36.2}$$

where v_i and v_g denote the value of a unit of the ith commodity and of a unit of gold respectively.

The exchange ratios of commodities cannot be correctly expressed in terms of the quantity of embodied labour; here, however, it is useful to maintain this hypothesis in order to show that it does not imply any necessary contradiction with the rejection of Say's Law.[3] Let us first consider a case of simple reproduction in which both workers' and capitalists' marginal propensity to consume is equal to one. The process at the macroeconomic level can be depicted by using a slightly modified version of the formula (36.1) above:[4]

$$M - \frac{C}{V} \ldots P \ldots \frac{C'}{V} M' \tag{36.3}$$

The capitalist class, in order to buy means of production and labour force (C), advances a money capital M, V being the velocity of circulation of money; MV is the monetary value of C. Through the process of production (P) capitalists produce commodities (C′) which embody a larger amount of labour than C. Capitalists can transform the total output C′ into money and realize all the labour embodied in it if all produced commodities are sold at their prices $p_i = v_i/v_g$ Given the velocity of circulation of money, V, the monetary value of C′ must be $M'V > MV$ and $(M' - M)V$ is the monetary value of the total surplus, that is, the monetary value of capitalists' aggregate profits. $M' > M$ is the amount of money which is required to make it possible to sell all produced commodities at their prices p_i. Thus, at the end of the process the capitalist class draws from circulation an amount of money M′ which is larger than the amount advanced.

Marx argued that this additional quantity of money $(M' - M)$ necessarily comes from the capitalist class itself which throws money into circulation to finance its consumption:

> it is the capitalist class itself that throws the money into circulation which serves for the realisation of the surplus-value incorporated in the

> commodities. But, *nota bene*, it does not throw it into circulation as advanced money, hence not as capital. It spends it as a means of purchase for its individual consumption.
>
> (Marx 1956: 338–9)[5]

At the end of each period, the capitalist class gets back the total amount of money advanced and, hence, also the money advanced to buy the social surplus. But where can capitalists initially find this additional money? Marx's answer is that the additional money is already in the hands of the capitalist class in the form of money hoards.[6] Marx assumed that capitalists own a quantity of money, M_T, which is equal to or larger than M′ (Marx 1956: 477). Only the amount M is used to buy means of production and hire the labour force at the beginning of the period; the quantity $(M_T - M)$ remains hoarded. But in order for the social surplus $(C' - C)$ to be sold, money has to be dishoarded and thrown into circulation.

Only if the surplus at its value is sold can capitalists realize their full money profits. In a case of simple reproduction, the whole surplus must be consumed by capitalists; therefore its monetary value, i.e. the monetary value of aggregate profits, is determined by the additional amount of money that capitalists throw into circulation to finance their consumption. In other words, aggregate profits are determined by capitalists' consumption decisions which, in turn, imply a decision to reduce their levels of money hoards. The capitalist class decides on its consumption before the actual realization of profits; such decisions are based on expected values, namely on expected profits. The capitalist 'advances to himself . . . money in anticipation of surplus-value still to be snatched by him; but in doing so he also advances a circulating medium for the realisation of surplus-value to be realised later'. How much is advanced depends on the 'customary or estimated revenue' (Marx 1956: 424).

In a case of expanded reproduction, the analysis is similar. The produced surplus may be sold and money profits realized if capitalists throw additional money into circulation. But, in expanded reproduction, not all the surplus may be consumed; it must be at least partly used to expand the scale of production. Therefore, part of the additional money put into circulation, say $(M' - M)_I$, is now spent on investment goods by capitalists and another part, say $(M' - M)_C$, is spent on consumption goods.[7] The value of total profits is

$$[(M' - M)_I + (M' - M)_C]\, V = (M' - M)\, V \qquad (36.4)$$

The monetary value of aggregate profits is the same as in the case of simple reproduction but profits now depend on two sets of decisions by capitalists: their investment and consumption decisions. In general, therefore, aggregate profits depend on capitalists' expenditure decisions which, in turn, imply a decision to reduce the level of money hoards.

There is, however, a significant difference between simple and expanded reproduction. In so far as simple reproduction is considered, the required amount of additional money (M′ − M) does not change over time since the produced surplus is necessarily constant. When expanded reproduction is considered, the surplus is growing over time and, consequently, a growing quantity of additional money is required to allow aggregate demand to keep pace with aggregate supply and aggregate monetary profits to grow. For Marx, the additional quantity of money may come from three different sources:

1 an increase in the velocity of circulation (a greater economy in the use of circulating money);
2 a decrease in capitalists' liquidity preference (the transformation of money hoards into circulating money);
3 an increase in the supply of money (increased production of gold) (see Marx 1956: 349–50).

Let us concentrate on the last two possibilities. To transform hoards into circulating money corresponds to a decrease in capitalists' liquidity preference, so capitalists as a whole must be willing to reduce their liquidity position. However, considering hoards and capitalists' propensity to throw them into circulation cannot represent a fully satisfactory solution in the case of expanded reproduction. If the quantity of money (gold) is given, dishoarding can represent only a temporary solution. If accumulation and growth proceed, the existing money hoards will be exhausted, and this leads to the conclusion that accumulation and growth must stop because of the scarcity of money unless the velocity of circulation keeps on growing indefinitely. In order to avoid this conclusion, it is necessary to allow for the possibility of increases in the total supply of money, the third case considered by Marx. If the capitalists' liquidity preference, the prices of commodities and the velocity of circulation of money as a medium of exchange do not change, the process of expanded reproduction can proceed if the supply of money grows at the same rate as the value of total production. If the capitalists' liquidity preference were to rise, while V remains constant, the increase in the supply of money would not imply the full realization of the growing surplus produced.

Both in the case of simple reproduction and in the case of expanded reproduction, if capitalists decide to advance an additional quantity of money (M″ − M) < (M′ − M), the level of aggregate profits would be negatively affected: aggregate monetary demand (M + M″)V, would fall short of aggregate supply (C′ = M′V) and either stocks of commodities would pile up or the prices of commodities would decrease. In any case, aggregate profits would be decreased. Their monetary value is (M″ − M)V which is less than (M′ − M)V, the monetary value of aggregate profits when all commodities are sold at their prices p_i.

The situation depicted above is a case of general overproduction of commodities due to an insufficient level of demand. Marx dealt with the problem of crises by starting from criticizing Ricardo, who had held that general gluts are impossible, that is to say, Say's Law holds. In Marx's analysis a general overproduction crisis is caused by an increase in the capitalists' propensity to hoard that amounts to a shift of aggregate demand from commodities to money:

> the supply of all commodities can be greater than the demand for all commodities, since the demand for the general commodity, money, exchange-value, is greater than the demand for all particular commodities, in other words the motive to turn the commodity into money, to realise its exchange-value, prevails over the motive to transform the commodity again into use-value.
>
> (Marx 1968: 505)

Aggregate demand falls short of aggregate supply and the economy suffers the simultaneous existence of unused productive capacity and unemployed labour.

The crucial question is why the capitalist class should increase its propensity to hoard. The answer is in the analysis of the motives for production and accumulation which characterize the behaviour of capitalist entrepreneurs. Entrepreneurs do not simply produce commodities in order to satisfy, directly or indirectly, their own needs; they start production and investment processes in order to make profits. The capitalist mode of production is a *monetary economy* in which production and investment processes are started in order to make profits:

> In reproduction, just as in the accumulation of capital, it is not only a question of replacing the *same* quantity of use-values of which capital consists, . . . but of replacing the value of the capital advanced along with the usual rate of profit (surplus-value). If, therefore, . . . the market prices of the commodities . . . fall far below their cost-prices, the reproduction of capital is curtailed as far as possible. Accumulation, however, stagnates even more. Surplus-value amassed in the form of money . . . could only be transformed into capital at a loss. It therefore lies idle as a hoard in the banks or in the form of credit money, which in essence makes no difference at all.
>
> (Marx 1968: 494)

Marx's concept of the capitalist mode of production is such that all relevant decisions of capitalists must be based on expectations. Capitalists make production and investment decisions within a market framework which cannot be known with certainty. The division of labour itself prevents any individual firm from knowing with certainty the market for its commodities. Thus, each firm has to make its decisions in an uncertain framework. Whenever capitalists expect that production and investment will give rise to 'insufficient' profits, they do not advance money to buy the means of production and hire workers; instead, they prefer to keep money idle, hoarded.

Only by taking account of these fundamental characteristics of the capitalist mode of production can we explain why the capitalists' propensity to hoard may increase and trigger off a general overproduction of commodities. Marx criticized Ricardo for abstracting from these essential aspects in analysing a capitalist economy:

> All the objections which Ricardo and others raise against overproduction etc. rest on the fact that they regard bourgeois production either as a mode of production in which no distinction exists between purchase and sale – direct barter – or as social production, implying that society, as if according to a plan, distributes its means of production and productive forces in the degree and measure which is required for the fulfilment of the various social needs, so that each sphere of production receives the quota of social capital required to satisfy the corresponding need.
>
> (Marx 1968: 529)

According to Ricardo, the production and sale of commodities generates an income which is either spent on consumption or saved. What is saved is, however, spent: it is invested to employ additional workers. In Ricardo's world, for every sale there is a corresponding purchase, so that production and investment cannot be limited by insufficient effective demand. In this context, money is merely a device to make the exchange of commodities simpler. Money income is never kept idle; people do not draw any utility from holding money idle. For Ricardo, exchange through money is not conceptually different from barter: 'Productions are always bought by productions, as by service; money is only the medium by which the exchange is effected' (Ricardo 1951: 1.291–2).

By allowing for the possibility that money is kept idle, Marx pointed out that a capitalist economy is essentially different from a barter economy; Say's Law ceases to be valid and general overproduction crises become *possible*. Further, by pointing out that capitalist production is carried out in order to make profits, Marx explained why the capitalist class may wish to keep money idle. Whenever capitalist producers expect that production and investment are not profitable, they keep money idle; this causes overproduction of commodities and unemployment of labour. The possibility to keep money idle, to hoard it, gives capitalist entrepreneurs the 'freedom' not to promote economic growth when it does not coincide with their private interests. Capitalist producers are not forced to act always in favour of the general interest.

Although Marx did not go beyond offering some interesting insights and suggestions,[8] his analysis can be enriched and generalized by introducing credit and the banking system. Once the financial sector is taken into consideration, the capitalist class is divided into two sectors: industrial and financial capitalists. Furthermore, the banks' liquidity preference becomes a crucial variable. In particular, an increase in the propensity to hoard of banks means that they are less willing to make their position less liquid by lending to industrial entrepreneurs. Changes in banks' liquidity preference may determine changes in the rate of interest or in the volume of loans at a given rate. In both cases, capitalists' expenditure will be affected. Thus, the level of aggregate profits in a growing economy depends on two sets of decisions: expenditure decisions by industrial capitalists and financing decisions by the banking system. In order for growing aggregate profits to be realized, the banking system as a whole must be willing initially to make its position less liquid.

Before turning to consider Keynes's position, two final observations concerning Marx's analysis are in order. First, it is worth stressing that here we have dealt only with Marx's analysis of the *possibility* of crises.[9] The reason why attention was focused on the possibility of crises is that we can find analogies between Marx's and Keynes's analyses only with respect to this aspect; their explanations of how such a possibility becomes actual are significantly different.[10] Second, although the demand for idle money plays an important role in his theory, Marx did not develop the analysis of the relation between changes in the demand for idle money and changes in the rate of interest. Furthermore, he did not pay much attention to the relation between the rate of interest and investment decisions. Changes in the propensity to hoard have a direct effect on the demand for commodities and labour and, hence, on their prices while investment decisions are essentially governed by other factors, for example expected profits, competition and technical innovations.

KEYNES'S OPINION OF MARX

If the problem of the relationship between Keynes and Marx were to be based only on Keynes's explicit position on Marx's economics, any question concerning Keynes's possible attitude toward Marx in a revised edition of *The General Theory* would be easy to answer: he would never have changed his highly negative opinion of Marx.

Keynes was not a scholar of Marx. In a letter to George Bernard Shaw in 1934 (*C.W.* XXVIII: 38), he said that he had 'looked into' *Das Kapital* and that he would read it again if Shaw promised to do the same. As there is no evidence that Shaw so promised, Keynes probably only 'looked into' Marx's book once.[11] Keynes's knowledge of Marx's economics was mainly based on secondary literature rather than on a direct acquaintance with the original writings of Marx. Joan Robinson was convinced that Keynes 'never managed to read Marx' (1973: ix) and that, in any case, he 'could never make head or tail of Marx' (1964: 96).[12] This, however, did not prevent Keynes from issuing trenchant judgements on Marx's economics in *The General Theory* and also before and after its publication.

In *The General Theory*, the book which was to 'knock away' Marxism,[13] Marx is quoted only three times. The first quotation, in a footnote (*C.W.* VII: 3n), is concerned with the definition of 'classical economics';[14] the other two quotations are more relevant but neither is very flattering to Marx. In criticizing his predecessors for having ignored the principle of effective demand, Keynes noted that the 'great puzzle of Effective Demand' had vanished from economics since Malthus, and only kept on living furtively in the 'underworlds' of Marx, Gesell and Major Douglas (*C.W.* VII: 32). In Chapter 23, Keynes expressed his conviction that the future will learn more from Gesell than from Marx; Gesell had tried to establish an 'anti-Marxian socialism' based on the rejection of the classical hypotheses that Marx had instead accepted (ibid.: 355).

These opinions are consistent with Keynes's opinions expressed both before and after *The General Theory.* Keynes always held that Marx's economic doctrine was flawed by serious logical contradictions although, sometimes, it may have contained interesting intuitions. In 1925, he wrote that Marx's *Das Kapital*, the bible of communism, was an 'obsolete economic textbook' which was 'not only scientifically erroneous but without interest or application for the modern world' (*C.W.* IX: 258). In 1934, Keynes wrote to George Bernard Shaw that his feelings about *Das Kapital* were the same as his feelings about the Koran; its 'dreary, out-of-date, academic controversialising' was 'extraordinarily unsuitable' to give inspiration to so many people and 'its contemporary *economic* value (apart from occasional but inconstructive and discontinuous flashes of insight) is *nil*' (*C.W.* XXVIII: 38). Finally, in 1942, after having read Joan Robinson's book on Marx's economics (Robinson 1942), Keynes had 'the feeling which I had before on less evidence, that he had a penetrating and original flair but was a very poor thinker indeed' (letter to Joan Robinson of 20 August 1942; quoted in Moggridge 1992: 470).

KEYNES'S ENTREPRENEUR ECONOMY

If we consider the more specific issues of effective demand and the critique of Say's Law, Keynes's opinion on the importance of Marx's contribution may have been negatively influenced by a book on trade cycles and value theory, written by McCracken in 1933. McCracken may have convinced Keynes that Marx's critique of Say's Law was inconsistent with his acceptance of the labour theory of value. Paradoxically, Joan Robinson may also have influenced Keynes's negative judgement of Marx. Joan Robinson's conviction that starting from Marx would have helped Keynes came quite late in the evolution of her thought (1964) and after she had been in close contact with Kalecki. Earlier, Joan Robinson was convinced that Marx was contradictory in his rejection of Say's Law, since he considered it as inapplicable only during crises (see, for example, Robinson 1942: 43–51, 1952: 79). It was only in 1953 that Joan Robinson became convinced that, for Marx, Say's Law never holds (see Robinson 1953: 264; see also Sardoni 1987: 66).

However, there is a stage in the development of Keynes's ideas in which he came rather close to Marx's critique of Say's Law. The basic elements of Keynes's critique of Say's Law in 1933 are also at the core of Marx's analysis. When in 1933 Keynes drafted several chapters of the book which was to become *The General Theory*, in particular he wrote a draft of the second and third chapters where the critique of the 'classical' doctrine and Say's Law is based on the distinction between a *co-operative economy*, a *neutral economy*[15] and an *entrepreneur* (or *monetary*) *economy*, that is, the capitalist economy in which 'we actually live'.[16] In this context, Keynes explicitly referred to Marx's analysis and recognized that the latter, starting from the formula M − C − M′, had pointed out the essential characteristic of capitalist economies which makes it possible to deal correctly with the issue of effective demand.

A co-operative economy, even though money is used for exchanges, is basically equivalent to a barter economy where the factors of production are rewarded by a share of the real output. In so far as factors of production are rewarded in agreed proportions, money is only a 'transitory convenience' which is used to buy a predetermined share of the output.[17] The same analytical results can be obtained even if less restrictive assumptions are made. If some factors do not use all their rewards to buy a share of current output but employ part of them to buy a share of pre-existing wealth, full employment is still attained, provided that the sellers of pre-existing wealth use, in turn, their proceeds to buy current output (*C.W.* XXIX: 77). The latter is an economy in which income may be spent on goods or saved by factors. Nevertheless, what is saved is spent; that is to say, all that is saved is invested.

For Keynes, 'classical economists' could hold that Say's Law applies and that full employment is ensured by assuming that capitalist economies behave *as if* they were co-operative economies. But capitalist economies are essentially different (*C.W.* XXIX: 78–9). Capitalist entrepreneurs start productive processes in order to earn a monetary profit, and not in order to produce more goods and employ more labour:

> An entrepreneur is interested, not in the amount of product, but in the amount of money which will fall to his share. He will increase his output if by so doing he expects to increase his money profit, even though this profit represents a smaller quantity of product than before.
> (*C.W.* XXIX: 82)

Entrepreneurs will direct money to production if they expect that to be profitable (in terms of money). If production is expected to be unprofitable, money is kept idle. As a result, less employment is offered by entrepreneurs: 'The choice . . . in deciding whether or not to offer employment is a choice between using money in this way or in some other way *or not using it at all*' (*C.W.* XXIX: 82; emphasis added).

Money is not current output, so that if the demand for it increases, while the demand for current output declines, there will be a decrease in employment. Money is the best store of value:

> Money in terms of which the factors of production are remunerated will 'keep' more readily than output which they are being remunerated to produce, so that the need of entrepreneurs to sell, if they are to avoid a running loss, is more pressing than the need of recipients of income to spend. This is the case because it is a characteristic of finished goods, which are neither consumed nor used but carried in stock, that they incur substantial carrying charges for storage, risk and deterioration, so that they are yielding a negative return for so long as they are held; whereas such expenses are reduced to a minimum approaching zero in the case of money.
>
> (*C.W.* XXIX: 86)[18]

The characteristics of money are such that buyers are not pressed to convert money into goods and entrepreneurs find it convenient to keep money instead of producing goods when they expect that demand will not be sufficient to make their production profitable. It is for these reasons that, in a capitalist economy, effective demand is likely to be insufficient to ensure the full-employment level of output(*C.W.* XXIX: 86–7).

It is in the description of how an entrepreneur economy functions that Keynes referred to Marx's formula $M - C - M'$:

> The distinction between a co-operative economy and an entrepreneur economy bears some relation to a pregnant observation made by Karl Marx, – though the subsequent use to which he put this observation was highly illogical. He pointed out that the nature of production in the actual world is not, as economists seem often to suppose, a case of $C - M - C'$, i.e. of exchanging commodity (or effort) for money in order to obtain another commodity (or effort). That may be the standpoint of the private consumer. But it is not the attitude of *business*, which is the case of $M - C - M'$, i.e. of parting with money for commodity (or effort) in order to obtain more money.
>
> (*C.W.* XXIX: 81)

Keynes did not explain why he regarded Marx's theoretical developments as illogical, but his reference to a book on value theory and trade cycles by McCracken (1933) may explain what he meant. McCracken had argued that

Marx's attempt to explain general overproduction crises due to a deficiency of effective demand was contradictory to his acceptance of the labour theory of value, as the latter implies the impossibility of having a general overproduction of commodities.[19]

However, we have seen above (pp. 263–7) that accepting the labour theory of value does not necessarily imply accepting Say's Law. In order for the law to hold it is also necessary to assume that money is demanded only as a means of circulation and that it is never kept idle in the form of hoards. In Marx's analytical framework, if the capitalists' liquidity preference increases because of pessimistic expectations concerning profits, effective demand falls short of aggregate supply and a general overproduction of commodities occurs. It is only in Ricardo's framework that the possibility to demand idle money is assumed away.

Thus, from this point of view, Marx's analysis shows significant similarities to Keynes's. Both criticized their respective predecessors for having treated capitalist economies as if they were essentially the same as barter (or co-operative) economies. Say's Law applies in an economy in which money is only a medium of exchange, a 'transitory convenience'. But in a capitalist economy money is also used as a store of value. The profitability of production and investment is the essential factor determining how money is used. If capitalists' expectations concerning profitability are pessimistic, the demand for idle money rises while the demand for goods and labour decreases. An increase in the demand for money is different from an increase in the demand for any other good. A larger demand for money determines a smaller demand for other goods and, hence, a decrease in the demand for labour. In fact, the increased demand for money gives rise to no increase (or no significant increase) in the level of employment in the production of money.

There is another element in common between Marx's approach and Keynes's critique in 1933. In both cases the critique of Say's Law is carried out within an analytical context in which neither the banking system nor the rate of interest play a role. It is capitalist entrepreneurs themselves who decide either to use money to produce and invest or to keep it idle. In other words, demand for idle money is directly determined by expected profits and not by expectations concerning the rate of interest which, in turn, plays a role in investment decisions. As I shall argue in the next section, the fact that, in 1933, Keynes did not deal with the relation between the demand for idle money and the rate of interest may be one of the factors which induced him to develop his analysis further and to turn away from Marx's approach.

FROM THE 1933 DRAFT TO *THE GENERAL THEORY*

By mid-1934, Keynes had abandoned his previous approach to the critique of Say's Law. In April, he had written to Kahn: 'I have been making rather extensive changes in the early chapters of my book' (*C.W.* XIII: 422). In a table of contents, written before the first proofs of *The General Theory* (October 1934), the chapters on the distinction between a co-operative and an entrepreneur economy had disappeared (*C.W.* XIII: 423–4).

In the letter to Kahn, 'classical' economists are no longer criticized for having assumed that a capitalist economy behaves like a co-operative economy, but for the assumption that aggregate demand is always equal to aggregate supply: 'The fundamental assumption of the classical theory, "supply creates its own demand", is that OW = OP *whatever* the level of O, so that effective demand is incapable of setting a limit to employment which consequently depends on the relation between marginal product in wage-good industries and marginal disutility of employment' (*C.W.* XIII: 422).[20] In *The General Theory*, Keynes followed the same line: 'the classical theory assumes . . . that the aggregate demand price (or proceeds) always accommodates itself to the aggregate supply price'; this inevitably leads to full employment because of competition among entrepreneurs: 'Say's Law, that the aggregate demand price of output as a whole is equal to its aggregate supply price for all volumes of output, is equivalent to the proposition that there is no obstacle to full employment' (*C.W.* VII: 26). Although Keynes still observed that the 'classical' assumption concerning the equality between aggregate supply and demand prices could be derived by assuming that a capitalist economy is essentially equivalent to a barter economy (*C.W.* VII: 20), the fundamental distinction between a co-operative economy and a capitalist economy ceased to play a central role. In my opinion, the basic reason why Keynes abandoned his previous line of criticism is because he was referring to a version of Say's Law which differed from the Ricardian version criticized by Marx.

In 1933, Keynes, like Marx, had criticized his predecessors for having assumed that a capitalist economy behaves like a barter economy. But Marx had an 'advantage' over Keynes: he could easily refer to Ricardo's explicit statements that a monetary capitalist economy is essentially the same as a barter economy and that all that is saved is always invested. Keynes instead found it much more difficult to point out passages from Marshall's or Pigou's works where equivalent statements were made as clearly and explicitly as those by Ricardo. After quoting a passage from Marshall's *Pure Theory of Domestic Values*, where it is explicitly said that all that is saved is necessarily invested, Keynes had to admit that it was difficult to find similar passages from Marshall's later work or in Pigou: 'The doctrine is never stated to-day in this crude form' (*C.W.* VII: 19; see also XXIX: 78–9 and XIII: 410).

Keynes had to deal with an interpretation of Say's Law that was not only less 'crude' but that also implied that the economy tends to a full-employment equilibrium, an implication which was foreign to classical political economy. The acceptance of Say's Law by Ricardo – and other classical economists – implied only that, in a country, any amount of capital can be used without facing any obstacle on the demand side (Ricardo 1951: 1.290–1), but this did not mean that the economy experiences full employment of *labour.*

If Say's Law is to imply full employment, it is necessary to assume that there is a process of wage adjustment which induces capitalist firms to vary their demand for labour as the wage varies in response to changes in the level of unemployment. Moreover, the functioning of such a process would require that another mechanism be at work: for every change in the level of employment (and income) there must be an adjustment process that brings investment and saving back to equality, namely variations of the interest rate. Ricardo never thought of such mechanisms; he simply assumed that all that is saved is invested.

In referring to Pigou's theory of unemployment, the target *par excellence* of his critique (*C.W.* VII: 279), Keynes argued: 'it is assumed that the rate of interest always adjusts itself to the schedule of the marginal efficiency of capital in such a way as to preserve full employment. Without this assumption Professor Pigou's analysis breaks down and provides no means of determining what the volume of employment will be' (*C.W.* VII: 274–5). Keynes always felt the necessity to demonstrate that variations in wages and the interest rate are not such as to ensure the achievement of full employment. He had been dealing with this issue since his 1932 draft chapters of *The General Theory* (*C.W.* XIII: 381–406). There, after having illustrated his interpretation of how the 'actual world' works, Keynes turned to considering what he regarded as his adversaries' predictable objections. For him, the level of output, and employment, essentially depends on investment, but it is not possible

> to apply this argument to the real world until we have disposed of two factors, which, in the judgment of traditional doctrine, enter in as equilibrating factors and altogether obviate the necessity of any such conclusion as that which we are propounding. The first of these is the reduction of the rate of wages; and the second is the automatic tendency in such conditions for a reduction in the rate of interest.
>
> (*C.W.* XIII: 389)

Also in the 1933 drafts, Keynes devoted his attention to the alleged existence of a mechanism which brings the economy back to full employment whenever it moves away from there. After having defined a co-operative economy and the sort of outcomes that it produces, Keynes pointed out that the same results can be obtained also in an economy where there is a class of entrepreneurs who start productive processes in order to sell the output for money (what Keynes called a *neutral economy*), provided that there exists a mechanism which makes the exchange value of the factors' money incomes always equal, at the aggregate level, to the proportion of output which would have been the factors' share in a co-operative economy (see *C.W.* XXIX: 78). This mechanism ensures that aggregate expenditure and aggregate cost always 'keep step' and, above all, that any factor that keeps employment at a lower level than full employment is adequately offset (*C.W.* XXIX: 91).

In *The General Theory* Keynes reached what he regarded as a satisfactory and thorough criticism of the neo-classical analysis of the mechanisms which ensure full employment: a decrease in money-wage rates does not necessarily yield a higher level of employment; the rate of interest, determined by monetary factors, does not work as the equilibrating mechanism of saving and investment. Monetary factors can keep the rate of interest at too high a level to allow enough investment to ensure full employment. This was, for Keynes, a more convincing and satisfactory critique of neoclassical orthodoxy. The critique was no longer based on the presumption of a tacit assumption that a capitalist economy is essentially the same as a co-operative economy, but it was based on the rejection of the traditional theory of the rate of interest. The rate of interest does not vary in such a way as to ensure S = I at the full-employment level of income.

KEYNES'S DISSATISFACTION WITH *THE GENERAL THEORY*

The General Theory was published in February 1936. As early as August of the same year Keynes was already convinced that his book required 're-writing and re-casting' and was planning to write some footnotes to the book.[21] Three years later, in the preface to the French edition of his book, Keynes again expressed the wish to rewrite it in a more clear-cut way. Keynes felt particularly dissatisfied with the excessively controversial nature of *The General Theory* which was due to his attempts to escape the old ideas and to the fact that he himself was at the junction point between the old 'classical' generation and the new generation:

> [I] have felt myself to be breaking away from . . . orthodoxy, to be in strong reaction against it, to be escaping from something, to be gaining an emancipation. And this state of mind on my part is the explanation of certain faults of the book, in particular its controversial note in some passages, and its air of being addressed too much to the holders of a particular point of view and too little *ad urbem et orbem.* I was wanting to convince my own environment and did not address myself with sufficient directness to outside opinion. Now three years later, having grown accustomed to my new skin and having almost forgotten the smell of my old one, I should, if I were writing afresh, endeavour to free myself from this fault and state my own position in a more clear-cut manner.
>
> (*C.W.* VII: xxxi)[22]

Keynes never went much beyond manifesting his dissatisfaction and never wrote the above-mentioned footnotes to *The General Theory*,[23] so that there does not exist direct evidence about the way in which he would have revised and improved the book. However, in speculating on Keynes's possible choices we may usefully refer to the articles that he wrote in 1937 after the publication of *The General Theory*: 'The General Theory of Employment' (*C.W.* XIV: 109–23); 'Alternative Theories of the Rate of Interest' (ibid.: 201–15); 'The "*Ex Ante*" Theory of the Rate of Interest' (ibid.: 215–23).[24] In these articles, written to answer a number of criticisms and misunderstandings of several commentators and reviewers of *The General Theory*, not only did Keynes restate analytical points already dealt with at length in 1936; he also introduced, or reintroduced, some aspects which had not been considered in *The General Theory*.

In 'The General Theory of Employment', Keynes expounded his notion of uncertainty and its difference from other conceptions in the clearest and most concise way,[25] he related the demand for money as a store of value to uncertainty about the future[26] and showed how these features of the world in which we actually live affect investment, which is therefore subject to fluctuations:

> It is not surprising that the volume of investment, thus determined, should fluctuate widely from time to time. For it depends on two sets of judgments about the future, neither of which rests on an adequate or secure foundation – on the propensity to hoard and on opinions of the future yield of capital assets.
>
> (*C.W.* XIV: 118)

In the following two articles, Keynes further elucidated his theory of the rate of interest and he specified his analysis of the demand for money by taking account of the 'finance motive'.[27] Moreover, Keynes reintroduced the analysis of the role of the banking system in the determination of the money supply and the rate of interest while, as is well known, in *The General Theory* he took the supply of money as exogenously given and did not analyse the role of banks, aspects which were central to his analysis in *A Treatise on Money*. He pointed out:

> the transition from a lower to a higher scale of activity involves an increased demand for liquid resources which cannot be met without a rise in the rate of interest, unless the banks are ready to lend more cash or the rest of the public to release more cash at the existing rate of interest. If there is no change in the liquidity position, the public can save *ex ante* and *ex post* and *ex* anything else until they are blue in the face, without alleviating the problem in the least – unless, indeed, the result of their effort is to lower the scale of activity to what it was before.

> This means that, in general, the banks hold the key position in the transition from a lower to a higher scale of activity. If they refuse to relax, the growing congestion of the short-term loan market or the new issue market, as the case may be, will inhibit the improvement, no matter how thrifty the public purpose to be out of their future incomes.
> (*C.W.* XIV: 222)

Although Keynes wrote his 1937 articles in order to contrast criticisms, objections and misunderstandings by interpreters of *The General Theory*, a general characteristic of these articles is that his theory is expressed in a clear and concise way by pointing out its essential analytical foundations and by drawing a clear-cut distinction between the positive analytical elements and the criticisms of orthodox economics. These articles represent a valuable indication of the lines along which Keynes could have recast his ideas in a revised edition of *The General Theory*. In this sense it is useful to compare Keynes's post-*General Theory* articles to his 1933 drafts in order to see whether there are common characteristics.

As I have argued above (pp. 272–5), Keynes abandoned his 1933 approach in order to provide what he regarded as a more satisfactory criticism of his closer predecessors. In doing so, he probably was to a certain extent unable to retain one important characteristic of the 1933 draft. Keynes's 1933 critique of Say's Law has the important merit of putting capitalist entrepreneurs' decisions at the centre-stage of his analysis. Aggregate outcomes depend on entrepreneurs' decisions concerning money, production and investment; these decisions are made in the light of the objective to make money profits and not to produce goods as such. This is the fundamental reason why entrepreneurs can decide to keep money idle and the economy can experience unemployment. In this way, the system's degree of liquidity preference is immediately and directly related to entrepreneurs' expectation of profit, which is the driving force in a capitalist economy.

In *The General Theory*, these fundamental elements of Keynes's vision of the capitalist economy do not disappear, but they are presented in a way which may lend itself to interpretations that are far from Keynes's spirit. Investment and production decisions, obviously, are related to entrepreneurs' expectations of profits but the relation between these decisions and the demand for money is more complex than in the 1933 draft. The exogenously given money supply and the liquidity preference of the public in general determine the rate of interest; this, along with entrepreneurs' long-term expectations, determines the level of investment, output and employment. The demand for 'idle money' is no longer directly related to entrepreneurs' expectations concerning profits but to the 'speculative motive', i.e. 'the object of securing profit from knowing better than the market what the future will bring forth' (*C.W.* VII: 170).

Keynes's analysis of money demand in *The General Theory* is carried out in a way in which the crucial role of entrepreneurs' drive for profits tends to disappear from the scene. Liquidity preference is explained on the basis of psychological factors and on the basis of financial speculators' behaviour; there are no longer capitalist entrepreneurs whose demand for idle money is related to their aim of maximizing profits and represents an immediate alternative to demand for goods and labour-force.

As a consequence of this, Keynes's analysis of money in *The General Theory* lends itself to interpretation more easily in terms of individuals' portfolio decisions *à la* Tobin (1958): the demand for money is considered as the demand for an asset like all the others (though more liquid) instead of a very special type of demand which can be explained by the inherent nature of capitalist economies.

However, the line of analysis that Keynes adopted in *The General Theory* also has some important advantages. First, in that way, Keynes was able to criticize better those who adopted a 'less-crude' version of Say's Law. In fact, in criticizing neoclassical economics, it is not sufficient to say that entrepreneurs may not invest and keep money idle; the objection that entrepreneurs would, however, be induced to invest and produce by variations in wages and the interest rate has to be answered. Keynes's analysis in *The General Theory* seems to respond to this analytical necessity. On the other hand, Keynes's 'less-crude' line of analysis in *The General Theory* was dictated not only by the need for a more satisfactory criticism of orthodox economics. Taking account of the existence of organized financial markets is an important analytic element for the explanation of the working of modern economies. In fact, one of the main drawbacks of the 1933 draft was the lack of an analysis of this important element.

After 1936 Keynes made an important step towards an analysis of modern capitalist economies. In his 1937 articles the analysis is carried out in such a way as to marry the fact that capitalist entrepreneurs' decisions are the crucial factor determining aggregate outcomes with the fact that money and financial markets are a decisive element of modern economies. While the central role of entrepreneurs' investment decisions is greatly emphasized, at the same time money and financial markets are clearly and explicitly treated as capitalist markets, i.e. markets where the main agents are capitalist entrepreneurs. This is largely due to the fact that Keynes abandoned the 1936 hypothesis of exogenous money and reintroduced banks. Banks are capitalist enterprises like industrial firms, and their decisions concerning liquidity are determined by their drive for profits. In this way, capitalist entrepreneurs' decisions and actions also play a decisive role in the determination of the rate of interest and, hence, of investment, output and employment. It is in this sense that the 1933 drafts could have been a useful reference for recasting Keynes's ideas in a revised edition of *The General Theory*. In these drafts – where Keynes went closer to Marx than ever – the analysis of the problem of effective demand hinges on a clear definition of the essential characteristics of a capitalist economy, where the drive for profits is at the core of all relevant decisions.

If we look at the intellectual process that brought Keynes from *A Treatise on Money* to the publication of *The General Theory*, we see that a characteristic of this process is that, while quite early on he perceived and outlined the basic laws of functioning of a capitalist economy, it took him much longer to provide what he considered a satisfactory criticism of orthodox economics. In 1932, for example, Keynes had already pointed out the crucial role of investment in the determination of income and employment but he had not yet provided convincing arguments against the orthodox objections to his analytical conclusions.

It seems that Keynes's struggle to escape old ideas did not have as much to do with his alternative understanding of the basic and essential characteristics of capitalist economies as with his attempts to develop a general model which was able to stand against the well-consolidated orthodox view. A few months after the publication of *The General Theory*, Keynes wrote to Harrod:

> To me, the most extraordinary thing regarded historically, is the complete disappearance of the theory of the demand and supply for output as a whole, i.e. the theory of employment, *after* it had been for a quarter of a century the most discussed thing in economics. One of the most important transitions for me, after my *Treatise on Money* had been published, was suddenly realising this. It only came after I had enunciated to myself the psychological law that, when income increases, the gap between income and consumption will increase – a conclusion of vast importance to my own thinking but not apparently, expressed just like this, to anyone else's. Then, appreciably later, came the notion of interest as being the meaning of liquidity preference, which became quite clear in my mind the moment I thought of it. And last of all, after an immense lot of muddling and many drafts, the proper definition of the marginal efficiency of capital linked up one thing with another.
>
> (Letter to Harrod of 30 August 1936, *C.W.* XIV: 85)[28]

Keynes's critique started with his perception that the crucial 'flaw' of neoclassical economics was its theory of money, a theory which could not be used to interpret capitalist economies: money is not a transitory convenience and, hence, a capitalist economy is *essentially* different from a barter economy. But Keynes also realized that this basic criticism had to be complemented by other arguments which were based on more solid textual evidence. In 1933, Keynes's general model was not developed in full detail: the analysis of the demand for liquidity was not fully elaborated; the theory of the rate of interest and the notion of marginal efficiency of capital were only outlined. This made Keynes's critique of Say's Law not solid enough to withstand the expected neoclassical objections. In accomplishing the task of providing a more satisfactory criticism of neoclassical economics, Keynes parted from Marx.

However, Keynes eventually became dissatisfied with his 'final product', the book published in 1936. We do not know how Keynes would have rewritten *The General Theory*, but his 1937 articles provide interesting insights and suggestions. In these articles, Keynes illustrated the fundamental elements of his analysis of a capitalist economy. In particular, he strongly stressed the fact that entrepreneurs' investment decisions are the crucial factor in the determination of income and employment and their fluctuations. Investment depends on the rate of interest which, in turn, is determined by the supply of and the demand for money, which are no longer variables that, as in *The General Theory*, simply depend on monetary authorities and on the liquidity preference of the public in general; banks now play a crucial role. Banks are capitalist enterprises like industrial firms; therefore capitalist entrepreneurs' decisions and actions in general come to play a decisive role in the working of capitalist economies.

Thus, in this sense, Keynes could have rewritten *The General Theory* by 'returning', at least partly, to his earlier approach, where the role of capitalist entrepreneurs was given centre-stage in the analysis of the world in which we actually live and the concern for the critique of the neoclassical model was less obtrusive. However, to allow for the possibility that Keynes could have gone back to his previous line of criticism is not to imply that he would have explicitly reconsidered Marx's contributions and arrived at a more favourable opinion of him. Keynes's ideological aversion to Marxism and his poor knowledge of Marx's original contributions seem to be strong arguments against the possibility that Keynes would have changed his mind about Marx's economics. For a more favourable attitude towards Marx's analysis of the capitalist process and his critique of Say's Law, we have to wait for the later opinions of Joan Robinson, the disciple of Keynes who was the one most exposed to Kalecki's influence.

NOTES

* This chapter is part of a research project on economic growth and market forms. A CNR grant for the project is gratefully acknowledged. The author also wishes to thank the editors for their helpful suggestions and advice.

1 'Kahn, at the "circus" where we discussed the *Treatise* in 1931, explained the problem of saving and investment by imagining a cordon round the capital-good industries and then studying the trade between them and the consumption-good industries: he was struggling to rediscover Marx's schema. Kalecki began at that point' (Robinson 1964: 95–6).

2 The monetary aspects of Marx's schemes of reproduction have been usually overlooked. Rosa Luxemburg's work is one of the few exceptions (see Luxem-

burg 1963: chs IV–IX). For a more detailed exposition of Marx's schemes, see Sardoni (1981, 1989).

3 As we shall see later, Keynes was probably induced to think that Marx's analysis was contradictory partly because Marx accepted the labour theory of value.

4 Here the velocity of circulation of money as a medium of exchange, V, is explicitly considered.

5 That the money required for the realization of capitalists' surplus has to be advanced by capitalists themselves is not paradoxical: 'For there are only two classes: the working class disposing only of its labour-power, and the capitalist class, which has a monopoly of the social means of production and money. It would rather be a paradox if the working class were to advance in the first instance from its own resources the money required for the realisation of the surplus-value contained in the commodities' (Marx 1956: 425).

6 In the first book of *Das Kapital* (1954: 134–41), Marx had argued that the existence of money hoards is a necessary requisite for a smooth process of circulation. See also Sardoni (1991: 223–4).

7 The capitalists' marginal propensity to consume must be less than 1, while the workers' propensity is still equal to one.

8 Marx was very interested in the working of the banking system and in the analysis of the factors which determine the rate of interest, but he did not succeed in providing a fully developed study of these issues. On Marx's analysis of the banking system, see Marx (1959: 338–613). For a more detailed exposition of Marx's analysis of the role of banks during a crisis, see also Sardoni (1987: 47–8, 78–83).

9 Marx was very careful to distinguish between the possibility and the actual occurrence of crises due to imbalances between supply and demand: 'factors which explain the possibility of crises by no means explain their actual occurrence' (Marx 1968: 502).

10 The main difference is that, for Marx, an imbalance between aggregate demand and supply inevitably gives rise to a general overproduction crisis whereas, for Keynes, it can also yield an 'underemployment equilibrium'. I have dealt with this issue in Sardoni (1987: esp. chs 4, 5 and 7).

11 In another letter to Shaw (1 January 1935), Keynes wrote that he had read the Marx–Engels correspondence, which did not lead him to change his mind on Marx (*C.W.* XXVIII: 42).

12 Recently, Thweatt (1983) and Behrens (1985) have argued that Keynes's acquaintance with Marx's work was greater than usually admitted. However, neither of them seems to provide enough evidence to disprove Joan Robinson's opinion.

13 In 1935, Keynes wrote to G.B. Shaw: 'To understand my state of mind . . . you have to know that I believe myself to be writing a book on economic theory, which will largely revolutionise . . . the way the world thinks about economic problems. When my theory has been duly assimilated and mixed with politics and feelings and passions, I can't predict what the final upshot will be in its effect on action and affairs. But there will be a great change, and, in particular, the Ricardian foundations of Marxism will be knocked away' (*C.W.* XXVIII: 42).

14 As is well known, Keynes also included Marshall, Edgeworth and Pigou among the classical economists. In order to avoid confusion the term classical in the Keynesian sense is, from now on, always in inverted commas.

15 On the notion of neutral economy, see pp. 274–5.

16 On the analytical importance of Keynes's 1933 drafts, see also Rotheim (1981) and Tarshis (1989).

17 'It is not necessary that the factors should receive their shares of the output in kind in the first instance; – the position is substantially the same if they are paid in money, provided they all of them accept the money merely as a temporary convenience, with a view to spending the whole of it forthwith on purchasing such part of current output as they choose' (*C.W.* XXIX: 76–7).

18 Keynes is here clearly referring to what he later was to call the 'essential properties of money' (*C.W.* VII: 222–44).

19 'It cannot be made too emphatic, that if value increases with quantity, the purchasing power increases with quantity, so there would always be demand if production were properly proportioned, and any evidence of lack of demand for any particular commodity gives automatic proof that demand exists for commodities that are not available. . . . Under the embodied labour theory of value, labour would still have wages sufficient for subsistence and reproduction, which was all that was possible under the Capitalistic Regime, and the more wares left in the hands of the employers the greater their wealth would be, so how could an increase in supply decrease the price?' (McCracken 1933: 55).

20 W is marginal prime cost, O is output and P is the expected selling price. In Keynes's theory, 'OW ≠ OP for *all* values of O, and entrepreneurs have to choose a value of O for which it *is* equal; – otherwise the equality of price and marginal prime cost is infringed. This is the real starting point of everything' (*C.W.* XIII: 422–3).

21 In a letter to Hawtrey of 31 August 1936, Keynes wrote: 'I am thinking of producing in the course of the next year or so what might be called *footnotes* to my previous book, dealing with various criticisms and particular points which want carrying further. Of course, in fact, the whole book needs re-writing and re-casting. But I am still not in a sufficiently changed state of mind as yet to be in the position to do that' (*C.W.* XIV: 47).

22 The controversial nature of *The General Theory* had caused him difficulties and incomprehension even with sympathetic readers like Harrod. See Harrod's letter to Keynes of 1 August 1935 (*C.W.* XIII: 530–4) and also Hicks's letter of 2 September 1936 (*C.W.* XIV: 72–4). Keynes's response to Harrod was that 'What some people treat as unnecessarily controversial is really due to the importance in my own mind of what I *used* to believe, and of the moments of transition which were for me personally moments of illumination. You don't feel the weight of the past as I do. . . . For experience seems to show that people are divided between the old ones whom nothing will shift and are merely amazed by my attempts to underline the points of transition so vital in my own progress, and the young ones who have not been properly brought up and believe nothing in particular' (*C.W.* XIV: 85).

23 Keynes did write a table of contents entitled 'Footnotes to "The General Theory"' (see *C.W.* XIV: 133–4).

24 Another important article for understanding the evolution of Keynes's ideas after *The General Theory* is 'Relative Movements of Real Wages and Output', written in 1939 (*C.W.* VII: 394–412).

25 'By "uncertain" knowledge, let me explain, I do not mean merely to distinguish what is known for certain from what is only probable. . . . The sense in which I am using the term is that in which the prospect of a European war is uncertain, or the price of copper and the rate of interest twenty years hence, or the obsolescence of a new invention, or the position of private wealth owners in the social system in 1970. About these matters there is no scientific basis on which to form any calculable probability whatever. We simply do not know'. But, despite our inability to know the future, we have to make decisions and,

therefore, 'behave exactly as we should if we had behind us a good Benthamite calculation of a series of prospective advantages and disadvantages' (*C.W.* XIV: 113–14).

26 '[O]ur desire to hold money as a store of wealth is a barometer of the degree of our distrust of our own calculations and conventions concerning the future. . . . The possession of actual money lulls our disquietude;, and the premium which we require to make us part with money is the measure of the degree of our disquietude' (*C.W.* XIV: 116).

27 'If by "credit" we mean "finance", I have no objection at all to admitting the demand for finance as one of the factors influencing the rate of interest. For "finance" constitutes . . . an additional demand for liquid cash in exchange for a deferred claim. It is, in the literal sense, a demand for money' (*C.W.* XIV: 209-10).

28 On Keynes's development of a general model after having arrived at his basic conclusions concerning the actual working of the economy, see also *C.W.* XIV: 212.

37

KEYNES, SCHUMPETER AND BEYOND

A non-reductionist perspective*

Alessandro Vercelli

> Do you not remember, I say, how, when you entered the realm of Lineland, you were compelled to manifest yourself to the King, not as a square, but as a line, because the Linear Realm had not Dimensions enough to represent the whole of you, but only a slice or section of you? In precisely the same way, your country of Two Dimensions is not spacious enough to represent me, a being of Three, but can only exhibit a slice or section of me, which is what you call a Circle.
>
> (Abbott 1884: 58)

INTRODUCTION

The main purpose of this chapter is to sketch a radical but it is hoped constructive critique of orthodox economics following the pathbreaking steps of Keynes and Schumpeter: radical, because the validity of orthodox theory will be confined to a limited sub-set of simple problems; constructive, because I shall try to point out a few methodological requisites for a more satisfactory economic theory, that is, a theory able to cope with the complex problems of a modern monetary economy.

The criticisms I am going to raise against orthodox theory may be seen as different aspects of a general charge of reductionsim. A reductionist theory may be defined as a theory which reduces the complexity of the phenomena studied in a distorted way; that is, in such a way as to impair the possibility of describing, explaining or forecasting important features of the above phenomena. This sort of pathological reductionism[1] must not be confused with the physiological procedures of reduction of complex phenomena to simple laws or principles which have often played a fundamental role in the development of science (see Agazzi 1991; Cornwell 1995; Weinberg 1995).

Borrowing the suggestive metaphors of E.A. Abbott in his well-known romance on the fantastic world of Flatland (1884), while the inhabitants of Lineland can see only points, and the inhabitants of Flatland can see only lines, we need a theory for a three-dimensional Spaceland (see the epigraph above). Otherwise the sphere that speaks in the epigraph is condemned to be perceived in a distorted way: as a plain circle in Flatland, or worse, as a simple line in Lineland.

This does not imply that a non-reductionist theory should be more complicated than a reductionist theory that refers to the same object. The theory of chaos which is part of the non-reductionist theory of 'complex dynamics' is a relatively simple theory as compared, for example, to the inter-temporal general equilibrium theory which is set in terms of classical dynamics. In other words, a non-reductionist theory does not deny the traditional methodological prescription that a simpler theory (or method), *ceteris paribus*, is better than a more complex theory, but claims that *reality* should not be oversimplified.

In most scientific disciplines we may often distinguish between a *reductionist* approach which aims to reduce complex phenomena to simple regularities, irreversible time to reversible time, dynamics to equilibrium, instability to stability, structural change to structural invariance, and so on, and an alternative *non-reductionist* approach which maintains that the above reductions miss or distort important aspects of actual phenomena, and give a fundamental role to complexity, irreversibility, disequilibrium and instability. The above (incomplete) list suggests that there are different forms of reductionism. They often come together, but this is not necessarily true. Here I shall consider only two of these forms which are particularly relevant for macroeconomics: dynamic reductionism, i.e. reduction of the dynamics of the economic system to classical dynamics; and structural reductionism, i.e. the reduction of the behaviour of the whole economy (as studied by macroeconomics) to the behaviour of its constituent parts (as studied by microeconomics).

Non-orthodox theory may assume two different forms: it may try to falsify altogether the received orthodox theory, as Copernican theory did with Ptolemaic theory, or it may generalize it as relativity theory did with Newtonian theory. Also, this second kind of scientific revolution may be radical, as the example of relativity theory shows, because it may relegate the validity of the received theory to a small sub-set of real phenomena.

In this chapter I shall be exclusively concerned with this second kind of non-orthodox economic theories, drawing inspiration from Keynes and Schumpeter. They share this way of conceiving of the relations between their theory and orthodox theory, though from apparently contrasting points of view. Keynes believes that 'classical' [2] theory applies only to a barter economy under full employment, but not to a monetary economy liable to unemployment equilibria, while Schumpeter believes that Walrasian economics applies only to the 'circular flow', characterized by economic routine, but not to the process of development, characterized by innovation and structural change. I intend to show that these two non-reductionist perspectives are complementary and should be integrated within a broader framework.

The structure of the chapter is as follows. I briefly reconstruct the evolution of dynamics that in my opinion has had profound implications for the evolution of most other disciplines, including economics (pp. 286–9). In particular, I examine the genesis and the basic features of classical reductionism which had, and still have, a profound influence upon orthodox economics through general equilibrium (hence forward GE) theory. I then rapidly sketch the genesis and the evolution of classical reductionism in economics (pp. 289–93). I breifly recall how slow and laborious was the struggle to give solid foundations to GE theory and why this problem is still unsettled and controversial. Finally, I briefly explore the nexus between microeconomics and macroeconomics (pp. 293–5). Since the reductionist approaches have not so far succeeded in giving solid foundations to macroeconomics, we have to reconstruct macroeconomic theory from a non-reductionist point of view in order to face the complex and dramatic problems of the actual economies. In order to succeed in this difficult task, Keynes and Schumpeter may still be an important source of inspiration (pp. 295–7). Concluding remarks follow. Since the aim of this chapter is to suggest in a very concise way a broad perspective on the evolution of macroeconomics, none of the argument is fully developed here. I just summarize, or hint at, arguments that I developed in more detail elsewhere (in particular, in Vercelli 1991, 1994, 1995a and 1995b).

THE EVOLUTION OF DYNAMICS

Let me start by rapidly sketching the fundamental stages of the evolution of dynamics, the science of motion through time. Dynamics is the scientific discipline, or sub-discipline, which has most influenced the evolution of the other disciplines, economics included. The way in which the relationships between rest and motion, equilibrium and disequilibrium, stability and instability, and the other basic dynamic concepts, are conceived deeply affects upon the most basic foundations of all scientific disciplines.

From a very general standpoint we may distinguish three stages in the evolution of dynamics in western thought. The first step is characterized by Aristotelian dynamics which ruled unchallenged for almost 2,000 years; only with the scientific revolution of the late Renaissance was Aristotelian dynamics rejected, to be gradually replaced by classical dynamics worked out by Galileo, Newton, Leibniz *et al.*; the third stage, which may be called *post-classical*, originated at the end of the nineteenth century from a few path-breaking contributions by Poincaré, Bruns and Hadamard which revealed the intrinsic limitations of classical dynamics and stimulated the emergence of new formal techniques and languages which have profoundly modified the conceptualization of dynamics (complex dynamics).

As is well known, Aristotelian dynamics distinguished four kinds of motion (corresponding to four kinds of causes): motion in space (or locomotion), genetic motion, formal motion and teleological evolution. According to Aristotelian dynamics, in the absence of external forces, terrestrial bodies stay still and celestial bodies maintain a steady circular motion.

The classical revolution radically modified Aristotelian dynamics by reducing the object of analysis exclusively to locomotion, eliminating the distinction between terrestrial and celestial bodies, and connecting the 'force' applied to a body to its acceleration instead of to its velocity. This reconceptualization came together with the elaboration of a new mathematical language which permits the exact calculus of the trajectories of physical bodies, just by knowing their initial position and impulse. Classical dynamics proved so successful that classical mechanics, based upon it, rapidly became the model for all scientific disciplines ('mechanism') until the end of the nineteenth century and beyond.

The scientific paradigm of classical mechanics is extremely reductionist, for a host of reasons:

1 the object of scientific analysis is reduced to locomotion. The role of the formal cause is restricted to the mathematical or geometrical form of the model. Genetic motion and teleological evolution are neglected as metaphysical;
2 stable equilibria become the basic reference of dynamics as they represent the relatively most invariant positions;
3 though the possibility of unstable equilibria is not denied, their relevance for scientific analysis is excluded, as they are considered ephemeral and unobservable positions. The virtual relevance of structural instability for scientific analysis is denied with similar arguments;
4 nature is considered as strictly deterministic; indeterminism is considered only the sign of residual human ignorance (Laplace);
5 time is conceived as fully reversible: natural laws are believed to be invariant with respect to time, while, by inverting the arrow of time, the trajectories of physical bodies change only direction and sign.

Classical dynamics showed the first symptoms of an irreversible but gradual crisis only at the end of the nineteenth century, when Poincaré and Bruns demonstrated the impossibility of proving the stability of the solar system through quantitative methods. The reason for that was clearly explained by Hadamard (1898) as a consequence of the structural instability of the solar system, which is typical of any complex dynamic system with more than three bodies. This impasse gave birth to new non-linear techniques for studying complex dynamic problems: in particular, qualitative methods (such as those developed by differential topology) and stochastic methods (such as those developed by ergodic theory). However, non-linear dynamics developed only very slowly, probably because the attention of physicists was distracted by the fascinating novelties of the beginning of the twentieth century (relativity and quantum theory), while the attention of mathematicians was captured by the developments of the new logicist and formalist schools led by Russell and Hilbert which reacted against the 'mathematics of time' that had characterized the formal developments of classical dynamics.

For many decades non-linear dynamics developed slowly and underground, mainly by applied mathematicians and engineers pushed by the exigencies of solving practical problems. A fully fledged theory of non-linear oscillations was developed in the 1920s in order to control and design radio circuits. However, it was only in the early 1970s that non-linear dynamics fully emerged from underground, attracting the attention of many scholars in different disciplines, under such imaginative labels as 'catastrophe theory', 'theory of chaos', 'theory of fractals', 'complex dynamics'.

The three stages of dynamics that I have rapidly examined are separated by two fundamental conceptual revolutions. The first revolution of the late Renaissance completely invalidated Aristotelian dynamics, which was fully inconsistent with classical dynamics. The second revolution, which has been progressively consolidated in this century, is much more ambiguous. The new developments of non-linear dynamics do not invalidate classical dynamics within the limits of its own assumptions, but they reduce dramatically the empirical scope of its assumptions. For different conditions, which represent the general case, classical dynamics turns out to be incorrect. Post-classical dynamics cannot be seen only as a marginal 'generalization' of classical dynamics but as a real reconceptualization of dynamics. This is so mainly for the following reasons:

1 the illusion that it may be possible to approximate any kind of dynamics through linear dynamics must be abandoned. Because of a marked sensitivity to initial conditions of most dynamic systems, any linear approximation would be profoundly misleading;
2 classical determinism is substituted by what could be called 'methodological indeterminism'. This does not necessarily imply ontological indeterminism; on the contrary, the theory of chaos is built upon deterministic assumptions. However, the properties of chaotic systems impose the use of stochastic methods for analysing and forecasting their dynamics;
3 the basic reference for analysing the dynamics of a system is no longer given by the traditional concept of stable equilibrium but by the much more complex concept of attractor. Only in extreme cases is an attractor characterized by a simple topology (fixed point or limit cycle). In most

cases attractors have a topology which is complex if not 'strange' (see, for example, Ruelle 1991: ch. 10);

4 confidence in the stability of equilibria fades away, since it is understood that the more complex is a system the less plausible is the stability of its equilibria;

5 the irreversibility of time is progressively recognized.

The evolution of the Aristotelian theory of locomotion and of classical dynamics was strictly intertwined with the evolution of mechanics. However, in the last two centuries dynamics progressively cut its original ties with mechanics and became an autonomous mathematical discipline applicable to any discipline. This has further increased its influence on the evolution of the scientific disciplines. Physical analogies have occasionally played a useful heuristic role but they have also proved to be misleading, while mathematical analogies are today considered much more universal and inspiring.

THE RISE OF ECONOMIC REDUCTIONISM AND ITS EVOLUTION

Adam Smith, the founding father of political economy, was not at all a reductionist. This is clearly revealed by the very title of his masterpiece (1776), as well as by its contents, in particular by his far-reaching approach which combines abstract reasoning with a broad historical perspective. Reductionist theory began to spread at the beginning of the nineteenth century. Ricardo defeated the non-reductionist Malthus by circumscribing the object of political economy to the distribution of a given product among alternative uses and conflicting social classes;[3] the French school of Bastiat and Say advocated individualistic foundations based on the tale of Robinson Crusoe and on barter equilibrium conditions; utilitarianism reduced the puzzle of rational decision to a mere calculus of pleasure and pains.

However, modern reductionism finds its fully fledged paradigm only with Walras. He was the first to succeed in applying the approach of classical physics to economics. For this feat he was defined by Samuelson as the 'Newton of political economy' and by Schumpeter as the greatest of economic theorists. However, Walras himself was unable to complete his ambitious theoretical plan. Notwithstanding his repeated efforts, he was not able to develop the dynamic part of the theory since he did not succeed in getting beyond the analysis of *tâtonnement* processes, so it is only the static part of mechanics which finds a systematic application to economics. This was considered a serious shortcoming by Walras himself as well as by the other main GE theorists of the first generation (Pareto, Wicksell, etc.). And this is the main reason why GE theory has almost been abandoned by the profession since the end of the first decade of the twentieth century. Most economists felt compelled to reach the conclusion that the static character of GE theory condemned it to sterility: how could we explain business cycles, inflation, unemployment and crises by resorting to such a static theory?

GE theory began to conquer the profession only when Hicks (1939) and Samuelson (1947b) succeeded in giving it proper dynamic foundations based on the principles of classical dynamics. It was clarified, in particular, that equilibrium is intrinsically a dynamic concept, and that its descriptive and predictive potential crucially depends on its stability. This led to the systematic study of the stability of GE. The first results obtained by Arrow and Hurwicz (1958) raised the hope that general equilibrium stability could obtain under quite general circumstances. Unfortunately, the counterexamples of Scarf (1960) and the theorem of Sonnenschein (1972) proved that there are basic features of market economies (such as complementarity among goods) that are inconsistent with the stability of equilibrium.

In the meantime, a new approach to GE theory developed which tried to leave time out of consideration altogether. This stream originated from the existence proofs suggested in the mathematical *Kolloquium* of Karl Menger held at the University of Vienna in the 1930s (see Ingrao and Israel 1990). The economists (e.g. Morgenstern) and the mathematicians (e.g. von Neumann) who participated in this research programme did not trust physical analogies and utilized new mathematical instruments based on Hilbertian formalism and French Bourbakism. The foundations in terms of classical mechanics were replaced by axiomatic foundations. The mathematics of time based on difference and differential equations was replaced by timeless mathematics based on abstract algebra and topology. The old physical reductionism was replaced by a neoreductionism based on timeless mathematics. The first fruit of this research programme is the famous book *Theory of Games and Economic Behaviour* (1944) by von Neumann and Morgenstern. The generalization by Nash (1951) of the proof of existence of an economy-wide equilibrium, based on the fixed-point theorem of Kakutani-Brower, opened the way to the first fully rigorous proof of existence of a GE given by Arrow and Debreu (1954). The gestation of this research programme culminated in the fundamental book by Debreu *The Theory of Value* (1959) which rapidly became the basic reference for the subsequent developments of GE theory.

The contradiction between the atemporal axiomatic foundations and the intertemporal problems implied by the applications of the theory to empirical phenomena is solved by disaggregating the goods according to a temporal index; that is, by considering the same good with different temporal indexes as if it represented different goods. In this approach time fully disappears as such, as it is reduced to a multiplication of the dimensions of the space of goods. The trouble is that this strategy of the spatialization of time (i.e. reduction of time to space) works only when markets are complete and the phenomena analysed are stationary.

Notwithstanding these serious shortcomings, the formalist approach to GE became very influential in the last two decades in all the articulations of economic theory, encouraging the adoption of a 'pure equilibrium method' (that is, a method according to which the positions of disequilibrium are not analysed, not even to provide dynamic foundations to the equilibrium positions). However, the absence of dynamic foundations produced a long series of awkward paradoxes that are not easily solvable in the frame of a formalist approach. Among them the following paradoxes may be briefly recalled:

1 GE theory assumes complete flexibility of prices that assures immediate convergence to market-clearing equilibrium, but perfect competition implies by definition that all the agents are price-takers, so that no one has the discretional power to modify prices (paradox of Arrow 1958). In order to justify and analyse price flexibility it is necessary to violate some of the axioms of the theory as, for example, the market-clearing condition or the perfect competition condition.
2 GE theory routinely assumes full informational efficiency of markets in the sense that observed prices fully reveal market fundamentals, but exactly for this reason no agent has any incentive to gather and elaborate information of this kind (paradox of Grossman and Stiglitz 1980). Also in this case, in order to justify the informational efficiency of competitive markets, it is necessary to violate some of the axioms of the theory which make sense only in equilibrium.
3 Rational expectations equilibria in purely speculative financial markets imply no trade even among diversely informed traders, since the equilibrium market price fully reveals the private information of each trader at zero trade for all traders (paradox of Tirole 1982). The problem may be circumvented only by modifying some of the axioms of the theory and assuming disequilibrium and/or weaker forms of rationality (see Sargent 1993).
4 New classical economics formulates the hypothesis of rational expectations in order to allow a sound process of policy appraisal (Lucas 1976). However, the rational expectations hypothesis precludes by definition the possibility of systematic mistakes, both *ex ante* and *ex post*, and therefore it is inconsistent with any change in economic policy not yet anticipated from the very beginning (paradox of Sims 1986a). To get round this paradox we should give up the hypothesis of rational expectations, at least in its strong version, allowing for systematic mistakes *ex post* and therefore permitting a genuinely unanticipated change in the economic environment.

These paradoxes point out not a *logical* contradiction in the model but a *semantic* incongruence in the axioms of the theory; that is, an incongruence among the meanings attributed to the axioms upon which the theory is based. These problems cannot be seen and solved in the framework of a formalist view of GE theory. We need proper dynamic foundations which permit the infusion of the necessary semantic contents into a GE model.

To sum up, the GE school is not at all homogeneous. I recalled the genesis of the basic conflict between a school of thought, which may be called formalist, that believes that axiomatic foundations are sufficient for GE theory (Debreu) and another school, which may be called anti-formalist, that belives that dynamic foundations are necessary for GE theory (Samuelson). These schools of thought have a completely different attitude towards time. The formalist school of Debreu maintains the primacy of syntactic foundations which is guaranteed by a correct axiomatization. The anti-formalist school does not deny that the syntactic coherence of a theory is a *necessary* condition for its consistency, but it does deny that it may be considered also a *sufficient* consistency condition since a second necessary condition is also required: the semantic congruence of the theory guaranteed by proper dynamic foundations. In other words, according to the anti-formalist school, any economic equilibrium should be not only logically coherent but also semantically meaningful, and this may be argued only in the framework of proper dynamic foundations.

At this point a further distinction should be introduced in the camp of the anti-formalist approach. The requisite of proper dynamic foundations for economic theory may have quite different implications according to the conception of dynamics adopted. According to the classical conception of dynamics, typical of the classical and neoclassical theory, the main emphasis is put upon the analysis of the stability of equilibria in order to justify their correct use, of equilibrium dynamics in order to study growth processes, and of cyclical oscillations of economies characterized by invariant structures. According to the post-classical point of view, attention should be given also to the methods and acquisitions of post-classical dynamics (theories of complexity, catastrophes, fractals, chaos, etc.) in order to explain the structural changes and the complex dynamics which characterize most economic systems.

Non-linear dynamics began to be applied to economics with a considerable lag which, however, was much shorter than that of classical dynamics. In a paper published in the first issue of *Econometrica* (1933) the physicist Le Corbeiller advertised the potential advantages for economics of non-linear dynamics, and about fifteen years later R.M. Goodwin published the first applications. However, very few economists took any interest in non-linear dynamics in the 1950s, 1960s and 1970s (notwithstanding important exceptions such as Kaldor and Hicks). Only in the 1980s did interest in non-linear dynamics begin to diffuse among economists in the wake of the new wave that was spreading in the natural sciences. This research programme, considered heterodox and not well founded by most mainstream economists, is progressively spreading in the field of cycle analysis (in particular, the study of long waves), technological change (evolution of technological paradigms), evolution of institutions (in particular, of financial institutions) and ecological economics.

MICRO AND MACRO

I touched upon the crucial role of dynamic reductionism in microeconomics. This form of reductionism also haunts macroeconomics. In addition, macroeconomics is characterized by a special kind of structural reductionism which has strongly affected its recent evolution: the reduction of macroeconomics to microeconomics.

The relations between the theory of macrophenomena and the theory of microphenomena has always been difficult in economics as in other scientific disciplines (physics, chemistry, biology, etc.) In economics, the conflict between the theory of relative prices (or theory of value) and the theory of absolute prices (or, more generally the theory of development, inflation and crisis in an entire economy) is as old as economic theory. Relative prices and the other microphenomena have always been related to demand and supply and/or to production inputs, while inflation, growth and crises have been brought back, at least since the sixteenth century, to some version of the quantity theory of money which remained almost completely unrelated to value theory. The conflict became even more radical with the neoclassical revolution. The theory of relative prices was founded on tastes, technology and endowments of productive factors. On the contrary, the theory of aggregate phenomena (inflation, development, cycles) continued to be based on some version of the aggregate 'exchange equation', though progressively more sophisticaed. The neoclassical theorists did not succeed in clarifying the nexus between 'the two faces of the moon' (see *G.T.*: 292). In the 1930s Keynes tries to solve the dilemma by founding a new discipline for the study of aggregate phenomena, conceived as completely autonomous from microeconomics. The new discipline, which was subsequently called macroeconomics, aims to be in many respects anti-reductionist. Keynes gives an important role to uncertainty, disequilibrium, instability, irreversible time, and so on. A conflict emerges therefore between reductionist microeconomics and anti-reductionist macroeconomics. The history of this conflict and of its attempted resolutions has been reconstructed many times (for a recent account, see Leijonhufvud 1992). Suffice it to recall that the most popular synthesis – the so-called neoclassical synthesis suggested by Modigliani, Samuelson and Patinkin – succeeded in reducing the tension between macro and micro only by giving an interpretation of Keynesian macroeconomics which is basically reductionist: uncertainty, irreversibility and instability do not retain any relevant roles. However, in this school macroeconomics keeps a somewhat autonomous status as the theory of the disequilibrium behaviour of macroeconomics. In the early 1970s there was a radical U-turn. The school of New Classical economists led by Lucas and Sargent suggested, and tried to implement, a radically reductionist research programme which fully denied any autonomy to macroeconomics relatively to GE microeconomics. In opposition to the school of New Classical economists, the school of New Keynesian economists has emerged with the aim to rescue the basic features of Keynesian macroeconomics and to assure compatibility with microeconomics by transforming this last discipline in a less reductionist direction.

In the course of the debate between different schools of macroeconomics a few arguments have been often repeated to support a reductionist approach:

1 The 'economic method' is reduced to the analysis of equilibrium positions: according to the extreme point of view maintained by New Classical economists, disequilibrium positions need not be considered by scientific analysis as they are unintelligible. However, the reduction to equilibrium makes sense only when disequilibrium dynamics does not affect the equilibrium itself. Whenever there is path-dependence or a multiplicity of equilibria, we cannot avoid a thorough analysis of disequilibrium behaviour. Moreover, a pure equilibrium method raises unsolvable paradoxes such as those which I mentioned before (see pp. 289–93).
2 There is only one stable equilibrium corresponding to full employment equilibrium. While Keynes had pointed out the possibility of a continuum of equilibria, all but one characterized by unemployment, the neoclassical synthesis considered only the full-employment equilibrium as stable, restoring the self-regulative character of a market economy. Unfortunately, the uniqueness of equilibrium is a very special case which is found only in the most simple dynamic systems (linear and/or of very low dimension).
3 Substantive rationality is assumed; that is, agents always succeed in maximizing their objective function. However, this point of view does not take account of the limits of human rationality. Limited rationality, as Simon (1982) suggested, leads to a different criterion of rationality: procedural rationality. In addition, both traditional paradigms of rationality (substantive and procedural rationality) neglect completely the specific aspects of human rationality: the capacity of controlling and designing the environment of human action.
4 Empirically relevant equilibria are considered stable, since unstable equilibria are considered non-observable. However, non-linear dynamics has clarified that both dynamic and structural stability are plausible only in very simple dynamic systems, which are unlikely to be able to mimic the actual behaviour of economic systems. In addition, dynamic stability may be in conflict with other basic requisites of reductionist analysis, notably

with determinacy. The suggested way out, that an equilibrium be conceived as a saddle-point, is an *ad hoc* solution which conflicts with the requisite of structural stability.

5 It is assumed that empirical phenomena are deterministic. Therefore, uncertainty is excluded or made irrelevant through *ad hoc* assumptions such as: certainty equivalence, rational expectations, stationarity and ergodicity of the relevant stochastic processes. Recent advances in probability theory and decision theory under uncertainty confirm the idea of Keynes and Knight that uncertainty cannot be reduced to risk (see for example, Kelsey and Quiggin 1992). In these cases the hypothesis of stationarity or ergodicity is unjustified.

In the light of this long list of unsolved problems we could wonder whether the reduction of macroeconomics to microeconomics is possible or even necessary. Before trying to answer this controversial question, we have to distinguish between 'unilateral reduction' of macroeconomics to microeconomics and 'unification' or 'reciprocal synthesis' of the two disciplines. The history of science suggests that all the most successful syntheses between scientific disciplines may be interpreted as the result of a process of reciprocally convergent assimilation between formerly autonomous disciplines. This sort of synthesis may eventually also materialize in the case of microeconomics and macroeconomics. But this synthesis is not yet mature. Past attempts have been conceived rather as 'unilateral reduction' of macroeconomics to microeconomics, and so far they have all failed. The neoclassical synthesis failed because, as was clearly proved by the 'Lucas critique', notwithstanding the strongly reductive interpretation of Keynesian disequilibrium behaviour, it still lacked proper microfoundations and so could be misleading for policy appraisal. However, New Classical economics is able to reduce macroeconomics to general equilibrium theory only under very strong assumptions which define away all the fundamental problems of macroeconomics. In particular, the crucial reference to a representative agent defines away any problem of co-ordination and makes meaningless the existence of money and even of trade itself.

Efforts to unify microeconomics and macroeconomics must be further pursued. We have learned a lot from past attempts but we should be aware that a general unification is still very far away. In the meantime we should not reject interesting macro theories for the reason that they lack fully fledged microfoundations.

KEYNES AND SCHUMPETER

The attempt to establish and develop a non-reductionist approach to macroeconomics may find an important source of inspiration in the path-breaking contributions of Keynes and Schumpeter.

Keynes rejected the classic assumption of a unique equilibrium at full employment, and maintained the plausibility of a plurality of equilibria, generally characterized by unemployment. He stressed the importance of concepts such as involuntary unemployment, which imply disequilibrium and irrationality according to classical economists; however, proper dynamic foundations of these concepts, foreshadowed by Keynes himself, confirm not only their scientific legitimacy but also their importance for understanding persistent unemployment. He underlined throughout his life the crucial importance of financial instability in a monetary economy. In the early works, up to the *Treatise on Money*, financial instability is interpreted as the expression of the dynamic instability of the full employment equilibrium, while in *The General Theory* attention shifted towards the structural instability of equilibrium positions; this is due to conventional long-term expectations which may be very reactive in a milieu characterized by strong uncertainty. Determinism is clearly rejected for economics, as for the other social disciplines, for which he foreshadows a very modern theory of probabilistic causality. Substantive rationality is also rejected since, under strong uncertainty, a sophisticated calculus of expected costs and benefits is considered impossible or completely unreliable. He is therefore open to admit the role of *prima facie* irrational drives in human decision, from the influence of alchemia and exoterism on Newton's thought to the impact of animal spirits of entrepreneurs on investment behaviour. However, he does not himself indulge in any form of irrationalism as his theory aims to persuade a rational audience in a rational way. Keynes's concept of rationality is much broader than that of substantive rationality typical of classical reductionism, and also broader than that of procedural rationality advocated by Simon; so he is able to explain in rational terms behaviours which would otherwise look irrational. His concept of rationality goes beyond the traditional adaptive notions of rationality, since it is also oriented towards the design and implementation of viable alternative institutional environments.

This is not to say that Keynes's approach as expounded in *The General Theory* is completely flawless. A few basic limitations have been lucidly captured by Schumpeter, who rightly stressed that the aggregative character and the short-run point of view of his approach prevented a thorough analysis of the capitalist process characterized by innovation and irreversible structural change (Schumpeter 1936).

Schumpeter assumed a non-reductionist point of view which is quite different from that of Keynes, but it may be shown that it is in many respects complementary to it. In consequence of a swarm of innovations, the pre-existing equilibrium becomes unstable and is actually destroyed by the process of innovation diffusion until eventually a new equilibrium materializes. The irreversible structural change induced by innovative entrepreneurs is the essential dimension of the capitalist process which is bound to be missed by Walrasian reductionism, and is missed – in his opinion – by Keynes himself.

Unfortunately, Schumpeter was unable fully to appreciate the positive side of *The General Theory* and the extent to which Keynes's theory was actually complementary to his own. Both Keynes and Schumpeter had reached the conclusion that, contrary to the received wisdom of reductionism, a monetary economy is structurally unstable. Keynes stressed the intertemporal structural flexibility induced by liquidity, while Schumpeter stressed the technological flexibility allowed by credit creation. In both cases the degree of structural stability is progressively augmented by increasingly sophisticated financial structures which enhance the intertemporal flexibility of the economic structure. However, while Keynes stressed the *pathological* aspects of financial flexibility which induce financial fragility, Schumpeter, on the contrary, stressed its *physiological* aspects, as a crucial permissive condition of innovation and development. These two aspects coexist in modern industrial economies and should be integrated in the analysis.[4] The Keynesian approach should be disaggregated and extended to the long period without sliding back into reductionism. On the other side, the Schumpeterian theory should be integrated with a theory of effective demand and financial instability under strong uncertainty: in such a theory, due to path-dependence, short-run fluctuations in aggregate demand may affect the long-run behaviour of the economy in an irreversible way.

Of course, a non-reductionist macroeconomic theory must not only look back to important sources of inspiration but must also look around and ahead. It must look around in order to understand the new features of the great contemporary problems: unemployment, financial instability, underdevelopment. It must look ahead into the distant future in order to anticipate the great global problems which may jeopardize the sustainability of development: in particular, those raised by environmental and demographic constraints.

CONCLUDING REMARKS

Classical reductionism, that is, the approach based on classical dynamics, was applied consistently to economic theory only very lately, almost three centuries after it was first applied in physics, that is, only in the 1940s when it was already beginning to decline in physics and in other natural sciences.

The non-reductionist (or, at least, less reductionist) point of view of nonlinear dynamics began to be applied in economics with a much shorter lag (slightly more than ten years), probably because of a very strong nonorthodox tradition which has always kept alive the instances neglected by mainstream reductionism.

The methodological crisis of classical reductionism came together with the international economic crisis and the ensuing frustration at the inability of macroeconomc theories to suggest efficient remedies. The orthodox theory reacted to this situation of crisis in two divergent ways.

One stream tried to enlarge the scope of the theory in a less reductionist direction (new Keynesian economics, new institutionalist economics, and so on). But, surprisingly, another stream went in the opposite direction, which might be called hyper-reductionist, working out an extreme form of reductionism. Even more surprisingly, this stream became the mainstream in the 1970s and the 1980s and is still very influential. The explanation of this success extends beyond the realm of economics and involves considerations drawn from the sociology and psychology of science. It was observed, for example, that the hyper-reductionist theory played the role of ideological support for neoliberism better than the rival theories in a period characterized by the crisis of both 'real Keynesianism' and Keynesian macroeconomics; probably it played also a role as psychological support for economists who were feeling more and more insecure about the intrinsic strength of their discipline and the range of its applicability to the real world.

This is not to deny that New Classical economics also played a constructive role in single sub-fields of economic analysis; unfortunately, its success has inhibited the search for a non-reductionist approach to macroeconomic problems. This search must be resumed with courage and must be pursued with energy in order to face the grave problems which haunt the world economy.

NOTES

* This chapter is based on the text of an invited lecture given at the University of Campinas (Brazil) which has subsequently been published in Portuguese (Vercelli 1994). I wish to thank G.C. Harcourt and all participants in the above seminar for their invaluable comments.

1 In a previous essay (Vercelli 1995a), I distinguished between the physiological and pathological manifestations of reductionism and anti-reductionism, and I argued that the dialectics between reductionism and anti-reductionism plays a constructive role in the development of science. Since in this chapter I am concerned neither with anti-reductionism nor with the physiological manifestations of reductionism, in order to simplify the terminology I shall use the word 'reductionism' in the specific sense of 'pathological reductionism'. The *non-reductionist* perspective advocated in this and in my previous work should not be confused with an *anti-reductionist* position, as it aims to avoid the pathological, or dogmatic, versions of both reductionism and anti-reductionism. Lack of space prevents a satisfactory treatment of these themes here.

2 In this chapter the word 'classical' will be used with the same meaning attributed to it by Keynes in *The General Theory*.

3 Though Ricardo's theory is less reductionist than that of Walras, it is more reductionist than that of Smith and Malthus, since the evolutionary problems of economic development are considered outside the scope of pure economic theory.

4 An interesting recent attempt at such a synthesis which builds on ideas of Keynes and Schumpeter is suggested in Morishima (1992).

38

KEYNES, KALECKI AND *THE GENERAL THEORY*

Peter Kriesler

> [W]ithout any contact either way, Michal Kalecki had found the same solution. . . . The interesting thing is that two thinkers, from completely different political and intellectual starting points, should come to the same conclusion. . . . I well remember my first meeting with Michal Kalecki – a strange visitor who was not only already familiar with our brand-new theories, but had even invented some of our private jokes. It gave me a kind of Pirandello feeling – was it he who was speaking or I?
>
> (Robinson 1964: 95)

In line with these comments by Joan Robinson, it is fairly well established that Keynes and Kalecki independently discovered the principle of effective demand. These two intellectual giants should have towered over twentieth-century economics. Their discovery showed, contrary to all previous economic thought with the possible exception of Marx[1] and 'the brave army of heretical . . . under-consumption[ists]',[2] that the economy would not necessarily generate full employment of all resources, especially not of labour. The reason for this was not some market 'imperfection', such as rigidity of prices or wages, but, rather, insufficient effective demand. In other words, fundamental to their respective visions of capitalist economies was the insight that there was no market mechanism that could guarantee full employment. Unemployment, far from being the result of a malfunction in the market mechanism, resulted from the way that markets worked. To achieve full employment, some exogenous injection of demand was required. Instead of the accolade due to them the contributions of Kalecki were largely ignored, especially in the mainstream, while those of Keynes were sanitized and introduced into the orthodoxy in a bastardized version with the emphasis on market imperfections[3]. Eventually even this version of Keynesianism was abandoned.

Despite the similarity of their conclusions as to the inability of market economies to generate full employment, Keynes and Kalecki emerged from entirely different backgrounds and from very different intellectual traditions.[4] Given the differences between the two, it is not suprising that there are important differences in their derivation of the analysis of effective demand.

In the first edition of *The General Theory*, there was no mention of Michal Kalecki. As Kalecki was unknown at that time outside Poland, this was entirely reasonable. However, given the importance of Kalecki's contribution to macroeconomic thought, and the admission by major Keynesian economists of its similarity to that of Keynes, it would be fruitful to speculate on the consequences of the influence of Kalecki on a second edition. This chapter will look at the contributions of and differences between these economists. In doing so, it will suggest ways in which incorporation of aspects of Kalecki's approach may be used to improve the analysis of *The General Theory*, so contributing to a second edition. However, in order to evaluate these contributions, they must be contrasted with the approaches of their predecessors, which is done in the next section. To approach the question of how a Kalecki-modified *General Theory* would look, it is necessary to outline briefly the main contributions of *The General Theory* as well as of Kalecki. Finally, a comparison of the two will be attempted, and suggestions as to a post-Kaleckian second edition of *The General Theory* will be made.[5]

Before continuing, it is important to note the ambivalent attitude of Keynes to Kalecki's contributions. His comments on the work of Kalecki varied from being dismissive and rude, on the one hand, to admiration on the other.[6] In some cases, he cites Kalecki to support his arguments,[7] and elsewhere he modified his analysis as a result of Kalecki's work [Keynes 1939c]. This indicates that Keynes was, at times, prepared to accept criticisms from Kalecki. Subsequently the people around Keynes, especially Joan Robinson, have argued that Kalecki's contributions could have supplemented many aspects of those of Keynes.[8] In other words, although it is not in fact likely that a second edition would have contained the modifications suggested in this chapter, it is possible.

THE PRE-KEYNESIAN THEORY

In discussing pre-Keynesian theory, we need to distinguish between classical and neoclassical economic analysis, although Keynes did not distinguish between them, lumping them together under his version of the term 'classical'. In discussing neoclassical analysis, there is little need to distinguish the pre-Keynesian and post-Keynesian versions, as there was no fundamental change as a result of *The General Theory*.[9]

Classical economics[10]

The main concern of the classical economists was in explaining the growth and accumulation of nations in historical time. To this purpose, they analysed the economy in terms of classes, believing that the determinants of distribution also determined the dynamics of the economy. Within this framework wages were taken as given at subsistence, so workers did not save. All investment (accumulation) came from profits. It was generally assumed that capitalists saved/invested all their profit. Unemployment was not considered to be a long-term problem due to some version of Say's Law, and the identification of acts of saving with investment, coupled with, in the case of Ricardo, a Malthusian mechanism. Although markets were assumed to be competitive, this should not be taken to be the same as the perfect competition of neoclassical economists. Rather, competition for the classical economists was associated with the tendency towards a uniform rate of profits. They did not distinguish between microeconomic and macroeconomic analysis, moving fairly easily between them. The distinction was not an operative one for either the classical economists or for Marx.[11]

Monetary and real variables were believed to be determined separately. In the financial sector, a version of the quantity theory linked the supply of money (in the form of gold) to the price level. The rate of interest was a real variable which equated saving and investment. There was little analysis of uncertainty or of the role of expectations.

Neoclassical economics

After the classical economists, the scope and method of economics changed. The focus became that of individuals maximizing at a moment of time. Economics became synonymous with price theory. Distribution and growth were relegated to secondary concerns.[12] The main point of the analysis was to show that flexible prices would clear markets. If there was unemployment, then the cause was rigid wages, which inhibited adjustment in the labour market, preventing the market-clearing price from being reached. In the loanable funds market, the 'natural' rate of interest equated saving (the supply of loanable funds) and investment (demand for those funds). Given the total level of employment, which was determined in the labour market, this market determined the division of that employment between the production of consumption and investment goods. As saving represented the supply of loanable funds, it was seen as being prior to investment. In other words, investment could not increase above the level determined by the supply of loanable funds.[13]

Employment, saving, investment, the rate of interest and relative prices were all determined within the real sector. The price level was seen as being a monetary variable determined within the monetary sector via the quantity theory. Accordingly, in the long run, the price level was seen as being exogenous to the real sector, being determined by the supply and demand for money. As a result, we had the neutrality of money in the long run, whereby monetary variables could not effect real variables, and vice versa.

According to Pigou, money is a veil. It is a surface phenomenon, having no real influence except that it can hide the underlying real story.[14] Economic agents see the economy through the veil of the monetary variables, which lie between the real variables and those agents. In other words, the perception of the economy was as if there was a box in which real variables were determined (including the rate of interest). In another box the monetary variables determined the inflation rate, with no connection between the boxes, at least in the long run. This can be represented as in Figure 38.1, where there are no connections between monetary and real variables.[15] In other words, monetary variables cannot affect real ones.

Most economists associated with 'neoclassical' general equilibrium deny any separate identity for macro theory, which is perceived as being some sort of aggregate of micro relations. Economists in this tradition, if they attempt to 'do macroeconomics', do so by deriving 'macroeconomic' results – such as non-market clearing equilibria – in general equilibrium models. By denying legitimacy to any 'holistic' approach[16] they reject the criticism, made by both Keynes and Kalecki, that there is a fallacy of composition involved in drawing macro conclusions from micro theory.[17] The underlying assumption behind this approach is that microeconomic theory is fundamental, while macroeconomic theory is only valid when derived from it.[18]

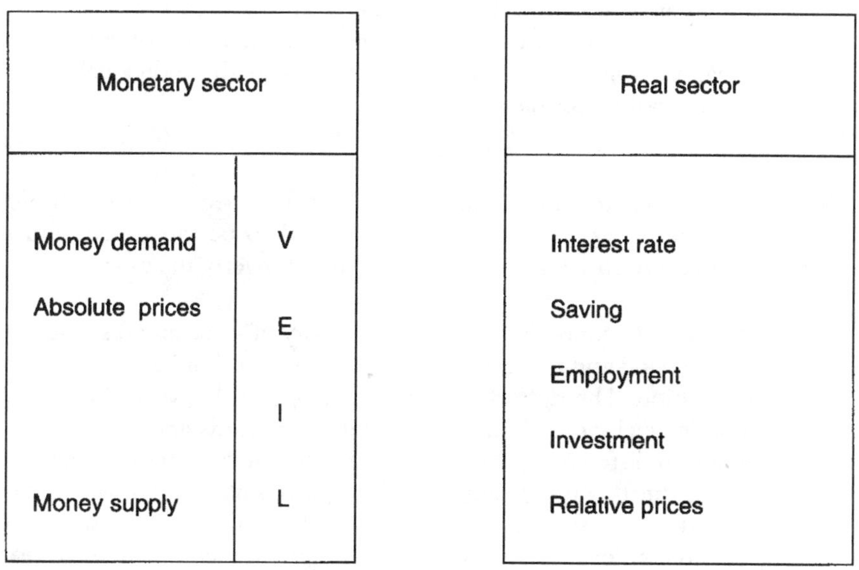

Figure 38.1 Relation between monetary and real sectors in neoclassical economics

THE GENERAL THEORY OF EMPLOYMENT, INTEREST AND MONEY

It was against this type of economic analysis that Keynes reacted. Like most path-breaking works, *The General Theory* contained a critique of the economic orthodoxy of the time, and the outline of a new approach to economics. The essence of Keynes's critique was in the logical idea of the fallacy of compositon:

> I have called my theory a *general* theory. I mean by this that I am chiefly concerned with the behaviour of the economic system as a whole . . . And I argue that important mistakes have been made through extending to the system as a whole conclusions which have been correctly arrived at in respect of a part of it taken in isolation.
>
> (Preface to French edition: *C.W.* VII: xxxii)[19]

In particular, he argued that the conventional theory errs in its treatment of the labour market, and of the saving–investment relation (*C.W.* VII: 84–5, 257–60).

The fallacy of composition becomes the basis for the distinction between micro and macro economics:

> Though an individual whose transactions are small in relation to the market can safely neglect the fact that demand is not a one-sided transaction, it makes nonsense to neglect it when we come to aggregate demand. This is the vital difference between the theory of economic behaviour of the aggregate and the theory of behaviour of the individual unit, in which we assume that changes in the individual's own demand do not affect his income.
>
> (*C.W.* VII: 85)

Keynes used this to argue that, instead of the neoclassical dichotomy between monetary and real analysis, these need to be integrated, and that the correct dichotomy was between micro and macro analysis:

> The division of economics between the theory of value and distribution on the one hand and the theory of money on the other hand is, I think, a false division. The right dichotomy is, I suggest, between the theory of the individual industry or firm and of the rewards and the distribution between different uses of a given quantity of resources on the one hand, and the theory of output and employment as a whole on the other hand. . . . as soon as we pass to the problem of what determines output and employment as a whole, we require the complete theory of monetary economy.
>
> (*C.W.* VII: 293)

Keynes, in this passage, argues for a micro–macro dichotomy. Macroeconomic theory explains the determination of total output and employment, while microeconomics explains the composition of that output. This is reiterated in the 'Concluding Notes' of *The General Theory*'s last chapter:

> If we suppose the volume of output to be given, i.e. to be determined by forces outside the classical scheme of thought, then there is no objection to be raised against the classical analysis of the manner in which private self-interest will determine what in particular is produced, in what proportions the factors of production will be combined to produce it, and how the value of the final product will be distributed between them. . . . To put the point more concretely, I see no reason to suppose that the existing system seriously misemploys the factors of production which are in use. . . . It is in determining the volume, not the direction, of actual employment that the existing system has broken down.
>
> *C.W.* VII: 378–9)

In other words, Keynes is arguing for the independence of microeconomic and macroeconomic factors. Macroeconomic factors, *by themselves*, explain the volume of employment and output, independent of microeconomic factors, which explain its composition. This passage also gives the basis of the micro–macro distinction used in the chapter. Microeconomic factors are taken as referring to those factors which determine price and output of individual firms and industries, in other words, they determine the composition of a given output and are determined by the structure of product markets. Macroeconomic factors, on the other hand, determine the volume of total output and employment. Keynes believed that this occurred independently of the microeconomic factors.[20]

Within the parameters defined for macroeconomic theory, Keynes identifies the main determinant of the level of employment as the level of effective demand. This, in turn, in a closed economy with no government is equal to the sum of expenditure on consumption and on investment.

Much has been written of Keynes's analysis of consumption and investment. It is important to note that his discussion of consumption is extremely sophisticated, and incorporates the basic ideas underlying all of the subsequent formulations of the consumption function.[21] The key determinant of consumption in the short run was, according to Keynes, not the rate of interest but, rather, the level of income. Although he did allow for the fact that incomes from different factors are associated with different marginal propensities to consume, this was never an important feature of his analysis.[22]

For Keynes, investment is determined by the marginal efficiency of capital and the rate of interest. Importantly, although, by definition, in equilibrium saving will equal investment, it is changes in income which equate them via the multiplier process, rather than the rate of interest:

> Keynes's intellectual revolution was to shift economists from thinking normally in terms of a model of reality in which a dog called savings wagged his tail labeled investment to thinking in terms of a model in which a dog called investment wags his tail called saving.
>
> (Meade 1975: 62)

The determination of the rate of interest, if it is no longer the price which equates saving and investment, was, as a result left 'in the air' (*C.W.* XIV: 212). For determination of the rate of interest Keynes looked at the money market: 'The rate of interest . . . is the "price" which equilibrates the desire to hold wealth in the form of cash with the available quantity of cash' (*C.W.* VII: 167).

In other words, Keynes believed that the rate of interest was mainly detemined in the monetary sector as the price that equates demand with a given supply of money. For Keynes, then, the rate of interest was determined by the level of nominal income, the liquidity preference schedule (which is based on underlying uncertainty), the money supply and the supply of substitute assets. As a result, the rate of interest no longer represents the reward for abstaining from consumption as it does in neoclassical theory, but becomes the reward for parting with liquidity.

So far, this discussion of the central principles of *The General Theory* has avoided explicitly discussing the underlying importance of expectations, which play a fundamental role in Keynes's analysis. Keynes makes it clear that most of the variables are 'expected' ones, with expectations and uncertainty playing a particularly important role in his analysis of money and of investment.[23]

In Keynes's analysis monetary and real variables cannot be separated, as they are in neoclassical theory. Money is not neutral, as his comments, quoted earlier, about the need to integrate monetary and real theory for the treatment of output and employment, indicate. The rate of interest, which is a monetary variable, together with the marginal efficiency of capital determines the level of investment, which in turn determines the level of both nominal and real income. These, in their turn, influence the rate of interest by their effect on the demand for money. The absolute price level also moves from being determined in the monetary sector to being determined in the real sector by costs of production (*C.W.* VII: 292–8). This is summarized in Figure 38.2. In other words, for Keynes monetary variables can affect real variables and real variables can affect monetary ones.

In Chapter 19, one of the key chapters of *The General Theory*, Keynes put his analysis together in considering the effects of changes in money-wages.[24] For a reduction in money-wages to increase employment, it would have to do so by increasing effective demand. To do this, according to

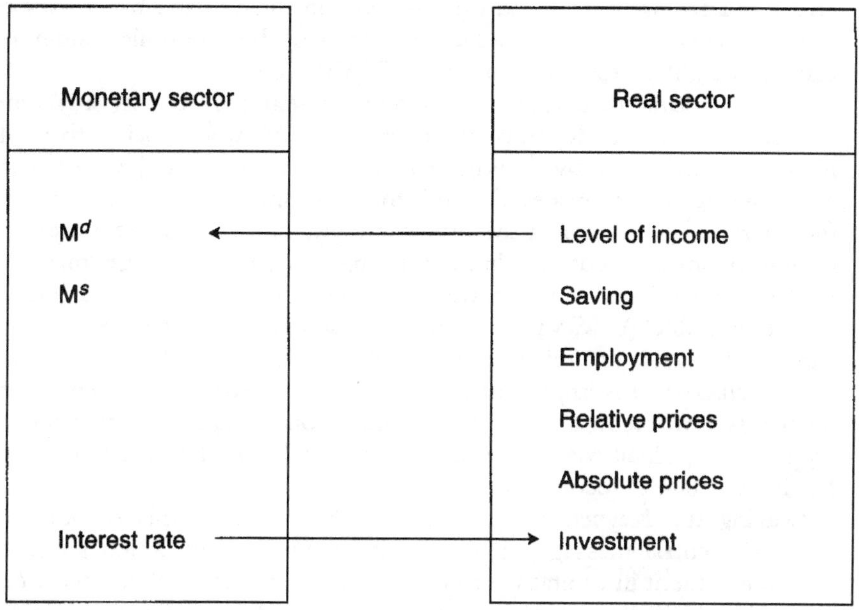

Figure 38.2 Relation between monetary and real sectors for Keynes

Keynes, it would need to operate on the exogenous variables and determining relations, namely the propensity to consume, the money supply, the marginal efficiency of capital schedule or the schedule for liquidity preference. Here Keynes notes that the fall in money-wages will redistribute income from wage-earners to other factors and from entrepreneurs to rentiers. The net effect of these is a likely fall in the propensity to consume. Its impact on investment depends on how it influences both general expectations and those of future wage changes. These, in turn, will impact on the marginal efficiency of capital. Keynes also notes that the increased burden of debt for some enterprises caused by the deflation 'may partly offset any cheerful reactions from the reduction of wages' (*C.W.* VII: 264), indicating the 'adverse effects on investment' of bankruptcy.

There is one important mechanism whereby the deflation caused by the reduction in wages may lead to increased employment, via the influence on the interest rate. The reduction in prices will lead to a reduction in nominal income, which reduces the transactions demand for money. This will reduce the rate of interest. With a given marginal efficiency of capital schedule, this will lead to an increase in investment, thereby increasing employment. This mechanism is referred to in the literature as the Keynes effect, and is the one way in which Keynes allows a reduction in money-wages to have a positive influence on employment: 'It is, therefore, on the effect of a falling wage – and price – level on the demand for money that those who believe in the self-adjusting quality of the economic system must rest the weight of their argument' (*C.W.* VII: 266).

Keynes warns that there are serious limitations to this adjustment mechanism. First, it depends on the quantity of money being fixed, and not being endogenously determined as a function of the level of wages, economic activity or prices. Second, the mechanism is equivalent to using monetary policy to expand the money supply, which would be a preferable option. In any case both are limited, in that a moderate change 'may prove inadequate, whilst an immoderate [one] might shatter confidence even if it were practicable' (*C.W.* VII: 267). In other words, the marginal efficiency of capital schedule is unlikely to remain stable during the deflationary process.

Nevertheless, it is important to note that the Keynes effect represents a mechanism whereby a reduction in the money-wage rate may increase employment, albeit via a very different mechanism from that envisaged by the neoclassical economists.

Leaving the Keynes effect aside for the moment, this demonstrates Keynes's central message, that there is no mechanism which guarantees full employment in capitalist economies. If it is achieved, then this is just a fluke. Involuntary unemployment is not caused by rigidities in money-wages or the rate of interest, but by the failure of effective demand.

Before continuing, it is necessary to examine an important modification which Keynes subsequently made to his analysis of the determination of the rate of interest. In 1937 Keynes published two replies to some of the critics of his analysis of interest in which he analysed an additional determinant of the demand for money. This was a demand for money to *finance* investment, which arises because 'planned investment – i.e. investment *ex ante* – may have to secure its "financial position" *before* the investment takes place; that is to say, before the corresponding saving has taken place' (*C.W.* XIV: 207). For Keynes the finance motive serves the same function as the other demands for money, and operates mainly through its influence on the rate of interest:

> [I]f the liquidity preference of the public . . . and of the banks are unchanged, an excess in the finance required by current *ex ante* output (it is not necessary to write 'investment', since the same is true of *any* output which has to be planned ahead) over the finance released by current *ex post* output will lead to a rise in the rate of interest. . . . Just as an increase in actual activity must . . . raise the rate of interest unless either the banks or the rest of the public become more willing to release cash, so . . . an increase in planned activity must have a similar, superimposed, influence.
>
> *C.W.* XIV: 220–1)

As a result, 'a heavy demand for finance can exhaust the market and be held up by lack of financial facilities on reasonable terms. . . . It is the supply of available finance which, in practice, holds up from time to time the onrush of "new issues"'(*C.W.* XIV: 210).

The importance of the discussion of the role of finance lies in its being a direct avenue in which Kalecki's analysis of the role of monetary considerations can be incorporated into *The General Theory*, as is discussed below (p. 312).

CRITICISMS OF *THE GENERAL THEORY*

In outlining the contributions of a Kalecki-influenced *General Theory* it is important to consider some of the limitations and criticisms of *The General Theory*. As is well known, *The General Theory* is an extremely controversial book, with much criticism being aimed at its central argument. This section will concentrate on criticisms that are valid, in the sense of accepting the basis of the Keynesian system. This is an important distinction to make, as many of the criticisms of the central tenets, particularly those associated with the neoclassical synthesis, ignore the essence of the Keynesian system. For example, those economists who stress the importance of rigid money-wages or of the liquidity trap as the mechanisms which prevent the achievement of full employment are ignoring *The General Theory* where both of these are explicitly ruled out as the causes of unemployment.[25]

One of the most important critics of Keynes's unemployment result was Pigou. He argued that if wealth were an argument in the consumption function, in addition to current income, then a reduction in wages would lead to full employment. This was due to the increase in the value of monetary assets caused by the wage deflation, which would, therefore, increase consumption and so restore full employment. Indeed, if the wage deflation continued long enough, then effective demand could not be deficient as one cent could buy a nation's GNP. This mechanism has been called the Pigou or real-balance effect. The most important response to this argument came from Kalecki in 1944. According to Kalecki, Pigou's analysis relies on the assumption of money supply exogeneity. In responding, Kalecki distinguished between 'inside' and 'outside' money. Inside money was the asset (cash and deposits) whose liability ('credits to persons and firms') is also held within the private sector. In this case, the reduction in prices will influence balance sheets, causing a redistribution between the holders of money and 'bank debtors', which will reduce the propensity to consume. With outside money, on the other hand, the asset (gold and currency) is held in the private sector, the offsetting liability is held outside the private sector, and therefore the redistribution will not decrease consumption. As a result, if the stock of outside money is relatively small, it would require a massive deflation to reduce saving sufficiently to generate full employment, and, in the process, 'wholesale bankruptcy and a confidence crisis' would overwhelm the Pigou effect (Kalecki 1944: 342–3).

The second major problem was identified with the analysis of investment in *The General Theory*, and particularly its static nature. Patinkin has noted that Keynes provided an analysis of the optimal capital stock, and not of the determination of the level of investment. Kalecki (in his review of *The General Theory*) argues that there was a logical flaw in Keynes's analysis of investment, 'the reason for this failure lies in an approach which is basically static to a matter which is by its nature dynamic' (Kalecki 1936: 231).

Consider the effect of a fall in the rate of interest. *Ceteris paribus*, this will lead to an increase in the level of investment, which will increase output and employment via the multiplier. According to Keynes, the main determinant of expectations of the future are current events. As a result, there will be an improvement in expectations which will shift the marginal efficiency of capital schedule outwards, and further increase investment. This will start the cumulative cycle again. The result of this is that, instead of Keynes providing a theory of unemployment equilibrium, Kalecki argued that it is really a theory of the business cycle.

The final criticisms of *The General Theory* are those discussed by Kaldor in a number of places, but in particular in his 'Limitations of *The General Theory*'. Kaldor identifies two major limitations:[26] first, that Keynes was 'unaware of the importance of imperfect competition to his theory' (Kaldor 1983b: 79);[27] and second, that Keynes treated the money supply as being fixed rather than as being endogenously determined. The endogenous money supply goes to the heart of two of the criticisms which allow full employment to be restored as a result of reductions in money-wages. Neither the Keynes effect nor the Pigou/real-balance effect will operate as a mechanism for increasing aggregate demand unless the money supply is exogenous, as the essence of both is that individual agents are left with excess money balances in their portfolios. It is the attempt to reduce these excess balances which restores full employment. However, if the money supply is treated as being endogenously determined, then there is no longer a channel for reductions in money-wages to increase employment.

KALECKI

In order to facilitate comparison with the discussion of Keynes in the previous section, it would have been useful to consider Kalecki's equivalent of *The General Theory*. However, even though there is no equivalent work of Kalecki, there is a certain continuity which runs through his analysis of capitalism. In particular, Kalecki's concern with the dynamic question of the determination of the business cycle will be considered in this section.

Kalecki also made criticisms, similar to those of Keynes, based on the fallacy of composition of orthodox economics in deriving conclusions related to 'the economy as a whole' based on individual experience.[28] They had similar views about the determination of employment, through the level of effective demand, determined by consumption and investment. Kalecki, like Keynes, rejected the role of the rate of interest in equilibrating saving and investment, but argued instead that they were equated by changes in the level and distribution of income caused by changes in the level of investment.[29]

This highlights an important distinction between the two writers. Kalecki's analysis was always in terms of classes – workers and capitalists – with the implication that the main determinant of people's economic relations was their role in production, and the constraints on their activities which this implied.[30] So workers are assumed to have a passive role, consuming all their income, while capitalists make investment, saving and consumption decisions influencing employment and prices. In other words, the classes are associated with different types of economic activity.[31] As a result, in Kalecki's work, the distribution of income is an important determinant of the level of income via, *inter alia*, its influence on the level of consumption. If wages are mainly consumed, while capitalists consume, save and invest, then changes in income and employment, according to Kalecki, also result from changes in distribution or from changes in capitalist expenditure decisions.[32] Further, unlike Keynes, who was mainly interested in the determination of output, Kalecki was concerned with the distribution of income for its implications for the living standards of the lower income groups.

Within this framework, employment and output are determined, as with Keynes, by consumption and investment demand. However, Kalecki's treatment of both components of aggregate demand varied substantially from that of Keynes. Using the Marxian reproduction schemes, Kalecki divided the economy into three sectors, on the basis of the nature of each sector's output.[33] Sector 1 produces capital goods; sector 2, capitalists' consumption goods; and sector 3, workers' consumption goods. The importance of this analytical division is the direct result of Kalecki's stress on distribution, as reflected in his use of the classical assumption that workers consume all their income. As a result, the output and employment of sector 3 are determined by the distribution of income between wage-earners and capitalists. As saving and investment come from capitalists, whose expenditure decisions are not limited by their current income, it is these expenditure decisions that determine both the output of sectors 1 and 2 and capitalist profits. Capitalist consumption can be decomposed into a stable (fixed) part and a part which is proportional to past profits. In other words, capitalist consumption, according to Kalecki, is determined by historical, not current, values. Investment determines the ouput of sector 1.

Although Kalecki saw investment as 'the central *pièce de résistance* of economics', it was the aspect of his work with which he was least satisfied, changing it continuously. Nevertheless, some constant themes recur. First, there is an emphasis on dynamic considerations in the analysis of the determinants of investment. Investment was seen as the least stable part of national income, and the main cause of cycles. Kalecki differentiated the investment decision from the resultant flow of investment, implying a lag between the decision and the resultant impact on aggregate demand, allowing for changes in 'entrepreneurial reactions' to explain differences between the two. The main determinants of investment were the ability of firms to finance investment internally, the size of the capital stock and profits. These, in turn, were determined by both the level and the rate of change of the level of economic activity. The rate of interest was not seen as being particularly significant, mainly because it was the long-term rate of interest which might influence investment decisions, and this did not exhibit 'marked cyclical fluctuations' (Kalecki 1990: 113).[34]

The financial sector's role in the investment process was through the medium of the availability of credit. This represents a substantial difference to Keynes, who stressed the role of the cost of finance rather than its availability, even after incorporating the finance motive. Kalecki's analysis of the determination of the rate of interest is similar to Keynes's discussion of the transactions demand. Kalecki distinguished between the short-term and the long-term rates of interest. The short-term rate of interest is determined by the value of transactions in the economy and the supply of money. An increase in the supply of money reduces the rate of interest. The long-term rate of interest, on the other hand, is a function of the expected short rate. According to Kalecki, as well as determining credit, banks controlled the money-creation process. It was their willingness to expand the money supply and extend credit which facilitated any expansion in investment. Similarly, if it was not forthcoming, it could constrain it. In other words, Kalecki argued that the supply of money was endogenously created in the private sector by banks. It is the response of the banking system to increased demand for money which determines the limits of the expansionary phase of the business cycle (Kalecki 1990: 13–14). In other words, in Kalecki's analysis it is banks, which are private sector firms, which determine changes in the money supply, depending on perceived profitability.[35]

According to Kalecki, the financial sector was as imperfectly competitive as the rest of the economy. It was this which explained the importance of internal finance to enable firms to expand (Kalecki 1937a).

For Kalecki, employment was determined by two separate factors. First, the expenditure decisions of capitalists determined the output of sectors 1 and 2. These were influenced by past profits and by both the level of economic activity and its rate of change. Second, factors associated with the mark-up determined the share of wages in national income. This, in conjunction with the level of output in sectors 1 and 2, determined employment and output in sector 3. This means that both micro and macro factors play a role in the determinantion of the level of output.

Like Keynes, investment for Kalecki plays a pivotal role in determining income. For Kalecki, this operates via its effect on the level of profits, which vary directly with changes in investment expenditure.

The relation between monetary and real sectors for Kalecki is represented in Figure 38.3. The main differences between Keynes and Kalecki in terms of the relations between sectors is the importance of availability of finance as the significant monetary variable, and the addition of distribution as a major real variable.

KEYNES AND KALECKI COMPARED

In order to understand both the similarities and the differences between Keynes and Kalecki, it is important to acknowledge the differences in their agendas. For Keynes:

> This book [*The General Theory*] is chiefly addressed to my fellow economists. . . . But its main purpose is to deal with difficult questions of theory, and only in the second place with the applications of this theory to practice. . . . Thus I cannot achieve my object of persuading economists to re-examine critically certain of their basic assumptions except by a highly abstract argument and also by much controversy. . . . I have thought it important, not only to explain my own point of view, but also to show in what respects it departs from the prevailing theory.
>
> (*C.W.* VII: xxi)

In other words, as was argued above, *The General Theory* is aimed at showng both the errors of the prevailing othodoxy and Keynes's own theory. To achieve this end, he was fundamentally concerned with showing the possibility of unemployment equilibrium and demonstrating that there was no

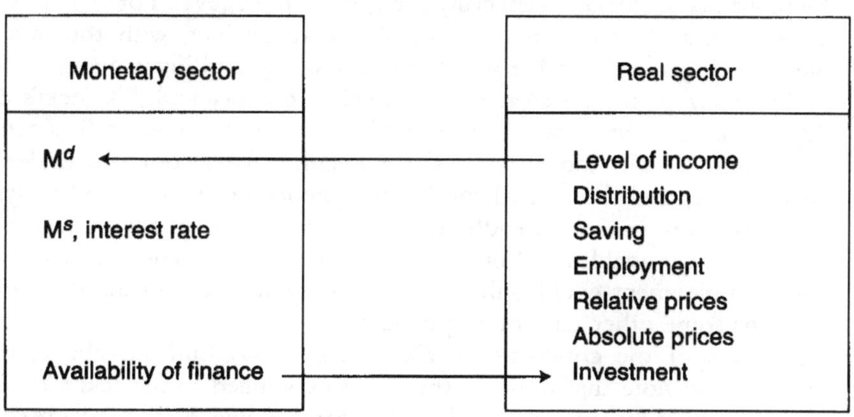

Figure 38.3 Relation between monetary and real sectors for Kalecki

mechanism within a market economy capable of restoring full employment. The analysis is concerned with abstract theory; policy consequences are only a secondary concern. This purpose should be contrasted with that of Kalecki, whose aim was not to engage in polemic with other economists but, rather, to attempt to understand the dynamics of capitalist economies, in particular, to provide an analysis of business cycles. As such, he was not concerned with making his ideas intelligible to the prevailing orthodoxy, but instead with drawng direct policy consequences. In addition, their different backgrounds played an important role in their different perceptions of the economy. Keynes came from an early study of philosophy and mathematics, entering economics by studying Marshall, and then engaged in applied work on currency, emerging as a monetary economist. Kalecki, on the other hand, never formally studied economics. His training was the result of early reading of Marxist economists in the under-consumptionist tradition, coupled with applied work on the Polish economy.[36] It was these which led him to the conclusions that capitalist economies were imperfectly competitive and subject to fluctuations, with unemployment being the norm.[37]

The work of Keynes and Kalecki, in many respects, represents a return to the focus and method of the classical economists. The interest in the macroeconomic question of the determination of output, as well as their approach, is reminiscent of classical theory. Kalecki, in particular, has resurrected the classical research agenda by placing distribution, growth and accumulation at the centre of economic analysis. In addition, the way in which he interrelates micro and macro theory, as well as his methodological use of historical time are very classical.[38] However, there are also some important differences. In particular, their denial of both Say's Law and the quantity theory means that Keynes and Kalecki developed alternative explanations of the determination of employment, the rate of interest, the monetary sector and especially the general price level. For the classical economists, real and monetary variables were distinct, with the rate of interest being a real variable which equates saving and investment.

This return to the classical approach helps to explain why Kalecki's and Keynes's insights were not used to modify neoclassical theory. In a sense, their approach was too alien to the conventional wisdom and undercut what has been called the 'hard core' of that theory. For neoclassical analysis, the neutrality of money and adherence to some version of Say's Law meant that monetary variables had no significant long-run influence on real ones, and unemployment could only be a temporary aberration caused by rigid wages or some other temporary phenomena.

In terms of the criticisms of *The General Theory* outlined above, it is interesting to note that none of them can be applied to Kalecki's version of the theory of effective demand. As has been argued, Kalecki assumed an endogenous money supply and, in fact, used this to reply to Pigou. This, of course, means that he had a different explanation for the determination of the rate of interest to that of Keynes.

It is well known that the starting point for Kalecki's analysis of output and employment was generally with the assumption of imperfect competition. He was extremely critical of the assumption of perfect competition, arguing that it was a 'dangerous myth'. This can be contrasted with Keynes, who was clearly dismissive of the analysis of imperfect competition, especially its implications for macroeconomic theory.[39]

At this stage it is appropriate to consider some of the main contrasts between Keynes and Kalecki. In order to bring these into sharper focus, their positions will also be compared to those of classical and neoclassical economists on a number of key issues. The numbers refer to Table 38.1 which summarizes the points of comparison.

The role of macroeconomics and of microfoundations (1) The early history of economics drew no distinction between macroeconomic and microeconomic analysis. Although the central concerns were with what we would now call macroeconomic questions, such as the determinants of growth and accumulation, these were seen to be stongly connected to the analysis of firms and prices. However, the 'marginal revolution' of the 1870s shunted the car of economics on to a different track. Microeconomic analysis became virtually synonymous with economics. The question of the determination of relative prices and quantities came to occupy the centre of the economic stage. Except for the discussion of monetary analysis of cyclical behaviour, macroeconomic analysis disappeared from the story. One of the major contributions of both Keynes and Kalecki was to restore macroeconomic analysis to an independent and important role in economic analysis. In particular, both relied on some form of fallacy of composition to illustrate the important principle that the behaviour of macroeconomic variables cannot be derived by simply aggregating up from the microeconomic level. However, on the question of microfoundations, Keynes paid little attention to micro considerations, including product markets.[40] His assumption of a given 'degree of competition' effectively rules out any role for imperfect competition. There is no real development of the microfoundations behind the analysis. Instead, Keynes concentrates on the role of financial markets, due to the importance of the rate of interest for investment decisions. In Kalecki, on the other hand, emphasis shifts away from financial markets to product markets, where determination of the mark-up has a direct bearing on employment via its role in determining the share of wages in national income:

> The importance of Kalecki's line of argument was in integrating the analysis of prices with the analysis of effective demand. Before Keynes, they were kept in two separate boxes; in America now the division between micro and macro theory is more complete than ever; but no

Table 38.1 Comparison of economic systems

	Micro/macro (1)	*Monetary/real* (2)	ΔY *equates* S & I (3)	*Monetary* R (4)	*Money supply endogenous* (5)	*Distribution (central role)* (6)	*Imperfect competition* (7)	*Uncertainty expectations* (8)
Classical	Yes	No	No	No	No	Yes	No	No
Kalecki	Yes	Yes	Yes	Yes	Yes	Yes	Yes	No
Keynes	No	Yes	Yes	Yes	No	No	No	Yes
Neoclassical	No	No	No	No	No	No	Yes	?

progress can be made with either until they are united in a truly *General Theory*.

(Robinson 1977: 190)

In other words, as has been argued above, the link between micro and macro is an important part of both classical and Kaleckian analysis, while Keynes maintained a dichotomy between them. The neoclassical economists, on the other hand, stressed the primacy of microeconomics.

Relations between monetary and real sectors (2–4) In both Keynes and Kalecki, monetary variables can affect real variables and real variables can affect monetary ones. In both cases the channel of transmission of the monetary sector is through investment. For Keynes, this is through the determination of interest rates, while for Kalecki, the main role of the monetary sector is to facilitate investment. For Kalecki, the role of financial markets lies in their ability to restrict the availability of finance and therefore provide constraints on investment.[41] However, if they do not do so, the friction which they create can constrain the economy. For both economists, changes in the level of income leads to changes in the transactions demand for money which, in turn, influences, albeit for different reasons, the rate of interest. This is in contrast to both classical and neoclassical economists, for whom there is an important dichotomy between these sectors. These distinctions are manifested in the mechanism which equilibrates saving and investment. For Keynes and Kalecki, these are equated by changes in the level of income, while the rate of interest is a monetary variable. For both classical and neoclassical economists, it is changes in the rate of interest which equates saving and investment, which, therefore, is a real variable.

Money supply (5) Keynes, in common with classical and neoclassical economists, assumed that the money supply was fixed, and determined by the central bank. For Kalecki, on the other hand, the banking sector as a whole consisted of imperfectly competitive private sector firms which could create money. Therefore, the money supply was endogenous to the private sector.

Distribution (6) Kalecki's analysis, like that of the classical economists, was always in terms of class, whereby distribution plays a key role in determining levels of output and employment. In neoclassical economics and in Keynes, distribution is a secondary consideration.

Imperfect competition/real wages (7) Because Keynes assumed diminished returns to be one of the great constants of economics (Keynes 1939c), an expansion of output would lead to a fall in real wages, as it pushes up cost of production and reduces the marginal product of labour. This inverse relation between real wages and employment enabled the neoclassicals to reclaim Keynesian economics in a bastardized version.[42] Kalecki, on the other hand, due partly to the assumption of constant returns, does not posit any definite relationship between changes in employment and changes in real wages. In other words, while Keynes, like the classical economists, implicitly assumes a competitive economy, Kalecki assumes an imperfectly competitive one. Modern neoclassical economics also considers the possibility of imperfect competition, and it has been implicated as an explanation for the existence of unemployment.

Uncertainty and expectations (8) Kalecki rarely dealt with the economic implications of expectations and uncertainty. In the few places in which he did, he hinted that he believed the main determinant of expectations of the future to be current events.[43] However, this is clearly not an adequate analysis, especially not when compared with the rich discussions on these issues of Keynes, in particular the importance of expectations for the determination of both the level of investment and the rate of interest.[44] These played a subordinate role in classical economics. Neoclassical economics, on the other hand, finesses the question. Either they follow Friedman and Savage in allowing for uncertainty but assuming that the distribution and mean are known, so that we are exactly certain of our uncertainty, or the assumption of 'rational' expectations is made so as effectively to dismiss expectations as an independent consideration.[45]

This discussion is summarized in Table 38.1 which allows a comparison to be made of the role of the issues discussed in classical and neoclassical economics, as well as their role in the analysis of Keynes and Kalecki.

CONCLUSIONS

Now that we have compared and contrasted the contributions of Keynes and Kalecki, we are in a position to see the extent to which incorporating some of Kalecki's insights into *The General Theory* would improve a second edition. As has been argued above (pp. 313–14) *The General Theory* was written as a polemical work, aimed at economists. As a result, its main purpose was theoretical and not 'practical'. A second edition could redress this. In particular, the incorporation of Kalecki's insights, which were practically orientated, provides an appropriate mechanism for this process. In addition, some of the concerns with the general theoretical statements could be addressed via such a new edition. Some of the more important changes can be summarized as follows:

1 The micro–macro and the real–monetary dichotomies: for the classical economists, there is no micro–macro dichotomy, but there is a real–monetary one. For neoclassical economists, macro does not matter, and there is a real–monetary dichotomy. For Keynes, while there is no real–

monetary dichotomy, there is a dichotomy between micro and macro; while for Kalecki there is neither a real–monetary nor a micro–macro dichotomy. In other words, for Kalecki, in order to explain the determinants of output and employment, micro and macro considerations, monetary and real factors all play a role. A Kalecki-inspired *General Theory* would keep the integration of the monetary and real sectors which are the cornerstones of Keynes's analysis of output. However, it would abolish the dichotomy between microeconomic and macroeconomic variables, allowing both to play a role in the determination of aggregate output and employment, through the role of distribution.

2 Similarly, the incorporation of the role of distribution and of imperfect competition would strengthen the microfoundations, which were a sad omission from the first edition.[46] In particular, following Kalecki, a primary role would be given to distribution, both as an important policy variable, and also as a key consideration in determining the level of effective demand.[47]

3 The incorporation of endogenous money, by allowing an important role for bank credit creation, would blunt the criticisms associated with the Keynes and the Pigou effects, as well as answering one of Kaldor's strongest criticisms.[48] In addition, it would allow a role for imperfections in financial markets,[49] and for the influence of the availability of finance on investment. Given the role finance had played in Keynes's writings subsequent to *The General Theory*, these would not involve substantial modifications.

4 Keynes's investment analysis would be modified in the manner discussed above, to incorporate dynamic concerns and explicitly introduce the importance of finance. At the same time, Keynes's insights into the nature and importance of uncertainty would be retained, but extended to the financial markets. As a result, the analysis of *The General Theory* would become dynamic and able to incorporate the important modifications which formed the heart of the Kaleckian system.

NOTES

* I should like to thank John Nevile and Trevor Stegman from the University of New South Wales, Joseph Halevi and Louis Haddad from the University of Sydney, Craig Freedman and Rod O'Donnell from Macquarie University, Mike White from Monash University and Geoff Harcourt from Cambridge University for their helpful comments. The paper on which this chapter is based was presented at the 8th HETSA Conference, and I should like to thank the participants for their useful suggestions.

1 See Sardoni (1987) and Chapter 36 in this volume.

2 *C.W.* VII: 370–1. See also p. 33n, where he refers to effective demand living only 'below the surface in the underworlds'.

3 'Keynes's version of the new theory was emasculated and wrapped up again in equilibrium and Kalecki's version was simply ignored' (Robinson 1977: 185).
4 It is not the purpose of this chapter to rehearse the debate of who got there first. Those interested in the question of the winner of the race are referred to Osiatynski (1990: 463–7) and Chapple (1991) and the references made there.
5 One important omission from the discussion is that of international considerations, which was largely neglected in the theoretical core of *The General Theory*. Both economists wrote extensively on this area, and reached similar conclusions about the implications of trade for domestic effective demand.
6 This is discussed in Kriesler (1988a, 1988b). In addition, see Keynes (1939) and Osiatynski (1990: 567–70).
7 See, for example, *C.W.* XIV 208n.
8 See, for example, Robinson (1964, 1977).
9 Neoclassical theory is here taken to refer to two branches of that theory. The first originated in Marshall, and was developed by Pigou. It was the Pigouvian version of the theory which Keynes attacked as representing the whole of neoclassical theory. The other branch is that which dominates the high theory of the discipline, and originated in the general equilibrium analysis of Walras. In particular, the versions of the theory developed from the end of the nineteenth century, which still dominate the discipline, are the ones referred to.
10 Clearly, in such a brief general discussion of the classical economists, a very broad brush has been used. This may not be fair to all members of the school. Rather, it is hoped to convey a rough guide to their treatment of the relevant issues.
11 See Kriesler (1996).
12 They were often analysed as part of the explanation of the business cycle, which explained short-run deviations from the long-run equilibrium position.
13 This, of course, is the famous Treasury view, against which Keynes reacted, and which has been resurrected in the modern form of complete 'crowding out'. There is evidence that the Treasury view may have been modified after 1929 (Clarke 1988).
14 This is the basis of the monetarist (Friedman) explanation for why there is a Phillips curve-type trade-off in the short run.
15 It should be noted that 'real' in this figure is used to explain variables determined in the 'real' sector, and is being contrasted to variables determined in the 'monetary' sector. This is a different dichotomy to that of nominal–real, which is referring to the role of price changes, not to the sector in which the variables are determined.
16 See, for example, Hahn (1984: 2) and Harcourt (1977: 375–6, 380).
17 See *C.W.* VII: Preface to the French edition, esp. pp. xxxii, xxxiii, and Chapter 19; Kalecki (1939a); Robinson (1951: 135–6) and Harcourt (1987a).
18 This is discussed in greater detail in Kriesler (1996).
19 All unacknowledged quotations are from *C.W.* VII.
20 Marris examines this proposition more carefully in Chapter 4 of Volume 1 of this work.
21 See Thomas (Chapter 9 in Volume 1 of this work).
22 *C.W.* VII: 262 and XIII: 369, 391. On this, see also Erdos (1977: 234); Kahn (1984: 134); Steindl (1985: 111); and Meek (1967: 187).
23 These are discussed in Howitt and in Kregel (Chapters 15 and 16, respectively, of Volume 1 of this work).
24 The title and analysis of this chapter give the lie to those economists who argue

that Keynes derived unemployment by assuming that money-wages are fixed. This is clearly nonsense.

25 Keynes's discussion of the influence of changes in money-wages on employment has already been noted. On the liquidity trap he comments: 'But whilst this limiting case might become practically important in the future, I know of no example of it hitherto' (*C.W.* VII: 207).

26 In fact, Kaldor notes four limitations, but one of these, Keynes's failure 'to deal with all the problems connected with international or interregional trade' (Kaldor 1983b: 83), is thrown into doubt by Davidson (Chapter 30 in this volume); while another, that Keynes's use of static analysis did not allow him to incorporate history and causality, are rejected by most of the literature, especially Joan Robinson.

27 See also Marris (Chapter 4 in Volume 1 of this work).

28 See, for example, Kalecki (1939a and 1954: 63).

29 See, for example, Kalecki (1954: 73) and Kriesler (1996).

30 See Kriesler (1996: section 5).

31 See Sawyer (1985: 188–9, 192–3). It should be noted that in a posthumously published paper, Kalecki (1971a) allowed a role for trade unions to influence the mark-up and hence real wages,

32 See, for example, Kalecki (1954: ch. 3); Kriesler (1987: ch. 7, and 1996).

33 One of the reasons Joan Robinson has argued that Kalecki's analysis of effective demand is more satisfactory than that of Keynes, is Kalecki's use of these schemas (Robinson 1964: 95–6; see also Kriesler and McFarlane 1993; and Sardoni, Chapter 36 in this volume).

34 For a more detailed discussion of the reasons why Kalecki did not believe that investment was interest-elastic, see Sawyer (1985: 50).

35 This assumption is made explicitly 'by assuming tacitly that the supply of money by the banks is elastic', (Kalecki 1971b: 159f). The mechanism of money creation is set out in detail in Kalecki (1933: 93–8). Keynes, in his work after *The General Theory*, seemed to be coming around to this position (see Dow and Sardoni, Chapters 28 and 36, respectively, in this volume).

36 See Kriesler (1988a).

37 See Kriesler and McFarlane (1993).

38 See Kriesler (1996).

39 See Kriesler (1988a).

40 Although he does cover himself in Chapter 2, when he sets out the classical postulates.

41 The unimportance of financial markets and the rate of interest in Kalecki's work can be gauged from the fact that the collection of essays which he chose as representing his 'main contributions to the theory of dynamics of capitalist economy' (Kalecki 1990: vii) contains no essays on the determination of the rate of interest, or of finance in general, except for the important paper on 'entrepreneurial capital and investment'.

42 Subsequently, in 1939 Keynes acknowledged statistical evidence of the likelihood of constant returns, and, therefore, that there is not necessarily an inverse relationship between real wages and employment. In that same article, Keynes (1939c) also acknowledges that the analysis of imperfect competition (including Kalecki's analysis) may play a more important explanatory role than he had previously admitted.

43 This does not mean that he never allowed a role for uncertainty. For example, in his 'The Principle of Increasing Risk' (Kalecki 1937a), he analyses the problems caused by risk for investment. However, there is no actual analysis

of uncertainty, it is simply assumed to be dependent on the size of the investment.

44 See Howitt and Kregel (Chapters 15 and 16, respectively, in Volume 1 of this work).

45 See Howitt and Hoover (Chapters 15 and 14, respectively, in Volume 1 of this work).

46 The importance of starting from imperfect competition for a second edition of *The General Theory* is discussed in Marris (Chapter 4 in Volume 1 of this work).

47 The links between distribution, consumption and effective demand are discussed in Thomas (Chapter 9 in Volume 1 of this work).

48 Dow (Chapter 28 in this volume) argues that the incorporation of endogenous money would not necessitate significant changes to the heart of the Keynesian system, and would, in fact, improve it.

49 See 'The Principle of Increasing Risk', reprinted in Kalecki (1939b).

39

ON LEIJONHUFVUD'S ECONOMICS OF KEYNES

Bruce Littleboy

INTRODUCTION

Axel Leijonhufvud's interpretation of Keynes has been met at various times by enthusiasm, denunciation and indifference. Interpreters of Keynes have extracted what they each regarded as integral to *The General Theory*. There is little effective communication between them. Alan Coddington (1976) identified three types of Keynesians: the reductionist, the fundamentalist and the hydraulicist. There are differences of substance, style and emphasis. Robert Clower and Axel Leijonhufvud are members of the first group.[1] The fundamentalist Post-Keynesians, Joan Robinson, Richard Kahn, Nicholas Kaldor, G.L.S. Shackle and Paul Davidson, are in the second; and Paul Samuelson and the neoclassical Keynesians, in the third. The variety of interpretation itself suggests that Keynes could have made himself clearer, but the phenomenon of multiple interpretation also arises with many other authors. In fact, portions of *The General Theory* partially support each construction.

In the famous 1937 *Quarterly Journal of Economics* article – the nearest thing we have to a second edition – Keynes pointed to the two central features of *The General Theory*: (a) uncertainty, a theme stressed by Shackle and many Post-Keynesians; and (b) the consumption function and multiplier, stressed by Axel Leijonhufvud. Elaboration of the meaning and significance of these two themes has proceeded largely independently, though Keynes gave them equal weight and regarded both as essential. Uncertainty can result in investment being unstable. Rather than its variations being offset by changes in comsumption, the multiplier moves consumption in the same direction. In principle, Leijonhufvud's views are as valid and valuable as Shackle's. Both have strengths and weaknesses. Each emphasizes only a part of Keynes's system and the two interpretations of Keynes can be better regarded, in many respects, as complementary.

This chapter examines the means by which Leijonhufvud sought to highlight the monetary foundations of the theory of effective demand. Many of his ideas (the missing auctioneer, liquidity constraints and financial buffers) have been absorbed more by mainstream economists than by fundamentalist Keynesians. The most obvious explanation – that Leijonhufvud sees Keynes through an orthodox lens – is not the best one. Leijonhufvud's 1968 book and subsequent important modifications are summarized. While his book was well received initially, [2] it has increasingly been attacked by the fundamentalists as a misreading of Keynes. Reasons for this rise and fall from favour are identified and appraised. Leijonhufvud's position is also explained and compared briefly with other views on Keynes's essential insights; namely, old-style Keynesian economics (subsumed under the neoclassical synthesis) and New Keynesian economics.

The basis of Leijonhufvud's 1968 position can be presented briefly. Less well known, and more important, at least if he and the fundamentalists are to be reconciled, are his later extensions and occasional retractions. Space limitations, however, prevent a full exegesis.

LEIJONHUFVUD'S APPROACH

The title of Leijonhufvud's (1968) book is its own abstract: *On Keynesian Economics and the Economics of Keynes.* The former, the textbook view, differs from the true Keynes in focus, emphasis and sometimes content. Paul Samuelson is often implicitly a target, and his reaction (1983) to Leijonhufvud is curt and dismissive. Leijonhufvud opposes the view that Keynes ultimately relies on rigid money-wages and prices with the liquidity trap in reserve. The former makes the aggregate supply curve (in P–Y space) flat and the latter makes the money-demand curve (and the LM curve) flat too. Textbooks claim that Classicists made the opposite, extreme assumption of vertical curves.

Emphasising the extremes of the elasticities misses Keynes's deeper contributions and also misrepresents Keynes's view on wages and interest rates, Leijonhufvud argues. Even the standard 45° income–expenditure diagrams and algebra (balanced budget multipliers and so on) are absent from *The General Theory* and invented by others afterwards (1968: 403).

The focus on elasticities renders both Keynes and the Classicists as being at two unrealistic extremes once common sense and empirical work show the curves typically to have intermediate slopes. To attribute to Keynes a flat LM and a steep IS curve virtually implies an advocacy of fiscal policy. Furthermore, since real balance effects operating on the IS curve would overcome even a liquidity trap, downward money-wage and price flexibility ultimately restores full employment. Classical theory returns in the long run by the back door. In the neoclassical–Keynesian model short-run prices are rigid, and, even if they fell, agents do not respond to the price incentives. Leijonhufvud regards all of this as a misrepresentation of Keynes's views on how individuals act and how the system behaves.

Leijonhufvud's reductionist account admittedly tends to be somewhat mechanistic itself, but it is not that the price system works impracticably slowly in grinding out full employment. Rather, perverse dynamics are unleashed when a money-using system is left to itself to react to a disturbance. The multiplier sends the system further away from full employment, and the associated liquidity constraints entrench a sub-optimal local equilibrium. Expectations do enter the picture, though. Pessimism can become deepened by the persistence of sluggish activity (1968: 380).

The theory and empirics of consumption nowadays incorporate liquidity constraints. While Keynes cited psychological principles to explain the split between consumption and saving, liquidity constraints can explain why income falls, which in turn causes both consumption and saving to fall. For some policy implications, which counteract Ricardian equivalence doctrines, see Boskin (1988).

Leijonhufvud's position can be better appreciated by comparing and contrasting it with others. Figure 39.1 shows the evolution of US mainstream Keynesianism from which Leijonhufvud largely stands apart.

Elements of Leijonhufvud's system have been selectively plucked out by the mainstream establishment perhaps, but the use and significance of his ideas have been passed over. Search theory and wage-stickiness, for example, have specific and limited roles to play in Leijonhufvud's writings, and involuntary, cyclical unemployment cannot be centrally founded on them. Involuntary unemployment induced by the multiplier might have been triggered by search unemployment, but is not made up of it. Leijonhufvud's stress on the multiplier and the lack of effective demand is largely missing from mainstream stories.

In Leijonhufvud, once you miss the boat, you are left stranded. Belated wage-cuts do not help, even if anyone knew what the new 'right' wage is. Absent also from neoclassical search-models is the crucial failure of interest rates to mesh saving and investment decisions. Unemployment in New Keynesianism (and, ironically, in Friedman, as Leijonhufvud (1981: 179) points out) is attributed to wage and price stickiness, to nominal inflexibilities in the labour and goods markets. As Peter Howitt (1990b: 1) notes: 'The reduction of the co-ordination problem to sticky prices is at the root of the decline of Keynesian economics.' Leijonhufvud insists that Keynes stressed the investment sector as the ultimate culprit: real investment and saving decisions are poorly co-ordinated by financial markets owing to uncertainties and speculation. Because Keynesians have drifted away from what they once stressed, they have left the terrain for New Classical and Austrian theory to occupy. While real business theory founded on voluntary (equilibrium) micro-incentives may be implausible, Keynes's original version based on involuntary (disequilibrium) multiplier-induced income effects could be more penetrative.

Investment is 'wrong' because investors and savers have no way of co-ordinating future consumption and production plans in the real world to bring about global utility maximization. Investment decisions are made in a world of Knightian uncertainty.[3] Investors do not know what savers want.

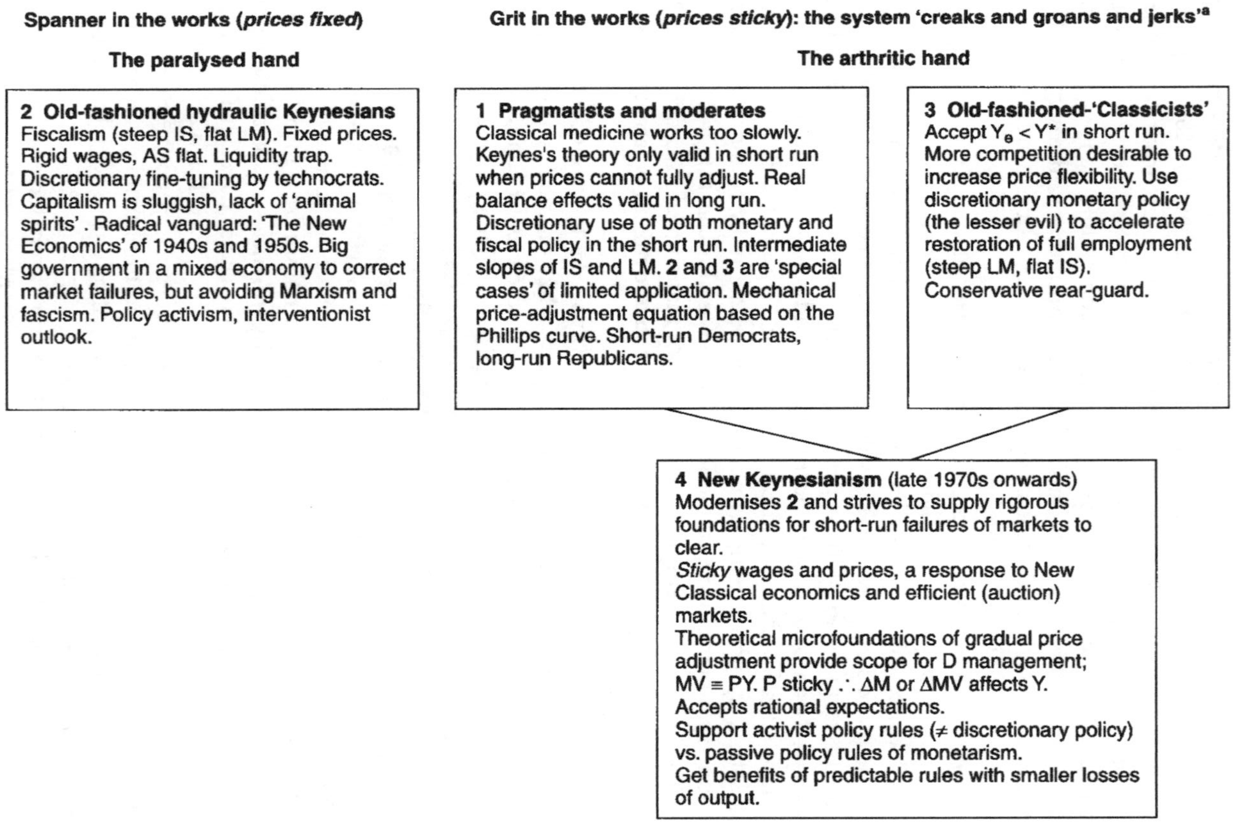

Figure 39.1 The mainstream view of Keynes-versus the Classics

Note: [a] *C.W.* XIII: 486.

Indeed, they receive false signals if thrift rises, as Chapter 16 of *The General Theory* shows.[4] Decisions by consumers to save now to consume more later are not communicated to the business sector, which simply sees a decline in sales and perversely infers that future sales prospects have worsened. Oddly, Leijonhufvud did not take the opportunity to point out that realized profits give rise to the effective power to finance investment internally, a favourite Post-Keynesian theme. Investment would then be more strongly pro-cyclical and amplify any perturbation.

Indeed, to compound the communications problem it is conceivable that the savers themselves do not know now exactly what they will want later.[5] This differs from the picture presented in the supposedly Keynesian textbooks in which the financial system is viewed as an efficient means by which loanable funds are allocated to investors (see Maclachlan 1993a: 140). Leijonhufvud (1968: 47) long ago expressed reservations about the neoclassical (full-employment) analysis of the co-ordination of borrowing and lending found in Gurley and Shaw (1960).

Nevertheless, anti-Classical results can stem from a focus on intertemporal malcoordination, and a worthwhile dialogue with the Austrians becomes possible (see Garrison 1985, and Snippe 1987). Leijonhufvud is entitled to his personal view (1981: 197) that Keynes was too dismissive of the Austrian concern over the structure, as distinct from the size, of investment. And one must accept Snippe's point that short-run unemployment emerges whenever total demand is too low, regardless of the consumption–investment split.

LEIJONHUFVUD AND THE FUNDAMENTALISTS: DIFFERENCES AND SIMILARITIES

Brevity requires that Leijonhufvud and the Post-Keynesian fundamentalists be compared and contrasted by a series of statements given in Table 39.1 without full textual support. Differences are, on examination, better regarded as matters of mere emphasis. Leijonhufvud (1968: 115 n. 5, 233, 355, 400, 400 n. 1) often has kind words for the 'British Keynesians' who often more accurately portrayed Keynes's views. Leijonhufvud's (1984) respect for Hicks the Elder also reflects some sympathy for fundamentalist doctrine. Given in Table 39.2 is a list of similarities between Leijonhufvud and the fundamentalists. Several items, indeed, may surprise some readers and would probably require some discussion and exegesis beyond that feasible here.

Before any reconciliation of Leijonhufvud and the Post-Keynesian fundamentalists can be effected, a number of misconceptions need to be dispelled.

The very notion of 'co-ordination failure' raises Post-Keynesian suspicions. Some Classical tendency towards full employment is apparently

Table 39.1 Differences in views on Keynes[6]

	Leijonhufvud	*Fundamentalists*
1	Simple, outside-money system with focus on cash constraints; exogenous M.	Sophisticated credit structures that allow for changes in expectations to affect total liquidity rapidly; endogenous M.
2	Integral that output markets and the demand for labour can be competitive (atomistic) and still malfunction.	Potential for misunderstanding is heightened in Keynes by his preserving elements of classical micro-theory.
3	Unions are relatively inactive and usually well-behaved, though they tether the money wage.	Wage-earners can provoke cost-push inflation, especially if endogenous M and industrial concentration apply.
4	Occasional reliance on wayward expectations, Knightian uncertainty and Arrow-type search-confusion.	Frequent and emphatic support of Knightian uncertainty, autonomous shifts in confidence, non-ergodics, historical time and irreversibility (path dependence).
5	Selective reference to institutional and social framework.	Focus on institutions as important to Keynes *vs* the classicists. Fundamental reforms to share markets and to wage-setting institutions are needed.
6	Views the *GT* more in conjunction with *Treatise on Money*.	Views *GT* more in conjuction with post–*GT* writings on uncertainty, finance motive and revolving credit.
7	Acceptance of stable speculative demand for money, but prefers to avoid regarding the dynamic liquidity preference theory as central; finance motive peripheral.	Centrality of liquidity preference theory, especially when finance motive incorporated; speculative demand is restless.
8	Sluggish expectational responses typical: realized exchanges signal effective demand.	Expectational over-reactions typical, and changes in confidence can change output before realized demand signals are sent or received.
9	Focus on means-of-exchange function of money to explain steps in the multiplier's mechanical dynamics.	The multiplier can be expectations-driven and instantaneous without the need for sequential changes in realized expenditure driving the process.
10	Focus on asset-demand for money to interrupt smooth flows from saving to investment: demand for money relatively stable, with some interest elasticity (though no liquidity trap).	Focus on *shifts* in speculative demand: changes in the *propensity* to hoard.
11	Focus on *false* signals due to realized liquidity constraints. Producers are forced to curtail output to meet the decline in demand. Consumers must reduce consumption when income falls.	Focus on *missing* signals – the future is empty and mute; indeed, current actions partly create it. Investors choose to curtail expenditure if they lose confidence. Producers choose to reduce output if lower realized sales are expected to persist.
12	Focus on objective realized signals.	Focus on subjective expectational factors.

Table 39.2 Similarities in views on Keynes's contribution[7]

1	Neither New nor Old Keynesian economics is faithful to Keynes.
2	Both reject hydraulic fine-tuning.
3	Shared scepticism over IS–LM.
4	Involuntary unemployment in the real world is not the workers' fault.
5	More wage and price flexibility would not reduce the amplitude of the trade cycle in the real world. Instability would be *worse* if money-wages were not sticky.
6	Common hostility to Walrasian general equilibrium theory as a means to analyse real-world economies.
7	Shared hostility to fix-price ('non-Walrasian') general equilibrium theory.
8	The invisible hand is unlikely to restore full employment in the face of a large disturbance.
9	Voluntary actions in the investment and the financial sectors can result in a persistent involuntary unemployment 'equilibrium' in the labour market.
10	Shared hostility to New Classical economics.

implicit in that Say's Law is being frustrated, or caused to fail, by some imperfection or inflexibility. New Keynesians sometimes speak of co-ordination failures and strategic complementarities, but they see persistent wage-price stickiness as integral (see Gordon 1990). Such distrust is largely unwarranted.

Probably, what Leijonhufvud calls 'malcoordination' or a 'co-ordination failure' fundamentalist Post-Keynesians would call 'perverse co-ordination' or 'socially sub-optimal co-ordination'. The system has settled into a sustained position (it has 'co-ordinated' itself) into the best state it can, given the lack of investment demand (and the state of liquidity preference). It is the lack of investment demand that is sub-optimal in a social sense.

But something surely has 'gone wrong' if some mutually beneficial trades are frustrated. If there were perfect information about future consumption plans and perfect co-ordination of output and expenditure, then there would be no involuntary unemployment, virtually by definition. Investment would equal full-employment saving.[8] Presumably, if investors could be assured that the output produced by a new machine would be sold profitably, they would not be too timid. Furthermore, if wealth-holders were not bearishly backward-looking but were willing instead to accept from investors whatever interest rate the auctioneer (or simultaneous-equation solver) computed as consistent with current full employment and with intertemporal co-ordination, all would be well in later periods too. In such a fantasy world, purchasing power would then not escape from the circular flow, if full-employment output were produced at the correct price vector. On top of this, if a full-employment solution to a system exists, being there of necessity involves co-ordination. There are no frustrated agents in a perfect world. Not being there *means* malcoordination in Leijonhufvud's language.

Leijonhufvud's reliance on search theory also creates the impression that some inflexibility or imperfection constitutes the essential problem. Again, Leijonhufvud has been misread. In Leijonhufvud, agents are more than just confused. They, more crucially, are constrained. They are not just forever making mistakes through ignorant choices. The multiplier is forcing them away from full employment even if they become wise after the event. Not that even this is likely: agents do not face an orderly, stable environment within which probabilistic estimates of a correct price vector can be made. They are confused and frustrated, not engaged in efficient search.

Some suspect that attributing contractions to an information failure makes the process voluntaristic and avoidable. For example even Solow (1984: 23) maintains:

> [T]he emphasis [in Leijonhufvud] on information is seriously misleading . . . It suggests that there is something knowable that, if known, would forestall macroeconomic malfunction. I suppose it would follow that macroeconomic policy could usefully be restricted to the production and dissemination of the missing information . . . One could equally say that the Second World War was an example of information failure: if Hitler had known what was going to happen, he would never have invaded Russia . . .

But fundamentalists also say 'we simply do not know' what actions will be justified by later events. In Leijonhufvud, everyone certainly knows they would rather be somewhere else. Initially, knowledge would (in an idealized Walrasian world) have helped, but not once we are trapped by real-world dynamics. Once you are overboard, you are bereft. Whether you jumped, tripped or were pushed matters little.

In no meaningful sense need real-world unemployment in Leijonhufvud be regarded as the fault of the worker. Only in a fantastic world of multilateral barter or perfect communication between workers and employers would an instantaneous wage-cut offset entrepreneurial pessimism. The failure of prices to adjust *instantly* to a new full-employment vector sets the multiplier going. Money-wage stickiness triggers the decline, but only at the very onset of the shock. Persistent unemployment is not caused by persistent wage-stickiness (as it is in New Keynesian models). Once the crucial moment has passed when a hypothetical money-wage cut would abort the downturn, the multiplier takes over. Belated wage cuts do not help overcome involuntary unemployment (Leijonhufvud 1968: 58, 67, 95 n. 23). We could, of course, argue that it is not obvious why belated wage cuts never work when the right instantaneous one always works. The concern here is with what Leijonhufvud says, not whether it makes full sense (see Littleboy 1990: 78–9 for details).

For the return of full employment, recognition of the necessity of a prior or simultaneous restoration of aggregate demand (whether by a shift in the investment or the consumption function) is in Leijonhufvud.[9] Mere knowledge of the 'correct' interest rate (and wage) is presumably inadequate. Bears must release liquidity and investors need to act.

Some criticisms of Leijonhufvud have resulted from his own one-sentence summaries of his position: 'In the Keynesian macrosystem the Marshallian ranking of price- and quantity-adjustment speeds is reversed' (1968: 52; italics removed). But anything less than instantaneous price flexibility (which would prevent false trading) is sufficient. Flow supplies of goods can clear and prices and quantities can fall together in Leijonhufvud's revised, or clarified, position (1983c: 197). (See Littleboy 1990: 68–9, 75 for further discussion.) Both Leijonhufvud and Clower are adamant that no Walrasian-style framework can explain real-world processes.[10] Pointing to the absence of the auctioneer is merely how unemployment is explained to a Walrasian.

Fundamentalists distrust conventional general equilibrium theory. It is difficult, if not impossible, to explain the very use of money in a Walrasian world within which economics essentially deals with solving specified equations simultaneously. In the real world, they say, there is uninsurable uncertainty. The equations do not exist for any auctioneer to solve. Leijonhufvud misses the point, it is claimed. Irreversible production commitments through time (with new goods and new technologies) cannot be analysed by exchanges based on fixed tastes and given opportunity sets. Money uniquely allows decisions to be deferred. More than the removal of the auctioneer separates Keynes from the Classicists. They have entirely different visions and analytical regimes. They cannot be mixed.

One might reply that money would be needed in a Walrasian exchange system if the transactions structure were specified appropriately. If each agent were instructed to deliver a specific bundle to a particular person, money would not be needed. But if the auctioneer simply cried out the price–quantity vector and, unlike a command economy, left the delivery details to the agents, then money (or, less efficiently, non-counterfeit coupons giving title to physical goods) makes the convergence to the vector less costly in terms of the cartage from stall to stall that is now saved. Furthermore, the transactions and exchange structures tend to evolve to reduce costs further. Intermediaries and inventory-holders evolve into being. And trade credit only becomes feasible later, once a history of mutual trust is established. (For early descriptions of how market networks come to evolve, that is, how the invisible hand acquires its flesh and bones, see Clower and Leijonhufvud 1975 and Clower 1977, 1993a.) Nowadays there is also a growing appreciation that in less-developed countries economic growth can depend on the sophistication of financial intermediation.

Of course, in Leijonhufvud, more is involved than the removal of the auctioneer. One-sentence summaries even of one's own book are bound to oversimplify. Leijonhufvud's overarching point is that mainstream economics pays no regard to the transactions structure (1968: 90). Money in fact necessarily plays the intermediary role. Leijonhufvud repudiates barter, or quasi-barter, models where all goods are perfectly liquid substitutes for money. In passing, he even acknowledges the Post-Keynesian point that price stability is desirable to underpin the use of currency-denominated contracts (1968: 108–9).

Another possible source of distrust could be Leijonhufvud's idea that Keynes exaggerated: subjected to small shocks, the system can automatically recover. The idea of self-corrective market forces within a corridor might not be attributable to Keynes – but Leijonhufvud never argued that it was. Keynes's faith in self-correction of macro shocks was arguably nil.[11] At times he even argued that the interest-rate mechanism would *never* work. For example, funds undesired by the investment sector would be absorbed by those in the consumption sector making losses owing to an increase in thrift (see Littleboy 1990: 173–80).

Nevertheless, Keynes was no socialist, as he would have been if he had believed that a capitalist system was utterly fragile. So, although Leijonhufvud does not attribute the corridor to Keynes, it is not necessarily contrary to Keynes's economic vision.[12] Work on corridor effects is still rather nascent, but see Howitt (1978) and Bernanke (1981).

Corridor analysis could have wide application, for example, in responding to New Classical real business cycle theory. Suppose you prick Robinson Crusoe's finger: you don't call for a surgeon; the body's natural restorative powers, far beyond the ability of any doctor to outperform or even design, do the job. But for a gunshot wound, intervention is necessary; waiting for the blood to clot and the bleeding to stop would be unwise. Doubtless, an equilibrium business cycle theorist could predict each spurt of blood and the sequential shut-down of vital organs. But, there is little to celebrate in a system responding 'efficiently' to false signals, however naturally they are produced. The body's natural dynamics depend on the scale of the injury.[13]

Leijonhufvud's approach invites policy applications. *Laissez-faire* performs some tasks well, but is ill-equipped to respond to a large-scale macroeconomic trauma. Consider any large structural shock, not necessarily confined to the investment sector. One sector makes losses, with no sector elsewhere making any offsetting profits. Resources in the loss-making sector are freed for use elsewhere, but why would they be taken up?

Indeed, if there are unemployment and gloomy business prospects generally, this is the very time that unemployed people lack the money in the hand to buy whatever some hypothetical new industry might supply. Structural adjustment requires a moderate degree of buoyancy in the economy overall. Slumps are not healthy environments for fledgling industries. Fundamentalists would presumably agree with this.

Furthermore, Leijonhufvud (see, for example, 1983d) must be allowed his personal judgements about the desirability of monetary rule nowadays. Keynes would hardly have supported an inflexible one in his day. But an attitude of rules with built-in flexibility to counter fluctuations in income hardly conflicts with Keynes's overall social vision, one could add.

Leijonhufvud has faded from prominence. Whether this owes more to fashion and accident than to well-informed judgement on the long-term value of his work is another question. Even Keynes's *General Theory* is regarded by many mainstream economists as ancient and irrelevant. And how influential are the fundamentalist Post-Keynesians outside their own circle?

Leijonhufvud is no polemicist. He rarely stands and fights. Neither can his insights be rendered by diagrams in undergraduate textbooks. Casual readers (and others) can easily confuse his contribution with mainstream search theory, fix-price general equilibrium theory and Patinkin's version of disequilibrium economics.[14]

Leijonhufvud is probably more politically conservative than most Post-Keynesians, and there is perhaps a cynical view in some circles that one's exegetical findings are coloured by one's political values to the point where the former is merely a mask for the latter.[15]

Fundamentalism and Leijonhufvud's reductionism are more distinct from other schools than they are from each other. Figure 39.2 reveals some family resemblances and outlines a reconciliation which is already being formed without the parties realizing it. Even Davidson (1981: 151) places Leijonhufvud adjacent to himself despite his (later) stinging critiques (for example, 1984).

SOME PHILOSOPHICAL AND METHODOLOGICAL ISSUES

Some Post-Keynesians (such as Roy Rotheim) regard the very notion of the specification of microfoundations – presumably whether Marshallian or Walrasian – as 'methodological individualism' which, by its nature (it is claimed) cannot deal with aggregate 'holistic' phenomena of an authentically 'macro' kind. Consider the fallacy of composition in scaling up the effects of an individual firm cutting the wage, or an individual household saving more. This is a very narrow view of methodological individualism and a correspondingly broad view of holism. If Ralph at a football game

The amputated hand

5 Fundamentalism

No Walrasian equilibrium can even be specified. The 'mechanism' is a fiction. The hand is invisible because it is not there. Unruly and restless expectations and fragile conventions dominate. Agents can lose confidence and stampede or just huddle together for security. The 'Chapter 12 Keynesians', Shackle, (sometimes) Davidson and Joan Robinson are anti-mechanistic and dislike 'Bastard Keynesians'. They stress ever-present potential instability. The future is unknow*able*. Knightian uncertainty differs from quantifiable, deterministic and statistical risk. Confidence and willingness to extend credit are essential. They are often accused of nihilism and excessive emphasis on individual and group irrationalities. Macro-instability is partly psychological and partly institutional.

The epileptic hand

6 Reductionism

The mechanism out of equilibrium sometimes goes mad when left to its own devices.

The auctioneer is a fiction: agents must fend for themselves, but the members of the crowd push each other further away from full employment.

False prices, trades and signals occur in disequilibrium. Robert Clower and Axel Leijonhufvud feature. Co-ordination breakdown is central. Dynamics depend on effective (money-backed or credit-backed) demand, not (Walrasian) notional demand.

Money effects exchanges. Deviation-amplification is due to the multiplier. Long-run recovery is problematic.

An Ecletic Reconciliation

The fumbling hand[a]

7 Neo-fundamentalism/fundamentalist reductionism

Expectations are often stable and conventions can be durable. The economy is tolerably stable (for the most part) but improvable output trends occur. Institutional reform and counter-cyclical stabilization via monetary or fiscal coarse-tuning (conceivably according to some activist rule) are desirable. Lack of full information and full rationality does not imply irrationality and incoherence. *Individuals* can remain reasonable even if the *system* is not, in terms of judging the macro outcomes produced. Actual (objective) declines in spending in one sector can have broadly predictable consequences elsewhere. Declines in investor confidence (IS shifts) might or might not induce sympathetic effects on financial bearishness (shifts in LM), depending on the size of the initial disturbance and the psychological environment.

Figure 39.2 Keynes's deeper revolution?

Note: [a] Perhaps Leijonhufvud himself coined a similar term (see Clower 1993b: 19).

stands up to get a better view, Bill and Beth behind him stand up too. Rapidly, a vast wedge of people stand up and the average person in it has, if anything, a worse view in practice. How methodological individualism is violated in this case is not apparent. The crowd rises because of the identifiable actions of specific agents. (Of course, cultural attitudes and the structure of the system of viewing within which individuals operate matter too. People behave differently at the opera.) Moving to macroeconomics, if particular investors lose confidence and if particular players in the financial sector are bearish when interest rates fall, then aggregate demand falls. Even if there are sociological and cultural grounds[16] underlying the actions of the investors and the bears, one could still in principle list the names and addresses of those individuals responsible; although, admittedly, socio-structural reform would be the likely long-term solution. (It is true that a contagion of sentiment through a group is in practice not always so conveniently studied by tracing the chain of infection from one individual to another.) The fallacy of composition stems, however, from errors of logic and observation, not the selection of methodological individualism as such. It is far from clear that explaining involuntary unemployment requires relying on the notion that 'the whole is more than the sum of its parts'.

As the fundamentalist tradition has unfolded, Keynes's broader philosophical position has come into focus. Leijonhufvud has little to say about uncertainty in *The General Theory* (let alone in the *Treatise on Probability*) and nothing to say about Keynes's papers for the Apostles (not readily available in 1968). So far as Keynes's political and social vision is concerned, Leijonhufvud (1981) places him, certainly by the time of *The General Theory*, slightly to the left of centre,[17] but he remarks that Keynes's 'socialisation of investment' in fixed capital (land, buildings, roads and railways) is 'not a very radical recommendation from today's standpoint' (p. 25.)[18] He was no heady advocate of the fiscal fix or caustic denunciator of monetary policy as portrayed by the textbooks of the neoclassical synthesis. There is so much controversy about Keynes's politics that perhaps Leijonhufvud cannot be too dogmatically judged. Indeed, O'Donnell (1989) sees Keynes as groping towards a new socialism.

Leijonhufvud reduces Keynes's vision to one where the machine can transmit false signals and operate under false instructions. The Newtonian clockwork can run amok and the hands can go in the wrong direction. We can regard mechanical metaphors as falling short of an appreciation of holistic and organic conceptions, but I make three points. First, much about an economy can meaningfully be understood in mechanistic and reductionist terms. If you are unemployed and without income, savings or credit, your consumption must fall. Second, it is part of Keynes's story that crucial components of the classical logic break down. The mechanics of interest-rate adjustment in the face of declining investment is an example. Third, it is true that parts of Keynes could be regarded as a blanket rejection of the mechanistic world view in so far as expectations are not governed by any deterministic process. Leijonhufvud, admittedly, tends to quarantine unruly expectations to 'trigger' – to use a mechanistic term – the initial 'shock'.

Nevertheless, mechanistic metaphors can well be helpful, even if incomplete.[19] In some ways economies are indeed like mechanisms. In others, not. Why must some (post–modern?) intellectuals insist on the purity of metaphor and the neoclassicists (modernists?) insist on the brutal simplicities that are required for formal consistency? For example, Shackle (1972: 218) insists that there is a deeply embedded contradiction in Keynes between the deterministic and the humanly creative. Practical people, however, are able to keep apparently conflicting perspectives in mind when dealing with the complexities of life. Both the subjective (confidence) and the objective (cash in hand) have their domains and they interact. Actual orders backed by spending power, or cash, need to be pumped through the body economic to keep it going. (Note the deliberately hydraulic metaphor.) And lives can be saved by a surgeon, a glorified plumber. For the full health of a complex human or social system, psychic healing may be needed too, but has Leijonhufvud (or anybody) ever denied that the institutional context, confidence and expectations crucially matter to an economy? And when realized results are poor, it is hard to preserve an optimistic outlook.

Leijonhufvud (1983a) also sees economics more as an art than a science, as do the fundamentalists. Things are not as simple to predict as both the hydraulicists and the mechanistic neoclassicists once asserted. And differences about how the world works – statements about overall vision rather than details of logic – are not amenable to mathematical dissection and proof.

There are also important methodological similarities between Leijonhufvud and Shackle. Both typically use words rather than mathematics. Neither is concerned with quantitative prediction but with a qualitative understanding of the pattern of events that capitalist systems exhibit when under duress. Both realize that the spontaneous and natural responses of agents to a disturbance need not be a smooth, calm and orderly adjustment to a new full-employment position. Market processes can drive a system away from some superior and sustainable level of output. There can be spontaneous disorder. Neither has faith in a total submission to market forces. They have much in common in terms of their general approach.

Indeed, recent discoveries in the philosophical foundations of Keynes's economics directly promote reconciliation of Leijonhufvud and the Post-Keynesians.[20] The so-called nihilism of some of the fundamentalist writers, especially Shackle, has faded from prominence with the realization that, under Knightian uncertainty, a rejection of the feasibility of instrumentally rational decision-making does not imply wildly unpredictable behaviour.

Reasonable behaviour is still possible even when there is uncertainty, and customs and conventions can moderate the individual's actions.[21] The potential volatility stemming from the absence of full information (or of accurately described probability distributions of contingent events) is thereby reduced. This gives greater scope for the unambiguous, but nevertheless notionally 'false', signals stemming from realized monetary exchanges. Sensible people tend to curtail output when realized demand falls. The stick behind (liquidity constraints) and the carrot ahead (expectations about the best course of action) work together.

Leijonhufvud focuses on inelastic expectations whereas fundamentalists more dramatically emphasize the overshooting of expectations, the excesses of optimism and pessimism of the financial and investment sectors. Either produces false price-and-quantity trades, however, so the upshot is the same. While Leijonhufvud says that it is wrong to focus on the extreme elasticities of the IS and LM curves, Shackle criticizes the elasticity fetishism of the mainstream more pointedly still. Shackle underlines the volatility of the curves and their propensity to shift suddenly and without warning or good cause. Some regard this, however, as nihilism.[22]

But Shackle's silence on the specifics of policy makes sense if one's vision is intended to hold general applicability in a world capable of both spontaneous order and spontaneous disarray as circumstances vary. (For non-nihilistic remarks by Shackle, see Littleboy 1990: 291, 307, n. 96). One is bound to be regarded as a one-sided anti-mechanist if provoked into a critique of a brazen, one-sided, mechanistic neoclassicism. And even if confidence can vanish without warning, the contractionary consequences can be predicted with reasonable reliability.

Besides, Shackle's view is not that all actions and prices are founded on fragile conventions. In the style of an evolutionary economist, Shackle (1972: 227) notes that some prices 'have stood at particular levels for some time [and] acquire thereby some sanction and authority. They are the "right" and even the "just" prices. But also they are the prices to which the society has adapted its ways and habits.'

As with the fundamentalists, there is a stong element of essentialism in Leijonhufvud. A common focus on the nature and causes of unemployment, and the natural concern with processes sets them apart form the neoclassical mainstream. To say that the multiplier is one over one minus the marginal propensity to spend is merely to give a mathematical expression for it. It does not explain what the multiplier is or how it works to amplify deviations (cf. Leijonhufvud 1968: 59).

Although Leijonhufvud uses Walrasian language to speak to Walrasians, his book is not a defence of general equilibrium theory, and it is an attack on its relevance to interpreting Keynes. Walrasian equilibrium is a conceptual benchmark. It is not a centre of gravitation for any real-world, money-using system. True data about future consumption, and investment yields, simply do not exist and would not be transmitted, and thus conceivably acted on, even if they did exist. Often fundamentalists are alienated by Leijonhufvud's use of Walrasian terminology. Perhaps they endorse the rather post-modern notion that a language determines the substance of the discourse rather than merely its style and emphasis. Some of us, however, still believe that a text has a reasonably definite meaning that transcends the limitations of any one language or system of beliefs.

CONCLUSION

What is the point, the reader may ask, of all this comparing, contrasting and reconciling? Why sift through moribund texts rather than participate in the work of building models capable of immediate, real-world application?[23] And why would the participants want to be reconciled? What is in it for the participants?[24] How can the scientific and persuasive power of their own approaches be enhanced by any united front against Classicism? These are good questions. I suppose much depends on whether you value truth for its own sake and on whether you believe that co-operation fosters intellectual progress more than conflict and misunderstanding do. Also, if we regard progress in broadly Lakatosian terms, in which false trails are explored and forgotten ones are rediscovered, then debates of the 1970s could still have currency. Post-Keynesians are quick to condemn others for following the wrong path in the distant past. Perhaps it is time to review their antagonism towards Leijonhufvud.

Even if Post-Keynesians and Leijonhufvud cannot see eye-to-eye on how best to present Keynes, economists generally can extract from their writings valuable insights for both theoretical and practical purposes. There is the risk here of sounding like an apologist for one side or the other. But if one party is going to disagree with the other, let it be over genuine differences and not over misperceptions repeated so often that they are held up as truths.

NOTES

1 Broadly sympathetic followers include Garretsen (1992) and Howitt (1990b). Incidentally, the term 'Post-Keynesian' (i.e. with a hyphen) is used throughout.
2 See Littleboy (1990: 55). Joan Robinson (1982), however, regarded Leijonhufvud (1981) as a step backwards.
3 Leijonhufvud (1968: 230).
4 Ibid.: 99, 258, 279.
5 Ibid.: 252. Rarely do classicists address the issue seriously. See Garrison (1985). Cf. the bizarre reasoning of Pigou (1936: 126).
6 Some points require sourcing:
3 Leijonhufvud (1968: 352) acknowledges the possibility of cost-push inflation

and (ibid.: 367–8) recognizes the historical character of the money wage. See also Leijonhufvud (1981: 181, n. 84).

4 The MEI shifts initially owing to sudden changes in investor confidence, but it is not violently unstable. Leijonhufvud (1968: 86, 340, 351, n. 28 – however, cf. p. 405). On Knightian risk versus uncertainty, see ibid.: 230, and on search theory, see ibid.: 76–8.

5 See ibid.: 228, 233. See also his account of Keynes's proposals on the 'socialisation of investment' (ibid.: 406–7).

6 See ibid.: 26, 401–13. Not only agents, but Keynes himself, are backward-looking!

7 See Leijonhufvud (1981: esp. 174, n. 65). Clower has always been even more scathing.

8 See Leijonhufvud (1968: 340, n. 11).

7 Supplied are references mostly to Leijonhufvud. Presumably no one doubts that fundamentalist Post-Keynesians hold these views.

1 Leijonhufvud (1983b: 214, n. 14, 219, 221, n. 20).

2 Although some fundamentalists see it as having a useful pedagogic role, especially if the finance motive is incorporated – Brothwell (1975); Davidson (1978) – Leijonhufvud ranges from hostile (1968: 30) – on doubtful grounds, it can be added (see Littleboy 1990: ch. 5) – to suspicious (1981: 147–51, 180).

3 Leijonhufvud (1968: 93–4, 336, 352, 408).

4 Ibid.: 37, 54n., 67, 108–9, 332.

5 See Littleboy (1990: 181).

6 Leijonhufvud (1983c: 197).

7 Leijonhufvud (1981: ch. 6).

8 Leijonhufvud, *passim*. This is part of what Leijonhufvud maintains is a 'Wicksell connection' (1981: ch. 7, esp. 133). See also 1968: 321.

9 Littleboy (1990: 181–2).

8 Secular stagnation is assumed away here. Investment opportunities, however, could dry up if (wealthy) savers have an instinctive urge to accumulate without consuming or if people's material wants reach some limit. One supposes that advocates of free markets would argue that falling nominal wages and prices and a shorter working week would automatically emerge to solve the problem.

9 But Leijonhufvud's drafting was less than ideal. See Littleboy (1990: 152). Its relevance is rather less clear in the strategic complementarity branch of New Keynesianism. Is some role for interest rate adjustment posited there?

10 Littleboy (1990: 181–2).

11 And compare Leijonhufvud (1981: 115, n. 24).

12 See Moggridge (1992: 433) for Keynes's view, admittedly in 1925, that free-market economics works tolerably 'nine times out of ten'. But he was then advocating public works programmes.

13 Cf. Leijonhufvud (1981: 334–5) and his ship analogy.

14 See Littleboy (1990: 24–8) for further discussion. Just because a fix-price theorist cites Clower or Leijonhufvud does not mean that either actually supports the approach.

15 Cf. Pareto's views on sociology in Finer (1966). Leijonhufvud (1985) is less cynical. He traces differences to rival social cosmologies.

16 See Lawson (1985a).

17 Note that Harrod's not entirely reliable biography was Leijonhufvud's source then.

18 Cf. Leijonhufvud (1981: 21–2). Keynes even held similar views in 1926.

19 One must be amused by Fritjof Capra (1983), who denounces the simple and orderly Newtonian, mechanistic world-view only to replace it with the more complex mechanistic one of Wiener. Cf. Leijonhufvud (1968: 396–7)! There is more to authentically holistic and organic processes than feedback loops and self-organization; but seeing the world in more complex terms, where natural processes do not yield the best outcomes, is surely an improvement, one supposes.

20 This area in the literature was beginning to flower when the manuscript of Littleboy (1990) was delivered to the publisher.

21 See Lawson (1985a); Littleboy (1990: pt 4).

22 See Coddington (1983: 61) and cf. Moggridge (1992: 145, a). Similar charges, incidentally, have often been made against Nietzsche, who was no nihilist. The absence of grounded, absolute truths was intended to point to the potential for positive human creativity, not engender indecision and despair. The world is only empty until humans, individually or in groups, fill it with their cultural or institutional creations. Cf. Littleboy (1990: 308, n. 108).

23 See Gerrard (1993).

24 See Guthrie (1993).

BIBLIOGRAPHY

Abbot, E.A. (1884) *Flatland: A Romance of Many Dimensions*, New York: Dover.

Abel, A. and Blanchard, O. (1986) 'The present value of profits and cyclical movements in investment', *Econometrica* 54: 249–73.

Ackley, G. (1961) *Macroeconomic Theory*, New York: Macmillan.

—— (1978) *Macroeconomics: Theory and Policy*, New York: Macmillan.

Adelman, I. (1991) 'Long term economic development', Working Paper no. 589, California Agricultural Station.

—— and Adelman, F. (1959) 'The dynamic properties of the Klein–Golberger model', *Econometrica* 27: 596–625.

Agazzi, E. (ed.) (1991) *The Problem of Reductionism in Science*, Dordrecht: Kluwer.

Aglietta, M. (1979) *Theory of Capitalist Regulation*, London: New Left Books.

Alston, W. (1964) *Dimensions of Meaning*, Englewood Cliffs, N.J.: Prentice Hall.

Amadeo, E.J. (1989) *Keynes's Principle of Effective Demand*, Aldershot, Hants: Edward Elgar.

—— (1992) 'Equilibrium unemployment in Keynes's *General Theory*: some recent debates', *Contributions to Political Economy* 11: 1–14.

—— (1994) 'Changes in output in Keynes's *Treatise on Money*', in J. Davis (ed.) *The State of Interpretation of Keynes*, Norwell, Mass.: Kluwer.

Ambler, E. (1985) *Here Lies: An Autobiography*, London: Weidenfeld & Nicolson.

Ambromovitz, M. *et al.* (eds.) (1958) *The Allocation of Resources: Essays in Honour of B.F. Haley*, Stanford, Calif: Stanford University Press.

Ambrose, A. (1979) *Wittgenstein's Lectures, Cambridge, 1932–35*, Oxford: Blackwell.

Ambrosi, G.M. (1976) 'Das Keynessche Portfoliomodell', *Diskussionsbeiträge des Fachbereichs*, Wirtschaftswissenschaften der Universität Konstanz.

Ancott, J. (ed.) (1983) *Analysing the Structure of Econometric Models*, New York: Martinus Nijhoff.

Andrews, P.W.S. and Brunner, E. (1975) *Studies in Pricing*, London: Macmillan.

Arestis, P. (ed.) (1988) *Contemporary Issues in Money and Banking*, London: Macmillan.

—— (1992) *The Post-Keynesian Approach to Economics*, Aldershot, Hants: Edward Elgar.

—— (ed.) (1993) *Money and Banking: Issues for the Twenty-first Century*, London: Macmillan.

—— and Chick, V. (eds) (1992) *Recent Developments in Post Keynesian Economics*, Aldershot, Hants: Edward Elgar.

—— and Dow, S.C. (eds) (1986) *On Money, Method and Keynes*, London: Macmillan.

—— and Howells, P. (forthcoming) 'Theoretical reflections on endogenous money: the problem with "convenience lending"', *Cambridge Journal of Economics*.

Arestis, P. and Marshall, M. (eds) (1995) *The Political Economy of Full Employment, Conservatism, Corporatism, and Institutional Change*, Aldershot, Hants: Edward Elgar.

—— and Sawyer, M. (eds) (1994) *The Elgar Companion to Radical Political Economy*, Aldershot, Hants: Edward Elgar.

Arrow, K.J. (1958) 'Toward a theory of price adjustment', in M. Abramovitz *et al.* (eds) *The Allocation of Economic Resources: Essays in Honour of B.F. Haley*, Stanford, Calif: Stanford University Press.

—— and Debreu, G. (1954) 'Existence of an equilibrium for a competitive economy', *Econometrica* 22: 265–90.

—— and Hahn, F.H. (1971) *General Competitive Analysis*, San Francisco: Holden-Day.

—— and Hurwicz, L. (1958) 'On the stability of competitive equilibrium', *Econometrica* 26: 522–52.

Aschauer, D. (1989) 'Is public expenditure productive?', *Journal of Monetary Economics* 24: 177–200.

Asimakopulos, A. (1971) 'The determination of investment in Keynes' model', *Canadian Journal of Economics* 4: 382–8.

—— (1977) 'Profits and investment: a Kaleckian approach', in G.C. Harcourt (ed.) *The Microeconomic Foundations of Macroeconomics*, London: Macmillan.

—— (1983a) 'The role of the short period: comment on Bharadwaj', in J.A. Kregel (ed.) *Distribution, Effective Demand and Internatonal Economic Relations*, London: Macmillan.

—— (1983b) 'Kalecki and Keynes on finance, investment and savings', *Cambridge Journal of Economics* 7: 221–33.

—— (1985) 'Keynes and Sraffa: visions and perspectives', *Political Economy* 1: 33–50.

—— (1988) 'Reply to Garegnani's comment', *Political Economy* 4: 259–62.

—— (1989) 'The nature and role of equilibrium in Keynes's *General Theory*', *Australian Economic Papers* 28: 16–28.

—— (1991) *Keynes's* General Theory *and Accumulation*, Cambridge: Cambridge University Press.

Aukurst, O. (1970) 'PRIM I: a model of the price and income distribution mechanism of an open economy', *Review of Income and Wealth* 16: 51–78.

Backhouse, R. (ed.) (1994) *New Perspectives on Economic Methodology*, London: Routledge.

Banerjee, A.V. (1992) 'A simple model of herd behaviour', *Quarterly Journal of Economics* 107: 797–807.

Bank of Canada (1991) 'The implementation of monetary policy in a system with zero reserve requirements', Discussion Paper 3, 6 Sept.

Baran, P.A. (1952) 'On the political economy of backwardness', *Manchester School of Economic and Social Studies* 20: 66–84.

—— (1957) *The Political Economy of Growth*, New York: Monthly Review Press.

—— and Sweezy, P.M. (1966) *Monopoly Capital*, New York: Monthly Review Press.

Baranzini, M. (ed.) (1982) *Advances in Economic Theory*, Oxford: Blackwell.

—— and Scazzieri, R. (eds) (1986) *Foundations of Economics: Structure of Inquiry and Economic Theory*, Oxford: Blackwell.

Barens, I. (1987) 'Geld und Unterbeschäftigung. John Maynard Keynes' Kritik der Selbstregulierungsvorstellung', *Volkswirtschaftliche Schriften*, Heft 368, Berlin: Duncker & Humblot.

—— (1988) 'Die (doppelte) Rolle des Geldes bei Keynes', in H. Hagemann and O. Steiger (eds) *Keynes'* General Theory *nach fünfzig Jahren*, Volkswirtschaftliche Schriften Heft 384, Berlin: Duncker & Humblot.

Barens, I. (1989) 'From the "banana parable" to the principle of effective demand: some reflections on the origin, development and structure of Keynes' *General Theory*', in D.A. Walker (ed.) *Perspectives on the History of Economic Thought*, Vol II, Aldershot, Hants: Edward Elgar.

—— (1990) 'The rise and fall of the "entrepreneur economy": some remarks on Keynes's taxonomy of economics', in D.E. Moggridge (ed.) *Perspectives on the History of Economic Thought*, Vol. IV: *Keynes, Macroeconomics and Method*, Aldershot, Hants: Edward Elgar.

Barnett, W.A. and Chen, P. (1988) 'The aggregation–theoretical monetary aggregates are chaotic and have strange attractors: an econometric interpretation of mathematical chaos', in W. Barnett, R. Ernst and W. Halbert (eds) *Dynamic Econometric Modelling*, Cambridge: Cambridge University Press.

Barnett, W.A. and Hinich, M. (1993) 'Has chaos been discovered with economic data?', in P. Chen and R. Day (eds) *Nonlinear Dynamics and Evolutionary Economics*, Oxford: Oxford University Press.

Barnett, W.A. and Singleton, K.J. (eds) (1986) *New Approaches to Monetary Economics: Proceedings of the Second International Symposium in Economic Theory and Econometrics*, Cambridge: Cambridge University Press.

Barrère, A. (ed.) (1988) *The Foundations of Keynesian Analysis*, Proceedings of a Conference held at the University of Paris I-Panthéon-Sorbonne, London: Macmillan.

Barro, R.J. (1978a) 'Unanticipated money, output, and the price level in the United States', *Journal of Political Economy* 86: 22–51.

—— (1978b) *The Impact of Social Security on Private Saving: Evidence from US Time Series*, Washington, D.C.: American Enterprise Institute.

—— (1980) 'A capital market in an equilibrium business cycle model', *Econometrica* 48: 1393–417.

—— (1989) 'Interest-rate targeting', *Journal of Monetary Economics* 23: 3–30.

—— (1994) 'The aggregate supply/aggregate demand model', *Eastern Economic Journal* 20 (1): 1–6.

—— and Gordon, D.B. (1983a) 'A positive theory of monetary policy in a natural rate model', *Journal of Political Economy* 91: 589–610.

—— and —— (1983b) 'Rules, discretion and reputation in a model of monetary policy', *Journal of Monetary Economics* 12: 101–21.

—— and Grilli, V. (1994) *European Macroeconomics*, Basingstoke, Hants: Macmillan.

—— and Grossman, H. (1976) *Money, Employment and Inflation*, Cambridge: Cambridge University Press.

Bartholomew, J. (1993) 'Least-squares learning and the stability of equilibria with externalities', *Review of Economic Studies* 60: 197–208.

Bateman, B.W. (1987) 'Keynes's changing conception of probability', *Economics and Philosophy* 3: 97–120.

—— (1990a) 'Keynes, induction and econometrics', *History of Political Economy* 22: 359–79.

—— (1990b) 'The elusive logical relation', in D.E. Moggridge (ed.) *Perspectives in the History of Economic Thought, Vol. IV, Keynes, Macroeconomics and Method*, Aldershot, Hants: Edward Elgar.

—— (1991) 'Das Maynard Keynes Problem', *Cambridge Journal of Economics* 15: 101–11.

—— (1994) 'Keynes uncertain revolution', unpublished book manuscript.

—— and Davis, J.B. (eds) (1991) *Keynes and Philosophy: Essays on the Origin of Keynes's Thought*, Aldershot, Hants: Edward Elgar.

Bauer, O. (1936) *Zwischen zwei Weltkriegen?*, Bratislava: Prager.

Bauer, P. (1945) 'Notes on Cost', *Economica* 12: 90–100.

Baumol, W.J. (1971) 'On the behavioural theory of the firm', in R. Marris and A. Wood (eds) *The Corporate Economy*, Cambridge, Mass.: Harvard University Press.
Baumol, W.J. (1977) 'Say's (at least) eight laws, or what Say and James Mill may really have meant', *Economica* 44: 145–61.
Bean, C.R. (1984) *The Estimation of 'Surprise' Models and the 'Surprise' Consumption Function*, Discussion Paper no. 191, London: London School of Economics: Centre for Labour Economics.
Beckerman, W. (ed.) (1986) *Wage Rigidity and Unemployment*, Baltimore, Md.: Johns Hopkins University Press.
Behrens, R. (1985) 'What Keynes knew about Marx', *Studi Economici* 26: 3–14.
Bell, D. and Kristol, I. (eds) (1981) *The Crisis in Economic Theory*, New York: Basic Books.
Bénabou, R. (1988) 'Search, price setting and inflation', *Review of Economic Studies* 55: 353–76.
—— (1992) 'Inflation and efficiency in search markets', *Review of Economic Studies* 59: 299–329.
Benassy, J. (1986) *Macroeconomics: An Introduction to the Non-Walrasian Approach*, London: Harcourt Brace Jovanovich.
Beranek, W. and Timberlake, R.H. (1987) 'The liquidity trap theory: a critique', *Southern Economic Journal* 54: 387–96.
Berg, L. (1994) 'Household savings and debts: the experience of the Nordic countries', *Oxford Review of Economic Policy* 10: 42–53.
Berle, A.A. and Means, G.C. (1932) *The Modern Corporation and Private Property*, New York: Macmillan.
Bernanke, B. (1981) 'Bankruptcy, liquidity and recession', *American Economic Review* 71: 155–9.
—— (1983) 'Irreversibility, uncertainty and cyclical investment', *Quarterly Journal of Economics* 98: 85–106.
Beveridge, W.H. (1936a) 'Employment theory and the facts of unemployment', unpublished MS. Held at British Library of Political and Economic Science, London.
—— (1936b) 'Supplementary notes on Keynes', unpublished MS. Held at British Library of Political and Economic Science, London.
Bhaduri, A. (1986) *Macroeconomics: The Dynamics of Commodity Production*, London: Macmillan.
—— (1996) 'Economic growth and the theory of capital: an evaluation of Joan Robinson's contribution', in C. Marcuzzo, L. Pasinetti and A. Roncaglia (eds) *The Economics of Joan Robinson*, London: Routledge, 200–6.
—— and Robinson, J. (1980) 'Accumulation and exploitation: an analysis in the tradition of Marx, Sraffa and Kalecki', *Cambridge Journal of Economics* 4: 103–15.
Bharadwaj, K. (1983) 'On effective demand: certain recent critiques', in J.A. Kregel (ed.) *Distribution, Effective Demand and International Economic Relations*, London: Macmillan.
Bhaskar, R. (1978) *A Realist Theory of Science*, Hemel Hempstead, Herts.: Harvester Press.
—— (1979) *The Possibility of Naturalism*, Hemel Hempstead, Herts.: Harvester Press.
—— (1986) *Scientific Realism and Human Emancipation*, London: Verso.
—— (1989) *Reclaiming Reality: A Critical Introduction to Contemporary Philosophy*, London: Verso.
Bhattacharjea, A. (1987) 'Keynes and the long-period theory of employment: a note', *Cambridge Journal of Economics* 11: 275–84.
Bikhchandani, S., Hirshleifer, D. and Welch, I. (1992) 'A theory of fads, fashion, custom and cultural change as informational cascades', *Journal of Political Economy* 100: 992–1026.

Black, F. (1970) 'Banking and interest rates in a world without money: the effects of uncontrolled banking', *Journal of Bank Research* 1: 8–20.

—— (1976) 'The dividend puzzle', *Journal of Portfolio Management* 2: 5–8.

—— (1987) *Business Cycles and Equilibrium*, Oxford: Blackwell.

Black, M. (1949) *Language and Philosophy: Studies in Method*, Ithica, N.Y.: Cornell University Press.

Blanchard, O. (1987) *Aggregate and Individual Price Adjustments*, Brookings Papers on Economic Activity no. 1, Washington, D.C.: Brookings Institution.

—— and Fischer, S. (1989) *Lectures on Macroeconomics*, Cambridge, Mass.: MIT Press.

—— and Kiyotaki, N. (1987) 'Monopolistic competition and aggregate demand', *American Economic Review* 77: 647–68.

Blatt, J. (1980) 'On the Frisch model of business cycles', *Oxford Economic Papers* 32: 467–79.

Blaug, M. (1980) *The Methodology of Economics*, Cambridge: Cambridge University Press.

Bleaney, M. (1976) *Underconsumption Theories: A History and Critical Analysis*, London: Lawrence & Wishart.

Blinder, A.S. (1976) 'Intergenerational transfers and life cycle consumption', *American Economic Review* 66: 87–93.

Bliss, C.J. (1987) 'Equal rates of profit', in J. Eatwell, M. Milgate and P. Newman (eds) *The New Palgrave: A Dictionary of Economics*, vol. 2, London: Macmillan.

Blundell, R. (1991) 'Consumer behaviour: theory and empirical evidence – a survey', in A.J. Oswald (ed.) *Surveys in Economics*, vol. II., Oxford: Blackwell, for the Royal Economic Society.

Boddy, R. and Crotty, J. (1975) 'Class conflict and macro policy: the political business cycle', *Review of Radical Political Economics*, Spring.

Boehm, S., Frowen, S. and Pheby, J. (eds) (1993) *Economics as the Art of Thought: Essays in Memory of G.L.S. Shackle*, London: Routledge.

Boitani, A. and Rodano, G. (eds) (1995) *Relazioni Pericolose. L'avventura dell'economia nella cultura contempporanea*, Bari: Laterza.

Boserup, M. (1969) 'A note on the prehistory of the Kahn multiplier', *Economic Journal* 79: 667–9.

Boskin, M. (1988) 'Consumption, saving and fiscal policy', *American Economic Review* 78: 401–7.

—— (ed.) (1979) *Economics and Human Welfare: Essays in Honour of Tibor Scitovsky*, New York: Academic Press.

Boulding, K. (1944) 'A liquidity preference theory of market prices', *Economica* 11: 55–63.

Bowles, S., Gordon, D. and Weisskopf, T. (1986) *Beyond the Wasteland*, New York: Anchor Press.

——, —— and —— (1989) 'Business ascendancy and economic impasse: a structural retrospective on conservative economics', *Journal of Economic Perspectives* 3: 107–34.

Bradford, W. (1993) 'Words and deeds: Keynes's "spectrum of appropriate languages" and the formation of macroeconomic theory and policy', University of Cambridge, mimeo.

Brady, M.E. (1993) 'J.M. Keynes's theoretical approach to decision-making under conditions of risk and uncertainty', *British Journal for the Philosophy of Science* 43, forthcoming.

—— and Lee, H.B. (1989a) 'Dynamics of choice behaviour: the logical relation between linear objective probability and nonlinear subjective probability', *Psychological Reports* 64: 91–7.

Brady, M.E. and Lee, H.B. (1989b) 'Is there an Ellsberg–Fellner paradox? A note on its resolution', *Psychological Reports* 64: 1087–90.

Brainard, W.C. and Tobin, J. (1968) 'Pitfalls in financial model building', *American Economic Review* 58: 99–122.

Braithwaite, R.B. (ed.) (1931) *The Foundations of Mathematics*, London: Routledge & Kegan Paul.

Branson, W.H. and Klevorick, A.K. (1969) 'Money illusion and the aggregate consumption function', *American Economic Review* 59: 832–43.

Brennan, G. and Waterman, A.M.C. (eds) (1994) *Economics and Religion: Are They Distinct?*, Boston, Mass.: Kluwer.

Brenner, Y.S., Reinders, J.P.G. and Spithoven, A.H.G.M. (eds) (1988) *The Theory of Income and Wealth Distribution*, Brighton: Wheatsheaf.

Brigham, E.F. and Gordon, M.J. (1968) 'Leverage, dividend policy and the cost of capital', *Journal of Finance* 23: 85–103.

Brock, W. (1986) 'Distinguishing random and deterministic systems', *Journal of Economic Theory* 40: 168–96.

——, Hsieh, D. and LeBaron, B. (1991) *Nonlinear Dynamics, Chaos and Instability*, Cambridge, Mass.: MIT Press.

Brothwell, J. (1975) 'A simple Keynesian's response to Leijonhufvud', *Bulletin of Economic Research* 27: 3–21.

—— (1983) 'Wages and employment: a reply to Maynard and Rose', *Journal of Post Keynesian Economics* 6: 101–4.

—— (1986) '*The General Theory* after fifty years: why are we not all Keynesians now?', *Journal of Post Keynesian Economics* 8: 531–47.

Brown, A.J. (1958) 'Inflation and the British Economy', *Economic Journal* 66: 449–63.

—— assisted by Jane Darby (1985) *World Inflation since 1950*, Cambridge: Cambridge University Press, for National Institute of Economic and Social Research.

Brown, C. (1992) 'Commodity money, credit money and the real balance effect', *Journal of Post Keynesian Economics* 15: 99–107.

Brunner, K. and Meltzer, A.H. (eds) (1976) *The Phillips Curve and Labour Markets*, Carnegie–Rochester Conference Series on Public Policy, vol. 1, Amsterdam: North-Holland.

—— and —— (1981) *The Costs and Consequences of Inflation*, Carnegie–Rochester Conference Series on Public Policy, Amsterdam: North-Holland.

Bruno, M. and Sachs, J.O. (1985) *Economics of Worldwide Stagflation*, Oxford: Blackwell.

Bryant, J. and Wallace, N. (1980) 'A suggestion for further simplifying the theory of money', Minneapolis: Federal Reserve Bank of Minneapolis and University of Minnesota, MS.

Buiter, W., Corsetti, G. and Roubini, N. (1993) 'Excessive deficits: sense and nonsense in the treaty of Maastricht', *Economic Policy* 16: 57–100.

Burch, S.W. and Werneke, D. (1975) 'The stock of consumer durables, inflation and personal saving decisions', *Review of Economics and Statistics* 57: 141–54.

Burda, M. and Wyplosz, C. (1993) *Macroeconomics: A European Text*, Oxford: Oxford University Press.

Burmeister, E. (1980) *Capital Theory and Dynamics*, Cambridge: Cambridge University Press.

Burns, A. and Mitchell, W. (1946) *Measuring Business Cycles*, New York: National Bureau of Economic Research.

Bush, J. (1994) 'Inflation obsession blinds policy makers to other ills', *The Times*, 25 August.

Bushaw, D.W. and Clower, R.W. (1957) *Introduction to Mathematical Economics*, Homewood, Ill.: Irwin.

Cagan, P. (1956) 'The monetary dynamics of hyperinflation', in M. Friedman (ed.) *Studies in the Quantity Theory of Money*, Chicago, Ill.: Chicago University Press.

Cairncross, Sir A. (1985) *Years of Recovery: British Economic Policy, 1945–51*, London: Methuen.

—— and Cairncross, F. (eds) (1992) *The Legacy of the Golden Age: The 1960s and their Consequences*, London: Routledge.

Campbell, J.Y. and Mankiw, N.G. (1989) 'Consumption, income and interest rates: reinterpreting the time series evidence', *NBER Macroeconomics Annual* 4: 185–216.

Capra, F. (1983) *The Turning Point*, London: Flamingo.

Carabelli, A. (1988) *On Keynes's Method*, London: Macmillan.

—— (1992) 'Organic interdependence and Keynes's choice of units in the *General Theory*', in B. Gerrard and J. Hillard (eds) *Philosophy and Economics of J.M. Keynes*, Aldershot, Hants: Edward Elgar.

Caravale, G.A. (ed.) (1991) *Marx and Modern Economic Analysis*, 2 vols, Aldershot, Hants: Edward Elgar.

Cardim de Carvahlo, F.J. (1990) 'Keynes and the long period', *Cambridge Journal of Economics* 14: 277–90.

—— (1992) *Mr Keynes and the Post Keynesians: Principles of Macroeconomics for a Monetary Production Economy*, Aldershot, Hants: Edward Elgar.

Cas, A. and Rymes, T.K. (1991) *On Concepts and Measures of Multifactor Productivity in Canada, 1961–80*, Cambridge: Cambridge University Press.

Caskey, J. and Fazzari, S. (1987) 'Aggregate demand contractions with nominal debt commitments: is wage flexibility stabilizing?', *Economic Enquiry* 25: 583–97.

—— and —— (1988) 'Price flexibility and macroeconomic stability: an empirical simulation analysis', Working Paper, St Louis, Mo.: Washington University, Department of Economics.

Caspari, V. (1989) 'Walras, Marshall, Keynes. Zum Verhältnis von Mikro- und Makroökonomie', *Volkswirtschaftliche Schriften*, Heft 387, Berlin: Duncker & Humblot.

Cassel, G. (1937) 'Mr Keynes' *General Theory*', *International Labour Review* 36: 437–45.

Chamberlain, T. and Gordon, M.J. (1989) 'Liquidity, profitability and long-run survival: theory and evidence on business investment', *Journal of Post Keynesian Economics* 11: 589–610.

Chamberlin, E. (1933) *The Theory of Monopolistic Competition*, Cambridge, Mass.: Harvard University Press.

Champernowne, D.G. (1964) 'Expectations and the links between the economic future and the present', in R. Lekachmann (ed.) *Keynes'* General Theory: *Reports of Three Decades*, New York: St Martin's Press.

Chang, W. and Smyth, D. (1971) 'The existence and persistence of cycles in a non-linear model: Kaldor's 1940 model re-examined', *Review of Economic Studies* 38: 37–44.

Chant, J. (1992) 'The new theory of financial intermediation', in K. Dowd and M.K. Lewis (eds) *Current Issues in Financial and Monetary Economics*, London: Macmillan.

Chapple, S. (1991) 'Did Kalecki get there first? The race for the *General Theory*', *History of Political Economy* 23: 243–61.

Chen, P. (1993) 'Searching for economic chaos: a challenge to econometric practice', in P. Chen and R. Day (eds) *Nonlinear Dynamics and Evolutionary Economics*, Cambridge: Cambridge University Press.

Chick, V. (1978) 'The nature of the Keynesian revolution', *Australian Economic Papers* 17: 1–20; reprinted in P. Arestis and S.C. Dow (eds) *On Money, Method and Keynes: Selected Essays*, London: Macmillan, 1992.

—— (1983) *Macroeconomics after Keynes: A Reconsideration of the* General Theory, London: Philip Allan and MIT Press.

—— (1984) 'Monetary increases and their consequences: streams, backwaters and floods', in A. Ingham and A.M. Ulph (eds) *Demand, Equilibrium and Trade: Essays in Honour of I.F. Pearce*, London: Macmillan; reprinted in P. Arestis and S.C. Dow (eds) *On Money, Method and Keynes, Selected Essays*, London: Macmillan, 1992.

—— (1986) 'The evolution of the banking system and the theory of saving, investment and interest', *Economics et sociétiés* 20: 111–26 (Monnaie et production 3); reprinted in P. Arestis and S.C. Dow (eds) *On Money, Method and Keynes, Selected Essays*, London: Macmillan, 1992.

—— (1987) 'Hugh Townshend', in J. Eatwell, M. Milgate and P. Newman (eds) *The New Palgrave: A Dictionary of Economics*, Vol. IV, London: Macmillan.

—— (1988) 'Sources of finance, recent changes in bank behaviour and the theory of investment and interest', in P. Arestis (ed.) *Contemporary Issues in Money and Banking*, London: Macmillan.

—— (1993a) 'Sources of finance, recent changes in bank behaviour and the theory of investment and interest', in P. Arestis (ed.) *Money and Banking: Issues for the Twenty-first Century*, London: Macmillan.

—— (1993b) 'The evolution of the banking system and the theory of monetary policy', in S.F. Frowen (ed.) *Monetary Theory and Monetary Policy: New Tracks for the 1990s*, London: Macmillan.

—— (forthcoming) 'Keynes-inspired contributions of Post-Keynesian economics', in V. Chick (ed.) *Keynes and the Post Keynesians*, London: Macmillan.

Chirinko, R.S. (1993) 'Business fixed investment spending: modelling strategies, empirical results and policy implications', *Journal of Economic Literature* 31: 1875–1911.

Church, K.B., Smith, P.N. and Wallis, K.F. (1994) 'Econometric evaluation of consumers' expenditure equations', *Oxford Review of Economic Policy* 10: 71–85.

Clark, C. (1945) 'Public finance and changes in the value of money', *Economic Journal* 55: 371–89.

Clarke, P. (1979) 'Investment in the 1970s: theory, performance and prediction', *Brookings Papers in Economic Activity* 1: 73–113.

—— (1988) *The Keynesian Revolution in the Making, 1924–36*, Oxford: Clarendon Press.

—— (1990) 'Hobson and Keynes as economic heretics', in M. Freeden (ed.) *Reappraising J.A. Hobson*, London: Unwin Hyman.

Clower, R.W. (1955) 'Competition, monopoly and the theory of price', *Pakistan Economic Journal* 5: 219–26.

—— (1960) 'Keynes and the Classics: a dynamic perspective', *Quarterly Journal of Economics* 74: 318–23.

—— (1965) 'The Keynesian counter-revolution: a theoretical appraisal', in F.H. Hahn and F.P.R. Brechling (eds) *The Theory of Interest Rates*, London: Macmillan.

—— (1967) 'A reconsideration of the microfoundations of monetary theory', *Western Economic Journal* 6: 1–33.

—— (1975a) 'Reflections on the Keynesian perplex', *Zeitschrift für Nationalökonomie* 35: 1–24.

Clower, R.W. (1975b) 'The obscurantist approach to economics: Keynes on Shackle', *Eastern Economic Journal* 2: 99–101.
—— (1977) 'The anatomy of monetary theory', *American Economic Review* 67: 206–12.
—— (1989) 'Keynes's *General Theory*: the Marshall connection', in D.A. Walker (ed.) *Perspectives in the History of Economic Thought*, Vol. II, Upleadon, Glos.: Edward Elgar.
—— (1990) 'Keynes's *General Theory*: a contemporary perspective', *Greek Economic Review* 12 (suppl.): 73–84.
—— (1991) 'Ohlin and *The General Theory*', in L. Jonung (ed.) *The Stockholm School of Economics Revisited*, New York: Cambridge University Press.
—— (1993a) 'Towards a reconstruction of economics', address to the annual meeting of the Canadian Economic Association, Ottawa, 5 June.
—— (1993b) 'The fingers of the invisible hand', mimeo.
—— (1993c) 'On truth in teaching macroeconomics', mimeo.
—— and Due, J.F. (1972) *Microeconomics*, Homewood, Ill.: Irwin.
—— and Leijonhufvud, A. (1975) in D.A. Walker (ed.) *Money and Markets*, Cambridge: Cambridge University Press, 1985.
—— and —— (1975) 'The coordination of economic activities: a Keynesian perspective', *American Economic Review* 65: 182–8.
Coates, J. (1990) 'Ordinary language economics: Keynes and the Cambridge philosophers', Cambridge University, unpublished PhD thesis.
—— (1996) *The Claims of Common Sense: Cambridge Philosophy and the Social Sciences*, Cambridge: Cambridge University Press.
Coddington, A. (1976) 'Keynesian economics: the search for first principles', *Journal of Economic Literature* 14: 1258–73.
—— (1982) 'Deficient foresight: a troublesome theme in Keynesian economics', *American Economic Review* 72: 480–7.
—— (1983) *Keynesian Economics: The Search for First Principles*, London: George Allen & Unwin.
Coen, R.M. (1971) 'The effect of cash flow on the speed of adjustment', in G. Fromm (ed.) *Tax Incentives and Capital Spending*, Washington, D.C.: The Brookings Institution.
Cohen, A.J. and Smithin, J. (eds) (1995) *Money, Financial Institutions and Macroeconomics*, Dordrecht: Kluwer.
Conard, J.W. (1959) *An Introduction to the Theory of Interest*, Berkeley, Calif.: University of California Press.
Conniffe, D. (1992) 'Keynes on probability and statistical inference and the links to Fisher', *Cambridge Journal of Economics* 16: 475–89.
Cooley, T.F., LeRoy, S.F. and Raymon, N. (1984) 'Econometric policy evaluation: a note', *American Economic Review* 74: 467–70.
Cooper, R. and John, A. (1988) 'Coordinating coordination failures in Keynesian models', *Quarterly Journal of Economics* 103: 441–63.
Cornwall, J. (1977) *Modern Capitalism: Its Growth and Transformation*, Oxford: Blackwell.
—— (1990) *The Theory of Economic Breakdown*, Armonk, N.Y.: M.E. Sharpe.
—— (1994) *Economic Breakdown and Recovery: Theory and Policy*, Armonk, N.Y.: M.E. Sharpe.
Cornwell, J. (ed.) (1995) *Nature's Imagination: The Frontiers of Scientific Vision*, Oxford: Oxford Press.
Costabile, L. and Rowthorn, R. (1985) 'Malthus's theory of wages and growth', *Economic Journal* 95: 418–37.

Cottrell, A. (1989) 'Price expectations and equilibrium when the interest rate is pegged', *Scottish Journal of Political Economy* 36: 125–40.

—— (1993) 'Keynes's theory of probability and its relevance to his economics: three theses', *Economics and Philosophy* 9: 25–51.

—— (1994) 'Keynes's vision and tactics', in J. Davis (ed.) *The State of Interpretation of Keynes*, New York: Kluwer.

—— and Lawlor, M.S. (1991) '"Natural rate" mutations: Keynes, Leijonhuvfud and the Wicksell connection', *History of Political Economy* 23: 625–43.

Cournot, A. (1838) *Recherches sur les principes mathématique de la théorie de la richesse*, English trans. N. Bacon and I. Fisher *Researches into the Mathematical Principles of the Theory of Wealth*, London: Macmillan, 1929.

Coveney, P. and Highfield, R. (1990) *Arrow of Time*, New York: Ballantine.

Cowen, T. and Kroszner, R. (1994) 'Money's marketability premium and the microfoundations of Keynes's theory of money and interest', *Cambridge Journal of Economics* 18: 379–90.

Crawley, K. (ed.) (1986) *The Collected Scientific Papers of Paul A. Samuelson*, Vol. 5, Cambridge, Mass., and London: MIT Press.

Cross, R. (1982) 'The Duhem–Quine thesis, Lakatos, and the appraisal of theories in macroeconomics', *Economic Journal* 92: 320–40.

Curtis, M. (1938) 'Saving and savings', *Quarterly Journal of Economics* 53: 623–6.

Cyert, R. and March, J. (1963) *A Behavioural Theory of the Firm*, Englewood Cliffs, N.J.: Prentice Hall.

Daly, V. and Hadjimatheou, G. (1981) 'Stochastic implications of the life-cycle–permanent-income hypothesis: evidence for the UK economy', *Journal of Political Economy* 89: 596–9.

Dalziel, P. (1996) 'The Keynesian miltiplier, liquidity preference and endogenous money', *Journal of Post Keynesian Economics*: 18: 311–31.

Dana, R. and Malgrange, P. (1983) 'The dynamics of a discrete version of a growth cycle model', in J. Ancott (ed.) *Analysing the Structure of Econometric Models*, New York: Martinus Nijhoff.

Darby, M.R. (1975) 'The financial and tax effects of monetary policy on interest rates', *Economic Enquiry* 13: 266–76.

Dardi, M. (1994) 'Kahn's theory of liquidity preference and monetary policy',*Cambridge Journal of Economics* 18: 91–107.

Darhendorf, R. (1995) *LSE: A History of the London School of Economics and Political Science, 1895–1995*, Oxford: Oxford University Press.

Darity, W., Jr (1985) 'On involuntary unemployment and increasing returns', *Journal of Post Keynesian Economics* 7: 363–73.

—— and Goldsmith, A.H. (1995) 'Mr. Keynes, the New Keynesians and the concept of full employment', in P. Wells (ed.) *Post Keynesian Economic Theory*, Boston, Mass.: Kluwer, 73–94.

—— and Horn, B.L. (1983) 'Involuntary unemployment reconsidered', *Southern Economic Journal* 49: 717–33.

—— and —— (1993) 'Rational expectations, rational belief and Keyne's *General Theory*', in W.J. Samuels and J. Biddle (eds) *Research in the History of Economic Thought and Methodology*, Greenwich, Conn. and London: JAI Press.

Dasgupta, P., Hart, O. and Maskin, E. (eds) (1992) *Economic Analysis of Markets and Games: Essays in Honour of Frank Hahn*, Cambridge, Mass.: MIT Press.

Davidson, J.E.H., Hendry, D.F., Srba, F. and Yeo, S. (1978) 'Econometric modelling of the aggregate time-series relationship between consumers' expenditure and income in the United Kingdom', *Economic Journal* 80 (September): 661–92.

Davidson, P. (1963) 'Public problems of the domestic crude oil history', *American Economic Review* 53: 85–108.

—— (1967) 'A Keynesian view of Patinkin's theory of employment', *Economic Journal* 77: 559–78.

—— (1972) *Money and the Real World*, London: Macmillan.

—— (1977) 'Money and general equilibrium', *Economie appliquée* 30: 542–63.

—— (1978) *Money and the Real World*, 2nd edn, London: Macmillan.

—— (1980) 'The dual faceted nature of the Keynesian revolution', *Journal of Post Keynesian Economics* 2: 291–313.

—— (1981) 'Post Keynesian economics: solving the crisis in economic theory', in D. Bell and I. Kristol (eds) *The Crisis in Economic Theory*, New York: Basic Books.

—— (1983) 'The marginal product is not the demand curve for labour and Lucas's labour supply function is not the supply of labour in the real world', *Journal of Post Keynesian Economics* 6: 105–17.

—— (1984) 'Reviving Keynes's revolution', *Journal of Post Keynesian Economics* 6: 561–75.

—— (1986) 'Finance, funding, saving and investment', *Journal of Post Keynesian Economics* 9: 101–11.

—— (1987) 'User cost', in J. Eatwell, M. Milgate and P. Newman (eds) *The New Palgrave: A Dictionary of Economics*, Vol. 4, London: Macmillan.

—— (1987–8) 'A modest set of proposals for resolving the international debt problem', *Journal of Post Keynesian Economics* 10: 323–38.

—— (1988) 'Endogenous money, the production process, and inflation analysis', *Economie appliquée* 41: 151–69.

—— (1989) 'Keynes and money', in R. Hill (ed.) *Keynes, Money and Monetarism: The Eighth Keynes Seminar*, held at the University of Kent at Canterbury, London: Macmillan.

—— (1991) 'Is probability theory relevant for uncertainty? A Post Keynesian perspective', *Journal of Economic Perspectives* 5: 129–44.

—— (1994) *Post Keynesian Macroeconomic Theory*, Aldershot, Hants: Edward Elgar.

—— and Smolensky, E. (1964) *Aggregate Supply and Demand Analysis*, New York: Harper & Row.

Davis, E.G. (1980) 'The correspondence between R.G. Hawtrey and J.M. Keynes on the *Treatise*: the genesis of output adjustment models', *Canadian Journal of Economics* 13: 716–24.

Davis, J.B. (1994a) *Keynes's Philosophical Development*, Cambridge: Cambridge University Press.

—— (ed.) (1994b) *The State of Interpretation of Keynes*, Norwell, Mass.: Kluwer.

—— (1996) 'Convergence in Keynes and Wittgenstein's later views', forthcoming in *European Journal of the History of Economic Thought.*

Davis, J.R. and Casey, F.J., Jr (1977) 'Keynes's misquotation of Mill', *Economic Journal* 87: 329–30.

Day, R. and Shaefer, W. (1985) 'Keynesian chaos, *Journal of Macroeconomics* 7: 277–95.

—— and —— (1987) 'Ergodic fluctuations in deterministic models', *Journal of Economic Behaviour and Organisation* 8: 339–61.

Deaton, A. (1978) 'Involuntary saving through unanticipated inflation', *American Economic Review* 68: 899–910.

—— (ed.) (1980) *Essays in the Theory and Measurement of Consumers' Behaviour*, Cambridge: Cambridge University Press.

—— (1992) *Understanding Consumption*, Oxford: Clarendon Press.

Debreu, G. (1959) *Theory of Value: An Axiomatic Analysis of Economic Equilibrium*,

Cowles Foundation Monograph no. 17, New Haven, Conn.: Yale University Press.

DeCoster, G., Labys, W. and Mitchell, D. (1992) 'Evidence of chaos in commodity futures prices', *Journal of Futures Markets* 12: 291–305.

de Gijsel, P. and Haslinger, F. (1988) 'Keynes' monetäre Begründung unfreiwilliger Arbeitslosigkeit. Anmerkungen zum 17. Kapitel der *General Theory*', in H. Hagemann and O. Steiger (eds) *Keynes'* General Theory *nach fünfzig Jahren, Volkswirtschaftliche*, Heft 384, Berlin: Duncker & Humblot.

Deleplace, G. (1987) 'Ajustement de marché et "taux d'intérêt spécifiques" chez Keynes et Sraffa', *Cahiers d'economie politique* (La 'Théorie Générale' de J.M. Keynes: un cinquantenaire), 214–15: 75–97.

DelMonte, A. (ed.) (1992) *Recent Developments in the Theory of Industrial Organisation*, London: Macmillan.

De Long, J.B. and Summers, L.H. (1986) 'Is increased price flexibility stabilizing?', *American Economic Review* 76: 1031–44.

De Marchi, N. and Morgan, M. (eds) (1994) 'Higgling: transactors and their markets in the history of economics', *History of Political Economy* 26 (suppl.): 184–225.

Desai, M. (1982) 'The task of monetary theory: the Hayek–Sraffa debate in a modern perspective', in M. Baranzini (ed.) *Advances in Economic Theory*, Oxford: Blackwell.

Dillard, D. (1948) *The Economics of John Maynard Keynes: The Theory of a Monetary Economy*, New York: Prentice Hall.

Dilworth, C. (ed.) (1992) *Intelligibility in Science*, special issue of *Poznan Studies in the Philosophy of the Sciences* 2: 319–54.

Dimand, R. (1988) *The Origins of the Keynesian Revolution*, Aldershot, Hants: Edward Elgar.

DiMatteo, M., Goodwin, R. and Vercelli, A. (eds) (1989) *Technological and Social Factors in Long Term Fluctuations*, New York: Springer Verlag.

Dirks, F.C. (1938) 'Retail sales and labor income', *Review of Economic Statistics* 20: 128–34.

Dirlam, J.B., Kaplan, A.D.H. and Lanzillotti, R.F. (1958) *Pricing in Big Business: A Case Approach*, Washington, D.C.: Brookings Institution.

Dixit, A. (1976) *The Theory of Equilibrium Growth*, London: Oxford University Press.

Dixon, H. (1987) 'A simple model of imperfect competition with Walrasian features', *Oxford Economic Papers* 39: 134–60.

Domar, E.D. (1946) 'Capital expansion, rate of growth and employment', *Econometrica* 14: 137–47.

—— (1947) 'Expansion and employment', *American Economic Review* 37: 34–55.

Dore, M. (1993) *The Macroeconomics of Business Cycles*, Oxford: Blackwell.

Dorfman, R., Samuelson, P.A. and Solow, R.M. (1958) *Linear Programming and Economic Analysis*, New York: McGraw-Hill.

Dow, A.C. and Dow, S.C. (1989) 'Endogenous money creation and idle balances', in J. Pheby (ed.) *New Directions in Post Keynesian Economics*, Aldershot, Hants: Edward Elgar.

Dow, J.C.R. and Saville, I.D. (1990) *A Critique of Monetary Policy: Theory and British Experience*, 2nd edn, Oxford: Oxford University Press.

Dow, S.C. (1985) *Macroeconomic Thought: A Methodological Approach*, Oxford: Blackwell.

—— (1990) 'Beyond dualism', *Cambridge Journal of Economics* 14: 143–58.

—— (1993) *Money and the Economic Process*, Aldershot, Hants: Edward Elgar.

Dow, S.C. (forthcoming) 'Knowledge, information and credit creation', in R.J. Rotheim (ed.) *New Keynesian Economics: A Post Keynesian Alternative*, London: Routledge.
—— and Hillard, J. (eds) (1995) *Keynes, Knowledge and Uncertainty*, Aldershot, Hants: Edward Elgar.
Dowd, K. and Lewis, M.K. (eds) (1992) *Current Issues in Financial and Monetary Economics*, London: Macmillan.
Downward, P. (1994) 'A reappraisal of case study evidence on business pricing: neoclassical and Post Keynesian perspectives', *British Review of Economic Issues* 16: 23–44.
Dreze, J. (1975) 'The existence of an exchange equilibrium under price rigidities', *International Economic Review* 16: 301–20.
Dunlop, J.T. (1938) 'The movement of real and money wage rates', *Economic Journal* 48: 413–34.
Dutt, A.K. (1986–7) 'Wage rigidity', *Journal of Post Keynesian Economics* 9: 279–90.
—— (1987) 'Keynes with a perfectly competitive goods market', *Australian Economic Papers* 26: 275–93.
—— (1992) 'Keynes, market forms and competition', in B. Gerrard and J. Hillard (eds) *The Philosophy and Economics of J.M. Keynes*, Aldershot: Edward Elgar.
—— and Amadeo, E.J. (1990a) *Keynes's Third Alternative? The Neo-Ricardian Keynesians and the Post Keynesians*, Aldershot: Edward Elgar.
—— and —— (1990b) 'Keynes's dichotomy and wage-rigidity Keynesianism', in D.E. Moggridge (ed.) *Perspectives in the History of Economic Thought*, Vol. 14, Aldershot, Hants: Edward Elgar.
Dybvig, P.H. and Ross, S.A. (1987) 'Arbitrage', in J. Eatwell, M. Milgate and P. Newman (eds) *The New Palgrave: A Dictionary of Economics*, Vol. 1, London: Macmillan.
Eatwell, J. (1983a) 'The long period theory of employment', *Cambridge Journal of Economics* 7: 269–85.
—— (1983b) 'Theories of value, output and employment', in J. Eatwell and M. Milgate (eds) *Keynes's Economics and the Theory of Value and Distribution*, London: Duckworth.
—— (1987) 'Own-rates of interest', in J. Eatwell, M. Milgate and P. Newman (eds) *The New Palgrave: A Dictionary of Economics*, Vol. 3, London: Macmillan.
—— and Milgate, M. (eds) (1983a) *Keynes' Economics and the Theory of Value and Distribution*, London: Duckworth.
—— and —— (1983b) 'Unemployment and the market mechanism', in J. Eatwell and M. Milgate (eds) *Keynes' Economics and the Theory of Value and Distribution*, London: Duckworth.
——, —— and Newman, P. (eds) (1987) *The New Palgrave: A Dictionary of Economics*, 4 vols, London: Macmillan.
Eckstein, O. (ed.) (1972) *The Econometrics of Price Determination*, Washington, D.C.: Board of Governors of the Federal Reserve System.
Edgeworth, F.Y. (1925) *Selected Papers in Political Economy*, London: Macmillan.
Eichner, A.S. (1976) *The Megacorp and Oligopoly*, Cambridge, Mass.: MIT Press.
Eisner, R. (1953) 'Guaranteed growth of income', *Econometrica* 21: 169–71.
—— (1958) 'On growth models and the neo-classical resurgence', *Economic Journal* 68: 707–21.
—— (1960) 'A distributed lag investment function', *Econometrica* 28: 1–29.
—— (1967) 'A permanent income theory for investment', *American Economic Review* 57: 363–90.
—— (1978) *Factors in Business Investment*, Cambridge, Mass.: Ballinger, for National Bureau of Economic Research.

Eisner, R. (1986) *How Real is the Federal Deficit?*, New York: The Free Press.

—— (1989) *The Total Incomes System of Accounts*, Chicago, Ill.: University of Chicago Press.

—— (1993a) 'US national saving and budget deficits', in G. Epstein and H. Gintis (eds) *The Political Economy of Investment, Saving and Finance: A Global Perspective*, A project of the World Institute for Development and Economic Research (WIDER), Helsinki: United Nations University.

—— (1993b) 'Sense and nonsense about budget deficits', *Harvard Business Review* 71: 99–111.

—— (1994a) 'Real government saving and the future', *Journal of Economic Behavior and Business Organisation* 23: 170–1.

—— (1994b) 'National saving and budget deficits', *Review of Economics and Statistics* 76: 181–6.

—— (1994c) *The Misunderstood Economy: What Counts and How to Count It*, Boston, Mass.: Harvard Business School Press.

—— (1996) 'US national saving and budget deficits', in G.A. Epstein and H. Gintis, *Macroeconomic Policy after the Conservative Era*, Cambridge: Cambridge University Press, 109–42.

—— and Chirinko, R.S. (1983) 'Tax policy and investment in major US macroeconomic econometric models', *Journal of Public Economics* 20: 139–66.

—— and Nadiri, M.I. (1968) 'Investment behavior and neo-classical theory', *Review of Economics and Statistics* 50: 369–82.

—— and —— (1970) 'Neoclassical theory of investment behaviour: a comment', *Review of Economics and Statistics* 52: 216–22.

—— and Pieper, P.J. (1984) 'A new view of the federal debt and budget deficits', *American Economic Review* 74: 11–29.

—— and Strotz, R.H. (1963) 'Determinants of business investment', in Commission on Money and Credits, *Impacts of Monetary Policy*, Englewood Cliffs, N.J.: Prentice Hall.

Ellsberg, D. (1961) 'Risk, ambiguity and the Savage axioms', *Quarterly Journal of Economics* 75: 643–69.

Elton, E.J. and Gruber, M.J. (1991) *Modern Portfolio Theory and Investment Analysis*, New York: John Wiley.

Emmanuel, A. (1972) *Unequal Exchange*, London: New Left Books.

Employment Policy, Cmd 6527 (1944), London: HMSO.

Epstein, G. and Gintis, H. (eds) (1993) *The Political Economy of Investment, Saving and Finance: A Global Perspective*, a project of the World Institute for Development and Economic Research (WIDER), Helsinki: United Nations University.

Erdos, P. (1977) 'A contribution to the criticism of Keynes and Keynesianism', in J. Schwartz (ed.) *The Subtle Anatomy of Capitalism*, Santa Monica, Calif.: Goodyear.

Eshag, E. (1963) *From Marshall to Keynes: An Essay on the Monetary Theory of the Cambridge School*, Oxford: Blackwell.

Fair, R.C. (1994) *Testing Macroeconomic Models*, Cambridge, Mass.: Harvard University Press.

Fama, E.F. (1978) 'The effects of a firm's investment and financing decisions on the welfare of its security holders', *American Economic Review* 68: 272–84.

—— (1980) 'Banking in the theory of finance', *Journal of Monetary Economics* 6: 39–57.

Favereau, O. (1988) 'Probability and uncertainty: "after all, Keynes was right"', *Economica* 10: 133–67.

Fazzari, S.M. (1982) 'The microeconomic dynamics of output and employment', Stanford University, unpublished PhD thesis.

Fazzari, S.M. (1985) 'Keynes, Harrod and the rational expectations revolution', *Journal of Post Keynesian Economics* 8: 66–80.

—— and Caskey, J. (1989) 'Debt commitments and aggregate demand: a critique of the neoclassical synthesis and policy', in W. Semmler (ed.) *Financial Dynamics and Business Cycles: New Perspectives*, Armonk, N.Y.: M.E. Sharpe.

—— and Mott, T. (1986) 'The investment theories of Kalecki and Keynes: an empirical study of firm data, 1970–82', *Journal of Post Keynesian Economics* 9: 141–206.

—— Hubbard, R.G. and Peterson, B.C. (1988) 'Financing constraints and corporate investment', *Brookings Papers on Economic Activity*, April: 141–95.

Feiwel, G.R. (ed.) (1985) *Issues in Contemporary Macroeconomics and Distribution*, London: Macmillan.

Felix, D. (1994) 'The Tobin tax proposal: background, issues and prospects', Working Paper no. 191, St. Louis, Mo.: Washington University.

Fender, J. (1981) *Understanding Keynes: An Analysis of* The General Theory, Brighton: Wheatsheaf.

Ferber, R. (1953) *A Study of Aggregate Consumption Functions*, New York: National Bureau of Economic Research.

—— (1966) 'Research in household behaviour', in *Surveys of Economic Theory*, Vol. III: *Resource Allocation*, London: Macmillan, for American Economic Association and the Royal Economic Society.

—— (1973) 'Consumer economics: a survey', *Journal of Economic Literature* 11: 1303–342.

Fetter, F.W. (1977) 'Lenin, Keynes and inflation', *Economica* 44: 77–80.

Fewings, D. (1979) *Corporate Growth and Common Stock Risk*, Greenwich, Conn.: JAI Press.

Finer, S.E. (1966) *Vilfredo Pareto: Sociological Writings*, London: Pall Mall Press.

Fischer, S. (1977) 'Long-term contracts, rational expectations, and the optimal money supply rule', *Journal of Political Economy* 85: 191–206.

—— (1981) 'Toward an understanding of the costs of inflation: II', in K. Brunner and A. Meltzer (eds) *The Costs and Consequences of Inflation*, Carnegie-Rochester Conference Series on Public Policy, Amsterdam: North-Holland.

Fisher, I. (1896) 'Appreciation and interest', *American Economic Association Publications* 3(11): 331–442.

—— (1907) *The Rate of Interest: Its Nature, Determination and Relation to Economic Phenomena*, New York: Macmillan.

—— (1911) *The Purchasing Power of Money*, New York: Macmillan.

—— (1920) *Stabilizing the Dollar*, New York: Macmillan.

—— (1930) *The Theory of Interest*, reprinted New York: Augustus M. Kelley, 1965.

Fitzgibbons, A. (1988) *Keynes's Vision: A New Political Economy*, Oxford: Clarendon Press.

Flanagan, R., Soskice, D. and Ulman, L (1983) *Unionism, Economic Stabilization and Incomes Policies: European Experience*, Washington, D.C.: Brookings Institution.

Flaschel, P. (1994) 'The stability of models of monetary growth with adaptive expectations or myopic perfect foresight', in W. Semmler (ed.) *Business Cycles: Theory and Empirical Methods*, London: Kluwer.

—— and Franke, R. (1992) 'Instability and price flexibility in generalized Tobin–Sargent models', Discussion Paper no. 259, Bielefeld: Universität Bielefeld.

Flavin, M. (1981) 'The adjustment of consumption to changing expectations about future income', *Journal of Political Economy* 89: 974–1007.

Foley, D. (1986) 'Stabilisation policy in a nonlinear business cycle model', in W. Semmler (ed.) *Competition, Instability and Nonlinear Cycles*, Berlin: Springer-Verlag.

Foley, D. (1987) 'Liquidity–profit rate cycles in a capitalist economy', *Journal of Economic Behaviour and Organisations* 8: 363–76.

—— (1988) 'Endogenous financial-production cycles', in W. Barnett, J. Geweke and K. Shell (eds) *Economic Complexity: Chaos, Sunspots, Bubbles and Nonlinearity*, Cambridge: Cambridge University Press.

Foster, G.P. (1986) 'The endogeneity of money and Keynes's *General Theory*', *Journal of Economic Issues* 20: 953–68.

Foster, J.B. (1986) *The Theory of Monopoly Capitalism: An Elaboration of Marxian Political Economy*, New York: Monthly Review Press.

Frank, M. and Stegnos, T. (1988) 'Some evidence concerning macroeconomic chaos', *Journal of Monetary Economics* 22: 423–38.

—— and —— (1989) 'Measuring the strangeness of gold and silver rates of return', *Review of Economic Studies* 56: 533–67.

Franke, R. and Semmler, W. (1991) 'Debt-financing of firms, stability and cycles in a dynamical macroeconomic growth model', in W. Semmler (ed.) *Financial Dynamics and Business Cycles*, Armonk, N.Y.: M.E. Sharpe.

Frankel, J.A. and Froot, K. (1991) 'Exchange rate forecasting techniques, survey data, and implications for the foreign exchange market', Working Paper in Economics 91–158, Berkely, Calif.: University of California.

Freeden, M. (ed.) (1990) *Reappraising J.A. Hobson*, London: Unwin Hyman.

Freedman, C. (1993) 'In defence of footnotes – a clarification of a misunderstanding of Keynes's definition of money', *Cambridge Journal of Economics* 16: 241–4.

Freimer, M. and Gordon, M.J. (1965) 'Why bankers ration credit', *Quarterly Journal of Economics* 79: 397–416.

Fried, J.S. and Howitt, P. (1983) 'The effects of inflation on real interest rates', *American Economic Review* 73: 968–80.

Friedman, B.M. and Hahn, F.H. (eds) (1990) *Handbook of Monetary Economics*, Amsterdam: North-Holland.

Friedman, M. (1953) 'The methodology of positive economics', in *Essays in Positive Economics*, Chicago, Ill.: University of Chicago Press.

—— (1956) *Studies in the Quantity Theory of Money*, Chicago, Ill.: Chicago University Press.

—— (1957) *A Theory of the Consumption Function*. Princeton, N.J.: Princeton University Press.

—— (1968) 'The role of monetary policy', *American Economic Review* 58: 1–17.

—— (1972) 'Comments on the critics', *Journal of Political Economy* 80: 906–50.

—— (1974) 'Comments on the critics', in R.J. Gordon (ed.) *Milton Friedman's Monetary Framework: A Debate with his Critics*, Chicago: University of Chicago Press.

—— (1992) *Money Mischief*, New York: Harcourt Brace Jovanovich.

—— and Meiselman, D. (1963) 'The relative stability of monetary velocity and the investment multiplier in the United States, 1897–1958', in Commission on Money and Credit, *Stabilization Policies*, Englewood Cliffs, N.J.: Prentice Hall.

Frisch, R. (1933) 'Propogation problems and impulse problems in dynamic economics', in *Essays in Honour of Gustav Cassel*, London: Allen & Unwin.

Fromm, G. (ed.) (1971) *Tax Incentives and Capital Spending*, Washington, D.C.: Brookings Institution.

Frowen, S.F. (ed.) (1993) *Monetary Theory and Monetary Policy: New Tracks for the 1990s*, London: Macmillan.

Frydman, R. and Phelps, E.S. (eds) (1983) *Individual Forecasting and Aggregate Outcomes: 'Rational Expectations' Examined*, New York: Cambridge University Press.

Furness, W.H. (1910) *The Island of Stone Money: Uap and the Carolines*, Philadelphia and London: J.B. Lippincott.

Galbraith, J.K. (1955) *The Great Crash 1929*, London: Hamish Hamilton.

—— (1975) *Money: Whence it Came, Where it Went*, London: André Deutsch.

Gardener, E.P.M. (1988) 'Innovation and new structural frontiers in banking', in P. Arestis (ed.) *Contemporary Issues in Money and Banking*, London: Macmillan.

Garegnani, P. (1978–9) 'Notes on consumption, investment and effective demand', 2 parts, *Cambridge Journal of Economics* 2: 335–53; 3: 63–82.

—— (1983) 'Two routes to effective demand', in J.A. Kregel (ed.) *Distribution, Effective Demand and International Economic Relations*, London: Macmillan.

—— (1988) 'Actual and normal magnitudes: a comment on Asimakopulos', *Political Economy, Studies in the Surplus Approach* 4: 251–8.

Garretsen, H. (1992) *Keynes, Coordination and Beyond: The Development of Macroeconomics and Monetary Theory since 1945*, Aldershot, Hants: Edward Elgar.

Garrison, R. (1985) 'Intertemporal coordination and the invisible hand: an Austrian perspective on the Keynesian vision', *History of Political Economy* 17: 309–19.

—— (1987) 'Full employment and intertemporal coordination: a rejoinder', *History of Political Economy* 19: 335–41

Gaynor, W.B. (1992) 'The transformation of the natural rate of interest into *The General Theory*'s state of long-term expectations', *Cambridge Journal of Economics* 16: 55–68.

Georgescu-Roegen, N. (1960) 'Mathematical proofs of the breakdown of capitalism', *Econometrica* 28: 225–43.

Gerrard, B. (1990) 'On matters methodological in economics', *Journal of Economic Surveys* 4: 197–219.

—— (1992) 'From *A Treatise in Probability* to *The General Theory*: continuity or change in Keynes's thought?', in B. Gerrard and J.V. Hillard (eds) *The Philosophy and Economics of J.M. Keynes*, Aldershot, Hants: Edward Elgar.

—— (1993) 'Book review', *Economic Analysis and Policy* 23: 94–5.

—— (1994a) 'Beyond rational expectations: a constructive interpretation of Keynes's analysis of behaviour under uncertainty', *Economic Journal* 104: 327–37.

—— (1994b) 'Animal spirits', in P. Arestis and M. Sawyer (eds) *The Elgar Companion to Radical Political Economy*, Aldershot, Hants: Edward Elgar.

—— (1995) 'Keynes, the Keynesians and the Classics: a suggested interpretation', *Economic Journal* 105: 445–58.

—— and Hillard, J. (1992) *The Philosophy and Economics of J.M. Keynes*, Aldershot, Hants: Edward Elgar.

Giblin, L.F. (1930) *Australia 1930*, Melbourne: Melbourne University Press.

Giddens, A. (1984) *The Constitution of Society*, Cambridge: Polity Press.

Gilboy, E. (1938) 'The propensity to consume', *Quarterly Journal of Economics* 53: 120–40.

—— (1939) 'The propensity to consume: reply', *Quarterly Journal of Economics* 53: 633–8.

Gillies, D.A. (1988) 'Keynes as a methodologist', *British Journal for the Philosophy of Science* 39: 117–29.

—— (1991) 'Intersubjective probability and confirmation theory', *British Journal for the Philosophy of Science* 42: 513–33.

Goldschlager, L.M. and Baxter, R. (1994) 'The loans standard model of credit money', *Journal of Post Keynesian Economics* 16: 453–77.

Goodhart, C.A.E. (1989) 'Has Moore become too horizontal?', *Journal of Post Keynesian Economics* 12: 29–34.

—— (1990) 'Dennis Robertson and the real business cycle theory: a centenary lecture', London: London School of Economics Finance Markets Group; reprinted in J. Presley (ed.) *Essays on Robertsonian Economics*, Basingstoke, Hants: Macmillan, 1992.

Goodhart, C.A.E. (1993) 'Can we improve the structure of financial systems?', *European Economic Review* 37: 269–91.

Goodwin, R. (1951) 'The non-linear accelerator and the persistence of business cycles', *Econometrica* 19: 1–17.

—— (1990) *Chaotic Economic Dynamics*, Oxford: Oxford University Press.

Gordon, D.M., Weisskopf, T.E. and Bowles, S. (1983) 'Long swings and the non-reproductive cycle', *American Economic Review*, 73(2): Papers and Proceedings 152–7.

Gordon, M.J. (1962) *The Investment, Financing and Valuation of the Corporation*, Homewood, Ill.: Irwin.

—— (1994) *Finance, Investment and Macroeconomics: The Neoclassical and a Post Keynesian Solution*, Aldershot, Hants: Edward Elgar.

—— and Gould, L.I. (1978) 'The cost of equity capital: a reconsideration', *Journal of Finance* 33: 849–61.

—— and Kwan, C.C. (1979) 'Debt maturity, default risk and capital structure', *Journal of Banking and Finance* 3: 313–29.

Gordon, R. (1982) 'Price inertia and policy ineffectiveness in the United States, 1890–1980', *Journal of Political Economy* 90: 1087–1117.

—— (ed.) (1986) *The American Business Cycle*, Chicago, Ill.: Chicago University Press.

—— (1990) 'What is the New-Keynesian economics?', *Journal of Economic Literature* 28: 1115–71.

Gossling, W.F. (1969) 'A note on user cost', *Manchester School of Economic and Social Studies* 37: 259–61.

Grandmont, J. and Laroque, G. (1986) 'Stability of cycles and expectations', *Journal of Economic Theory* 40: 138–51.

Grassberger, P. and Proccaccia, I. (1983) 'Characterisation of strange attractors', *Physical Review Letters* 50: 346–9.

Grassl, W. and Smith, B. (eds) (1986) *Austrian Economics: Historical and Philosophical Background*, New York: New York University Press.

Graziani, A. (1984) 'The debate on Keynes's finance motive', *Economic Notes of Monte dei Paschi di Siena* 1: 5–33.

Greenfield, R. and Yeager, L. (1983) 'A laissez-faire approach to monetary stability', *Journal of Money, Credit and Banking* 15: 302–15.

—— and —— (1986) 'Competitive payments systems: comment', *American Economic Review* 76: 848–9.

—— and —— (1989) 'Can monetary disequilibrium be eliminated?', *Cato Journal* 9: 405–21.

——, Woolsey, W.W. and Yeager, L.B. (1995) 'Is direct convertibility impossible?', *Journal of Money, Credit and Banking* 27: 293–7.

Groenewegen, P. (1995) *A Soaring Eagle: Alfred Marshall, 1842–1924*, Aldershot, Hants: Edward Elgar.

Grossman, S.J. and Stiglitz, J.E. (1980) 'On the impossibility of informationally efficient markets', *American Economic Review* 66: 246–53.

Gunning, P. (1985) 'Causes of unemployment: the Austrian perspective', *History of Political Economy* 17: 223–44.

Gurley, J.G. and Shaw, E.S. (1960) *Money in a Theory of Finance*, Washington, D.C.: Brookings Institution.

Guthrie, W. (1993) 'Book review', *Southern Economic Journal* 59: 546–7.

Haavelmo, T. (1958) 'What can static equilibrium models tell us?', *Economic Enquiry* 12: 27–34.

Haberler, G. (1941) *Prosperity and Depression*, New York: McGraw-Hill.

Hadamard, J. (1898) 'Les surfaces à courbures opposées et leur lignes géodésiques', *Journal de mathématiques pures et appliquées* 4: 27–73.

Hadjimatheou, G. (1987) *Consumer Economics after Keynes: Theory and Evidence of the Consumption Function*, London: Wheatsheaf.

Hagemann, H. and Steiger, O. (eds) (1988) *Keynes's* General Theory *after Fifty Years*, Berlin: Duncker & Humblot.

Hahn, F.H. (1965) 'On some problems of proving the existence of equilibrium in a monetary economy', in F.H. Hahn and F.P.R. Brechling (eds) *The Theory of Interest Rates*, London: Macmillan.

—— (1973) 'On the foundation of monetary theory', in M. Parkin (ed.) *Essays in Modern Economics*, London: Longman; reprinted in F.H. Hahn, *Equilibrium and Macroeconomics*, Oxford: Blackwell, 1984.

—— (1980) 'General equilibrium theory', *Public Interest* 58 (special issue): 123–8.

—— (1982) *Money and Inflation*, Oxford: Blackwell.

—— (1984) *Equilibrium and Macroeconomics*, Oxford: Blackwell.

—— (1985) *Money, Growth and Stability*, Oxford: Blackwell.

—— (1988) 'Liquidity', *Handbook of Monetary Economics*, II, Amsterdam: North Holland Press.

—— (ed.) (1989) *The Economics of Missing Markets, Information, and Games*, Oxford: Clarendon Press.

—— (1991) 'The next hundred years', *Economic Journal* 101: 47–50.

—— (1992a) 'Reflections', *Royal Economic Society Newsletter* no. 77: 5.

—— (1992b) 'Answer to Backhouse: Yes', *Royal Economic Society Newsletter* no. 78: 5.

—— and Brechling, F.P.R. (eds) (1965) *The Theory of the Rate of Interest*, London: Macmillan.

—— and Solow, R.M. (1986) 'Is wage flexibility a good thing?', in W. Beckerman (ed.) *Wage Rigidity and Unemployment*, Baltimore, Md.: Johns Hopkins University Press.

—— and —— (1996) *A Critical Essay on Modern Macroeconomic Theory*, Oxford: Blackwell.

Hahnel, R. and Sherman, H. (1982) 'The rate of profit over the business cycle', *Cambridge Journal of Economics* 6: 185–94.

Hall, R. and Hitch, C. (1939) 'Price theory and business behaviour', *Oxford Economic Papers* 2: 12–45.

Hall, R.E. (1978) 'Stochastic implications of the life-cycle–permanent-income hypothesis: theory and evidence', *Journal of Political Economy* 86: 971–87.

—— (1982) 'Explorations in the gold standard and related policies for stabilizing the dollar', in R.E. Hall (ed.) *Inflation: Cause and Effects*, Chicago, Ill.: University of Chicago Press.

—— (1983) 'Optimal fiduciary monetary systems', *Journal of Monetary Economics* 12: 33.

Hamouda, O.F. and Smithin, J.N. (eds) (1988) *Keynes and Public Policy after Fifty Years*, Vol. 2: *Theories and Method*, Aldershot, Hants: Edward Elgar.

Hansen, A.H. (1938) *Full Recovery or Stagnation?*, New York: W.W. Norton.

—— (1953) *A Guide to Keynes*, New York: McGraw-Hill.

Hansen, L.P. and Sargent, T.J. (1980) 'Estimating and formulating dynamic linear rational expectations models', reprinted in R. Lucas and T. Sargent (eds) *Rational Expectations and Econometric Practice*, London: George Allen & Unwin, 1981.

Hansson, B. (1985) 'Keynes's notion of equilibrium in *The General Theory*', *Journal of Post Keynesian Economics* 7: 332–41.

Harcourt, G.C. (1959) 'Pricing policies and inflation', *Economic Record* 35: 133–6; reprinted in P. Kerr (ed.) *The Social Science Imperialists: Selected Essays*, London: Routledge, 1982.

—— (1965) 'The accountant in a golden age', *Oxford Economic Papers* 17: 66–80; reprinted in C. Sardoni (ed.) *On Political Economists and Modern Political Economy: Selected Essays of G.C. Harcourt*, London: Routledge, 1992.

—— (1972) *Some Cambridge Controversies in the Theory of Capital*, London: Cambridge University Press.

—— (1976) 'The Cambridge controversies: old ways and new horizons – or dead end?', *Oxford Economic Papers* 28: 25–65; reprinted in C. Sardoni (ed.) *On Political Economists and Modern Political Economy: Selected Essays of G.C. Harcourt*, London: Routledge, 1992.

—— (ed.) (1977) *The Microeconomic Foundations of Macroeconomics*, London: Macmillan.

—— (1981) 'Marshall, Sraffa and Keynes: incompatible bedfellows?', *Eastern Economic Journal* 5: 39–50; reprinted in C. Sardoni (ed.) *On Political Economists and Modern Political Economy: Selected Essays of G.C. Harcourt*, London: Routledge, 1992.

—— (1982) *The Social Science Imperialists: Selected Essays*, ed. P. Kerr, London: Routledge.

—— (1983) 'Keynes' college bursar view of investment: comment on Kregel', in J.A. Kregel (ed.) *Distribution, Effective Demand and International Economic Relations*, London: Macmillan.

—— (1984) 'Reflections on the development of economics as a discipline', *History of Political Economy* 16: 489–517; reprinted in C. Sardoni (ed.) *On Political Economists and Modern Political Economy: Selected Essays of G.C. Harcourt*, London: Routledge, 1992.

—— (ed.) (1985) *Keynes and his Contemporaries: The Sixth and Centennial Keynes Seminar held at the University of Kent at Canterbury (1983)*, London: Macmillan.

—— (1987a) 'The legacy of Keynes: theoretical models and unfinished business', in D.A. Reese (ed.) *The Legacy of Keynes: Nobel Conference XXII*, San Francisco, Calif.: Harper & Row, 1–22; reprinted in C. Sardoni (ed.) *On Political Economists and Modern Political Economy: Selected Essays of G.C. Harcourt*, London: Routledge, 1992.

—— (1987b) 'Bastard Keynesianism', in J. Eatwell, M. Milgate and P. Newman (eds) *The New Palgrave: A Dictionary of Economics*, Vol. 1, London: Macmillan.

—— (1990) 'On the contributions of Joan Robinson and Pierro Sraffa to economic theory', in M. Berg (ed.) *Political Economy in the Twentieth Century*, London: Philip Allan; reprinted in C. Sardoni (ed.) *On Political Economists and Modern Political Economy: Selected Essays of G.C. Harcourt*, London: Routledge, 1992.

—— (1992) 'Introduction', in C. Sardoni (ed.) *On Political Economists and Modern Political Economy: Selected Essays of G.C. Harcourt*, London: Routledge.

—— (1993) *Post-Keynesian Essays in Biography: Portraits of Twentieth Century Political Economists*, London: Macmillan.

—— (1994a) 'Kahn and Keynes and the making of *The General Theory*', *Cambridge Journal of Economics* 18: 11–23.

—— (1994b) 'The structure of Tom Asimakopulos's later writings', in G.C. Harcourt, A. Roncaglia and R. Rowley (eds) *Income and Employment in Theory and Practice*, London: Macmillan.

—— and Kenyon, P. (1976) 'Pricing and the investment decision', *Kyklos* 29:

449–77; reprinted in C. Sardoni (ed.) *On Political Economists and Modern Political Economy: Selected Essays of G.C. Harcourt*, London: Routledge, 1992.

Harcourt, G.C. and O'Shaughnessy, T.J. (1985) 'Keynes's unemployment equilibrium: some insights from Joan Robinson, Piero Sraffa and Richard Kahn', in G.C. Harcourt (ed.) *Keynes and his Contemporaries*, London: Macmillan.

—— and Sardoni, C. (1994) 'Keynes's vision: method, analysis and "tactics"', in J.B. Davis (ed.) *The State of Interpretation of Keynes*, Dordrecht: Kluwer.

——, Karmel, P.H. and Wallace, R.H. (1967) *Economic Activity*, Cambridge: Cambridge University Press.

——, Roncaglia, A. and Rowley, R. (eds) (1994) *Income and Employment in Theory and Practice*, London: Macmillan.

Harcourt, W. and Sardoni, C. (trs) (1993) 'Piero Sraffa: "Monetary Inflation in Italy during and after the war"', *Cambridge Journal of Economics*, 17: 7–26.

Harris, S.E. (ed.) (1947) *The New Economics: Keynes's Influence on Theory and Policy*, New York: Alfred A. Knopf.

Harrod, R.F. (1937) 'Mr Keynes and traditional theory', *Econometrica* 5: 74–146.

—— (1939) 'An essay in dynamic theory', *Economic Journal* 49: 14–33.

—— (1947) 'Keynes, the economist', in S.E. Harris (ed.) *The New Economics: Keynes's Influence on Theory and Policy*, New York: Alfred A. Knopf.

—— (1948) *Towards a Dynamic Economics*, London: Macmillan.

—— (1951) *The Life of John Maynard Keynes*, London: Macmillan; 2nd edn, 1963.

—— (1959) 'Domar and dynamic economics', *Economic Journal* 69: 451–64.

—— (1963) *The Life of John Maynard Keynes*, London: Macmillan.

Hart, O. (1982) 'A model of imperfect competition with Keynesian features', *Quarterly Journal of Economics* 97: 109–38.

Hassard, J. (ed.) (1990) *Sociology of Time*, London: Macmillan.

Hawtrey, R.G. (1937a) *Capital and Employment*, London: Longmans.

—— (1937b) 'Alternative theories of the rate of interest', *Economic Journal* 47: 436–43.

—— (1952) *Capital and Employment*, 2nd edn, London: Longmans.

Hayek, F.A. von (1928) 'Das intertemporale Gleichgewichtssystem der Preise und die Bewegung des "Geldwerts"', *Weltwirtschaftliches Archiv* 28: 33–79.

—— (1931) *Prices and Production*, London: Routledge.

—— (1932) 'Money and capital: a reply', *Economic Journal* 42: 237–49.

—— (1941) *The Pure Theory of Capital*, Chicago, Ill.: University of Chicago Press.

—— (1978) *New Studies in Philosophy, Politics, Economics and the History of Ideas*, London: Routledge & Kegan Paul.

Hébert, R.F. (1987) 'Isnard, Achylles Nicolas', in J. Eatwell, M. Milgate and P. Newman (eds) *The New Palgrave: A Dictionary of Economics*, Vol. 2, London: Macmillan.

Heckscher, E.F. (1931) *Merkatilsmen*, 2 vols, Stockholm: P.A. Norstedt; authorized trans. Mendel Shapiro, as *Mercantilism*, London: Allen & Unwin, 1935; rev. edn. New York: Macmillan, London: Allen & Unwin, 1955.

Heering, W. (1991) 'Geld, Liquiditätsprämie und Kapitalgüternachfrage. Studien zur entscheidungstheoretischen Fundierung einer Monetären Theorie der Produktion', in *Studien zur monetären Ökonomie*, Vol. 10, Regensburg: Transfer Verlag.

—— (1993) 'Analytische Aspekte einer Monetären Theorie des Outputs', in H.J. Stadermann and O. Steiger (eds) *Der Stand und die Nächste Zukunft der Geldforschung.* Festschrift für Hajo Riese zum 60. Geburtstag, Volkswirtschaftliche Schrifen Heft 424, Belrin: Dincker & Humblot.

Hegeland, H. (1954) *The Multiplier Theory*; reprinted New York: A.M. Kelley, 1966.

Heller, W. (ed.) (1986) *Essays in Honor of Kenneth Arrow*, Vol. 2, Cambridge: Cambridge University Press.

—— and Starr, R.M. (1979) 'Capital market imperfection, the consumption function and the effectiveness of fiscal policy', *Quarterly Journal of Economics* 93: 455–63.

Hellwig, F.M. (1993) 'The challenge of monetary theory', *European Economic Review* 37: 215–42.

Hempel, C.G. (1939) 'Vagueness and logic', *Philosophy of Science* 6: 178.

—— (1965) *Aspects of Scientific Explanation*, New York: Free Press.

Hendry, D.F. (1983) 'Econometric modelling: the consumption function in retrospect', *Scottish Journal of Political Economy* 30: 193–220.

—— (1994) 'HUS revisited', *Oxford Review of Economic Policy* 10: 86–106.

—— and von Ungern-Sternberg, T. (1980) 'Liquidity and inflation effects on consumers' expenditure', in A.S. Deaton (ed.) *Essays in the Theory and Measurement of Consumers' Behaviour*, Cambridge: Cambridge University Press.

——, Muellbauer, J. and Murphy, A. (1990) 'The econometrics of DHSY', in J.D. Hey and D. Winch (eds) *A Century of Economics: 100 Years of the Royal Economic Society and the* Economic Journal, Oxford: Blackwell.

Hey, J.D. and Winch, D. (eds) (1990) *A Century of Economics: 100 Years of the Royal Economic Society and the* Economic Journal, Oxford: Blackwell.

Heymann, D. and Leijonhuvfud, A. (1995) *High Inflation*, Oxford: Clarendon Press.

Hicks, J.R. (1936) 'Mr Keynes's theory of employment', *Economic Journal* 46: 138–252.

—— (1937) 'Mr Keynes and the "Classics": a suggested interpretation', *Econometrica* 5: 147–59.

—— (1939) *Value and Capital*, Oxford: Oxford University Press.

—— (1950) *A Contribution to the Theory of the Trade Cycle*, Oxford: Oxford University Press.

—— (1965) *Capital and Growth*, Oxford: Oxford University Press.

—— (1967) *Critical Essays in Monetary Theory*, Oxford: Clarendon Press.

—— (1974) *The Crisis in Keynesian Economics*, New York: Basic Books.

—— (1982) *Money, Interest and Wages*, Oxford: Blackwell.

Hill, R. (ed.) (1987) *Keynes, Money and Monetarism: The Eighth Keynes Seminar held at the University of Kent at Canterbury*, London: Macmillan.

Hobsbawm, E. (1994) *The Age of Extremes*, London: Michael Joseph.

Hobson, J.A. (1932a) *From Capitalism to Socialism*, London: Hogarth Press.

—— (1932b) 'The world's economic crisis', *The Nation*, 20 July: 53.

—— (1934) 'Under-production and under-consumption', *New Statesman and Nation*, 24 March: 443.

—— (1938) *Confessions of an Economic Heretic*, with an introd. by M. Freeden, Brighton: Harvester Press, 1976.

Holden, A. (ed.) (1986) *Chaos*, Princeton, N.J.: Princeton University Press.

Holden, G.R. (1938a) 'Mr Keynes' consumption function and the time preference postulate', *Quarterly Journal of Economics* 52: 281–96.

—— (1938b) 'Rejoinder', *Quarterly Journal of Economics* 52: 709–12.

Hoover, K. (1988) *The New Classical Macroeconomics*, Oxford: Blackwell.

Howard, D.H. (1978) 'Personal saving behavior and the rate of inflation', *Review of Economics and Statistics* 60: 547–54.

Howard, M.C. and King, J.E. (1992) *A History of Marxian Economics*, Vol. II: *1929–90*, London: Macmillan.

Howitt, P. (1978) 'The limits to stability of a full-employment equilibrium', *Scandinavian Journal of Economics* 80: 265–82.

Howitt, P. (1986) 'The Keynesian recovery', *Canadian Journal of Economics* 19: 626–41.

—— (1988) 'Wage flexibility and employment', in O.F. Hamouda and J.N. Smithin (eds) *Keynes and Public Policy after Fifty Years*, Vol. 2: *Theories and Method*, Aldershot, Hants: Edward Elgar.

—— (1990a) 'Deterministic outcomes with multiple equilibria', unpublished.

—— (1990b) *The Keynesian Recovery, and Other Essays*, Ann Arbor, Mich.: University of Michigan Press.

—— (1992) 'Interest rate control and nonconvergence to rational expectations', *Journal of Political Economy* 100: 776–800.

—— (1995) 'Cash in advance, microfoundations in retreat', in K. Velupillai (ed.) *Inflation, Institutions and Information*, London: Macmillan.

—— and McAfee, R.P. (1992) 'Animal spirits', *American Economic Review* 82: 493–505.

Howrey, E.P. and Hymans, S.H. (1978) 'The measurement and determination of loanable-funds saving', *Brookings Papers on Economic Activity*, 655–85.

Hudson, H. (1957) 'A model of the trade cycle', *Economic Record* 33: 378–89.

Huth, T. (1989) *Kapital und Gleichgewicht. Zur Kontroverc zwischen neoKlassischer und neoricardianischer Theorie des allgemeinen Gleichgewichts*, Marburg: Metropolis-Verlag.

Hutt, W.H. (1974) *A Rehabilitation of Say's Law*, Athens: Ohio University Press.

Hymans, S.H. (1970) 'Consumption: new data and old puzzles', *Brookings Papers on Economic Activity* 117–26.

Ingham, A. and Ulph, A.M. (eds) (1984) *Demand, Equilibrium and Trade: Essays in Honour of I.F. Pearce*, London: Macmillan.

Ingrao, B. and Israel, G. (1990) *The Invisible Hand: Economic Equilibrium in the History of Science*, Cambridge, Mass.: MIT Press.

Jaffe, W. (1956) *English Translation of Walras'* Elements, London: Allen & Unwin.

Jäggi, C.M. (1986) *Die Makroökonomik von J.M. Keynes*, Berlin: Springer Verlag.

Jarsulic, M. (ed.) (1985) *Money and Macro Policy*, Boston, Mass.: Kluwer-Nijhof.

—— (1989) 'Endogenous money and credit cycles', *Journal of Post Keynesian Economics* 12: 35–48.

—— (1993a) 'A nonlinear model of the pure growth cycle', *Journal of Economic Behaviour and Organisation* 22: 133–51.

—— (1993b) 'Complex dynamics in a Keynesian growth cycle model', *Metroeconomica* 44: 43–64.

Johnson, H.J. (1951) 'Some Cambridge controversies in monetary theory', *Review of Economic Studies* 19: 90–104.

Jöhr, W.A. (1937) '"Verbrauchsneigung" und "Liquiditätsvorliebe". Eine Auseinandersetzung mit J.M. Keynes', *Jahrbücher für Nationalökonomie und Statistik*, 146: 641–62.

Jones, R. and Ostroy, J.M. (1984) 'Flexibility and uncertainty', *Review of Economic Studies* 51: 13–32.

Jonung, L. (ed.) (1991) *The Stockholm School of Economics Revisited*, New York: Cambridge University Press.

Jorgensen, D.W. (1963) 'Capital theory and investment behaviour', *American Economic Review* 53(May): 247–59.

—— and Siebert, C.D. (1968) 'A comparison of alternative theories of investment behaviour', *American Economic Review* 58: 681–712.

—— and Stephenson, J.A. (1967) 'Investment behavior in US manufacturing', *Econometrica* 35: 169–220.

Juster, F.T. and Taylor, L.D. (1975) 'Towards a theory of saving behavior', *American Economic Review* 65(May): 203–9.

Juster, F.T. and Wachtel, P. (1972) 'Inflation and the consumer', *Brookings Papers on Economic Activity* 71–121.

Kahn, R.F. (1929) 'The economics of the short period', Fellowship Dissertation, King's College, Cambridge; 1st English edn, London: Macmillan, 1989.

—— (1931) 'The relation of home investment to unemployment', *Economic Journal* 41: 173–98.

—— (1959) 'Exercises in the analysis of growth', *Oxford Economic Papers* 2: 143–56.

—— (1971) 'Notes on the rate of interest and the growth of firms'; reprinted in R.F. Kahn, *Selected Essays on Employment and Growth*, Cambridge: Cambridge University Press. 1972: 208–32.

—— (1972) *Selected Essays on Employment and Growth*, Cambridge: Cambridge University Press.

—— (1984) *The Making of Keynes's 'General Theory'*, Cambridge: Cambridge University Press.

Kaldor, N. (1939–40) 'Speculation and economic stability', *Review of Economic Studies* 7: 1–27.

—— (1955–6) 'Alternative theories of distribution', *Review of Economic Studies* 23: 83–100.

—— (1957) 'A model of economic growth', *Economic Journal* 67: 591–624.

—— (1960) 'Keynes's theory of own-rates of interest', in N. Kaldor (ed.) *Essays on Economic Stability and Growth*, London: Duckworth.

—— (1966) 'Macroeconomic theory and income distribution', *Review of Economic Studies* 33: 309–19.

—— (1970) 'The new monetarism', *Lloyds Bank Review* April: 1–18.

—— (1980) 'Monetary policy in the United Kingdom', in *Memoranda on Monetary Policy: Evidence to the Treasury and Civil Service Committee*, London: HMSO.

—— (1982) *The Scourge of Monetarism*, Oxford: Oxford University Press.

—— (1983a) 'Keynesian economics after fifty years', in D. Worswick and J. Trevithick (eds) *Keynes and the Modern World*, Cambridge: Cambridge University Press.

—— (1983b) 'Limitations of *The General Theory*', in F. Targetti and A. Thirlwall (eds) *Further Essays on Economic Theory and Policy*, London: Duckworth.

—— and Mirrlees, J. (1962) 'A new model of economic growth', *Review of Economic Studies* 29: 174–92.

Kalecki, M. (1933) 'Essays on the business cycle theory'; reprinted in J. Osiatynski (ed.) *Collected Works of Michal Kalecki*, Vol. I: *Capitalism: Business Cycles and Full Employment*, Oxford: Clarendon Press.

—— (1936) 'Some remarks on Keynes's theory'; reprinted in J. Osiatynski (ed.) *Collected Works of Michal Kalecki*, Vol. I: *Capitalism: Business Cycles and Full Employment*, Oxford: Clarendon Press, 1960.

—— (1937a) 'The principle of increasing risk', *Economica* 4: 440–7; reprinted in J. Osiatynski (ed.) *Collected Works of Michal Kalecki*, Vol. I: *Capitalism: Business Cycles and Full Employment*, Oxford: Clarendon Press.

—— (1937b) 'A theory of the business cycle', *Review of Economic Studies* 4: 77–97.

—— (1938) 'The determinants of the distribution of the national income', *Econometrica* 6: 97–112.

—— (1939a) 'Money and real wages, Part I (theory)'; translated from the Polish in M. Kalecki, *Studies in the Theory of Business Cycles, 1933–39*, Oxford: Blackwell, 1969.

—— (1939b) *Essays in the Theory of Economic Fluctuations*, London: George Allen & Unwin.

—— (1943) *Studies in Economic Fluctuations*, London: George Allen & Unwin.

Kalecki, M. (1944) 'Professor Pigou on "The Classical Stationary State": a comment', *Economic Journal* 54: 131–2.
—— (1954) *Theory of Economic Dynamics*, New York: Rinehart.
—— (1968) 'Trend and business cycle reconsidered', *Economic Journal* 78: 263–76.
—— (1969) *Studies in the Theory of Business Cycles, 1933–1939*, Oxford: Blackwell.
—— (1971a) 'Class struggle and distribution of national income', *Kyklos* 24: 1–9; reprinted in M. Kalecki, *Selected Essays on the Dynamics of The Capitalist Economy (1933–70)*, Cambridge: Cambridge University Press.
—— (1971b) *Selected Essays on the Dynamics of the Capitalist Economy (1933–70)*, Cambridge: Cambridge University Press.
—— (1990) 'Three systems', in J. Osiatynski (ed.) *Collected Works of Michal Kalecki*, Vol. I, Oxford: Clarendon Press.
—— (1991) *Collected Works of Michal Kalecki*, Vol. II: *Capitalism: Economic Dynamics*, ed. J. Osiatynski Oxford: Clarendon Press.
Kelsey, D. and Quiggin, J. (1992) 'Theories of choice under ignorance and uncertainty', *Journal of Economic Surveys* 6: 133–53.
Keynes, J.M. (1904) 'Ethics in relation to conduct', unpublished mimeo, King's College Library, Cambridge University.
—— (1919) *The Economic Consequences of the Peace*, London: Macmillan; *C.W.* II.
—— (1921) *A Treatise on Probability*, London: Macmillan; *C.W.* VIII.
—— (1922) 'The forward market in foreign exchanges', *Manchester Guardian Commercial* (Reconstruction Supplement) 20 April: 11–18.
—— (1923) *A Tract on Monetary Reform*, London: Macmillan; *C.W.* IV.
—— (1925) *La Riforma Monetaria*, Italian trans. P. Sraffa, Milan: Fratelli Treves Editori.
—— (1926) *The End of Laissez-faire*, Edinburgh: Neill; *C.W.* IX: 272–94.
—— (1928) *Britain's Industrial Future: Being the Report of the Liberal Industrial Inquiry*, Ernest Benn.
—— (1930a) *A Treatise on Money: The Pure Theory of Money*, London: Macmillan; *C.W.* V.
—— (1930b) *A Treatise on Money: The Applied Theory of Money*, London: Macmillan; *C.W.* VI.
—— (1933a) 'A monetary theory of production' in *Der Stand und die nächste Zukunft der Konjunkturforschung: Festschrift für Arthur Spiethoff*; reprinted in *C.W.* XIII: 408–11.
—— (1933b) *The Means to Prosperity*, London: Macmillan; *C.W.* IX: 335–66.
—— (1933c) Letter to Marcus Wallenburg, Keynes Papers, King's College, Cambridge, File L/33.
—— (1933d) *Essays and Sketches in Biography*, London: Macmillan.
—— (1934) 'Poverty in plenty: is the economic system self-adjusting?', *The Listener*, 21 Nov: 850–1; *C.W.* XIII: 485–92.
—— (1936) *The General Theory of Employment, Interest and Money*, London: Macmillan; *C.W.* VII.
—— (1937a) 'Alternative theories of the rate of interest', *Economic Journal* 47: 241–52; *C.W.* XIV: 201–15.
—— (1937b) 'The "ex ante" theory of the rate of interest', *Economic Journal* 47: 663–9; *C.W.* XIV: 215–26.
—— (1937c) 'The General Theory of Employment', *Quarterly Journal of Economics* 51: 209–23; *C.W.* XIV: 109–23.
—— (1937d) 'The theory of the rate of interest', in A.D. Gayer (ed.) *The Lessons of Monetary Experience: Essays in Honour of Irving Fisher*, reprinted in *Readings in the Theory of Income Distribution*, Philadelphia, Pa: Blakiston, 1946; *C.W.* XIV: 101–8.

Keynes, J.M. (1938a) 'Mr Keynes' consumption function: reply', *Quarterly Journal of Economics* 52: 708–9; *C.W.* XIV: 268–70.

—— (1938b) 'Mr Keynes' consumption function: further note', *Quarterly Journal of Economics* 53: 160; *C.W.* XIV: 268–70.

—— (1938c) 'D.H. Robertson on Mr Keynes and "finance": a comment', *Economic Journal* 48: 318–22; *C.W.* XIV: 229–33.

—— (1939a) 'Mr Keynes on the distribution of incomes and "propensity to consume": a reply', *Review of Economic Statistics* 21: 129; *C.W.* XIV: 270–1.

—— (1939b) 'Professor Tinberg's method', *Economic Journal* 49: 558–68; *C.W.* XIV: 306–18.

—— (1939c) 'Relative movements of real wages and output', *Economic Journal* 49: 34–51; *C.W.* VII: 394–412.

—— (1939d) 'The process of capital formation', *Economic Journal* 49: 569–74; *C.W.* XIV: 278–85.

—— (1940a) '[On a method of statistical business-cycle research] Comment', *Economic Journal* 50: 154–6; *C.W.* XIV: 318–20.

—— (1940b) *How to Pay for the War*, London: Macmillan; *C.W.* IX: 367–439.

—— (1971–89) *The Collected Writings of John Maynard Keynes* [*C.W.*] ed. D.E. Moggridge, Vols I–XXX, London: Macmillan.

—— (1971) *A Tract on Monetary Reform*, in *The Collected Writings of John Maynard Keynes* Vol. IV, London: Macmillan.

—— (1972a) *Essays in Persuasion*, in *The Collected Writings of John Maynard Keynes*, Vol. IX, London: Macmillan.

—— (1972b) *Essays in Biography*, in *The Collected Writings of John Maynard Keynes*, Vol. X, London: Macmillan.

—— (1973a) *The General Theory of Employment, Interest and Money* in *The Collected Writings of John Maynard Keynes*, Vol. VII, London: Macmillan.

—— (1973b) *A Treatise on Probability*, in *The Collected Writings of John Maynard Keynes*, Vol. VIII, London: Macmillan.

—— (1973c) *The General Theory and After. Part I: Preparation*, in *The Collected Writings of John Maynard Keynes*, Vol. XIII, London: Macmillan.

—— (1973d) *The General Theory and After. Part II: Defence and Development*, in *The Collected Writings of John Maynard Keynes*, Vol. XIV, London: Macmillan.

—— (1979) *The General Theory and After: A Supplement*, in *The Collected Writings of John Maynard Keynes*, Vol. XXIX, London: Macmillan.

—— (1980) *Activities, 1940–46*, in *The Collected Writings of John Maynard Keynes*, Vol. XXVII, London: Macmillan.

—— (1981) *Activities, 1929–31: Rethinking Employment and Unemployment Policies*, in *The Collected Writings of John Maynard Keynes*, Vol. XX, London: Macmillan.

—— (1983a) *Economic Articles and Correspondence – Academic*, in *The Collected Writings of John Maynard Keynes*, Vol. XI, London: Macmillan.

—— (1983b) *Economic Articles and Correspondence: Investment and Editorial*, in *The Collected Writings of John Maynard Keynes*, Vol. XII, London: Macmillan.

—— and Henderson, H. (1929) 'Can Lloyd George do it? ', in *The Collected Writings of John Maynard Keynes*, Vol. IX, London: Macmillan.

King, J.E. (1981) 'Perish commerce! Free trade and underconsumption in early British radical economics', *Australian Economic Papers* 20: 235–57.

—— (1983) 'Utopian or scientific? A reconsideration of the Ricardian socialists', *History of Political Economy* 15: 345–73.

—— (1994a) 'J.A. Hobson's macroeconomics: the last ten years (1930–40)', in J. Pheby (ed.) *Free-thought in Economics and Politics*, London: Macmillan.

King, J.E. (1994b) 'Aggregate supply and demand analysis since Keynes: a partial history', *Journal of Post Keynesian Economics* 17: 3–31.

—— (ed.) (1996) *An Alternative Macroeconomic Theory: The Kaleckian Model and Post-Keynesian Economics*, Boston, Mass.: Kluwer.

—— and Regan, P. (1988) 'Recent trends in labour's share', in Y.S. Brenner, J.P.G. Reinders and A.H.G.M. Spithoven (eds) *The Theory of Income and Wealth Distribution*, Brighton: Wheatsheaf.

Kirman, A. (1989) 'The intrinsic limits of modern economic theory: the emperor has no clothes', *Economic Journal* 99 (suppl.): 126–39.

—— (1992) 'Whom or what does the representative individual represent? ', *Journal of Economic Perspectives* 6: 117–36.

Kiyotaki, N. and Blanchard, O. (1987) 'Monopolistic competition and the effects of aggregate demand', *American Economic Review* 77: 647–67.

Klamer, A. (1984) *The New Classical Macroeconomics: Conversations with the New Classical Economists and their Opponents*, Brighton: Harvester.

Klausinger, H. (1991) *Theorien der Geldwirtschaft. Von Hayek und Keynes zu neueren Ansätzen*, Volkswirtschaftliche Schriften Heft 407, Berlin: Duncker & Humblot.

—— (1993) 'Keynes und die Postkeynsianer zur Produktionselastizität des Geldes – Eine Kritik', in H.J. Stadermann and O. Steiger (eds) *Der Stand und die nächste Zukunft der Geldforschung. Festschrift für Hajo Riese zum 60. Geburtstag*, Volkswirtschaftliche Schriften Heft 424, Berlin: Duncker & Humblot.

Kleiman, E. (1989) 'The cost of inflation', Working Paper, Jerusalem: Hebrew University.

Klein, L. (1947) *The Keynesian Revolution*, New York: Macmillan.

—— (1950) *Economic Fluctuations in the United States, 1921–41*, New York: John Wiley.

—— and Goldberger, A. (1955) *An Econometric Model of the United States, 1929–52*, Amsterdam: North-Holland.

Knight, F.H. (1921) *Risk, Uncertainty and Profit*, Chicago, Ill.: Chicago University Press.

—— (1937) 'Underemployment and Mr Keynes' revolution in economic theory', *Canadian Journal of Economics and Political Science* 3: 100–23.

Kopke, R. (1985) 'The determinants of investment spending', *New England Economic Review* July/Aug: 19–35.

Koslowski, P. (ed.) (1985) *Economics and Philosophy*, Tubingen: Siebeck.

Kregel, J.A. (1976) 'Economic methodology in the face of uncertainty: the modelling methods of Keynes and the Post-Keynesians', *Economic Journal* 86: 209–25.

—— (1980) 'Markets and institutions as features of a capitalist production system', *Journal of Post Keynesian Economics* 3: 32–48.

—— (1981) 'On distinguishing between alternative methods of approach to the demand for output as a whole', *Australian Economic Papers* 20: 63–71.

—— (1982) 'Money, expectations and relative prices in Keynes' monetary equilibrium', *Economie appliquée* 35: 449–65.

—— (1983a) 'Effective demand: origins and development of the notion', in J.A. Kregel (ed.) *Distribution, Effective Demand and International Economic Relations*, London: Macmillan.

—— (1983b) 'The microfoundations of the "Generalisation of *The General Theory*" and "bastard Keynesianism": Keynes' theory of employment in the long and short period', *Cambridge Journal of Economics* 7: 343–61.

—— (1983c) 'Budget deficits, stabilisation policy and liquidity preference: Keynes's post-war policy proposals', in F. Vicarelli (ed.) *Keynes's Relevance Today*, London: Macmillan.

Kregel, J.A. (ed.) (1983d) *Distribution, Effective Demand and International Economic Relations*, London: Macmillan.

—— (1984) 'Expectations and rationality within a capitalist framework', in E.J. Nell (ed.) *Free Market Conservatism: A Critique of Theory and Practice*, London: Allen & Unwin.

—— (1984–5) 'Constraints on output and employment', *Journal of Post Keynesian Economics* 7: 139–52

—— (1985a) 'Hamlet without the prince: Cambridge macroeconomics without money', *American Economic Review* 75: 133–9.

—— (1985b) 'Harrod and Keynes: increasing returns, the theory of employment and dynamic economics', in G.C. Harcourt (ed.) *Keynes and his Contemporaries: The Sixth and Centennial Keynes Seminar held at the University of Kent at Canterbury, 1983*, London: Macmillan, 66–88.

—— (1988) 'The multiplier and liquidity preference: two sides of the theory of demand', in A. Barrère (ed.) *The Foundations of Keynesian Analysis*, proceedings of a conference held at the University of Paris I-Panthéon-Sorbonne, London: Macmillan.

—— (1994) 'Causality and real time in Asimakopulos's approach to saving and investment in the theory of distribution', in G.C. Harcourt, A. Roncaglia and R. Rowley (eds) *Income and Employment in Theory and Practice*, London: Macmillan.

Kreps, D.M. (1992) 'Static choice and the presence of unforeseen contingencies', in P. Dasgupta, O. Hart and E. Maskin (eds) *Economic Analysis of Markets and Games: Essays in Honour of Frank Hahn*, Cambridge, Mass.: MIT Press.

Kriesler, P. (1987) *Kalecki's Microanalysis: The Development of Kalecki's Analysis of Pricing and Distribution*, Cambridge: Cambridge University Press.

—— (1988a) 'Keynes and Kalecki on method', School of Economics Discussion Paper 88/14, University of New South Wales.

—— (1988b) 'The methods of Keynes and Kalecki', in H. Hagemann and O. Steiger (eds) *Keynes's General Theory after Fifty Years*, Berlin: Duncker & Humblot.

—— (1996) 'Microfoundations: a Kaleckian perspective', in J. King (ed.) *An Alternative Macroeconomic Theory: The Kaleckian Model and Post-Keynesian Economics*, Boston, Mass.: Kluwer.

—— and McFarlane, B. (1993) 'Michael Kalecki on capitalism', *Cambridge Journal of Economics* 17: 215–35.

Kuenne, R.E. (1977) 'Money, capital and interest in intertemporal general equilibrium theory', *Economie appliquée* 30: 617–38.

Kuhn, T.S. (1953) *The Copernican Revolution*, New York: Vintage Books.

—— (1962) *The Structure of Scientific Revolutions*, Chicago, Ill.: University of Chicago Press.

Kurihara, K.K. (ed.) (1954) *Post Keynesian Economics*, London: Allen & Unwin.

—— (1956) *Introduction to Keynesian Dynamics*, London: Allen & Unwin.

Kurz, H.D. (1983) 'What is wrong with Keynesian economics? Comment on Bharadwaj', in J.A. Kregel (ed.) *Distribution, Effective Demand and International Economic Relations*, London: Macmillan.

—— (1995a) 'Über "natürliche" und "künstliche" Störungen des allgemeinen wirtschaftlichen Gleichgewichts: Friedrich August Hayeks monetäre Überinvestitionstheorie in *Preise und Produktion*', in *Vademecum zu einem Klassiker der Marktkoordination*, Düsseldorf: Verlag Wirtschaft und Finanzen.

—— (1995b) 'The Hayek–Keynes–Sraffa controversy reconsidered', University of Graz, unpublished MS.

Kydland, F.E. and Prescott, E.C. (1977) 'Rules rather than discretion: the inconsistency of optimal plans', *Journal of Political Economy* 85: 473–91.

Kydland, F.E. and Prescott, E.C. (1982) 'Time to build and aggregate fluctuations', *Econometrica* 50: 1345–69.

Lachmann, L.M. (1986a) *The Market as an Economic Process*, Oxford: Blackwell.

—— (1986b) 'Austrian theory under fire: the Hayek–Sraffa duel in retrospect', in W. Grassl and B. Smith (eds) *Austrian Economics: Historical and Philosophical Background*, New York: New York University Press.

Laidler, D. (1983) 'Misconceptions about the real bills doctrine and the quantity theory: a comment on Sargent and Wallace', Research Report no. 8314 University of Western Ontario, Dept of Economics.

—— (1990a) 'Alfred Marshall and the development of monetary economics', in J.K. Whitaker (ed.) *Centenary Essays on Alfred Marshall*, Cambridge: Cambridge University Press, 44–78.

—— (1990b) *Taking Money Seriously*, London: Philip Allan.

Lange, O. (1938a) 'The rate of interest and the optimal propensity to consume', *Economica* NS 5: 12–32.

—— (1938b) 'Saving in process analysis', *Quarterly Journal of Economics* 53: 620–2.

—— (1942) 'Say's Law: a restatement and criticism', in O. Lange, F. McIntyre and T.O. Yntema (eds) *Studies iin Mathematical Economics and Econometrics, in Memory of Henry Schultz*, Chicago, Ill.: University of Chicago Press.

——, McIntyre, F. and Yntema, T. (eds) (1942) *Studies in Mathematical Economics and Econometrics, in Memory of Henry Schultz*, Chicago, Ill.: University of Chicago Press.

Latsis, S.J. (ed.) (1976) *Method and Appraisal in Economics*, Cambridge: Cambridge University Press.

Lavoie, M. (1985) 'Credit and money: the dynamic circuit, overdraft economics, and Post-Keynesian economics', in M. Jarsulic (ed.) *Money and Macro Policy*, Boston, Mass.: Kluwer-Nijhof.

—— (1992) *Foundations of Post Keynesian Economic Analysis*, Aldershot, Hants: Edward Elgar.

Lawlor, M.S. (1994a) 'The historical context of Keynes's views on financial markets', in N. de Marchi and M. Morgan (eds) *Higgling: Transactors and Their Markets in the History of Economics* (History of Political Economy series, Vol. 26, suppl.), Durham, N.C.: Duke University Press, 184–225.

—— (1994b) 'The own-rates framework as an interpretation on *The General Theory*: a suggestion for complicaitng the Keynesian theory of money', in J.B. Davis (ed.) *The State of Interpretation of Keynes*, Dordrecht: Kluwer.

—— and Horn, B.L. (1992) 'Notes on the Sraffa–Hayek exchange', *Review of Political Economy* 4: 317–40.

——, Darity, W., Jr and Horn, B.L. (1987) 'Was Keynes a chapter two Keynesian?', *Journal of Post Keynesian Economics* 10: 516–28.

Lawson, T. (1985a) 'Uncertainty and economic analysis', *Economic Journal* 95: 909–27.

—— (1985b) 'Keynes, prediction and econometrics', in T. Lawson and H. Peseran (eds) *Keynes' Economics: Methodological Issues*, London: Croom Helm.

—— (1987) 'The relative/absolute nature of knowledge and economic analysis', *Economic Journal* 97: 951–70.

—— (1989) 'Realism and instrumentalism in the development of econometrics', *Oxford Economic Papers* 41: 236–58.

—— (1990a) 'Review of *Keynes: Philosophy, Economics and Politics*', *Economic Journal* 100: 987–9.

—— (1990b) 'Realism, closed systems and expectations', International School of Economic Research workshop paper: presented at Certosa di Pontignani, Siena, Italy.

Lawson, T. (1991) 'Keynes and the analysis of rational behaviour', in R.M. O'Donnell (ed.) *Keynes as the Philosopher Economist*, London: Macmillan.
—— (1993) 'Keynes and convention', *Review of Social Economy* 51: 174–200.
—— (1994a) 'Why are so many economists opposed to methodology?', *Journal of Economic Methodology* 1: 105–33.
—— (1994b) 'A realist theory for economics', in R. Backhouse (ed.) *New Perspectives on Economic Methodology*, London: Routledge.
—— (1994c) 'Critical realism and the analysis of choice, explanation and change', *Advances in Austrian Economics* 1: 3–30.
—— (1995a) 'A realist perspective on contemporary economic theory', *Journal of Economic Issues* 29: 1.
—— (1995b) 'Economics and expectations', in S.C. Dow and J. Hillard (eds) *Keynes, Knowledge and Uncertainty*, Cheltenham, Glos.: Edward Elgar.
—— and Pesaran, H. (eds) (1985) *Keynes' Economics: Methodological Issues*, London: Croom Helm.
Le Corbeiller, Ph. (1933) 'Les systèmes autoentretenus et les oscillations de relaxation', *Econometrica* 1: 28–32.
Leijonhufvud, A. (1968) *On Keynesian Economics and the Economics of Keynes: A Study in Monetary Theory*, London: Oxford University Press.
—— (1969) *Keynes and the Classics: Two Lectures on Keynes' Contribution to Economic Theory*, London: Institute of Economic Affairs.
—— (1981) *Information and Coordination: Essays in Macroeconomic Theory*, New York: Oxford University Press.
—— (1983a) 'Book review', *Journal of Economic Literature* 21: 107–10.
—— (1983b) 'Keynesianism, monetarism and rational expectations: some reflections and conjectures', in R. Frydman and E.S. Phelps (eds) *Individual Forecasting and Aggregate Outcomes*, Cambridge: Cambridge University Press.
—— (1983c) 'What would Keynes have thought of rational expectations?', in D. Worswick and J. Trevithick (eds) *Keynes and the Real World*, Cambridge: Cambridge University Press.
—— (1983d) 'Constitutional constraints on the monetary powers of government', *Economia della Scelte Pubbliche* 2: 87–100.
—— (1984) 'Hicks on time and money', *Oxford Economic Papers* 36 (suppl.): 26–46.
—— (1985) 'Ideology and analysis in macroeconomics', in P. Koslowski (ed.) *Economics and Philosophy*, Tubingen: Siebeck.
—— (1992) 'Keynesian economics: past confusions, future prospects', in A. Vercelli and N. Dimitri (eds) *Macroeconomics: A Survey of Research Strategies*, London: Oxford University Press.
Lekachman, R. (ed.) (1964a) *Keynes'* General Theory: *Reports of Three Decades*, London: Macmillan.
—— (1964b) *Keynes and the Classics*, Boston, Mass.: D.C. Heath.
Leontief, W. (1954) 'Mathematics in economics', *Bulletin of the American Mathematical Society* 60: 215–33.
Lerner, A.P. (1934) 'The concept of monopoly and the measurement of monopoly power', *Review of Economic Studies*, 1(2): 157–75.
—— (1943) 'User cost and prime user cost', *American Economic Review*, 33: 131–2.
—— (1944) *The Economics of Control: Principles of Welfare Economics*, New York: Augustus M. Kelley.
—— (1952) 'The essential properties of interest and money', *Quarterly Journal of Economics* 66: 172–93.
—— (1962) 'Own-rates and the liquidity trap', *Economic Journal* 72: 449–52.

LeRoy, S.F. (1994) 'On policy regimes', in K.D. Hoover (ed.) *Macroeconometrics: Developments, Tensions, Prospects*, Dordrecht: Kluwer.

—— and Singell, Larry D. Jr (1987) 'Knight on risk and uncertainty', *Journal of Political Economy* 95(2): 394–406.

Lévy, P. (1991) 'Keynes aprés Sraffa et Hayek: les origins trompeuses du chapitre 17 de la *Théorie Général.* Commentaire sur Gary Mongiovi', *Economie appliquée* 44: 153–9.

Lewis, D. (1969) *Convention: A Philosophical Study*, Cambridge, Mass.: Harvard University Press.

Lewis, M.K. (1990) 'Liquidity', in John Creedy (ed.) *Foundations of Economic Thought*, Oxford: Blackwell.

Lewis, W.A. (1949) *Overhead Costs*, London: Unwin University Books.

Lim, S.K. (1990) 'Keynes's long-period theory of employment: the evidence against', *The Manchester School of Economic and Social Studies* 58: 66–73.

Lindahl, E. (1929) 'Prisbildningspoblements uppläggning från kapitalteoretisk synpunkt', *Economisk tidskrift* 31: 31–81.

—— (1939) *Studies in the Theory of Money and Capital*, New York: Rhinehart.

Lipsey, R.G. (1972) 'The foundations of the theory of national income: an analysis of some fundamental errors', in M. Peston and B.A. Corry (eds) *Essays in Honour of Lord Robbins*, London: Weidenfeld & Nicolson.

—— and Stone Tice, H. (eds) (1989) *The Measurement of Saving, Investment and Wealth*, Chicago, Ill.: University of Chicago Press.

Lipton, P. (1991) *Inference to the Best Explanation*, London: Routledge.

Littleboy, B. (1990) *On Interpreting Keynes: A Study in Reconciliation*, London: Routledge.

—— (1994) 'The foregotten common sense of Keynes', *WISER* (Whitlam Institute for Social and Economic Research) 2: 29–32.

Long, J. and Ploesser, C. (1983) 'Real business cycles', *Journal of Political Economy* 91: 39–69.

Lorenz, H.W. (1987) 'Strange attractors in a multisectoral business cycle model', *Journal of Economic Behaviour and Organisation* 8: 397–411.

Lubell, H. (1947) 'Effects of redistribution of income on consumers' expenditure', *American Economic Review* 37: 157–70.

Lucas, R.E., Jr (1972a) 'Econometric testing of the natural rate hypothesis', in O. Eckstein (ed.) *The Econometrics of Price Determination*, Washington, D.C.: Board of Governors of the Federal Reserve System, 50–9.

—— (1972b) 'Expectations and the neutrality of money', *Journal of Economic Theory* 4: 103–24.

—— (1973) 'Some international evidence on output–inflation tradeoffs', *American Economic Review* 63: 326–34.

—— (1975) 'An equilibrium model of the business cycle', *Journal of Political Economy* 83: 1113–34.

—— (1976) 'Econometric policy evaluation: a critique', in K. Brunner and A.H. Meltzer (eds) *The Phillips Curve and Labour Markets*, Carnegie-Rochester Conference Series on Public Policy, Vol. 1, Amsterdam: North-Holland, 19–46.

—— (1977) 'Understanding business cycles', in Karl Brunner and Alan H. Meltzer (eds) *Stabilization of the Domestic and International Economy*, Carnegie-Rochester Conference Series on Public Policy, Vol. 5, Amsterdam: North-Holland; reprinted in Robert E. Lucas, Jr, *Studies in Business-Cycle Theory*, Oxford: Blackwell, 1981: 215–39.

—— (1980) 'Two illustrations of the quantity theory of money', *American Economic Review* 80: 1005–14.

Lucas, R.E., Jr (1981) *Studies in Business Cycle Theory*, Oxford: Blackwell.
—— (1986) 'Adaptive behaviour and economic theory', *Journal of Business* 59: 401–26.
—— (1987) *Models of Business Cycles*, Oxford: Blackwell.
—— (1988a) 'Money demand in the United States: a quantitative review', *Carnegie-Rochester Series on Public Policy* 29: 137–68.
—— (1988b) 'On the mechanics of economic development', *Journal of Monetary Economics* 22 (July): 3–42.
—— (1990) 'Liquidity and interest rates', *Journal of Monetary Theory* 50: 237–64.
—— and Sargent, T.J., Jr (1979) 'After Keynesian macroeconomics', *Federal Reserve Bank of Minneapolis Review* Spring: 1–16; reprinted in R.E. Lucas, Jr and T.J. Sargent, Jr, *Rational Expectations and Econometric Practice*, London: George Allen & Unwin, 1981: 295–319.
—— and —— (1981) *Rational Expectations and Econometric Practice*, London: George Allen & Unwin.
Lutz, F. and Hague, D.C. (eds) (1961) *The Theory of Capital*, London: Macmillan.
—— and Lutz, V. (1951) *The Theory of Investment of the Firm*, New York: Greenwood Press.
Luxemburg, R. (1963) *The Accumulation of Capital*, London: Routledge & Kegan Paul.
McCallum, B.T. (1985) 'Bank deregulation, accounting systems of exchange and the unit of account: a critical review', *Carnegie-Rochester Conference Series on Public Policy* 23: 13–46.
—— (1986) 'Some real issues concerning interest rate pegging, price level determinacy, and the real bills doctrine', *Journal of Monetary Economics* 17: 135–60.
McCloskey, D.N. (1983) 'The rhetoric of economics', *Journal of Economic Literature* 21: 481–517.
—— (1986) *The Rhetoric of Economics*, Brighton, Wheatsheaf.
McCloughry, R. (1982) 'Neutrality and monetary equilibrium: a note on Desai', in M. Baranzini (ed.) *Advances in Economic Theory*, Oxford: Blackwell.
McCracken, H.L. (1933) *Value Theory and Business Cycles*, New York: Falcon Press.
MacDougall, G.D.A. (1936) 'The definition of prime and supplementary costs', *Economic Journal* 46: 4430–61.
McKinnon, R.I. (1990) 'Interest rate volatility and exchange rate risk: new rules for a common monetary standard', *Contemporary Policy Studies* 8: 10.
Maclachlan, F.C. (1993a) *Keynes's General Theory of Interest: A Reconsideration*, London: Routledge.
—— (1993b) 'Austrian and Post Keynesian interest rate theory: some unexpected parallels', in G. Mongiovi and C. Rühl (eds) *Macroeconomic Theory: Diversity and Convergence*, Aldershot, Hants: Edward Elgar.
Madan, D.P. and Owings, J.C. (1988) 'Decision theory with complex uncertainties', *Synthese* 75: 25–44.
Maddison, A. (1964) *Economic Growth in the West*, London: Allen & Unwin, for the 20th Century Fund.
—— (1982) *Phases of Capitalist Development*, Oxford: Oxford University Press.
Majewski, R. (1988) 'The Hayek challenge and the origins of Chapter 17 of Keynes' *General Theory*', in H. Hagemann and O. Steiger (eds) *Keynes'* General Theory *nach fünfzig Jahren*, Volkswirtschaftliche Schriften Heft 384, Berlin: Duncker & Humblot.
Mäki, U. (1992) 'On the method of isolation in economics', in C. Dilworth (ed.) *Intelligibility in Science*, special issue of *Poznan Studies in the Philosophy of the Sciences* 2: 319–54.

Makowski, L. (1989) 'Keynes' liquidity preference theory: a suggested reinterpretation', in F.H. Hahn (ed.) *The Economics of Missing Markets, Information, and Games*, Oxford: Clarendon Press.
Malinvaud, E. (1972) *Lectures on Microeconomic Theory*, Amsterdam: North Holland.
—— (1977) *The Theory of Unemployment Reconsidered*, Oxford: Blackwell.
—— (1980) *Profitability and Unemployment*, Cambridge: Cambridge University Press.
Mankiw, N. (1985) 'Small menu costs and large business cycles: a macroeconomic model of monopoly', *Quarterly Journal of Economics* 100: 529–39.
—— (1988) 'Imperfect competition and the Keynesian cross', *Economics Letters*, 26: 7–13.
—— (1989) 'Real business cycles: a New Keynesian perspective', *Journal of Economic Perspectives* 3: 79–90.
—— (1992) 'The reincarnation of Keynesian economics', *European Economic Review* 36: 559–65.
—— and Romer, D. (eds) (1991) *New Keynesian Economics*, Cambridge, Mass.: MIT Press.
—— and Shapiro, M.D. (1985) 'Trends, random walks and tests of the permanent income hypothesis', *Journal of Monetary Economics*, 16 (June): 165–74.
Marcuzzo, M. (1994) 'R.F. Kahn and imperfect competition', *Cambridge Journal of Economics* 18: 25–39.
——, Pasinetti, L. and Roneaglia, A. (eds) (1996) *The Economics of Joan Robinson*, London: Routledge.
Marglin, S. and Schor, J. (1990) *The Golden Age of Capitalism*, Oxford: Oxford University Press.
Margolit, A. (1976) 'Vagueness in vogue', *Synthese* 33: 211–21.
Marris, R. (1964) *The Economic Theory of Managerial Capitalism*, London: Macmillan.
—— (1972) 'Why economics needs a theory of the firm', special issue of *Economic Journal* 82: 321–52.
—— (1991) *Reconstructing Keynesian Economics with Imperfect Competition*, Aldershot, Hants: Edward Elgar.
—— (1992) 'R.F. Kahn's fellowship dissertation: a missing link in the history of economic thought', *Economic Journal* 102: 1235–43.
—— and Mueller, D. (1980) 'The corporation and competition', *Journal of Economic Literature* 18: 32–63.
—— and Wood, A. (eds) (1971) *The Corporate Economy*, Cambridge, Mass.: Harvard University Press.
Marschak, J. (1939) 'Personal and collective budget functions', *Review of Economic Statistics* 21: 69–74.
—— (1942) 'Economic interdependence and statistical analysis', in O. Lange (ed.) *Studies in Mathematical Economics and Econometrics*, Chicago, Ill.: University of Chicago Press.
Marshall, A. (1871) 'Money', reprinted in J. Whittaker (ed.) *The Early Writings of Alfred Marshall*, 2 vols, London: Macmillan, 1975.
—— (1889) *The Pure Theory of Foreign Trade: Domestic Values*, reprinted London: London School of Economics, 1930.
—— (1895) *Principles of Economics*, 3rd edn, London: Macmillan.
—— (1920) *Principles of Economics*, 8th edn, London: Macmillan.
Marx, K. (1904) *A Contribution to the Critique of Political Economy*, trans from 2nd German edn by N.I. Stone, Chicago, Ill.: Charles H. Kerr.
—— (1954) *Capital*, Book I, Moscow: Progress Publishers.
—— (1956) *Capital*, Book II, Moscow: Progress Publishers.
—— (1959) *Capital*, Book III, Moscow: Progress Publishers.

Marx, K. (1968) *Theories of Surplus-Value*, Part II, Moscow: Progress Publishers.
Matthews, R.C.O. (1991) 'Animal spirits', in J.G.T. Meeks (ed.) *Thoughtful Economic Man: Essays on Rationality, Moral Rules and Benevolence*, Cambridge: Cambridge University Press.
Meade, J.E. (1975) 'The Keynesian revolution', in M. Keynes (ed.) *Essays on John Maynard Keynes*, Cambridge: Cambridge University Press.
—— (1993) 'The relation of Mr Meade's relation to Kahn's multiplier', *Economic Journal* 103: 664–5.
Meek, R.L. (1967) 'The place of Keynes in the history of economic thought', in *Economics, Ideology and Other Essays*, London: Chapman & Hall.
Meeks, J.G.T. (1991a) 'Keynes on the rationality of decision procedures under uncertainty: the investment decision', in J.G.T. Meeks (ed.) *Thoughtful Economic Man: Essays on Rationality, Moral Rules and Benevolence*, Cambridge: Cambridge University Press.
——— (ed.) (1991b) *Thoughtful Economic Man: Essays on Rationality, Moral Rules and Benevolence*, Cambridge: Cambridge University Press.
Meltzer, A.H. (1988) *Keynes's Monetary Theory: A Different Interpretation*, Cambridge: Cambridge University Press.
Merton, R.C. (ed.) (1972) *The Collected Scientific Papers of Paul A. Samuelson*, Vol. 3, Cambridge, Mass., and London: MIT Press.
—— and Samuelson, P.A. (1974) 'Fallacy of the log-normal approximation to optimal portfolio decision making over many periods', *Journal of Financial Economies* 1: 67–94.
Metzler, L.A. (1943) 'Effects of income distribution', *Review of Economic Statistics* 25: 49–57.
—— *et al.* (1948) *Income, Employment and Public Policy: Essays in Honor of Alvin H. Hansen*, New York: W.W. Norton.
Meyer, J.R. and Kuh, E. (1957) *The Investment Decision: An Empirical Study*, Cambridge, Mass.: Harvard University Press.
Milgate, M. (1977) 'Keynes on the "Classical" theory of interest', *Cambridge Journal of Economics* 1: 307–15.
—— (1979) 'On the origin of the notion of "intertemporal equilibrium"', *Economica* 46: 1–10.
—— (1982) *Capital and Employment: A Study of Keynes's Economics*, London: Academic Press.
—— (1987) 'Keynes' *General Theory*', in J. Eatwell, M. Milgate and P. Newman (eds) *The New Palgrave: A Dictionary of Economics*, Vol. 2, London: Macmillan.
Millar, J.R. (1972) 'The social accounting basis of Keynes' aggregate supply functions', *Economic Journal* 82: 600–11.
Miller, E.M. (1984) 'Bank deposits in the monetary theory of Keynes', *Journal of Money, Credit and Banking* 16: 242–6.
Miller, M.H. (1988) 'The Modigliani–Miller propositions after thirty years', *Journal of Economic Perspectives* 2: 99–120.
—— and Modigliani, F. (1961) 'Dividend policy, growth, and the valuation of shares', *Journal of Business* 34: 411–33.
—— and —— (1966) 'Some estimates of the cost of capital to the electric utility industry, 1954–57', *American Economic Review* 56: 333–91.
Miller, M. and Williamson, J. (1987) *Targets and Indicators: A Blueprint for the International Coordination of Economic Policy*, Washington, D.C.: Institute for International Economics.
Mini, P. V. (1991) *Keynes: Bloomsbury and the General Theory*, New York: St Martins Press.

Minsky, H. (1959) 'A linear model of cyclical growth', *Review of Economics and Statistics* 41: 133–45.
—— (1975) *John Maynard Keynes*, New York: Columbia University Press.
—— (1976) *John Maynard Keynes*, London: Macmillan.
—— (1978) 'The financial instability hypothesis: a restatement', *Thames Papers in Political Economy*, Autumn.
—— (1982) *Inflation, Recession and Economic Policy*, Brighton: Wheatsheaf.
Mishkin, F.S. (1976) 'Illiquidity, consumer durable expenditure and monetary policy', *American Economic Review* 66: 642–54.
—— (1977) 'What depressed the consumer? The household balance sheet and the 1973–75 recession', *Brookings Papers in Economic Activity* 1: 123–64.
—— (1982) 'Does anticipated monetary policy matter? An econometric investigation', *Journal of Political Economy* 82: 22–51.
Mittermaier, K.H.M. (1986) 'The hand behind the invisible hand: dogmatic and pragmatic views on free markets and the state of economic theory', unpublished PhD dissertation, University of Witwatersrand.
Modigliani, F. (1944) 'Liquidity preference and the theory of interest and money', *Econometrica* 12: 45–88.
—— (1949) 'Fluctuations in the saving ratio: a problem in economic forecasting', *Social Research* 14: 413–20.
—— (1975) 'The life cycle hypothesis of saving twenty years later', in M. Parkin and A.R. Nobay (eds) *Contemporary Issues in Economics*, Manchester: Manchester University Press.
—— (1977) 'The monetarist controversy; or, should we forsake stabilisation policies?', *American Economic Review* 67: 1–19.
—— and Ando, A. (1957) 'Tests of the life-cycle hypothesis of savings', *Bulletin of the Oxford Institute of Economics and Statistics* 19: 99–124.
—— and Brumberg, R. (1954) 'Utility analysis and the consumption function: an interpretation of cross-section data', in K.K. Kurihara (ed.) *Post-Keynesian Economics*, London: Allen & Unwin.
—— and Miller, M.H. (1958) 'The cost of capital, corporation finance, and the theory of investment', *American Economic Review* 48: 261–97.
—— and —— (1963) 'Corporate income taxes and the cost of capital: a correction', *American Economic Review* 53: 433–43.
—— and Steindel, C. (1977) 'Is a tax rebate an effective tool for stabilization policy?', *Brookings Papers on Economic Activity* 1: 175–203.
Moggridge, D.E. (ed.) (1990) *Perspectives in the History of Economic Thought: Keynes, Macroeconomics and Method*, Aldershot, Hants: Edward Elgar.
—— (1992) *Maynard Keynes: An Economists's Biography*, London: Routledge.
Mongiovi, G. (1990) 'Keynes, Sraffa and Hayek: on the origins of Chapter 17 of the *General Theory*', *Economie appliquée* 43: 131–56.
—— and Rühl, C. (eds) (1993) *Keynes'* General Theory *nach fünfzig Jahren*, Berlin: Duncker & Humblot.
Moore, Basil J. (1988) *Horizontalists and Verticalists: The Macroeconomics of Credit Money*, Cambridge: Cambridge University Press.
—— (1994) 'The demise of the Keynesian multiplier: a reply to Cottrell', *Journal of Post Keynesian Economics* 17: 121–34.
Moore, G.E. (1903) *Principia Ethica*, Cambridge: Cambridge University Press.
Moore, G.E. and Zarnowitz, V. (1986) 'Major changes in cyclical behaviour', in R. Gordon (ed.) *The American Business Cycle*, Chicago: Chicago University Press.

Morgan, D.P. (1991) 'New evidence firms are financially constrained', *Federal Reserve Bank of Kansas City Quarterly Review* 76: 5.

Morishima, M. (1992) *Capital and Credit: A New Formulation of General Equilibrium Theory*, Cambridge: Cambridge University Press.

Mott, T. (1985–6) 'Towards a Post-Keynesian formulation of liquidity preference', *Journal of Post Keynesian Economics* 8: 222–32.

Muellbauer, J. (1983) 'Surprises in the consumption function', *Economic Journal Conference Papers* 93: 34–49.

—— (1994) 'The assessment: consumer expenditure', *Oxford Review of Economic Policy* 10: 1–41.

Mullineux, A., Dickinson, D. and Peng, W. (1993) *Business Cycles*, Oxford: Blackwell.

Mummery, A.F. and Hobson, J.A. (1889) *The Physiology of Industry*, reprinted New York: Augustus M. Kelley, 1989.

Muth, J.F. (1960) 'Optimal properties of exponentially weighted forecasts', *Journal of the American Statistical Association* 29: 299–306.

—— (1961) 'Rational expectations and the theory of price movements', *Econometrica* 29: 315–35.

Nagatani, H. and Crowley, K. (eds) (1977) *The Collected Scientific Papers of Paul A. Samuelson*, Vol. 4, Cambridge, Mass., and London: MIT Press.

Nash, J.F. (1951) 'Non-cooperative games', *Annals of Mathematics* 54: 286–95.

Neftci, S. (1984) 'Are economic time series asymmetric over the business cycle?', *Journal of Political Economy* 92: 307–28.

Negishi, T. (1979) *Microeconomic Foundations of Keynesian Macroeconomics*, Amsterdam: North-Holland.

Nell, E.J. (1983) 'Keynes after Sraffa: the essential properties of Keynes' theory of interest and money: comment on Kregel', in J.A. Kregel (ed.) *Distribution, Effective Demand and International Economic Relations*, London: Macmillan.

—— (ed.) (1984) *Free Market Conservatism: A Critique of Theory and Practice*, London: Allen & Unwin.

Neumann, J. von and Morgenstern, O. (1944) *Theory of Games and Economic Behaviour*, Princeton, N.J.: Princeton University Press.

Ng, Y.K. (1980) 'Macroeconomics with non-perfect competition', *Economic Journal* 90: 479–92.

—— (1986) *Mesoeconomics*, Brighton: Wheatsheaf.

Nickell, S. and Layard, R. (1985) 'The causes of British unemployment', *National Institute Economic Review* 111: 62–85.

Niehans, J. (1978) *The Theory of Money*, Baltimore, Md: Johns Hopkins University Press.

Nikaido, H. (1975) *Monopolistic Competition and Effective Demand*, Princeton, N.J.: Princeton University Press.

O'Donnell, R. (1982) *Keynes: Philosophy and Economics: An Approach to Rationality and Uncertainty*, PhD dissertation, University of Cambridge.

—— (1989) *Keynes: Philosophy, Economics and Politics. The Philosophical Foundations of Keynes's Thought and their Influence on his Economics and Politics*, London: Macmillan.

—— (1990a) 'An overview of probability, expectations, uncertainty and rationality in Keynes's conceptual framework', *Review of Political Economy* 2: 253–66.

—— (1990b) 'Keynes on mathematics: philosophical foundations and economic applications', *Cambridge Journal of Economics* 14: 29–47.

—— (1990c) 'Continuity in Keynes's conception of probability', in D.E. Moggridge (ed.) *Perpsectives in the History of Economic Thought: Keynes, Macroeconomics and Method*, Aldershot, Hants: Edward Elgar.

O'Donnell, R. (1991a) 'Keynes on probability, expectations and uncertainty', in R.M. O'Donnell (ed.) *Keynes as Philosopher-Economist*, London: Macmillan.
—— (1991b) 'Keynes on mathematical economics and econometrics: some new evidence', Research Paper 344, School of Economic and Financial Studies, Macquarie University.
—— (ed.) (1991c) *Keynes as Philosopher-Economist*, London: Macmillan.
—— (1992) 'The unwritten books and papers of J.M. Keynes', *History of Political Economy* 24: 767–817.
—— (1995a) 'A supplementary edition of J.M. Keynes's writings: rationale, nature and significance', *History of Economics Review* 23, Winter: 61–73.
—— (1995b) 'The genesis of the only diagram in *The General Theory*', Macquarie Economics Research Papers, Macquarie University.
OECD (1978) *Towards Full Employment and Price Stability*, Paris: OECD.
—— (1994a) *Economic Outlook*, Paris: OECD.
—— (1994b) *Labour Force Statistics*, Paris: OECD.
Ohlin, B.G. (1937a) 'Some notes on the Stockholm theory of savings and instrument, Parts I and II', *Economic Journal* 47: 53–69, 221–40.
—— (1937b) 'Alternative theories of the rate of interest', *Economic Journal* 47: 423–7.
Okun, A. (1975) 'Inflation: its mechanics and welfare costs', *Brooking Papers on Economic Activity* 2: 366–73.
—— (1981) *Prices and Quantities*, Princeton, N.J.: Princeton University Press.
Ono, Y. (1994) *Money, Interest and Stagnation*, Oxford: Clarendon Press.
Orcutt, G.H. and Roy, A.D. (1949) *A Bibliography of the Consumption Function*, Cambridge: Department of Applied Economics, mimeo.
Orléan, A. (1989) 'Mimetic contagion and speculative bubbles', *Theory and Decision* 27: 63–92.
Orzech, Z.B. and Groll, S. (1991) 'Otto Bauer's business cycle theory: an integration of Marxian elements', *History of Political Economy* 23: 745–63.
O'Shaughnessy, T.J. (1983) 'On a long-period interpretation of the principle of effective demand', unpublished PhD dissertation, King's College, Cambridge.
—— (1984) 'Short-period and long-period interpretations of the principle of effective demand', Jesus College, Cambridge, mimeo.
Osiatynski, J. (ed.) (1990) *Collected Works of Michael Kalecki.* Vol. 1: *Capitalism: Business Cycles and Full Employment*, Oxford: Clarendon Press.
Panico, C. (1985) 'Market forces and the relationship between the rate of interest and the rate of profits', *Contributions to Political Economy* 4: 37–60.
—— (1987) 'The evolution of Keynes's thought on the rate of interest', *Contributions to Political Economy* 6: 53–61.
—— (1988a) *Interest and Profit in the Theories of Value and Distribution*, London: Macmillan.
—— (1988b) 'Sraffa on money and banking', *Cambridge Journal of Economics* 12: 7–28.
Park, M.S. (1994) 'Long period', in P. Arestis and M. Sawyer (eds) *The Elgar Companion to Radical Political Economy*, Aldershot, Hants: Edward Elgar.
Parkin, M. (1990) *Economics*, Reading, Mass.: Addison-Wesley.
—— and Nobay, A.R. (eds) (1975) *Contemporary Issues in Economics*, Manchester: Manchester University Press.
Pasinetti, L.L. (1962) 'Rate of profit and income distribution in relation to economic growth', *Review of Economic Studies* 29: 267–79.
—— (ed.) (1974) *Growth and Income Distribution: Essays in Economic Theory*, Cambridge: Cambridge University Press.

Pasinetti, L.L. (ed.) (1980) *Essays in the Theory of Joint Production*, New York: Columbia UniversityPress.
—— (1981) *Structural Change and Economic Growth: A Theoretical Essay on the Dynamics of the Wealth of Nations*, Cambridge: Cambridge University Press.
—— (1986) 'Theory of value: a source of alternative paradigms in economic analysis', in M. Baranzini and R. Scazzieri (eds) *Foundations of Economics: Structure of Inquiry and Economic Theory*, Oxford: Blackwell.
—— (1993) '*Structural Economic Dynamics*: *A Theory of the Economic Consequnce of Human Learning*, Cambridge: Cambridge University Press.
—— *et al.* (1966) 'Symposium on "Paradoxes in Capital Theory"', *Quarterly Journal of Economics* 80: 503–83.
Patinkin, D. (1965) *Money, Interest and Prices: An Integration of Monetary and Value Theory*, New York: Harper & Row.
—— (1972a) 'Interest', in D. Patinkin (ed.) *Studies in Monetary Economics*, New York: Harper & Row.
—— (ed.) (1972b) *Studies in Monetary Economics*, New York: Harper & Row.
—— (1976a) *Keynes's Monetary Thought: A Study of its Development*, Durham, N.C.: Duke University Press.
—— (1976b) 'Keynes and econometrics: on the interaction between the macroeconomics revolutions of the interwar period', *Econometrica* 44: 1091–1123.
—— (1978) 'Keynes' misquotation of Mill', *Economic Journal* 88: 341–2.
—— (1982) *Anticipations of* The General Theory*?*, Chicago, Ill.: University of Chicago Press.
—— (1989) *Money, Interest and Prices*, abridged 2nd edn, Cambridge, Mass.: MIT Press.
—— (1990) 'On different interpretations of *The General Theory*', *Journal of Monetary Economics* 26: 205–43.
Peston, M. and Corry, B.A. (eds) (1972) *Essays in Honour of Lord Robbins*, London: Weidenfeld & Nicolson.
Pheby, J. (ed.) (1989) *New Directions in Post Keynesian Economics*, Aldershot, Hants: Edward Elgar.
—— (ed.) (1994) *Free-thought in Economics and Politics*, London: Macmillan.
Phelps, E.S. (1967) 'Phillips curves, expectations of inflation and optimal unemployment over time', *Economica* 34: 254–81.
—— and Taylor, J.B. (1977) 'Stabilizing powers of monetary policy under rational expectations', *Journal of Political Economy* 85: 163–90.
Phillips, A.W.H. (1958) 'The relationship between unemployment and the rate of change of money wages in the United Kingdom, 1861–1957', *Economica* NS 25: 283–99.
Phillips, H. (1924) 'The theory of social economy, by Gustav Cassel', *Economic Journal* 34: 235–41.
Pigou, A.G. (1936) 'Mr J.M. Keynes' *General Theory of Employment, Interest and Money*', *Economica* 3: 115–32.
Pindyck, R.S. (1991) 'Irreversibility, uncertainty and investment', *Journal of Economic Literature* 29: 1110–48.
Pissarides, C.A. (1978) 'Liquidity considerations in the theory of consumption', *Quarterly Journal of Economics* 92: 279–96.
Pollin, R. (1991) 'Two theories of money supply endogeneity: some empirical evidence', *Journal of Post Keynesian Economics* 13: 366–96.
Ponsard, C. (1985) 'Fuzzy sets in economics: foundation of soft decision theory', *Management Decision Support Systems* 83.
Prendennis (1992) *Observer*, 21 June.

Presley, J. (ed.) (1992) *Essays in Robertsonian Economics*, Basingstoke, Hants: Macmillan.

Purvis, D. (1971) 'Introducing useful money into a growth model', *Canadian Journal of Economics* 4 (August): 374–81.

Quine, W. (1960) *Word and Object*, Cambridge, Mass.: MIT Press.

—— (1981) *Theories and Things*, Cambridge, Mass.: Belknap Press.

—— (1987) *Quiddities*, Cambridge, Mass.: Belknap Press.

Ramsey, F.P. (1922) 'The Douglas proposals', *Cambridge Magazine* 10: 74–6.

—— (1926) 'Truth and probability', reprinted in R.B. Braithwaite (ed.) *The Foundations of Mathematics*, London: Routledge & Kegan Paul, 1931.

—— (1978) *Foundations of Mathematics*, London: Routledge & Kegan Paul.

Ramsey, J., Sayers, C. and Rothman, P. (1990) 'The statistical properties of dimension calculations using small data sets: some economic applications', *International Economic Review* 31: 991–1020.

Rappaport, P. (1992) 'Meade's general theory model: stability and the role of expectations', *Journal of Money, Credit and Banking* 24: 356–69.

Reddaway, W.B. (1936) '*The General Theory of Employment, Interest and Money* [review]', *Economic Record*, 12: 28–36.

—— (1966) 'Rising prices for ever?', *Lloyds Bank Review*, July.

—— (1983) 'How useful are Keynesian ideas in the 1980s?', *Proceedings of the British Academy* 69: 263–78.

—— (1992) *Portfolio Management for Not-for-profit Institutions*, London: Institute for Public Policy Research.

Reese, D.A. (ed.) (1987) *The Legacy of Keynes*, Nobel Conference XXII, New York: Harper & Row.

Remenyi, J. (1991) *Where Credit is Due*, London: IT Publications.

Riach, P.A. (1995) 'Wage-employment determination in a Post Keynesian world', in P. Arestis and M. Marshall (eds) *The Political Economy of Full Employment: Conservatism, Corporatism, and Institutional Change*, Aldershot, Hants.: Edward Elgar.

Ricardo, D. (1951–73) *Works and Correspondence of David Ricardo*, ed. P. Sraffa and M. Dobb, 11 vols, Cambridge: Cambridge University Press.

Ricci, G. and Vellupillai, K. (eds) (1988) *Growth Cycles and Multisectoral Economics: The Goodwin Tradition*, New York: Springer-Verlag.

Richardson, D.R. (1986) 'Asimakopulos on Kalecki and Keynes on finance, saving and investment', *Cambridge Journal of Economics* 10: 191–9.

Richardson, G.B. (1990) *Information and Investment: A Study of the Working of the Competitive Economy*, 2nd edn, New York: Oxford University Press.

Richter, R. (1990) *Geldtheorie*, 2nd rev. edn, Berlin: Heidelberg.

Roberts, D.L. (1978) 'Patinkin, Keynes, and aggregate supply and demand analysis', *History of Political Economy* 10: 549–76.

Robertson, D.H. (1926) *Banking Policy and the Price Level*, New York: Augustus M. Kelley.

—— (1936) 'Some notes on Mr Keynes' *General Theory of Employment*', *Quarterly Journal of Economics*, 51: 168–91.

—— (1937) 'Alternative theories of the rate of interest', *Economic Journal* 47: 428–36.

—— (1938a) 'Mr Keynes and "finance"', *Economic Journal* 48: 314–18.

—— (1938b) 'Mr Keynes and "finance"', *Economic Journal* 48: 555–6.

—— (1957–9) *Lectures on Economic Principles*, 3 vols, London: Staples Press.

—— (1966) *Essays on Money and Interest*, London: Fontana.

Robinson, J. (1933) *The Economics of Imperfect Competition*, London: Macmillan.

Robinson, J. (1936) 'The long period theory of employment', *Zeitschrift für Nationalökonomie* 7: 74–93.

—— (1937) *Essays in the Theory of Employment*, London: Macmillan.

—— (1941) 'Marx on unemployment', *Economic Journal* 51: 234–48.

—— (1942) *An Essay on Marxian Economics*, London: Macmillan.

—— (1951–79) *Collected Economic Papers* [*C.E.P.*], Oxford: Blackwell; general index published 1980.

—— (1951) 'Marx and Keynes', in *Collected Economic Papers*, Vol. I, Oxford: Blackwell.

—— (1952) 'The model of an expanding economy', reprinted in *C.E.P.* II, 2nd edn: 74–8.

—— (1953) *On Re-reading Marx*, reprinted in *C.E.P.* IV: 247–68.

—— (1956) *The Accumulation of Capital*, London: Macmillan.

—— (1960) *Collected Economic Papers*, Vol. II, Oxford: Blackwell.

—— (1961a) 'Prelude to a critique', *Oxford Economic Papers* 13: 53–8.

—— (1961b) 'Own-rates of interest', *Economic Journal* 71: 596–600.

—— (1962a) '*The General Theory* after twenty-five years', *Economic Journal* 72: 690–2.

—— (1962b) *Essays in the Theory of Economic Growth*, London: Macmillan.

—— (1964) 'Kalecki and Keynes', in *C.E.P.* III, 2nd edn: 92–9.

—— (1965) 'Piero Sraffa and the rate of exploitation', *New Left Review*, 31: 128–34; reprinted as 'A reconsideration of the theory of value', *C.E.P.* III: 173–81.

—— (1971a) *Economic Heresies*, New York: Basic Books.

—— (1971b) 'The second crisis in economic theory', in *C.E.P.* IV.

—— (ed.) (1973) *After Keynes*, Oxford: Blackwell.

—— (1974) 'History versus equilibrium', *Thames Papers in Political Economy*, reprinted in *C.E.P.* V: 48–58.

—— (1975a) *Collected Economic Papers*, Vol. II, 2nd edn, Oxford: Blackwell.

—— (1975b) *Collected Economic Papers*, Vol. III, 2nd edn, Oxford: Blackwell.

—— (1977) 'Michal Kalecki', reprinted in C.E.P. V: 184–96.

—— (1979) *Collected Economic Papers*, Vol. V, Oxford: Blackwell.

—— (1980) 'Time in economic theory', *Kyklos* 33: 219–29.

—— (1980, 1985) 'Spring cleaning', mimeo; reprinted as 'The theory of normal prices and the reconstruction of economic theory', in G.R. Feiwel (ed.) *Issues in Contemporary Macroeconomics and Distribution*, London: Macmillan, 1985: 157–65.

—— (1982) 'Shedding darkness', *Cambridge Journal of Economics* 6: 295–6.

Rogers, C. (1989) *Money, Interest and Capital*, Cambridge: Cambridge University Press.

—— (1990) 'The nature and role of equilibrium in Keynes's *General Theory*: an alternative perspective', University of Adelaide, unpublished mimeo.

—— (1993) 'Review of Cardim de Carvalho (Ferdinand J.), *Mr Keynes and The Post Keynesians*', *Economic Journal* 103: 1317.

—— (1994) 'Michael Lawlor's own-rates interpretation of *The General Theory*', in J.B. Davis (ed.) *The State of Interpretation of Keynes*, Dordrecht: Kluwer.

—— (1995) 'Post Keynesian monetary theory and the principle of effective demand', in A.J. Cohen and J. Smithin (eds) *Money, Financial Institutions and Macroeconomics*, Dordrecht: Kluwer.

Rosch, E. (1975) 'Family resemblances: studies in the internal structure of categories', *Cognitive Psychology* 7: 573–605.

Rose, H. (1967) 'On the nonlinear theory of the employment cycle', *Review of Economic Studies* 34: 153–73.

Ross, S.A. (1988) 'Comment on the Modigliani–Miller propositions', *Journal of Economic Perspectives* 2: 127–33.

Ross, S.A., Westerfield, R., Jordan, B. and Roberts, G. (eds) (1993) *Fundamentals of Corporate Finance*, Burr Ridge, Ill.: Irwin.

Rostow, W.W. (1980) *Why the Rich Get Richer and the Poor Slow Down*, Austin, Tex.: University of Texas.

Rotheim, R.J. (1981) 'Keynes's monetary theory of value (1933)', *Journal of Post Keynesian Economics* 3: 568–85.

—— (1993) 'On the indeterminacy of Keynes's monetary theory of value', *Review of Political Economy* 5: 197–216.

—— (ed.) (forthcoming) *New Keynesian Economics: A Post Keynesian Alternative*, London: Routledge.

Rousseas, S. (1986) *Post-Keynesian Monetary Economics*, Basingstoke, Hants: Macmillan.

Rowthorn, R. (1981) 'Demand, real wages and economic growth', *Thames Papers in Political Economy*, Spring.

Ruelle, D. (1991) *Chance and Chaos*, Princeton, N.J.: Princeton University Press.

Runde, J. (1990) 'Keynesian uncertainty and the weight of arguments', *Economics and Philosophy* 6: 275–92.

—— (1991) 'Keynesian uncertainty and the stability of beliefs', *Review of Political Economy* 3: 125–45.

—— (1993) 'Shackle on probability', in S. Boehm, S. Frowen and J. Pheby (eds) *Economics as the Art of Thought: Essays in Memory of G.L.S. Shackle*, London: Routledge.

—— (1994a) 'Keynesian uncertainty and liquidity preference', *Cambridge Journal of Economics* 18: 129–44.

—— (1994b) 'Keynes after Ramsey: in defence of *A Treatise on Probability*', *Studies in the History and Philosophy of Science* 25: 97–121.

—— (1994c) 'The Keynesian probability-relation: in search of a substitute', in J. Davis (ed.) *The State of Interpretation of Keynes*, Dordrecht: Kluwer.

—— (1995) 'Chances and choices: some notes on probability and belief in economic analysis', *Monist*: 78: 97–121.

Russell, B. (1923) 'Vagueness', *Australasian Journal of Psychology and Philosophy* 1: 90.

Rymes, T.K. (1980) 'Sraffa and Keynes on interest rates', *Carleton Economic Papers*, Ottawa: Carleton University.

—— (1987) 'Keynes's lectures, 1932–35: notes of students', *Carleton Economics Papers*, Ottawa: Carleton University.

—— (1989a) *Keynes's Lectures, 1932–35: Notes of a Representative Student*, London: Macmillan; Ann Arbor, Mich.: University of Michigan Press.

—— (1989b) 'The theory and the measurement of the nominal output of banks, sectoral rates of saving and wealth in the national accounts', in R.G. Lipsey and H. Stone Tice (eds) *The Measurement of Saving, Investment and Wealth*, Chicago, Ill.: University of Chicago Press.

—— (1989c) 'Keynes's lectures, 1932–35: notes of students', *Carleton Economics Papers*, Ottawa: Carleton University.

—— (1994) 'Keynes and knowledge', in G. Brennan and A.M.C. Waterman (eds) *Economics and Religion: Are They Distinct?*, Boston, Mass.: Kluwer.

Salter, W.E.G. (1960) *Productivity and Technical Change*, Cambridge: Cambridge University Press; 2nd edn, with Addendum by W.B. Reddaway, 1966.

Samuels, W.J. and Biddle, J. (eds) (1993) *Research in the History of Economic Thought and Methodology*, Greenwich, Conn., and London: JAI Press.

Samuelson, P.A. (1939) 'A synthesis of the principle of acceleration and the multiplier', *Journal of Political Economy* 47: 786–97.

—— (1946) '*The General Theory*, *Econometrica* 14: 187–200.

Samuelson, P.A. (1947a) '*The General Theory* (3)', in S.E. Harris (ed.) *The New Economics: Keynes's Influence on Theory and Policy*, New York: Alfred A. Knopf.
—— (1947b) *Foundations of Economic Analysis*, Cambridge, Mass.: Harvard University Press.
—— (1948) *Economics: An Introductory Analysis*, New York: McGraw-Hill.
—— (1966–86) *The Collected Scientific Papers of Paul A. Samuelson*, 5 vols, ed. J.E. Stiglitz (Vols 1 and 2, 1966), R.C. Merton (Vol. 3, 1972), H. Nagatani and K. Crowley (Vol. 4, 1977), K.Crowley (Vol. 5, 1986), Cambridge, Mass. and London: MIT Press.
—— (1983) 'Sympathy from the other Cambridge', *Economist* 287: 21–5.
Sardoni, C. (1981) 'Multisectoral models of balanced growth and the Marxian schemes of expanded reproduction', *Australian Economic Papers* 20: 383–97.
—— (1987) *Marx and Keynes on Economic Recession*, Brighton, Sussex: Wheatsheaf.
—— (1989) 'Some aspects of Kalecki's theory of profits: its relationship to Marx's schemes of reproduction', in M. Sebastiani (ed.) *Kalecki's Relevance Today*, London: Macmillan, 206–19.
—— (1991) 'Marx and Keynes: the critique of Say's Law', in G.A. Caravale (ed.) *Marx and Modern Economic Analysis*, Aldershot, Hants: Edward Elgar, 219–39.
—— (1992a) 'Market forms and effective demand: Keynesian results with perfect competition', *Review of Political Economy* 4: 377–95.
—— (ed.) (1992b) *On Political Economists and Modern Political Economy: Selected Essays of G.C. Harcourt*, London: Routledge.
Sargent, T.J. (1978) 'Estimation of dynamic labour demand schedules under rational expectations', in R.E. Lucas, Jr and T.J. Sargent, Jr, *Rational Expectations and Econometric Practice*, London: George Allen & Unwin, 429–500.
—— (1979) *Macroeconomic Theory*, Orlando, Fla.: Academic Press.
—— (1981) 'Interpreting economic time series', *Journal of Political Economy* 89: 213–48.
—— (1984) 'Autoreggressions, expectations and policy advice', *American Economic Review* 74: 408–15.
—— (1993) *Bounded Rationality in Macroeconomics*, Oxford: Clarendon Press.
—— and Wallace, N. (1973) 'Rational expectations and the dynamics of hyperinflation', *International Economic Review* 14: 328–50.
—— and —— (1975) '"Rational" expectations: the optimal monetary instrument and the optimal money supply rule', *Journal of Political Economy* 83: 241–54.
—— and —— (1976) 'Rational expectations and the theory of economic policy', *Journal of Monetary Economics* 2: 169–83.
Sawyer, M. (1985) *The Economics of Michal Kalecki*, London: Macmillan.
—— (1992a) 'The relationship between Keynes's macroeconomic analysis and theories of imperfect competition', in B. Gerrard and J. Hillard (eds) *The Philosophy and Economics of J.M. Keynes*, Aldershot, Hants: Edward Elgar.
—— (1992b) 'On imperfect competition and macroeconomic analysis', in A. DelMonte, *Recent Developments in the Theory of Industrial Organisation*, London: Macmillan.
Sayers, C. (1987) 'Diagnostic tests for nonlinearity in time series data: an application for the work stopping series', University of Houston, mimeo.
Scarf, H. (1960) 'Some examples of global instability of the competitive equilibrium', *International Economic Review* 1: 157–72.
Schefold, B. (1979) 'Fixes Kapital als Kuppelprodukt und die Analyse der Akkumulation bei unterschiedlichen Formen des technischen Fortschritts', in *Gesellschaft, Beiträge zur Marxistischen Theorie 13*, Edition Suhrkamp, Vol. 692, Frankfurt: Suhrkamp.

Schefold, B. (1980) 'Fixed capital as a joint product and the analysis of accumulation with different forms of technical progress', in L.L. Pasinetti (ed.) *Essays in the Theory of Joint Production*, New York: Columbia University Press.

—— (1987) 'Joint production in linear models', in J. Eatwell, M. Milgate and P. Newman (eds) *The New Palgrave: A Dictionary of Economics*, Vol. 2, London: Macmillan.

—— (1991) 'Einleitung zur Neuausgabe von Irving Fisher *The Nature of Capital and Interest*', in B. Schefold (ed.) *Irving Fisher* The Nature of Capital and Interest. *Vademecum zu einem Klassiker der Zinstheorie*, Düsseldorf: Verlag Wirtschaft und Finanzen.

—— (1995a) 'Die Relevanz der Cambridge-Theorie für die ordnungspolitische Diskussion', in B. Schefold (ed.) *Wirtschaftsstile*. Band 2: *Studien zur ökonomischen Theorie und zur Zukunft der Technik*, Frankfurt a.M.: Fischer Taschenbuch Verlag.

—— (1995b) 'Überlegungen zu einer neowalrasianischen, marshallianischen und klassischen Mikrofundierung der Theorie der effectiven Nachfrage', in B. Schefold (ed.) *Wirtschaftsstile*. Band 2: *Studien zur ökonomischen Theorie und zur Zukunft der Technik*, Frankfurt a.M.: Fischer Taschenbuch Verlag.

Scheinkman, J. and LeBaron, B. (1989) 'Nonlinear dynamics and stock returns', *Journal of Business* 62: 311–37.

Schinasi, B. (1981) 'A nonlinear dynamic model of short-run fluctuations', *Review of Economic Studies* 48: 649–56.

Schnadt, N. and Whittaker, J. (1993) 'Inflation-proof currency? The feasibility of variable commodity standards', *Journal of Money, Credit, and Banking* 25: 214–21.

—— (1995) 'Is indirect convertibility impossible?', *Journal of Money, Credit, and Banking* 27: 297–8.

Schneider, M. (1987) 'Underconsumption', in J. Eatwell, M. Milgate and P. Newman (eds) *The New Palgrave: A Dictionary of Economics*, Vol. 4, London: Macmillan.

Schumpeter, J.A. (1911) *Theorie der wirtschaftlichen Entwicklung*, Leipzig: Duncker & Humblot; English trans. in *The Theory of Economic Development*, Oxford: Oxford University Press, 1934.

—— (1936) 'Review of Keynes's *General Theory*', *Journal of the American Statistical Association* 31: 791–5.

—— (1942) *Capitalism, Socialism and Democracy*, New York: Harper & Row.

—— (1946a) 'Keynes and statistics', *Review of Economics and Statistics* 28: 194–6.

—— (1946b) 'John Maynard Keynes, 1883–1946', *American Economic Review* 36: 495–518.

—— (1954) *History of Economic Analysis*, London: Allen & Unwin.

Schwartz, J. (ed.) (1977) *The Subtle Anatomy of Capitalism*, Santa Monica, Calif.: Goodyear.

Scott, A.D. (1953) 'Notes on user cost', *Economic Journal* 63: 368–84.

Sebastiani, M. (ed.) (1989) *Kalecki's Relevance Today*, London: Macmillan.

Selgin, G.A. and White, L.H. (1994) 'How would the invisible hand handle money?', *Journal of Economic Literature* 32: 1718–49.

Semmler, W. (ed.) (1986) *Competition, Instability and Nonlinear Cycles*, New York: Springer-Verlag.

—— (1987) 'A macroeconomic limit cycle with financial perturbations', *Journal of Economic Behaviour and Organisation* 8: 469–95.

—— (ed.) (1989) *Financial Dynamics and Business Cycles: New Perspectives*, Armonk, N.Y.: Sharpe.

Shackle, G.L.S. (1951) 'Twenty years on: a survey of the theory of the multiplier', *Economic Journal* 59: 241–60.

Shackle, G.L.S. (1955) *Uncertainty in Economics and Other Reflections*, Cambridge: Cambridge University Press.
—— (1965) *A Scheme of Economic Theory*, Cambridge: Cambridge University Press.
—— (1967) *The Years of High Theory*, Cambridge: Cambridge University Press.
—— (1972) *Epistemics and Economics*, Cambridge: Cambridge University Press.
—— (1974) *Keynesian Kaleidics*, Edinburgh: Edinburgh University Press.
—— (1979) *Imagination and the Nature of Choice*, Edinburgh: Edinburgh University Press.
—— (1983) 'An interview with G.L.S. Shackle', *Austrian Economics Newsletter* 4: 1, 5–8.
Shapiro, N. (1995) 'Markets and mark-ups: Keynesian views', in S. Dow and J. Hillard (eds) *Keynes, Knowledge and Uncertainty*, Aldershot, Hants: Edward Elgar.
Shepherd, A., Turk, J.S. and Silbertson, A. (eds) (1983) *Microeconomic Efficiency and Macroeconomic Performance*, Oxford: Philip Allan.
Sherman, H. (1991) *Business Cycles*, Princeton, N.J.: Princeton University Press.
Shove, G.F. (1942) 'The place of Marshall's *Principles* in the development of economic theory', *Economic Journal* 52: 294–329.
Sichel, D. (1991) 'Business cycle duration dependence: a parametric approach', *Review of Economics and Statistics* 73: 254–60.
Simmons, G.F. (1963) *Introduction to Topology and Modern Analysis*, New York: McGraw-Hill.
Simon, H.A. (1957) *Models of Man*, New York: John Wiley.
—— (1959) 'Theories of decision making in economics and behavioural science', *American Economic Review* 49: 253–83.
—— (1976) 'From substantive to procedural rationality', in S.J. Latsis (ed.) *Method and Appraisal in Economics*, Cambridge: Cambridge University Press.
—— (1982) *Models of Bounded Rationality*, Cambridge, Mass.: MIT Press.
——, Egidi, M., Marris, R. and Viale, R. (1992) *Economics, Bounded Rationality and the Cognitive Revolution*, Aldershot, Hants: Edward Elgar.
Sims, C.A. (1982) 'Policy analysis with econometric modes', *Brookings Papers on Economic Activity* 1: 107–52.
—— (1986a) 'A rational expectations framework for short run policy analysis', in W.A. Barnett and K.J. Singleton (eds) *New Approaches to Monetary Economics: Proceedings of the Second International Symposium in Economic Theory and Econometrics*, Cambridge: Cambridge University Press.
—— (1986b) 'Are forecasting models usable for policy analysis?', *Federal Reserve Bank of Minneapolis Quarterly Review* 10: 2–15.
Skidelsky, R. (1983) *John Maynard Keynes*. Vol. I: *Hopes Betrayed, 1883–1920*, London: Macmillan.
—— (1989) 'Keynes and the state', in D. Helm (ed.) *The Economic Borders of the State*, Oxford: Oxford University Press.
—— (1992) *John Maynard Keynes*. Vol. II: *The Economist as Saviour, 1920–1937*, London: Macmillan.
—— (1995a) 'The role of ethics in Keynes's economics', in S. Brittan and A. Hamlin (eds) *Market Capitalism and Moral Values*, Aldershot, Hants: Edward Elgar.
—— (1995b) 'J.M. Keynes and the quantity theory of money', in M. Blaug *et al. The Quantity Theory of Money*, Aldershot, Hants: Edward Elgar.
Skott, P. (1989) 'Effective demand, class struggle, and economic growth', *International Economic Review* 30: 231–47.
Slutsky, E. (1927) *The Summation of Random Causes as the Source of Cyclical Processes*,

Vol. III, no. 1, Moscow: Conjuncture Institute; reprinted in *Econometrica* 5 (1937): 105–46.

Smith, A. (1776) *An Enquiry into the Nature and Causes of the Wealth of Nations*, reprinted New York: Modern Library, 1937.

Smithson, M. (1988) 'Fuzzy sets theory and the social sciences: the scope for application', *Fuzzy Sets and Systems* 26: 12–15.

Snippe, J. (1987) 'Intertemporal coordination and the economics of Keynes: comment on Garrison', *History of Political Economy* 19: 329–41.

Snower, D. (1984) 'Imperfect competition, underemployment and crowding out', *Oxford Economic Papers* 36: 177–99.

Solow, R.M. (1956) 'A contribution to the theory of economic growth', *Quarterly Journal of Economics* 70: 65–94.

—— (1957) 'Technical change and the aggregate production function', *Review of Economics and Statistics*, 39: 312–20.

—— (1984) 'Mr Hicks and the Classics', *Oxford Economic Papers* 36: 13–25.

—— (1986) 'Monopolistic competition and the multiplier', in W. Heller (ed.) *Essays in Honour of Kenneth Arrow*, Vol. 2, Cambridge: Cambridge University Press.

Sonnenschein, H. (1972) 'Market excess demand functions', *Econometrica* 40: 549–63.

—— (1987) 'Oligopoly and game theory', in J. Eatwell, M. Milgate and P. Newman (eds) *The New Palgrave: A Dictionary of Economics*, Vol. 3, London: Macmillan.

Soper, C.S. (1956) 'The supply curve in Keynesian economics', *South African Journal of Economics* 24: 1–8.

Speight, A.E.H. (1990) *Comsumption, Rational Expectations and Liquidity: Theory and Evidence*, Hemel Hempstead, Herts.: Harvester Wheatsheaf.

Springer, W.L. (1977) 'Consumer spending and the rate of inflation', *Review of Economics and Statistics* 59: 299–306.

Sraffa, P. (1932a) 'Dr Hayek on money and capital', *Economic Journal* 42: 42–53.

—— (1932b) 'A rejoinder', *Economic Journal* 42: 249–51.

—— (1960) *Production of Commodities by Means of Commodities: Prelude to a Critique of Economic Theory*, Cambridge: Cambridge University Press.

—— (1961) 'Comment', in F. Lutz and D.C. Hague (eds) *The Theory of Capital*, London: Macmillan, 305–6.

—— (1962) 'Production of commodities: a comment', *Economic Journal* 72: 477–9.

—— (1993) 'Monetary inflation in Italy during and after the war', trans. W.J. Harcourt and C. Sardoni, *Cambridge Journal of Economics* 17: 7–26.

Stadermann, H.J. and Steiger, O. (eds) (1993) *Der Stand und die nächste Zukunft der Geldforschung*, Berlin: Duncker & Humblot.

Staehle, H. (1937) 'Short-period variations in the distribution of incomes', *Review of Economic Statistics* 19: 133–43.

—— (1938) 'New considerations on the distribution of incomes and the propensity to consume (partly in reply to Mr Dirks)', *Review of Economic Statistics* 20: 134–41.

—— (1939) 'A rejoinder', *Review of Economic Statistics* 21: 129–30.

Stanners, W. (1993) 'Is low inflation an important condition for high growth?', *Cambridge Journal of Economics* 17: 79–107.

Startz, R. (1989) 'Monopolistic competition as a foundation for Keynesian macroeconomic models', *Quarterly Journal of Economics* 104: 738–52.

Steindl, J. (1952) *Maturity and Stagnation in American Capitalism*, Oxford: Blackwell.

—— (1985) 'J.M. Keynes: society and the economist', in F. Vicarelli (ed.) *Keynes's Relevance Today*, London: Macmillan.

Stiglitz, J.E. (ed.) (1966) *The Collected Scientific Papers of Paul A. Samuelson*, Vols 1 and 2, Cambridge, Mass., and London: MIT Press.
—— (1984) 'Price rigidities and market structure', *American Economic Review* 74 (proceedings): 350–5.
—— (1988) 'Why financial structure matters', *Journal of Economic Perspectives* 2: 121–6.
—— (1993) 'New and old Keynesians', *Journal of Economic Perspectives* 7: 43–4.
—— and Weiss, A. (1981) 'Credit rationing in markets with imperfect information', *American Economic Review* 71: 393–410.
Stigum, B.P. (1990) *Towards a Formal Science of Economics: The Axiomatic Method in Economics and Econometrics*, Cambridge: Mass.: MIT Press.
Stone, R. (1978) *Keynes, Political Arithmetic and Econometrics*, Proceedings of the British Academy, Vol. 64, Oxford: Oxford University Press.
—— (1991) 'The ET interview', *Econometric Theory* 7: 85–123.
—— and Stone, W.M. (1938) 'The marginal propensity to consume and the multiplier: a statistical investigation', *Review of Economic Studies* 6: 1–24.
Strachey, J. (1935) *The Nature of Capitalist Crisis*, London: Victor Gollancz.
Studart, R. (1995) *Investment Finance in Economic Development*, London: Routledge.
Suits, D.B. (1963) 'The determinants of consumer expenditure: a review of present knowledge', in *Impacts of Monetary Policy: Commission on Money and Credit*, Englewood Cliffs, N.J.: Prentice Hall.
Summers, L. (1986) 'Some skeptical observations on real business cycle theory', *Federal Reserve Bank of Minneapolis Quarterly Review* Autumn: 23–7.
Swan, T.W. (1956) 'Economic growth and capital accumulation', *Economic Record* 32: 334–61.
Sweezy, P.M. (1942) *The Theory of Capitalist Development*, New York: Oxford University Press.
—— (1963) 'The first quarter century', in R. Lekachmann (ed.) *Keynes'* General Theory, London: Macmillan.
—— (1991) '*Monopoly Capital* after twenty-five years', *Monthly Review* 43(7): 52–7.
Sylos-Labini, P. (1956) *Oligopoly and Technical Progress*; English trans. Cambridge, Mass.: Harvard University Press, 1969.
—— (1987) 'Oligopoly', in J. Eatwell, M. Milgate and P. Newman (eds) *The New Palgrave: A Dictionary of Economics*, Vol. 3, London: Macmillan.
Targetti, F. and Kinda-Hass, B. (ed. and trans.) (1982) 'Kalecki's review of Keynes' *General Theory*', *Australian Economic Papers* 21: 244–60.
—— and Thirlwall, A.P. (eds) (1983) *Further Essays on Economic Theory and Policy*, London: Duckworth.
Tarshis, L. (1939) 'Changes in real and money wages', *Economic Journal* 49: 150–4.
—— (1948) 'An exposition of Keynesian economics', *American Economic Review* 38: 261–72.
—— (1979) 'The aggregate money supply function in Keynes's *General Theory*', in M.J. Boskin (ed.) *Economics and Human Welfare: Essays in Honor of Tibor Scitovsky* New York: Academic Press.
—— (1989) 'Keynes's cooperative economy and his aggregate supply function', in J. Pheby (ed.) *New Directions in Post Keynesian Economics*, Aldershot, Hants: Edward Elgar.
Terzi, A. (1986–7) 'The independence of finance from saving: a flow of funds interpretation', *Journal of Post Keynesian Economics* 9: 188–97.
Tew, B. (1953) 'Keynesian accountancy', *Yorkshire Bulletin of Economic and Social Research* 5: 147–53.
Thirlwall, A.P. (1979) 'The balance of payments constraint as an explanation of

international growth rate difference', *Banca Nazionale del Lavoro Quarterly Review* 128: 45–53.

Thomas, J.J. (1989) 'The early econometric history of the consumption function', *Oxford EconomicPapers* 41: 131–49.

—— (1992) 'Income distribution and the estimation of the consumption function: an historical analysis of the early arguments', *History of Political Economy* 24: 153–81.

Thomas, R.L. (1993) *Introductory Econometrics: Theory and Applications*, 2nd edn, London: Longman.

Thrift, N. (1990) 'The making of a capitalist time consciousness', in J. Hassard (ed.) *Sociology of Time*, London: Macmillan.

Thweatt, W.O. (1983) 'Keynes on Marx's *Das Kapital*', *History of Political Economy* 15: 617–20.

Timlin, M.F. (1942) *Keynesian Economics*, Toronto: University of Toronto Press.

Tinbergen, J. (1940) 'On a method of stastical business-cycle research: a reply', *Economic Journal* 50: 141–54.

Tirole, J. (1982) 'On the possibility of speculation under rational expectations', *Econometrica* 50: 1163–81.

Tobin, J. (1955) 'A dynamic aggregative model', *Journal of Political Economy* 63(1): 103–15.

—— (1958) 'Liquidity preference as behaviour towards risk', *Review of Economic Studies* 25: 65–86.

—— (1969) 'A general equilibrium approach to monetary theory', *Journal of Money, Credit, and Banking* 1: 15–29.

—— (1972) 'Inflation and unemployment', *American Economic Review* 62: 1–19.

—— (1975) 'Keynesian models of recession and depression', *American Economic Review* 65: 195–202.

—— (1978) 'A proposal for international monetary reform', *Eastern Economic Journal* 4: 153–9.

—— (1980a) *Asset Accumulation and Economic Activity: Reflections on Contemporary Macroeconomic Theory*, Oxford: Blackwell.

—— (1980b) 'Are New Classical models plausible enough to guide policy?, *Journal of Money, Credit, and Banking* 12: 788–99.

—— (1982) 'Money and finance in the macroeconomic process', *Journal of Money, Credit and Banking* 14: 171–204.

—— (1983) 'Comment', in J. Trevithick and D. Worswick (eds) *Keynes and the Modern World*, Cambridge: Cambridge University Press.

——— (1987) 'Fisher, Irving', in J. Eatwell, M. Milgate and P. Newman (eds) *The New Palgrave: A Dictionary of Economics*, Vol. 2, London: Macmillan.

—— (1988) 'The future of Keynesian economics', *Eastern Economic Journal* 12: 347–58.

—— (1993) 'Price flexibility and output stability: an old Keynesian view', *Journal of Economic Perspectives* 7: 45–65.

—— (1994) 'Price flexibility and output stability: an old Keynesian view', in W. Semmler (ed.) *Business Cycles: Theory and Empirical Methods*, Boston, Mass.: Kluwer Academic.

Torr, C.S.W. (1992) 'The dual role of user cost in the derivation of Keynes's aggregate supply function', *Review of Political Economy* 4: 1–17.

Torre, V. (1977) 'Existence of limit cycles and control in complete Keynesian systems by theory of bifurcations', *Econometrica* 45: 1457–66.

Townend, J.C. (1976) 'The personal saving ratio', *Bank of England Quarterly Bulletin* 16: 53–73.

Townshend, H. (1937) 'Liquidity-premium and the theory of value', *Economic Journal* 47: 157–69.
Trautwein, H.M. (1993) 'A fundamental controversy about money: Post-Keynesian and new monetary economics', in G. Mongiovi and C. Rühl (eds) *Macroeconomic Theory: Diversity and Convergence*, Aldershot, Hants: Edward Elgar.
Treasury and Civil Serviced Select Committee (1993) *The Role of the Bank of England*, Committee Reports Vols I and II, London: HMSO.
Trevithick, J. (1992) *Involuntary Unemployment: Macroeconomics from a Keynesian Perspective*, Hemel Hempstead, Herts.: Harvester Wheatsheaf.
—— (1994) 'The monetary prerequisites for the multiplier: an adumbration of the crowding-out hypothesis', *Cambridge Journal of Economics* 18: 77–90.
—— and Worswick, D. (eds) (1983) *Keynes and the Modern World*, Cambridge: Cambridge University Press.
Tuchscherer, T. (1979) 'Keynes' model and the Keynesians: a synthesis', *Journal of Post Keynesian Economics* 1: 96–109.
Turvey, R. (1965) 'Does the rate of interest rule the roost?', in F. Hahn and F.P.R. Brechling (eds) *The Theory of the Rate of Interest*, London: Macmillan.
Tutin, C. (1988) 'Intérêt et ajustement: le débat Hayek–Keynes (1931–32)', *Economie appliquée* 41: 247–87.
United Nations (UN) (1993) *System of National Accounts*, New York: UNO.
United States Bureau of Census (1959) *Statistical Abstract of the United States, 1959*, Washington, D.C.: USGPO.
van der Ploeg, F. (1983) 'Predator–prey and neoclassical models of cyclical growth', *Zeischrift für Nationalökonomie* 43: 235–56.
van Fraassen, B.C. (1989) *Laws and Symmetry*, Oxford: Clarendon Press.
Velupillai, K. (ed.) (1995) *Inflation, Institutions and Information*, London: Macmillan.
Vercelli, A. (1991) *Methodological Foundations of Macroeconomics: Keynes and Lucas*, Cambridge: Cambridge University Press.
—— (1994) 'Por una macroeconomia nao reductionista: una perspectiva de longo prazo', *Economia e Sociedade* 3: 3–19.
—— (1995a) 'Economia e fisica', in A. Boitani and G. Rodano (eds) *Relazioni Pericolose. L'avventura dell'economia nella cultura contemporanea*, Bari: Laterza.
—— (1995b) 'Coherence, meaning and responsibility in the language of economics', paper presented at the conference on 'The Language of Science' at the University of Bologna, 25–27 October 1995, forthcoming in the *Proceedings of the Conference*.
——— and Dimitri, N. (eds) (1992) *Macroeconomics: A Survey of Research Strategies*, Oxford: Oxford University Press.
Vicarelli, F. (1984) *Keynes: The Instability of Capitalism*, New York: Macmillan.
—— (ed.) (1985) *Keynes's Relevance Today*, London: Macmillan.
Viner, J. (1936) 'Mr Keynes on the causes of unemployment', *Quarterly Journal of Economics* 51: 147–67.
Walker, D.A. (1984) *Money and Markets*, Cambridge: Cambridge University Press.
—— (1987a) 'Edgeworth versus Walras on the theory of tatonnement', *Eastern Economic Journal* 13: 155–65.
—— (1987b) 'Leon Walras', in J. Eatwell, M. Milgate and P. Newman (eds) *The New Palgrave, A Dictionary of Economics*, Vol. 4, London: Macmillan.
—— (ed.) (1989) *Perspectives in the History of Economic Thought*, Vol. II, Aldershot, Hants.: Edward Elgar.
Wallace, N. (1983) 'A legal restrictions theory of the demand for money and the role of monetary policy', *Federal Reserve Bank of Minneapolis Quarterly Review*, Winter: 1–7.

Wallis, K.F., Andrews, M.J., Bell, D.N.F., Fisher, P.G. and Whitley, J.D. (1984) *Models of the UK Economy: A Review by the ESRC Macroeconomic Modelling Bureau*, Oxford; Oxford University Press.

——, Fisher, P.G., Longbottom, J.A., Turner, D.S. and Whitley, J.D. (1986) *Models of the UK Economy: A Fourth Review by the ESRC Macroeconomic Modelling Bureau*, Oxford: Oxford University Press.

——, Andrews, M.J., Fisher, P.G., Longbottom, J.A. and Whitley, J.D. (1987) *Models of the UK Economy: A Fifth Review by the ESRC Macroeconomic Modelling Bureau*, Oxford: Oxford University Press.

Walras, L. (1874) *Elements of Pure Economics*, trans and annotated W. Jaffe, Homewood, Ill.: Richard D. Irwin, 1954.

Warming, J. (1932) 'The financing of public works: a note', *Economic Journal* 42: 492–5.

Wärneryd, K. (1989) 'Legal restrictions and the evolution of the media of exchange', *Journal of Institutional and Theoretical Economics* 145: 613–26.

—— (1990) 'Legal restrictions and monetary evolution', *Journal of Economic Behaviour and Organisation* 13: 117–24.

Weil, P. (1990) 'Nonexpected utility in macroeconomics', *Quarterly Journal of Economics* 105: 29–42.

Weinberg, S. (1995) 'Reductionism redux', *New York Review of Books* 42: 39–42.

Weintraub, R. (1979) *Microfoundations*, Cambridge: Cambridge University Press.

Weintraub, S. (1949) *Price Theory*, New York: Pitman.

—— (1956) 'A macroeconomic approach to the theory of wages', *American Economic Review* 46: 835–56.

—— (1957) 'The micro foundations of aggregate demand and supply', *Economic Journal* 67: 455–70.

Weisskopf, T. (1979) 'Marxism crisis theory and the rate of profit in the post-war US economy', *Cambridge Journal of Economics* 3: 340–77.

Wells, P. (ed.) (1995) *Post Keynesian Economic Theory*, Boston, Mass.: Kluwer.

Wennerberg, H. (1967) 'The concept of family resemblance in Wittgenstein's later philosophy', *Theoria* 33: 107–32.

Westin, R.B. (1975) 'Empirical implications of infrequent purchase behavior in a stock adjustment model', *American Economic Review* 65: 384–96.

Whitaker, J. (1975) *The Early Writings of Alfred Marshall: 1867–90*, 2 vols, New York: Free Press.

White, L. (1984) 'Competitive payments systems and the unit of account', *American Economic Review* 74: 699–712.

—— (1986) 'Competitive payments systems: reply', *American Economic Review* 76: 850–3.

—— (1987) 'Accounting for non-interest bearing currency: a critique of the legal restrictions theory of money', *Journal of Money, Credit, and Banking* 19: 448–56.

—— (1989) *Competition and Currency: Essays on Free Banking and Money*, New York: New York University Press.

Whitley, J. (1994) *A Course in Macroeconomic Modelling and Forecasting*, Hemel Hempstead, Herts.: Harvester Wheatsheaf.

Wickens, M.R. and Molana, H. (1984) 'Stochastic life cycle theory with varying interest rates and prices', *Economic Journal Conference Papers* 94: 133–47.

Wicksell, K. (1935) *Lectures on Political Economy*, 2 vols, New York: Macmillan.

—— (1936) *Interest and Prices: A Study of the Causes Regulating the Value of Money*, London: Macmillan.

Wiggins, S. (1990) *Introduction to Applied Nonlinear Dynamical Systems and Chaos*, New York: Springer-Verlag.

Williamson, J. (1987) 'Exchange rate management: the role of target zones', *American Economic Review* 77: 200–4.

Winnett, A. (1992) 'Some semantics of endogeneity', in P. Arestis and V. Chick (eds) *Recent Developments in Post Keynesian Economics*, Aldershot, Hants: Edward Elgar.

Winslow, T. (1986) 'Keynes and Freud: psychoanalysis and Keynes's account of the "animal spirits" of capitalism', *Social Research* Winter: 549–78.

Wittgenstein, L. (1921) *Tractatus Logico-philosophicus*; English trans. D. Pears and B. McGuiness, New York: Routledge & Kegan Paul, 1961.

—— (1953) *Philosophical Investigations*, Oxford: Blackwell; 2nd edn rev., 1958.

—— (1974) *Letters to Russell, Keynes and Moore*, Oxford: Blackwell.

—— (1975) *Philosophical Remarks*, trans. R. Hargreaves and R. White, Chicago, Ill.: Chicago University Press.

Wojnilower, A.M. (1980) 'The central role of credit crunches in recent financial history', *Brookings Papers on Economic Activity* 2: 277–326.

Wolf, A. (1986) 'Quantifying chaos with Lyapunov exponents', in A. Holden (ed.) *Chaos*, Princeton, N.J.: Princeton University Press.

Wood, A. (1975) *A Theory of Profits*, Cambridge: Cambridge University Press.

Woodford, M. (1990) 'The optimum quantity of money', in B.M. Friedman and F.H. Hahn (eds) *Handbook of Monetary Economics*, Amsterdam: North-Holland.

—— (1992) 'Self fulfilling expectations and fluctuations in aggregate demand', in N.G. Mankiw and D. Romer (eds) *New Keynesian Economics*, Vol. 2, Cambridge, Mass.: MIT Press.

Worswick, G.D.N. (1991) *Unemployment: A Problem of Policy*, Cambridge: Cambridge University Press, for the National Institute of Economic and Social Research.

—— and Trevithick, J. (eds) (1983) *Keynes and the Modern World*, Cambridge: Cambridge University Press.

Wray, L.R. (1990) *Money and Credit in Capitalist Economies: The Endogenous Money Approach*, Aldershot, Hants: Edward Elgar.

—— (1991) 'Boulding's balloons: a contribution to monetary theory', *Journal of Economic Issues* 25: 1–20.

Yang, R.-S. and Brorsen, W.B. (1993) 'Nonlinear dynamics of daily futures prices: conditional heteroskedasticity or chaos?', *Journal of Futures Markets* 13(2): 175–91.

Yeager, L.B. (1989) 'A competitive payments system: some objections considered', *Journal of Post Keynesian Economics* 11: 370–7.

Young, W. (1987) *Interpreting Mr Keynes: The IS–LM Enigma*, London: Polity Press.

Zadeh, L. (1973) 'Outline of a new approach to the analysis of complex systems and decision processes', *Institute of Electrical and Electronics Engineers Transactions on Systems, Man, and Cybernetics* SMC-3: 28–44.

—— (1975) 'Fuzzy logic and approximate reasoning', *Synthese* 30: 407–28.

Zarnowitz, V. (1992) *Business Cycles: Theory, History, Indicators, and Forecasting*, Chicago, Ill.: Chicago University Press.

—— and Moore, G. (1986) 'Major changes in cyclical behaviour', in R. Gordon (ed.) *The American Business Cycle*, Chicago, Ill.: Chicago University Press.

Zeitlin, I. (1967) *Marxism: A Re-examination*, New York: Van Nostrand.

Zellner, A., Huang, D.S. and Chau, L.C. (1965) 'Further analysis of the short-run consumption function with emphasis on the role of liquid assets', *Econometrica* 33: 571–81.

NAME INDEX

SUBJECT INDEX